WOOD ART TODAY 2

JEFFREY B. SNYDER, EDITOR

Schiffer Publishing Ltd
4880 Lower Valley Road Atglen, Pennsylvania 19310

Dedication

To Mary Alice Snyder and James J. Snyder. Thanks Mom and Dad for all you do and for all your guidance and encouragement. You are two of the angels in my life that make the journey so much more rewarding!

Other Schiffer Books by Jeffrey B. Snyder
Art Jewelry Today 2. ISBN: 9780-7643-3065-0. $50.00
Ceramics Today. ISBN: 9780-7643-3465-8. $50.00
Ironwork Today 2. ISBN: 9780-7643-3064-3. $50.00
Printmakers Today. ISBN: 9780-7643-3462-7. $50.00

Other Schiffer Books on Related Subjects
Dona Z. Meilach. *Wood Art Today.* ISBN: 0764319124. $59.95

Library of Congress Control Number: 2009944168

Cover and book designed by: Bruce Waters
Type set in Trajan Pro BT/New Gothic BT

ISBN: 978-0-7643-3463-4
Printed in Hong Kong

Published by Schiffer Publishing Ltd.
4880 Lower Valley Road
Atglen, PA 19310
Phone: (610) 593-1777; Fax: (610) 593-2002
E-mail: Info@schifferbooks.com

For the largest selection of fine reference books on this and related subjects, please visit our web site at **www.schifferbooks.com**
We are always looking for people to write books on new and related subjects. If you have an idea for a book please contact us at the above address.

This book may be purchased from the publisher.
Include $5.00 for shipping.
Please try your bookstore first.
You may write for a free catalog.

In Europe, Schiffer books are distributed by
Bushwood Books
6 Marksbury Ave.
Kew Gardens
Surrey TW9 4JF England
Phone: 44 (0) 20 8392 8585; Fax: 44 (0) 20 8392 9876
E-mail: info@bushwoodbooks.co.uk
Website: www.bushwoodbooks.co.uk

CONTENTS

Acknowledgments

I thank the artists and galleries who assisted in this project. Without their efforts, this book would not have been possible. Special thanks need to be made of the following galleries that passed along my call for artists.

del Mano Gallery: *www.delmano.com*
Hana Coast Gallery: www.hanacoast.com
Ironwood Gallery: www.ironwoodgallery.com
Northwest Fine Woodworking: www.nwfinewoodworking.com

I also thank those who chose to help anonymously. Their humility is profound and their guidance is much appreciated

Finally, I thank my publisher, co-workers, church, friends, and family, who keep my spirits up and the books coming.

Introduction

Around the world and throughout time, wherever there have been trees, sharp implements, and individuals with artistic talent, wood art has been created. The varieties of wood used, forms created, and techniques employed have grown as the centuries rolled by. Today wood art spans a broad range of woods, forms, and techniques, representing the unique visions and inspirations of today's artists. This book provides a sampling of the works of fine wood artists employing many techniques and creating many forms of art. All of the artists create unique, one-of-a-kind artworks.

This book presents a sampling from the vast and impressive range of wood art created during the first decade of the twenty-first century. The artists are presented alphabetically, allowing readers to review the range of each artist's work together. The artists introduce the subject and speak for themselves through their impressive work.

Use the resources presented at the back of the book, and contact the galleries and the artists to learn about their most recent work, for this field and these artists are on the move, evolving new styles continually. Excitement in this field is growing, tree by tree.

The Artists and Their Work

Michael Bauermeister

Augusta, Missouri, www.michaelbauermeister.com

Artist's Statement

I make sculptural forms out of wood using traditional, and some not-so-traditional, techniques. Many of my pieces are based on vessel shapes from various cultures as well as the natural vessels of pods, seeds, shells, and husks. I find these comforting forms to be an easy way to start into a sculptural idea both for me and for the viewer. Then, with trust and confidence gained, we can explore the resulting wooden poetry.

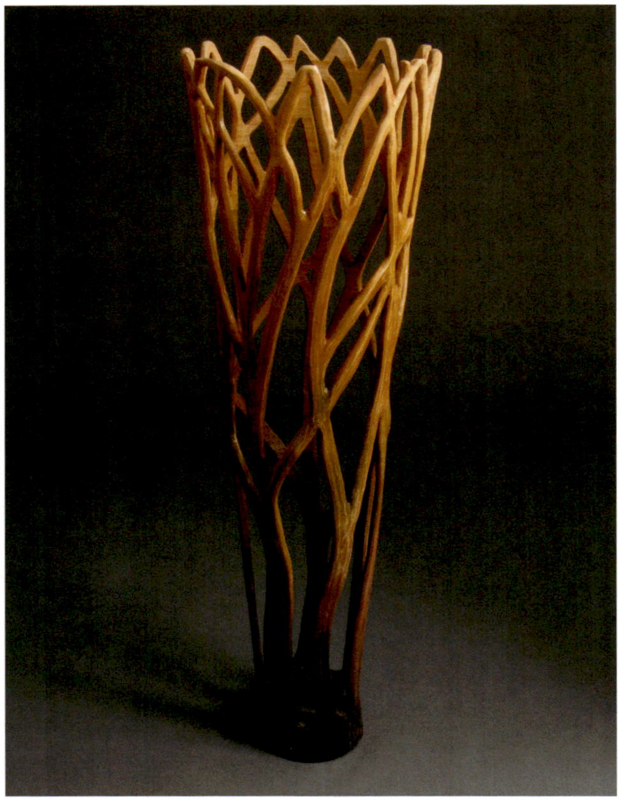

Michael Bauermeister. *Circle of Seven Sycamores*. Sycamore, 50" x 16" x 16".

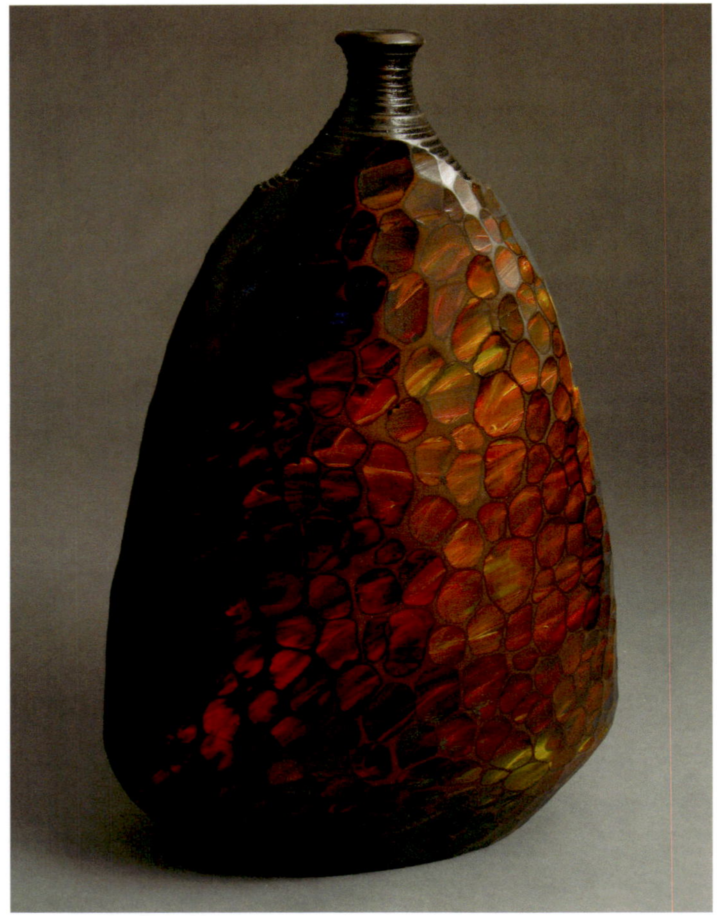

Michael Bauermeister. *Paint Bottle*. Linden, paint, 30" x 18" x 10".

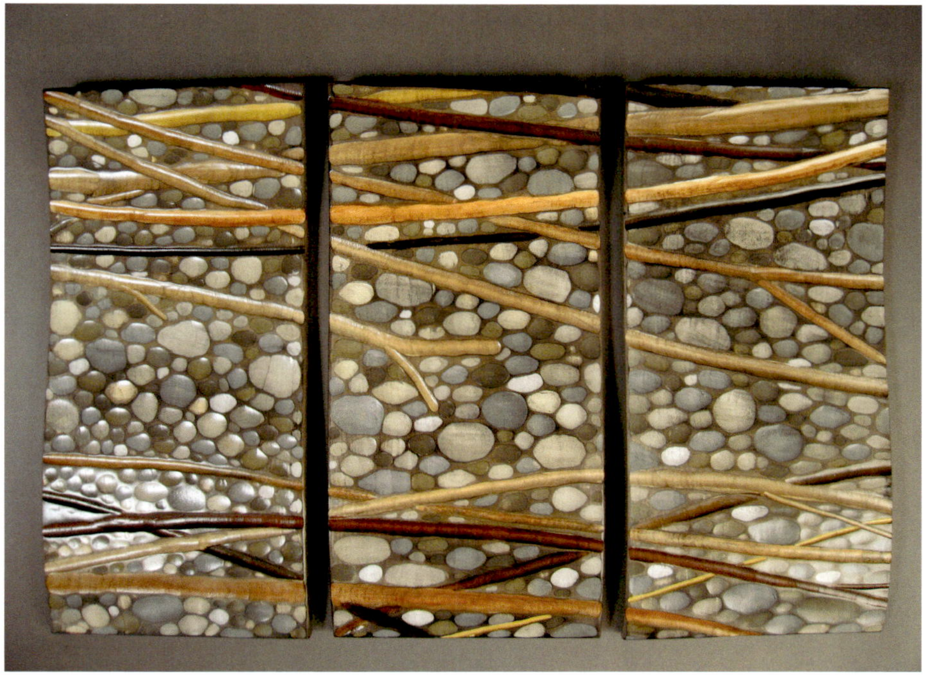

Michael Bauermeister. *Sticks and Stones*. Three panel triptych, linden, paint, stain, 25" x 38".

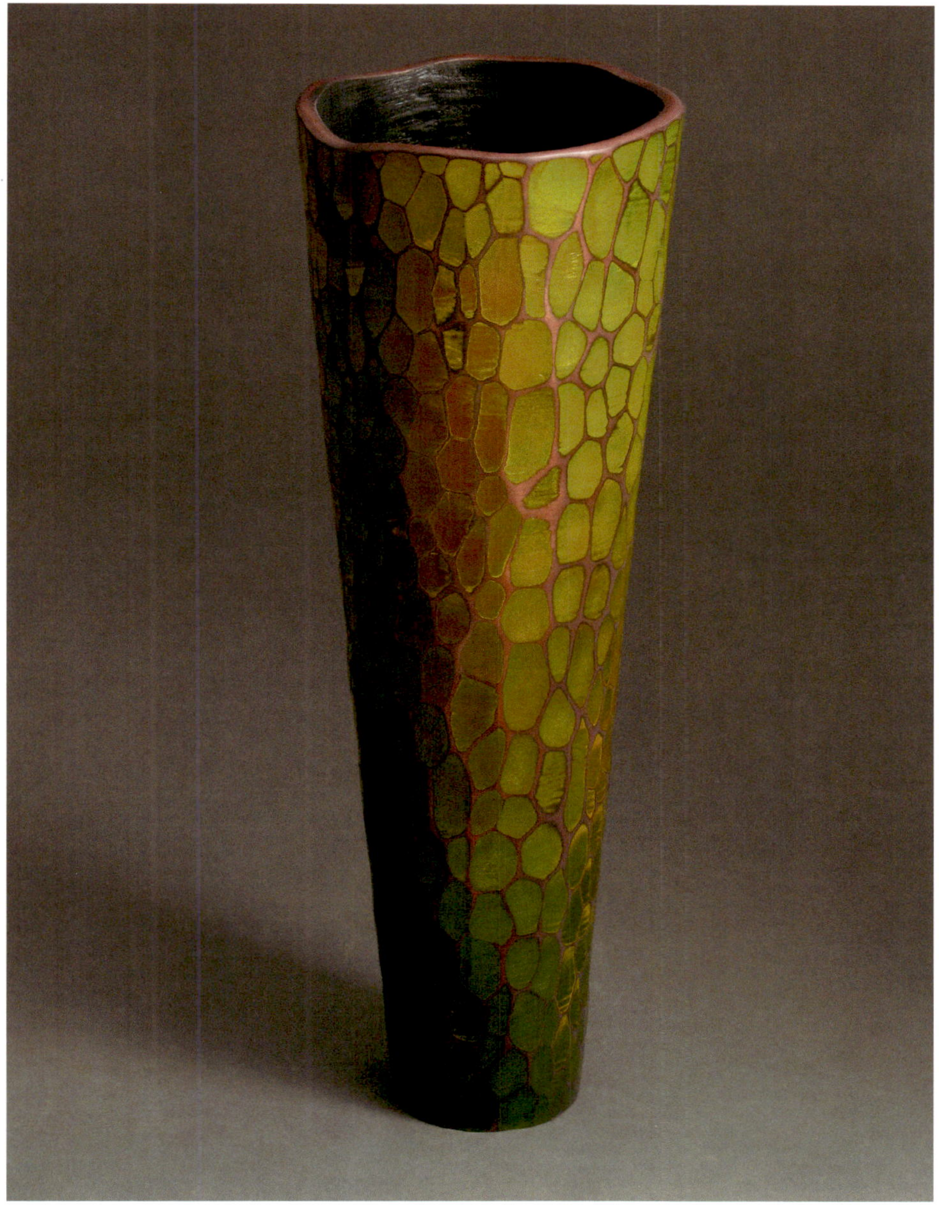

Michael Bauermeister. *Green Cup*. 2008. Linden, tinted lacquer, 33" x 11" x 11".

Jerry Bennett

Huntsville, Texas, jbennettart@sbcglobal.net

Artist's Statement

While some of my work is abstract, I prefer to represent the human spirit in some way. Picasso's approach to "representation" – presenting the *essence* of an entire subject at once – and the fluidity of Lino Tagliapietra's glass art, have found their way into my work. I seek to engage my audience, and it is my goal that none walk away unaffected.

Individual Artwork

On and On

I am drawn to works that are fluid and dynamic. I came across a work by Jose de Rivera, a sculptor who worked in steel. His piece, *Construction #190* with varying diameters and fluid curves, floored me. Although static, it exhibits an energy and fluidity as if it is forever moving. I had to figure out a way to utilize the same aesthetic concept in wood. *On and On* is the result. Its construction required borrowing a little from centuries old techniques and some new. A steel or brass armature is formed to the desired shape, and an external skin of segmented wood layers is applied. Each layer is turned individually to the correct diameter and tapered to follow the design. Any shape is possible with this process; however, success depends on being meticulous in the design and execution of the armature.

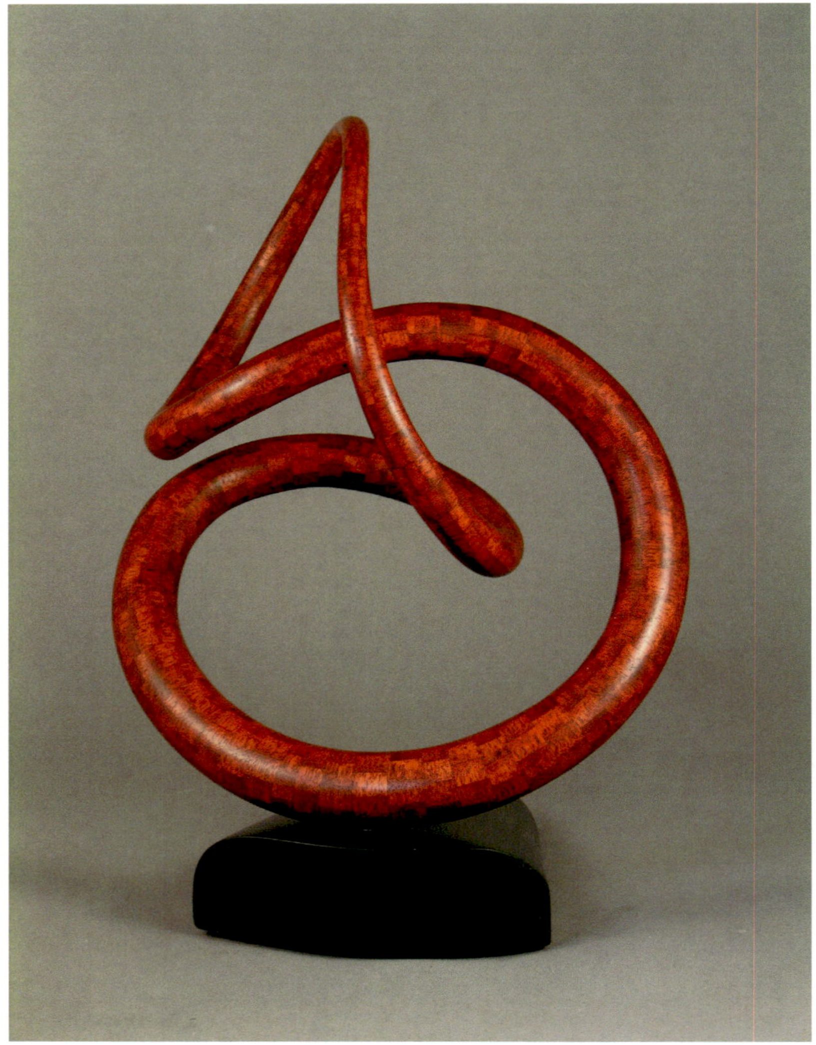

Jerry Bennett. *On and On.* Mahogany, maple, brass, acrylic paint, 15 1/2" h x 11" x 11".

Serenade

My life-long passion for music was sure to find its way into my art, and did! Having discovered the ability to represent fluidity and motion with *On and On,* the natural progression was to apply it to a plucked string. Serenade was based on the guitar. The components of the guitar are repositioned in a playful way to impart a unique personality. From any vantage point, one can experience its full essence.

Works with such dynamic components created a new challenge – shipping! I found that the best solution was to have the strings, neck, top, and base disconnect, and shipped in 3 form-fitted crates.

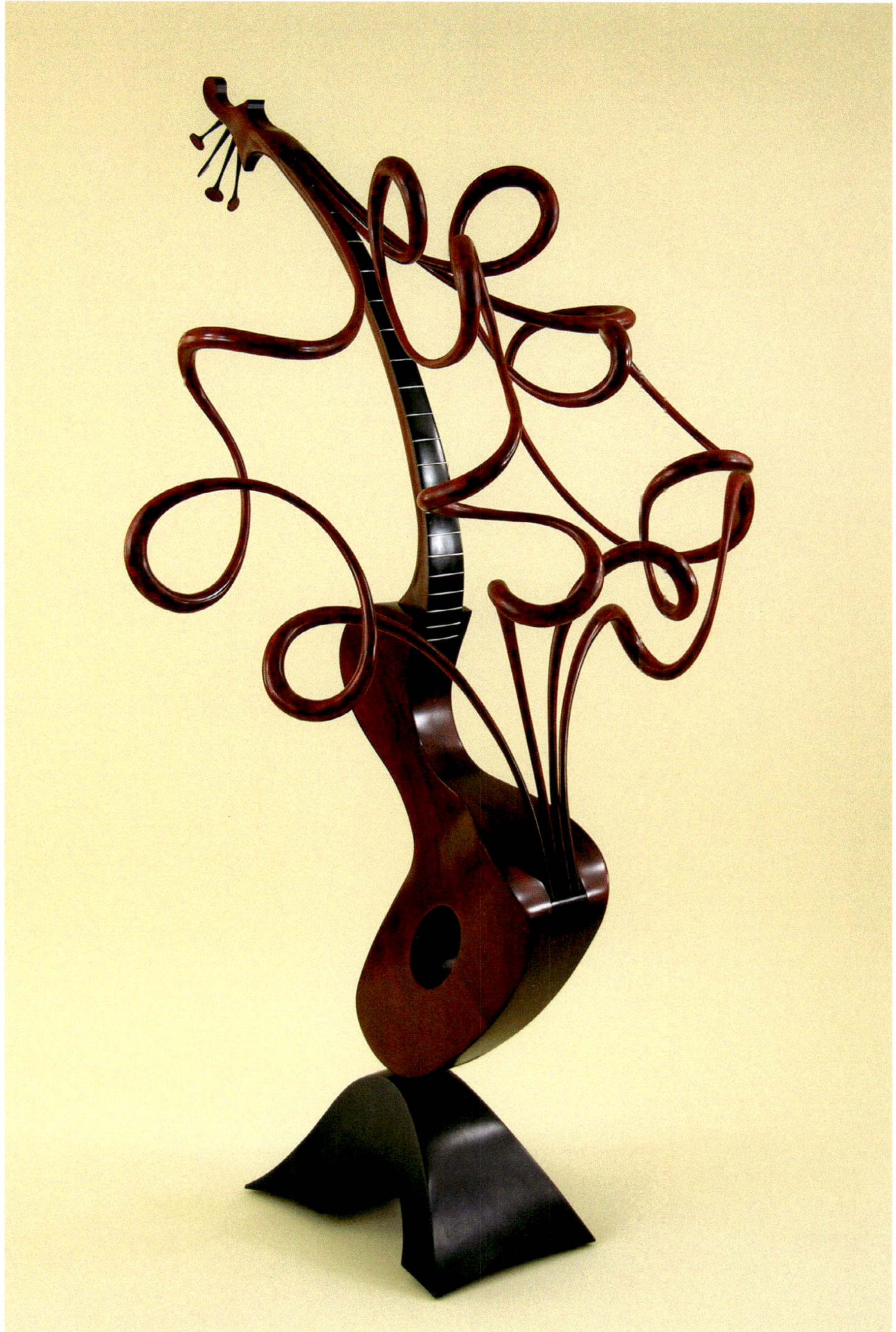

Jerry Bennett. *Serenade.* Mahogany, ebony, nickel fret wire, maple, brass, 6' h x 3-1/2' x 3-1/2'.

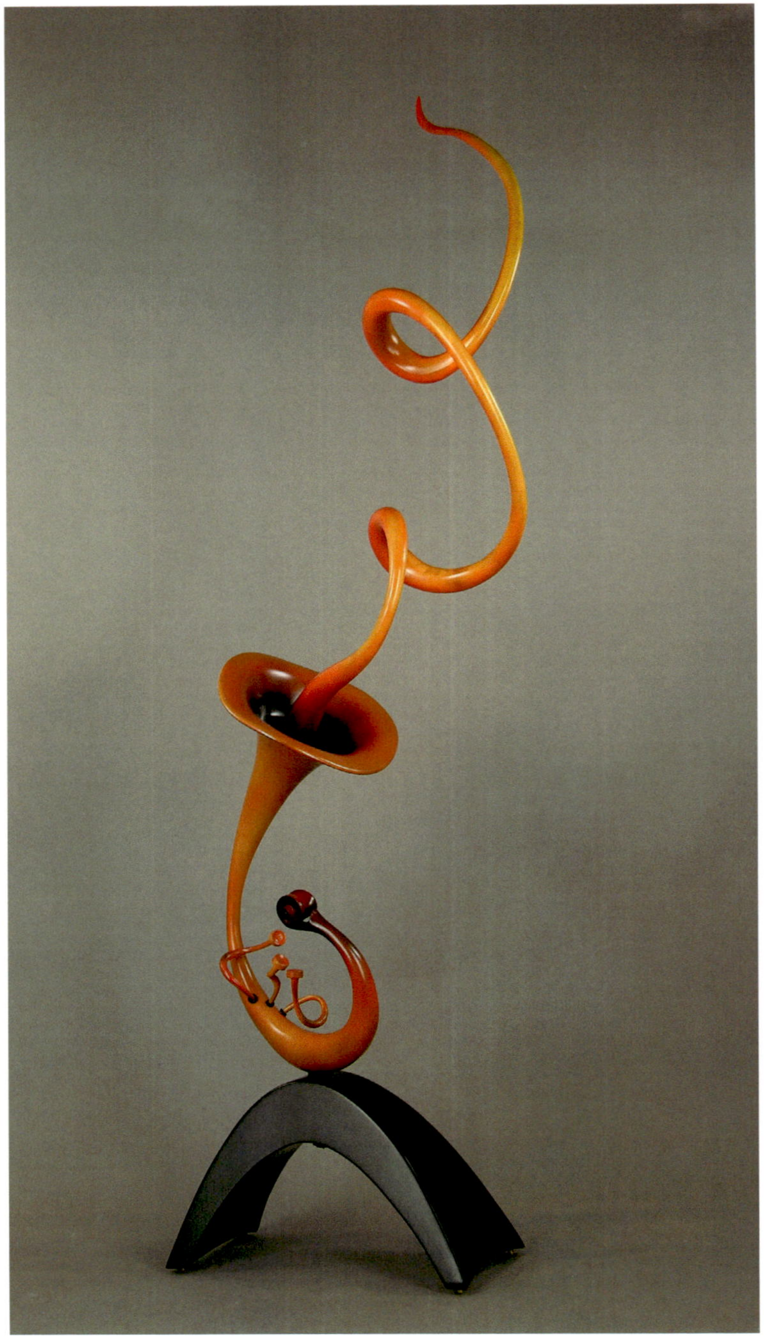

Late Night Solo

Bringing fluidity of form to music emanating from other musical instruments led to the creation of *Late Night Solo*. In this case, I could apply the process not only to the sound coming from the horn, but also to the horn itself. Being a little playful with the subject, I threw in a violin scroll at the bottom where the mouthpiece goes. I take considerable license with shape and never depict an instrument true to form. My musical work is really about presenting the *essence* of music and not the instruments.

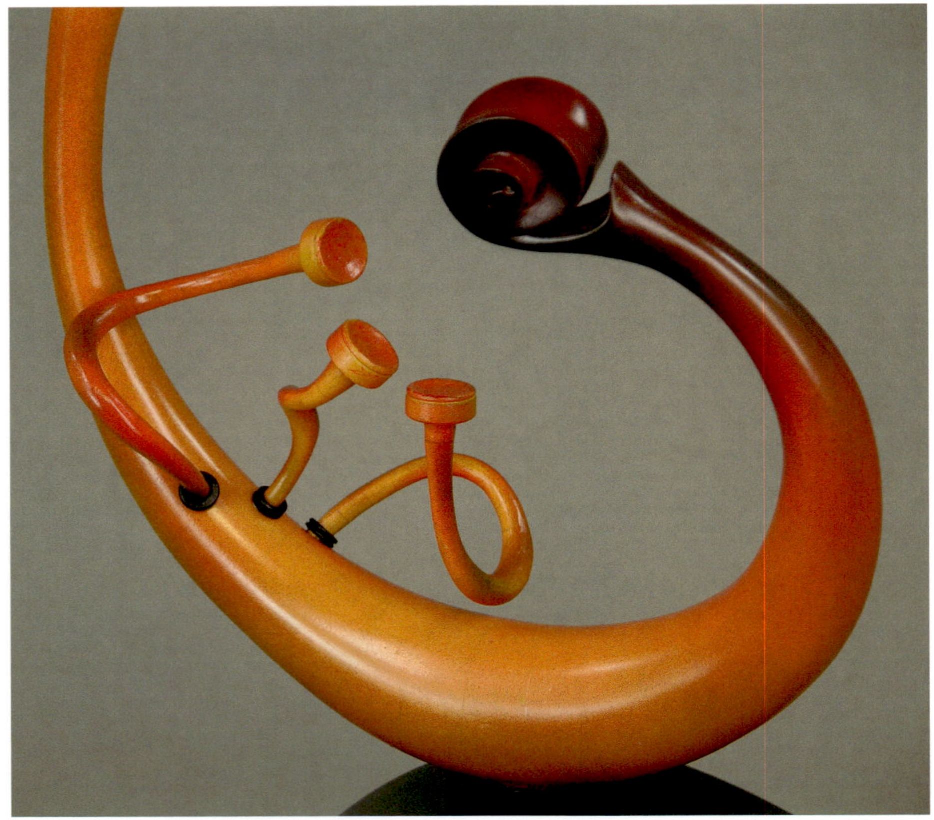

Jerry Bennett. *Late Night Solo.* Yellowheart, ebony, maple, steel, brass, acrylic paint, 42" h x 17" x 11".

Jonathan Benson

Lorton, Virginia, www.bensonfurniture.com

Artist's Statement

My work is both functional and non-functional and is made primarily from wood. I often explore the energy and forces of nature. I am fascinated with hurricanes, thunderstorms, tornados, and earthquakes, and the energy that drives them. I can capture a sense of this energy in a unique way by combining bent and curved pieces of wood and lathe turned elements. My pieces seem to be moving without actually having any moving parts. Wood stays my primary medium because I love the way it works, looks, and the infinite variety of species and grain patterns that naturally occur. I often spend as much time finding, selecting, and determining just how to cut the wood to best utilize the grain, as I do making the rest of the piece, but this to me is as much a part of the hunt as perfecting the design.

Individual Artwork

The Hurricane

The idea for this piece came from my interest in weather systems and how they form. I try to capture the energy and power of nature in my work. I want to bring as much energy as possible to the piece without having any moving parts. I have often incorporated earthquakes, hurricanes, storms, and geologic upheavals into my designs. The actual construction of this piece had to wait until I had the opportunity to develop the proper technique for constructing a curved panel that curves back on itself. I wanted to add several innovative techniques to the traditional techniques. The technique involved placing several thin layers of wood together inside a vacuum bag and the wrapping it around a form.

The wood was also selected and matched to create a motion that brings the viewer's eye into the piece. The turned cylinder of wood in the center of this table forms the eye of the Hurricane. The way the eye is split and shifted adds an unexpected sense of energy that gives a sense that the object may be pulling apart.

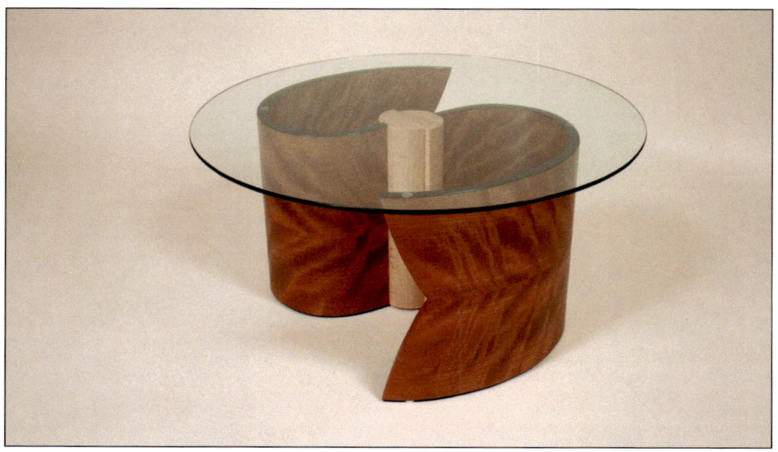

Jonathan Benson. *The Hurricane.* Motteled makore, curly maple with a glass top, 17" h. x 36" d.

The Wave

This piece pushes the boundaries of wood bending. It took a few years and several attempts to find a way to create this shape consistently. This piece was a culmination of a process that stretched over ten years or so of tinkering around when I had the time.

There is a strong sense of motion and energy in this piece. Force seems to be pushing in from the ends to create this "W" shape. There are just a few simple shapes here because I wanted to pare this idea down to its essence. I have made far more complicated tables based on similar ideas that were not nearly as successful as this design.

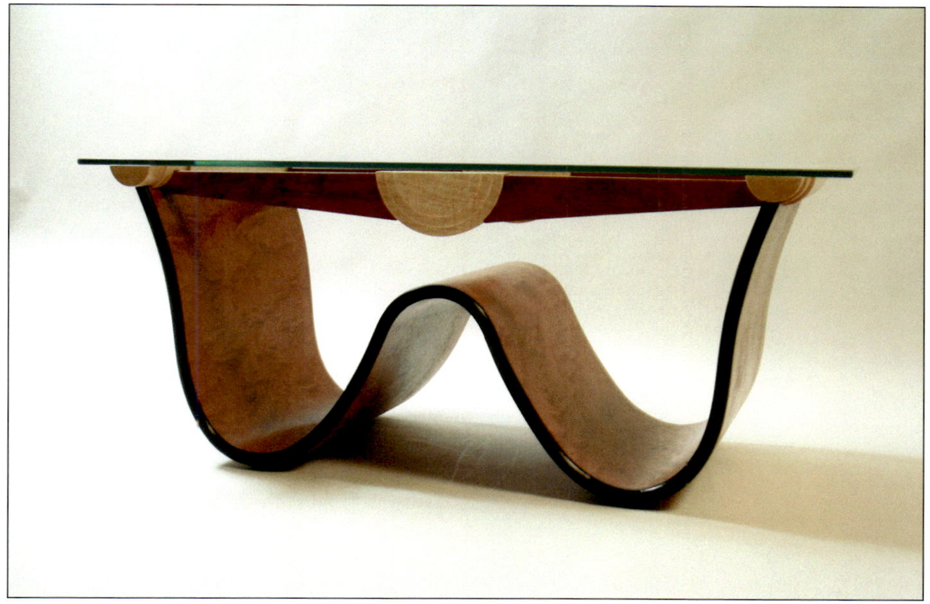

Jonathan Benson. *The Wave*. Waterfall bubinga, curly maple, and glass.

Dixie Biggs

Gainesville, Florida, http://dixiebiggs.com/

Artist's Statement

I grew up with a love of carving and a fascination for working with wood. My interest in woodturning began in 1979 when I taught myself to use a wood lathe so I could duplicate a chess set my grandfather had made. My work has evolved from that initial experience.

Although each piece begins on the lathe, I see this as a starting point for further development. I create the surface of my work using various carving tools, both hand-held and power driven. Often the wood will dictate what surface texture I use.

Having a degree in Agriculture, much of my work incorporates a botanical theme. I find a great deal of inspiration in the shapes, textures, and simple beauty found in nature. My sculptural pieces create a restful place for my turned work. What I strive to evoke in my pieces is a sense of tranquility that a quiet walk in the woods can bring.

I experience a great deal of excitement watching a piece take shape. I never know what I am going to find once I get below the bark of a log. Sometimes there is buried treasure! It is such a thrill when I find unexpected swirls, burls, patterns, and colors. I love finding wood that others have discarded and breathing new life into it. I feel I have accomplished this when someone can't resist picking up a piece of my work and caressing it.

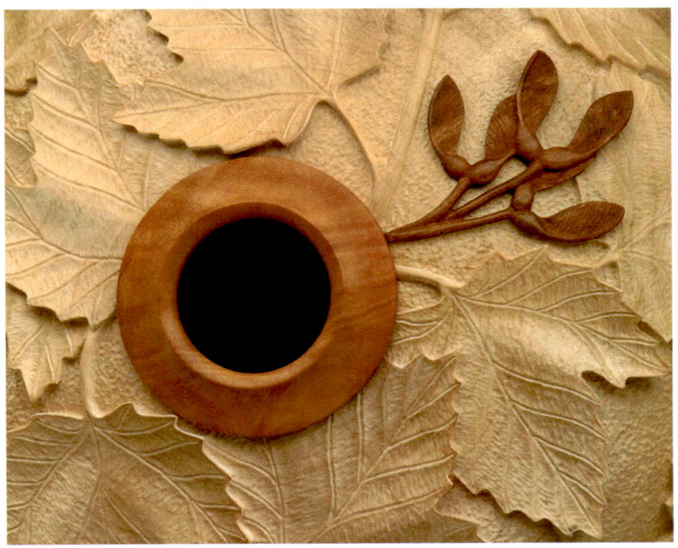

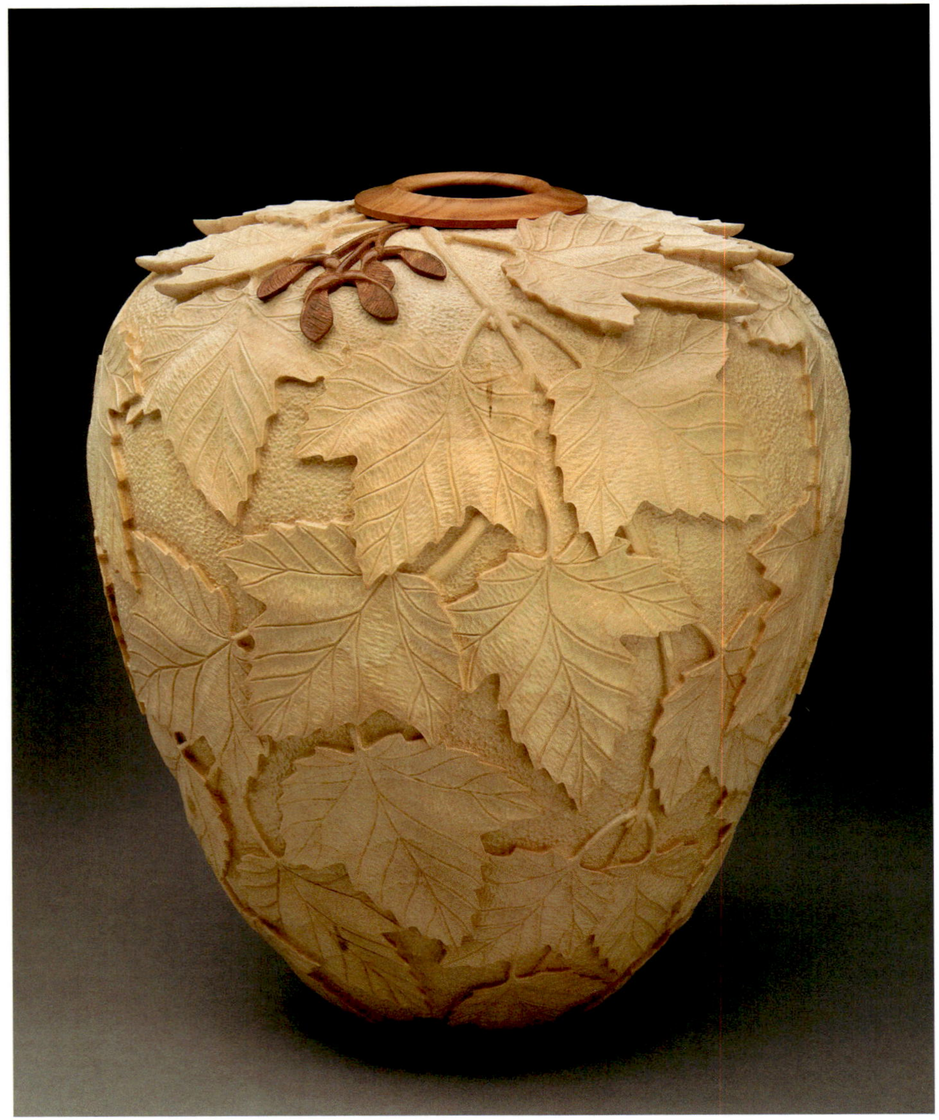

Dixie Biggs. *Between Earth & Sky.* 2007. Open vessel made of maple and madrone, turned and then carved holly vessel and base with a touch of pink ivory berries, 12" h x 10" d. *Photo by Randy Batista.*

The vessel was first turned from a solid piece of fresh cut maple. Once the wood was dry I inset a piece of madrone that would become the seeds. Then the weeks of carving began.

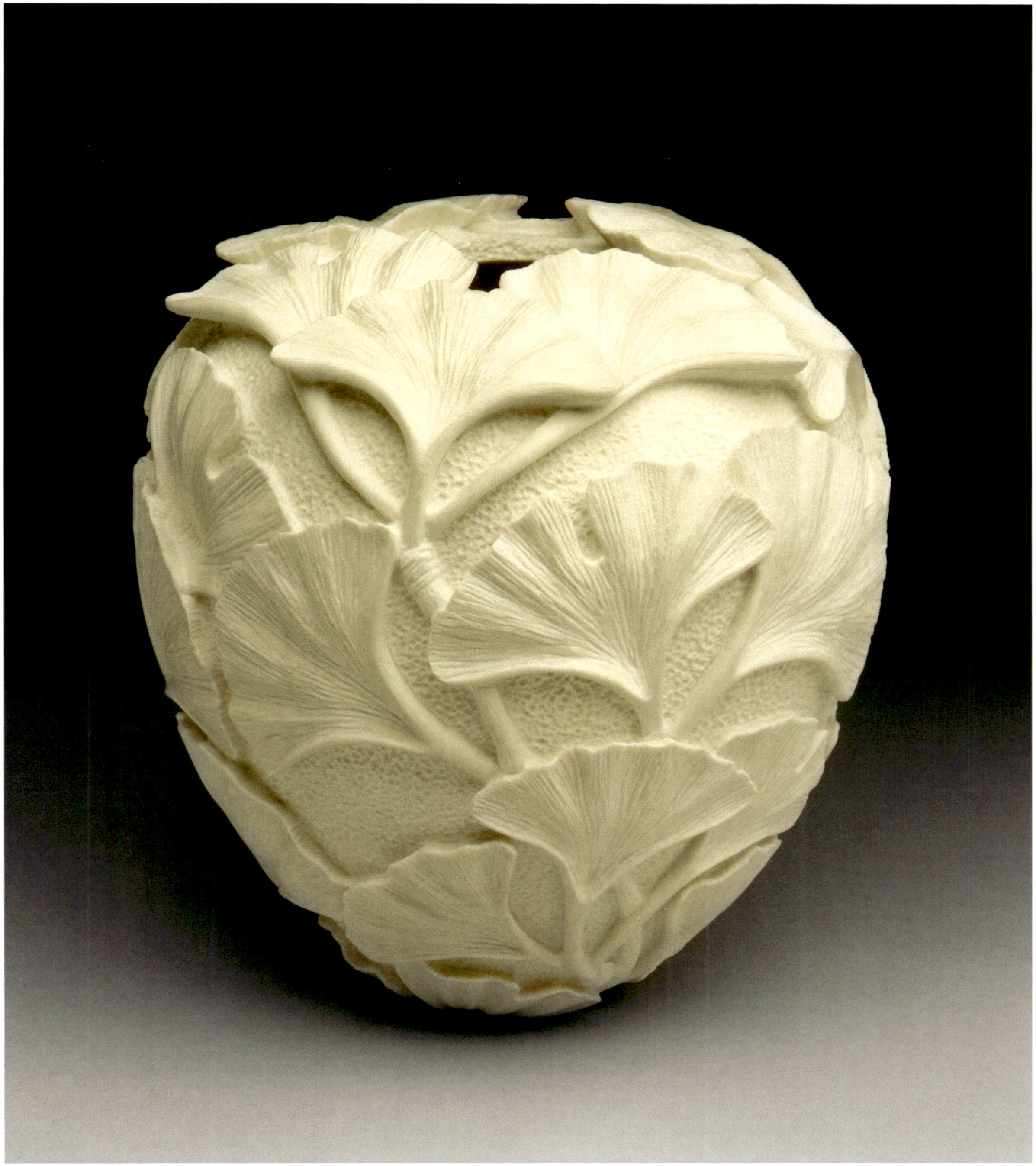

Dixie Biggs. *Harmony.* 2007. Open vessel made from bleached Jacaranda, I first turn the vessel and then once it's dry I do the carving. 6" h x 5.5" d. *Photo by Randy Batista.*
Sometimes my pieces reference the actual trees that supplied the material. In celebration of the essence of the tree I "wrap" the vessels in a protective covering of carved leaves.

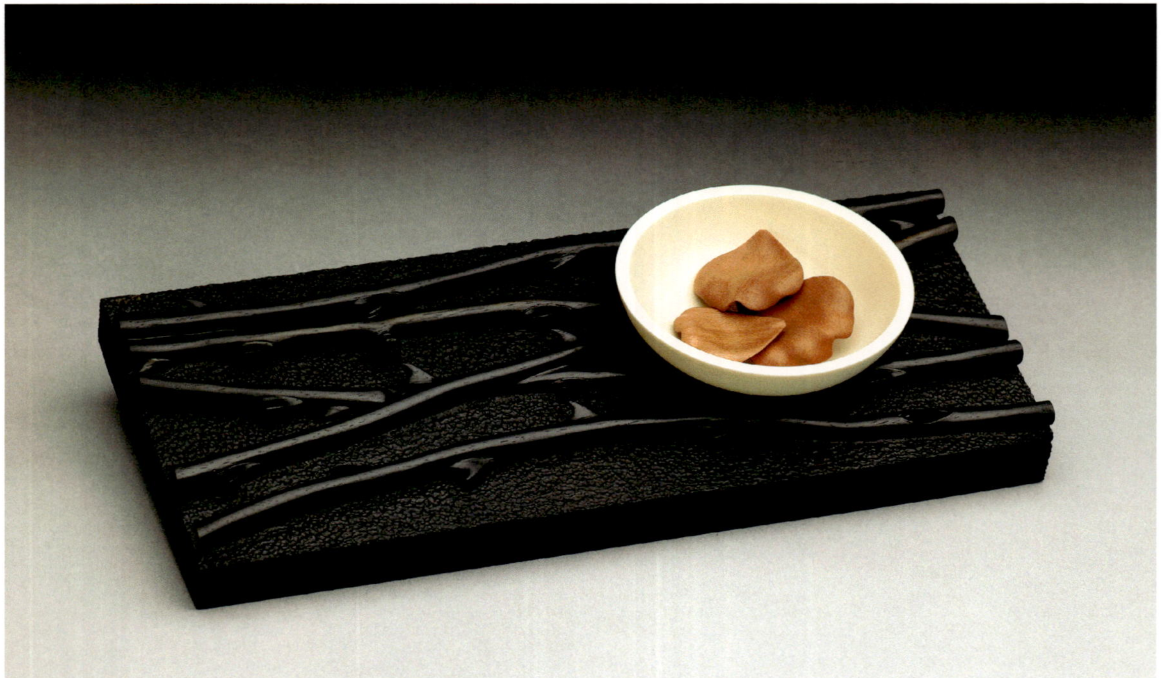

Dixie Biggs. *Petals & Thorns*. 2007. Sculptural piece made from ebony, holly and dogwood, turned holly bowl resting on carved ebony base with carved rose petals made from dogwood, 2" h x 4" w x 9" l. *Photo by Randy Batista*

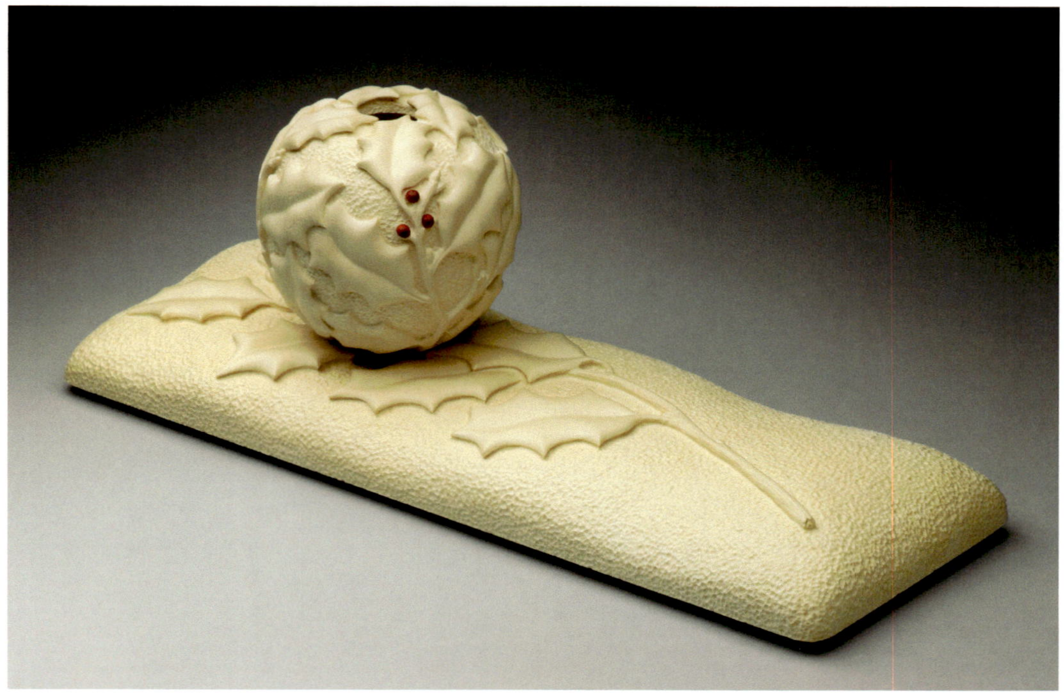

Dixie Biggs. *Winter's Grace*. 2009. Sculptural piece made of holly and pink ivory, 4" h x 4" w x 11" l. *Photo by Randy Batista*

Brian Bortz

Durham, North Carolina, bbortz@yahoo.com

Artist's Statement

A piece of my furniture begins in the design phase, and if it is a commission piece, it is a collaborative effort between the clients and myself. My current work blends vibrant, exotic wood veneers with a hint of the Art Deco era of the 1920s and '30s. If I'm pigeon-holed into defining my style I call it, "Contemporary Art Deco." My "Freeform Marquetry" mixes woods along organic and geometric lines using marquetry techniques for contrast, complement, tone, and color. This technique is most evident in my *River Series* work, which represent a topical view of a meandering river (with an occasional island thrown in!) going through the piece. The rivers all start as drawings on plywood, which are then freehand cut on a band saw or a scroll saw – *no patterns or templates are used* so exact duplication of a piece is impossible, resulting in a truly unique piece of furniture. Mated pairs (such as a pair of side tables) are stacked and cut at the same time, thus producing the same river pattern.

I do not use stains or dyes to change the color of wood; if I'm going for a specific blend of color, tone, and figure I search for woods that naturally have the characteristics I desire. I pay very close attention to color and figure and select the most distinctive pieces to be used in the most visible area of the furniture. My furniture is built with fine, domestic hardwoods, accented by highly figured exotic woods and veneers, creating a piece of furniture that invites attention longer than just a few moments...

All my furniture is made by hand, using only basic power tools – hand tools such as planes, chisels, and scrapers are used daily in my studio. I usually have at least one assistant working with me on larger pieces and performing some of the basic milling and sanding of smaller pieces. I complete all the marquetry work, more complex milling, and all finishing jobs on every piece I create. I use time-tested strong joinery in my work whenever possible. I use a variety of finishing techniques selected to best accent the naturally occurring figure in the wood, with all prominent touchable surfaces being hand-polished to produce a silky feel.

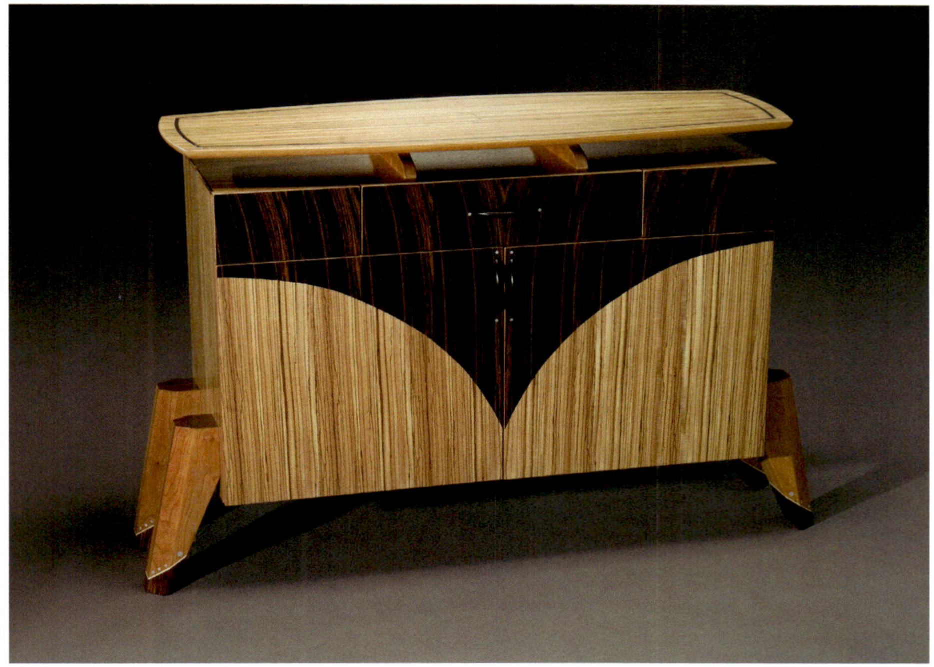

Brian Bortz. Buffet/Entertainment Center 3. 2009. Made of ebony, zebrawood, cherry and white mother of pearl, wood marquetry and shell inlay, 56" x 19 x 36" (L x W x H). *Photographer: Greg Plachta*

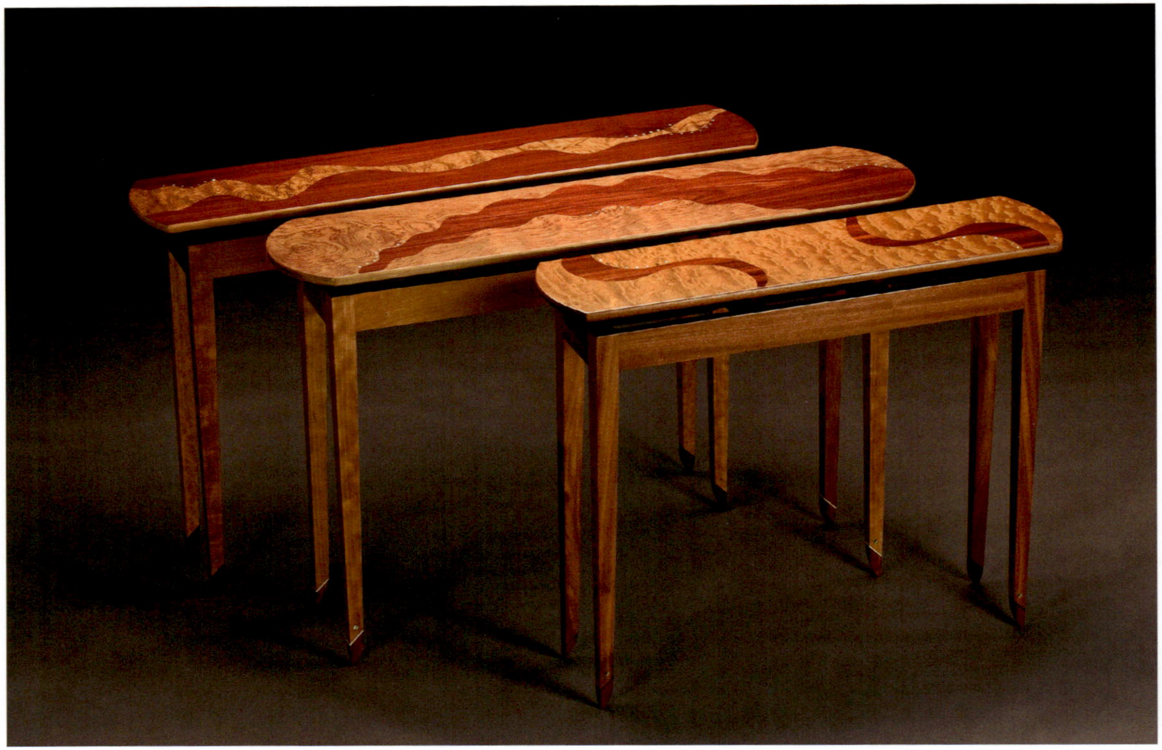

Brian Bortz. Console Tables. 2009. Variety of woods and shell, wood marquetry and shell inlay, measurements variable. *Photographer: Greg Plachta*

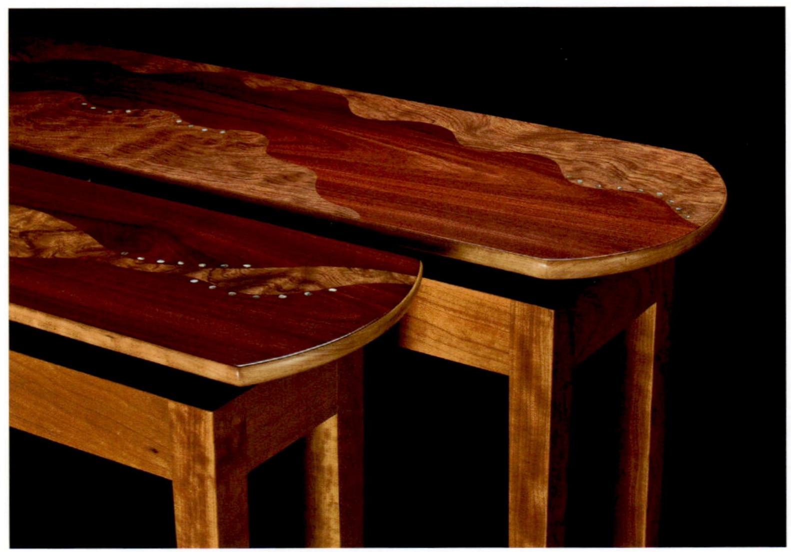

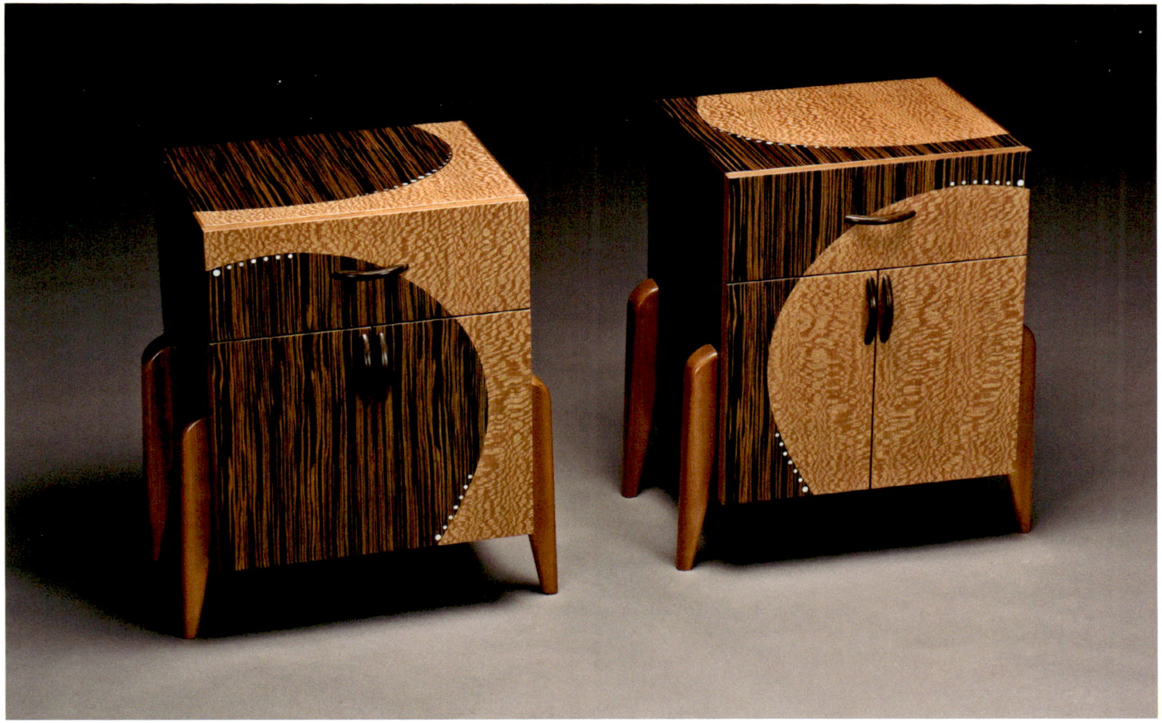

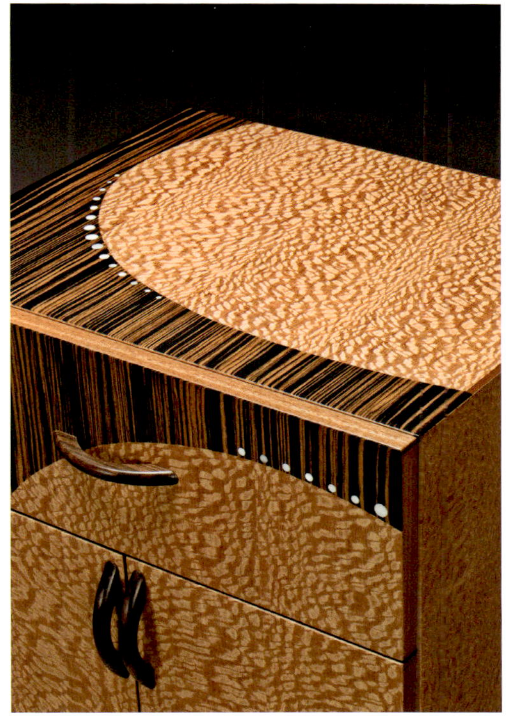

Brian Bortz. Opposition Cabinets. 2009. Made of eco-ebony, lacewood, sapele, and white mother of pearl, wood marquetry and shell inlay, 19" x 15" x 27" (L x W x H). *Photographer: Greg Plachta*

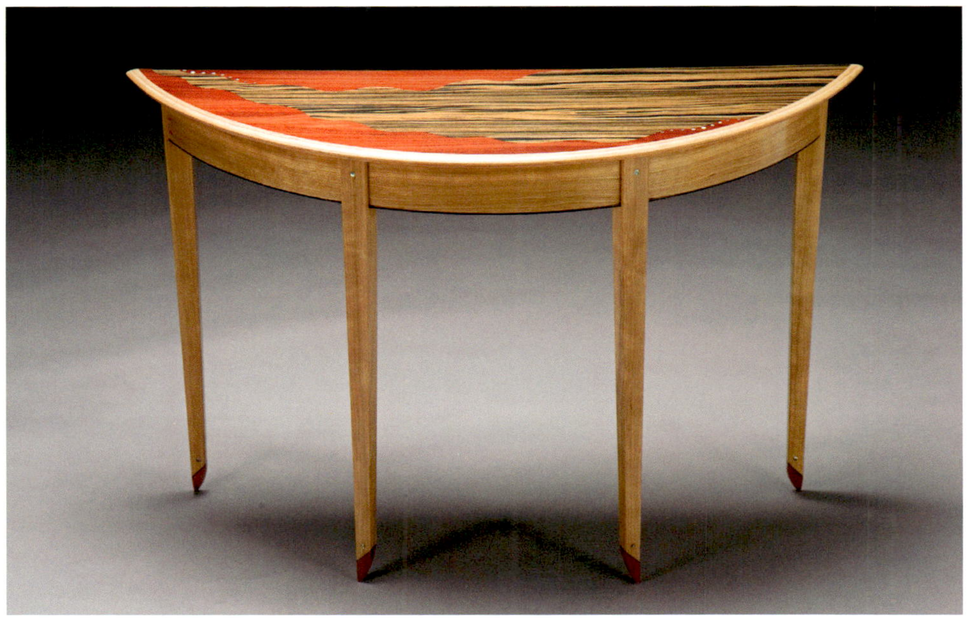

Brian Bortz. Roman Candle Demilume. 2009. Made of eco-ebony, bloodwood, cherry, and abalone shell, wood marquetry and shell inlay; bent laminated continuous piece front apron, 44" x 16" x 30" (L x W x H). *Photographer: Greg Plachta*

Pam Bowman

admin@pambowman.com

Artist's Statement

The rhythms, routines and rituals of life interest me. Repetitive and labor-intensive processes are used in my work to portray the tasks of living, the steady and continual efforts of life. An integral part of the work is the compulsive nature of process – repetitive methods symbolic of memory, ceremony, and ritual.

Materiality is one of the most obvious things about my work. I am attracted to natural materials and fibers – materials that relate to the earth and the lives of women throughout time. The gathering of materials is both intuitive and compulsive, yet the choices are carefully made in order to reinforce concepts and give meaning to the work.

There are also other forces that I blend in my work. Ideals are of necessity tempered by pragmatism. Practiced technical experience must be combined with creativity. My goal is to create installations that blend concepts and materials, ideals and realities, experience and creativity, resulting in the emergence of spirit.

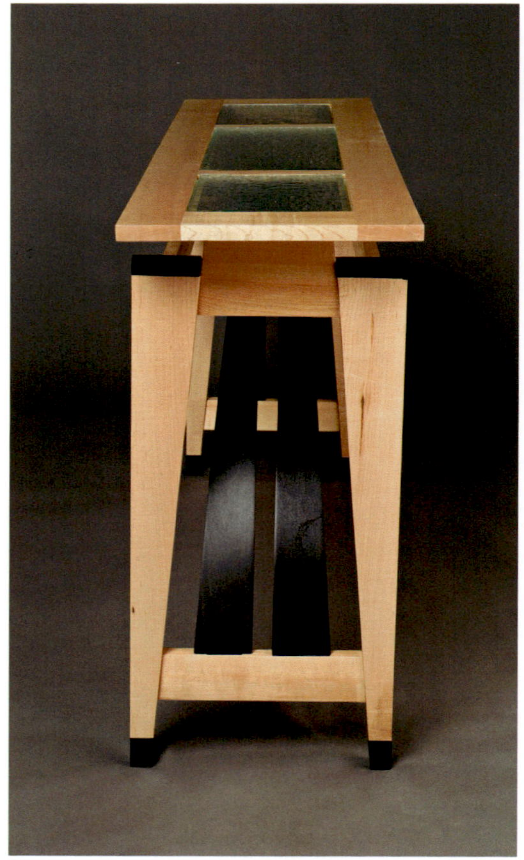

Pam Bowman. *The Color of Water.* 2005. Sofa table. *Photography by Tyler Marshall*

Individual Artwork

The Color of Water

The design of this sofa table, with its deceptively simple curves and angles, is influenced by Modernism. A view from the end of the table shows tapered legs and rails that frame a double arch spanning the length of the table. Above the legs and the arch is negative space that creates the illusion of a floating tabletop.

The table was first designed and drawn using CATIA. Then, it was built with traditional joinery and materials; the table also has roots in time-honored and established woodworking conventions. Mortise and tenon joints are used throughout the piece. The light color of quarter sawn and bird's-eye maple is contrasted with African blackwood caps at the top and bottom of each leg.

Two unique features of the design are the arches and the glass. The double arch in the center of the table was bent on its horizontal axis. This is complimented by a slight curve that was cut into the outside edges relative to the vertical axis. The inside edges of each arch remain parallel to each other.

The tabletop has three panels of inset glass. Three layers of glass were fused together for each panel. By painting kiln wash onto the shelf of the electric kiln, texture was added to the glass while fusing it. The fused glass is artistic in its own right but it also allows a view of the arches below. The combination of creative design with traditional joinery and materials gives this table significant and enduring merit.

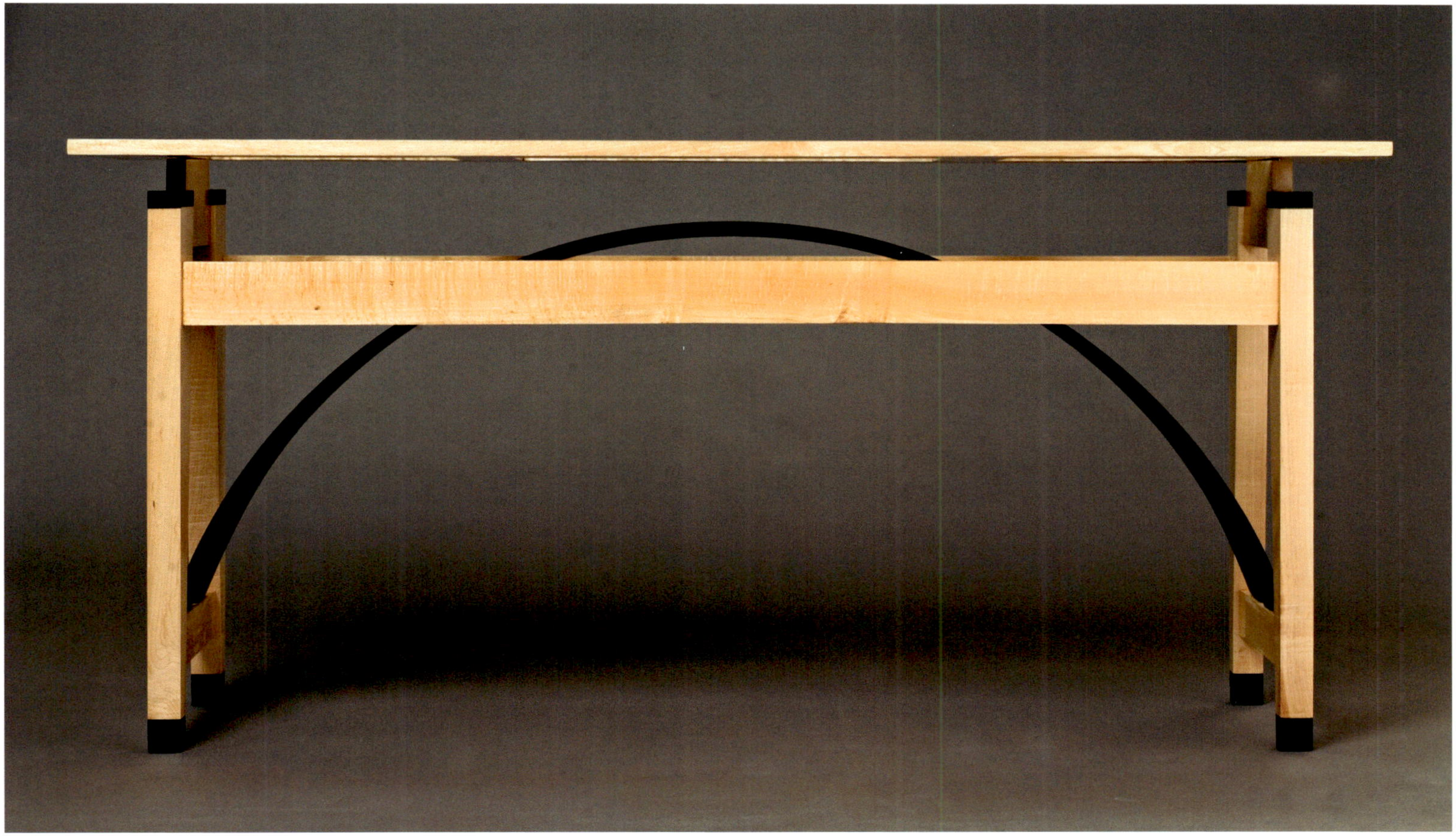

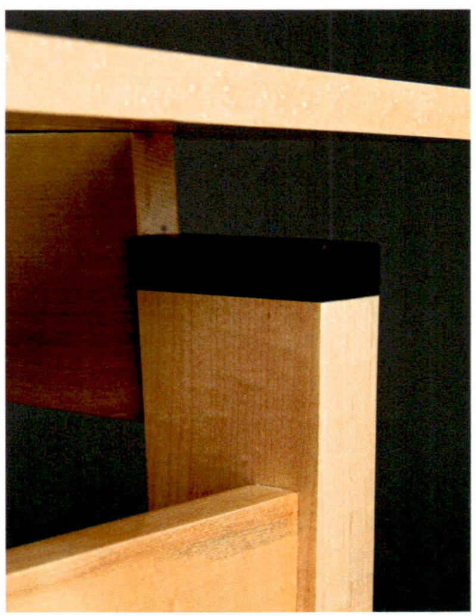

Pam Bowman. *The Color of Water.* 2005. Detail of the blackwood cap on the upper leg. *Photography by Tyler Marshall*

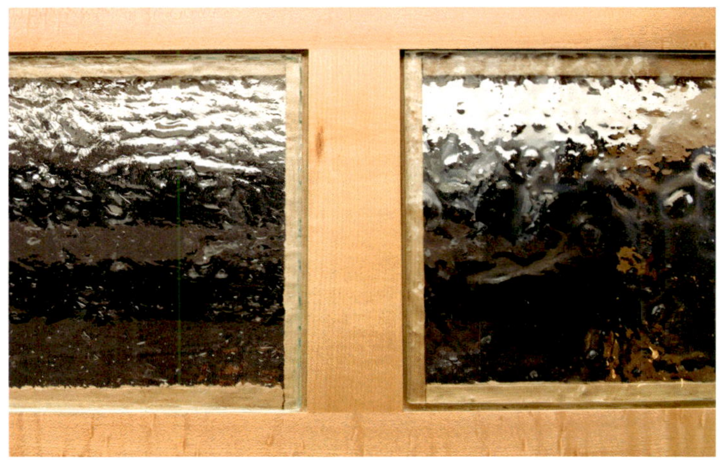

Pam Bowman. *The Color of Water.* 2005. Detail of the fused glass top. *Photography by Tyler Marshall*

Michael Brolly

Philadelphia, Pennsylvania, brollywood@aol.com

Artist's Statement

Michael Brolly is a woodturner/sculptor who creates a wide range of artwork, including whimsical sculptures, and works with children in the woodshop at Moravian Academy. Brolly's work is imbued with a sense of wonder, and humor, that is accessible to a diverse audience.

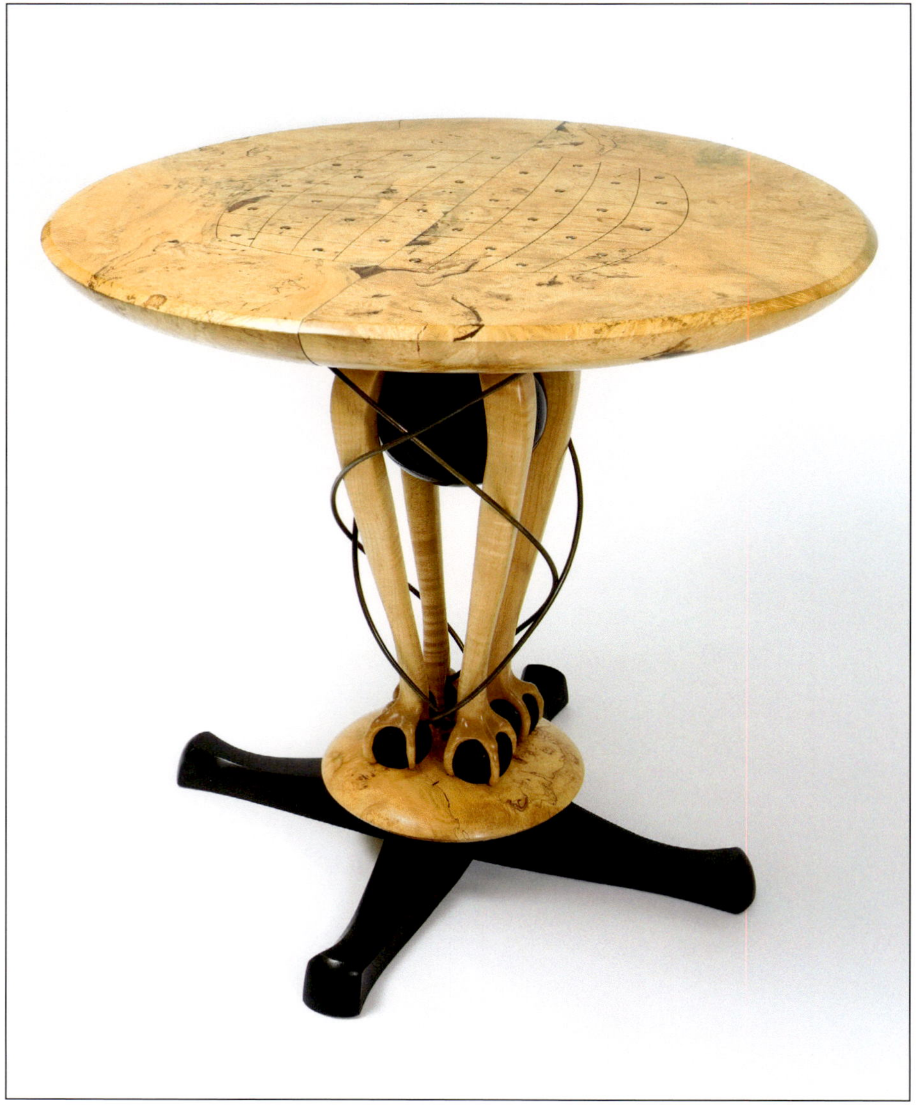

Michael Brolly. Game Table. 2003. Wood, turned and carved, 32" d. x 31" h. The top is maple burl with a lazed engraved morphed Chess Board with 1/2" d. bronze pins marking alternating squares. The large ball underneath is glass and the spiraling stabilizers are 1/2" bronze rod. The ball and claw feet rest on an ebonized mahogany cross brace. (right and opposite page)

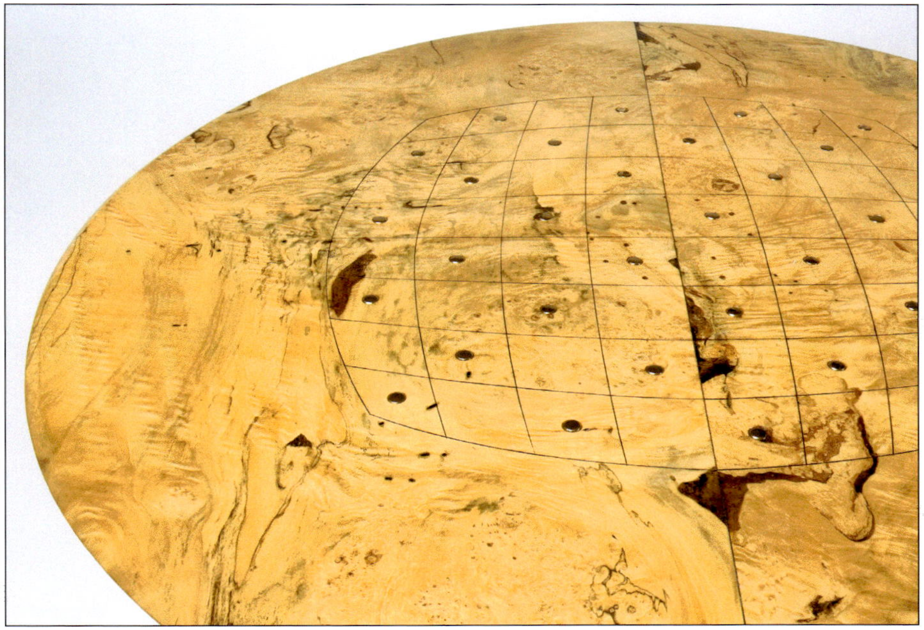

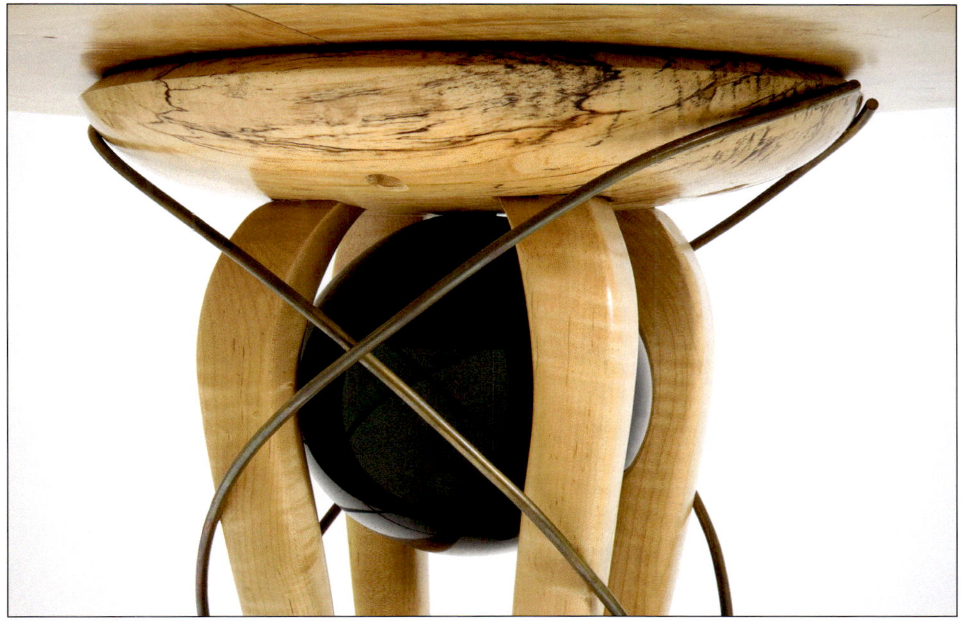

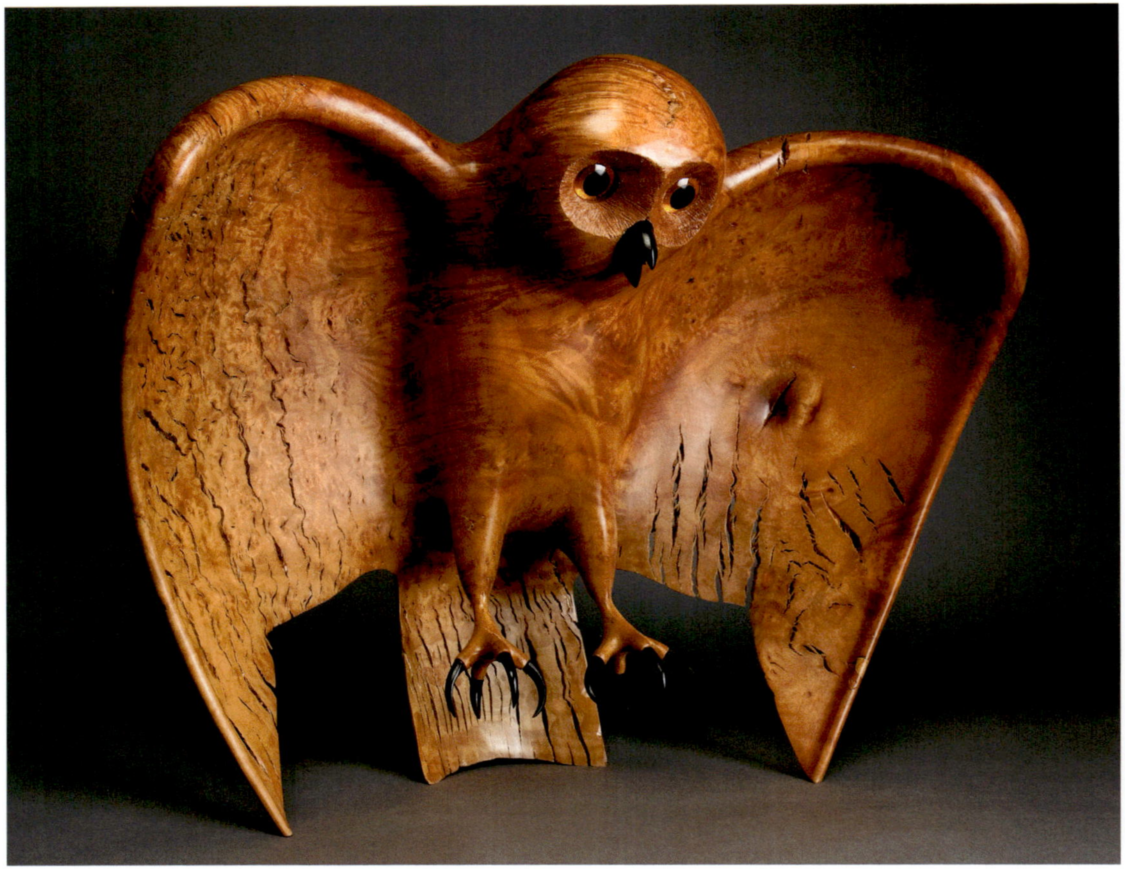

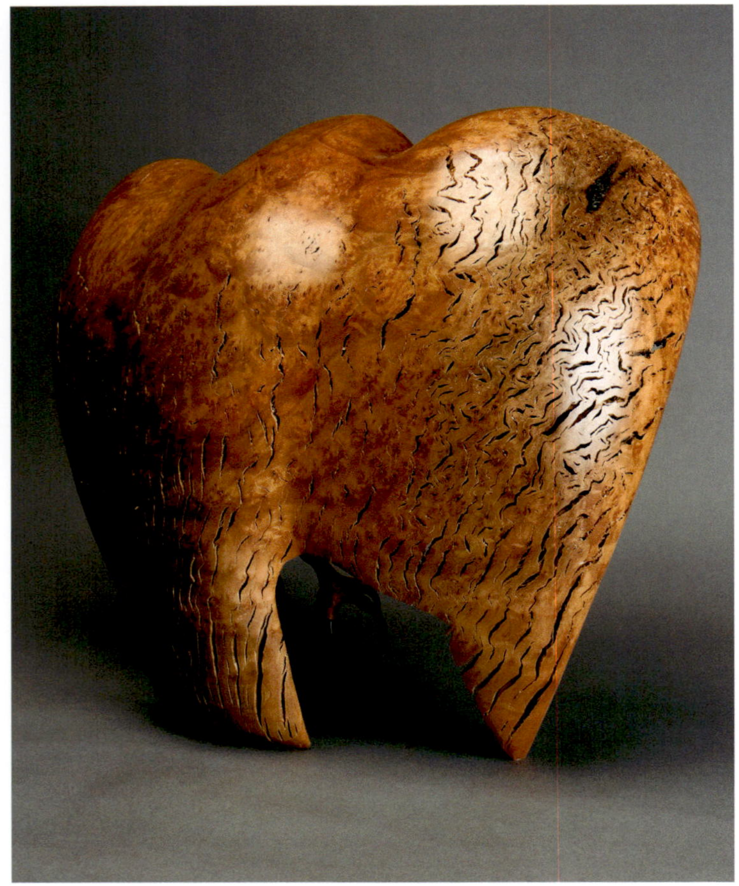

Michael Brolly. Owl. 2005. Wood, turned and carved, 20" w x 19" h x 8" d. Eyes are light gathering plastic with ebony pupils and 23 K gold leaf (for reflecting the light back out). Talons and beak are also ebony and the body is improperly dried madrone burl. *Photographer: Donna Chiarelli*

Christian Burchard

www.burchardstudio.com

Artist's Statement

I find my self much intrigued by the wild and expressive possibilities that working with wood that is highly unstable offers. My process is experimental, unpredictable.

I use wood from the roots of the madrone tree, which grows in the Northwest. I strive to let its history and energy be part of my work. Transforming, reducing, abstracting.

Comparing it to black and white photography, I remove the color and focus on the spirit, the essence of the objects. I treasure their quiet simplicity.

Individual Artwork

Wood

I work just about exclusively with Pacific madrone from the Arbutus family. My favorite parts are the burls that grow within the roots of these trees. They are harvested for the veneer market and I use the rejects from this harvest.

These burls often weigh many thousands of pounds. To be able to use them, the dirt and rocks have to be removed; then they can be cut into useable blocks.

By working with wet wood with a high water content (up to 20% of its volume) and by cutting or turning my forms very thin (to about an 1/8th of an inch), I take advantage of and encourage the changes that occur as the wood dries. As the water evaporates and leaves the cells and the space between the cells, the wood shrinks. Depending on how those cells were aligned in its structure, some very dynamic changes occur.

Tools

I work with a variety of tools. The chainsaw is used for most of the wood preparation, but also for sculptural pieces. Here the marks that are left are dramatic and forceful. The lathe is used for round forms, mainly in a series I call "Baskets." Tool marks here are subtle and soft.

In my current series of wall sculptures, called 'Fragments' and 'Torsos' I work with the band saw and a horizontal band saw mill to cut large blocks of madrone burl into very thin panels. The saw leaves subtle lines across the surface of the wood. I dry these panels slowly over a period of weeks, sometimes months, in a controlled environment, allowing them to take on their final shape, while minimizing the chances of cracking.

Surface

When they have finished drying, I sandblast and bleach them. The sandblasting cleans and softens them. Like a lot of my other work, I bleach the panels white to expose what is within. I compare this to Black and White photography. I remove most of the color to simplify, to focus on the structure and the undulations and textures that occurred through the drying process.

Sometimes it feels obvious how a particular panel wants to be used, at other times it takes me a while to read it, feel it, ask what it wants from me, so that I can do my part. Many are discarded.

I mount these thin slices of wood on the wall. At times, I display them as single objects, but mostly I assemble them into larger groups, all cut from the same block of green wood. I am interested in their interactions and the spaces between them. I enjoy the way their shapes and textures flow together and create a whole. When mounted and with proper lighting, beautiful shadows appear on the wall, extending the form in varying degrees of grey.

Baskets

In the *Baskets* series, I use a very simple form turned on the lathe in varying sizes, turned very thin to let the wood speak at its fullest. The movement of the wood during the drying is contained by this simple form. Each basket is different from the next. Here too, tool marks are left. Edges are burnt. Sometime the wood out of the actual root system of the madrone tree is used, resulting in extreme distortion. By displaying them in multiples in varying sizes, I create families, relationships.

Nature

To be working this closely with nature is a blessing, but also often overwhelming. It is a struggle. At times I find myself needing to put my foot down, to control the outcome of my work, only to find that I trampled something beautiful. At other times I feel overwhelmed, scared: What is needed here of me, how can I match the beauty of this living thing? How am I to know when to be loud and when to be quiet?

Panels

When I am working with the panels, I am looking for certain patterns – patterns that are know to us, from nature, landscapes, maps or bodies and birds. I want a pattern or image that elicits a visceral response. How come a piece of wood is looking like a torso or the flight of birds?

When the image is quiet enough to have some space for me, it becomes a canvas and I can add to or change the direction of the energy.

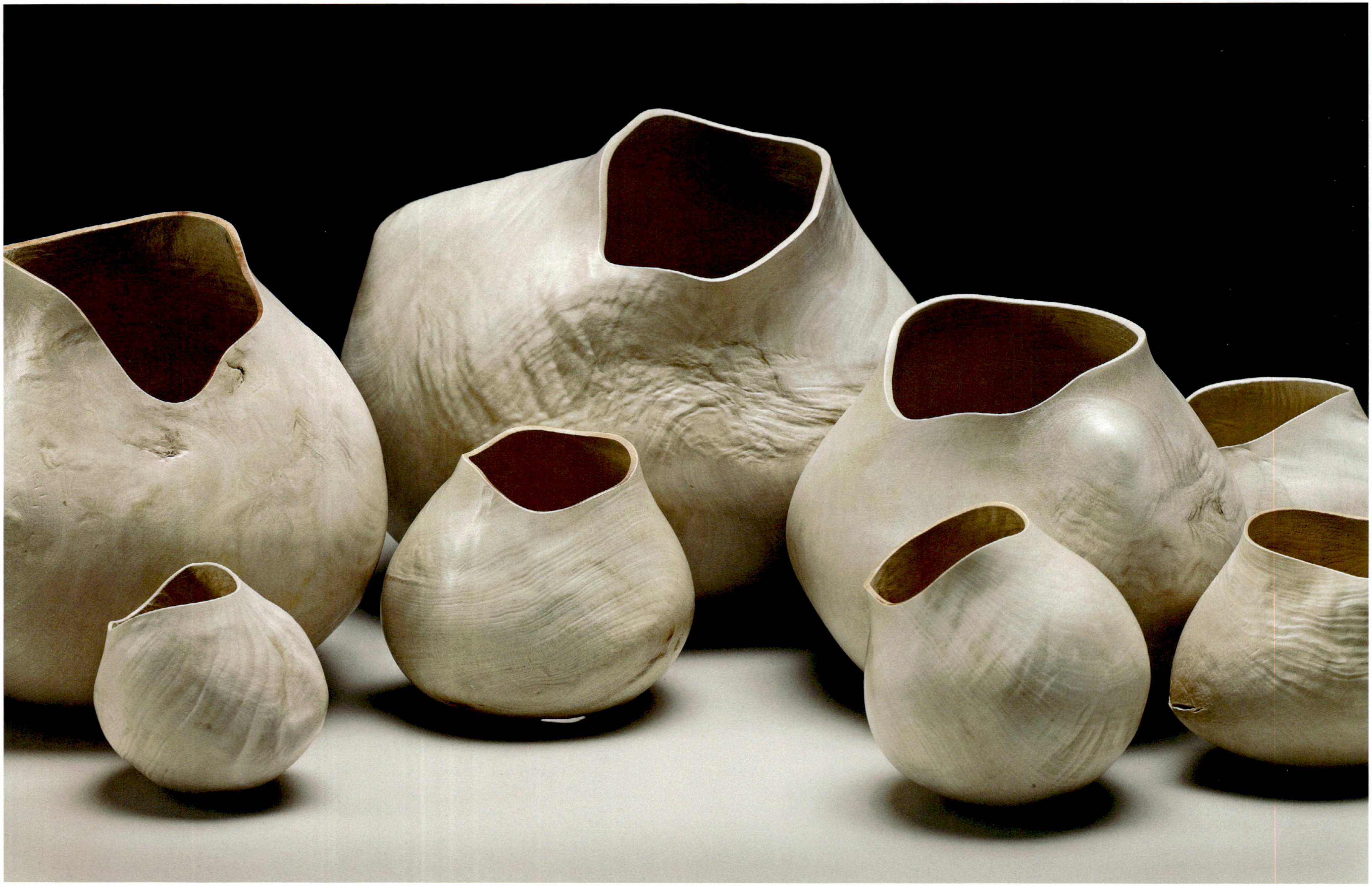

Christian Burchard. *White Basket Group.* 2006. Bleached madrone burl, 13" to 2" d.

Christian Burchard. *Rocks & Trees #5*. 2008. Bleached madrone burl, flat and hollow forms, 15" x 17" x 7".

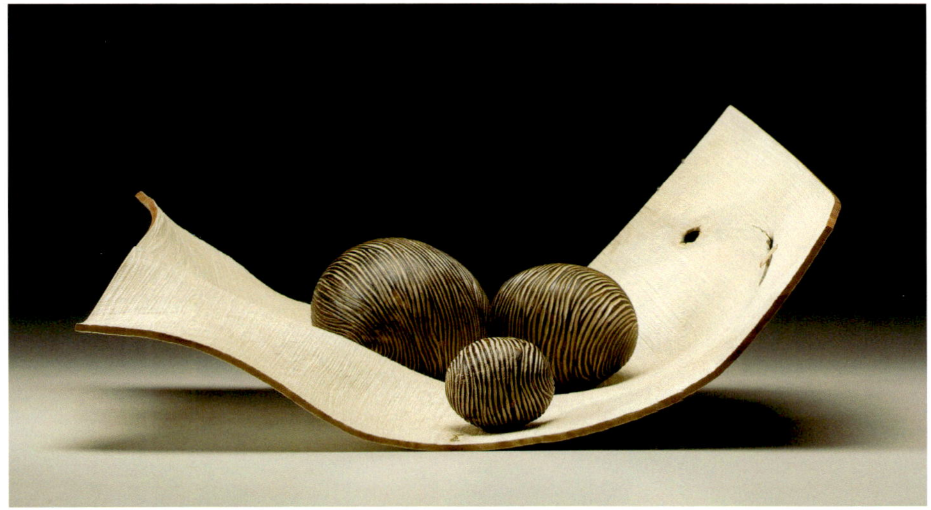

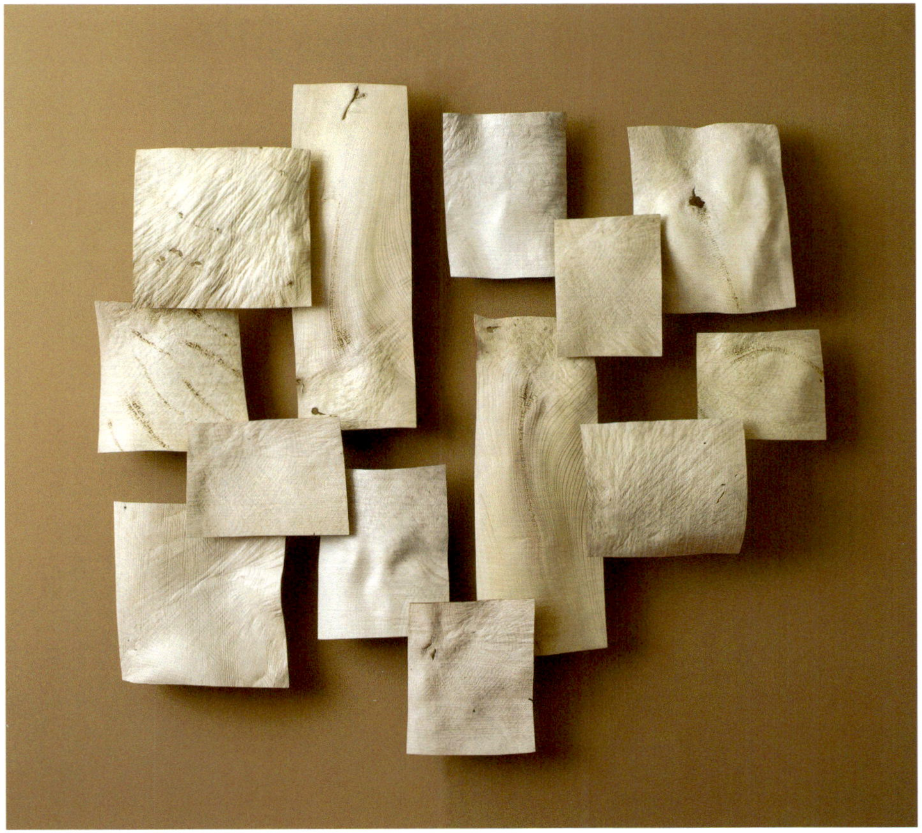

Christian Burchard. *Memories of Moments of Intimate Connections.* 2008. Bleached madrone burl, 58" wide x 54" tall x 7" deep,

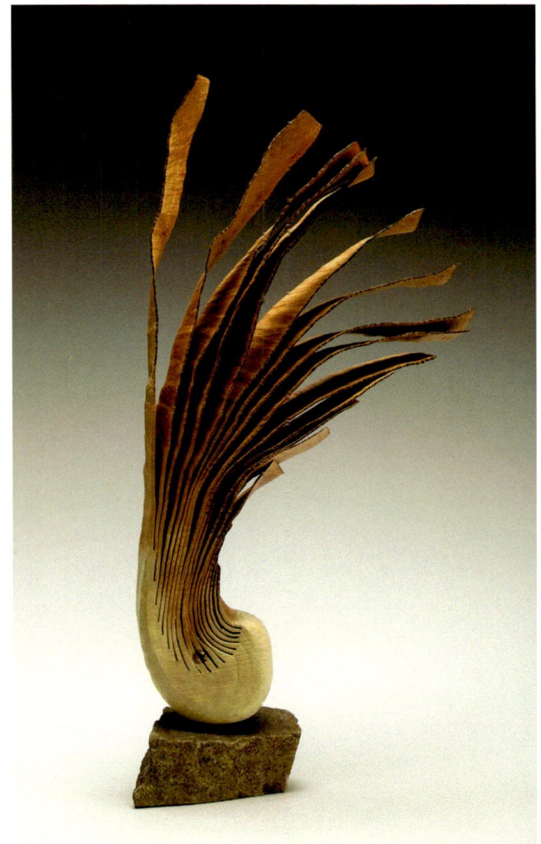

Christian Burchard. *Wrestling with the Riddle #2.* 2009. Madrone burl, 30" x 6" x 8".

Tom Calhoun

www.worldwoodworks.com

Artist's Statement

Tom's search for meaning in life carries over into his daily woodworking. Finding the proper balance between design and the inherent beauty of wood requires conscious effort. The process can start with the physical labor of felling and milling trees into usable lumber, and continues through design, execution, and finishing; he has been known to produce pages of sketches in the process of refining and engineering an initial inspiration, "My work is deeply satisfying because it is a craft that keeps me physically, mentally, and aesthetically active."

The use of limited and diminishing resources of indigenous Hawaiian woods requires an effort to remain "pono" (which roughly translates as "correct behavior"). This has developed into an involvement in protecting and encouraging the survival of native plants, thereby helping the Hawaiian Culture to also continue, which, in turn, led to a major role in the restoration of *Mo'olele"*, Maui's forty-three foot double hulled sailing canoe during the mid-1990s.

Individual Artwork

The two *Series Nexus* pieces are number 4 and 5 of a series I started in October of 2008. The nexus refers to the ancient belief that trees were the connecting point between earth, water, and the heavens.

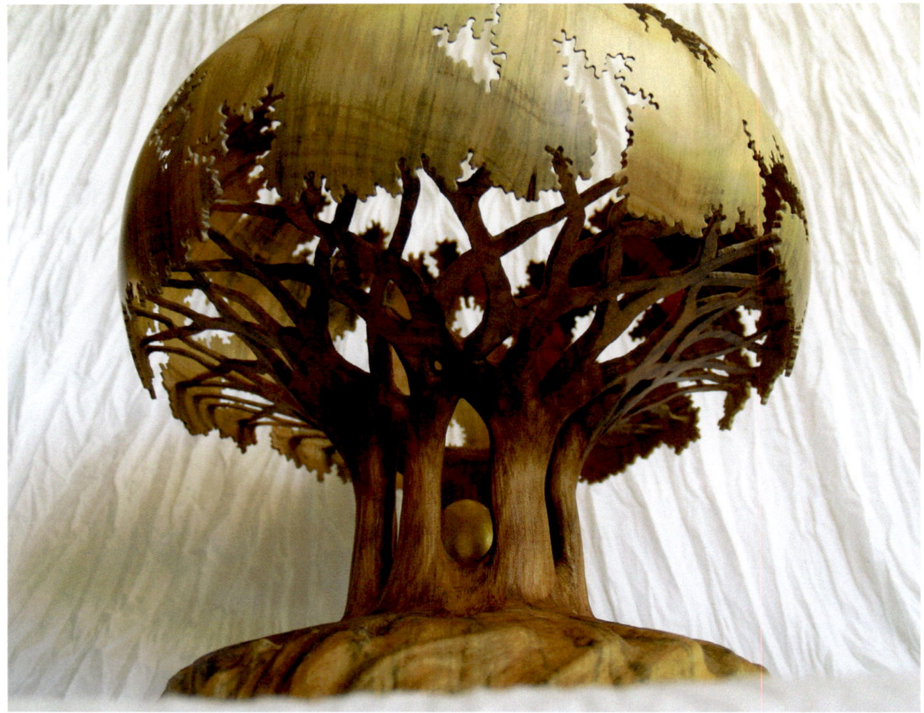

Tom Calhoun. *Nexus 4* is subtitled *The Tangled Roots of the Bodhi Tree.* It is made of Norfolk pine, turned and carved, with an egg cast in epoxy resin and gilded with 22K gold leaf, 16" d x 15" h. (above and opposite page)

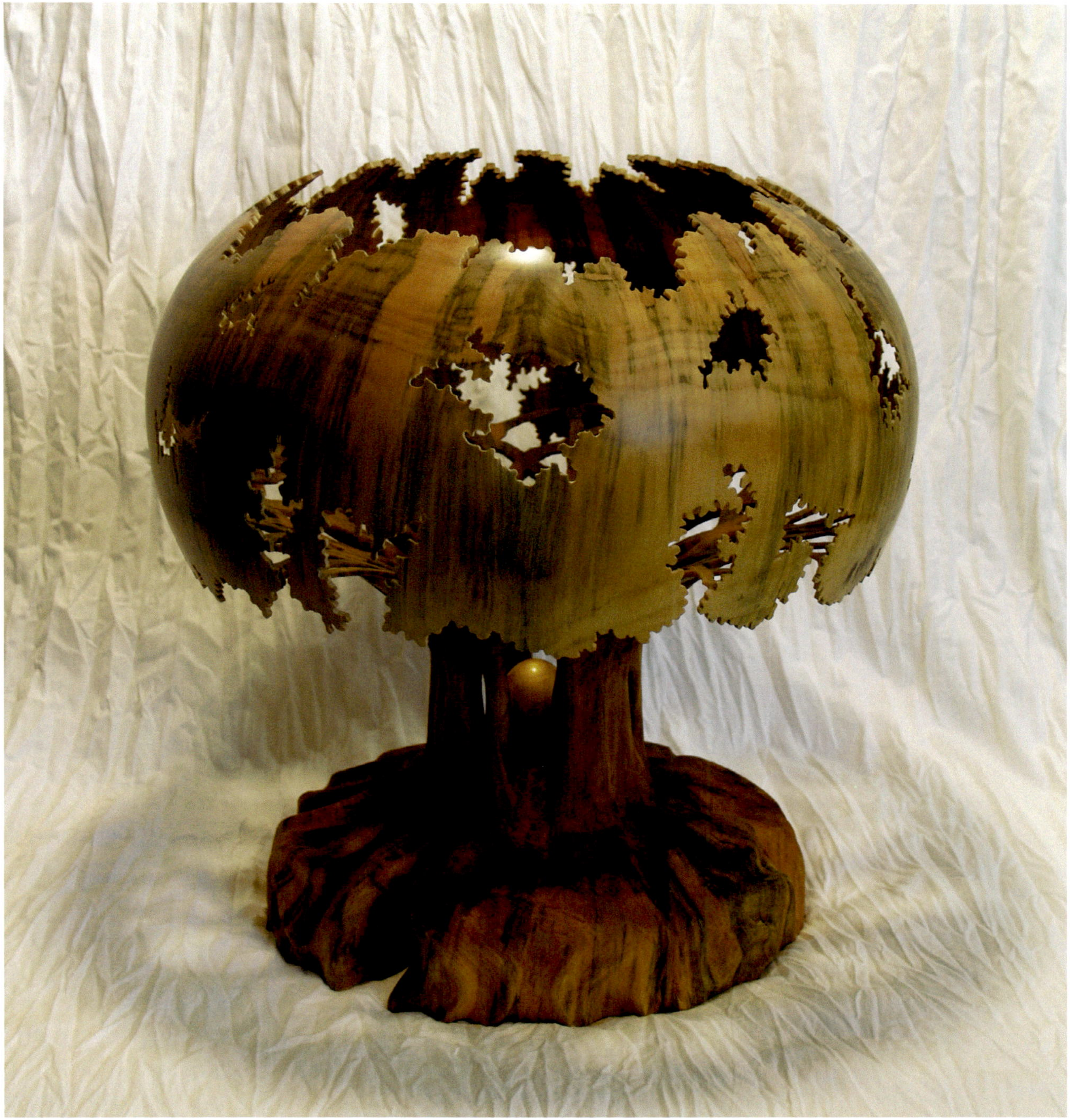

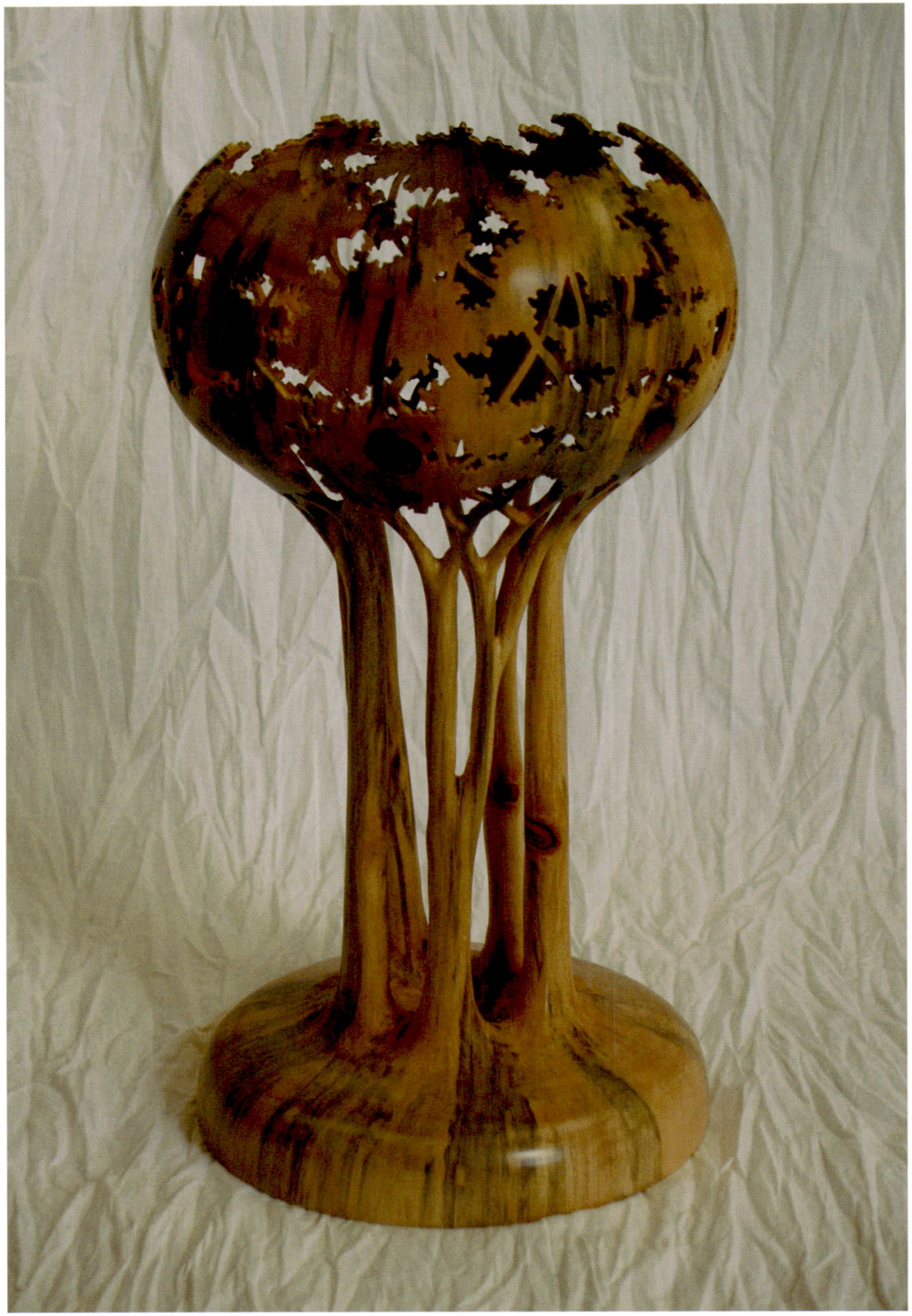

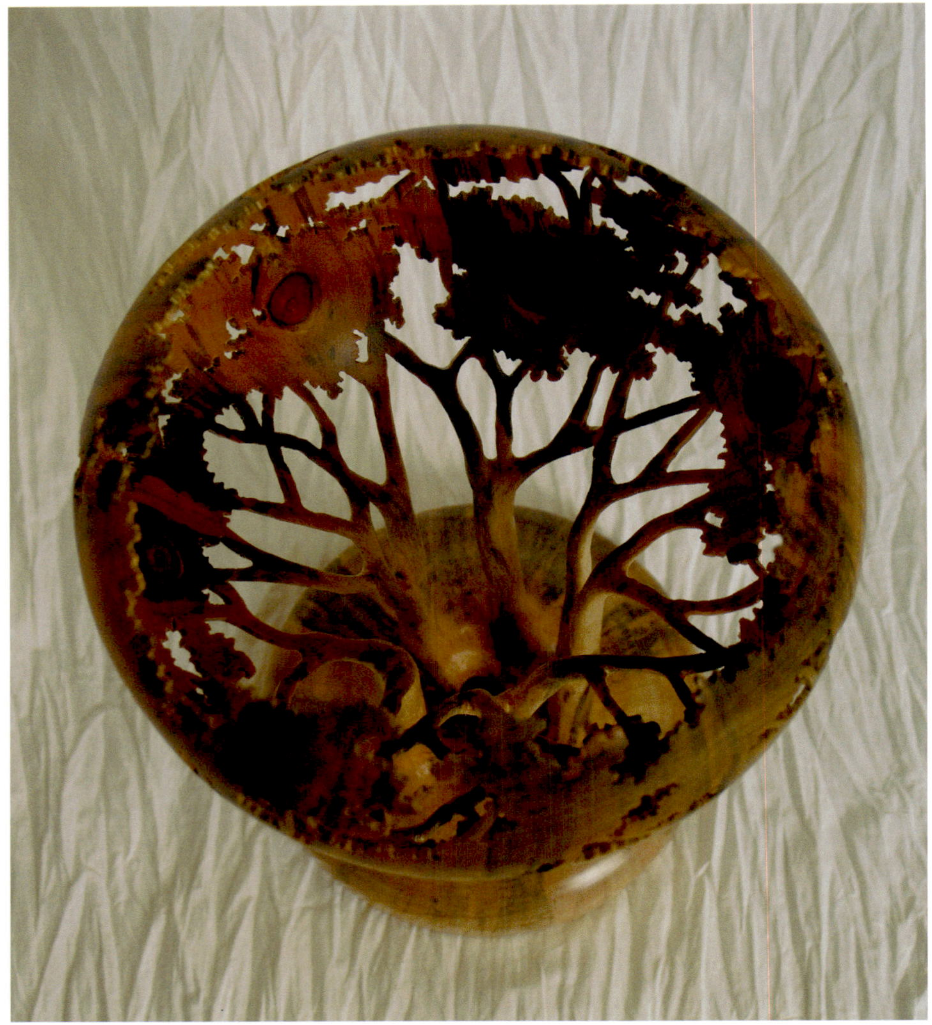

Tom Calhoun. *Nexus 5* is subtitled *Along the Apian Way*, and was my homage to the umbrella pines that are so common along this ancient Roman roadway, turned and carved Norfolk pine, 9 1/2" d x 18" h.

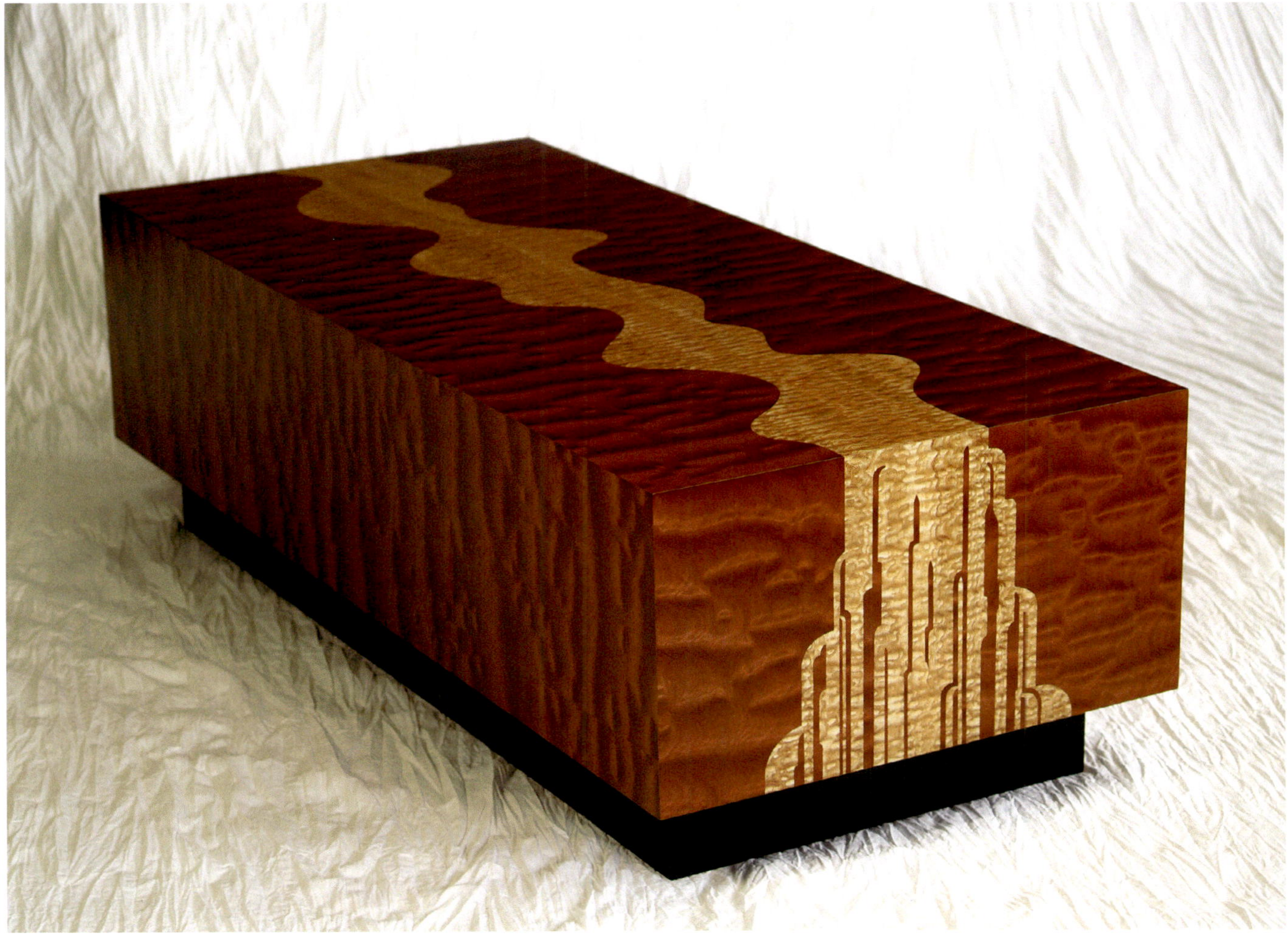

Tom Calhoun. *Waterfall,* 22" w x 51" l x 16" h.

Waterfall was my foray into bringing a little Art Nouveau movement into what is basically an Art Deco style piece, albeit very clean and modern. The waterfall ends were somewhat tedious, but the real challenge was cutting the tamo ash "river" into the makore with the huge quilt. The switchback curves preclude the use of "machine" methods as they always result in some amount of offset, so all of it had to be cut by hand, complicated by the use of such highly figured veneers.

Marilyn Campbell

Ontario, Canada, www.marilyncampbell.ca

Artist's Statement

Although nature has long been an inspiration, I have in recent years become interested in bringing a more classic, cultured look to my vessels. The current black and white series began with a book of vintage and contemporary handbags. I felt the bold designs and strong geometrical elements shown in the bags would work well in the split vessel form, using line, contrast, and texture to create the compositions. As the series developed and both the vessels and stands evolved, the pieces began to take on aspects of human forms, of clothing and fashion. My intention is for the vessels to evoke images of grand social events set back in an era when elegance and style were the cultural ideal. I want the viewer to think of the golden age of Art Deco, tuxes, tails, top hats, and formal gowns. Although similar in format, each vessel is different and named to reflect the "personality" I see in it.

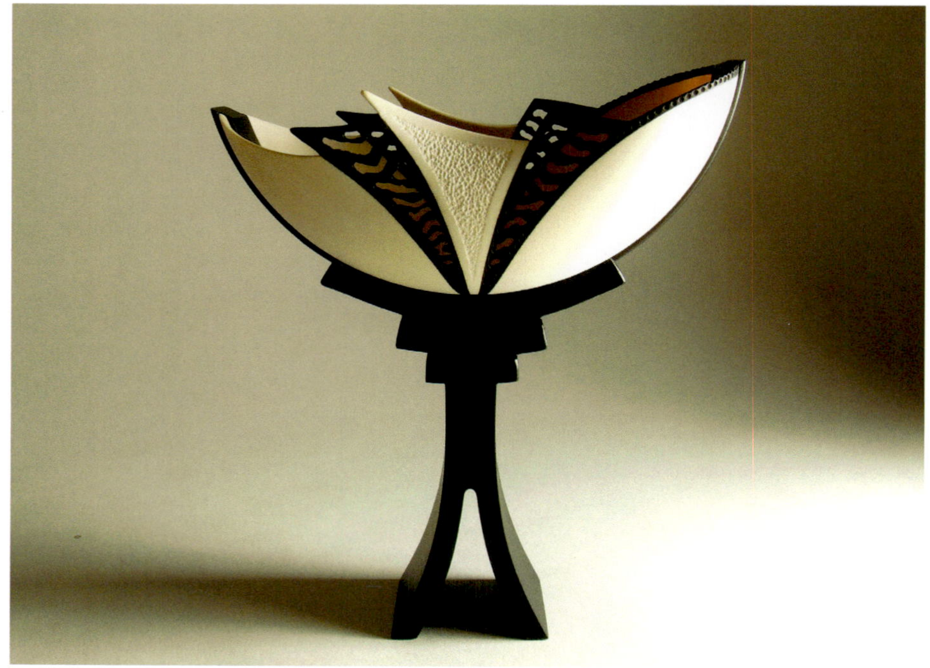

Marilyn Campbell. *Bon Vivant.* 2008. Split-bowl turning, resin inlay, vessel: holly, epoxy, paint; stand: purpleheart, epoxy, paint, 6 1/2" h x 5 1/2" w x 2 1/2" d.

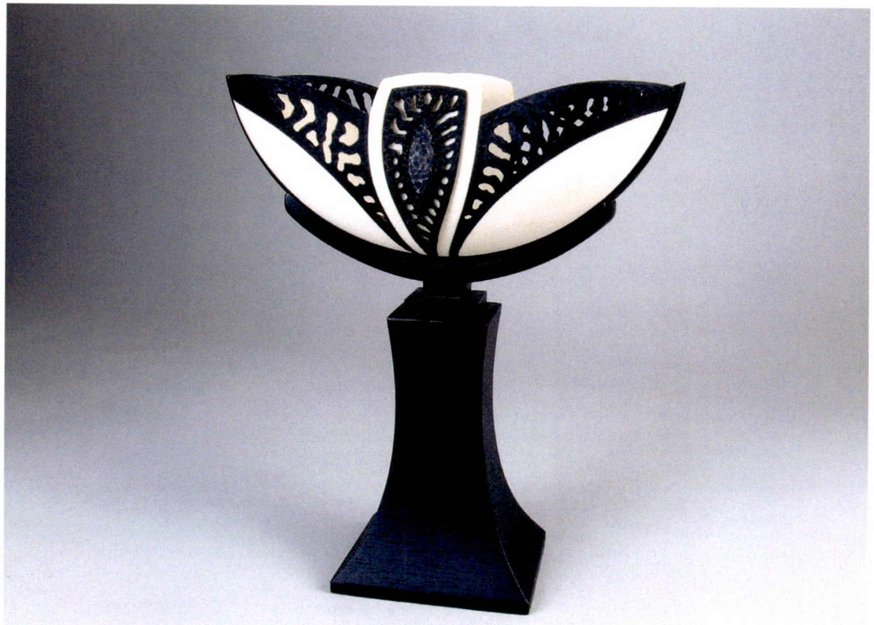

Marilyn Campbell. *Cameo.* 2008. Split-bowl turning, resin inlay and overlay, vessel: holly, epoxy, paint; stand: purpleheart, epoxy, paint, 6 3/4" h x 5 1/2" l x 2 1/2" d.

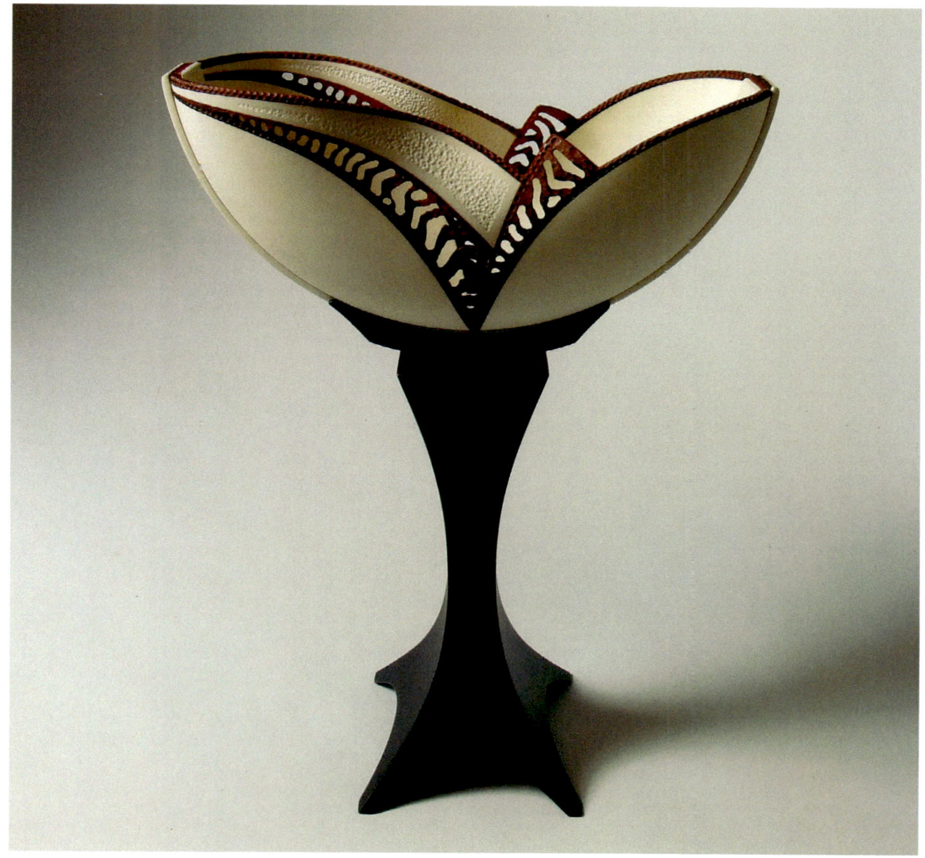

Marilyn Campbell. *The Red Queen.* 2009. Split-bowl turning, resin inlay, vessel: holly, epoxy, paint; stand: holly, epoxy, paint, 8 1/4" h x 6" w x 2 1/2" d.

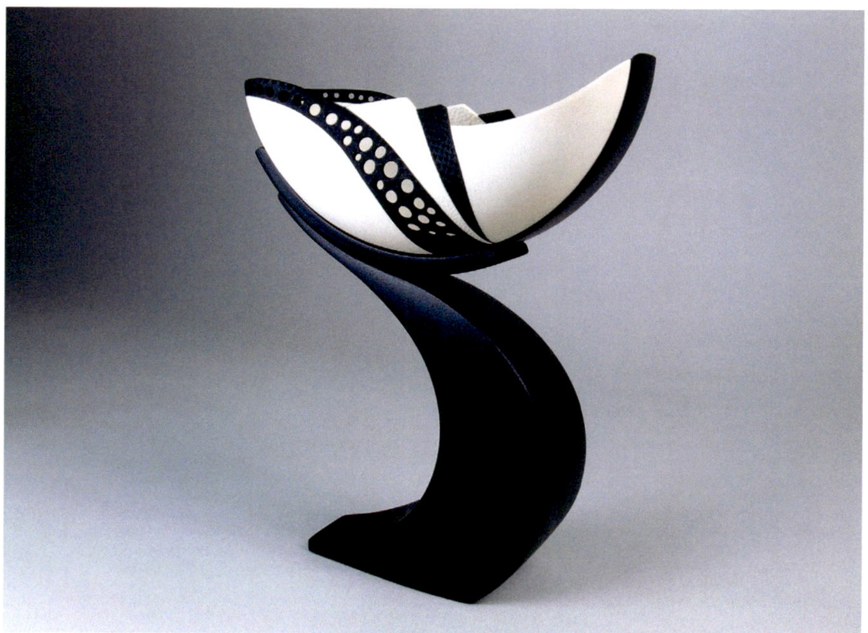

Marilyn Campbell. *Coquette.* 2008. Split-bowl turning, resin inlay, vessel: holly, epoxy, paint; stand: purpleheart, epoxy, paint, 7 1/2" h x 5 1/4" w x 2 1/2".

Christopher W. Cantwell

Oakhurst, California

Artist's Statement

I use well over 100 species of wood and about a dozen kinds of shell from around the world. I am best known for my unique inlay techniques. I also include carving, constructing, turning, and many other techniques to get the forms I want. The colors of the materials in the works are natural. I work to bring out the best in the beautiful, natural materials I work with. I usually start with a concept of my own that grows and changes as a work gains a life and voice of its own.

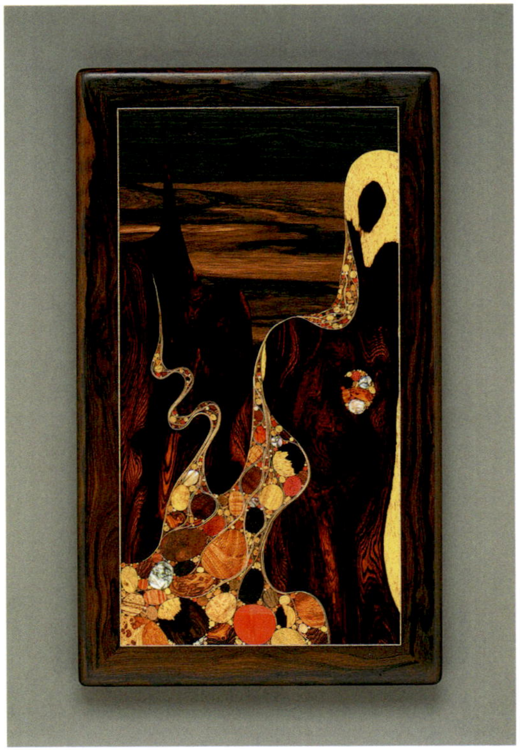

Christopher W. Cantwell. *Snow Melt. Series #15.* 2001. Ziricote, parakingwood, ebony, wenge, cocobolo, tulipwood, walnut, Macassar ebony, purpleheart, granadillo, maple, zebrawood, satinwood, ambonia burl, pink ivorywood, verawood, snakewood, pau ferro, chakte kok, abalone shell, partridgewood, bocote, ziricote, black bull hoof, flamewood, African blackwood, Palo Escrito, paua shell, 8" x 14" x 1". *Photographer: George Post*

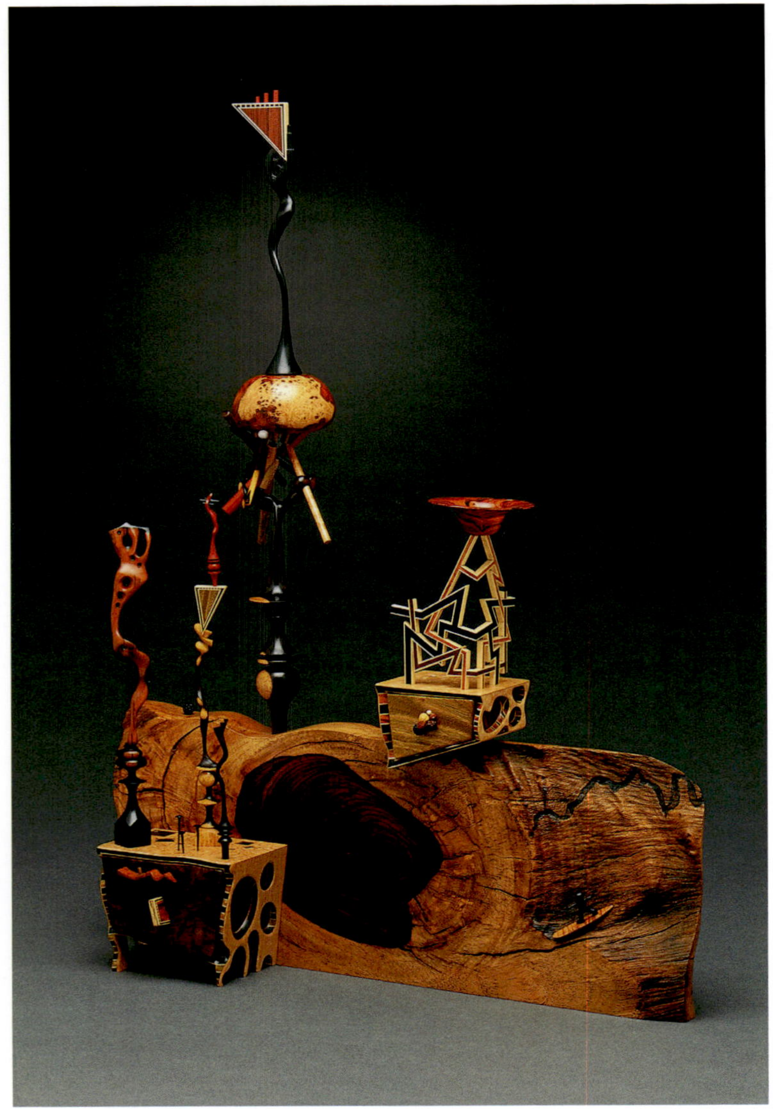

Christopher W. Cantwell. *Trinity.* 2001. Nicaraguan rosewood, walnut, ambonia burl, verawood, tulipwood, parakingwood, Macassar ebony, ebony, maple, pink ivorywood, snakewood, partridgewood, koa, black bull hoof, African blackwood, 15" x 4" x 18". *Photographer: George Post.*
This piece is about the Holy Trinity and contains my testimony as a Christian; so, if you see me at a show, ask me about it.

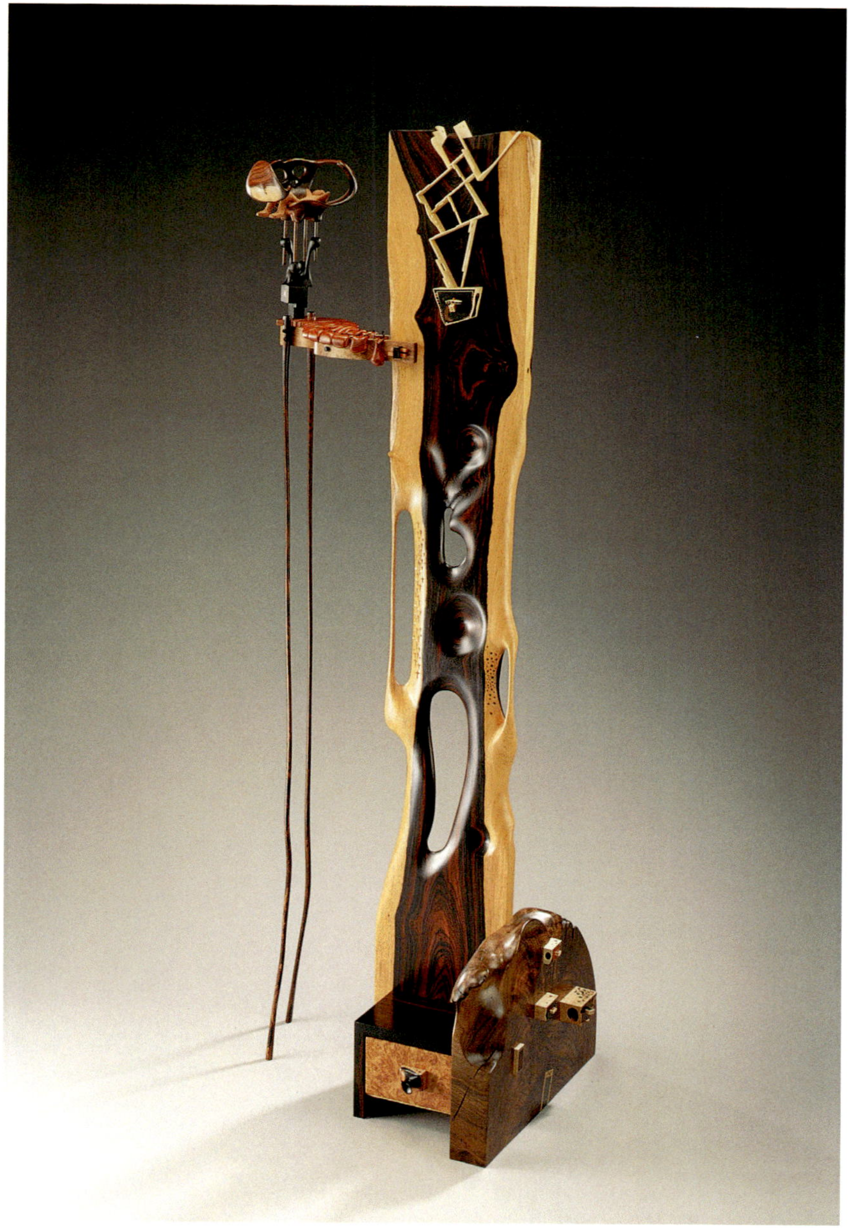

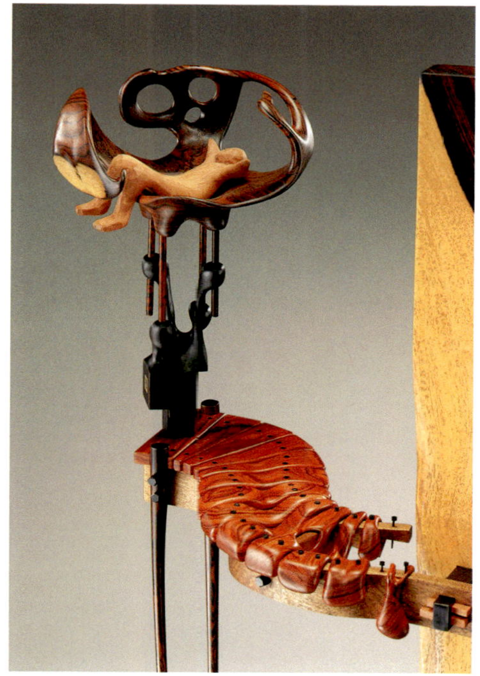

Christopher W. Cantwell. *Walk.* 2002. Cocobolo, walnut, Macassar ebony, amboyra burl, Brazilian kingwood, Mexican kingwood, tulipwood, ebony, black acacia, holly, chakte kok, African blackwood, rosewood, birch plywood, pink ivorywood, maple, purpleheart, felt, screws, red oil paint, pau shell, 61" x 21" x 17". *Photographer: Hap Sakwa*

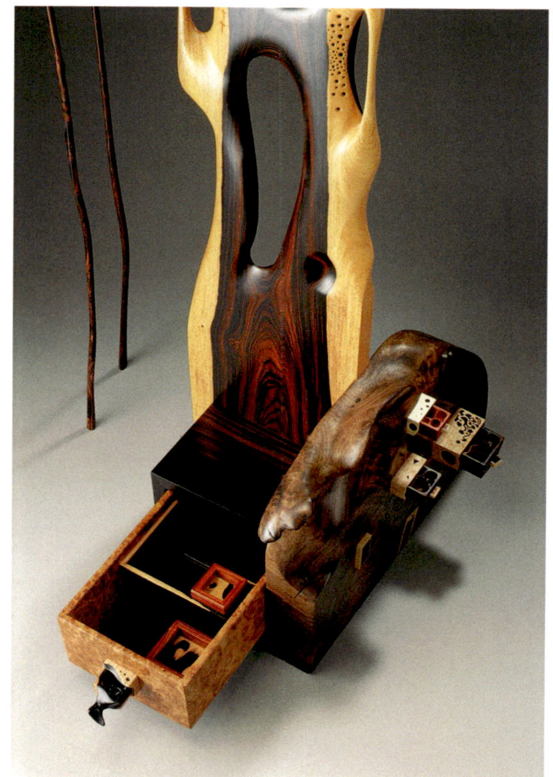

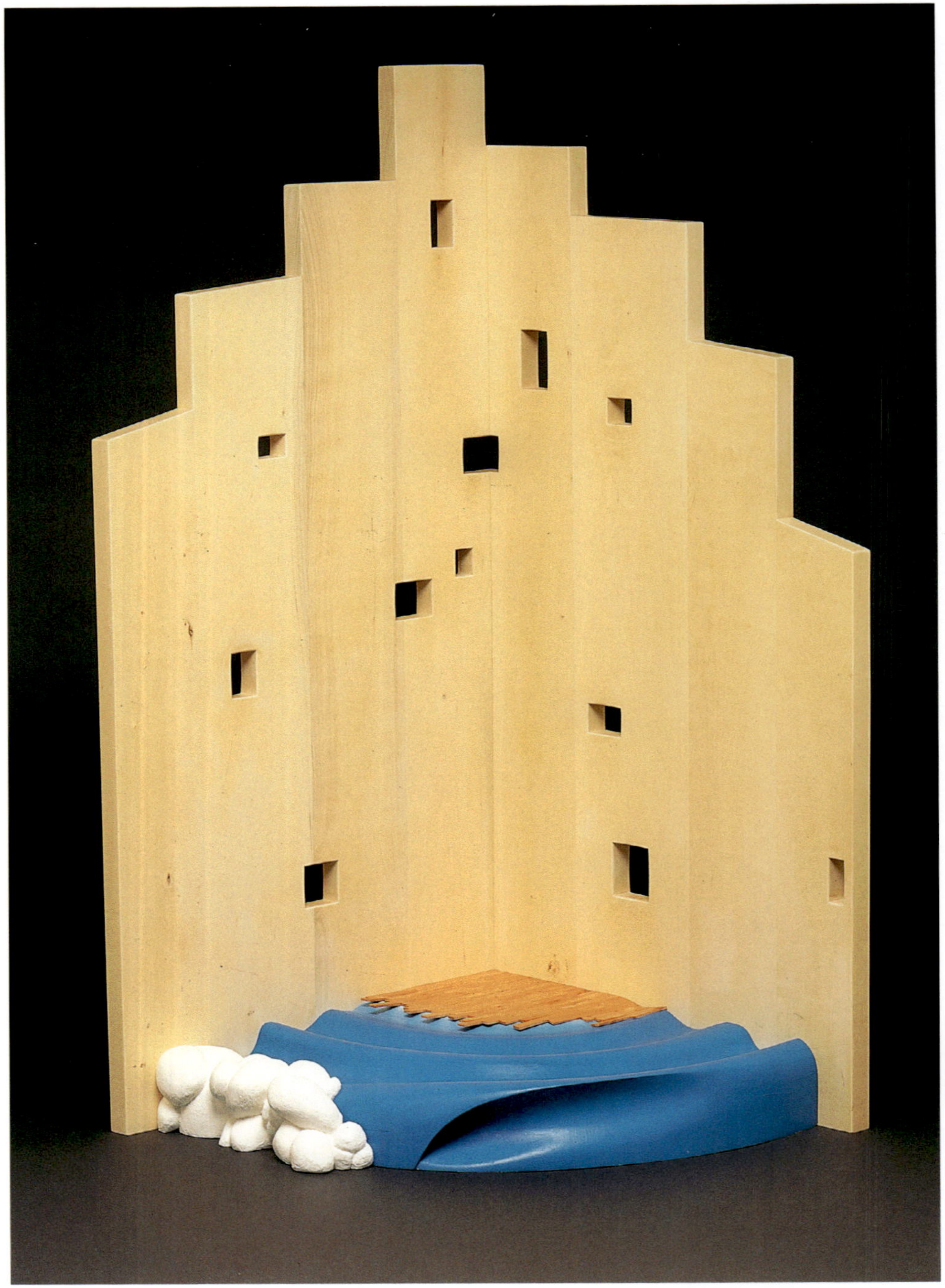

Christopher W. Cantwell. *Something Strange Has Happened to Me. Series #1.* 2003. Holly, birch plywood, Pacific yew, gesso, acrylic paint, 19" x 19" x 39". *Photographer: George Post*

KIP W. CHRISTENSEN

Provo, Utah

Artist's Statement

I feel fortunate that I was introduced to turning at the relatively young age of twenty-one and have been able to participate in the remarkable renaissance of woodturning that has taken place during the past thirty years. While I enjoy general machine and hand woodworking, my preference is toward turning and I have tried to develop some level of versatility through experimenting with a wide range of turned projects and techniques including bowls, vessels, boxes, hollow turning, surface decoration, and production work. I have found countless hours of satisfaction quietly working in my studio. I still lose track of time as hours easily go by unnoticed.

In producing my work, my first focus is on form, then I look to add areas of interest that may be achieved in any number of ways. However, for aesthetic work particularly, and even for most of the functional turning I do, form is the primary focus. There seems to be no other redeeming quality that has the power to compensate for poor form.

I have learned to appreciate the early, often mediocre pieces that mark the progression of my work. The first few pieces I turned became gifts to my mother. Perhaps only she could look me in the eye and honestly say she thought they were wonderful. Years later, when I realized how crude those early pieces were, I gathered them up, destroyed them, and replaced them with more refined pieces. My mother never forgave me for that, and I have come to regret it as well.

I have been fortunate to associate with many of the world's top turners. These are people of great creative and technical talent. Among this group I have made many good friends and have been positively influenced by their work and friendship.

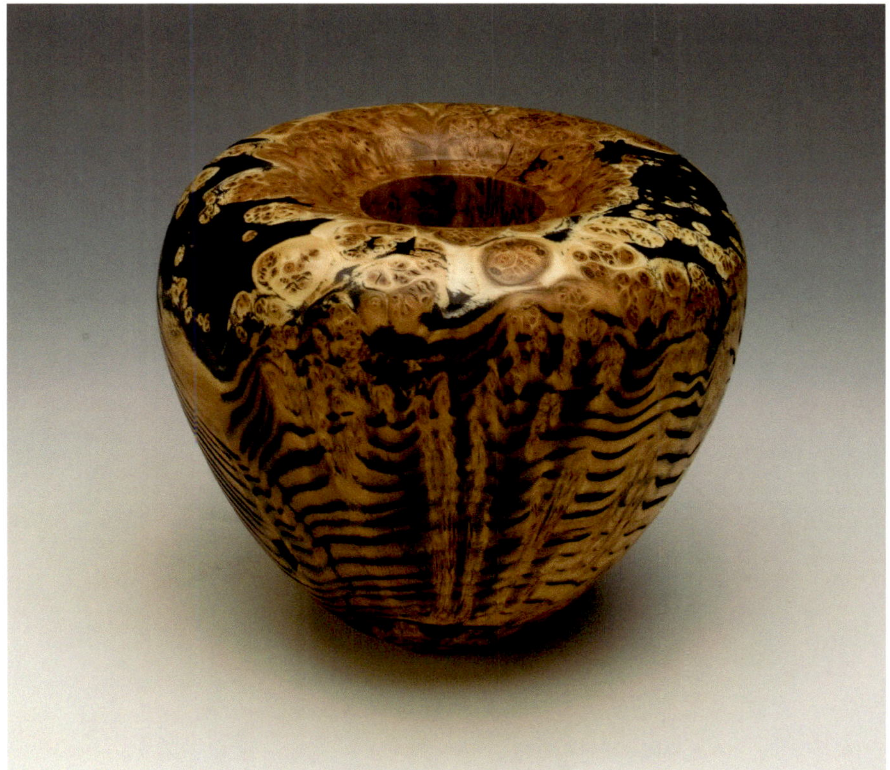

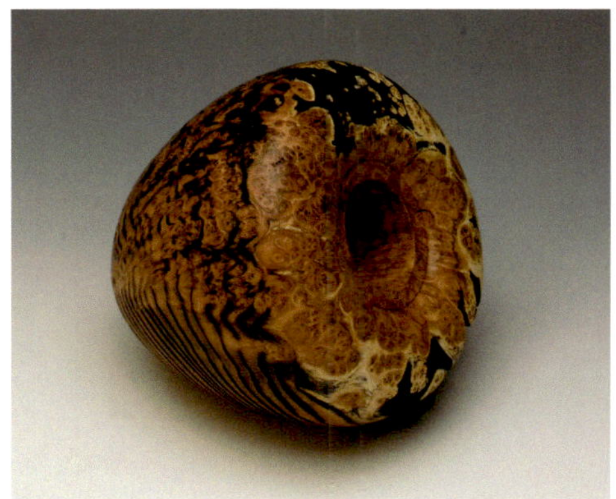

Kip W. Christensen. *Blackened Sepulcher.* 2009. Russian olive burl, turning, sandblasting, ebonizing, sanding, and finishing, 5" h x 5.75" d. *Photographer: Kip Christensen.*
The *Blackened Sepulcher Series* was inspired by the remarkable stone structures in Bryce Canyon, Utah.

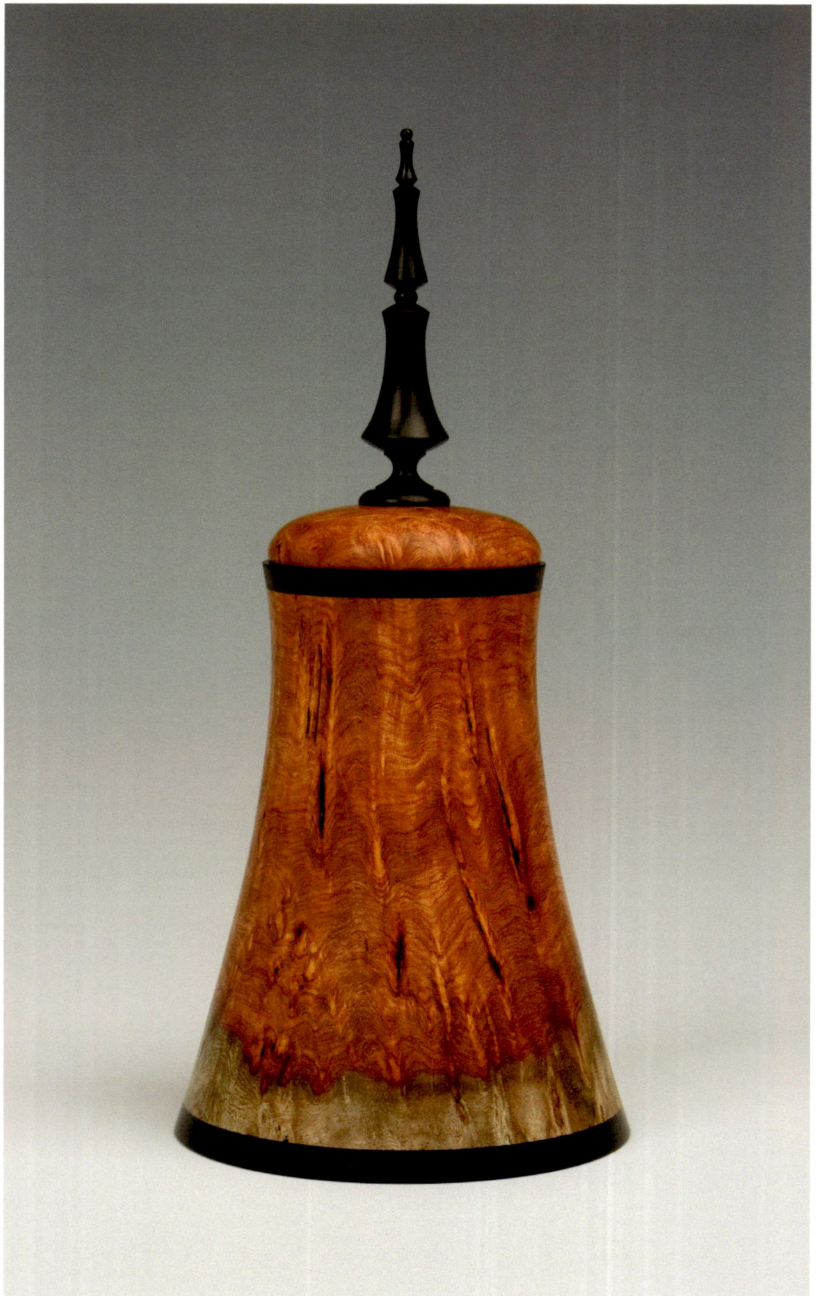

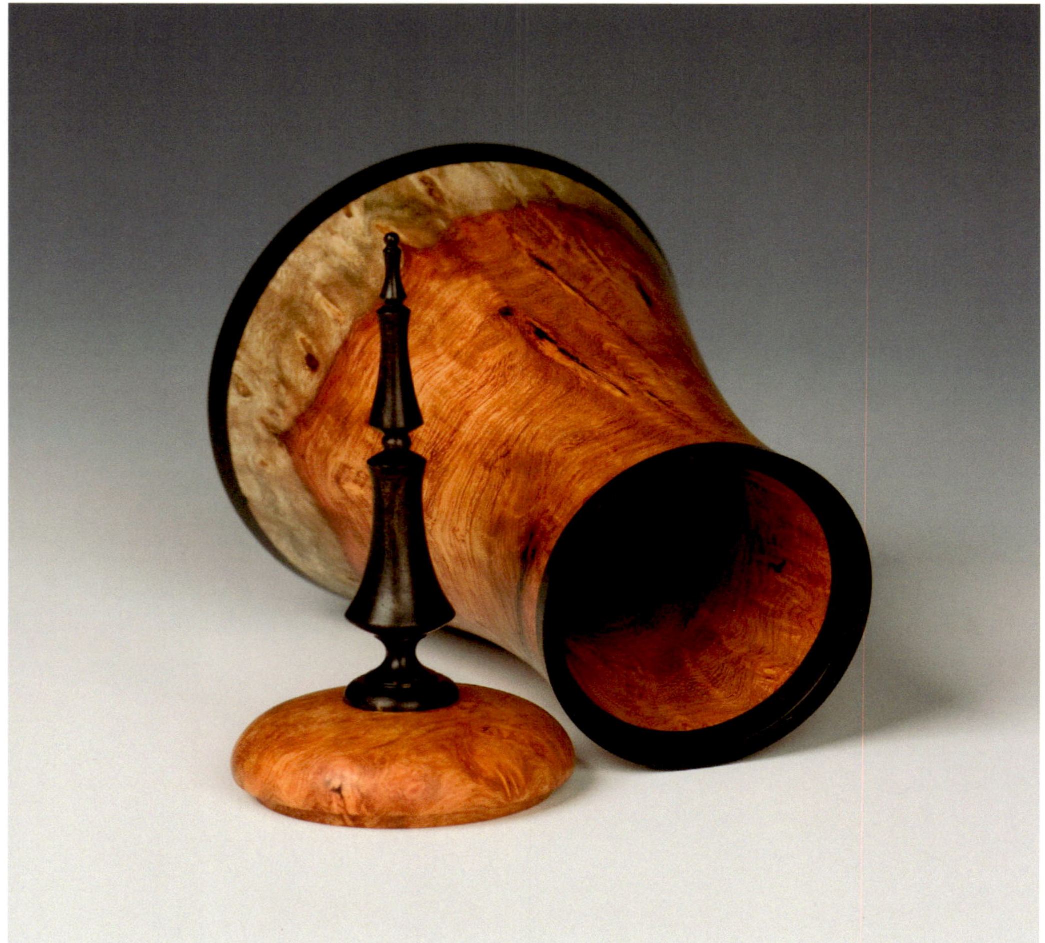

Kip W. Christensen. *Tower Box.* 2009. Amboyna burl, African blackwood, turquoise, 6.5" h x 2.75" d. *Photographer: Kip Christensen.*
The *Tower Box Series* is turned using a variety of commercial and homemade chucks to secure and give access to various parts of the piece during the turning process. Two subtle surprises can be found inside the piece—a decorative spiral of chatterwork applied to the inside bottom, and a small turquoise cabochon inset on the underneath side of the lid.

Hunt Clark

Sparta, Tennessee, clarkmcclary@yahoo.com

Artist's Statement

Each of these sculptures is a result of an intense exploration between movement and space. A bulb jutting out or a sudden sharp angle disrupting otherwise fluid forms imposes a sense of space in time. I draw on the biomechanics of nature to create shapes that suggest motion. As a result, these forms tend to have a functional—even corporeal—feel. My shapes frequently mimic forms that have evolved to facilitate movement.

I developed an unconventional technique using a chain saw and other specialized tools that allows me to test the limits of the medium to create sculptures that, though static, retain a sense of fluid movement. When I approach the wood, I generally have a concept in mind. The material carries its own particular limitations, but my intention is to explore my original idea as fully as possible.

The tools I use give me the freedom to impose a structure on the piece. The freedom manifests itself in the feeling that rather than carving out a space, I'm actually displacing the weight of the form, that wood is malleable, that it can be made to rise and fall, can be pushed or pulled.

With every new piece I investigate more deeply the relationship between motion, space, and form. The thinness and consistency of these sculptures defines my decisions.

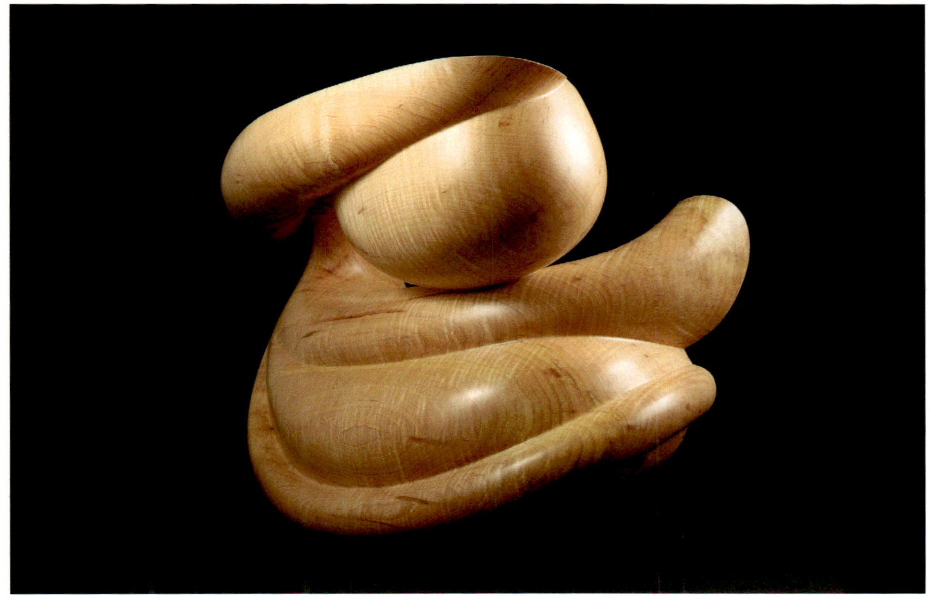

Hunt Clark. *Cms2-06.* 2006. Curly maple.

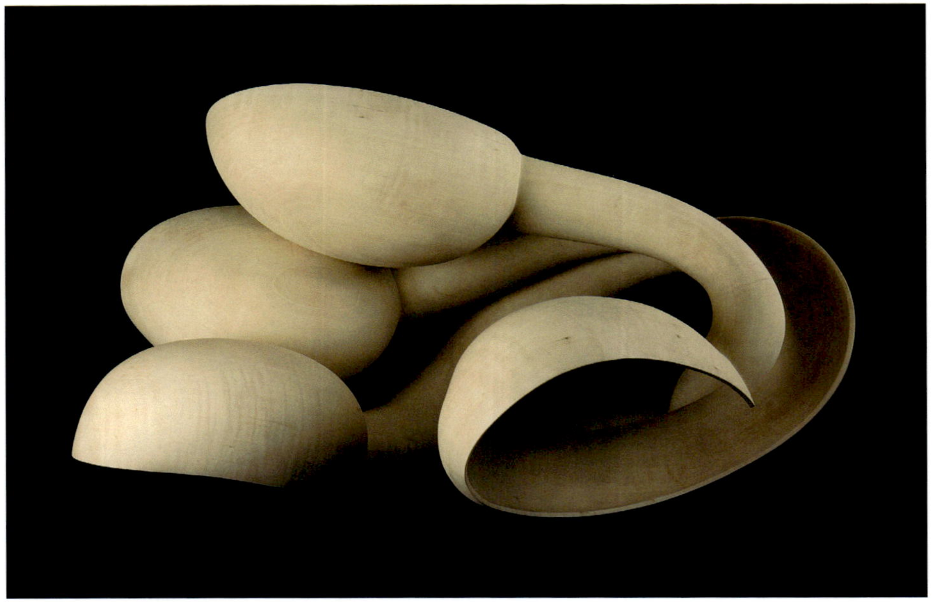

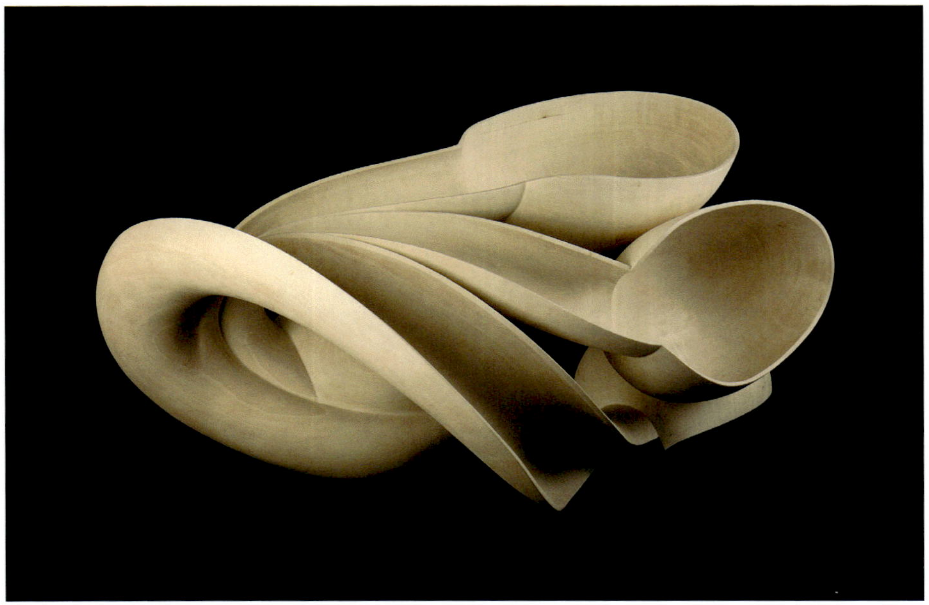

Hunt Clark. *Bpn2-08.* 2008. Bleached pear. *Stephen Keeble and Karen Depew Collection*

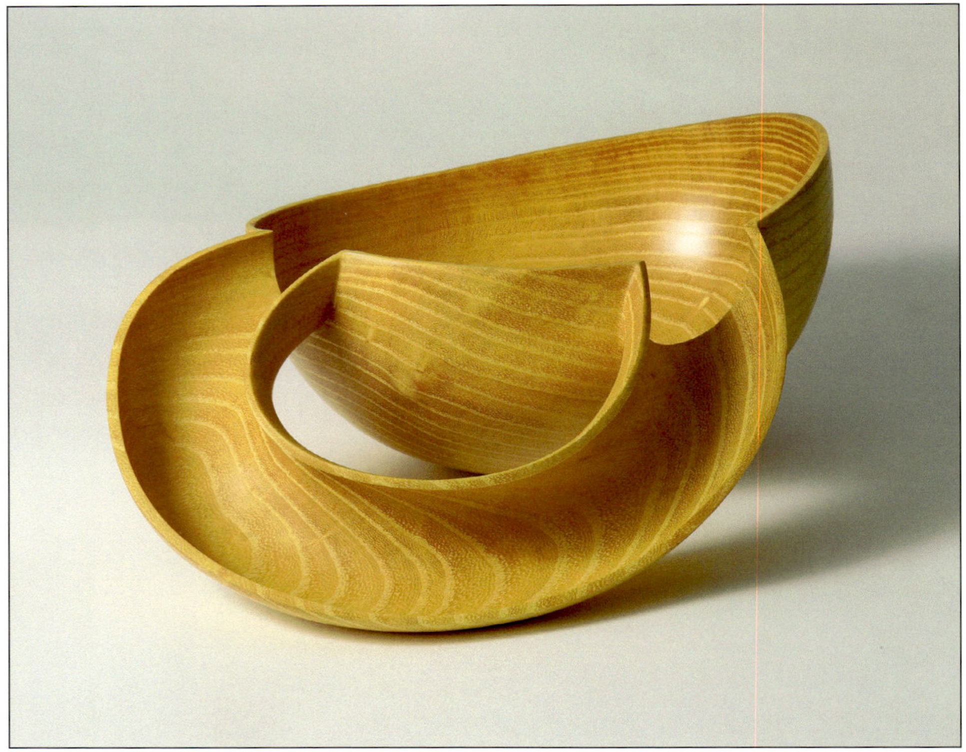

Hunt Clark. *On3-08.* 2008. Osage orange. *Mark Lindquist Collection*

Ronald Cook

Santa Cruz, California, www.roncookstudios.com

Artist's Statement

Ronald Cook creates one-of-a-kind American and European stringed folk instruments based on historical and contemporary designs. His skilled craftsmanship is shaped by a desire to integrate his love of music, art, and history with the profound beauty and rich resonance of tone woods to create distinctive works of art and music. He uses a combination of recycled, salvaged, and sustainably harvested woods.

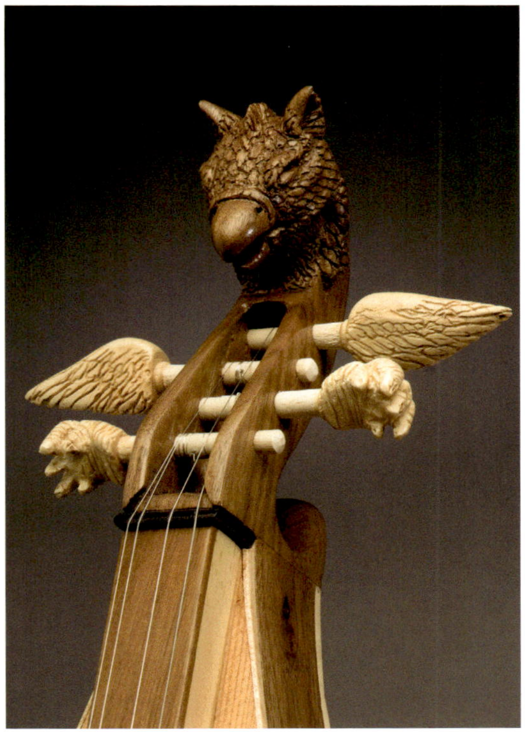

Ronald Cook. Mountain Dulcimer: *The Gryphon*. Back side: Eastern black walnut; head & tailpiece: hand-carved black walnut; top: Douglas fir (125+ year old first growth wood salvaged from a demolished Portland, Oregon, warehouse; fingerboard: pine with Eastern black walnut; tuning pegs: hand-carved maple; 35" l x 6" w x 3" d. *Photographer: Paul Schraub Photography*

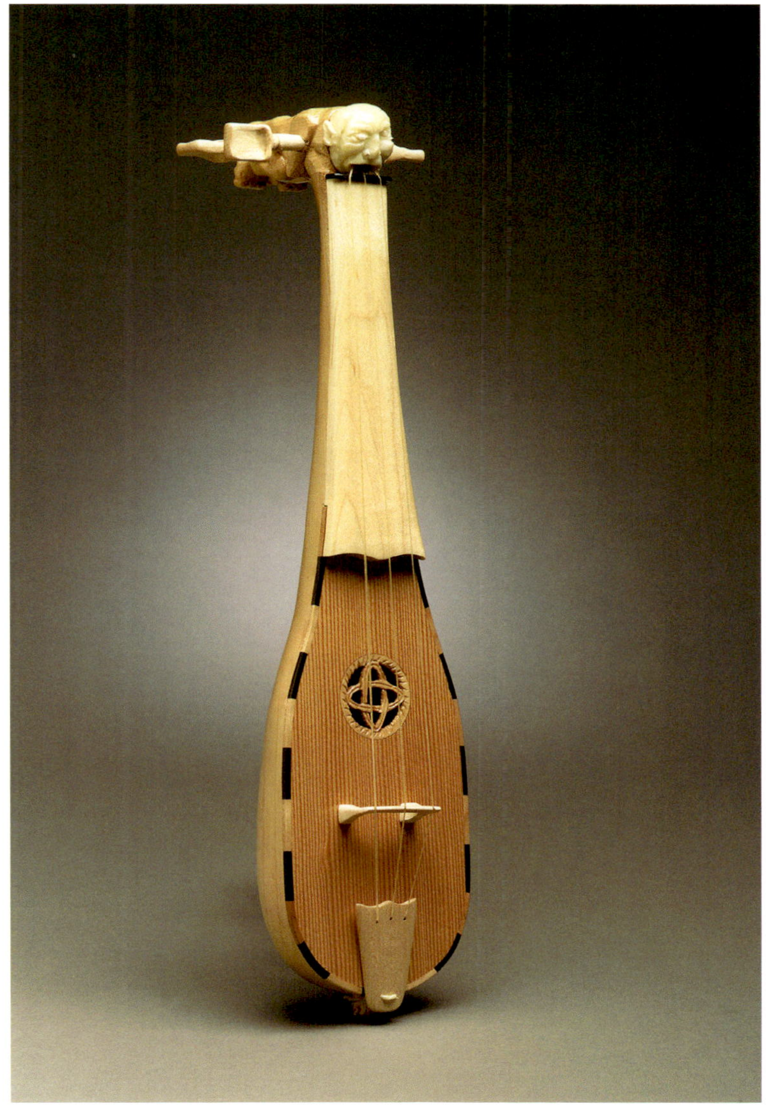

Ronald Cook. Tenor Rebec: *Quasimodo*. Body, neck: hand-carved maple; head: hand-carved maple and tagua nut; top: Douglas fir (125+ year old first growth wood salvaged from a demolished Portland, Oregon, warehouse); bridge, tailpiece, rosette: hand-carved maple; binding: maple with recycled ebony (from keys of a destroyed piano); 21" l x 5" w x 3.5" d. *Photographer: Paul Schraub Photography*

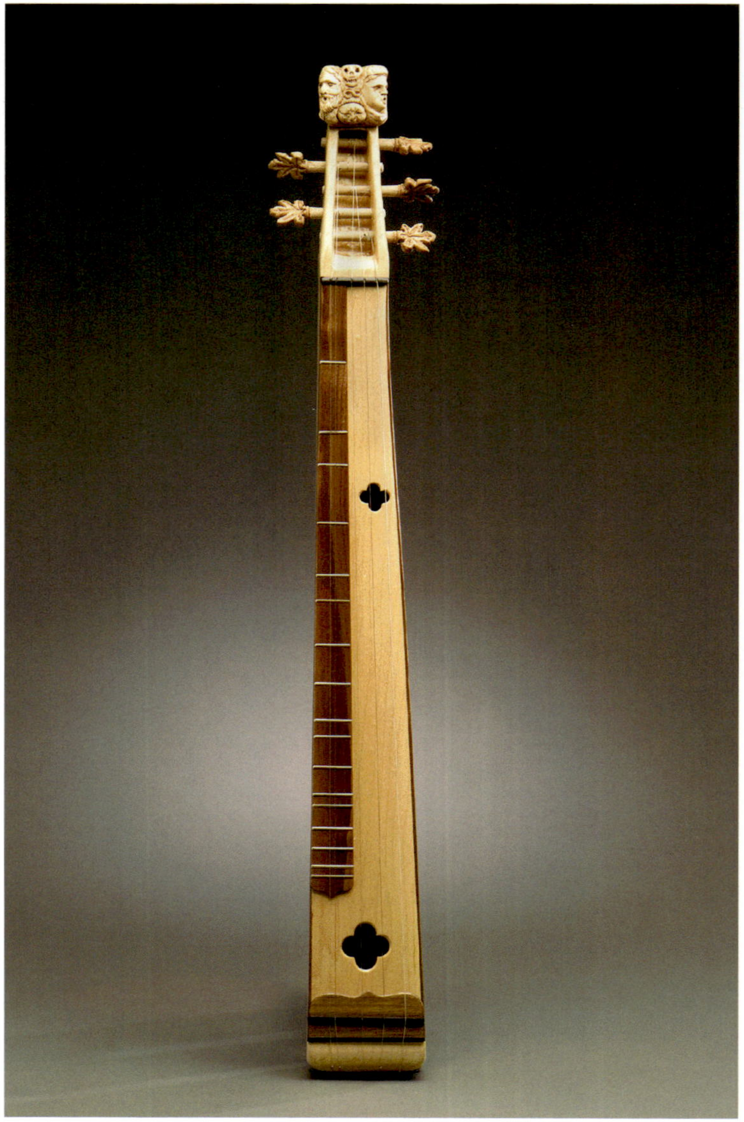

Ronald Cook. Epinette des Vosges *Man, Woman, Birth, Death, Infinity*. Body: maple with Eastern black walnut fingerboard and trim; head: hand-carved maple; tuning pegs: hand-carved salvaged pear wood; 30" l x 4" 2 x 2.5" d. *Photographer: Paul Schraub Photography*

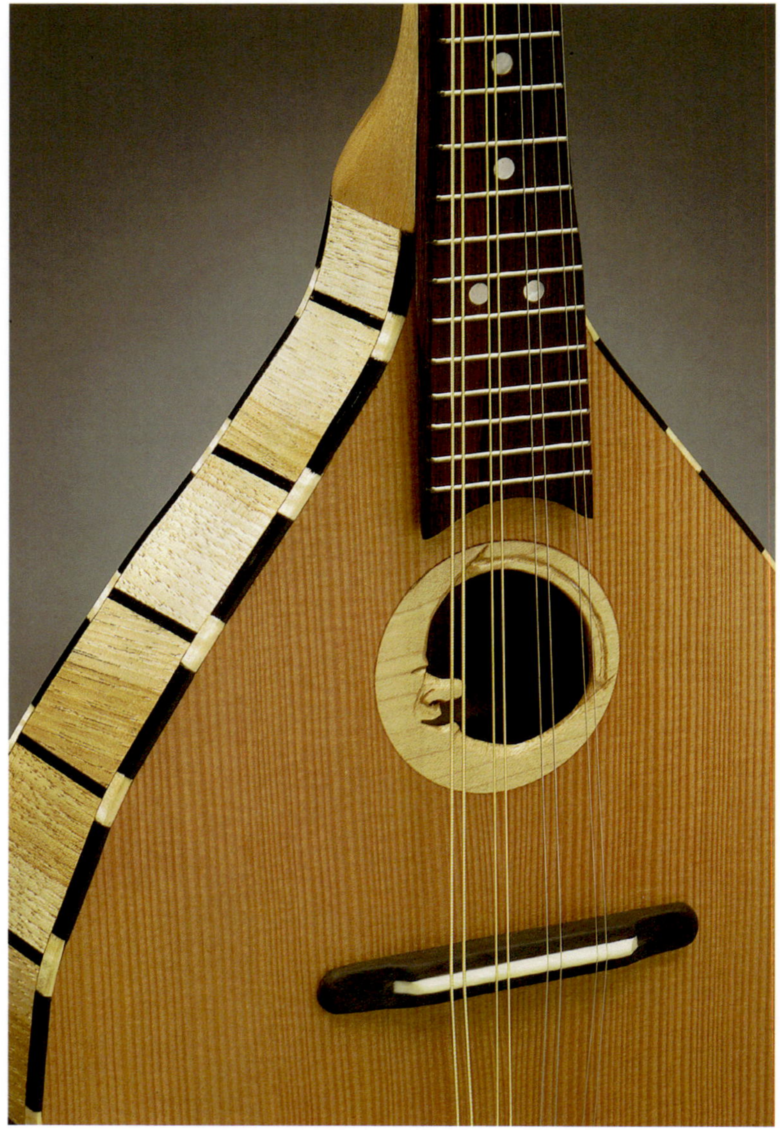

Ronald Cook. Mandolin *The Jester*. Back: pecan; sides and binding: pecan pieces with maple and recycled ebony (from keys of a destroyed piano); top: Douglas fir (125+ year old first growth wood salvaged from a demolished Portland, Oregon, warehouse; fingerboard: Indonesian Rosewood; neck and head: maple with hand-carved tagua nut; 24" l x 9" w x 3" d. *Photographer: Paul Schraub Photography*

Stephen Courtney

Venice, California, www.stephencourtney.com

Artist's Statement

From the initial sketch, refinement in design, and through the process of millwork, these are the lines that in balance, scale, and proportion, preoccupy my mind's eye. Working with curves, angles, or just clean, straight lines – there is nowhere to hide a compromise of craft or flaw in design. When the elements of design, coupled with the skills of craft, are integrated successfully, a piece can appear almost simple. Often this simplicity conceals a complex design, the unseen challenges demanded of tools and materials.

Modern and progressive is the way I like furniture the most, dynamic and different. Furniture as art...as sculpture, with purpose, utility, and function. Useful objects of art designed to enrich, to elevate the living experience, and summons a sense of spirit and beauty to the human environment.

Although primarily a woodworker, I respond to the mix, the union of materials such as stone, metal, and hides. Color brings life. Humor brings spirit. I try to build both into a design without a sense of "gimmick" or, more importantly, without compromising the architectural and structural integrity of the piece.

Inspiration? I am in awe of the design and technique of architect John Lautner. I marvel at his work with gravity, his cleverness with the element of cantilever. Tracing the evolution of modern furniture, I am amazed at the awesome body of work funneled through the Herman Miller house. Designers George Nelson, Isamu Noguchi, Verner Panton, and Charles and Ray Eames remain as legends.

Today is a great day to have a hand or interest in furniture as an art form. In urban and rural workshops and studios across America, talented artists, craftsmen and women are busy creating innovative designs, expressing their art through the language of furniture. I am glad to have a voice amongst them.

Individual Artwork

3-legged Desk

The big question was, will the walnut-wrapped wood veneer desk stand with just three legs? It wasn't until the full-scale piece was built and tested that I knew that the single foot, set beneath the bank of drawers, would support the extended overhang of the cantilevered desktop. Omitting the front left leg creates freedom of movement to shift in and out from a seated position. The *avante garde* design was created with 16/4 solid stock. Hard-rock maple legs were unconventionally mounted to the angled sides of the desk using concealed inserted metal mounts.

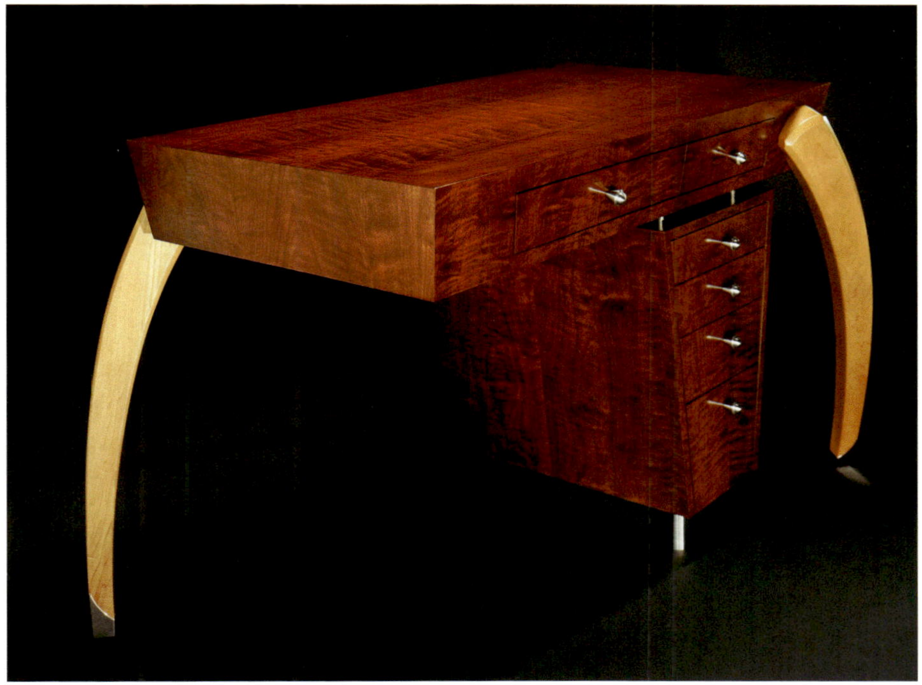

Stephen Courtney. *3-legged Desk*. Walnut swirl veneer, maple legs, glass, stainless steel, 34" h x 81" w x 24" d.

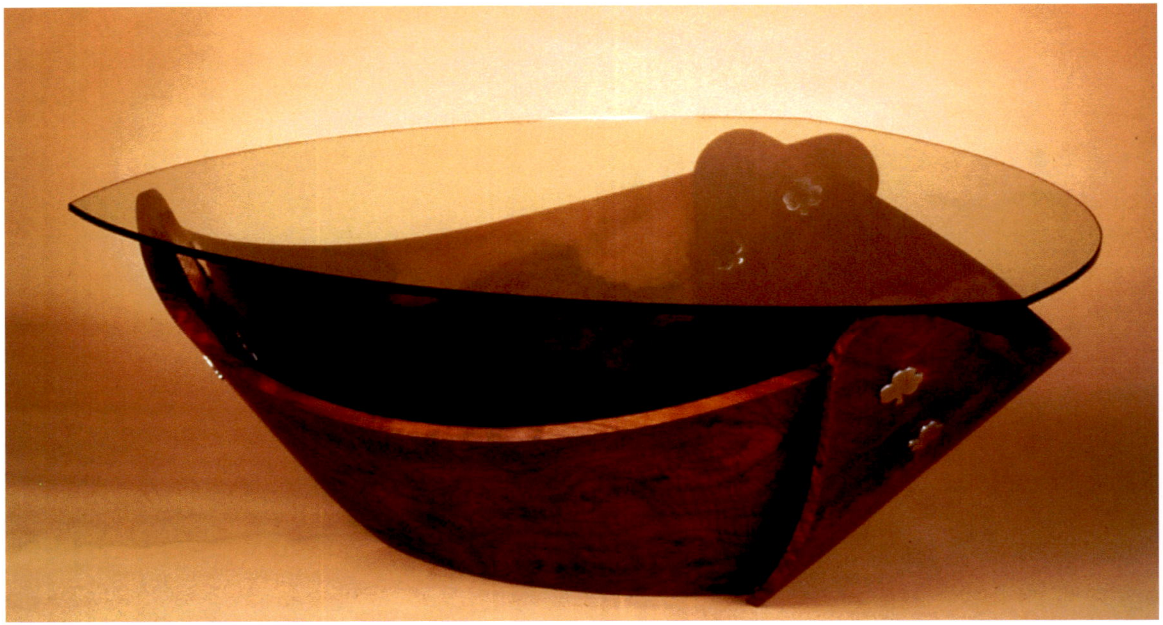

Stephen Courtney. *Cloverleaf Coffee Table*. Figural walnut, glass, stainless steel shamrocks, 17" x 48" d.

Cloverleaf Coffee Table

The three elements that make up the integrated walls were achieved after multiple mockups and much trial and error. Once the correct leaning angles were figured out and the three leaves were united, the word heard throughout the wood shop was "Eureka." The shield shaped glass top, with an eased edge, sits with stability upon the intersecting ears, appearing like a basket.

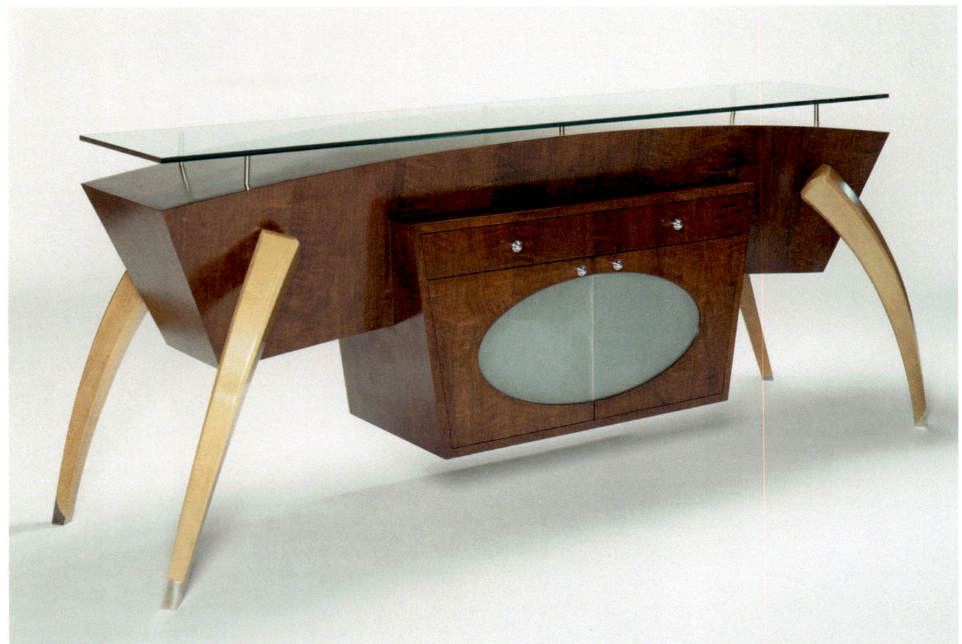

Stephen Courtney. *Neeld Console*. Walnut veneer, maple legs, glass, stainless steel, 81" w x 36" h x 28" d.

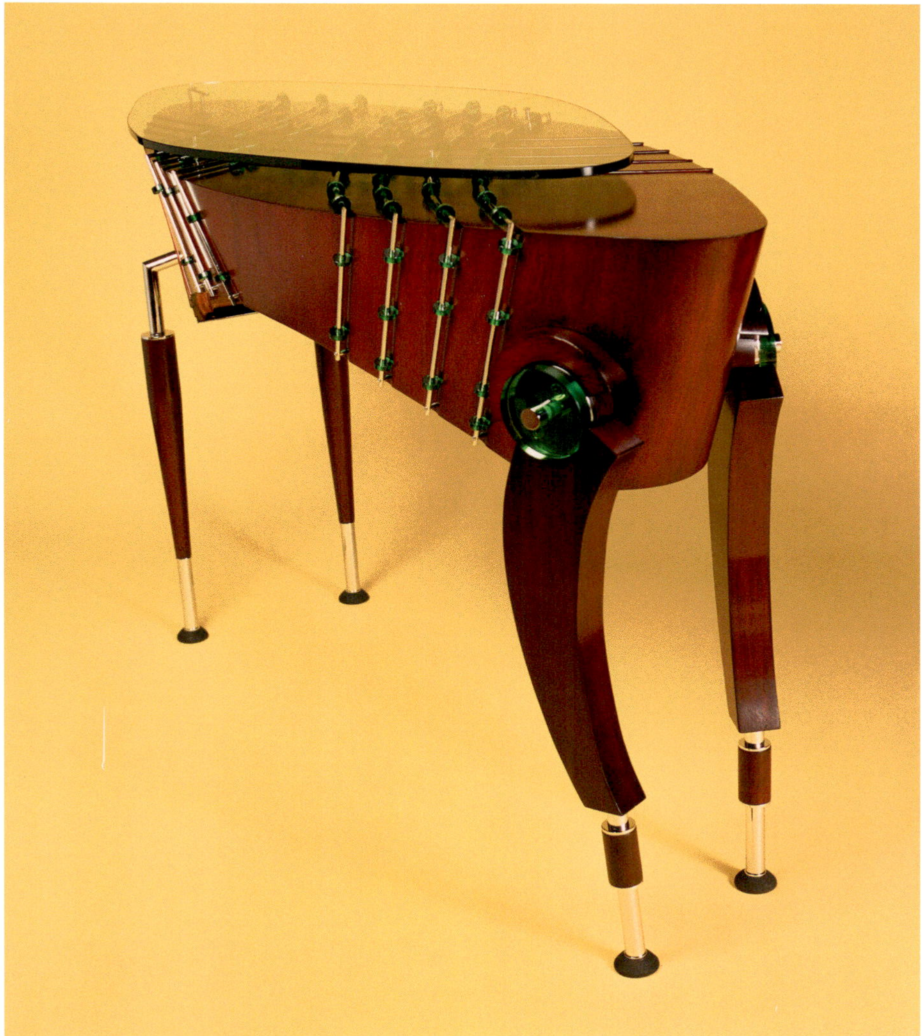

Stephen Courtney. *Metropolis Console.* Mahogany, stainless steel, glass, 61" w x 39" h x 25" d.

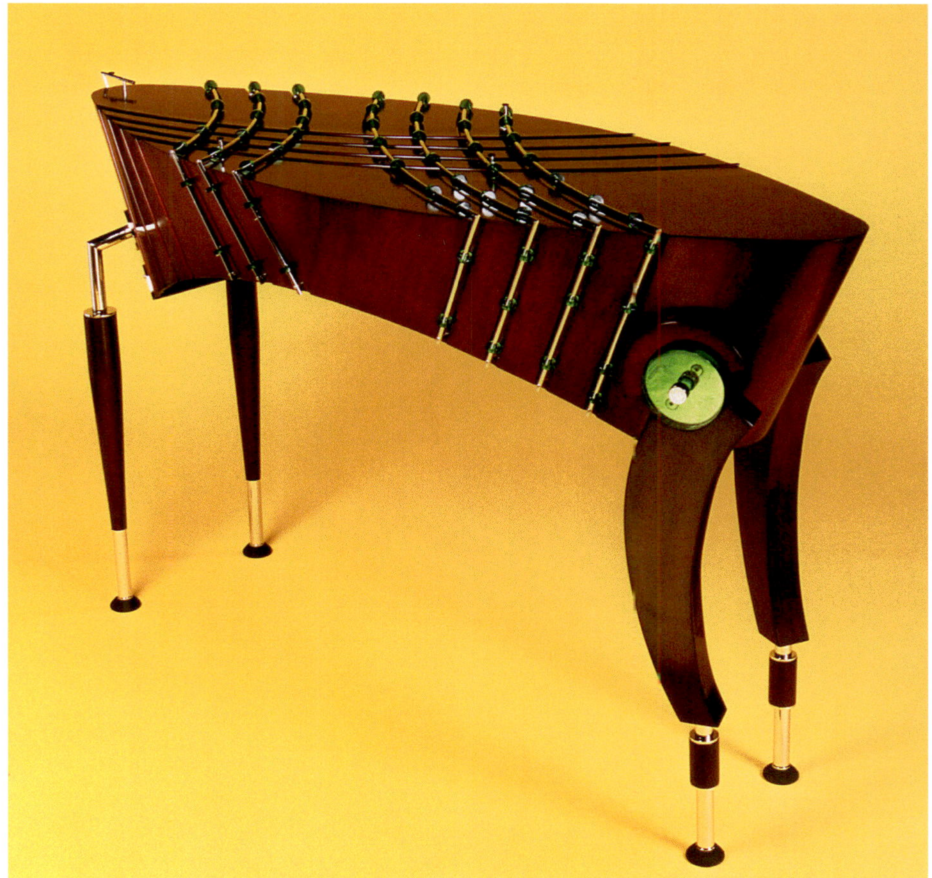

Jonathan Cox

Provo, Utah

Artist's Statement

Although I describe my work as contemporary and Asian influenced, I enjoy incorporating abstract and modern ideas along with my own personal style. The most important aspects of my work do not just include flowing lines and function; my main foci are grain harmony, structural integrity, and finish execution. Not only do I desire that each piece of furniture that I make be appealing to the eye and touch, I want my work to last generations for everyone to enjoy.

Individual Artwork

Double Black Cherry

This unique king-size bed was carefully made to reveal hand-cut joinery and negative space. Its double head and footboard design was created with mortise and tenon construction. Through wedged tenons hold the top to the bedposts and chattered blackwood pins reinforce the panels. The double tenon construction of the side rails goes completely through the first panel of the head and footboard, and then half way into the second panel. They are then wedged into place with African blackwood.

Butterfly inlays reinforce the joints of the cross-hatched panels. The rear panels are veneered with curly maple. Three-stage touch activated xenon lamps are inlaid into the headboard. The bed was finished with Waterlox tung oil.

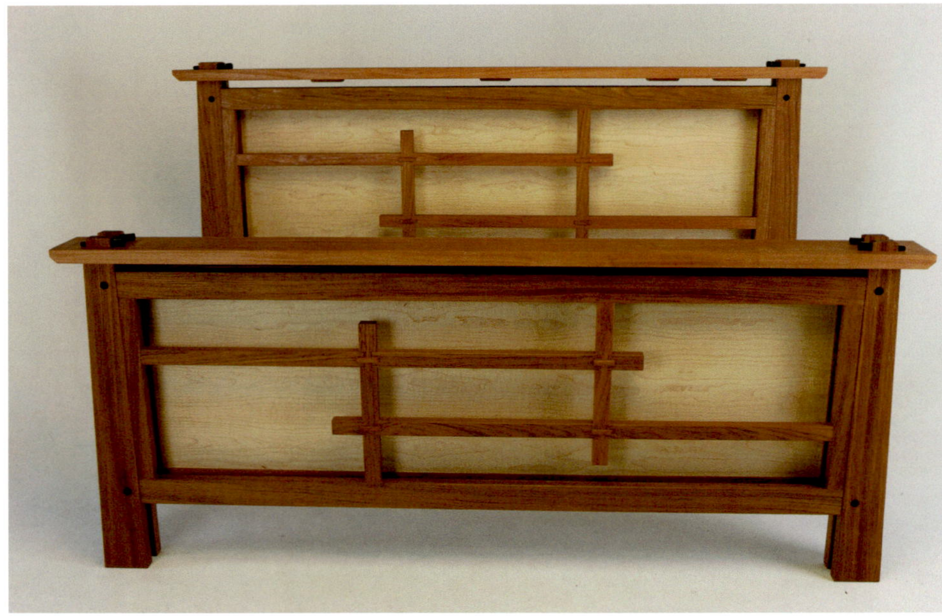

Jonathan Cox. *Double Black Cherry*. 2008. Jatobá, curly maple veneer, African black-wood, tung oil, xenon lights, headboard: 7" deep x 86" w x 55" h; footboard: 7" deep x 86" w x 38" h. *Photographer: Mark Louis Weinberg*

Ribbon Stripes

Based on the idea of a cabinet on a stand, *Ribbon Stripes* displays the careful use of book-matched grain and hand joinery. The cabinet's sides are fastened to its top with half-blind dovetails and the rear frame and panel keeps it square. The doors include pinned through tenons. The latticework on the doors uses half lap joinery.

The table's rigid joinery includes mitered mortise and tenon construction, blind dovetails for the upper divider, and a double tenon for the lower divider. The drawer uses half-blind dovetails and a Spanish cedar bottom for a cinnamon-like aroma.

Ribbon Stripes was sanded to 600 grits and finished with Waterlox tung oil and wax.

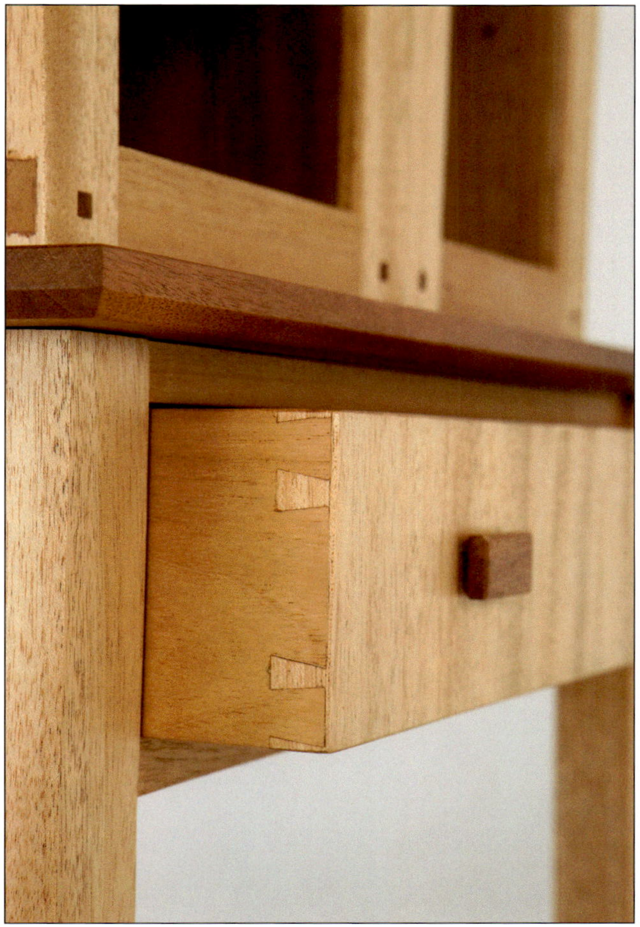

Jonathan Cox. *Ribbon Stripes*. 2007. African mahogany, genuine mahogany, Spanish cedar, Waterlox, wax, 16" deep x 22" w x 66" h. *Photographer: Mark Louis Weinberg*

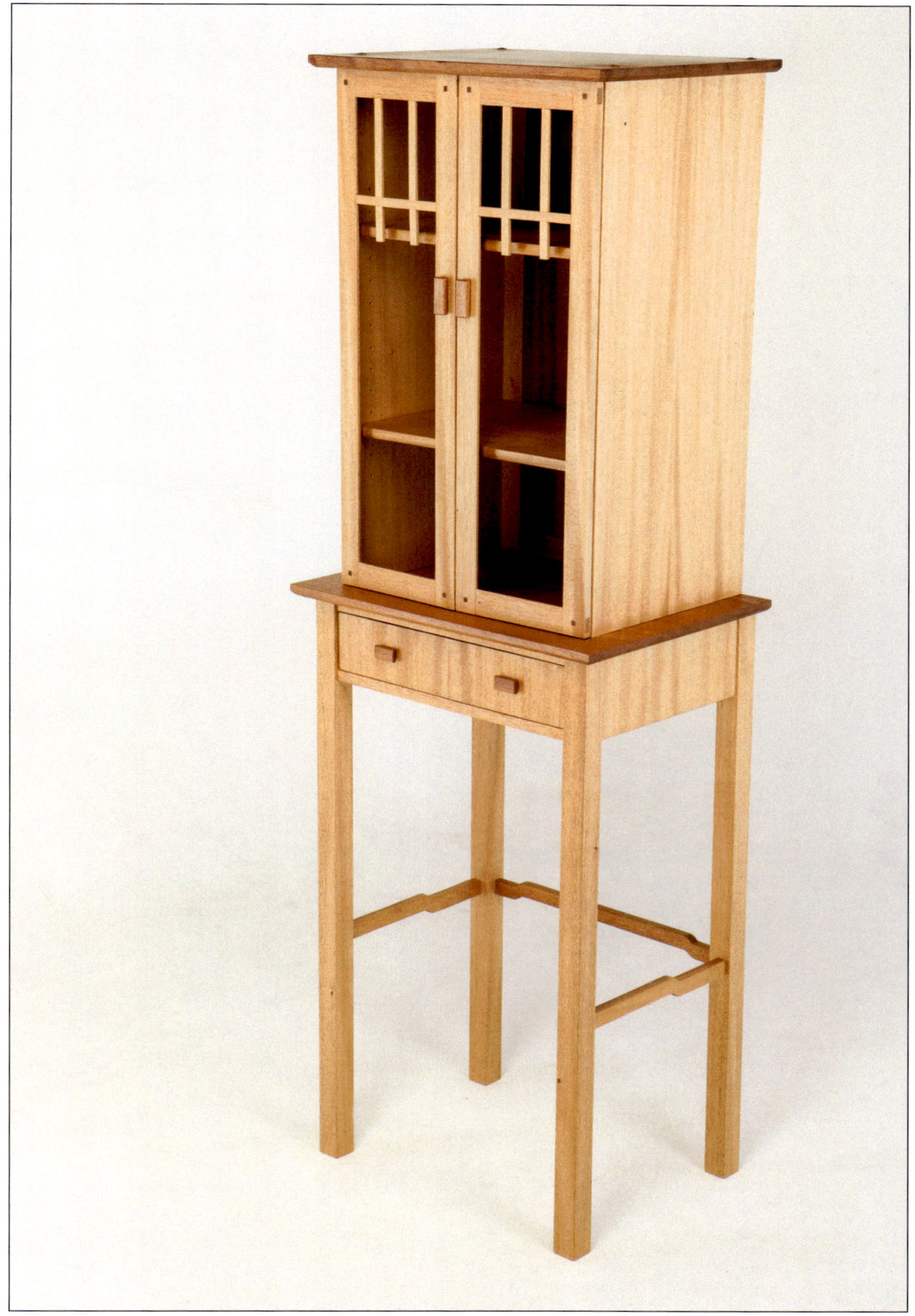

Split Personality

Split Personality is a living room table characterized by its large live edge split top and cantilevered pedestal base. The table includes a careful selection of granadillo curly hard maple, cocobolo, and purpleheart. The base is made using an ancient Japanese floor construction joint called *Yatoi Hozo Sashi*. It is a post and pole joint that includes four beams that insert into one location on a post. This joint was normally used to connect foundational posts to floor joists in Japanese shrines. Each beam in the *Yatoi Hozo Sashi* joint has five separate tenons that mortise into a post face or edge. The beams are reinforced with two long cocobolo floating tenons that are pinned and wedged for added rigidity. The foot structure of the base is assembled with two perpendicular half-lapped feet. The feet attach to the pedestal by a pinned double bridle joint. The granadillo top is attached to the pedestal with a through double-wedged tenon that juxtaposes the carved sapwood. The table was finished with Waterlox tung oil and Renaissance wax.

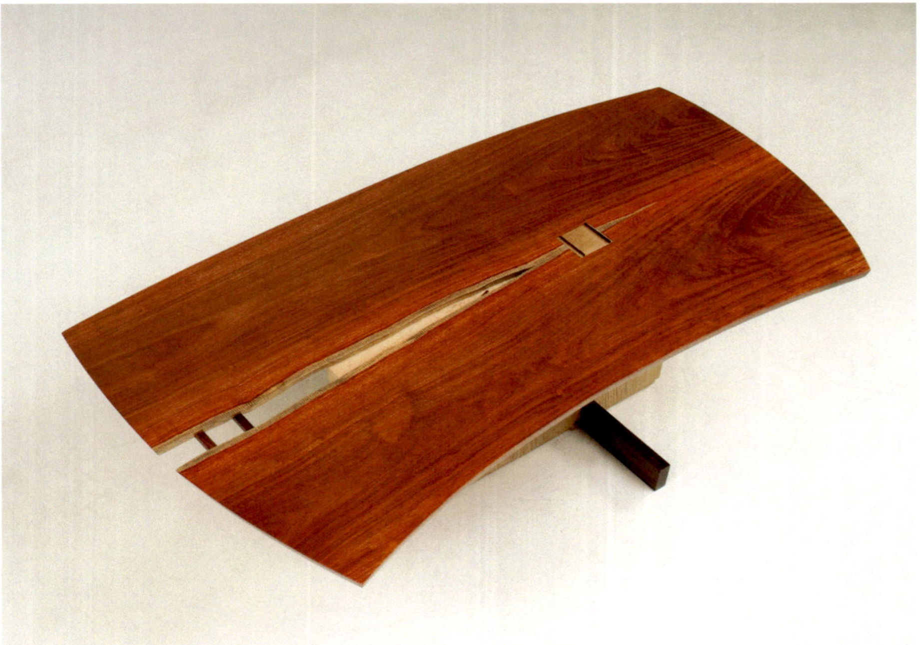

Jonathan Cox. *Split Personality*. 2009. Granadillo, curly hard maple, cocobolo, purpleheart, tung oil, 24" w x 48" l x 17" h. *Photographer: Weston Colton*

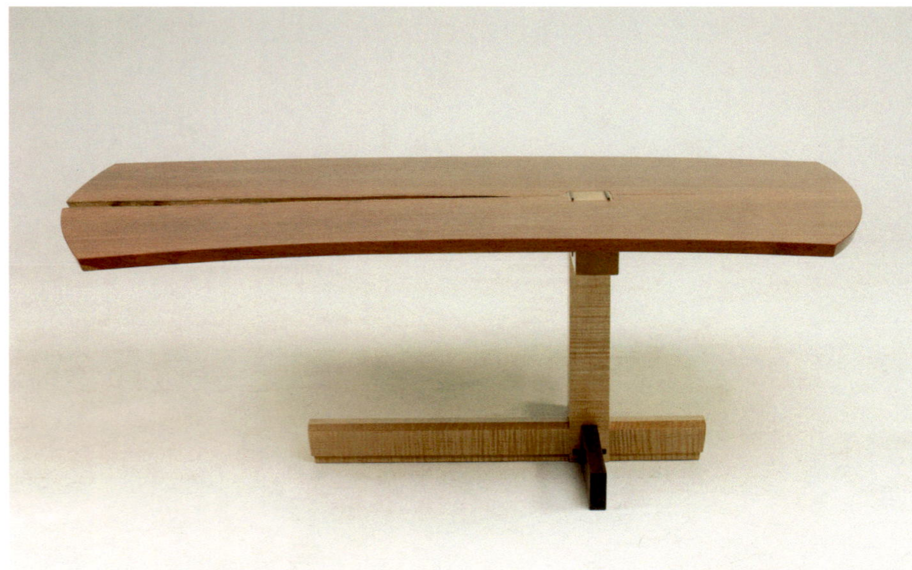

Derek Secor Davis

Boulder, Colorado, www.dereksecordavis.com

Artist's Statement

My life and my work are greatly influenced by the natural world. I live and work in a rural, mountainous area and spend a great deal of time in a quiet and wild setting. My forms are an interpretation and organic conglomeration of what I see in my daily life. Any look at nature reveals a world that is remarkable in its precarious balance and inevitable disintegration and change. This ever changing world is a constant source of inspiration for me as I create pieces that are either in an unlikely state of balance, are showing signs of fracture and disintegration, or are indicative of weathering and erosion. I am interested in simple, elemental forms that can be a metaphor for humankind's relationship to nature. Similarly, I am drawn to cast off, weathered industrial items that serve as a contrast to my natural elements and are representative of the influence of man in nature. I find in the relationship and presence of both these organic and industrial forms an elusive and mysterious essence that speaks of the ongoing metamorphosis of our world.

Individual Artwork

A Table of Thanksgiving

This table is a large console table that utilizes forms reminiscent of the gourds and pods of Thanksgiving time. This table is constructed from a large salvaged piece of American elm placed upon some carved and painted poplar which in turn is built upon a steel armature.

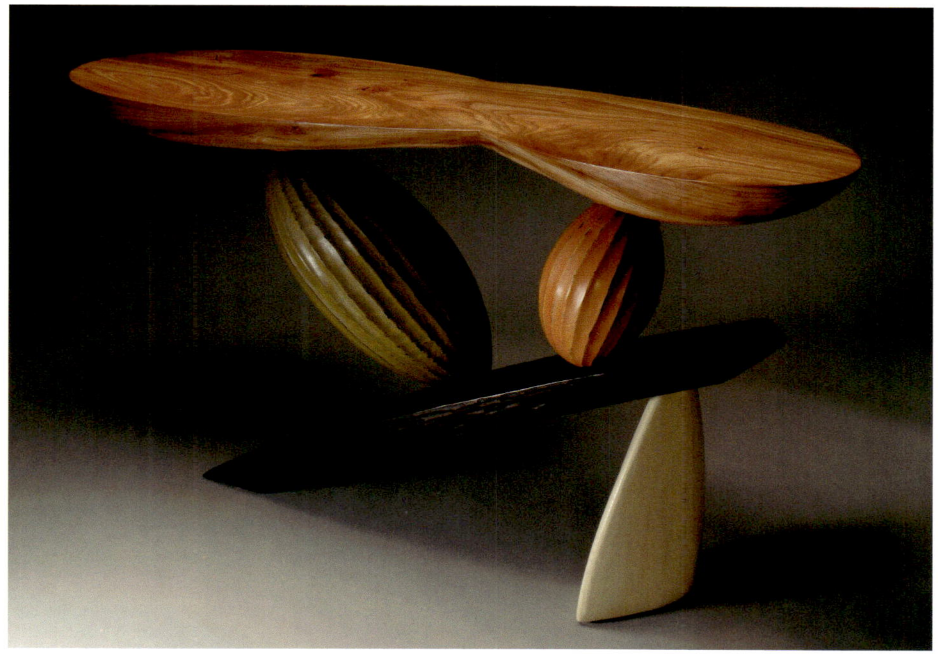

Derek Secor Davis. *A Table of Thanksgiving.* 2004. Gourd forms support top, urban salvaged elm & poplar, milk paint, traditional carving with steel armature, 33" x 17" x 64". *Photo by John Bonath, Maddog Studio*

In the Realm of the Senses

This table is a whimsical piece about the essence of life. What came first, the egg or the being? The curve or the desire? Also a tribute to the Japanese film director Nigish Oshima from whose 1976 film I took the title for this table.

The tabletop surface consists of cottonwood branches that are inlaid in a surface of pigmented epoxy. This is accomplished by first tacking with glue the branches to a substrate. Over this is poured a thin layer of pigmented epoxy. When this has cured, the surface is sanded and leveled, which reveals the branches that have been buried in the epoxy.

Spring Bench

An exterior bench for the type of person who likes a little bounce out of life. This bench is constructed from a large found spring that came from a local mine, reclaimed redwood, a found steel pipe, and some cast concrete. I couldn't resist creating a piece that would utilize the stiff bounce of this massive spring. Likewise it takes a rather massive individual to get much bounce out this bench, but it is possible!

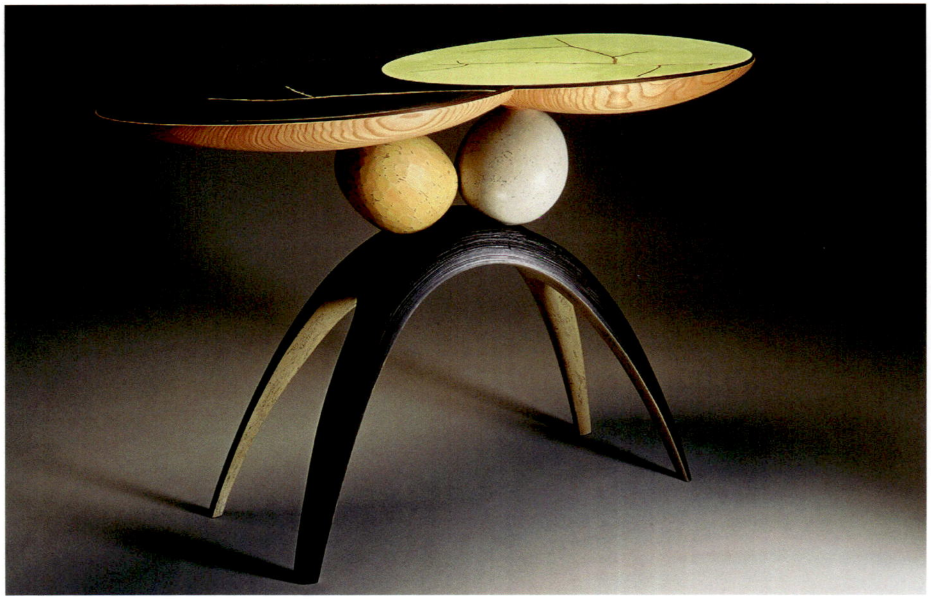

Derek Secor Davis. *In The Realm of the Senses.* 2004. Sculptural forms support top, pigmented epoxy, cottonwood branches, white ash, poplar, fir, acrylic, traditional carving, pigmented epoxy, 35" x 19" x 48". *Photo by John Bonath, Maddog Studio*

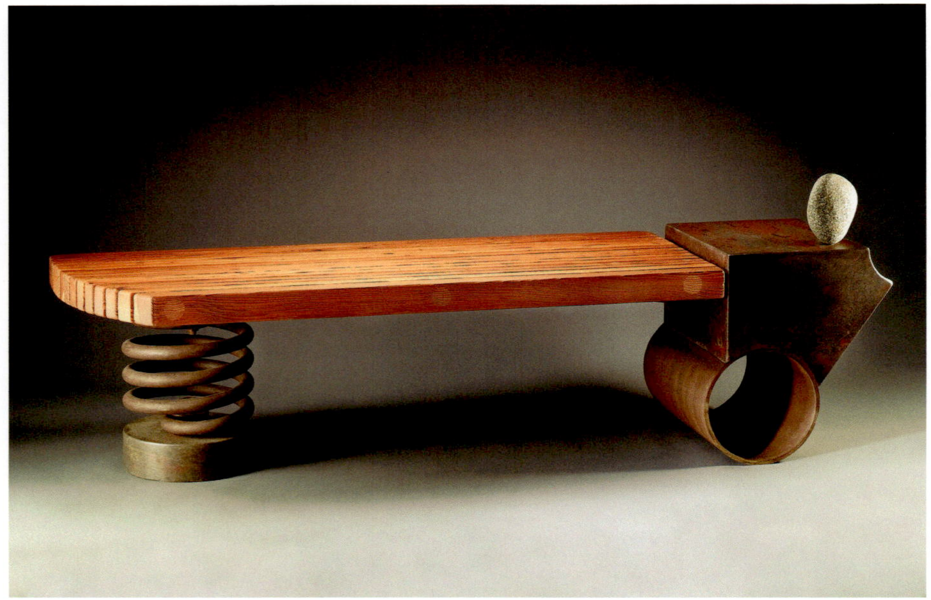

Derek Secor Davis. *Spring Bench.* 2005. Found objects support top, reclaimed redwood, found steel, concrete, stone, traditional woodworking with cast concrete, 28" x 22" x 73". *Photo by Tim Benko*

Welcome Back

This incidental table was designed to be placed in the middle of a large loft. The desire was for the piece to make a striking visual statement and to stand both literally and figuratively on its own. The table is constructed of cast concrete in the base (for stability) and painted wood sculptural elements supporting a tabletop make of stacked plywood with a myrtlewood burl as the finish top.

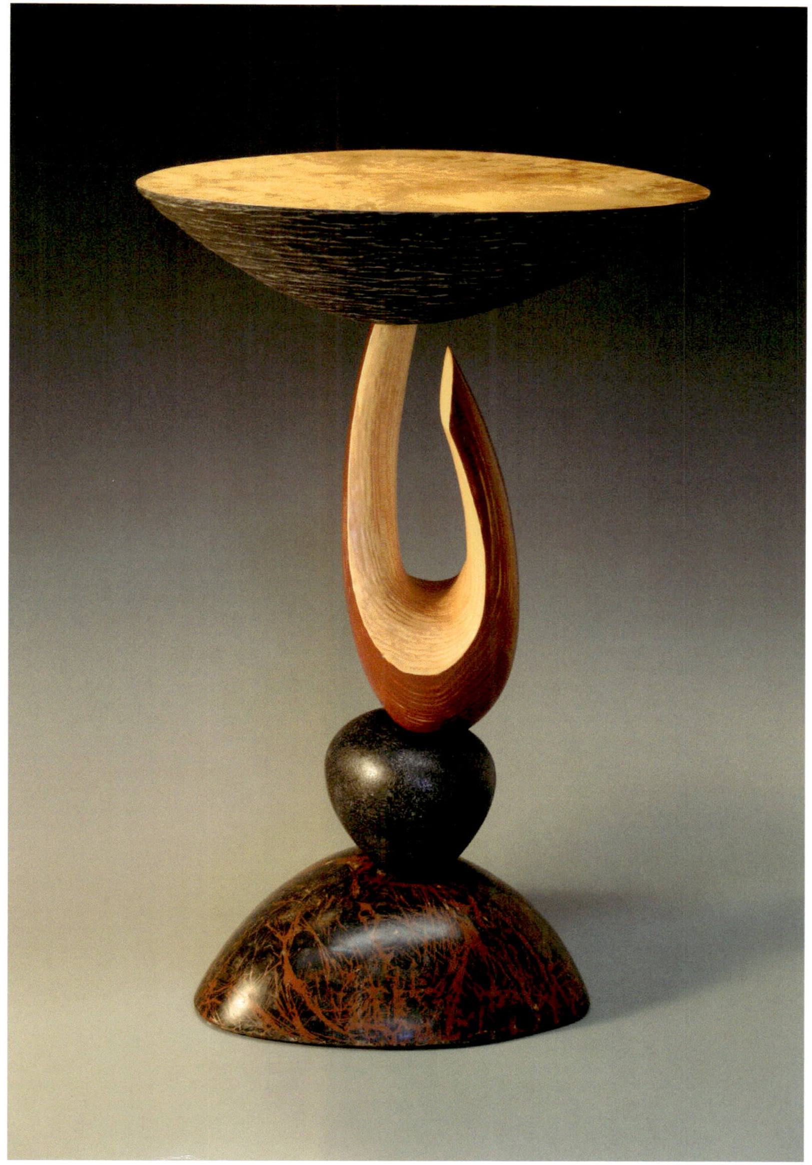

Derek Secor Davis. *Welcome Back.* 2007. Sculptural forms support wooden top, myrtlewood veneer, fir, milkpaint, cast concrete, traditional carving with cast concrete, 42" x 26" x 17". *Photo by Derek Secor Davis*

Jack de Vos

Wungong WA, Australia, www.jackdevos.com

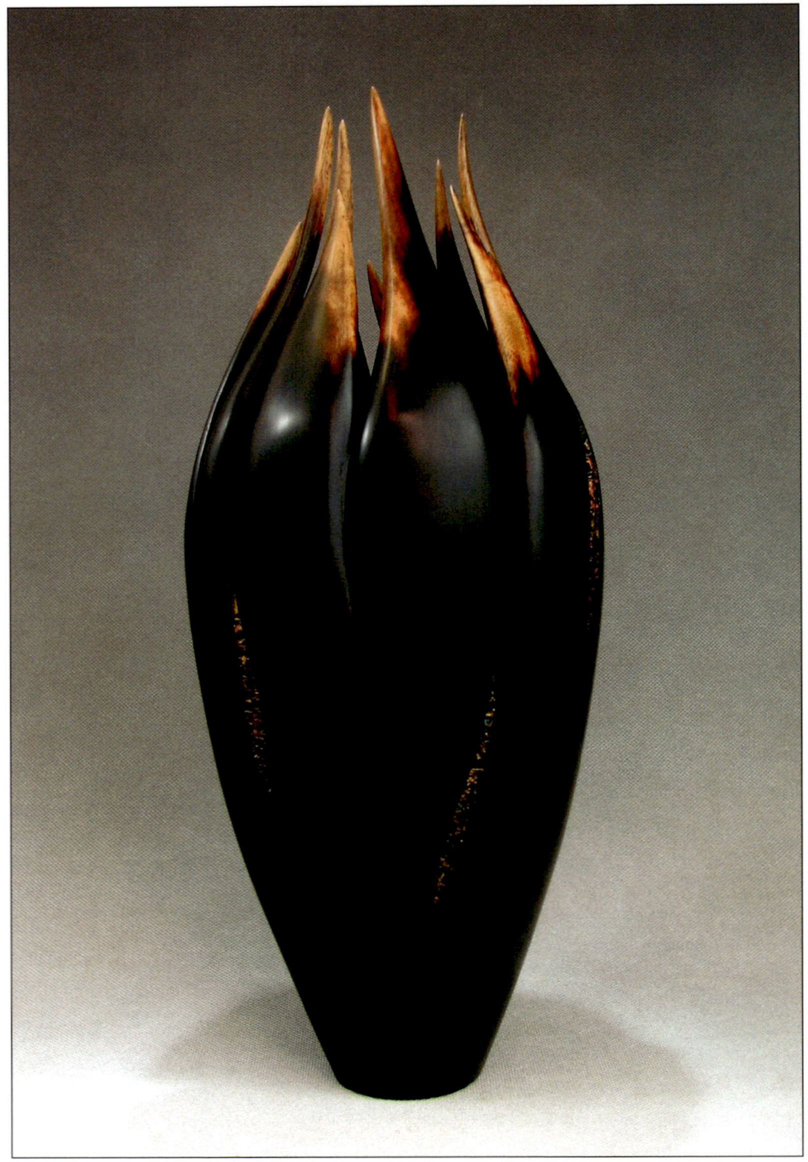

Artist's Statement

I have an acute awareness that the wood, and the trees it comes from, as well as the talent one has to craft fine pieces, are God given. In my artistic pieces I aim to reflect my appreciation for the majestic beauty of God's creation. As a result, most of my artistic pieces are inspired by nature.

Individual Artwork

Charred Remains

The Australian bush or forest is unique, for though these forests are often ravaged by fires they are not destroyed by them as is often the case with northern hemisphere forests. Instead, new growth burst out of the fire-charred branches and in several years all appears as before. Seeds lying dormant for years, benefiting from the heat and smoke, spring into life and soon the undergrowth is lusher than ever. Nonetheless, the scars of previous fires remain evidence of the toughness and resilience of the Australian bush.

Charred Remains is what you see after a destructive fire, charred pieces of branches reaching heavenward in a cry of anguish.

Jack de Vos. *Charred Remains.* 2008. Hollow vessel, marri, turned and carved, 410 x 170 diam.

Maryville Series

On the 7th of February 2009, now known as "Black Saturday," several bushfires were burning 100km north of Melbourne in the state of Victoria. Melbourne suffered the hottest day in its history on that Saturday, with some parts of the tinder-dry state reaching 48C. The fatal factor was the wind, with gusts of 100km/h fanning flames, transforming small fires into infernos. The different fires linked up to become an unstoppable fire-front; as a result over 120,000 hectares, or 300,000 acres, were destroyed at the cost of 173 lives and a loss of well over 200 homes.

Marysville, a popular mountain hamlet of 550 people, was all but wiped off the map with a loss of thirty-five lives.

The *Marysville* pieces attempt to capture some of the elements of this disaster.

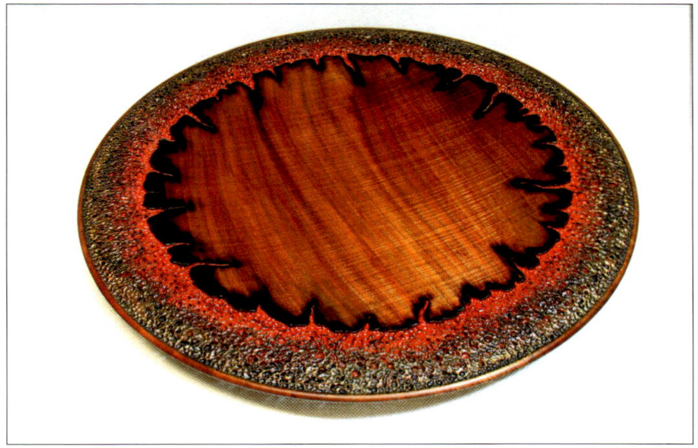

Jack de Vos. *Marysville – Devastation.* 2009. Platter, Tasmanian blackwood, turned and carved, 440 x 40.

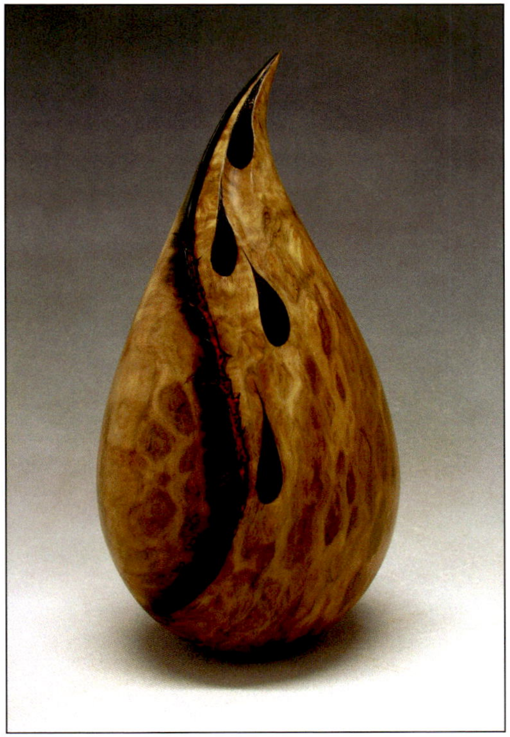

Jack de Vos. *Marysville – Vale of Tears.* 2009. Hollow vessel, birdseye bluegum, turned and carved, 370 x 165.

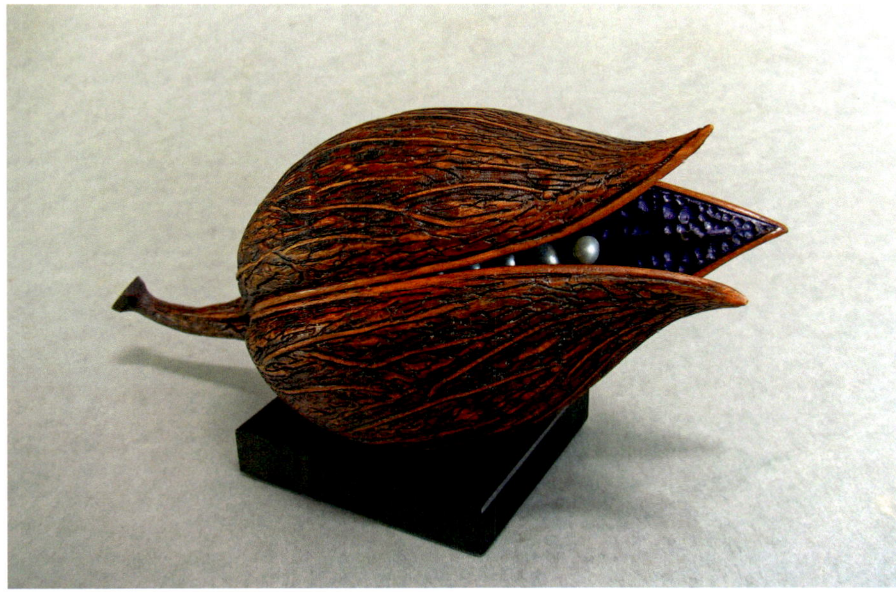

Jack de Vos. *Trinitas.* 2009. Seedpod, sheoak, turned and carved, 150 x 75.

Seedpod Series

The *Seedpod Series* are pieces inspired by flowers or seedpods.

The *Trinitas Pod* has cultured pearls as "seeds." A challenging piece, the blank was first cut into three equal pieces with a common meeting point in the center, then glued together using a paper joint that could be split once the piece was turned and hollowed. The inside of each separate section was then dimpled, painted, and the pearls attached; then all three sections were permanently glued together, the outside textured and stained.

MARK DEL GUIDICE

Norwood, Massachusetts, www.markdelguidice.com

Artist's Statement

As a Studio Furniture maker in the twenty-first century, I find myself working at the intersection of art, craft, and design. It is the history, traditions, and skills of these melding disciplines that influences my vision and informs my unique approach to furniture.

Working independently, and with a true love of labor, I have been developing my visual concepts into completed pieces through a process of sketching, writing, large drawings, model making, and mock ups. What comes of this is finely crafted furniture with a strong emphasis on form, surface, and content that is distinctive and not derivative of other styles and makers.

To further enhance my individual approach, I incise carve markings that are intuitive hieroglyphs, intended to evoke personal interpretations from each viewer; they are a response to the inundation of images from our visually sophisticated world – symbols from symbols. Additionally, I carve notable quotations in Morse code. Utilizing the code from a visual perspective rather than its essentially audible form allows me to add subtle content to the focus of each piece.

It is my intent that through my process of exploration and personalization a fresh perspective will result that reveals my unique creative vision and my passion for the medium of furniture.

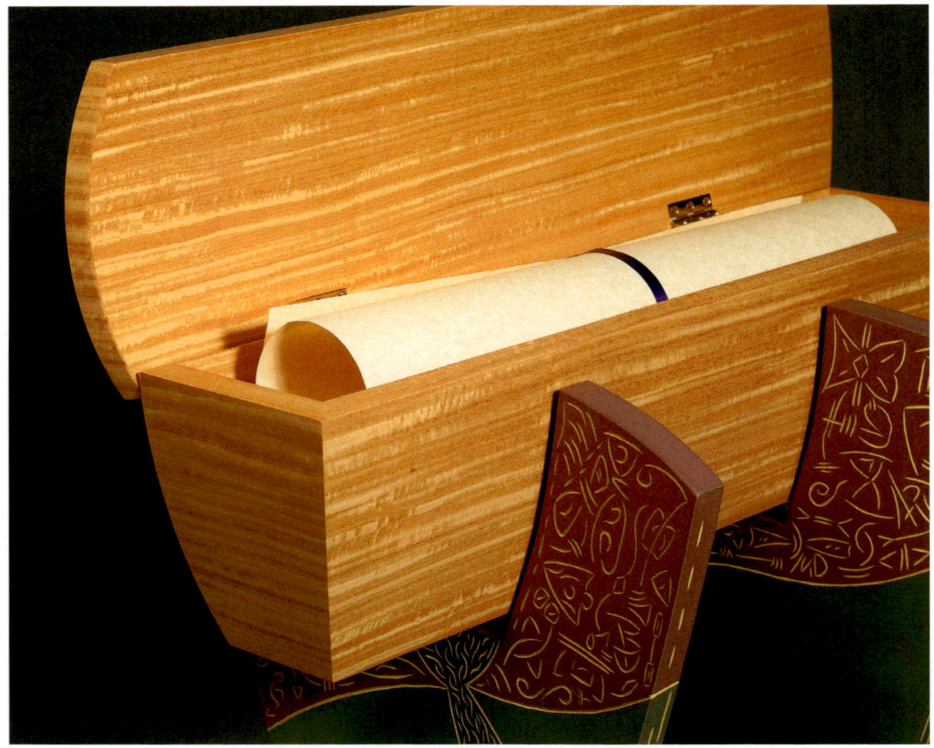

Mark Del Guidice. *Never the Same Again.* 2009. Sculptural box holding the degree that transformed me. Morse code on edges reads, "Mind to Hand to Mind to Hand..." Satinwood, bubinga, pau amarello, incise carved & milk painted basswood, lacquer, 20" H x 23" W x 14" D. (above and opposite page)

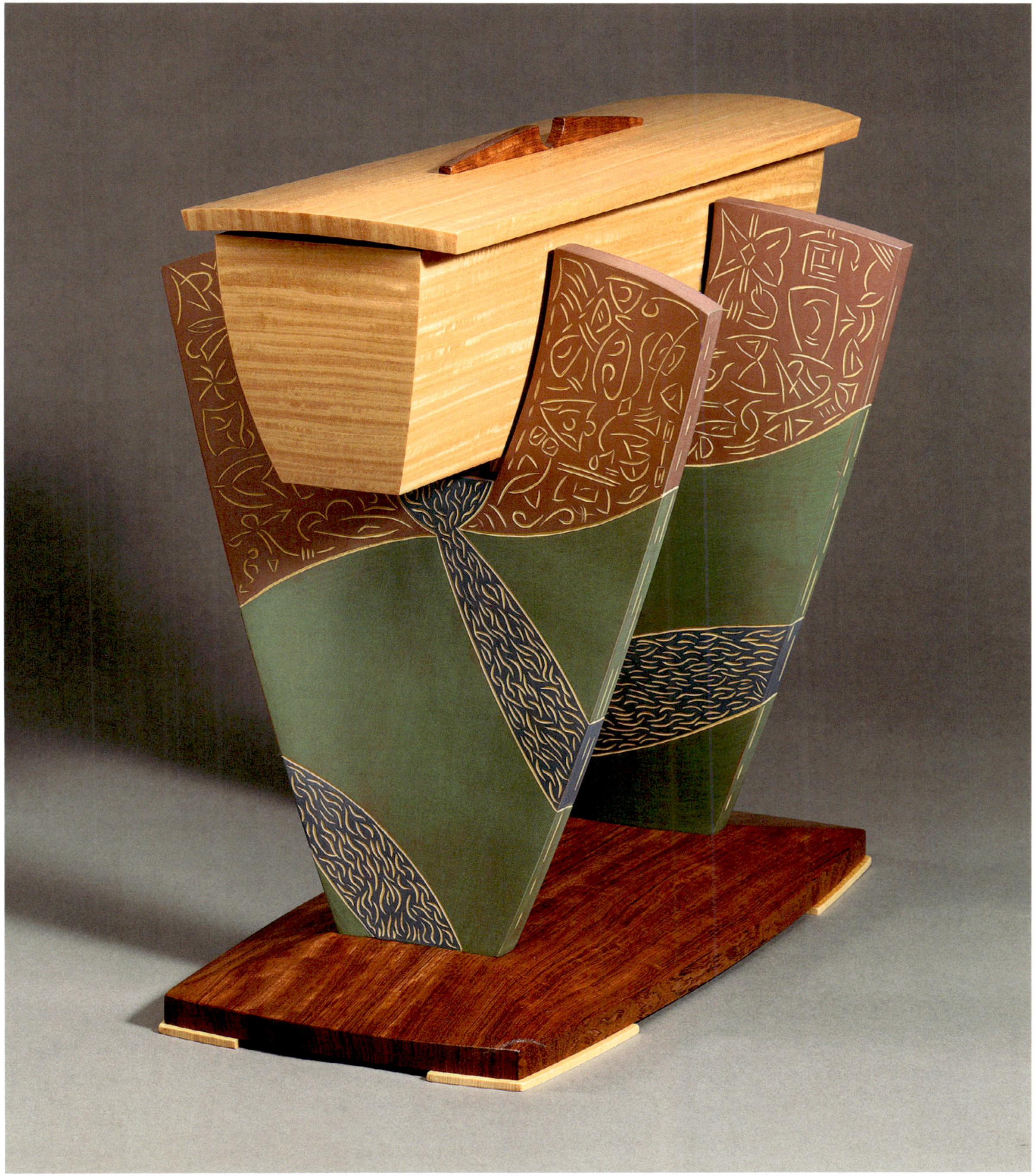

Cindy Drozda

Boulder, Colorado, www.cindydrozda.com

Artist's Statement

Lidded containers have fascinated me since I was a child hiding secret treasures; today they are my most creatively stimulating body of work. My work choreographs pure classic form with burl patterns. I complete the piece with a delicate hand-turned blackwood finial, creating a lidded vessel with elegant presence and lively personality. A jewel hidden under the lid reminds us of the treasure that life reveals when we make the effort to look deeper within.

Individual Artwork

Lidded Vessels and Containers

My vessels are turned on a lathe from a solid piece of wood. The rough chunk of wood is mounted to the machine, and a hand held chisel shapes the spinning piece. Specialized hook-shaped tools are used to hollow out the interior of the vessel. Hollowing is a time consuming process, working by feel, checking frequently with calipers, and coaxing all of the wood chips out of the small opening.

After the unseasoned (green) piece of wood is turned to its rough shape, it is dried until all of the tree sap in the cells has evaporated. I use a variety of drying techniques since each type of wood reacts differently. The rough turned piece may be boiled for a couple of hours in a big pot of water, or dried slowly in a paper bag, before finishing the drying in a specially made kiln. As the wood dries, it shrinks, distorts, and sometimes cracks. At this point some of the rough pieces don't survive. After it is completely dry, the vessel is remounted to the lathe, turned to its final shape, and sanded to a high polish.

I finish the completed vessel with hand rubbed oil and wax for waterproof protection. Because the wood is completely seasoned in Colorado's dry climate, and the vessel is turned with a consistently thin wall, the piece should not crack or change its shape even if it is taken to live in a wetter or drier environment.

When creating a lidded container, I often will decorate the piece with precious metals, gemstones, or 23k gold leaf. The application of gold leaf is known as "gilding," and has been used to decorate furniture, picture frames, signs, architectural components, religious artifacts, books, and other highly prized works since the Middle Ages. I use a traditional gilding technique of applying a "gold size" varnish, which the gold leaf adheres to, and finish with a burnishing style referred to as "engine turning." Since pure gold doesn't tarnish, there is no protective coating over the gold to impair its brilliance.

Despite my best efforts to control it, wood remains a living material with its own personality! My pieces develop their own character as they age.

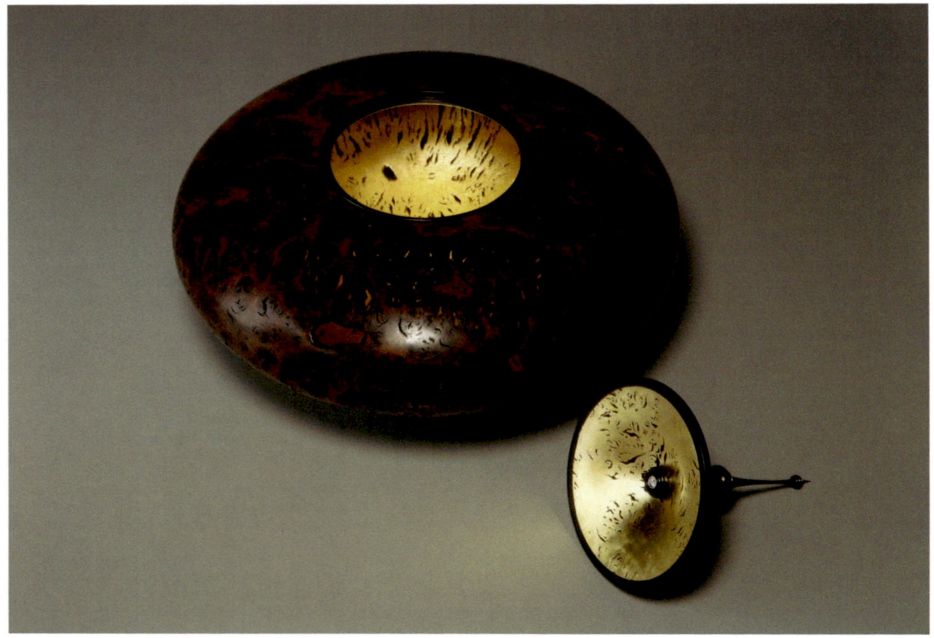

Cindy Drozda. *Treasure of the Ancient Maya.* 2004. Lidded vessel, Mexican chechen burl, African blackwood, 5pt diamond in 14KW, 23K gold leaf, 9.7" x 8.7". *Photographer: Tim Benko, Benko Photographics* (above and opposite page)

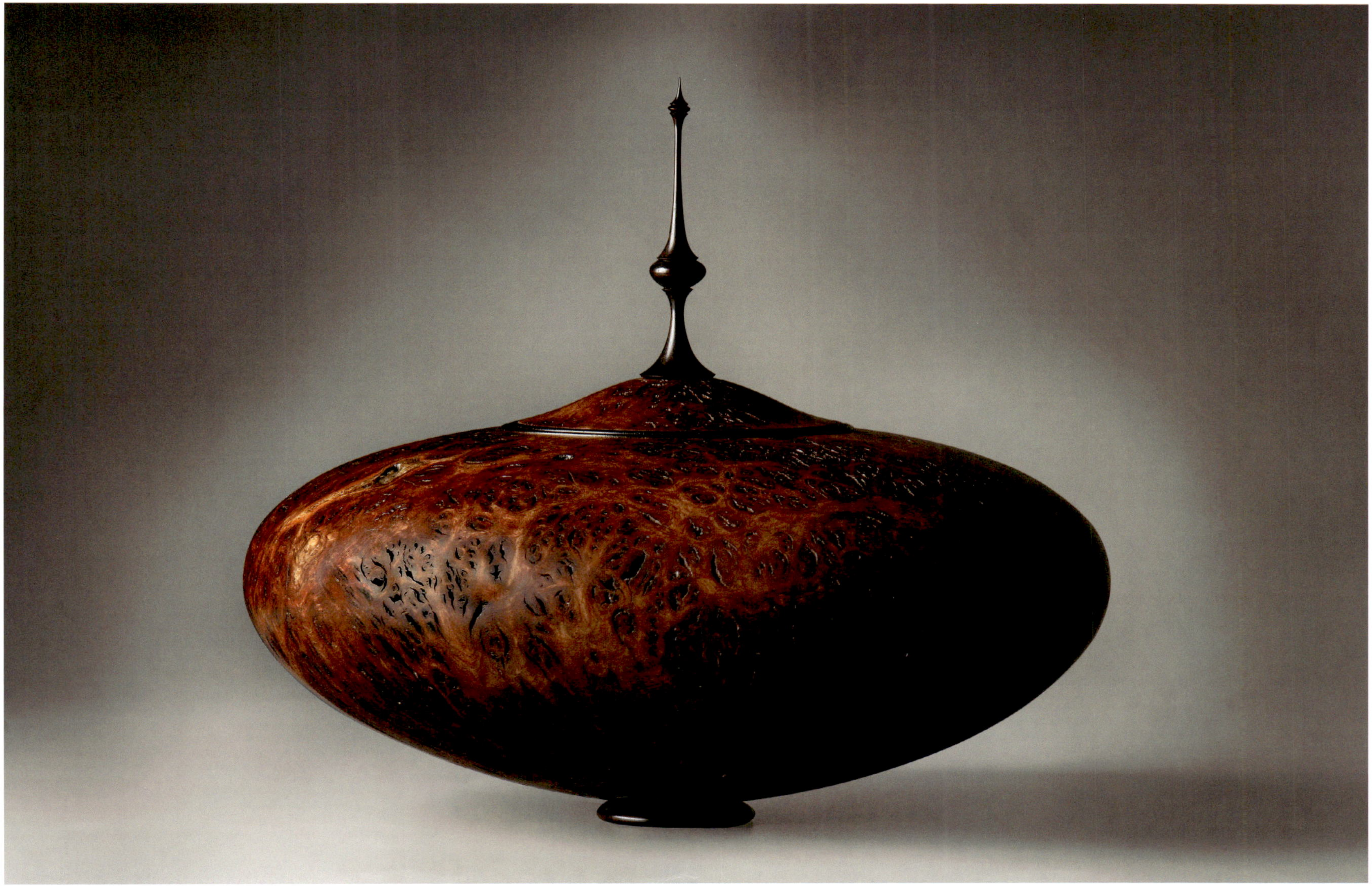

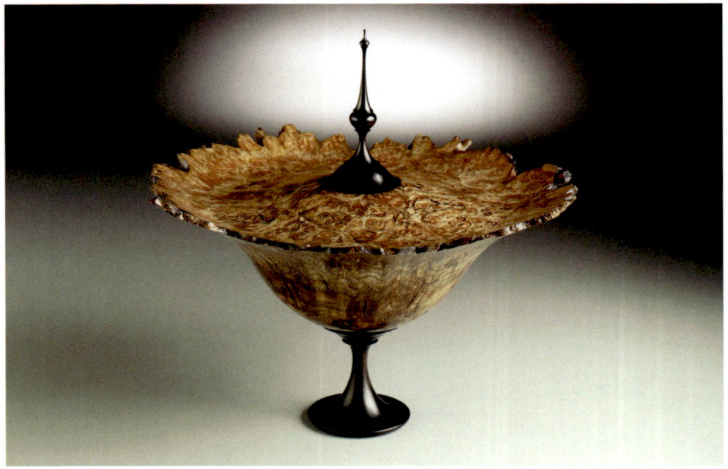

Cindy Drozda. *Inanna. Goddess Series.* 2005. Lidded vessel, Mexican chechen burl, African blackwood, akoya pearl in 14K, 8.3" x 7.8". *Photographer: Tim Benko, Benko Photographics*

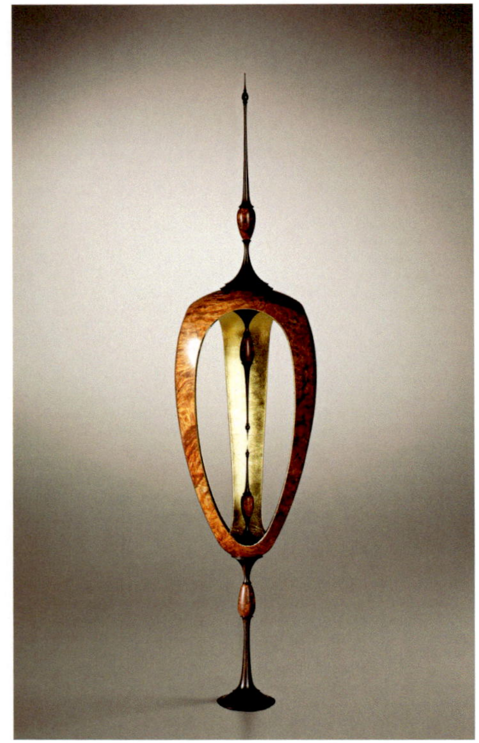

Cindy Drozda. *Seeds Of Change.* 2008. Triangular lidded vessel, amboyna burl, African blackwood, 4pt colored diamonds, 23K gold leaf, 4.5" x 20.5". *Photographer: Tim Benko, Benko Photographics*

Goddess Series Lidded Vessels

My *Goddess Series* celebrates balance in our world, of right brain and left brain, warrior and nurturer. In creating these pieces I express my own search for balance in my life as I honor the synergy of the mythical goddess.

I created this series after reading two very powerful books, Dan Brown's *The DaVinci Code*, and Leonard Schlain's *The Alphabet vs the Goddess*. Schlain's book in particular made me aware of the importance of what Goddess energy represents, in our culture and in each of us as individuals.

The mythical Goddess, as the giver of birth and life, has helped to give my work new life at a time when I was feeling frustrated. *Goddess Series* pieces are named after goddesses from the mythology of cultures worldwide.

The natural edged pieces remind me of an oyster's shell, and are named for ocean goddesses.

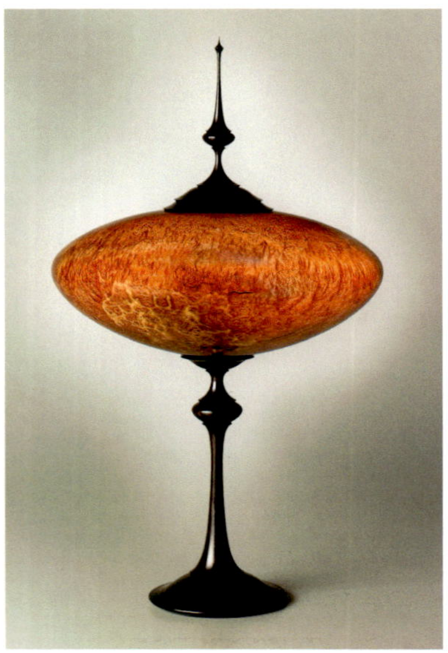

Cindy Drozda. *Pele, Hawaiian Goddess of Fire. Goddess Series*. 2005. Lidded vessel, red mallee burl. African blackwood, 6mm garnet in 14K gold, 9" x 15.8". *Photographer: Tim Benko, Benko Photographics*

Seeds Of Change Lidded Vessel

My own life is in a period of great change. As I journey through the "Change Of Life," I become aware of changes all around me. *Seeds Of Change* represents these changes, in our country's leadership, in the economy and therefore in my business, in our environment, in my life, and especially in my artwork. When designing a complex composition like *Seeds Of Change*, it is very evident how every change that is made changes everything else – in art as in life.

Seeds Of Change is a multi-axis turning made from a solid piece of amboyna burl wood, and accented with African blackwood finials and pedestal. The vessel is a small blackwood bowl underneath the lid. The open interior is gilded with 23k gold leaf and two 4pt diamonds hidden inside represent life's hidden treasures.

George Dubinsky

www.georgedubinsky.com

Artist's Statement

Furniture, Sculpture, Design

I am a designer. Deeply rooted in craft, I strive to build authentic objects that stimulate the dialogue and experience between human and object. Designing and making furniture has become a way for me to express ideas using furniture objects as a vehicle for conceptual thought. I intend to create a more personal conversation with the objects by giving them personality. Carefully considered design allows for various levels of investigation.

Individual Artwork

Stash Cabinet

I have always respected fine, solid wood casework. In my eyes a solid wood cabinet with finely fitted doors and piston fit drawers is the test that separates the men from the boys. Case pieces have a long history of secret compartments to hide valuables. The *Stash Cabinet* is a two-piece collection case with a secret compartment. By pressing a flush wooden button on top of the case, the spring-loaded drawer will pop out of the side of the case, revealing the secret compartment. Dovetails, half blind dovetails, and wedged tenons hold this case together.

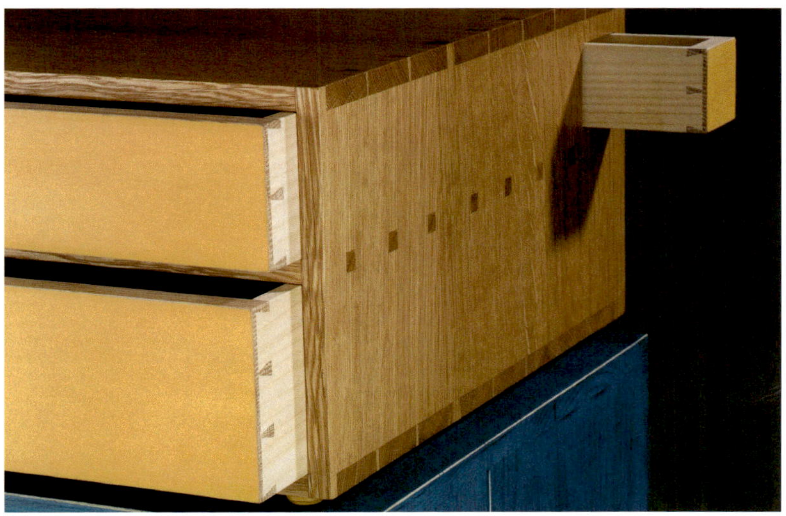

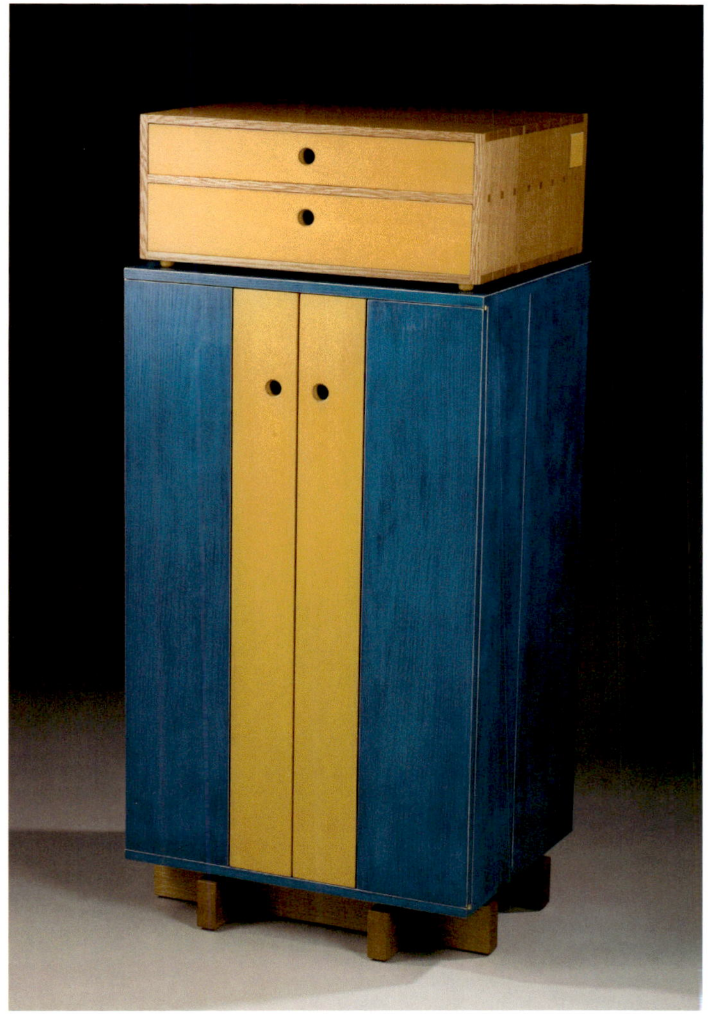

George Dubinsky. *Stash Cabinet.* 2006. Ash, white oak, milk paint, 16" d x 20" w x 47" h. *Photographer: Mark Johnson*

Haystack Chair

I love to be inspired by my working environment. With an inspirational setting I typically like to work with little concrete direction. For me it's all about developing a loose idea by working through it as organically as I can.

A few years ago I had the great pleasure of assisting a class taught by Eck Follen at Haystack School of Craft. During the two-week class I made this chair that I call *Haystack Chair*. The forms were inspired by granite rock formations that line Maine's coast; one formation in particular that I caught myself sketching in my notebook resembled a funky little chair. While searching for material to build my new little chair I stumbled across replacement decking planks that the maintenance guys were using to fix the extensive deck walkways that spread throughout the school. By building a frame and cutting thin strips of wood I was able to capture the volumetric quality of the rock while utilizing a material that spoke to the environment that fueled the design process.

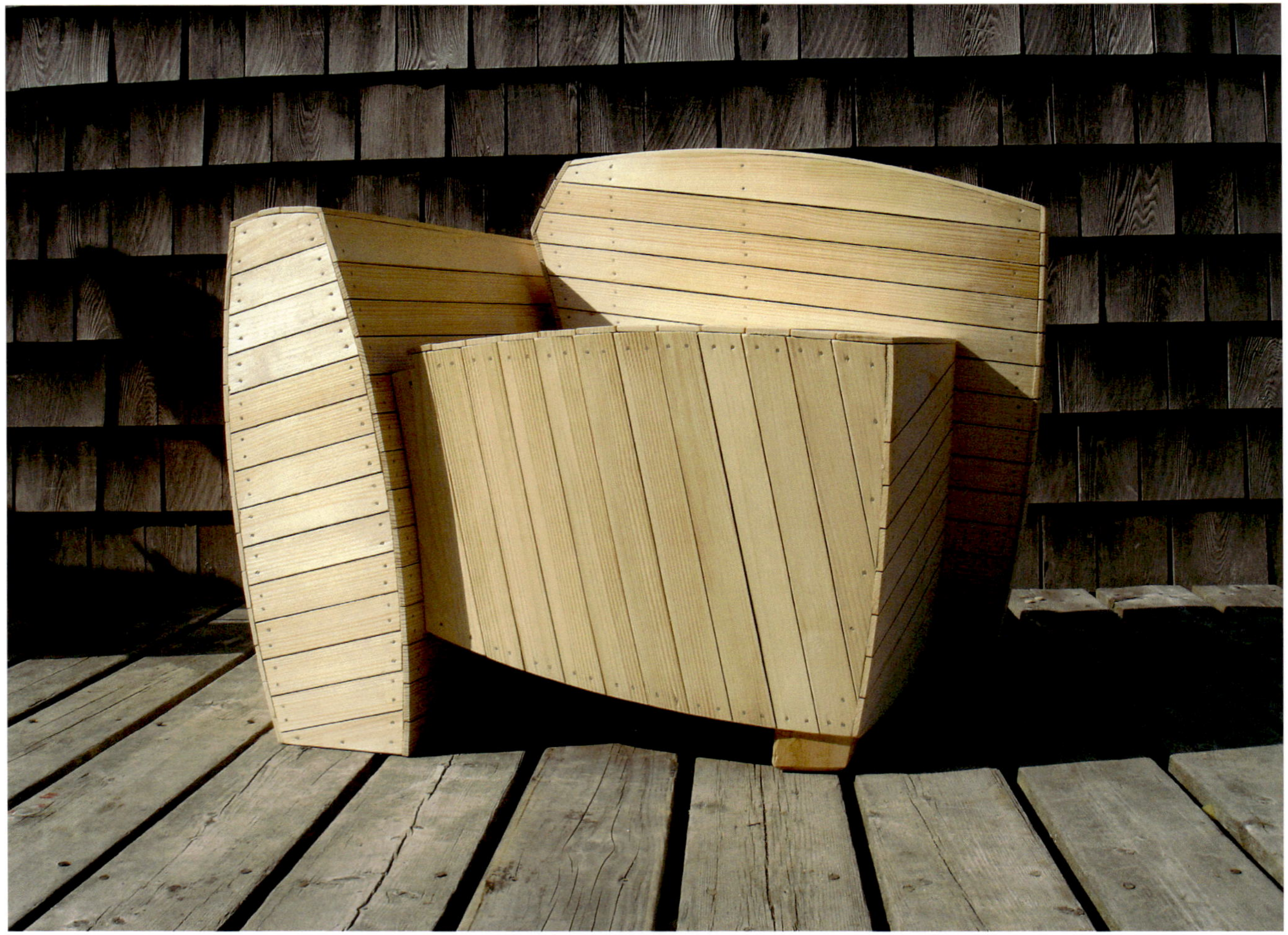

George Dubinsky. *Haystack Chair.* 2007. Decking material, 23" d x 25" w x 25" h.

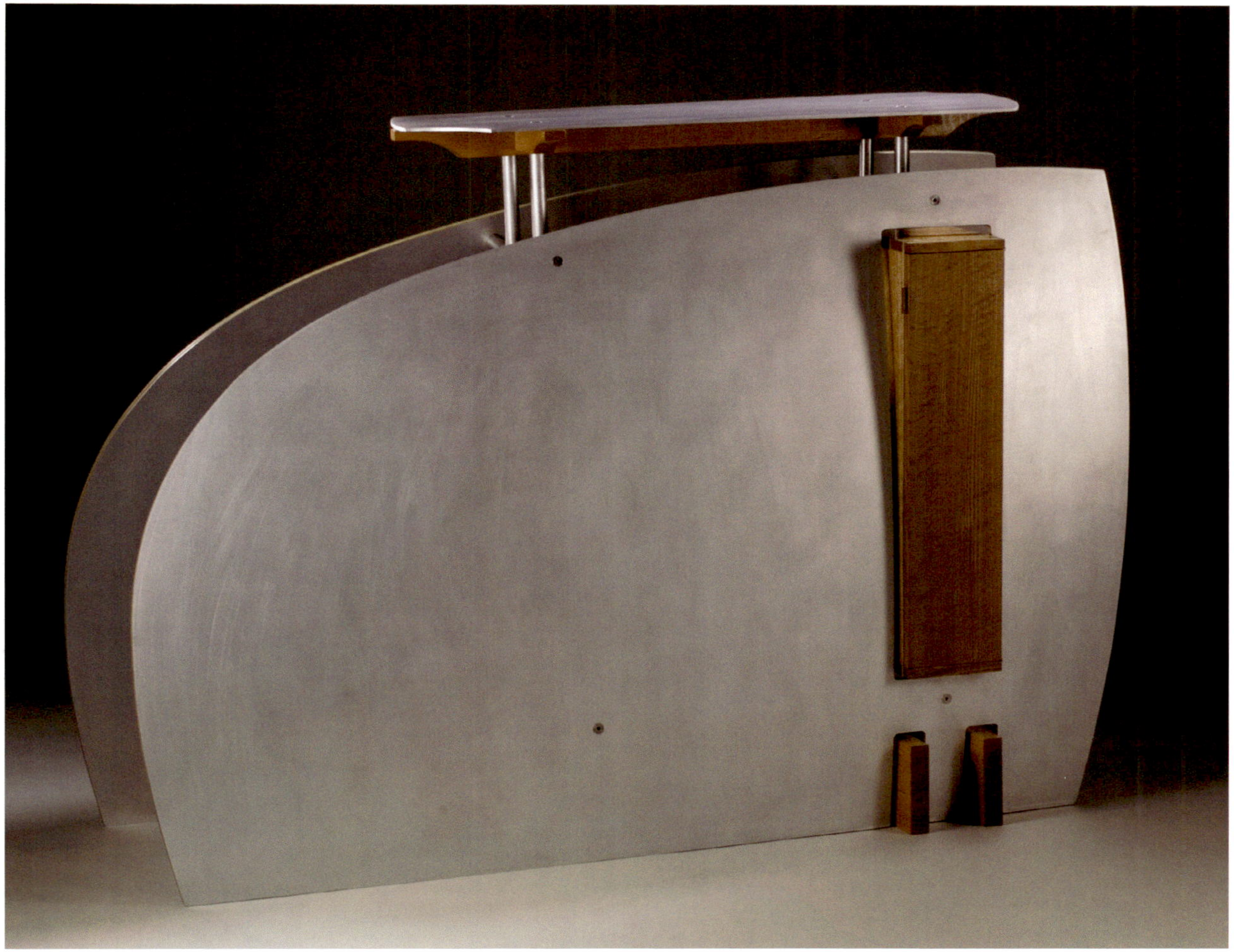

George Dubinsky. *Wine Case*. 2008. Oak, molded plywood, aluminum, 20" d x 54" w x 40" h.
Photographer: Mark Johnson

Wine Bar

The wine bar is an exploration of form and structure as well as a sculptural contrast of new and old construction techniques. The piece was a commission and serves a level of functional purpose. A cabinet for holding three bottles of wine and glasses as well as a table that creates a place to display one piece from the clients craft collection.

My intent is to contrast new and old craft. Old being represented by elements constructed in white oak held together by cutting traditional joinery, allowing the material to hold itself together. The new represented by elements constructed in molded plywood and aluminum. The molded plywood is made from large sheets of birch veneer bound by layers of PVA glue; a two-part epoxy holds the aluminum skin to the curved wooden sheets. The framework connecting all elements is TIG wielded from machined aluminum rod.

On paper the design was simple, two subtle curved laminated sheets intersected by a simple dovetail cabinet, an aluminum top supported by a white oak frame all held together with a three-piece aluminum structure. It was a wonderful learning experience to bounce from one way of working to a complete extreme, all on the same project. This piece acts as a model representing how the old acts as a foundation for the new.

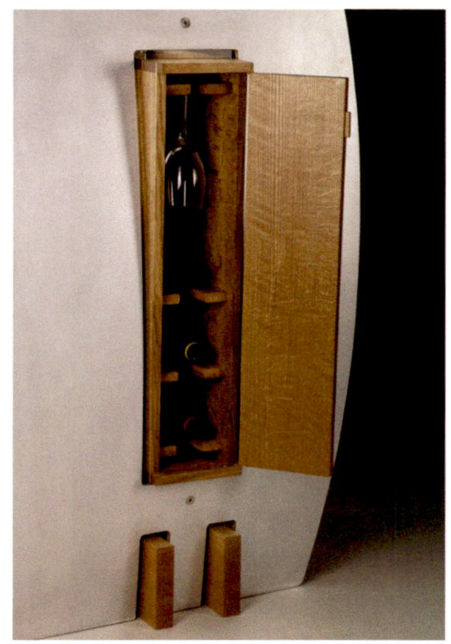

Dennis Elliott

Cape Coral, Florida, www.denniselliott.com

Artist's Statement

I was born in London, England, in 1950 and became a professional musician by the age of sixteen. I met my wife, Iona, in the United States, and married her in London in 1972. That Christmas I was given a lathe attachment for my Black & Decker drill, by my wife, and began what I thought then to be my hobby.

I feel a tremendous importance and responsibility each time I begin a new piece. Pondering a burl that was once a living part of a tree, I treat the cutting of it like a diamond. Knowing this piece of wood was and can be again a thing of beauty, I'm obliged to the wood, and it's not obliged to me.

When I look at the surface of the wood it seems to dictate what form it should be. The piece I turn could probably outlive me, thus, I know how important what I make might be.

In creating music, you're creating out of thin air. There's no material that you're working with when you begin. It's like magic, appearing from thin air. When you're working with a solid object like a piece of tree, you can only do it once. The responsibility is therefore greater than creating a new song, which can be wiped out and started again.

Playing music on stage is instantaneous. Any movement you make is done and gone. It's just a feeling at that time. If someone asked me "why did you play that thing at that part" after the show or performance I would say, what part? There's no magic at one part. The whole thing is what really matters. I feel in turning wood the importance is in the whole piece, not the part. Not the neck, the bead, or the foot.

Turning wood for me began as an outlet, fun in just using the lathe. I could spend hours, as my wife would say, making "toothpicks." Now, woodturning challenges me and I find myself in the midst of the beginning of my future!

Individual Artwork

Sculpted Vessels

Over the last ten or more years, my focus seems to have lingered on making pieces that are interesting to touch and strangely have the appearance of looking rather old and well worn by time. Some have abstract markings and appear to be of some ancient or Indian inspiration, but I have never studied anything like that so I guess I just like the effect!

Although I use carving techniques and sometimes burn and scorch these markings with an open flame, many of these "accents" are created without too much thought as to where they are placed, since I do not want the piece to look too contrived.

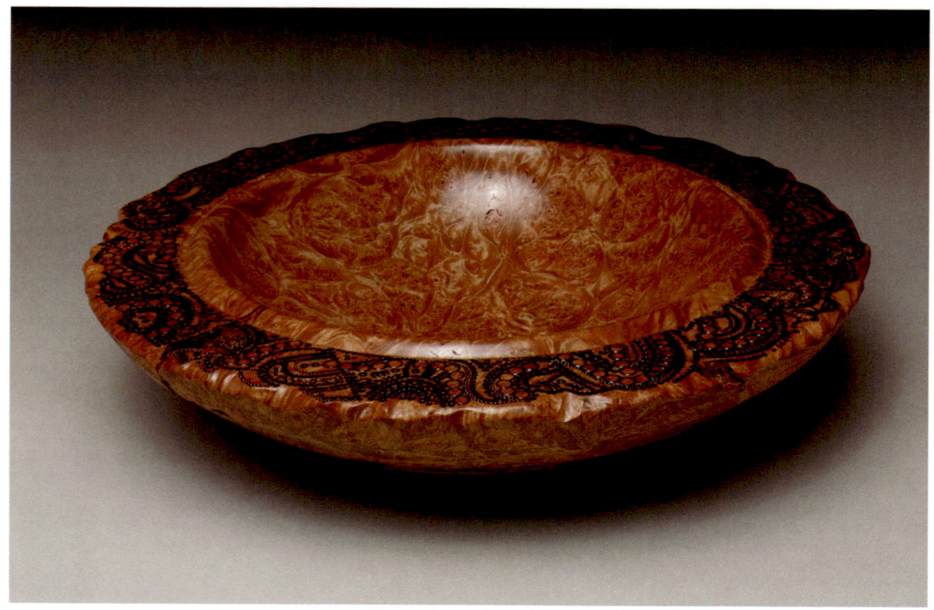

Dennis Elliott. *Presentation Bowl.* Bigleaf maple burl, turned, carved, & burned, 5" h x 19 1/4" d. *Photo taken by David Peters courtesy of del Mano Gallery*

Gemini Series

The term Gemini, in this instance, simply refers to the piece having two distinctly different faces. The typical Gemini consists of a base, a stainless steel rod, and the actual Gemini.

The whole concept of this series is to be able to rotate the piece whenever one wishes, so as to give it a different look. The *Gemini Vortex* becomes an object of interactive art, in the fact that the viewer has many choices as to how the piece is displayed, and the freedom to make changes at any time. I feel this involves the viewer in the actual artistic process.

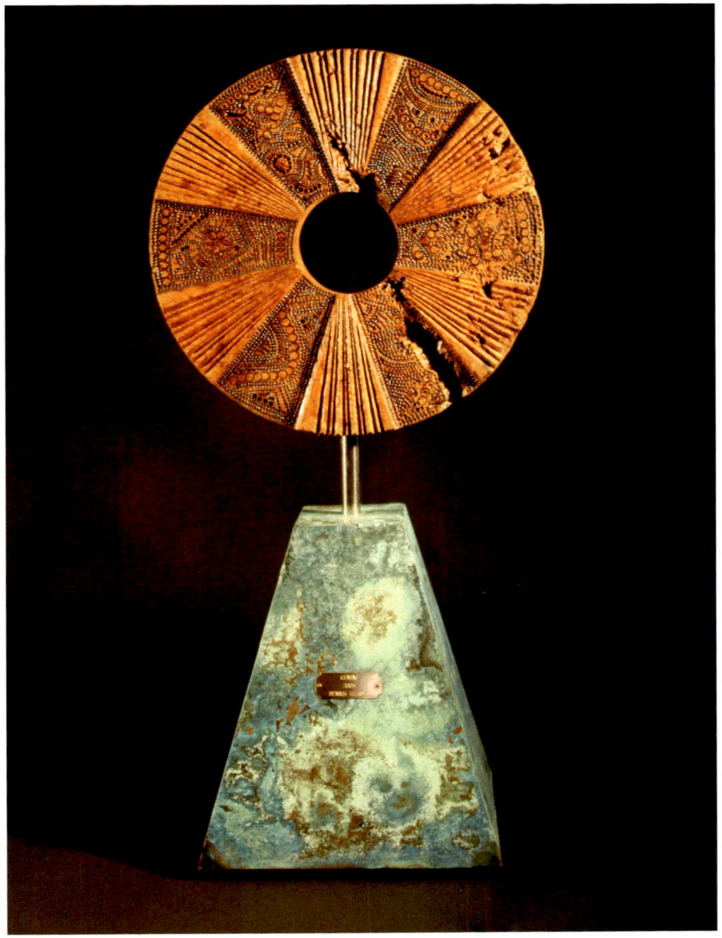

Dennis Elliott. *Gemini.* Bigleaf maple burl & copper with blue patina, turned, carved, & burned, 32 1/4" h x 15" w x 12" deep. *Photographer: Iona S. Elliott*

Wall Sculptures

My making "Wall Sculptures" really evolved from simple platters. These platters were turned and carved into table centerpieces. They were quite large and I decided to route a keyhole in the back, so that when someone would want to use the table, they could, if they wished, hang the platter on the wall. They were quite decorative and displayed nicely that way.

I started to receive slabs of ample burl from my supplier that were far too large for platters, so I decided to eliminate any preference of them being functional, and started making the pieces solely for wall hangings; this meant that I could have a lot more going on in the work, more content, freedom, and expression. I have explored this series over a thirteen year period and have used other materials such as metal, alabaster, semi-precious stones, and avonite to add contrasting texture and movement to the piece as well as carving and burning.

People rarely touch a painting, but my "Wall Sculptures" are three dimensional, and I encourage people to touch them.

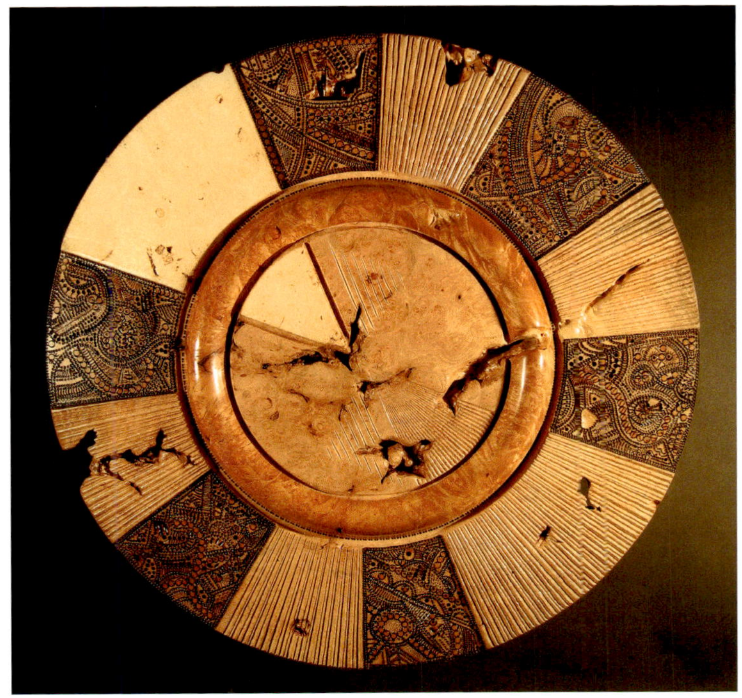

Dennis Elliott. *Covering Your Bases.* Bigleaf maple burl, turned, carved, & burned, 32" h x 32" d. *Photographer: Iona S. Elliott*

Framed Wall Sculptures

I have been making Wall Sculptures for many years now and they have gone through many changes as far as design and process is concerned, but I have never thought to frame one until I received a slab of maple burl in one of my shipments of wood that was just too thin to go through the normal routine of first flattening the back and then remounting it in the lathe to work on the face. It was just too thin, so I decided to make a nice frame for it and leave the back unfinished. The first was a prototype and would be a nice experiment and maybe I would learn something in the process.

The result so impressed me, and everyone that saw the finished piece, that I decided to continue with the series. Some of the smaller pieces really benefit from this as it seems to draw attention to them and it also frees me from my self imposed minimum size of about thirty-six inches for a Wall Sculpture as I feel that by that very term it should be something quite substantial and anything less is just too small.

The background or "Field" of the frame is a black rubberized coating that really makes the piece "pop," especially when mounted on a white wall. I am also using a cleat system on the back of the frame that allows it to be easily installed and removed and yet hold the piece flat against the wall.

Now I find myself wanting to frame even the very large pieces, but that is a decision that can be put off until the piece is finished as the original process is back in play and they can be displayed framed or unframed and this gives me, or indeed the buyer, the freedom to choose.

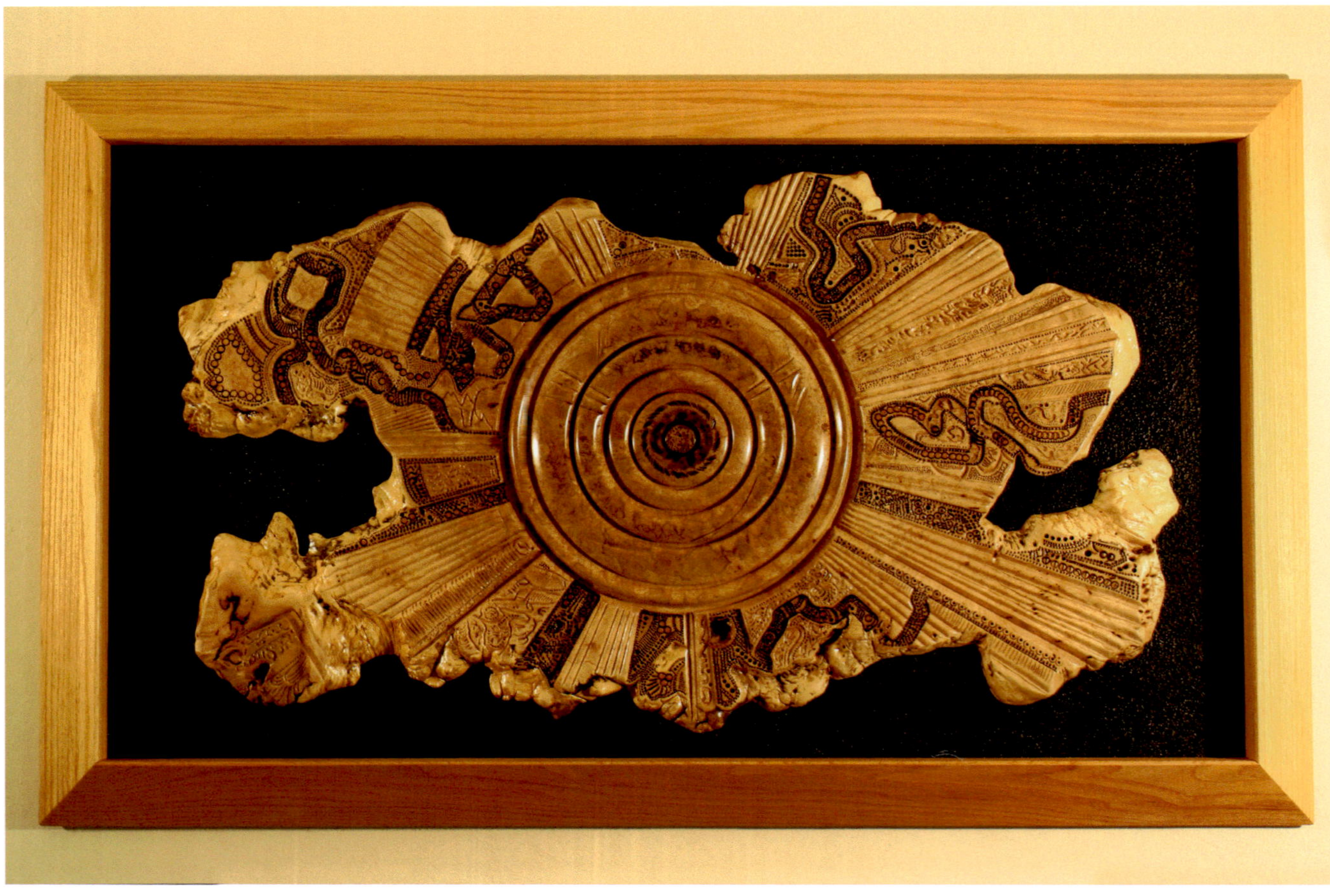

Dennis Elliott. Framed Wall Sculpture. Bigleaf maple burl with oak frame, turned, carved, & burned, 36 1/2" h x 60 1/4" w x 2 3/4" deep. *Photographer: Iona S. Elliott*

Charles Faucher

New Ipswich, New Hampshire, www.CharlesFaucher.com

Artist's Statement

My bowl and geometric forms involve a great deal of cutting and assembling before shaping. That is usual for segmented forms. What is different here, and is the energy driving all of my work, is the way I assemble. I do not build vertically. I move horizontally, or sideways. The heart of the process is a vintage Logan machine lathe with a 7.375" swing, which allows me to mill inside and outside diameters to metal working tolerances. I assemble various exotic woods into rings and then fit the rings inside or outside each other to a tolerance of .006 to create a range of effects. There are two-dimensional graphics or three-dimensional forms depending on how the rings are manipulated. The rings can also be assembled on multiple centers, resulting in a range of effects that are full of energy and surprise.

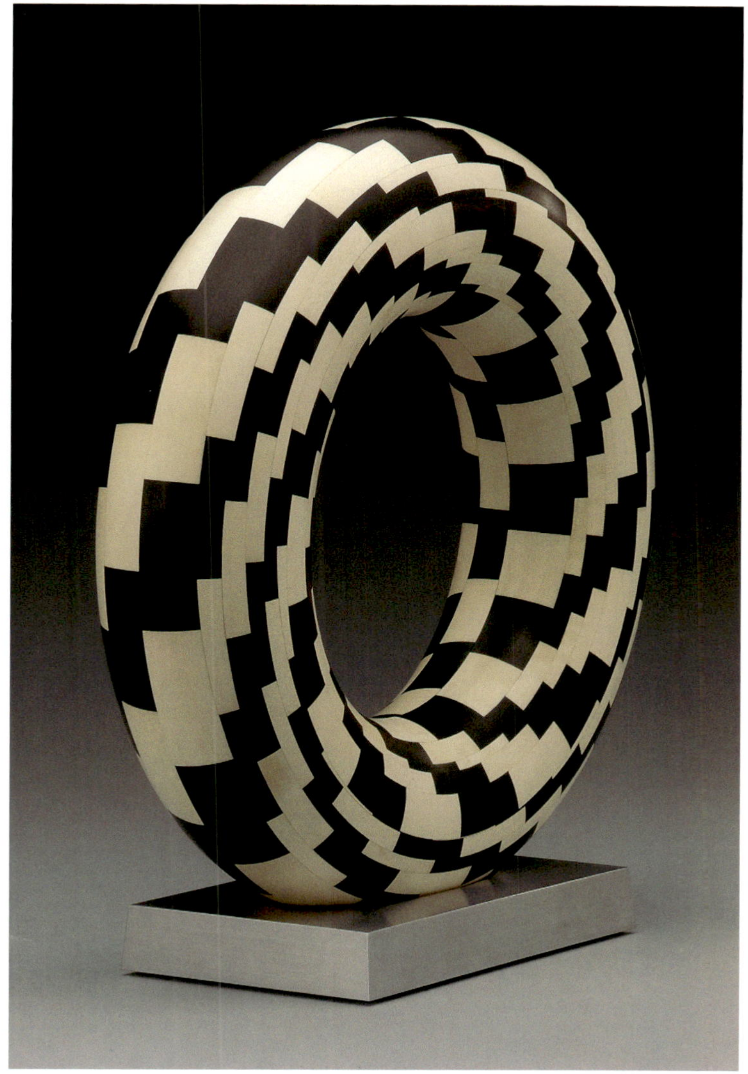

Charles Faucher. *Raging Torus*. 2009. Turned hollow geometric object, holly and ebony; aluminum base, segmented and assembled on multiple centers, 10" d x 2.50" w. *Photographer: Dean Powell*

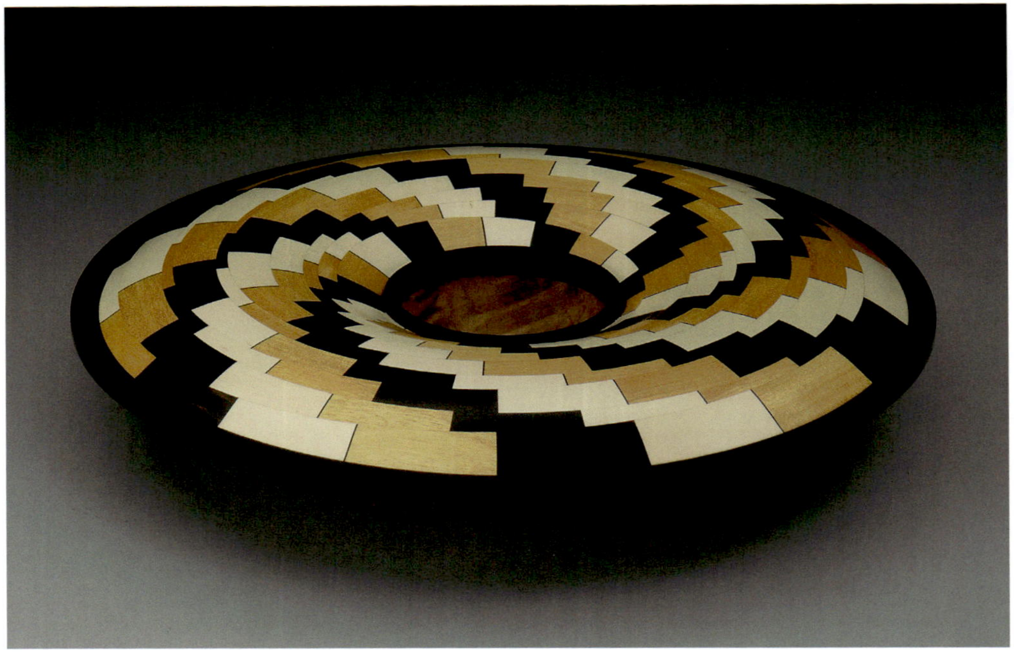

Charles Faucher. *Yellow Spiral*. 2009. Small bowl with large lip, myrtle, yellowheart, holly, and ebony, segmented and assembled on multiple centers, 14.50" d x 2" h. *Photographer: Dean Powell*

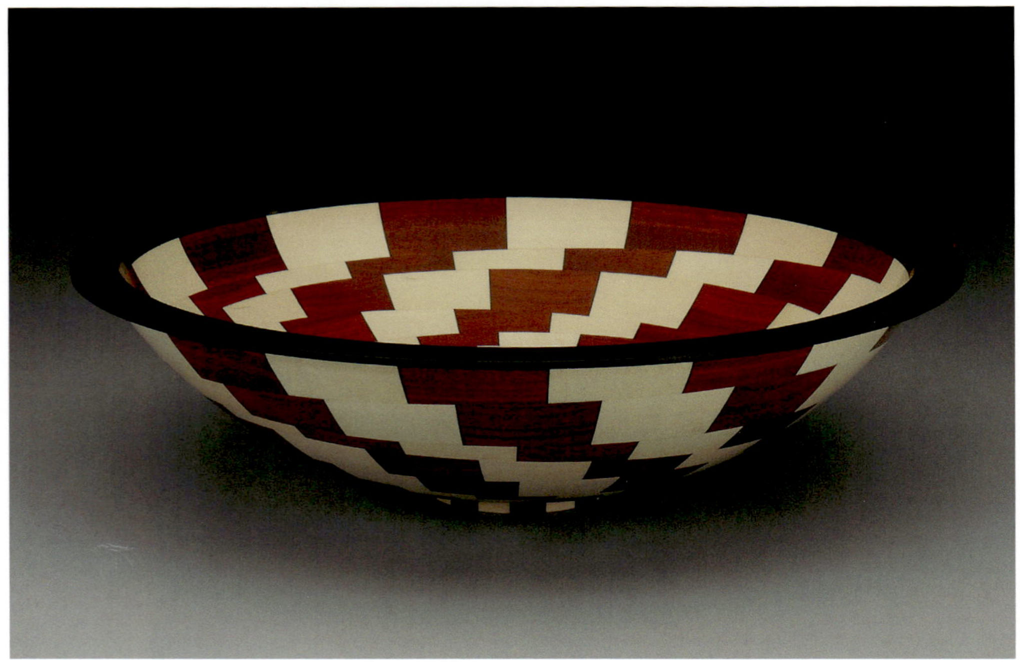

Charles Faucher. *Zig Zag*. 2009. Large bowl, ebony, holly, and bloodwood, segmented and assembled on multiple centers, 14.25" d x 5" h. *Photographer: Dean Powell*

Harvey Fein

www.harveyfein.com

Artist's Statement

If asked, those who know would say that I'm in love with the mechanics of things. I need to know how things work. While in college, I earned spending money as a mechanist and used to imagine that when I retired I'd work in a machine shop again, for fun.

But a much better future announced itself to me when, in 1997, a friend gave me a wooden bowl he had made, and then showed me how he had made it. Holding the gouge in my hand for the first time, I knew that this was for me. I bought my first lathe that very afternoon.

As I moved away from imitating the many generous teachers and critics I encountered both in person, on the page, and on video, I saw that my creativity and my skills as a machinist and a maker (I have been manufacturing window treatments for forty-five years) were showing up in my turnings. What started out as a desire to find a way to insert pieces of a contrasting wood in the rim of an open-form bowl, eventually evolved into the fixture that enables me to make the work that I do now.

Somewhere along the way, I came up with five elements that I try to put into my work: craft, form, mystery, surface decoration, and integration. In each piece I make I strive for the melding of these elements. The craft element I have developed over many years. The form is mostly proscribed by the golden mean. The lathe and the jig add the mystery while the jig cuts, wood grain or added materials add the surface decoration. Picking and choosing which elements go into a piece is the integration. Just because I can doesn't mean that I should.

The mechanical process, which is so familiar to me, has been incomparably enriched and deepened by the addition of the aesthetic concerns involved in making a successful piece in wood. It pleases me a lot to think that in looking at my work you might experience some of the joy I have in making it.

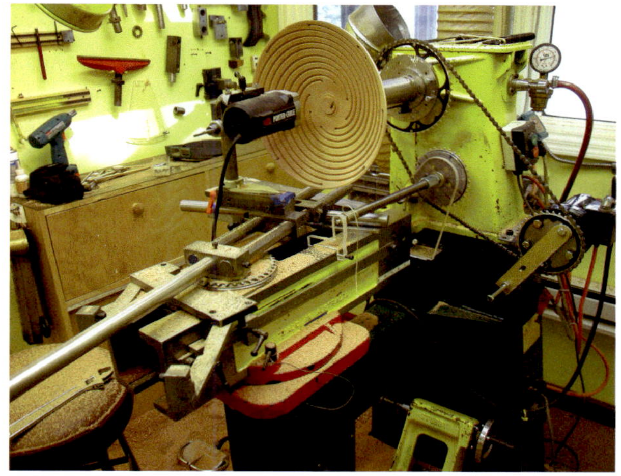

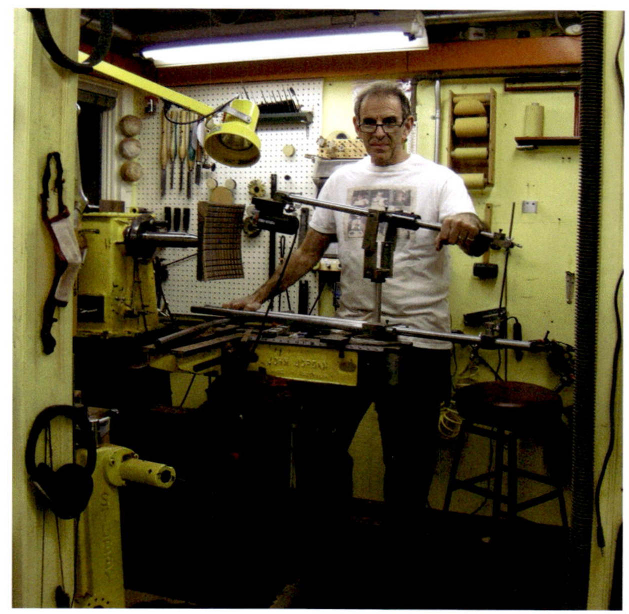

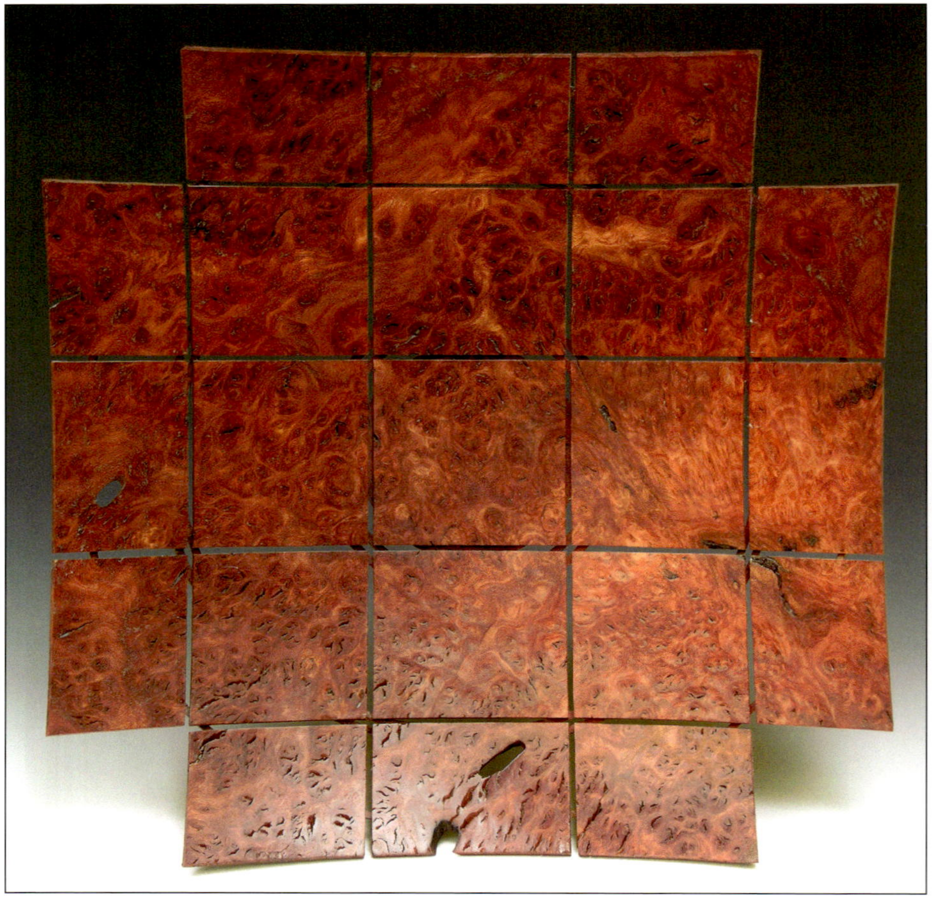

Harvey Fein. *MAD.* Jarrah burl, 14 1/4" x 14 1/4" x 1 3/4" h.

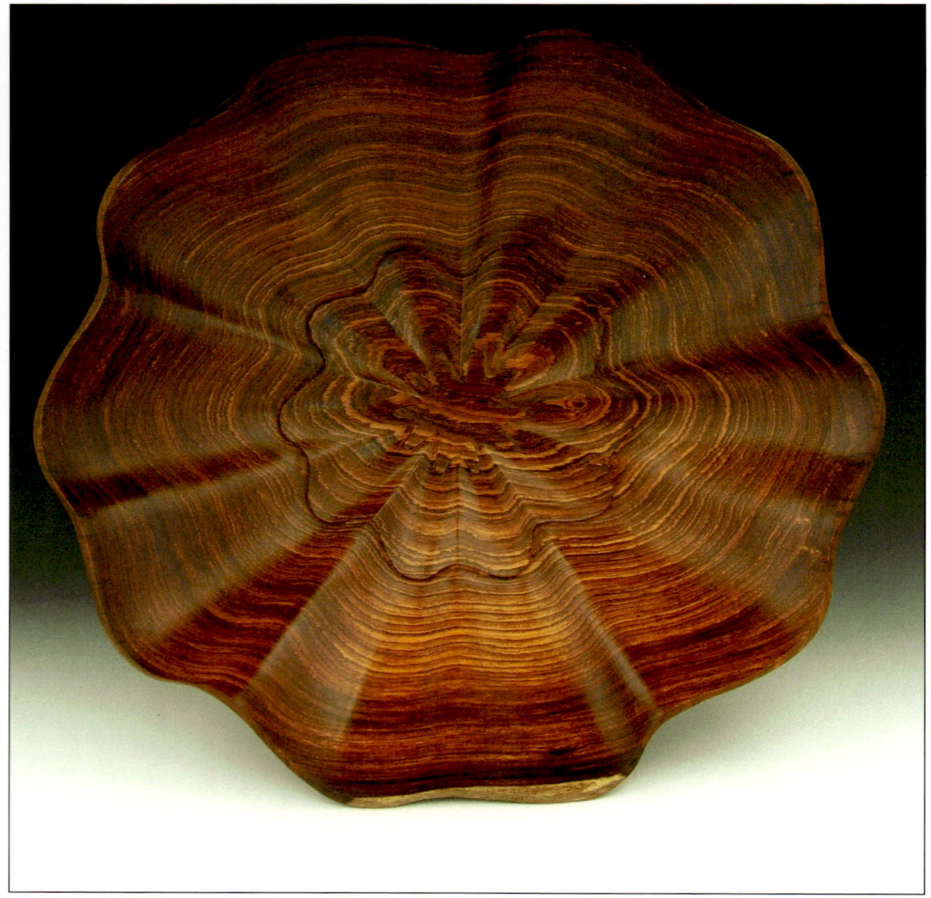

Harvey Fein. *09-26-08.* Cocobolo, 19" d x 3 1/2 h.

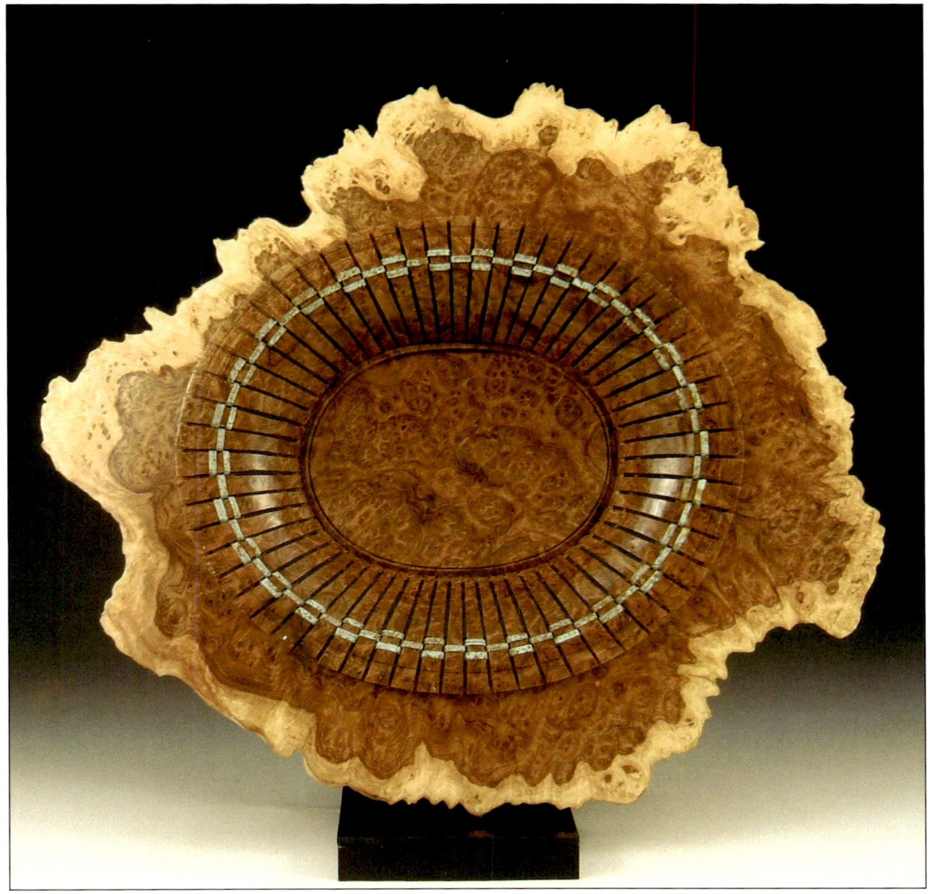

Harvey Fein. *02-22-09.* Concinna burl, 19" x 16" x 2 1/4" h.

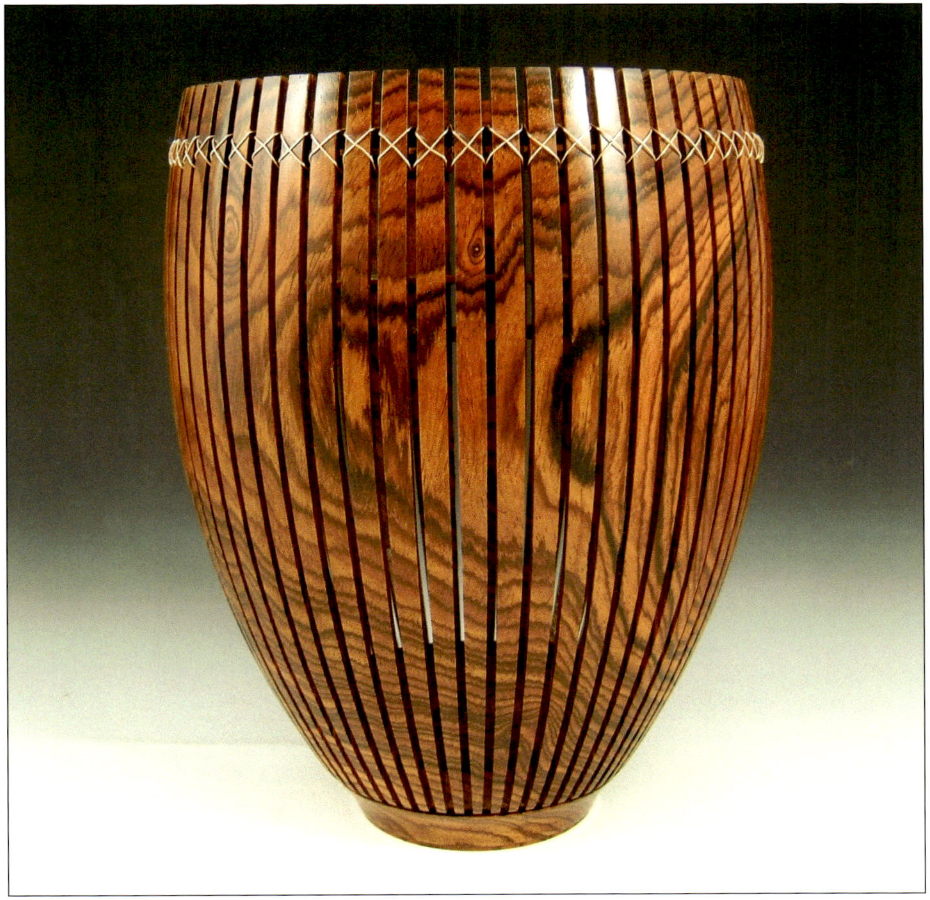

Harvey Fein. *02-02-09.* Cocobolo, copper wire, 7 3/4" d x 11 1/2 h.

Rue Ann Flanders

Indianapolis, Indiana

Artist's Statement

My artistic focus on woodworking incorporates sculptural, decorative design in colors and finishes that enliven the natural elements of the wood. The flowing shapes, the consistent use of spheres, and bright colors are inspired by the playfulness of youth.

Using wood as my medium reflects my appreciation of a natural material capable of being transformed into organic and architectural shapes. These shapes can be both visually entertaining and functional. The transformation can result in whimsical furniture when architectural or abstract sculpture when organic. Repeating these shapes and adding colors throughout each piece visually unites the work and completes the theme.

Every piece of work begins with a series of sketches, progresses to the model stage, which is possibly the most important stage as this is where the kinks are worked out, then to construction, and finally to finishing. With the utilization of various techniques such as oxidized metal leafing, or faux painting, the finishing can take as much time as the construction, but it's this detail that adds to the uniqueness of my work.

When I complete a piece, I not only experience accomplishment but I truly enjoy what I have created. The real test, however, is seeing the smiles of others when they see my work. It's then that I know I have achieved my goal.

Individual Artwork

Sphere Cabinet

The *Sphere Cabinet* combines functionality, whimsy, and kinetic movement. In designing this piece, I wanted the colors to be bold and different and the shapes to be fun. Since the design carries a ball theme, it seemed only natural to add movement by allowing the balls in the doors to spin.

The body of the cabinet was constructed out of a sheet of maple plywood using a v groove router bit and "folding" the wood similarly to folding a box.

There are two drawers curved in the shape of a grand piano. The pulls incorporate balls as well to continue the theme inside the cabinet. Half balls were used as spacers between the legs and the cabinet, and between the curved half circles in the upper pediment. Wooden triangles, spaced strategically, add contrast and interest.

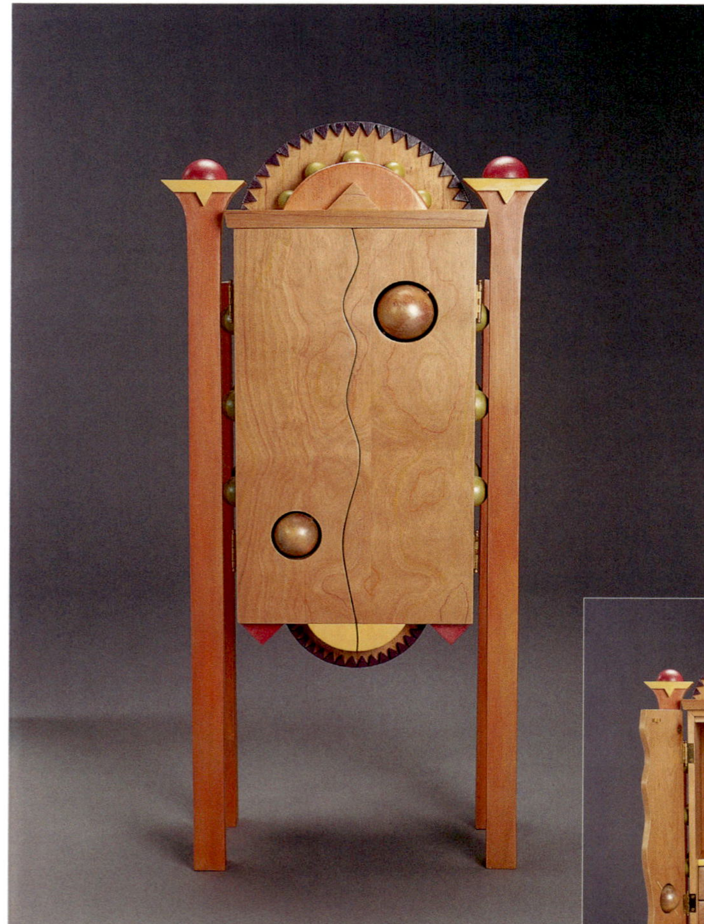

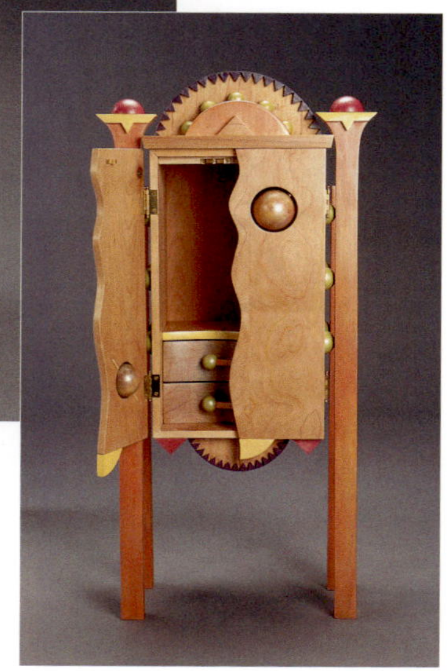

Rue Ann Flanders. *Sphere Cabinet.* 2005. Table top cabinet, maple veneer plywood and poplar wood, 36" h x 12" w x 12" d. *Photographer: Steve Cassidy*

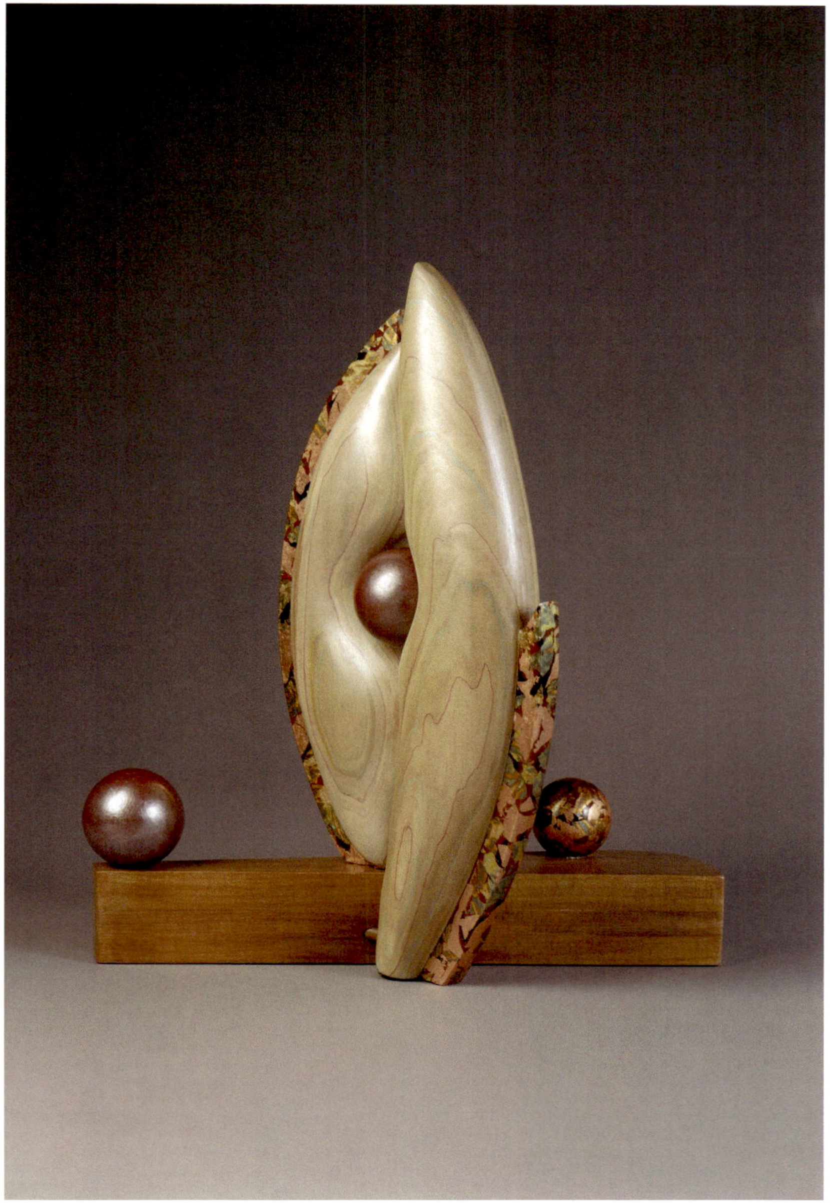

Levels of Balance

This sculpture shows the interaction between organic shapes of growth and change, and static shapes of metal and spatial relationships. It stands 21" high with the base spanning 19".

After the concept for this sculpture was mentally formed, I progressed to drawings, then the construction of models using clay, and finally moved to the wood itself. At the wood stage, the process begins with blocks of poplar glued together to get the bulk needed for shaping. The softness of poplar and its compatibility with paint made it a good choice for this project. Once glued, I roughed out the piece on the band saw and then went to an angle grinder to finish the shape.

When you reach a certain point in the construction, the design usually alters as the sculpture starts telling you what to do to finish it. This happened with this sculpture once the vertical pieces were complete. It was only then that I could determine the shape of the base and the logistics of making it stand on its own.

Metal was used to secure the floating ball in the middle and to secure the vertical sculpture to the base. The "wings" and balls were painted in multi-color Japan paint, then sporadically covered with metal leaf. The colors of the paint were carried throughout the wood grain to visually marry the segments together.

Rue Ann Flanders. *Levels of Balance I.* 2007. Wood sculpture, 21" h x 19" l. *Photographer: Steve Cassidy*

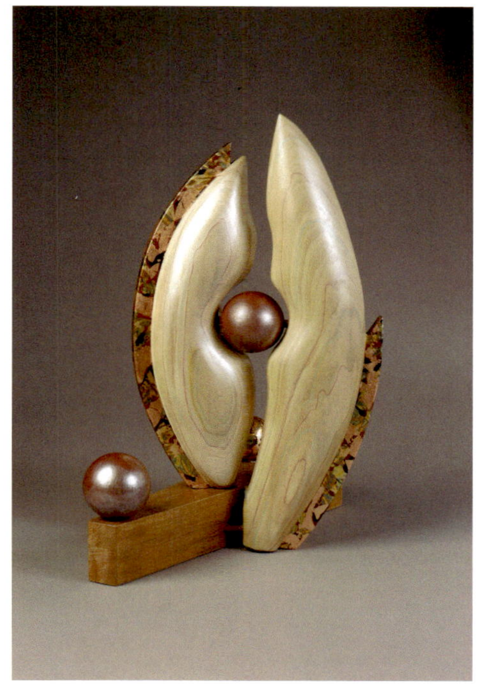

Liam Flynn

Limerick, Ireland, www.liamflynn.com

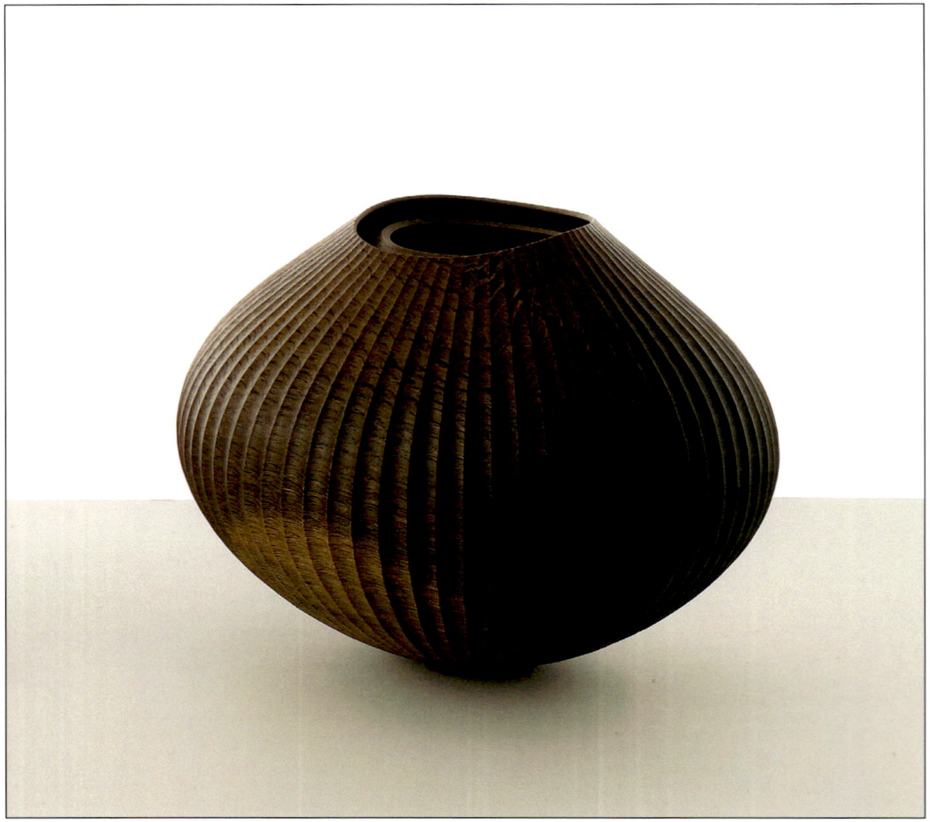

Liam Flynn. Inner Rimmed Vessel. Fumed oak, turned & carved, 34 cm w x 26 cm h.

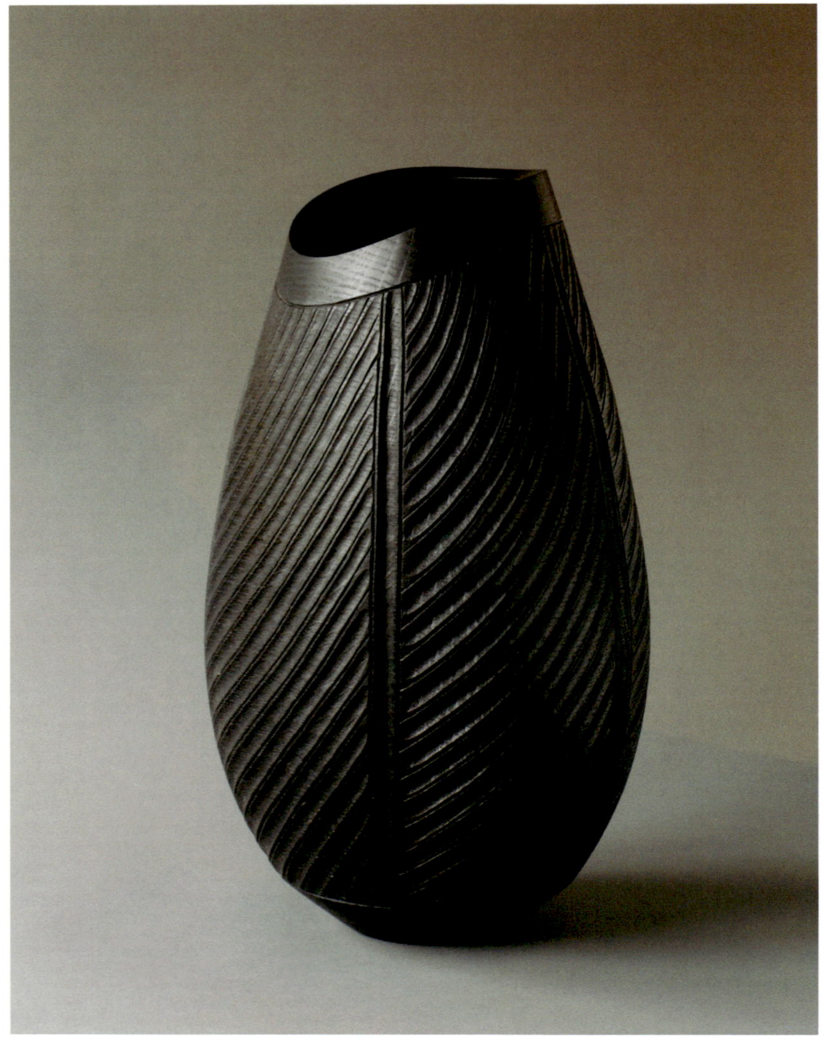

Liam Flynn. Inner Rimmed Vessel. Ebonised oak, turned & carved, 32 cm h. *Collection of the V&A Museum London*

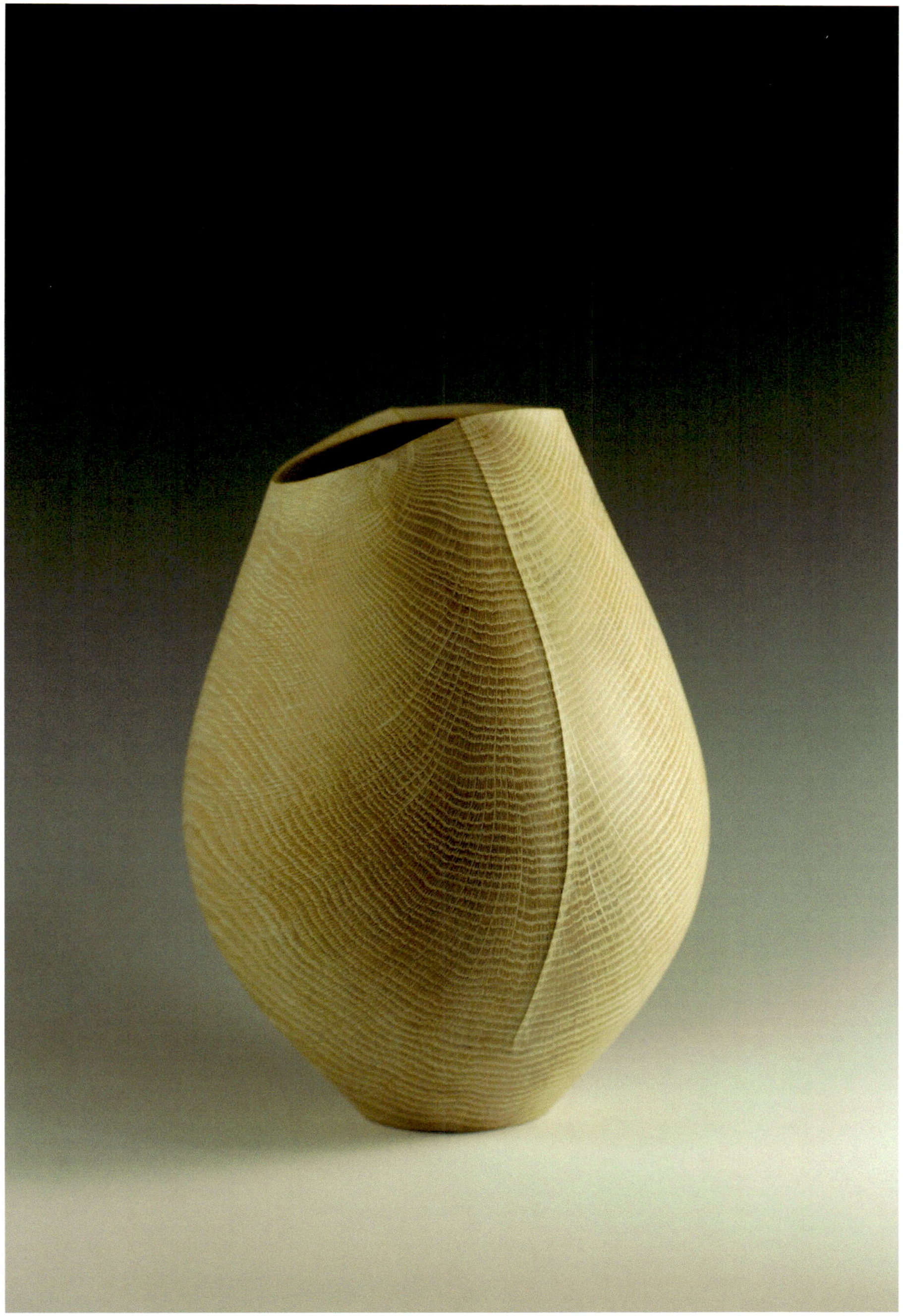

Liam Flynn. Inner Rimmed Vessel with Spine. Oak, turned & carved, 35 cm h. *Irish Government Embassies Collection*

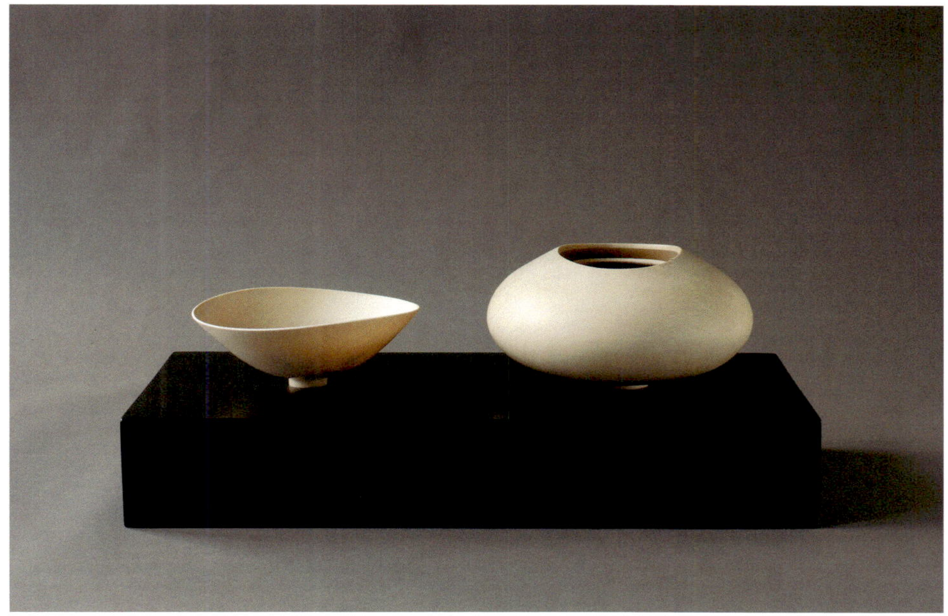

Liam Flynn. *Still Life with Holly.* Turned, 35 cm w.

MARK FRANK

Los Osos, California, www.lavaman.com

Artist's Statement

While watching a glowing sunset reflect onto snow-capped mountains, I try to experience the moment fully. Letting my thoughts fill with the unique beauty after a day of collecting, I endeavor to bring these inspiring memories home. For as long as I can remember, I have had a passion for nature. In college I studied art and ecology, disciplines that only deepened my connection with, and reverence for, this beautiful planet. Through the pieces I create as an artist, I strive to reveal this insight, and give others that same sense of wonderment.

In this way, my creative process truly begins in the forest where I personally collect each piece of wood, an ancient form of *krummholz* ponderosa pine. Upon sculpting through the often hundred years to an inch ring pattern, I expose the tree's thousand-year history. The finished sculpture looks naturally formed, but a closer look will reveal where I have merged artistic composition and the elegant symmetries found in the twisted patterns of the wood. Since sculpting exposes a tree's growth ring pattern, you can follow where I have followed grain and color. And because I integrate the unique forms in each piece of wood, every sculpture is truly one-of-a-kind. In some cases, molds are taken from the more interesting shapes, and resin prototypes constructed for casting in metal. It can take hundreds of hours to perfect a medium-sized wood sculpture, and my production is limited to only a handful of finished pieces each year.

Just as viewing clouds evoke thoughts different to each viewer and impart an appreciation of nature, it is my wish these sculptures will do the same—connecting us all, through art, to each other and to our amazing world.

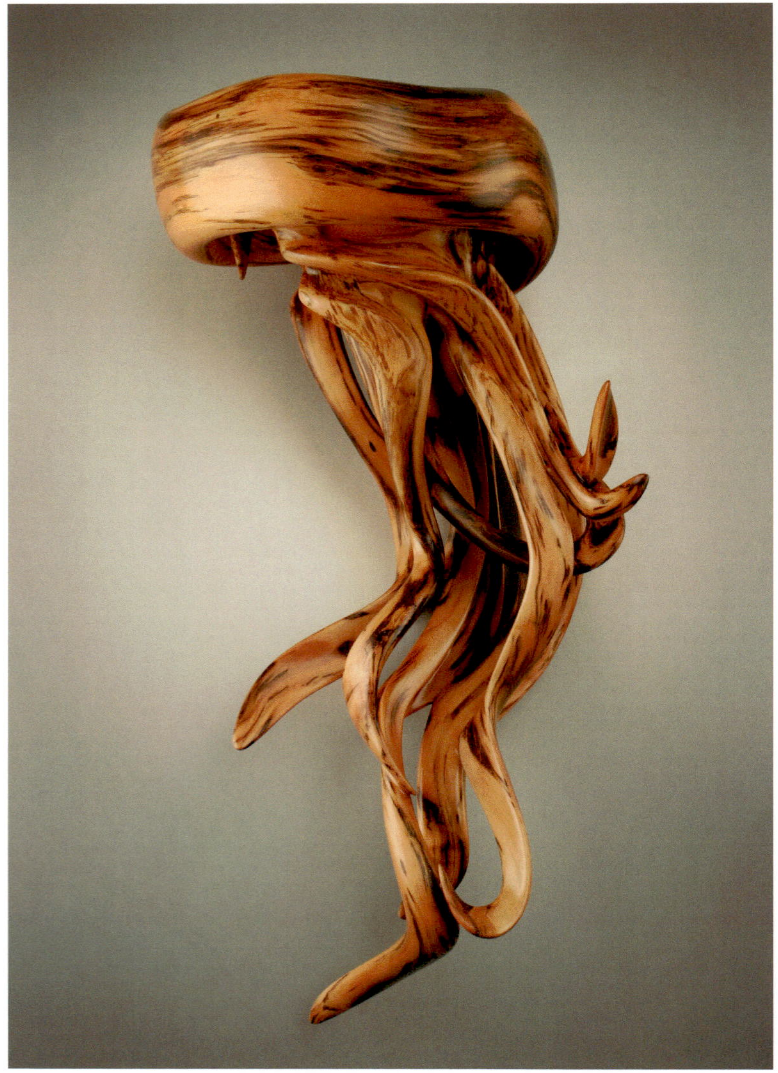

Mark Frank. *M565.* Ponderosa pine, 21" w x 43" h x 16 1/2" d. *Photograph by Ron Bez*

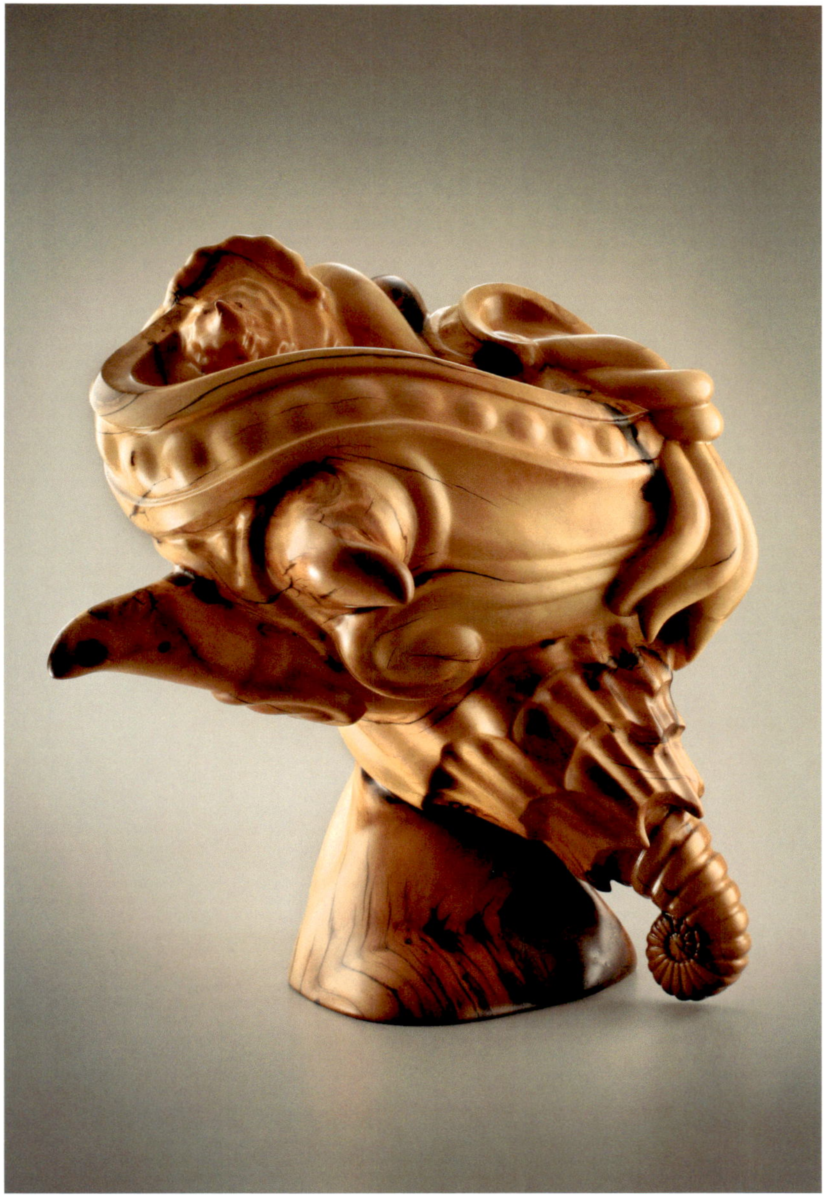

Mark Frank. *M575.* Ponderosa pine, 28 1/2" w x 32" h x 22" d.
Photograph by Ron Bez

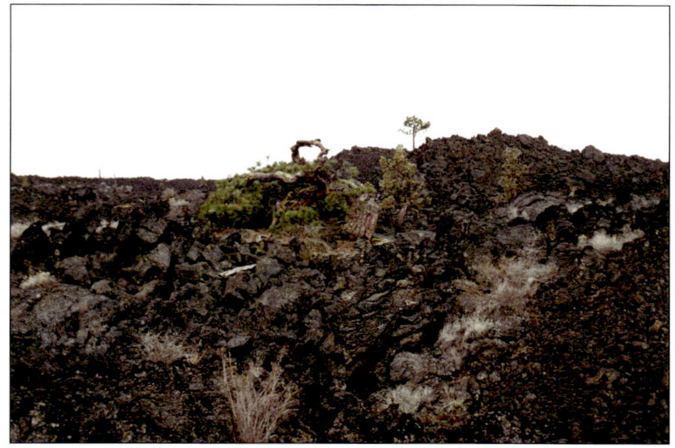

Millennium Tree. *Photograph by Mark Frank*

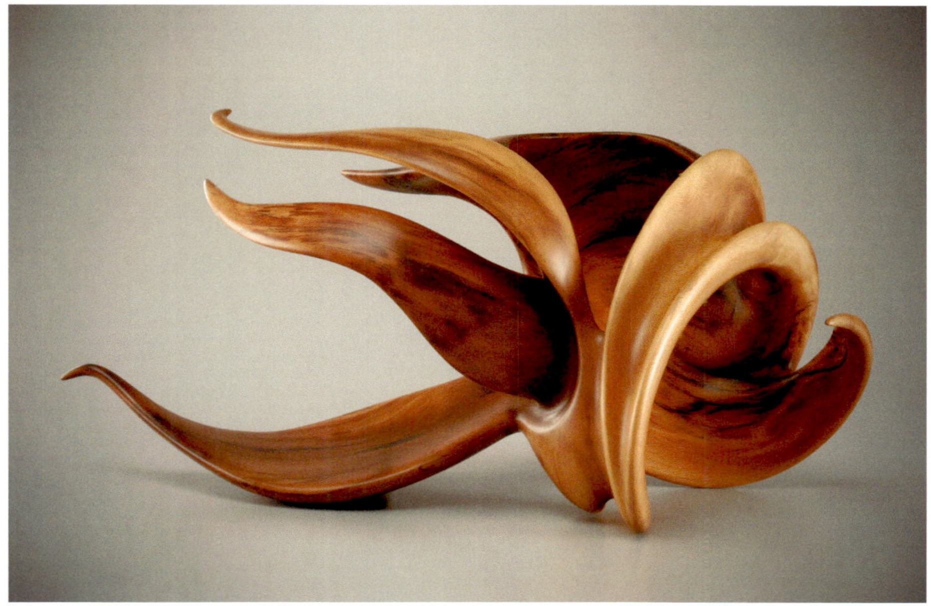

Mark Frank. *Millennium.* Ponderosa pine, 22" w x 10 1/2" h x 9 1/2" d.
Photograph by Ron Bez

Dewey Garrett

Livermore, California, dgarrett@panix.com

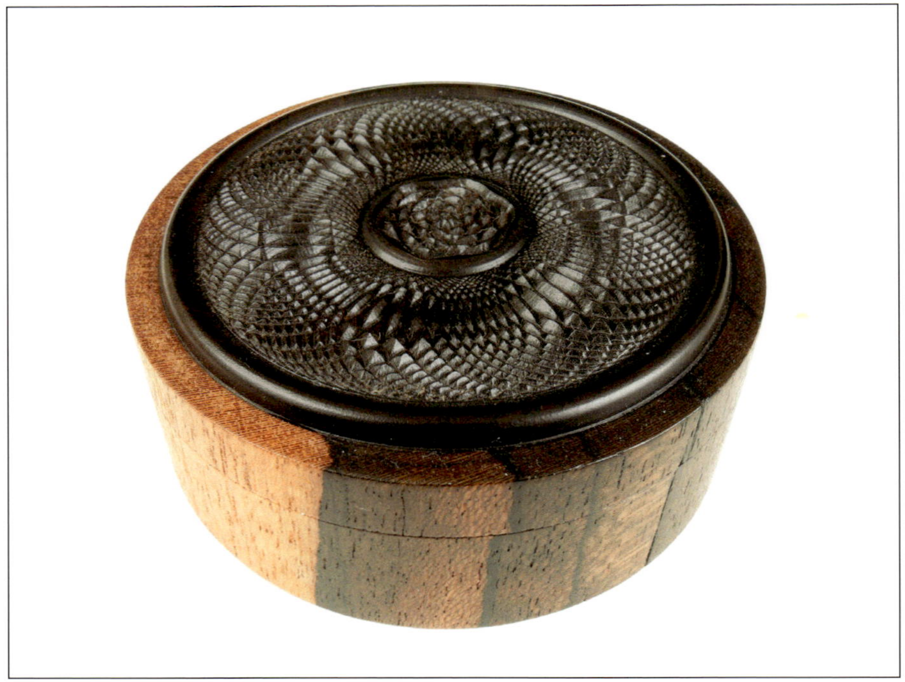

Artist's Statement

Ornamental Turning

Ornamental turning is an old and specialized branch of turning with a unique and interesting history. Paralleling the development of the plain turning lathe, advanced practitioners developed complex machines to produce highly decorative work. The art form was popular with the aristocracy of Europe and interested George III of England, Louis XVI of France, and Peter the Great of Russia.

I am currently making small boxes following the traditions of the field. The work is quite demanding in the precision required for the pattern work and in the extreme attention to detail needed for the many steps in the process. In addition to the unlimited possibilities for design, I've found new ways to make mistakes, but each completed work adds to the learning process and my design repertoire.

The traditional materials for ornamental turning are ivory and hard, fine-grained woods like boxwood and especially African blackwood. Ivory is no longer a candidate for new work and after years of woodworking, I've developed mild allergies to woods of the Dalbergia genus that includes blackwood. Though I can use the wood with extra care, the problem has motivated me to seek alternatives. In my search, I've found some very useful resins that I can cast to make cylindrical blocks that become the raw material for my boxes. This 'faux ivory" material has an appearance similar to ivory and excellent machining properties that are important for the patterns and the fine-pitch screw threads used on boxes.

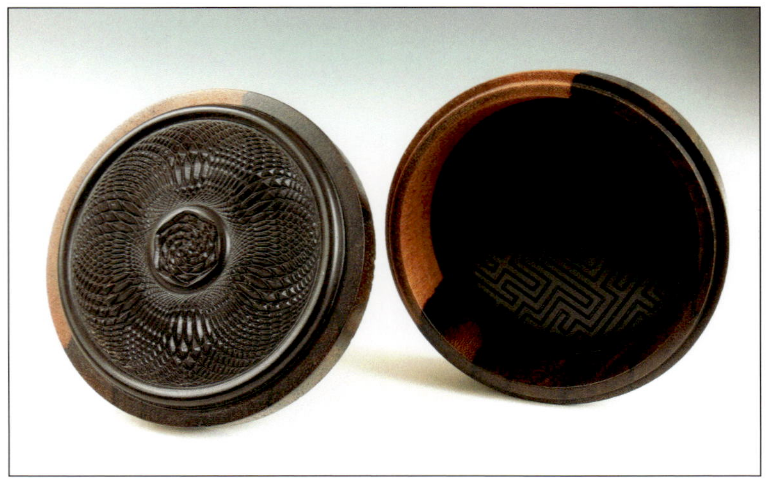

Dewey Garrett. *Grace Box.* 2009. Wooden box, xiricote and African blackwood, hand turned then decorated on ornamental turning engine, 1.5" h x 3.5" d. The top pattern is a classic pattern of ornamental turning after a design by the Reverend W. A. Grace of Great Britain; the interior patterns include mazes and other that were made possible with my computer-driven ornamental turning engine.

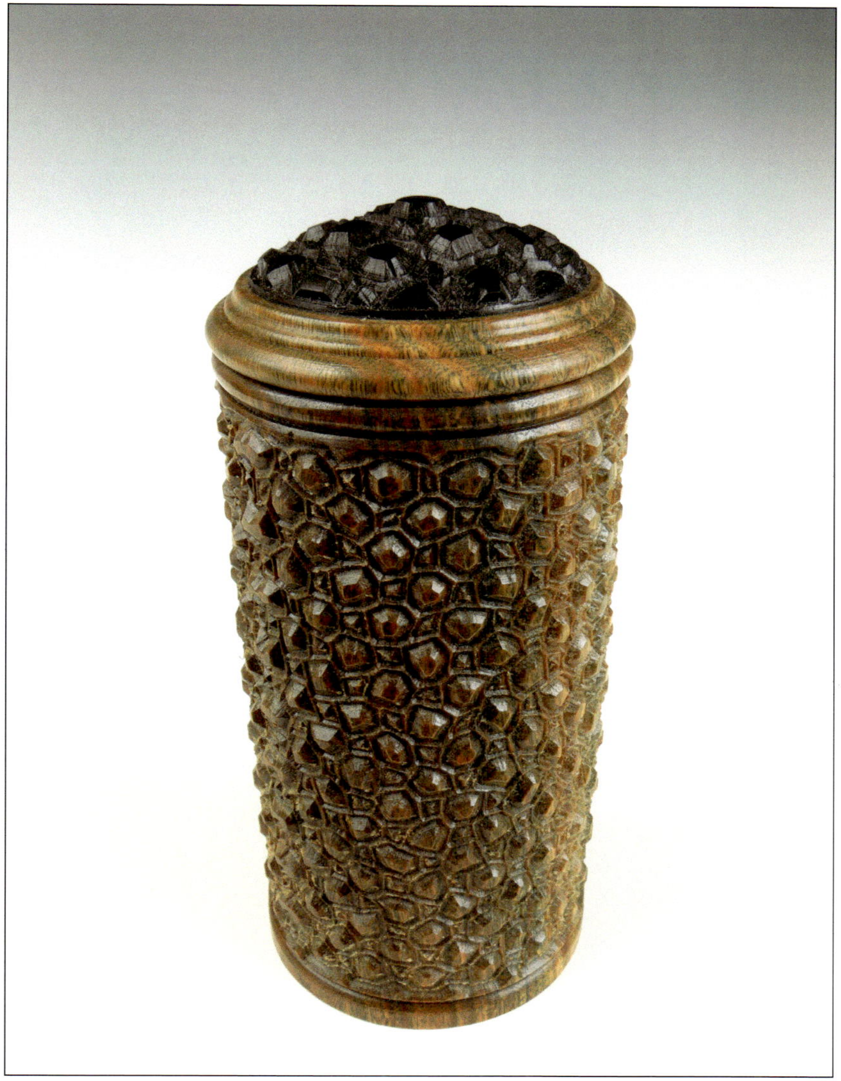

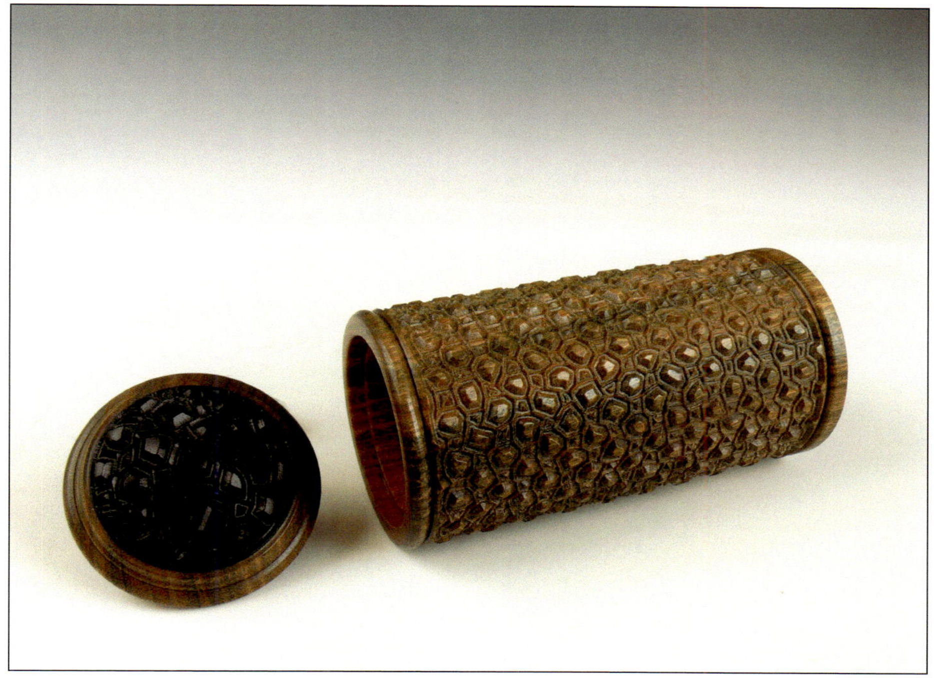

Dewey Garrett. *Stones Box.* 2009. Wooden box, lignum vitae and African blackwood, hand turned then decorated on ornamental turning engine, 4.5" h x 2" d. The stones patterns include an ordered pattern that is a departure from conventional ornamental turning.

David Groth

http://davidgroth.net/

Artist's Statement

Sculpting in myrtlewood washed up along the Pacific Northwest beaches is a journey that begins by reclaiming timbers between storms and after rivers have flooded. Next, working intuitively, I allow the form to evolve as I carve. When a piece starts growing, I grow with it. I have no preconceptions. By working in this way, each new sculpture becomes an act of discovery. I find this intuitive approach challenging and rewarding because of the complete and undivided focus and concentration it requires. It calls for my total involvement with the creative process unfolding at hand. The resulting artwork reveals every step of this personal journey and leads to insights my intellect wouldn't visualize. Over the years I've grown to especially respect and appreciate the character woven into each individual sculpture, transforming reclaimed tree to finished carving.

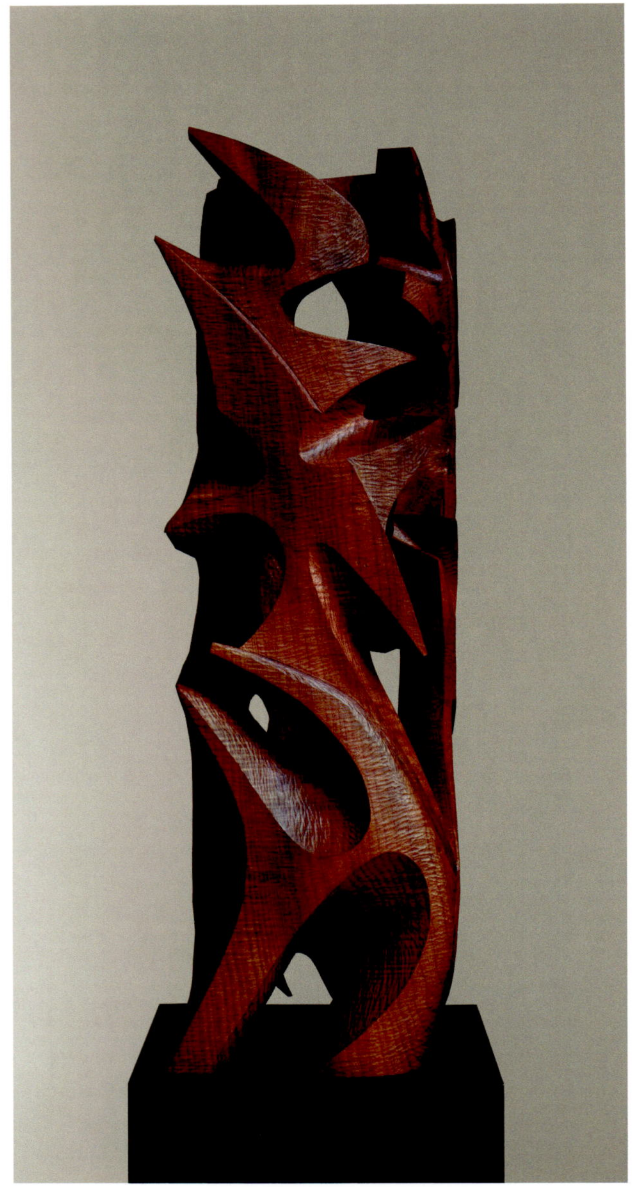

David Groth. *Lizard Skin*. 2006. Free standing sculpture, myrtlewood, 40" h x 16" w x 14.75" l.

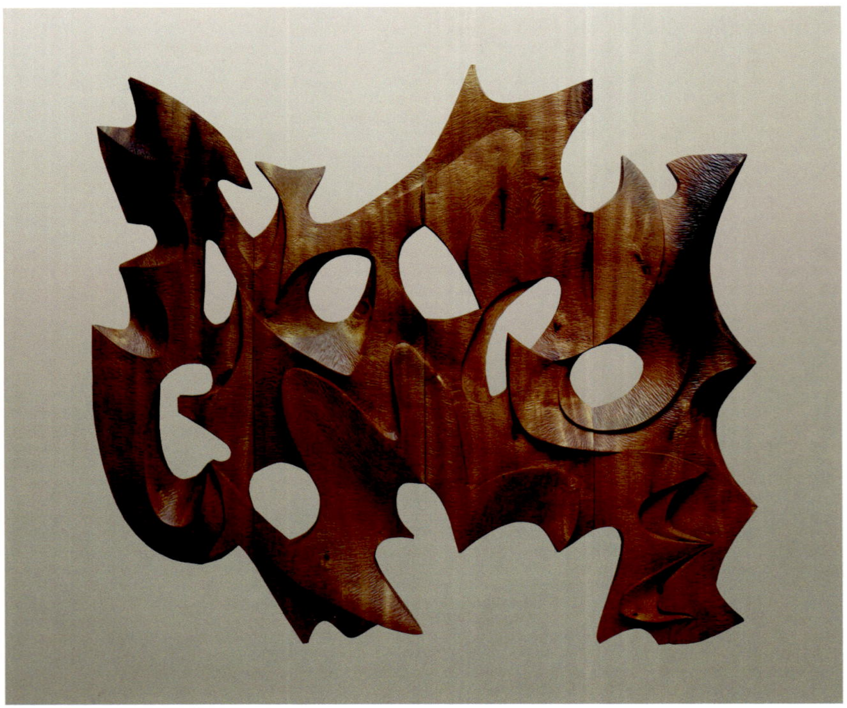

David Groth. *Marinus.* 2007. Wall sculpture, myrtlewood, 50.25" h x 56" w x 5.25" l.

David Groth. *Shuriken Shield.* 2009. Carved table, myrtlewood, 22.5" h x 24" w x 30" l.

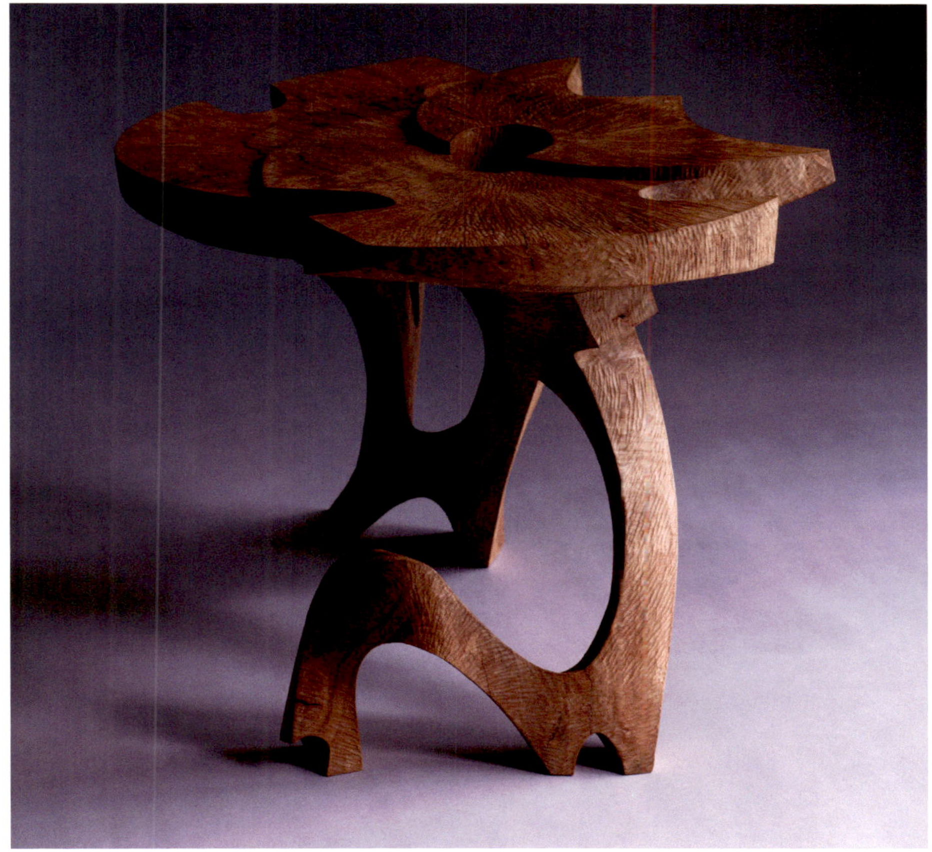

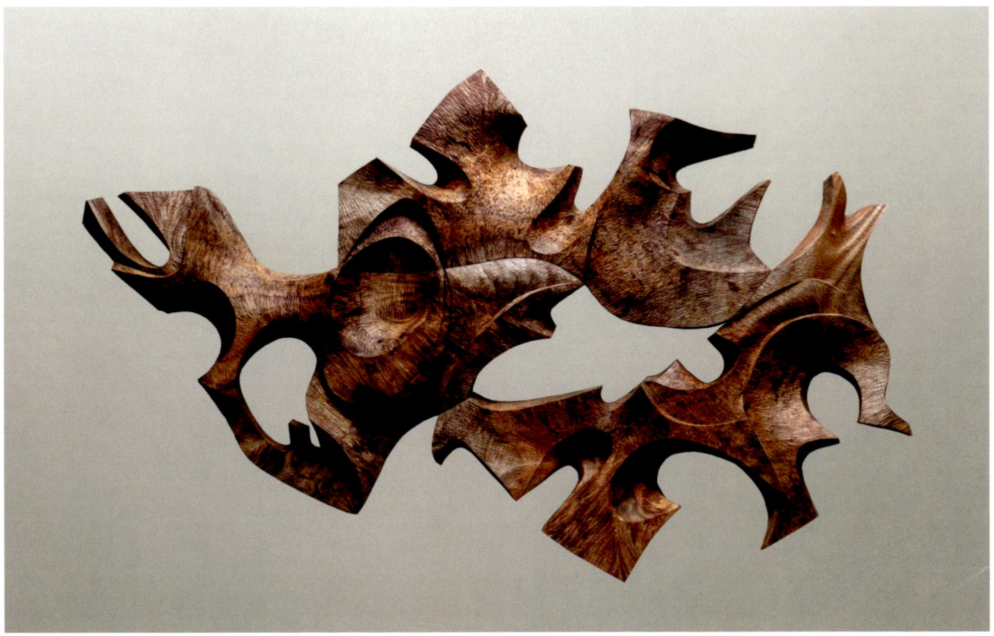

David Groth. *Stegosaurus.* 2007. Wall sculpture, myrtlewood, 42.5" h x 67.375" w x 6" l.

Scott Grove

Rochester, New York, www.scottgrove.com

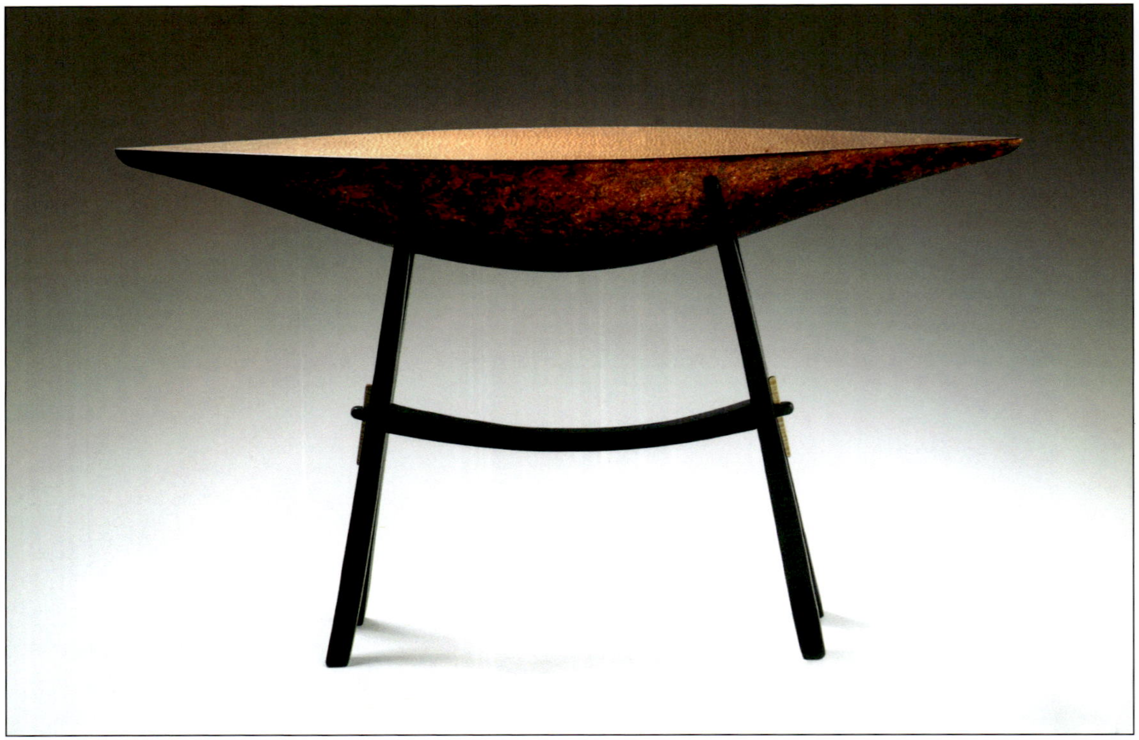

Scott Grove. *Eidelbaub Jr. (Bob).* Pommele sapele, ebonized oak, composite, copper polychrome finish, pinned mortise tendon, 60" x 12" x 35".

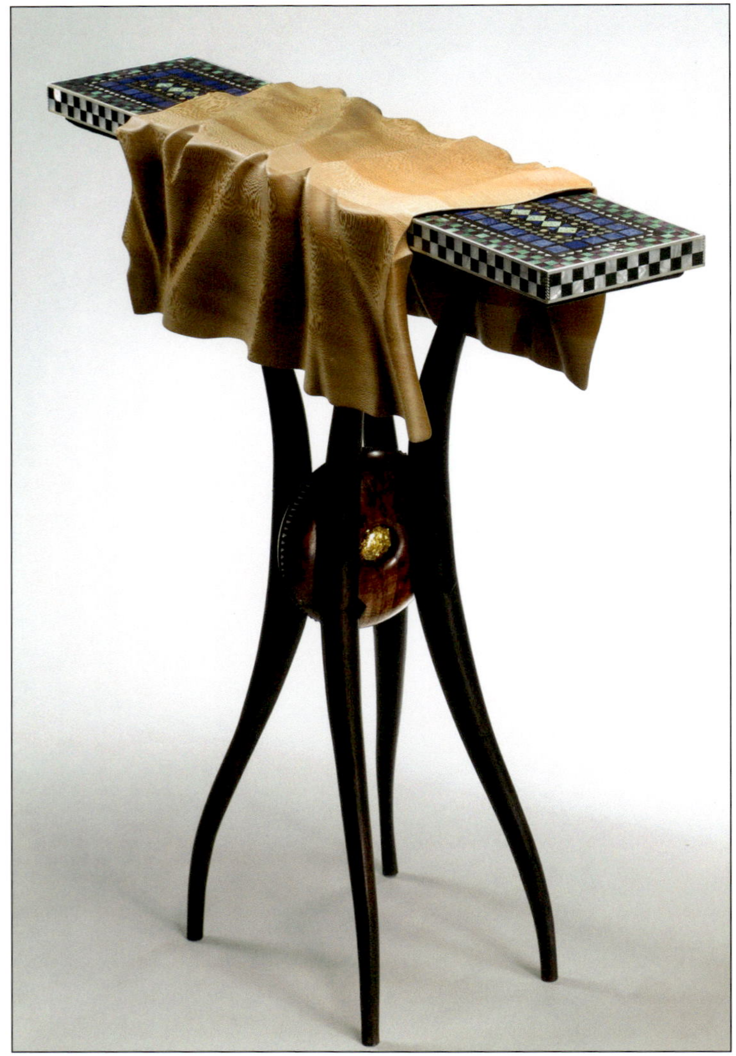

Scott Grove. *Polyidol.* American sycamore, walnut burl, steam bent oak, sterling silver, variety of gems; amber, amethysts, onyx, mother of pearl, malachite, gold stone, turquoise.

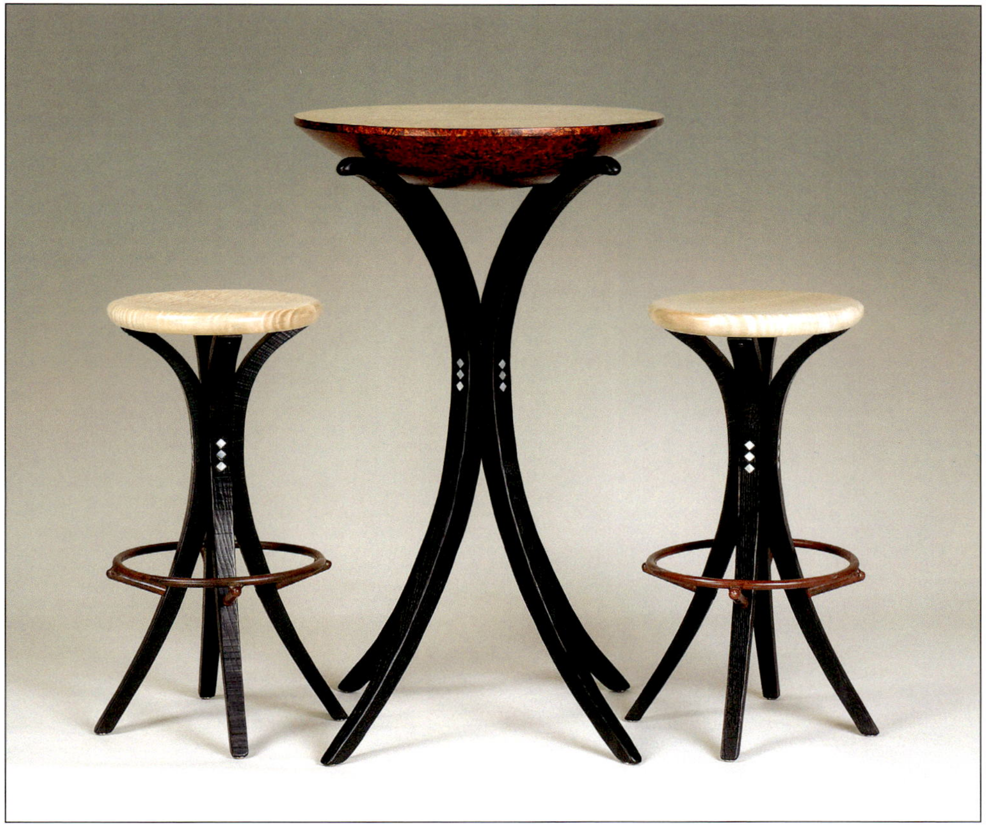

Scott Grove. *Kim.* Café table, mappa burl, steam bent oak, poplar, polychrome finish, mother-of-pearl, 24" d x 42".
Scott Grove. *Louie.* Stool, curly maple, steam bent oak, mother-of-pearl, steel, 14" d x 30".

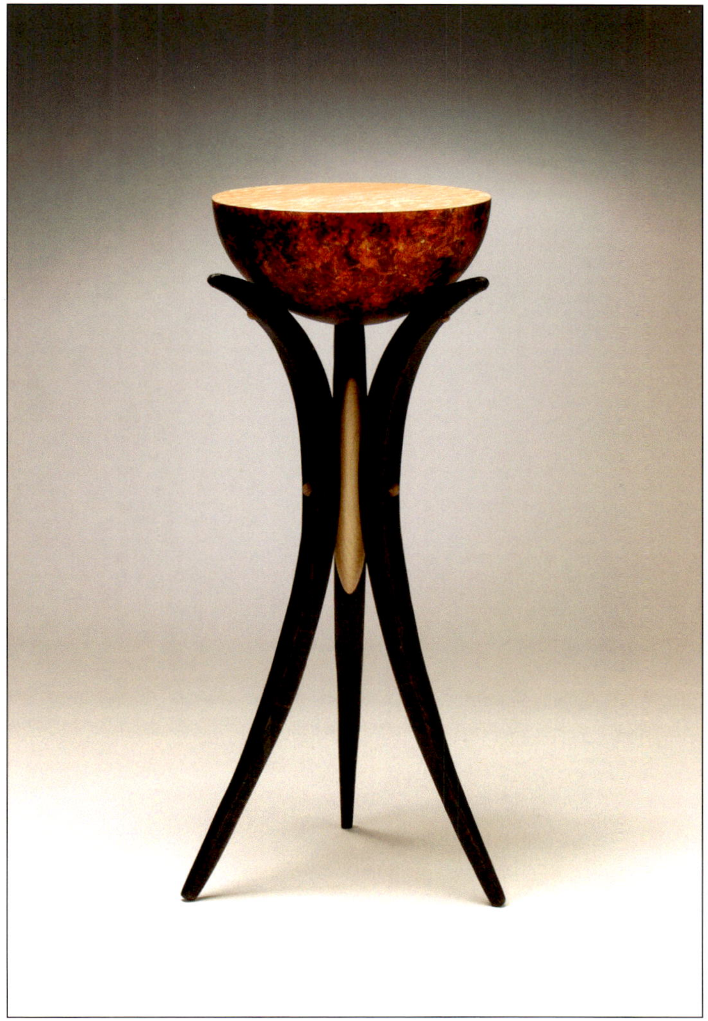

Scott Grove. *Victoria.* Pedestal, quilted maple, copper, polychrome firish, 12" d x 32" h.

Glen G. Guarino

Cedar Grove, New Jersey, www.guarinofurnituredesign.com

Artist's Statement

I hope my furniture speaks clearly, in a language that conveys a sense of the person behind the art; of someone who loves the creative process and respects the beauty of the material from which it is made. As each viewer moves a hand along the lines of the work, I want them to sense the skill and love for the craft needed to create it.

For me each new design is a small adventure, exploring my imagination and the potential of the material. Like craftsmen of the past, I prefer to perform my work using fine hand tools instead of relying on machines that may technically speed completion, but limit the scope of the design. Machines, while certainly useful at times, can create an artificial distance between the artist and the material. My hands-on approach allows me to let the simplicity of the design reveal itself, creating a piece that imparts serenity and calm, reflecting the tree's grace and strength. As each design becomes real and tangible, I get a sense of a tree evolving into a new life as a useful piece of art. I'm grateful to be the catalyst for this rebirth.

Ultimately, I hope people will want to own my art, make it part of their personal living space, use it, enjoy it, and then hand it down to their loved ones.

Individual Artwork

Reclining Figure

I presented the clients with eight or so designs from which they chose *Reclining Figure*. I knew it would be the most difficult to do. Watching them look at all the different design sketches, I could see they loved it. I asked myself, how am I going to make this crazy design?

Reclining Figure proved to be a very time consuming project with a number of construction challenges. Each small piece of wood had to have an angle chopped on each end, and then a compound band saw cut was made on both the inside and outside to conform to a pattern that showed the shape of the compound curve. Gluing each small piece of the stack down and against the adjoining piece without a flat surface to hold a clamp proved to be the crux of the construction challenges. The scraping and sanding to final shape of the inside curve also proved to be time consuming. The table is finished with many coats of Tung oil varnish.

In the end, the hard work was worth it because the piece was so well received.

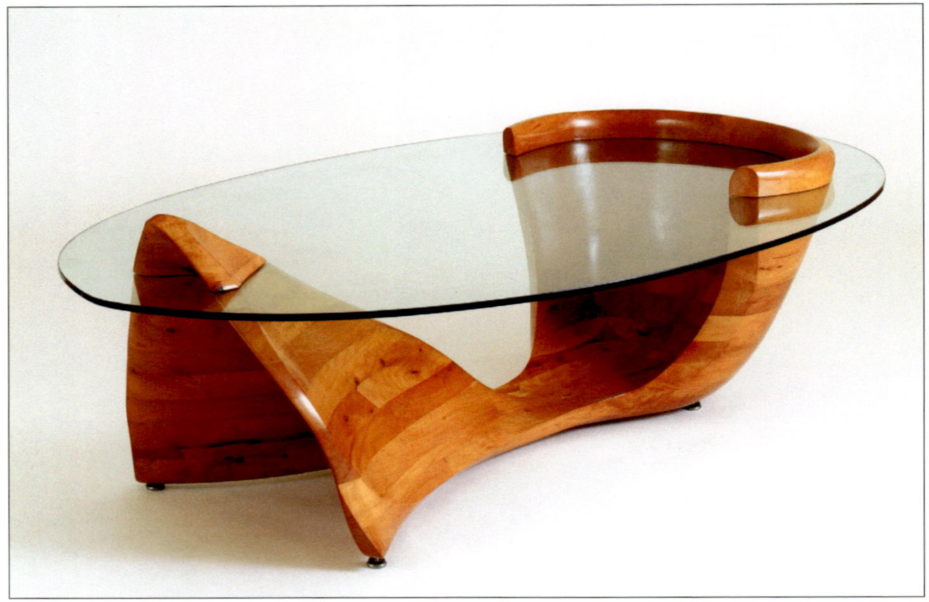

Glen G. Guarino. *Reclining Figure.* 2000. Coffee table, Swiss pear wood and glass, traditionally joined and carved, 21" h x 61" w x 28" deep. *Photographer: Rich Russo*

Flower Mirror

The clients who own *Flower Mirror* were frequent guests to a local gallery I was showing my work in. A table and mirror combination on display caught their attention and they expressed an interest in buying it, but then decided to pass on the sale. Several days later they called the gallery owner to discover the table and mirror had been sold to another couple. After talking to the gallery owner, they contacted me and through the gallery commissioned a mirror. At the time, they were both involved in the arts, she a still life painter who loves flowers and he owned an advertising company. I designed a few flower designs and they liked this variation the most. The spot I hung the piece was perfect. The soft curves allowed the light to dance across the surface of the wood, highlighting the wonderful grain. When I returned home my wife said they had called and asked if I would call them. I hoped nothing was wrong as I called. On the contrary, they loved the mirror and wanted me to design another piece! They became collectors of my work.

Arts & Crafts Radiator Cover

The Arts and Crafts movement began in England and the United States in the later part of the nineteenth century. My interpretation takes the clean lines a bit further by making pieces look lighter and adding a delicacy that showcases the material and craftsmanship.

I designed the original mirror and radiator cover for a foyer in our home. The house was trimmed in chestnut when built in 1927. Chestnut is a durable and decorative wood with a lovely warm tone. Shedua, which is sometimes referred to as mutenye, offers a nice surprise in color contrast. I used chestnut boards I had taken out of a built in. I had to burn off five coats of paint, but I felt it was worth it and I could not allow myself to throw the wood out. The Arts and Craft pieces were a real pleasure to do because the wood is so easy to work with. I enjoyed every moment of the process and I often receive complements from people visiting our home.

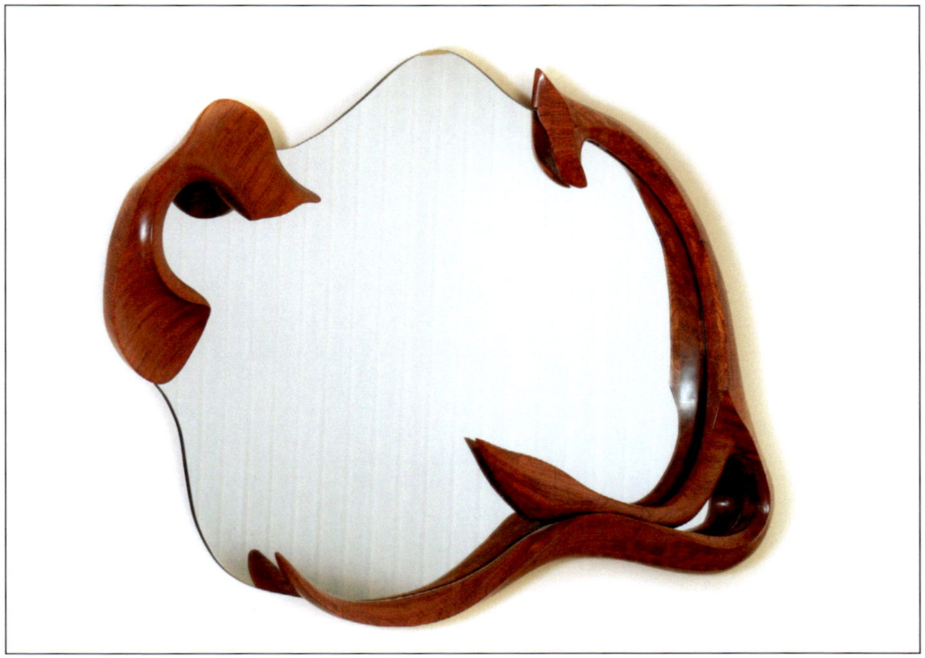

Glen G. Guarino. Flower Mirror. 2001. Bubinga, stacked and carved, 33" h x 64" w x 3" deep. *Photographer: Rich Russo*

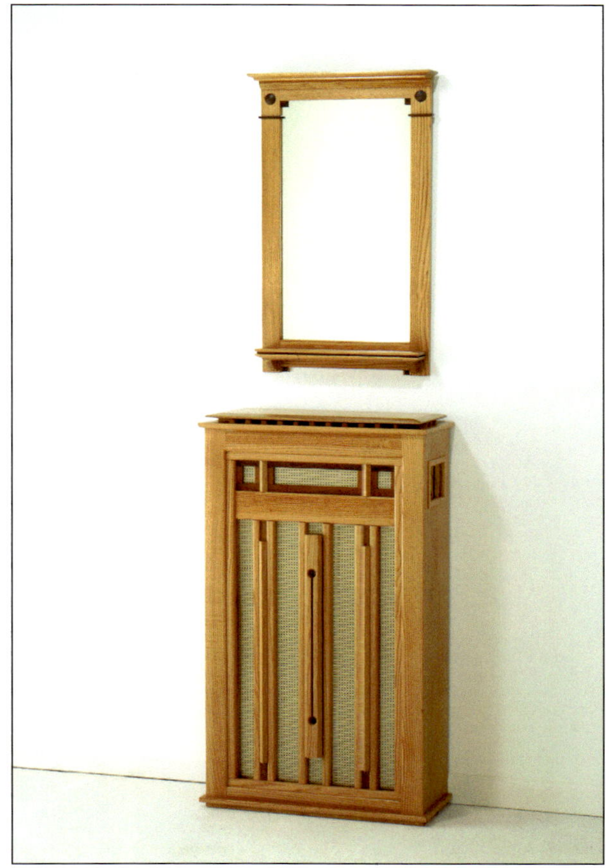

Glen G. Guarino. Arts & Crafts Radiator Cover. 2006. Chestnut and shedua, traditionally joined, 43" h x 24" w x 11"deep. *Photographer: Rich Russo*

In Tune

When I design for a client, I always develop several designs. The designs usually represent two or more different directions, giving the clients more choices. *In Tune* was a close second that I felt would be a great one to do and show around.

On my lumber rack I had a couple of thick curly maple boards that I was saving for about a dozen years, just waiting for the right design that would show off the beautiful grain. The legs and stretchers were first band sawed and then hand-shaped with spoke shaves and scrapers. The challenge was to make all four legs look identical. The ebony I used to accent the design was rescued from an old dump located next to a sawmill twenty-five years ago that I save for special pieces and use sparingly.

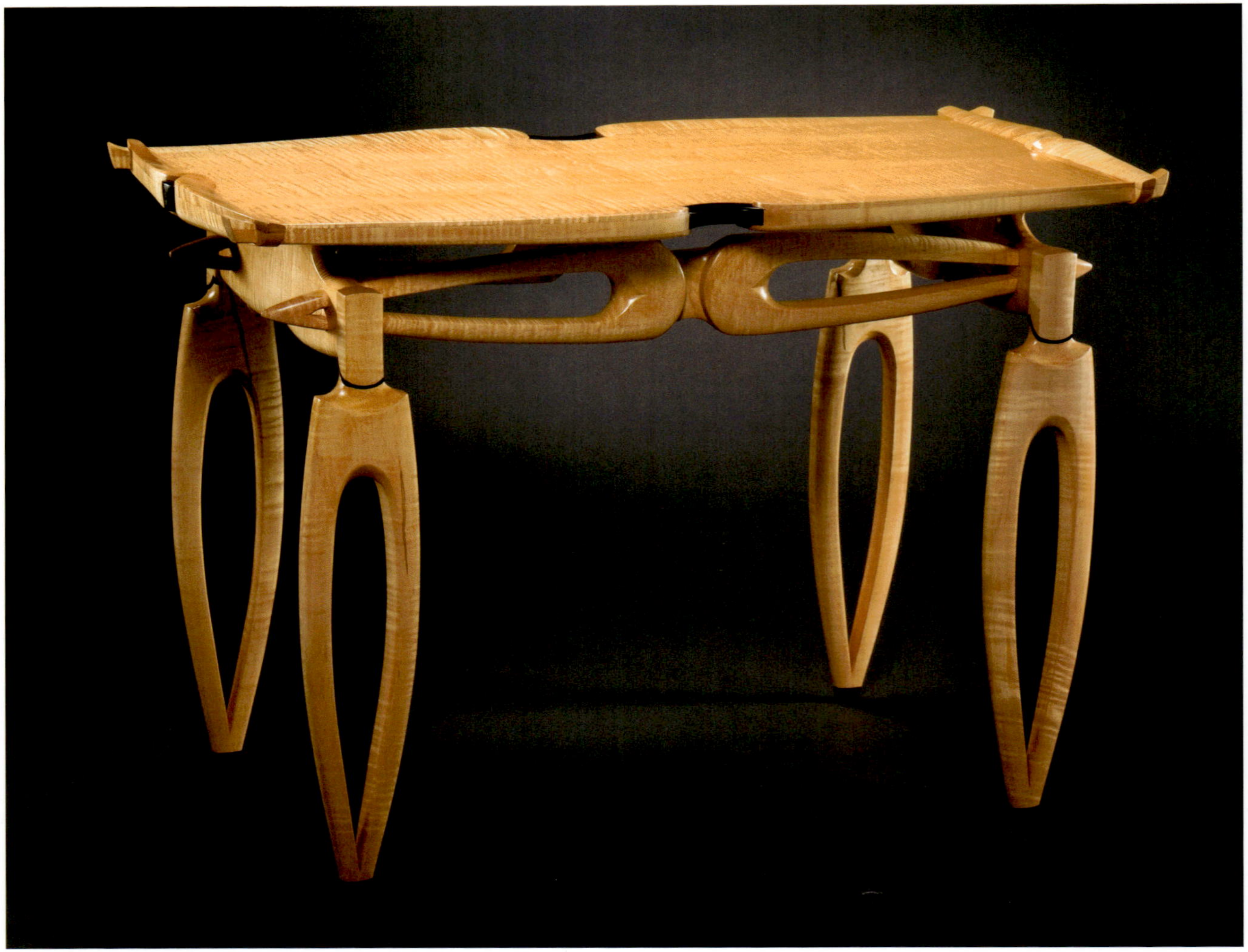

Glen G. Guarino. *In Tune.* 2009. Table, maple and ebony, traditionally joined and carved, 35" h x 52" w x 25" deep. *Photographer: Rich Russo*

Philippe Guillerm

Rockland, Maine

Artist's Statement

Art and music are more direct languages than spoken or written words could ever be, and my sculptures sing. I've always wanted to send a message that could be accessible to all. My goal is that a person who is walking on the street, very busy, will stop and take a few minutes of his time to appreciate my work and understand my message.

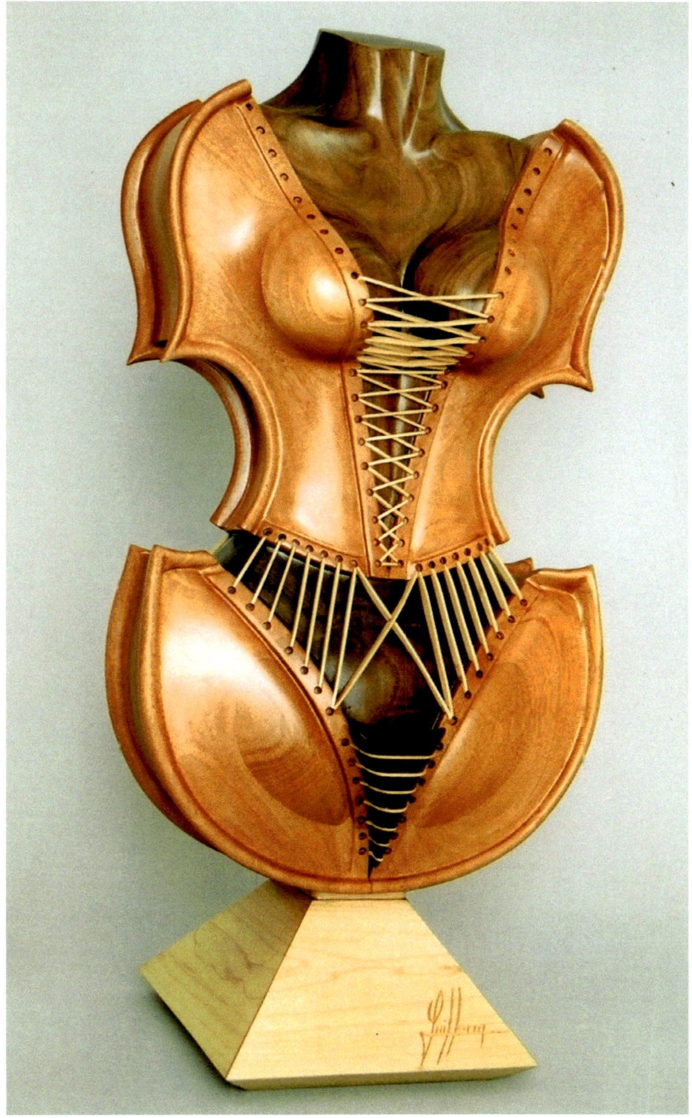

Philippe Guillerm. *Laces.* 2002. Wood sculpture, mahogany, walnut, and maple, 35" x 17" x 12".

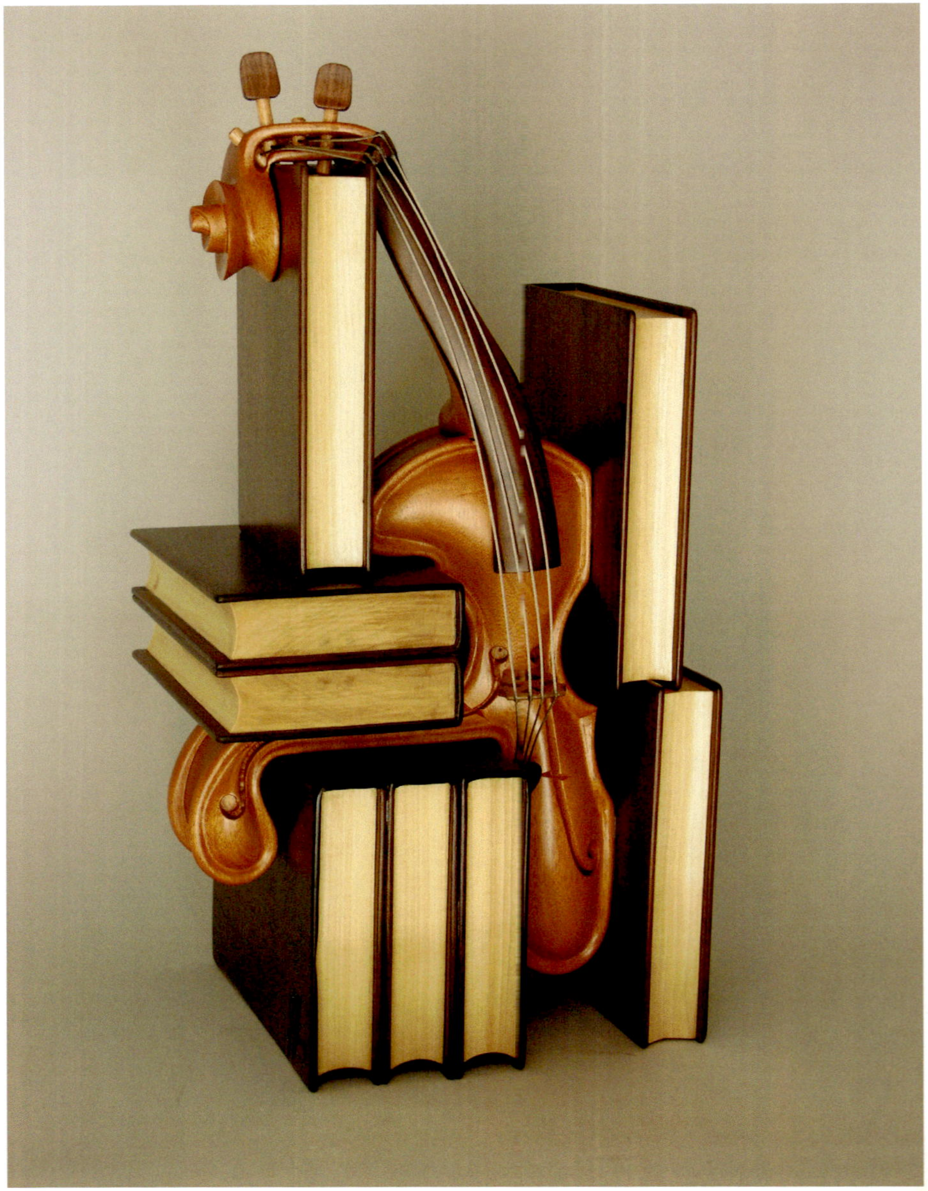

Philippe Guillerm. *Education.* 2007. Wood sculpture, mahogany, walnut, and maple, 22" x 15" x 7".

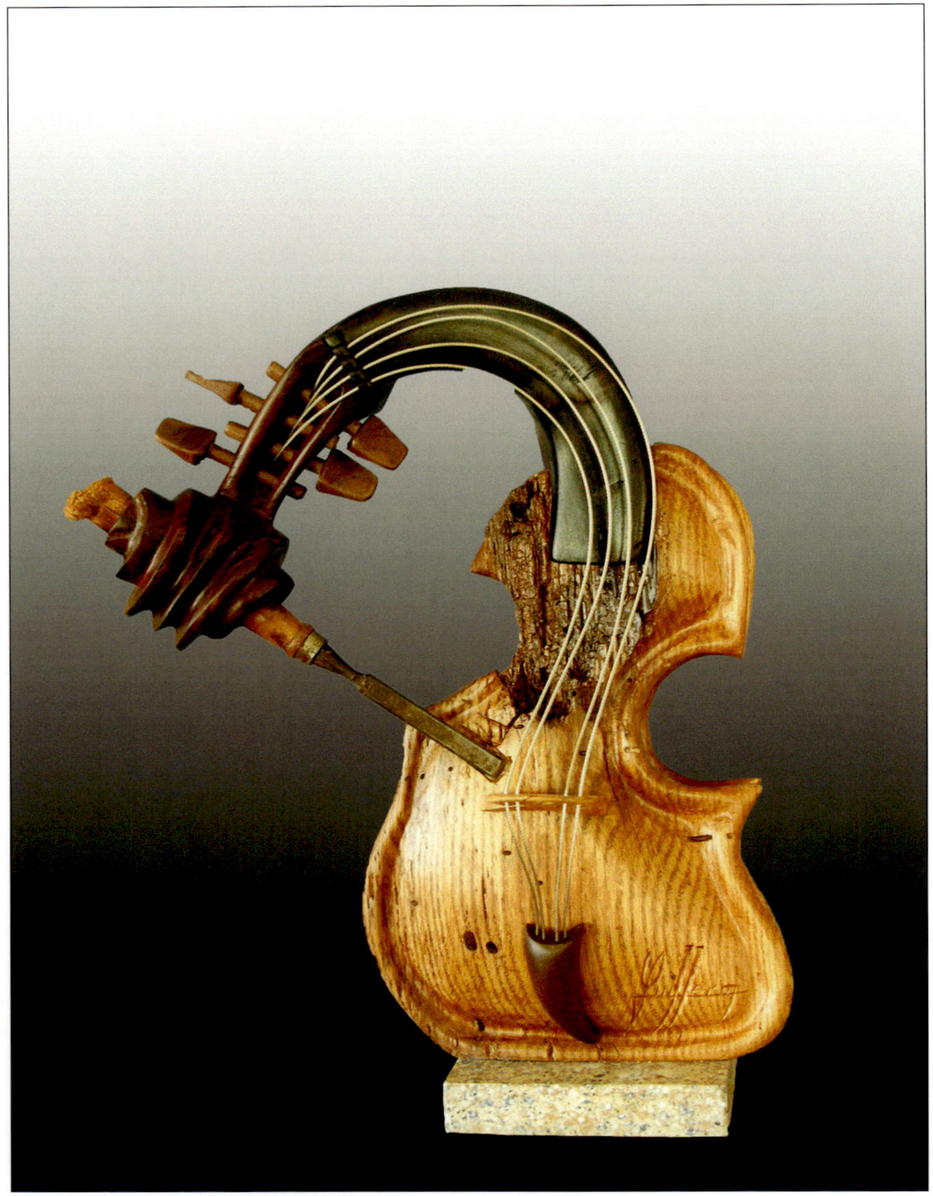

Philippe Guillerm. *Self Taught*. 2008. Wood sculpture, oak, maple, and walnut, 22" 15" x 5".

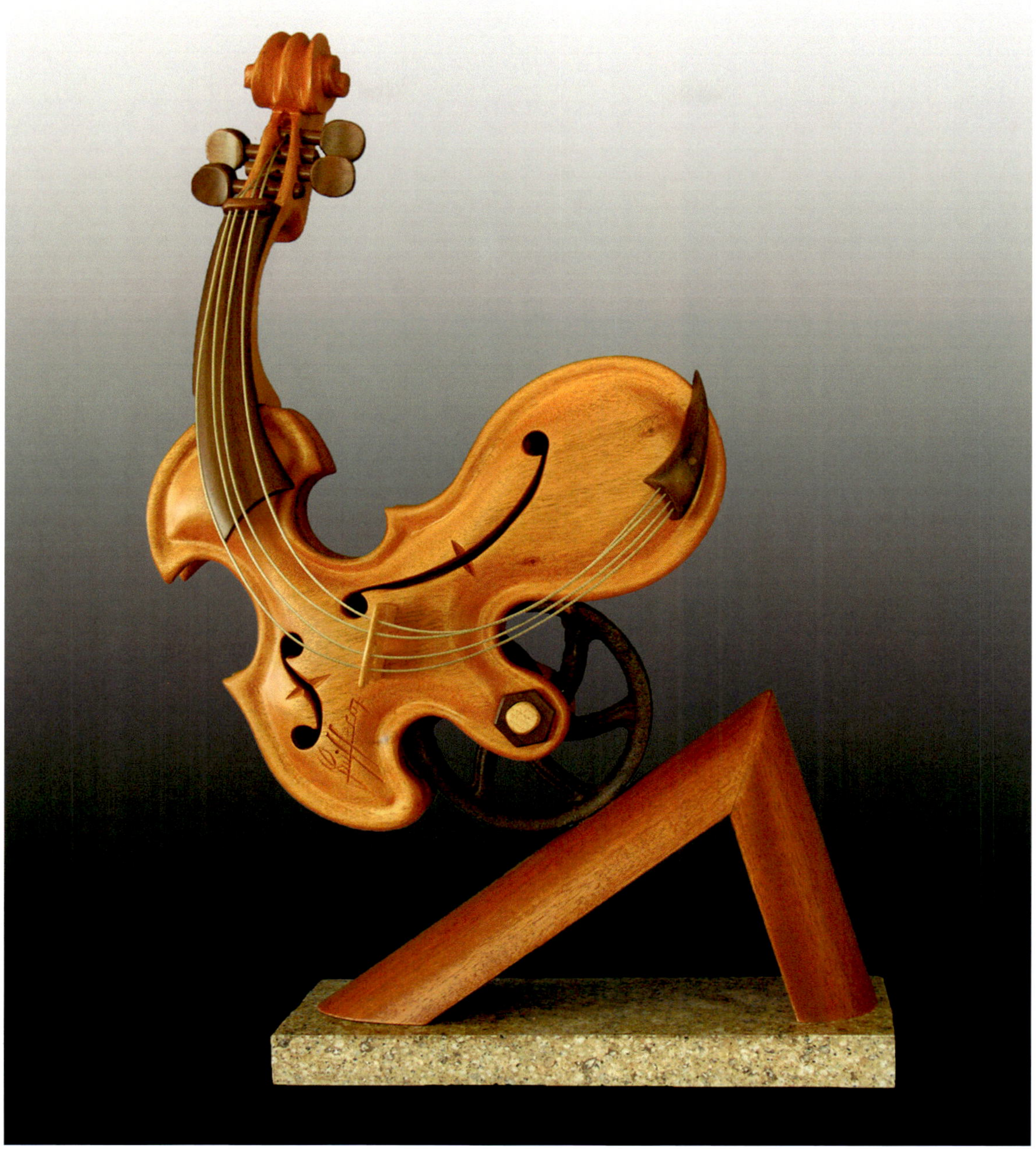

Philippe Guillerm. *Presto*. 2008. Wood sculpture, mahogany, walnut, and maple, steel, 20" x 17" x 5".

Nicola Henshaw

www.nicolahenshaw.co.uk

Artist's Statement

My work is interactive and tactile, soft gouged, sanded or filed textures in the wood are as important as the form and color of each piece I make. An element of fun is integral to my work; it is great to see people's faces as they hear a story that has inspired a design of a chair. It is not only the shape of an animal or bird that intrigues me, but their habits – the way a duck ruffles its feathers or a heron preens. I spend many a chilly day at the zoo, observing and sketching the precise waddle of a crocodile or the exact stance of a wart hog.

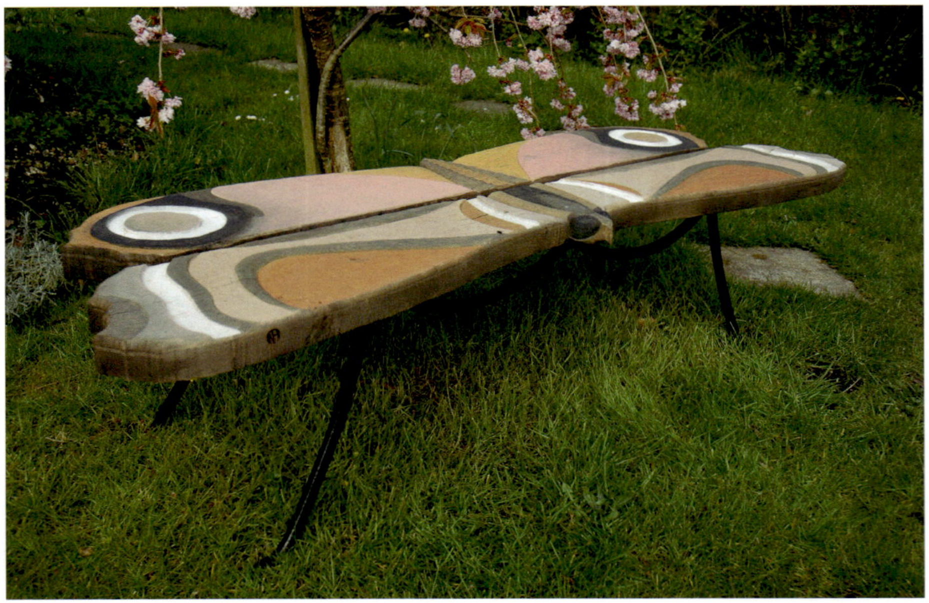

Nicola Henshaw. *Butterfly Bench*. 2009. Carved new forest oak and steel, stained with oil-based colors, 165 x 48 x 43cm. *Photographer: Mark Curzon.* I was commissioned to make a series of different butterfly benches for a private butterfly sanctuary.

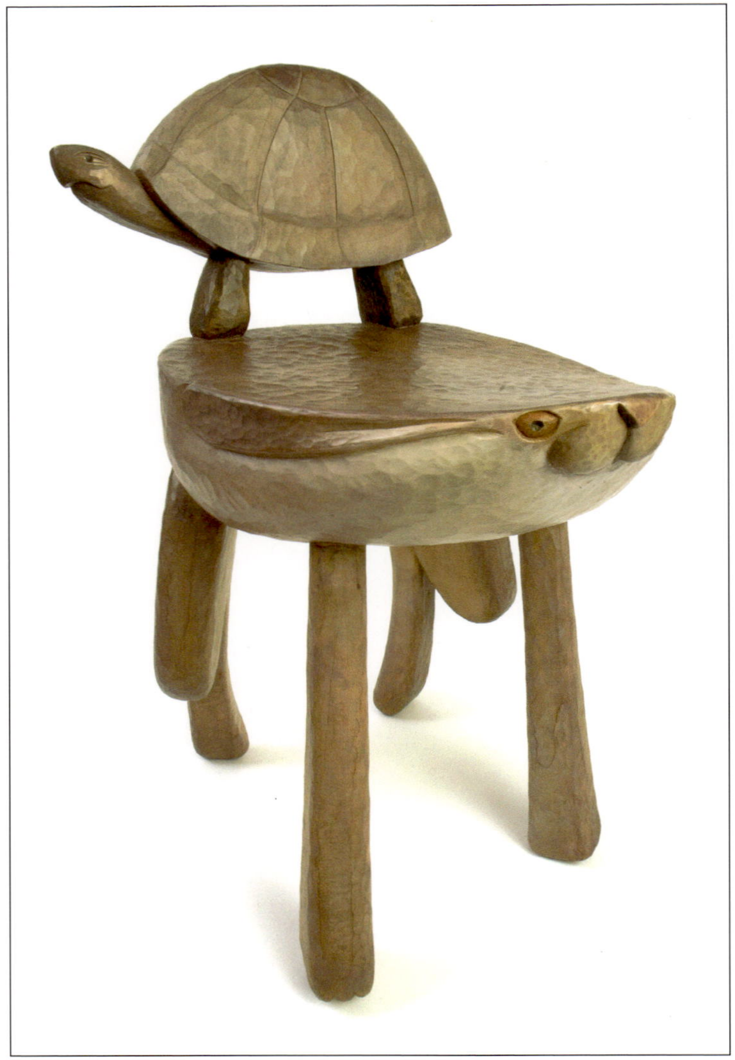

Nicola Henshaw. *Hare and Tortoise Chair*, based on the Aesop fable "The Hare and the Tortoise." 2008. Carved in English lime wood, stained with spirit-based colors, sealed with wax, 50 x 50 x 70cm. *Photographer: Mark Curzon*

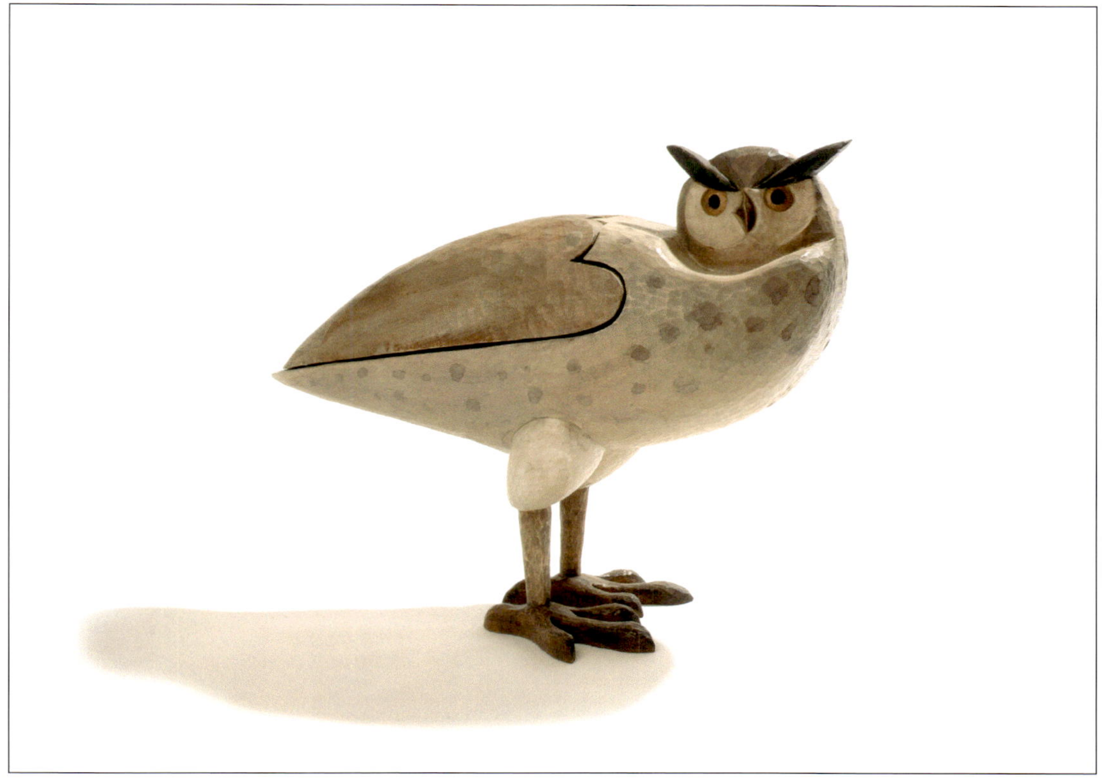

Nicola Henshaw. *Owl Box*, based on the proverb, "The owl is king of the night." 2009. Box in the shape of a standing owl with hinged wings, carved English lime wood and silver leaf, stained with spirit-based colors, and sealed with wax, the wings of the owl hinge open to reveal a silver leaf moon, 60 x 35 x 50cm. *Photographer: Mark Curzon*

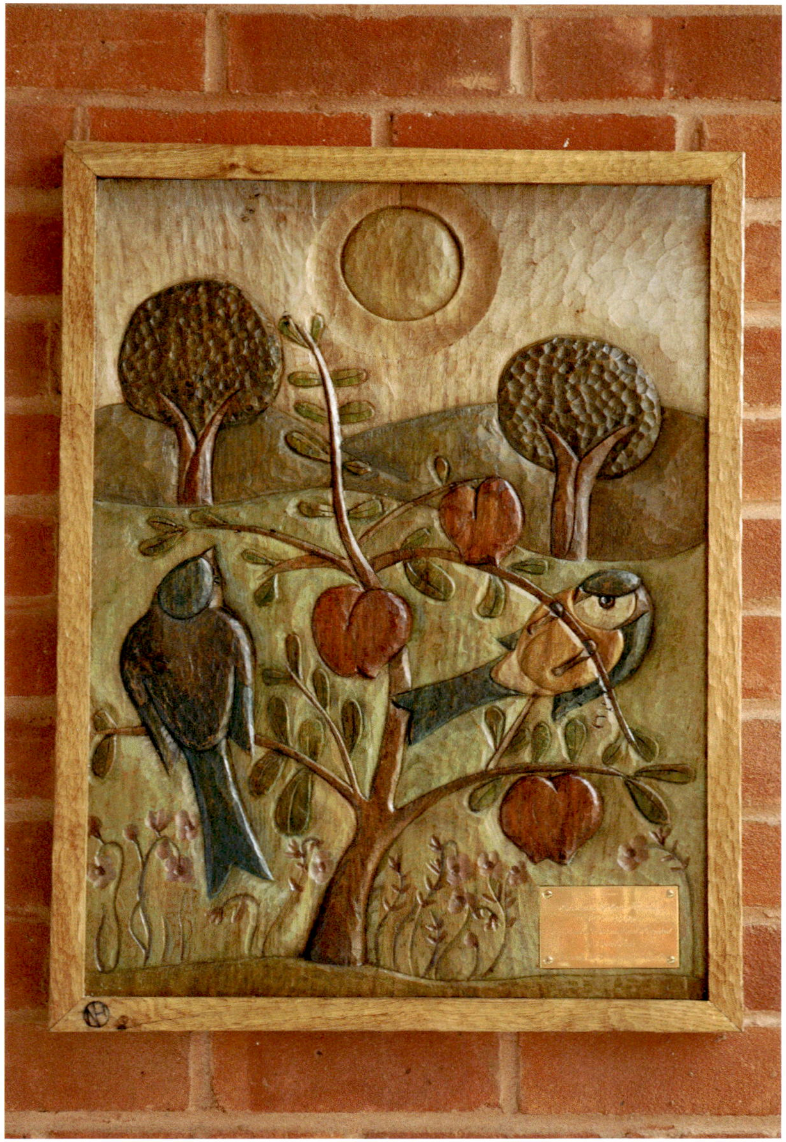

Nicola Henshaw. *Kiss of the Sun Panel,* based on the poem, "A kiss of the sun for pardon/ A song of the birds for mirth/ You are nearer god's heart in a garden/ than anywhere else on earth." 2007. Panel illustrating birds in an apple tree with sun, carved new forest oak, stained with spirit-based colors, and sealed with wax, 60 x 90cm. *Photographer: Mark Curzon*

WILLIAM HUNTER

Rancho Palos Verdes, California
www,hunter-studios.com

Artist's Statement

It's a conundrum... how to use words to describe a body of work whose essence is abstract and process is on a non-verbal, often sub-conscious level. Subtractive sculpting is a spontaneous, unspoken dialogue between the work and me. It is a meditative process of imagination, appraisal, and decision that springs from an idea and is put into motion.

My work is meant to spark an elusive emotion, awaken a memory, and explore the spiritual and metaphysical dimensions of our lives. I use the vessel – humanity's oldest and richest metaphor – as a vehicle. Through subtractive sculpting and deconstruction, I'm building a visual language to express this emotional sub-context and elicit a contemplative response.

I've always been concerned with implied kinetics and giving my pieces a new life through the illusion of motion. Early on I started with texturing and light disc sculpting to manipulate surface in order to change the energy of the vessel, affecting the surface in an almost painterly way. Then I started sculpting deeper into the pieces, adding gesture to the surface treatments, which gave me more voices and new ways to allude to motion. The next exploration was carving through the walls of the pieces, which began a dialog of interior and exterior, light and shadow, positive and negative, and again expanded my sculptural vocabulary with the vessel. Then I took some of these same forms and cut them completely apart and gave them a new freedom. This deconstruction of the vessel gave me new ways to activate space, work with interplay, and allow the cut spirals to leave the realm of the vessel and explore abstract energy.

My approach is to work in the realm where the scientific and poetic merge. I can get there only when my eye, hand, and soul are in perfect harmony with my materials and motive.

Individual Artwork

Infinity's Echo

This piece was created for a Collector's of Wood Art show titled *Presence of Absence.* The show concerned artist's use of negative space as a major voice in the work. I not only like the negative space aspect of the piece but I particularly enjoy that the elements themselves seem to bend space, allude to infinity, and almost defy gravity.

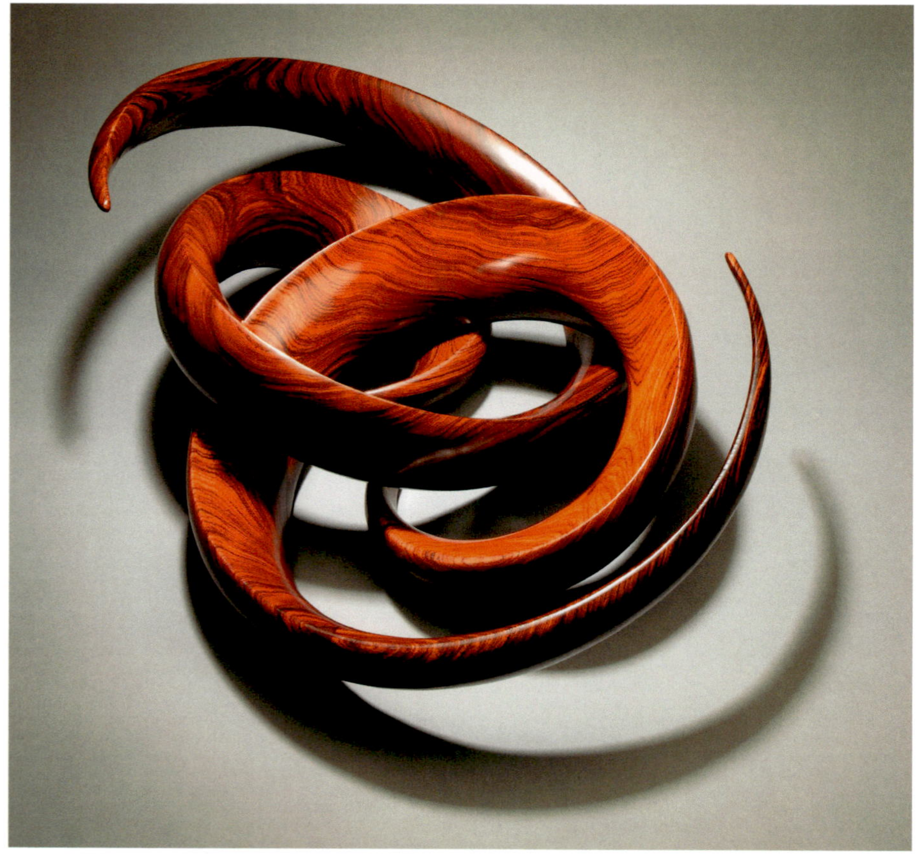

William Hunter. *Infinity's Echo.* 2006. Cocobolo, two piece double helix, 14 1/2" h x 23" w x 16" d. *Photographer: Alan Shaffer*

Enso: Within and Without

There is a centuries-old Zen philosophy expressed as "enso." Brush strokes embody the concepts "within" as the circle, "without" as the square. This piece of circle and square has also a third Zen vessel... the one that isn't there. When I set the vessel on top of the empty square, completing it, the negative space is in the form of a lipped vessel. Within and without, thrice!

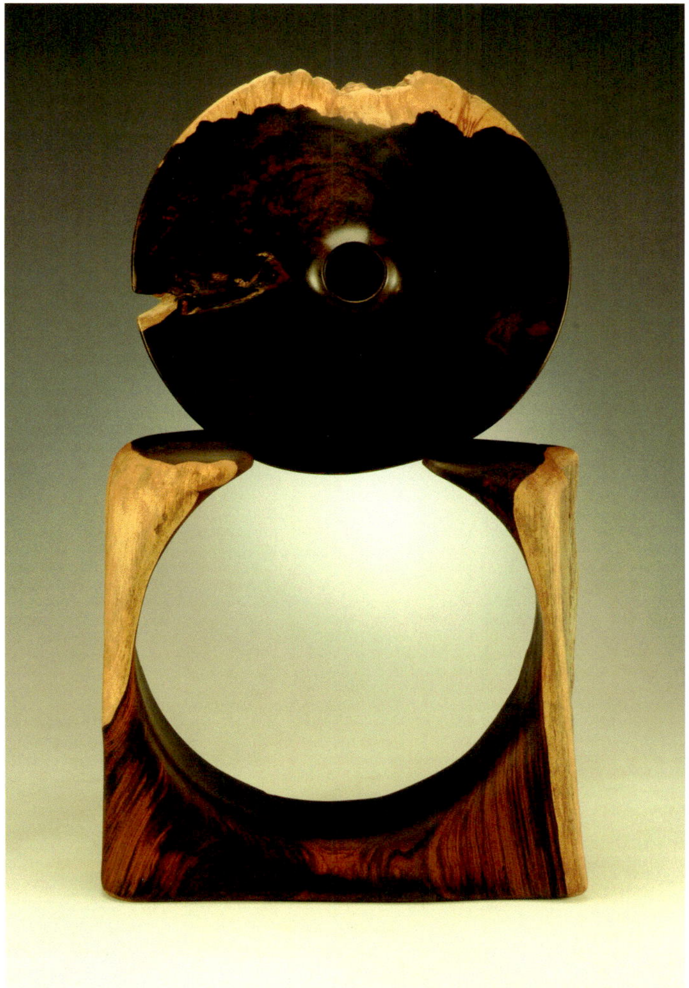

William Hunter. *Enso: Within and Without.* 2008. Cocobolo, variable: 23" h x 18" w x 16" d, 35" h x 18" w x 5 1/2" d. *Photographer: Tony Cunha*

Spheres of Transformation

There is dichotomy in the aspect of this piece and yet it is integrated as one. The Sphere's source is mysterious, celestial, and meteoric. The Circle is lean, encompassing, and protecting the sphere. The tension springs from our irresistible desire to complete the circle, to make it whole.

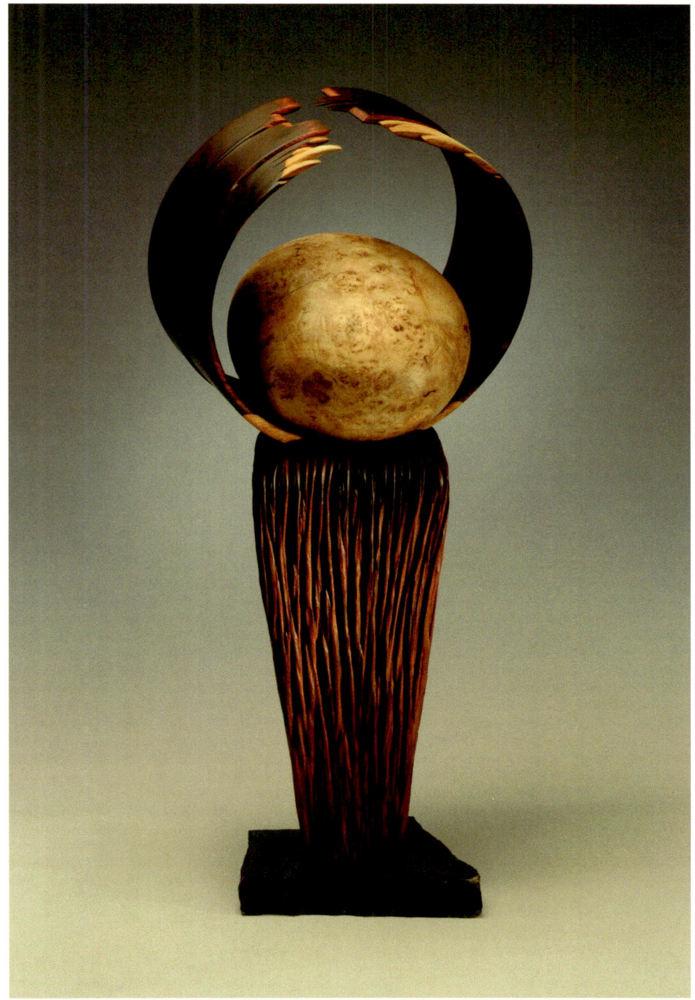

William Hunter. *Spheres of Transformation.* 2008. Cocobolo & maple burl, 3' h x 16" w x 13" d. *Photographer: Tony Cunha*

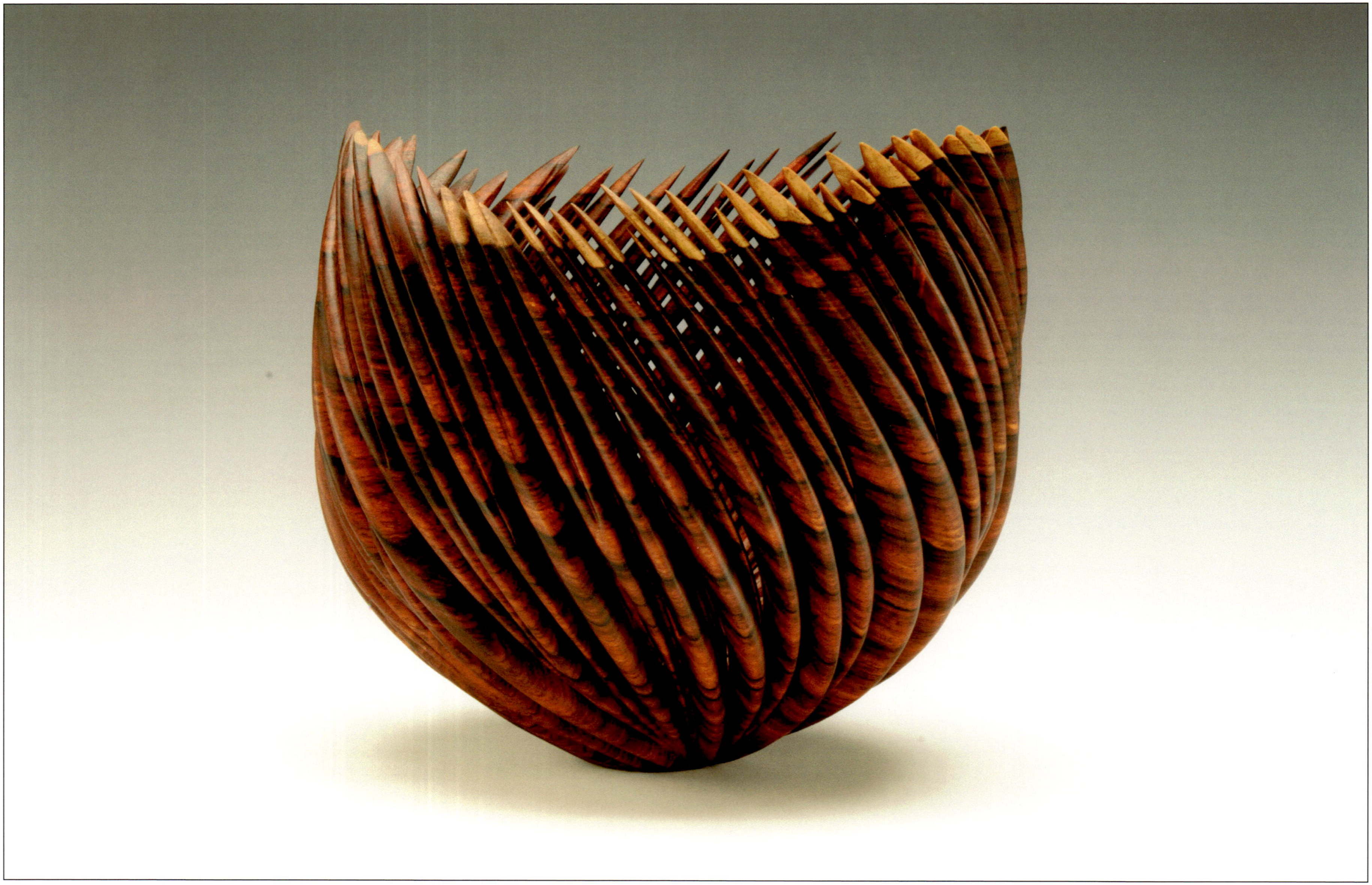

William Hunter. *Stirring Breezes.* 2009. Cocobolo with sap tips, 9 1/2" h x 10" d. *Photographer: Tony Cunha*

Janel Jacobson

Harris, Minnesota, www.janeljacobson.com

Individual Artwork

Dragonfly

When I saw the block of quilted maple, I knew that it would become the water underneath a dragonfly. I saw the rippling chatoyance of the wood grain as the movement of water. The undulating surface was shaped with a belt sander, using files and hand sanding to complete the form. The glossy finish was achieved by multiple, very thin applications of a rubbing oil finish, with a few final applications of an oil urethane topcoat to provide a more durable surface.

The dragonfly and reeds were carved from a single piece of Pacific madrone, which was a particularly challenging carving to complete. Once colored using tube watercolors, several thinly sprayed coats of semi-gloss lacquer were applied.

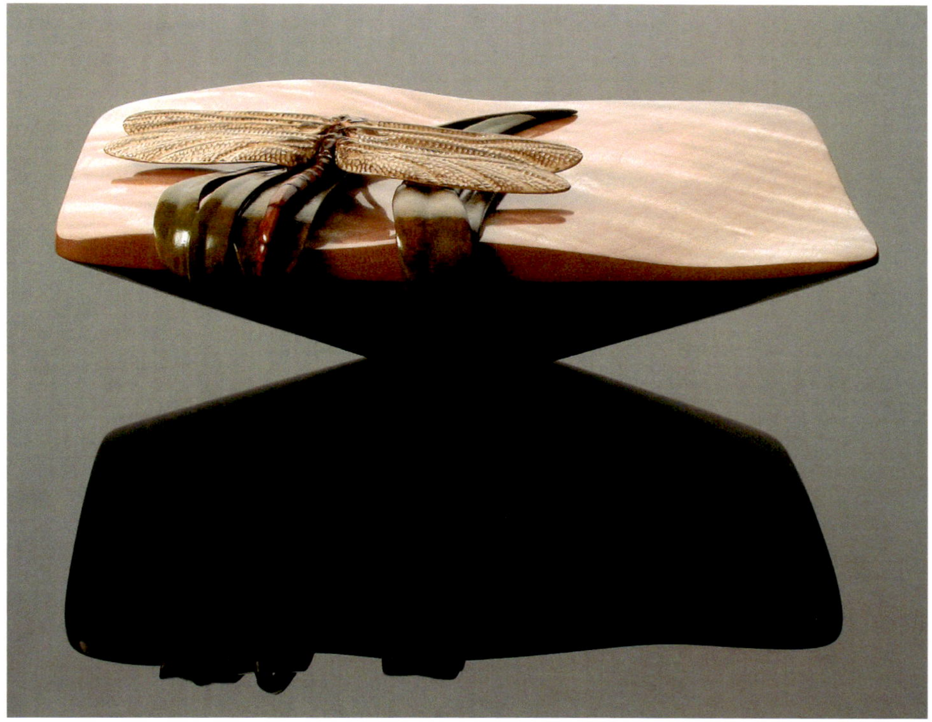

Janel Jacobson. *Dragonfly.* 2005. Small sculptural form, quilted maple base; Pacific madrone - dragonfly & water grass, 6.0" x 4.9" x 2.2", 15.3 x 11.3 x 5.5 cm.

Summer Singer

The Cicada on an apple tree branch was carved from boxwood. The slender legs were carved, creating openings underneath its body, and much attention was paid to the characteristic details of this beautiful insect, as well as the apple branch. The color was achieved by using a palette of artist oil paints.

When a branch is used in a composition with insects or critters, one may consider it as a background element. I feel that the branch is as important to the whole piece as is the creature upon it. Much care is taken to represent the branches and leaves as elements that are as identifiable as the carved creatures.

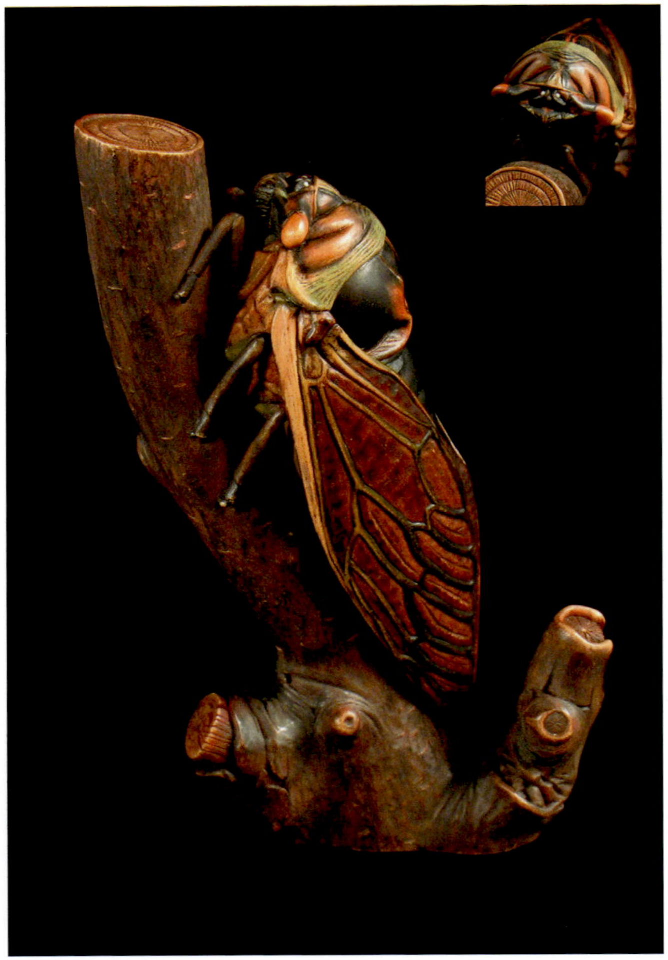

Janel Jacobson. *Summer Singer.* 2006. Small sculptural form, boxwood, 3.6" x 1.8" x 0.75", 9.3 x 4.6 x 2.0 cm.

Mouse & Pumpkin Seeds

The Japanese boxwood (*asama tsuge*) was a gift from Japanese netsuke carver, Sakai Masami. The mouse and pumpkin are a single piece of wood, while the eyes are inlaid horn and the seeds are mammoth tusk. Colored with artist oil paints.

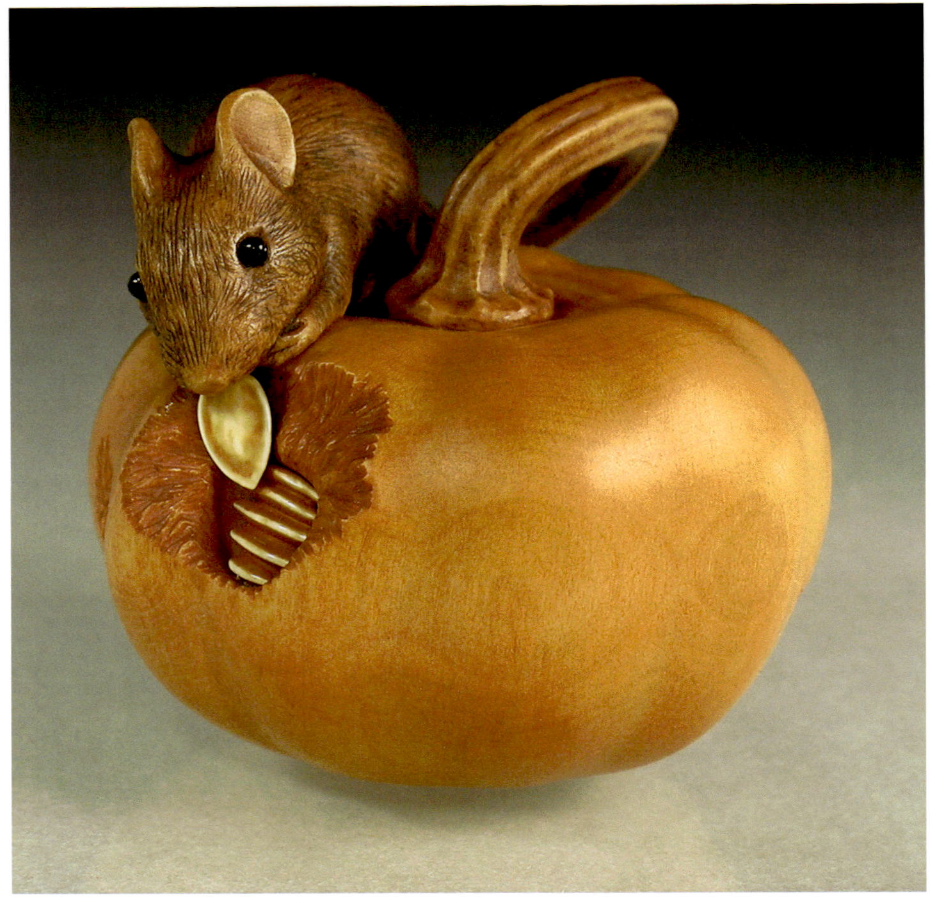

Janel Jacobson. *Mouse & Pumpkin Seeds.* 2007. Small sculpture – netsuke, 1.7" x 1.5" x 1.5", 4.3 x 3.8 x 3.8 cm.

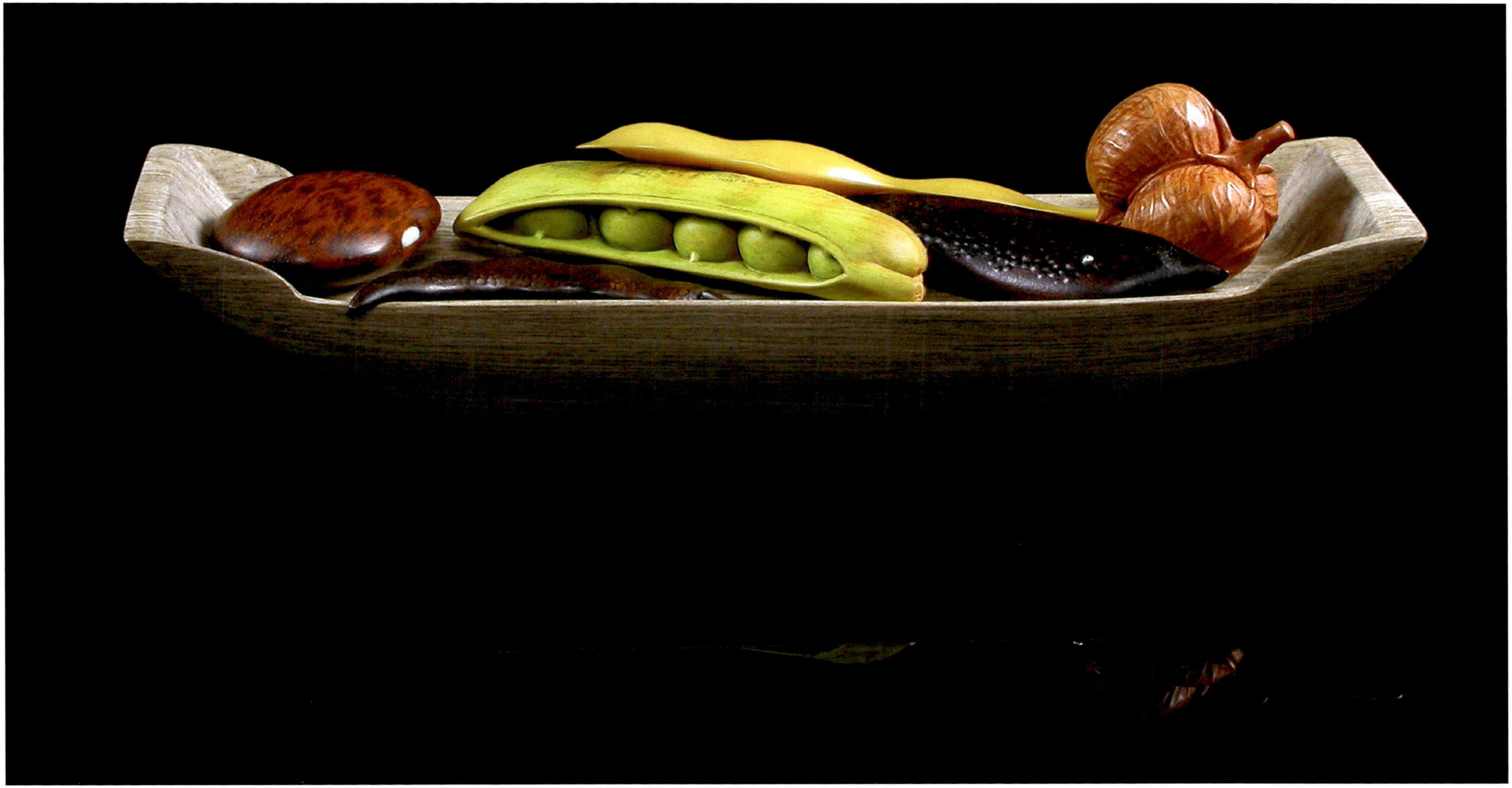

Janel Jacobson. *Pods & Seeds* - Collection 2. Tray, persimmon (from Meryl Salen), 5.0" x 1.5" x 1.0", 12.8 x 3.8 x 2.5 cm.

Douglas W. Jones & Kim Kulow-Jones

www.randomorbitstudio.com

Artists' Statement

We strive to build furniture and decorative objects that are elegant and imaginative, sophisticated yet playful. Though wood is our primary medium, we typically use a combination of materials, textures, curving surfaces, and rich colors to express our ideas. We trained as artists and craftspeople, but we seek to maintain an openness and immediacy towards materials like those found in folk art. Rediscovering a sense of lost or hidden beauty while encouraging a sustainable future is our ultimate goal.

Sometimes our work incorporates found or recycled objects directly; recent pieces make reference to familiar forms such as boats and other nautical themes. We use a variety of techniques, including woodturning, bending, shaping, carving, painting, and concealed joinery to create a balance of form, texture, and color.

Individual Artwork

Taproot

This sculpture evolved from repeating shapes in my sketchbook. In three-dimensional form, the shapes became more about balance, the interplay of weight and lightness. They also include my usual interests of color and pattern to activate the surface.

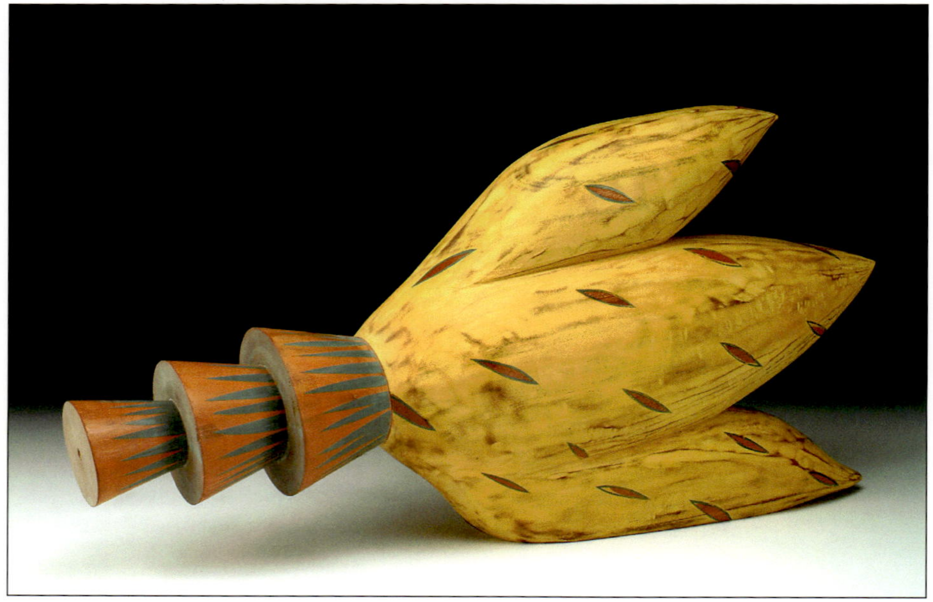

Kim Kulow-Jones. *Taproot.* 2003. Wood and paint, 20" h x 37" l x 7" w.
Photographer: Jerry Anthony

Nautical Bench

This bench is one of a pair designed for a private residence in Vermont. The goal was to create a visually compelling seating area for a circular, 80 square foot space at the top of a stairway. I sought to echo the curving architecture and complement the spectacular views of Lake Champlain visible through the windows above. The imagery is intended to evoke nautical themes as well as drawing on the traditions of formal seating. The benches are constructed of mahogany slats over a bent plywood armature, sandwiched between solid mahogany frames. The legs are turned and shaped and the armrest is shaped and carved, with a spiral hand rest. Each bench mirrors the other.

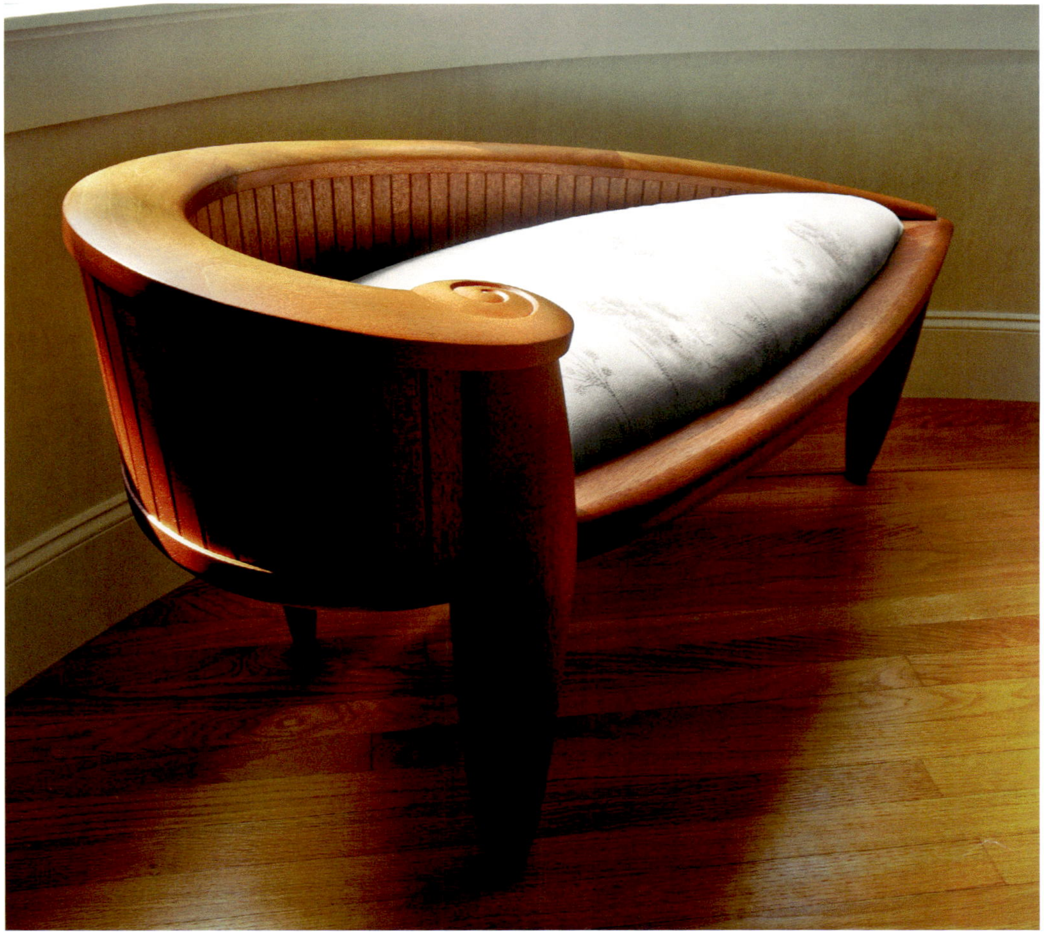

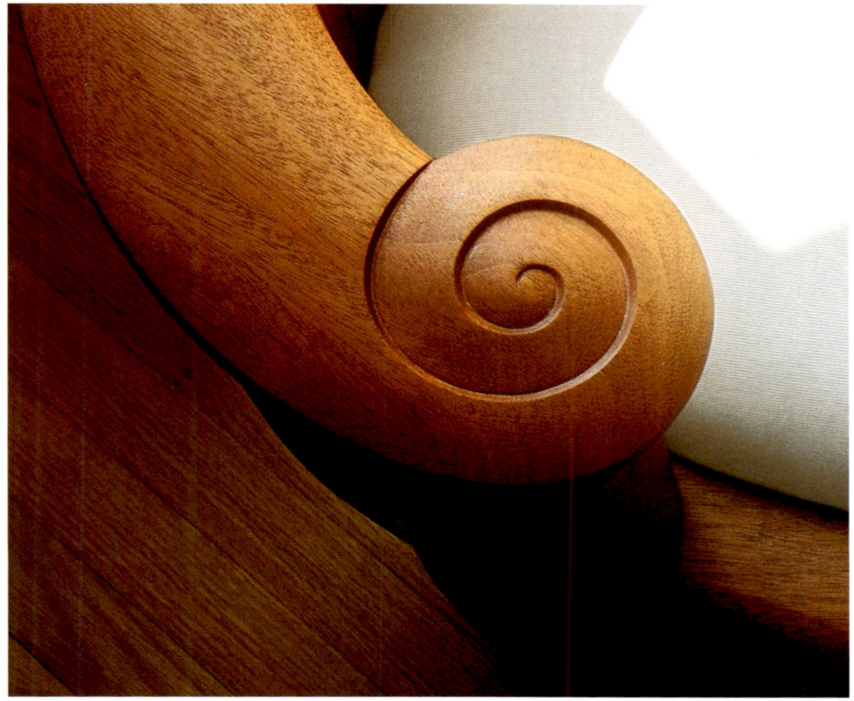

Douglas W. Jones. *Nautical Bench.* 2004. Mahogany, plywood, fabric, 28" x 51" x 23". *Photographer: Susan Teare*

Chess Set

This is our interpretation of a chess set using our own abstracted designs for each of the traditional pieces. Carved, painted, and textured pieces, painted mahogany board, turned and carved feet.

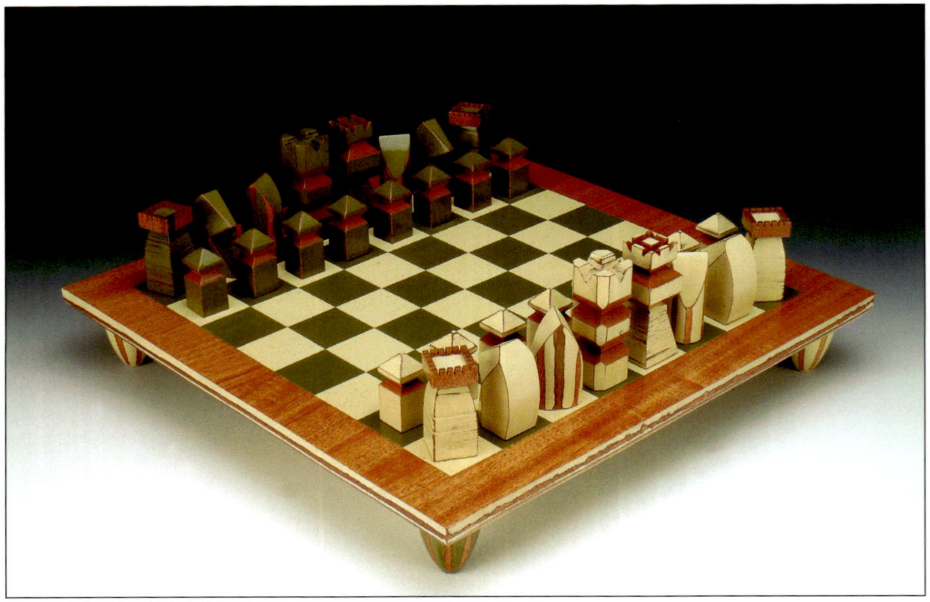

Douglas W. Jones and Kim Kulow-Jones. Chess Set. 2005. Mahogany, milk paint, 7" x 19.5" x 19.5". *Photographer: Jerry Anthony*

Boat Bench

Commissioned by the Museum of International Folk Art for the show, *A Chair for All Reasons*. The bench design grew out of a remembrance of an early experience with rowboat construction. Bent laminations of wood surround an interior framework. Milk paint and brass details.

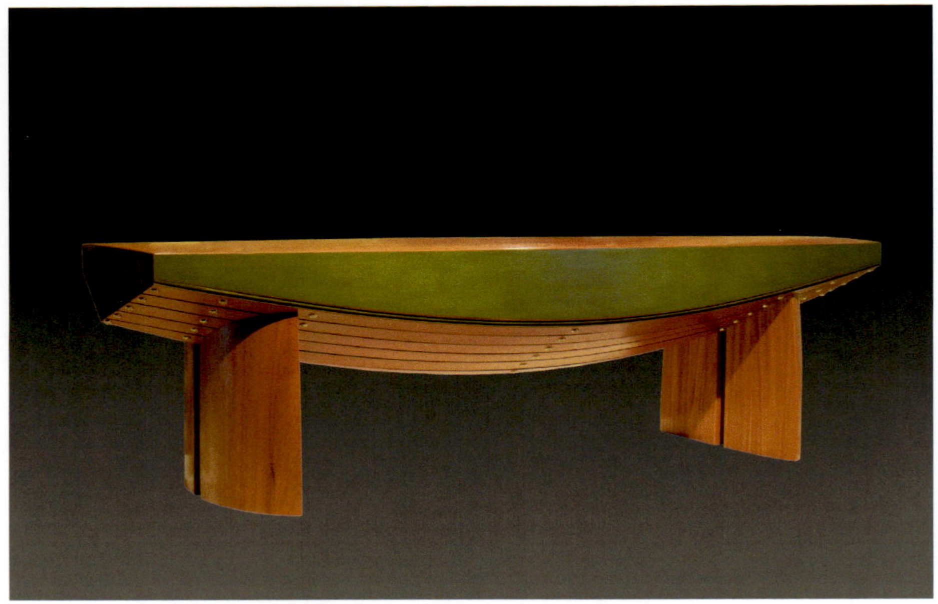

Douglas W. Jones and Kim Kulow-Jones. *Boat Bench.* 2009. Mahogany, milk paint, brass screws, 17" x 60" x 19". *Museum of International Folk Art, Santa Fe, New Mexico. Photo by: Blair Clark*

JOHN JORDAN

Cane Ridge, Tennessee,
www.johnjordanwoodturning.com

Artist's Statement

The pieces I make are simple but finely detailed vessels. Manipulating the color and patterns in the wood to complement the form, and the texturing and carving to create visual and tactile contrasts are important parts of the process and the result. What I feel is most important is the intangible quality that the piece is "right" that comes with putting emotion and feeling into the work. A simple object can be very powerful and emotional just for what it is. These pieces are simply decorative vessels that reflect my interest in surface textures/contrasts and form and the personal responses that I have to them, which I suspect are similar to the feelings that makers of decorative objects have felt for thousands of years.

Many of the woods that I use are from the dump, construction sites, etc. I find great satisfaction in creating elegant objects from material once destined to be buried or burned.

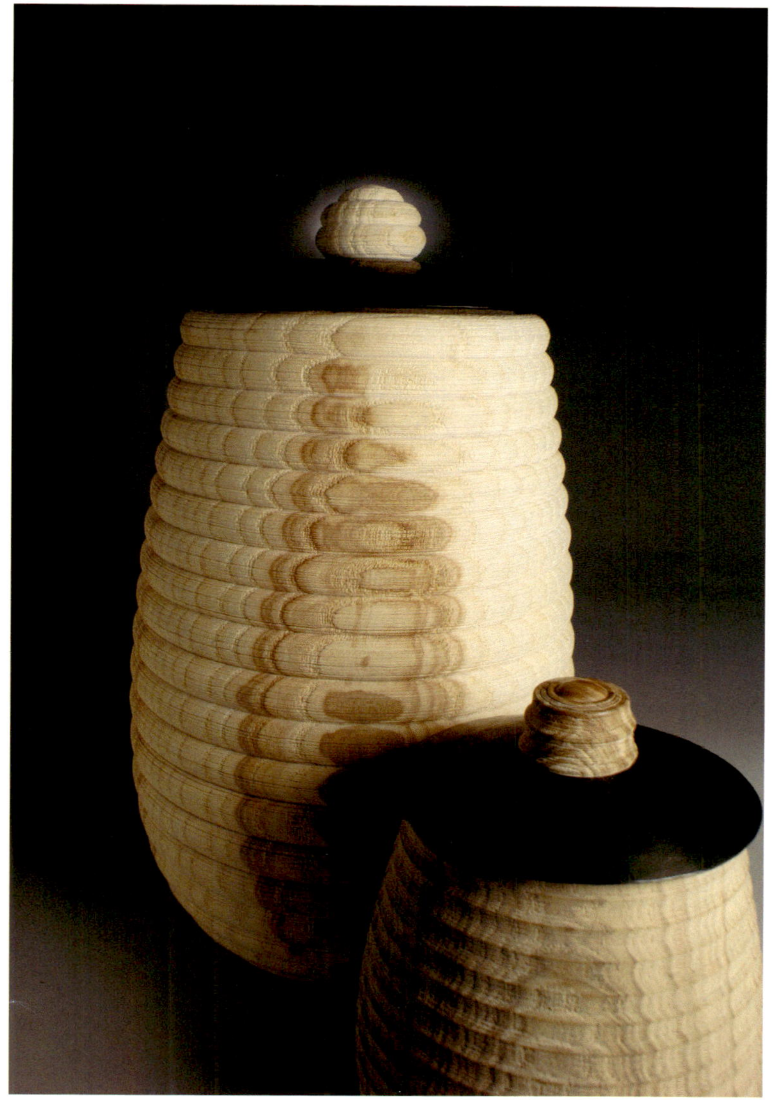

John Jordan. Ash Jars. 2007. Turned, carved ash, hammered steel, 11" x 7", 6" x 4".

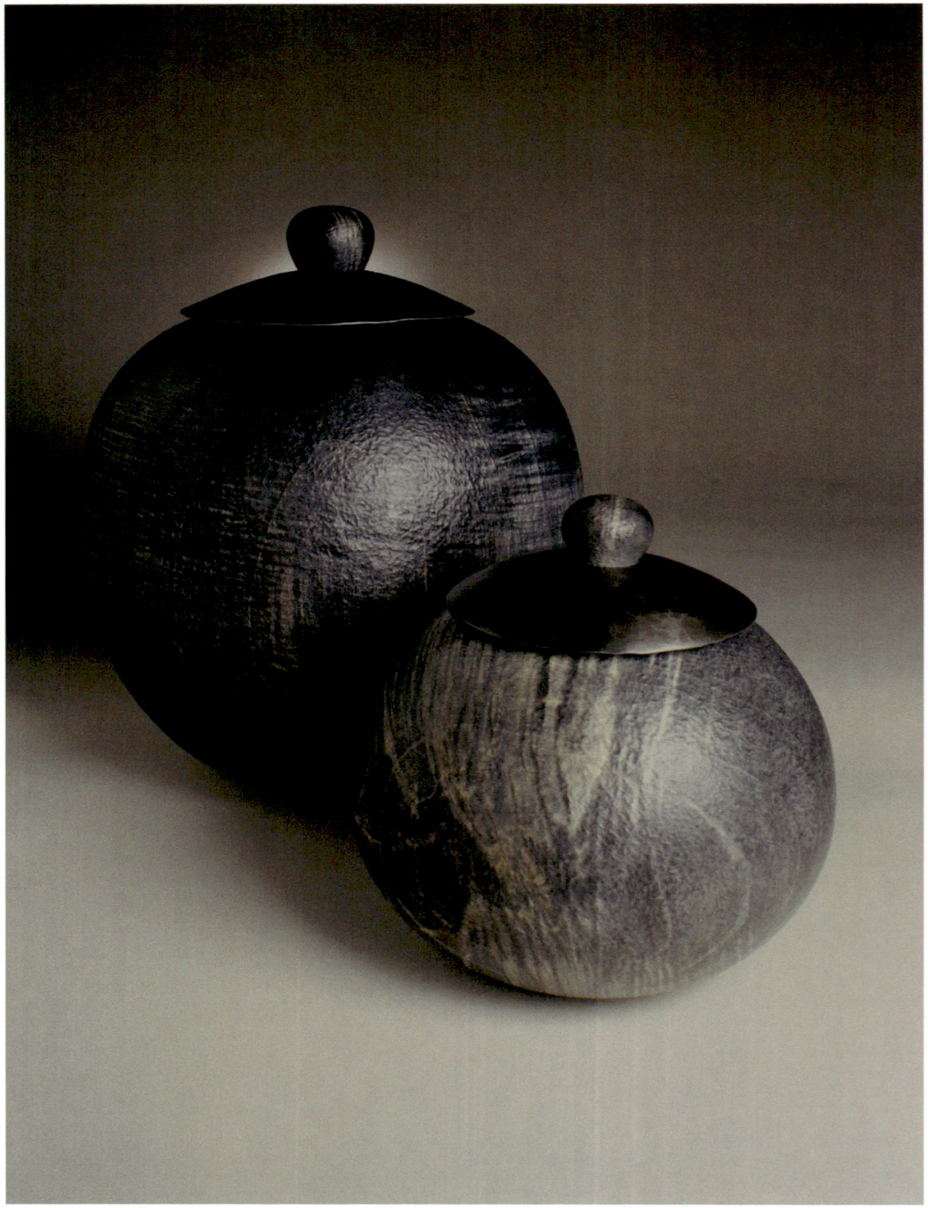

John Jordan. Black Jars. 2007. Turned, carved, dyed maple, hammered steel, 10" x 8", 6" x 5".

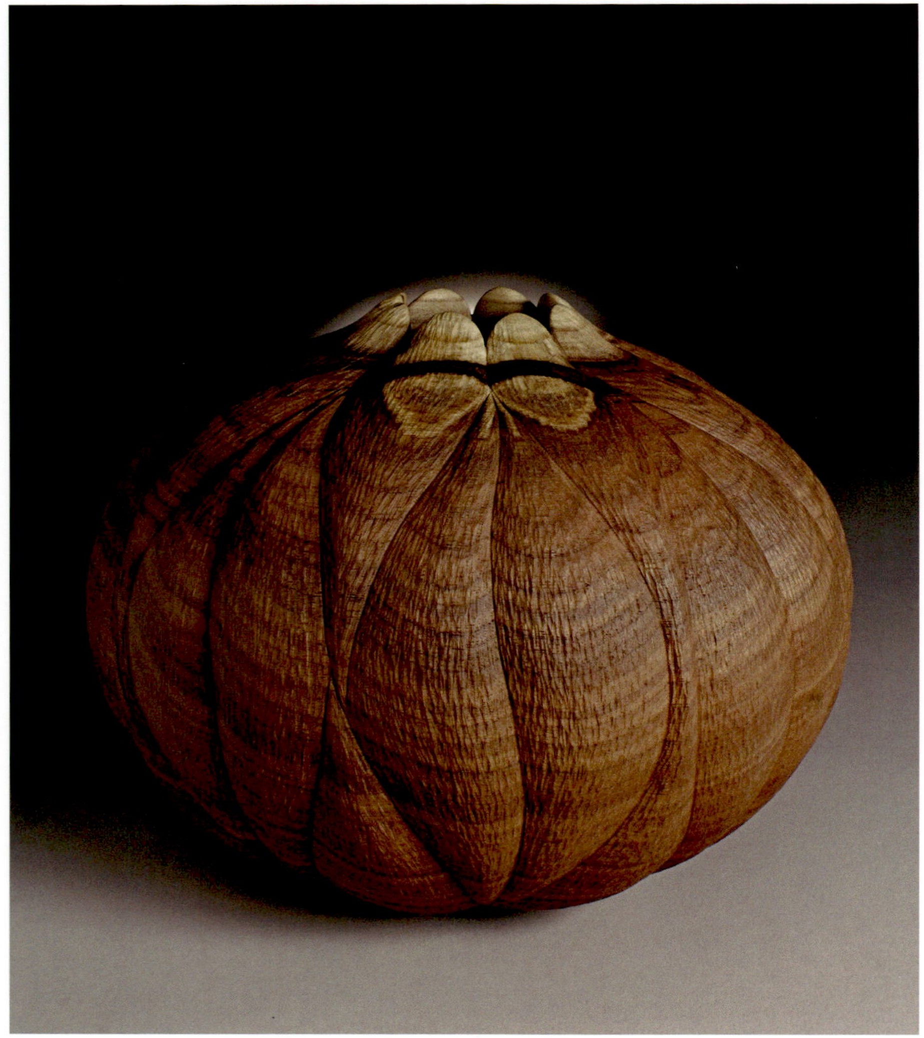

John Jordan. Walnut Vessel. 2008. Turned, carved walnut, 9" x 8".

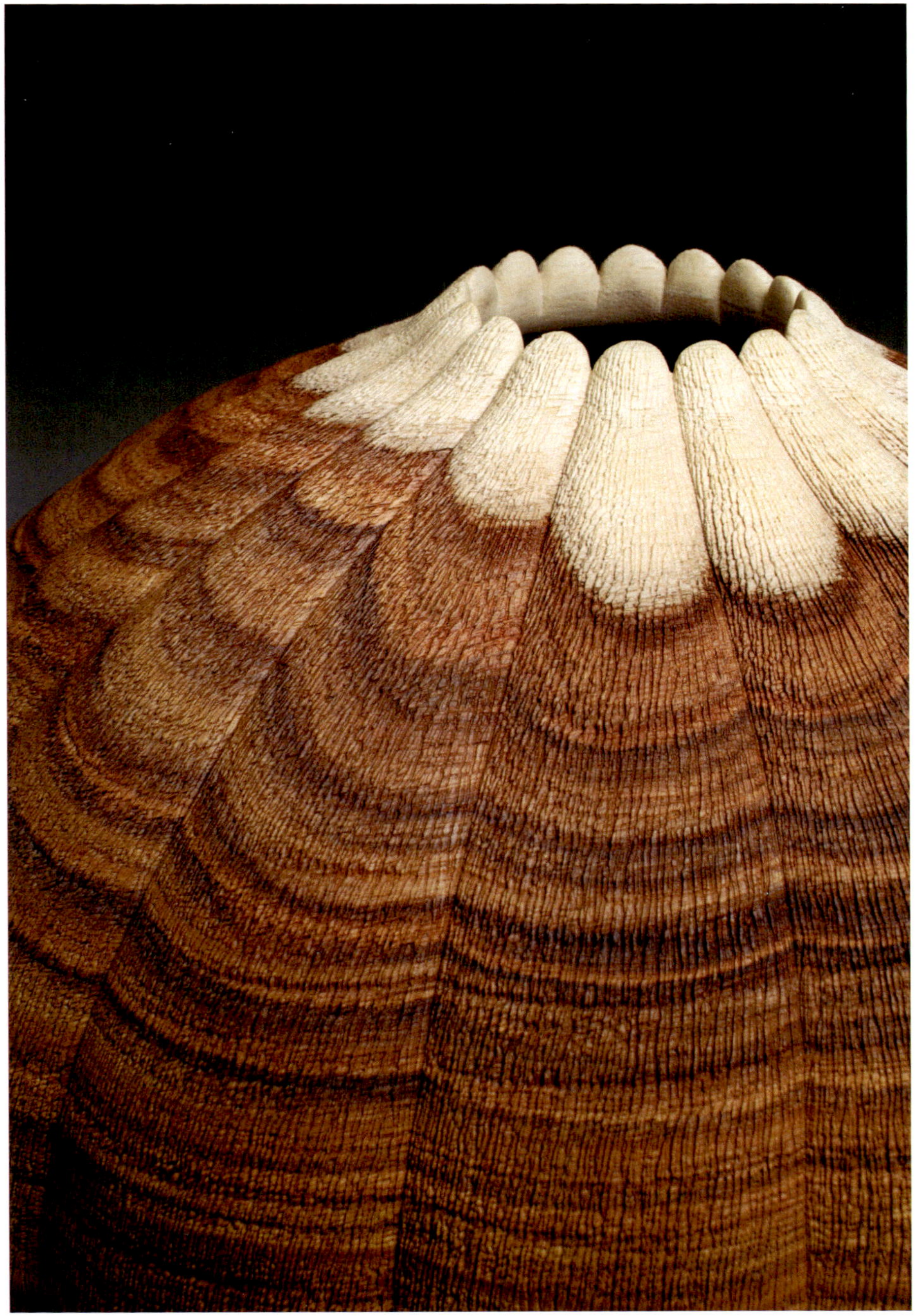

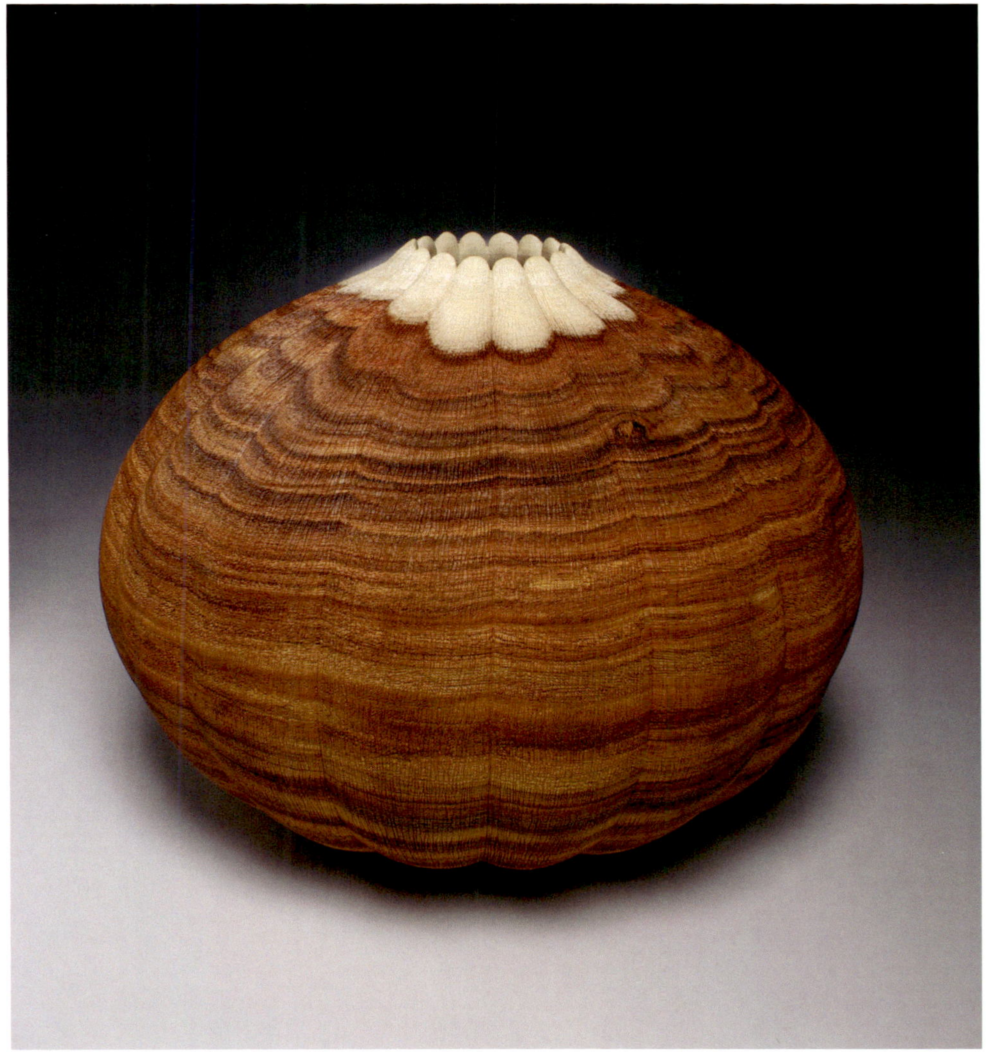

John Jordan. Rosewood Vessel. 2009. Turned, carved rosewood, 11" x 9".

Christine Kaiser

www.christinekaiser.com

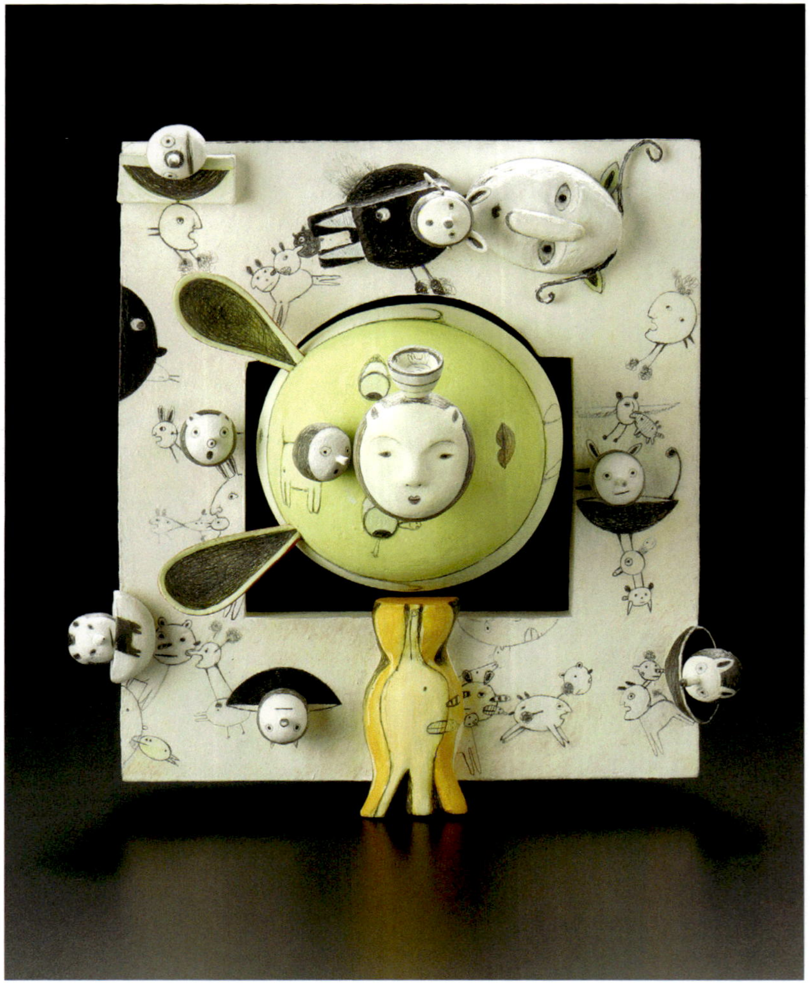

Christine Kaiser. *Not Yet.* 2008. Paint, basswood, graphite, basswood planks cut on band saw, shaped with a belt sander and rotary tool, carved with a rotary tool, painted with water based paints, graphite and pencil, 12" x 11" x 8". *Photographer: John Polak*

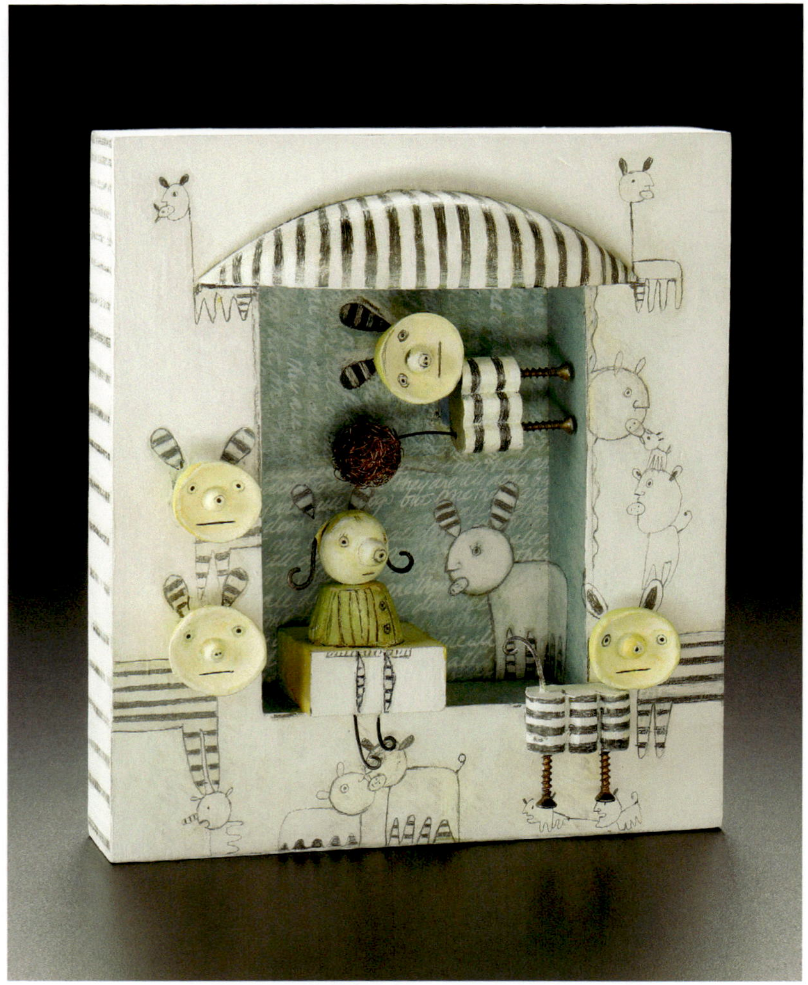

Christine Kaiser. *They are all dogs but me.* 2007. Paint, basswood, pine, graphite, wire, screws, basswood and pine planks cut on band saw, shaped with a belt sander and rotary tool, carved with a rotary tool, painted with water based paints, graphite and pencil. Fabricated wire elements and screws added, 11" x 10" x 2". *Photographer: John Polak*

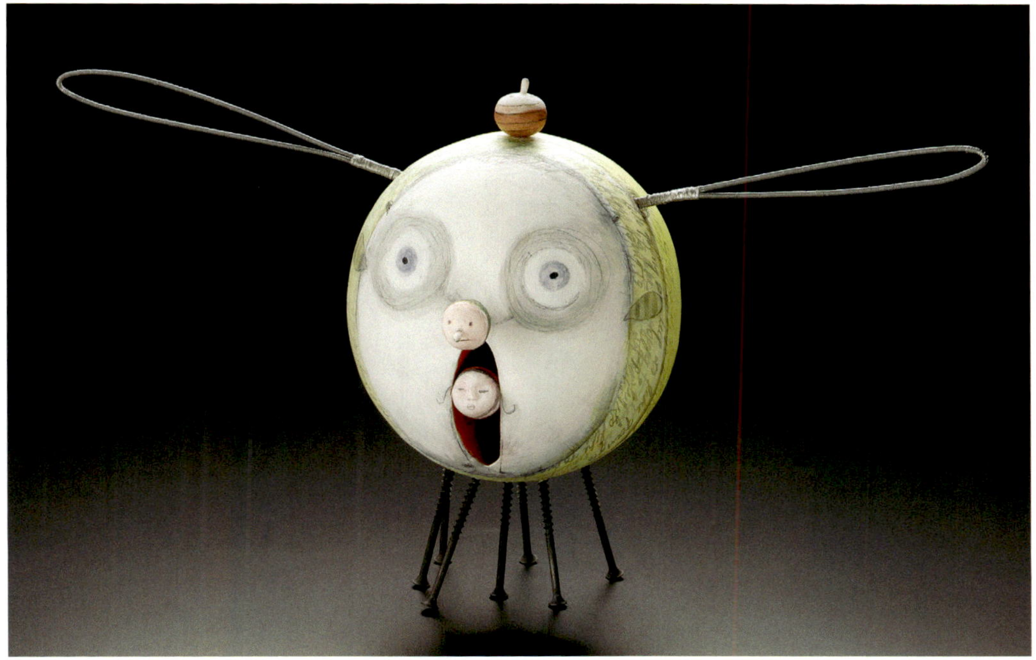

Christine Kaiser. *Its just like going to sleep.* 2007. Paint, basswood, graphite, wire, screws, basswood planks cut on band saw, shaped with a belt sander and rotary tool, carved with a rotary tool, painted with water based paints, graphite and pencil. Fabricated wire elements and screws added, 15" x 16" x 8". *Photographer: John Polak*

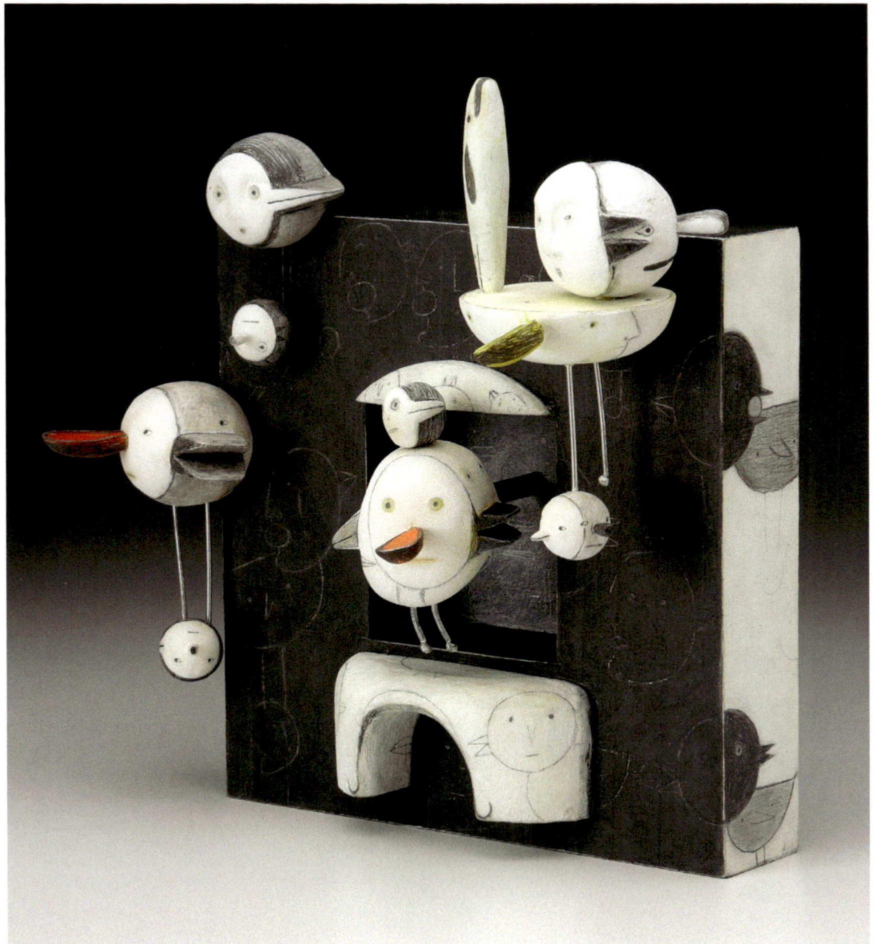

Christine Kaiser. *Take me.* 2008. Paint, basswood, graphite, wire, silver solder, basswood planks cut on band saw, shaped with a belt sander and rotary tool, carved with a rotary tool, painted with water based paints, graphite and pencil. Fabricated wire elements added, 11" x 10" x 6". *Photographer: John Polak*

Ronald G. Koehler

Cleveland, Mississippi, koehler@tecinfo.com

Individual Artwork

Balanced Diet Series

I try to put a little humor in my work and sometimes use a play on words as in the case of the *Balanced Diet Series*. This series grew out of a vegetable and food toy vehicle series from several years ago. Experimentation with common, ordinary tools produced interesting food textures. Drilling slightly into the surface of wood with several different sizes of drill bits produced a bread-like textured surface. A bush hammer (a stone carving tool similar to a meat tenderizing tool) produced a hamburger-like texture. These surfaces were enhanced with paint to make interesting *trompe l'oeil* food items. Some of the works in this series contain unlikely components, but are well balanced with lots of fiber.

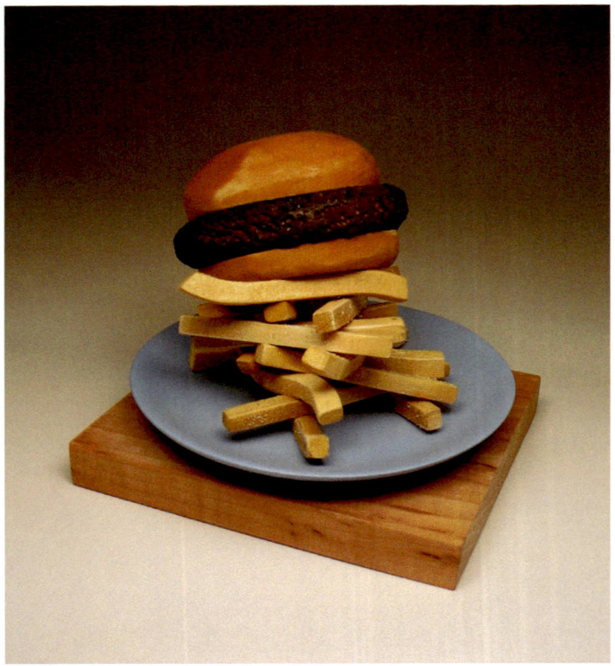

Ronald G. Koehler. *Balanced Burger & Fries.* 2008. Wood, paint, carved, 5" x 7" x 7".

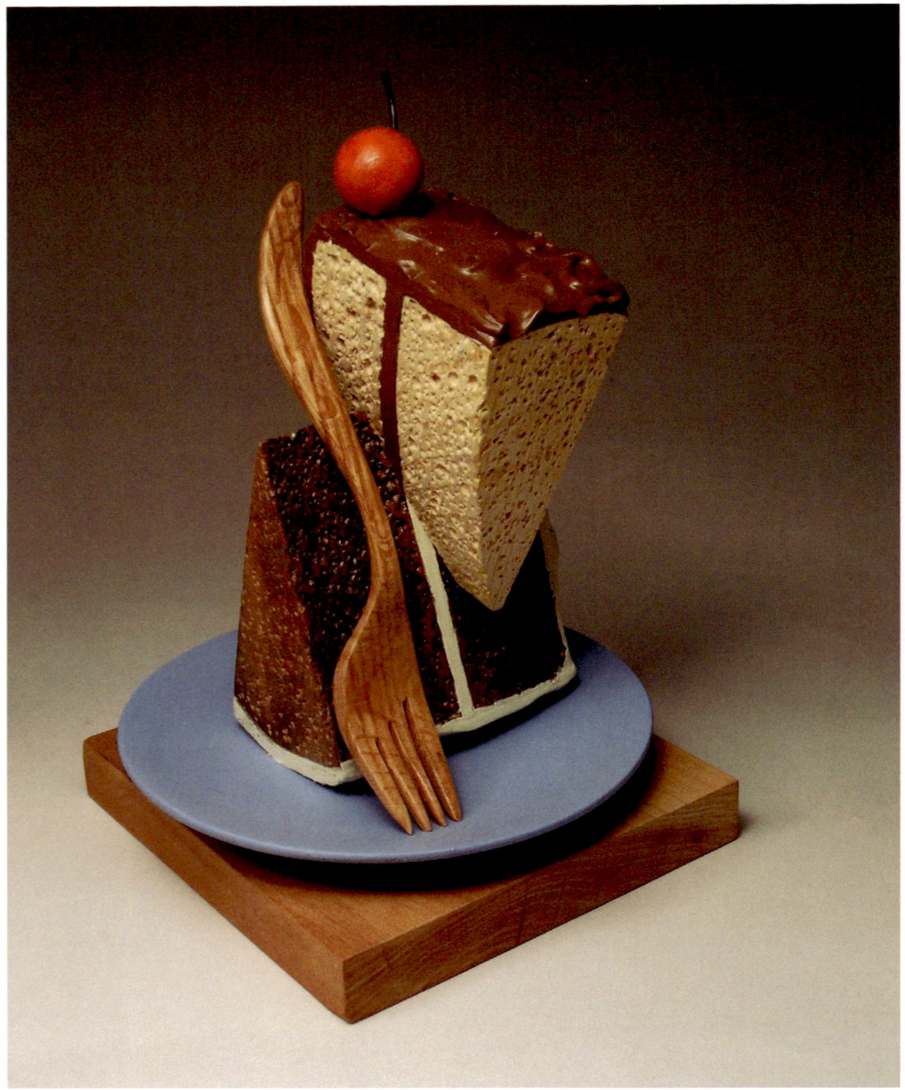

Ronald G. Koehler. *Balanced Cake with Fork.* 2009. Wood, paint, carved, 8" x 7" x 7".

Brush Series

Most of my recent work has been composed of individual units pertaining to the visual symbol of the paint brush. This series includes a "Dadaist" reference by mass-producing a readymade object. Although the shape chosen more closely resembles a house painting brush, the visual connection between the brush and creativity is a genuine one.

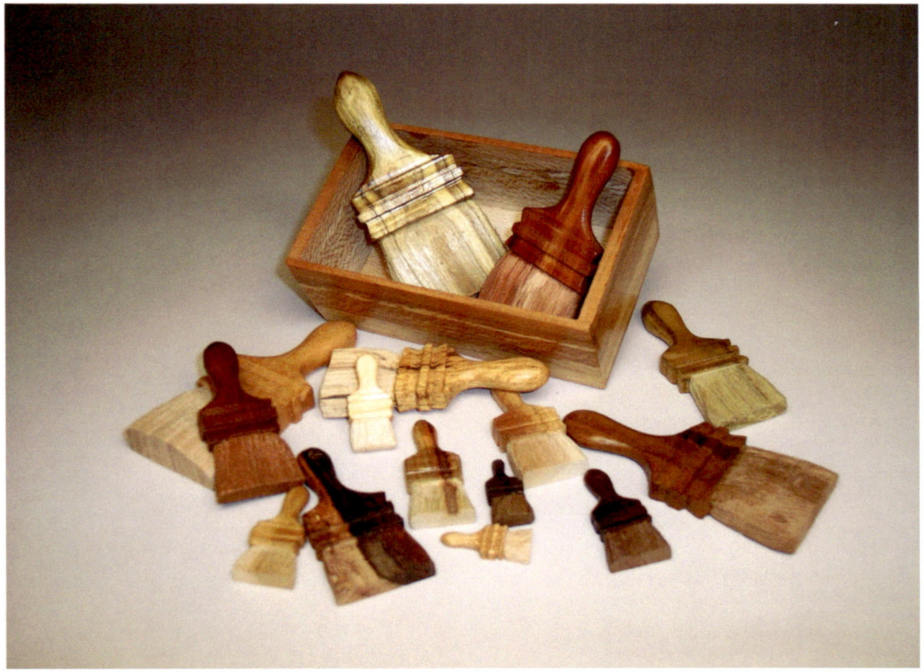

Ronald G. Koehler. *Box of Brushes*. 2006. Wood, carved, 4" x 6" x 3".

Tool Series

I have always been fascinated with tools and how things are made. The shapes are sawn out of wood and carved to look like the individual tools and painted with a graphite patina, which gives them a metallic-look.

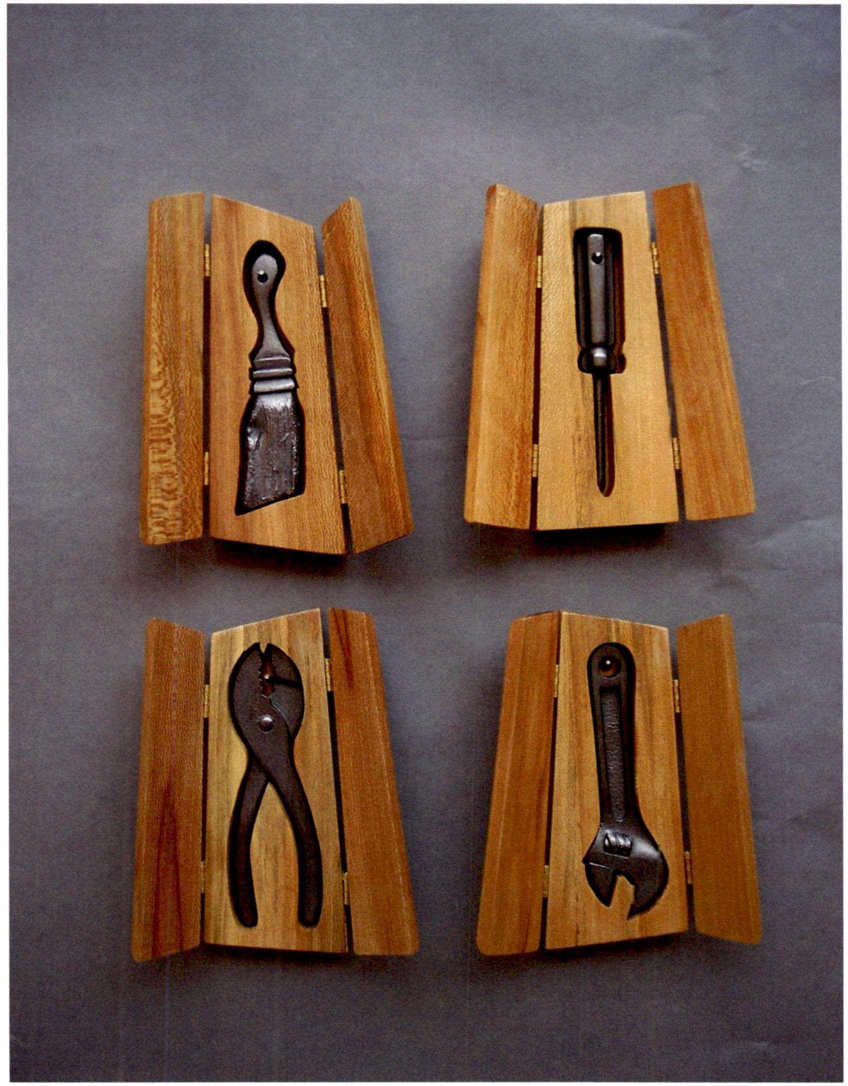

Ronald G. Koehler. Tool Boxes-set #6. 2008. Wood with graphite patina, carved, 20" x 16" x 2".

Ron Layport

Pittsburgh, Pennsylvania, ronlayport@Verizon.net

Individual Artwork

Voices from the Rim

From canyon rims of the Colorado Plateau, and throughout the Rio Grande Basin, come voices of ancient peoples—ancient makers—speaking in a language of vessel forms so powerful, so connected to the earth, that one can actually experience a thousand years of humankind.

This vessel reflects upon that continuum, and upon my place in it.

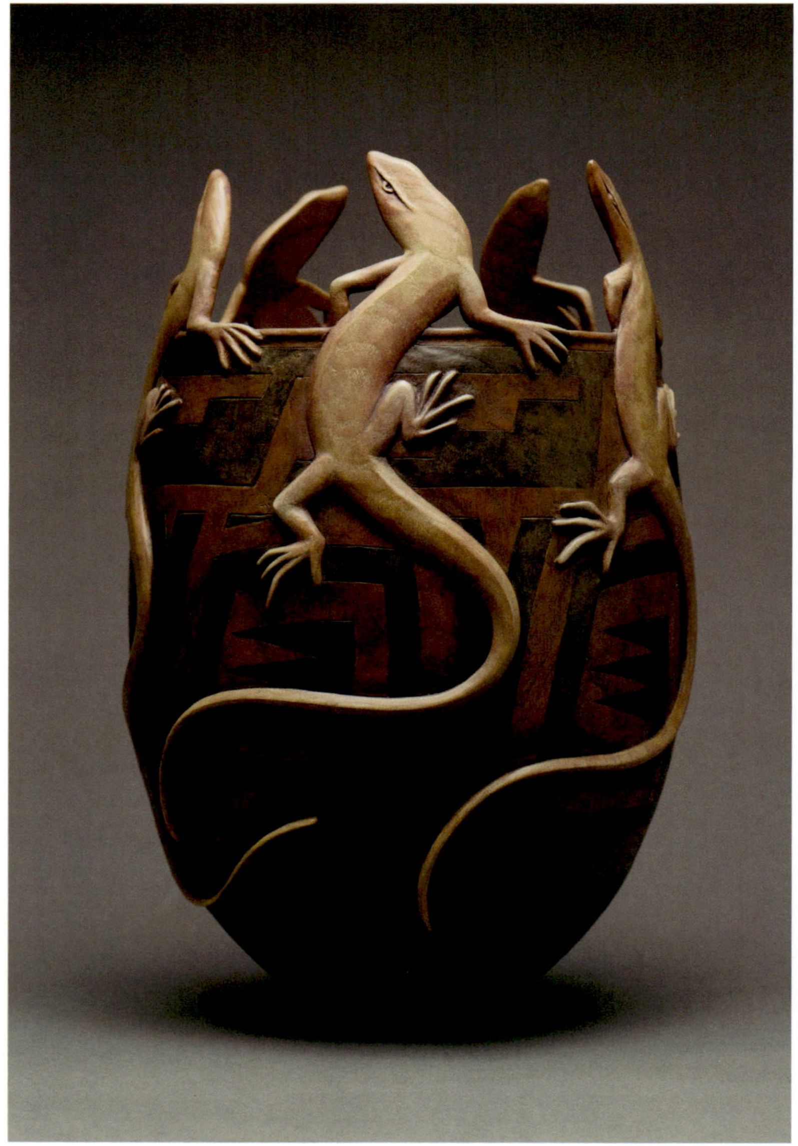

Ron Layport. *Voices from the Rim.* 2008. Ash, pigment, turned, sculpted, pigmented wood vessel, 12" h x 7.75" d.

Masque Of Eos, Goddess of the Dawn

Part of an ongoing series, *Vessels From A Distant Dance*, exploring the turned vessel form as a ceremonial or spirit mask, a container of the spirit. Negative space is used to add visual complexity and a sense of air to the sculpted form.

This is the largest and most open of the series thus far. I've coaxed the log beyond the point of reason.

Ron Layport. *Masque Of Eos, Goddess of the Dawn.* 2008. Sycamore, maple, steel, pigment, turned, sculpted, pigmented mask on stand, 21" w x 6.50" d, 11" h x 21" w x 6.50" d.

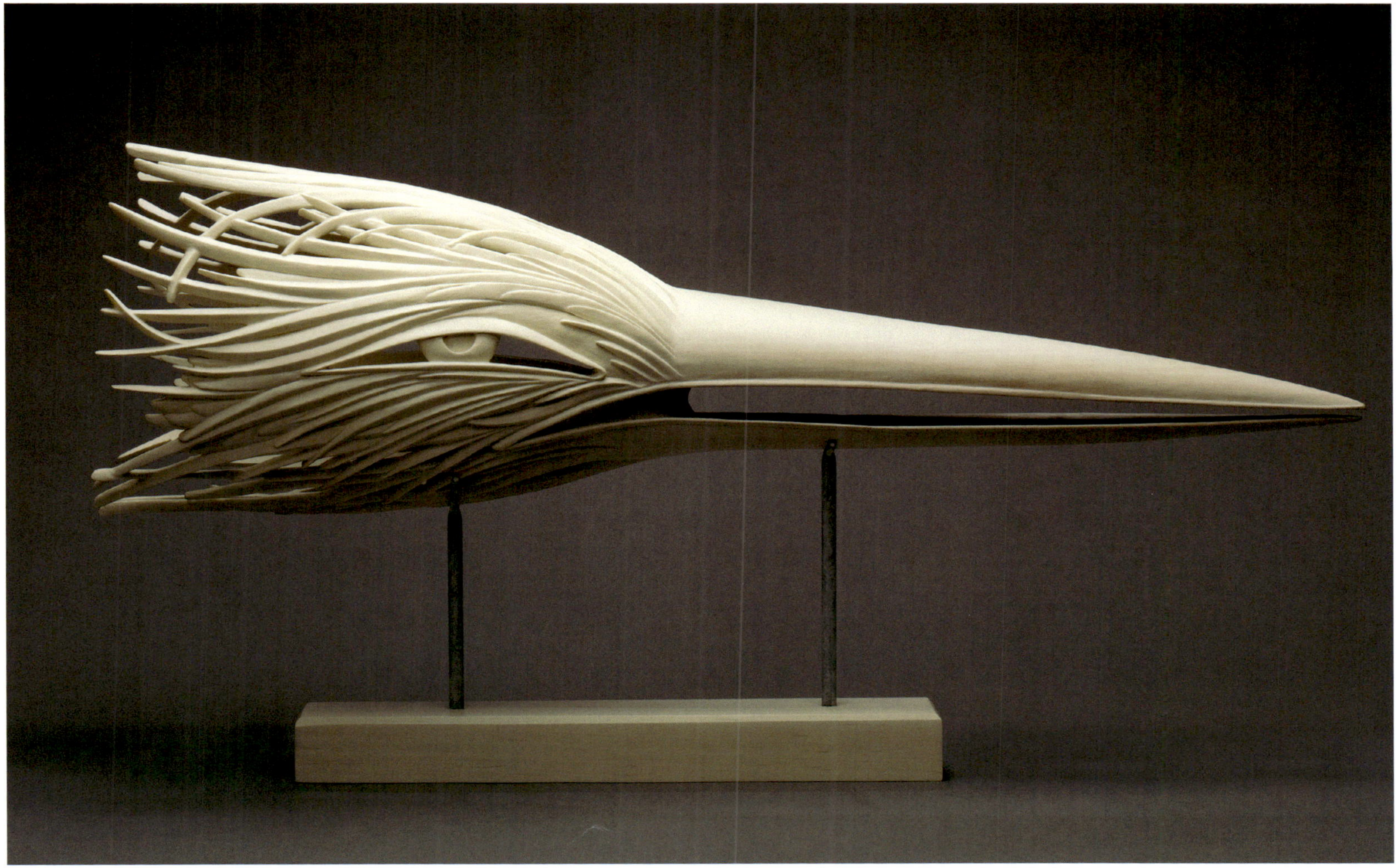

Spirits of the Light

This is a painting...a sculptural bowl form...a metamorphic journey...from a 90-pound slab to a nearly weightless "canvas." The dragonfly symbolizes growth and change, illumination and enlightenment. Its color transformation, through the reflection and refraction of light, is a reminder that we too can be transformed in powerful, imaginative ways, if we so choose. *Spirits of the Light* is intended as a wall sculpture, to embrace variations in light throughout the day.

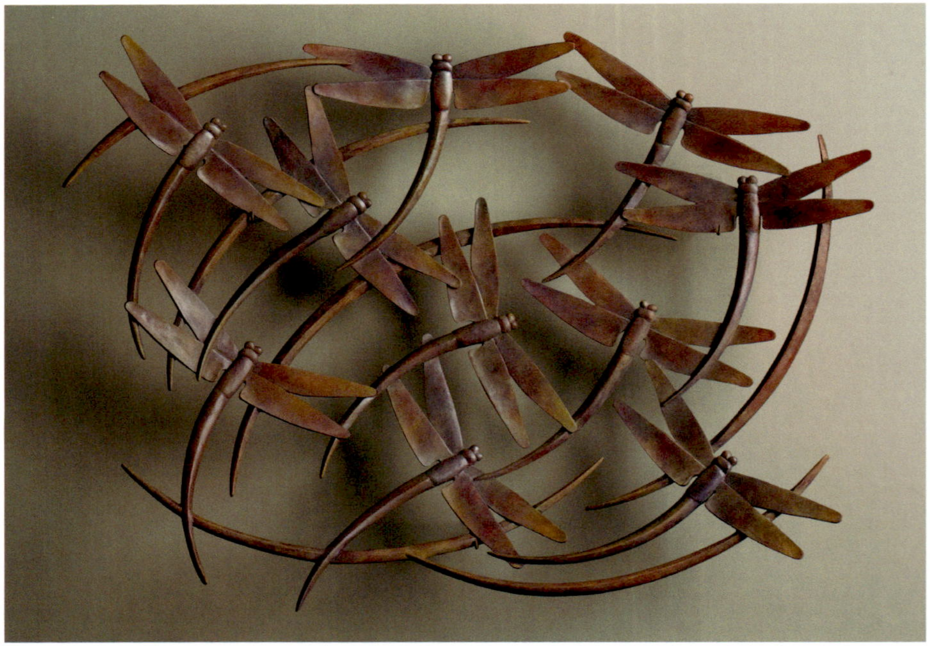

Ron Layport. *Spirits of the Light.* 2009. Maple, pigment, turned, sculpted, pigmented wall piece (includes mounting brackets), 21" h x 27.5" w x 4" d.

Wolf Chorus

The wolf chorus is once again celebrated throughout the valley of the Yellowstone. The term "wolf chorus" refers to the howling harmonies that summon the pack for the hunt.

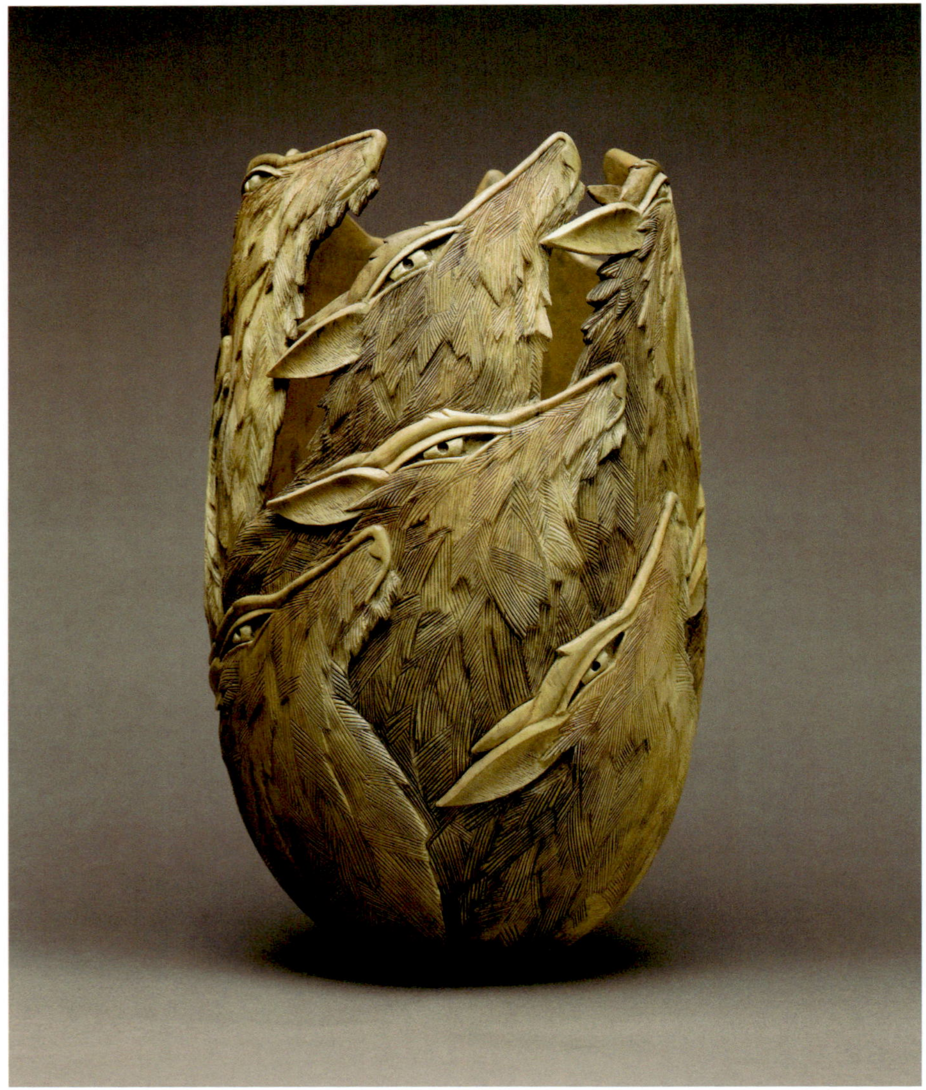

Ron Layport. *Wolf Chorus.* 2009. Tulip poplar, pigment, turned, sculpted, pigmented wood vessel, 14.25" h x 8.25" d.

Po Shun Leong

www.poshunleong.com

Artist's Statement

My statements, like moving targets, are always changing, but the following is a constant. You are never too old to play around with wood and should not be afraid to experiment. The value of the events along the way rather than an unreachable destination can open us to new ideas.

Individual Artwork

Constellation, Dining Table

Overlooking the ocean next to an east-facing window, this breakfast table waits for the early sun. The suns rays penetrate openings to the interior, bringing a Jon Kuhn glass sculpture to life. Swirling spheres representing a constellation of planets support the glass top. Looking within the interior of the table, the glass sculpture is mounted on a tower in an imaginary city. At night, the inner city can be illuminated by hidden light. Mainly mahogany and many other woods, laminated, band sawn, and carved.

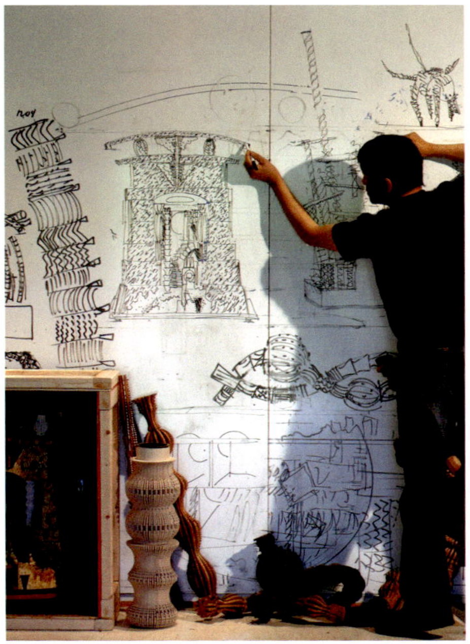

Po Shun Leong. *Drawing*. 2009. Rarely do I draw to work out ideas. Most of my designs are created spontaneously by playing around with material, forms, bit of thought, and the help of woodworking machines. Adjustments or drastic design changes made on the spot seem to work well for me, rather than adhering to rigid, preconceived plans.

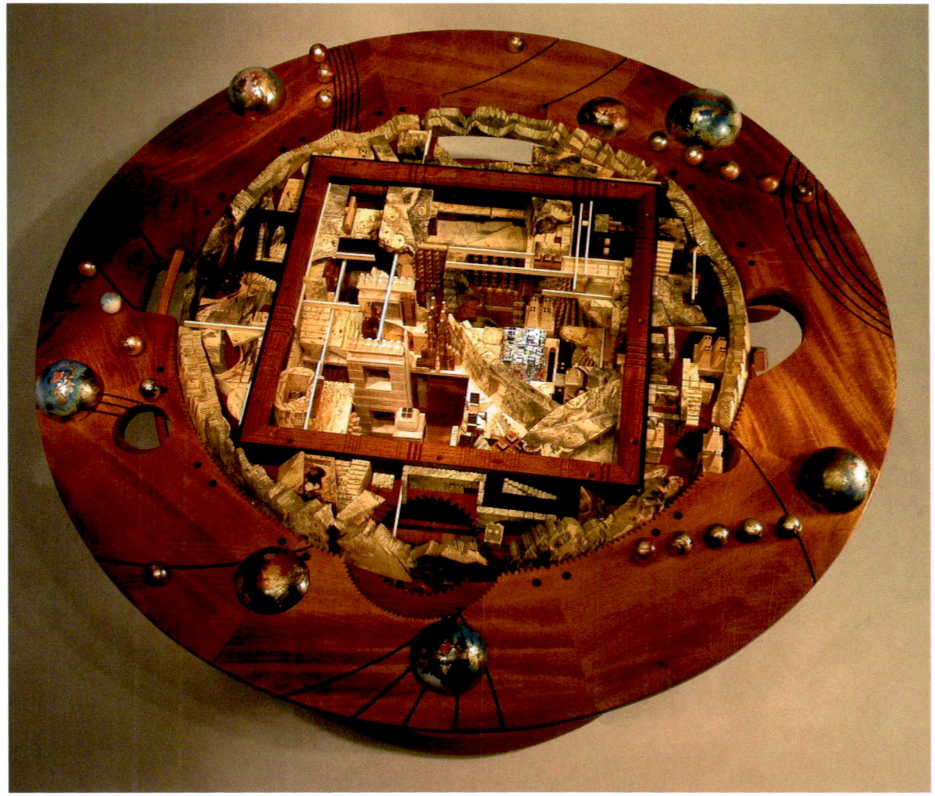

Po Shun Leong. *Constellation, Dining Table*. 2006. The glass top has been removed to show the imaginary inner city in the detail shot. 32" h x 54" d.

Fortune Cookie Stool

This stacking stool was inspired by the way a fortune cookie is folded. Pure design is about the reduction of parts to the simplest element in order to function. A flat piece of plywood can be bent into a strong, three-dimensional structure by forming it in a vacuum mold.

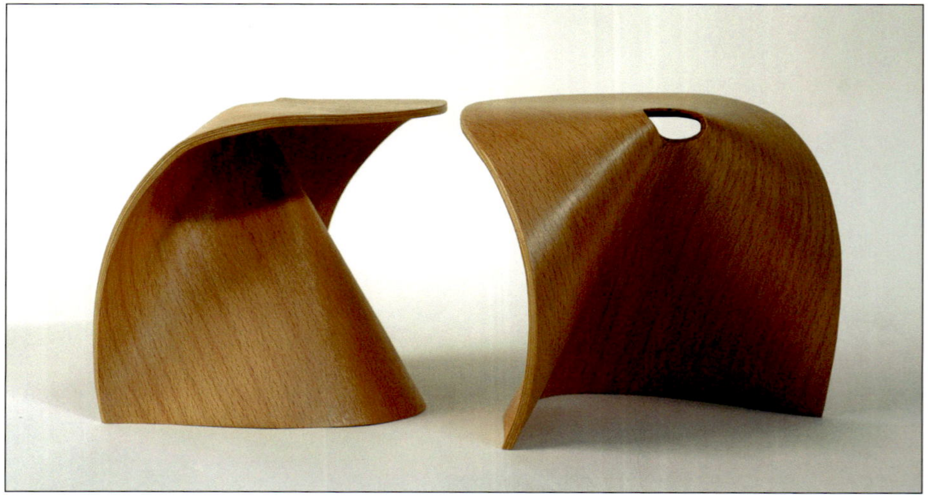

Po Shun Leong. *Fortune Cookie Stool*. 2008.

Ancient Ruins Box

It is a box inspired from the legendary places of the world, like Mont Saint-Michel or some lost horizon. Your eyes and hands do the traveling. Secret chambers add to the drama. For contrast, texture or color I used cherry, zebrawood, maple, wenge, ebony, pink ivory wood, narra, pernambuco, buckeye burl, and cocobolo. Most of the structure is assembled from precut band sawn components.

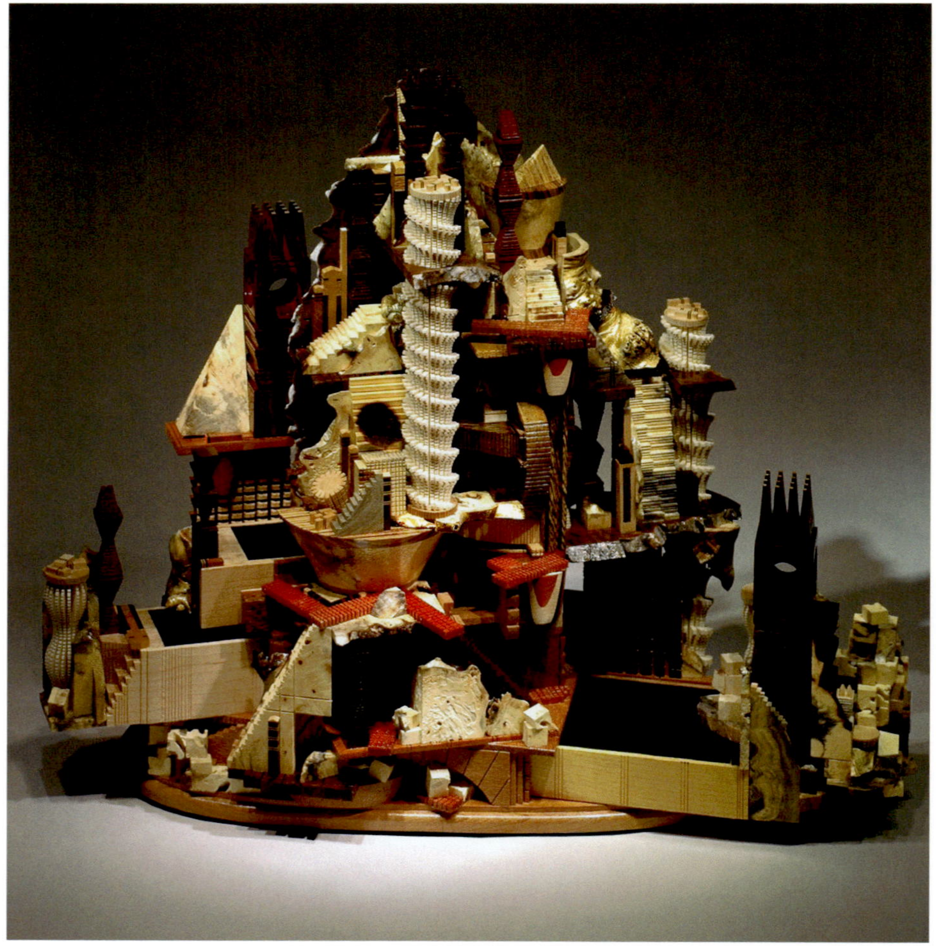

Po Shun Leong. *Ancient Ruins Box*. 2009. Showing the sliding drawers open. 24" h x 20" w x 10" d.

Bloom

This is about walking through the California desert when the flowers explode into bloom. This sculptural object was made of bleached maple with a band saw. The method to make parts follows: Thin straight wood strips (think flat fettuccine) are individually glued tightly around 1/4" to 1/2" diameter wood dowels. It takes from fifteen to thirty strips to cover a single dowel. Some patience and a steady hand are required.

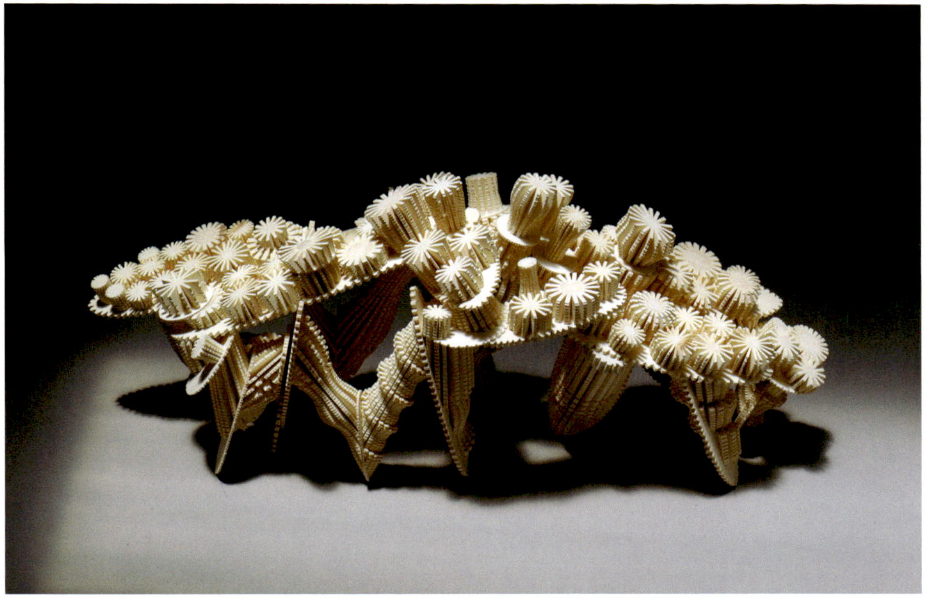

Po Shun Leong. *Bloom*. 2009. 9.75" h x 24" w x 7.5" d.

Landscape Box

This box is inspired from the legendary places of the world, like Machu Picchu or the cliff dwellings of Mesa Verde. The ruins, stairs, and secret spaces are intended to set off a train of thought and a journey backwards again and again. Built in illumination brings the theatrical interior to life. On the front surface, the squiggly shapes are from scraps of a compressed wood waste structural "I" beam that my neighbor conveniently threw over the fence. For contrast, texture or color in the carvings I used Philippine mahogany, maple, wenge, ebony, pink ivory wood, narra, pernambuco, buckeye burl and cocobolo, all carved with a band saw. Having plenty of pre-carved elements ready to assemble is like preparing the ingredients for a Chinese feast.

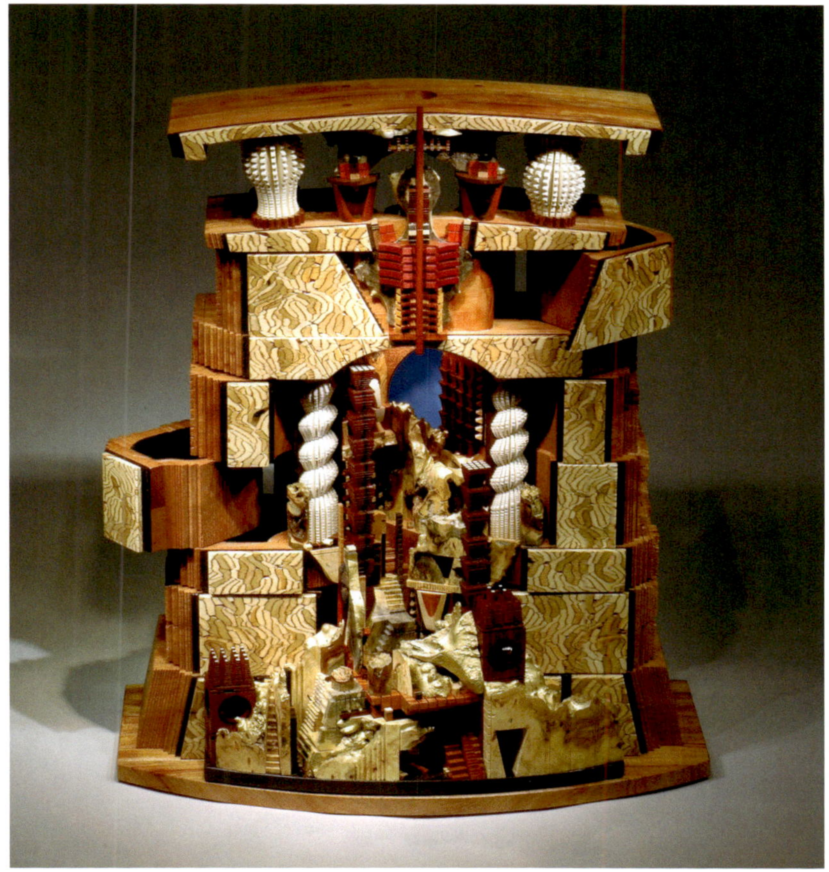

Po Shun Leong. *Landscape Box.* 2009. 28.5" h x 21" w x 13.5" d.

Robert Levin

Burnsville, North Carolina, www.robertlevin.com

Artist's Statement

Over the years I have been working on a series of pieces that have marked a departure from my studio glass work. These began by using glass, wood, and other materials in a very basic, visceral way. I have always felt intuitively that materials carry their own metaphors, or a resonance to a more emotional level, and have used this as a point of departure. In these pieces, it seems important to maintain the integrity of the various materials, to let them "speak for themselves." Some of the pieces are largely the result of an interest in using these materials together, and in how the working process can leave its own documentation: the wood charred by the once-hot glass, showing the creative and destructive possibilities of fire within the same moment; or the ways in which other materials may be bent or constricted. I continually find certain themes emerging: with many of the pieces, the working process has involved an exploration of pressure and constraint, balance and gesture.

There is also an element of craftsmanship in these pieces that speaks of the importance of the materials themselves, as well as the importance of the hand that acts upon them. Often the work has begun by following a fairly intuitive path dictated by a sense of form, balance, or an exploration of how forms and materials might work together. But, inevitably, I see other themes cropping up. So there is a sense of having a dialog with the work, of learning about some hidden aspects of my own sensibilities by having made a tangible object. For me, this dialog is an important aspect of the exploration involved with the work.

Some pieces have been informed by other concerns, which for me have connotations of constraint, including the ways in which we place limits around our own experiences. A few of the pieces are somewhat whimsical, while others have a more serious or mystical connotation. Some of the sculptures use the image of the bridge, perhaps as a metaphor for how we can span the gaps or walls that we create. It also seems to me that art acts as a bridge between the invisible and the visible, between thoughts and form. My most recent sculptures have been wall pieces that are influenced by my interest in African art, and include much more carving and the evidence of the hand & tools working on the wood.

In all of these pieces, I've created problems for myself to solve; hopefully, the pieces offer solutions to problems while at the same time raising more questions. I want them to be ambiguous and evocative at the same time.

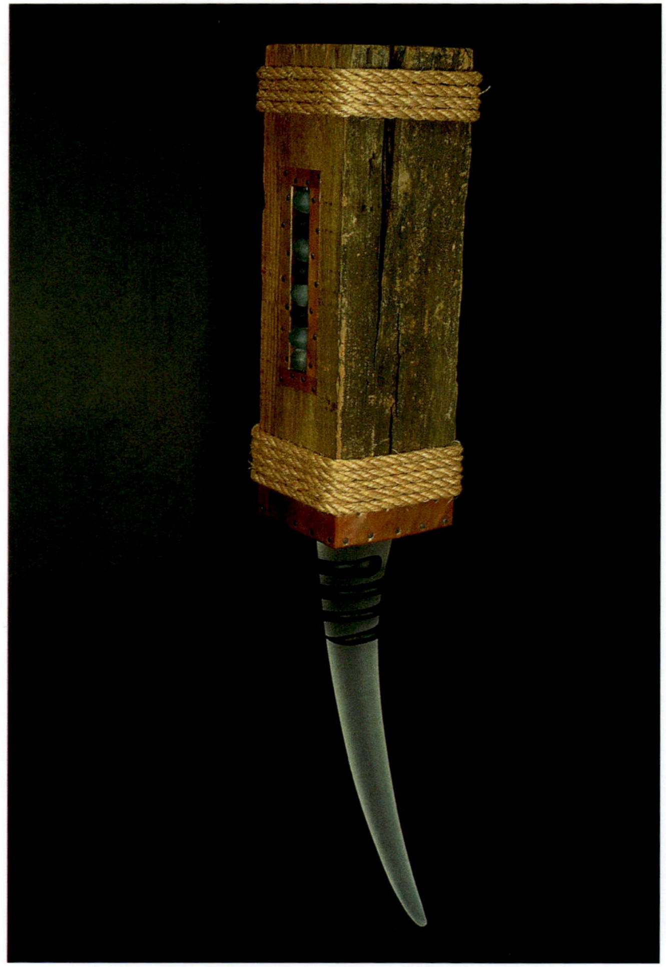

Robert Levin. *Kincho.* 2001. Wood, glass, rope, 41" h x 22" x 13".

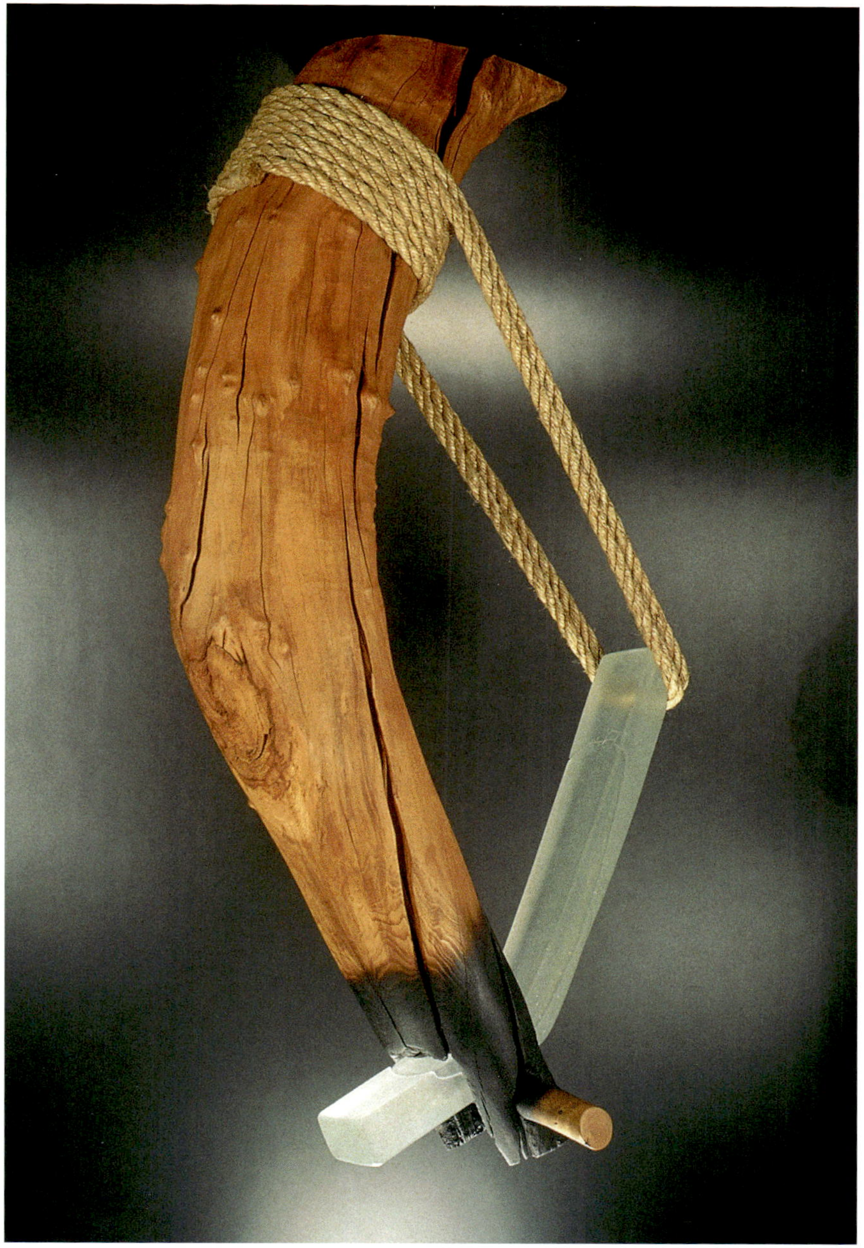

Robert Levin. *Oak Bridge.* 2001. Wood, glass, rope, gold leaf, 12" h x 32.5" x 12.5".

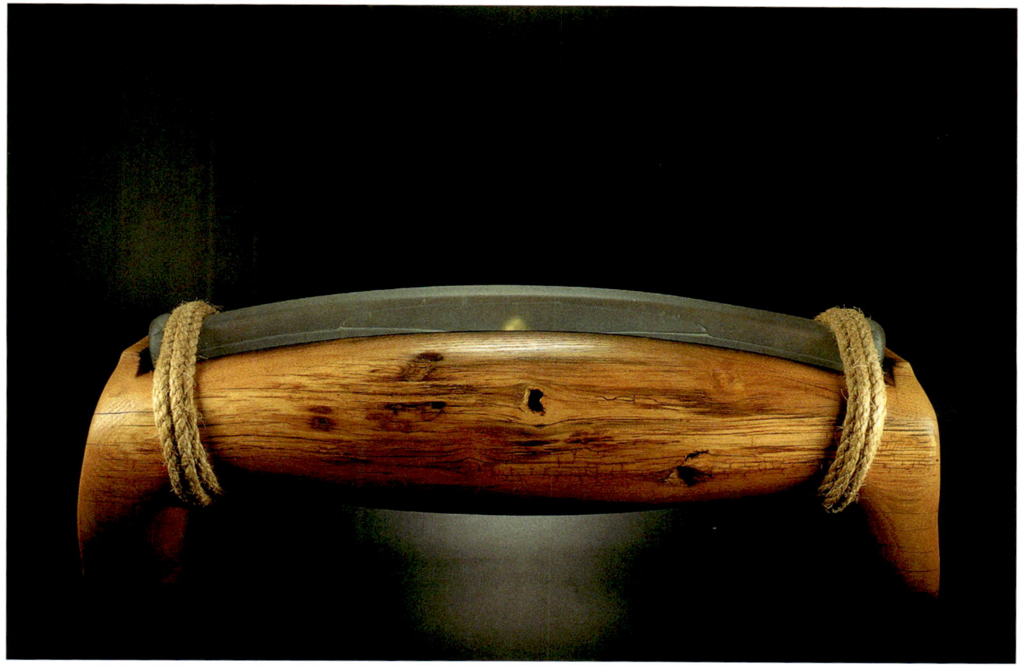

Robert Levin. *Tusk.* 2001. Wood, glass, rope, 38" h x 41" x 12".

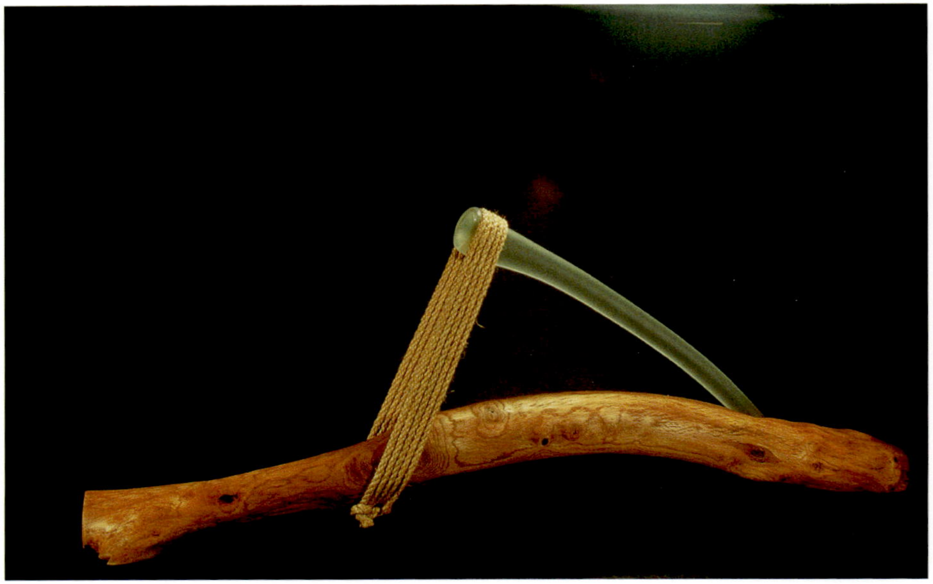

Robert Levin. *Diviner.* 2001. Wood, glass, rope, copper, 33" h x 6.5" x 9.75".

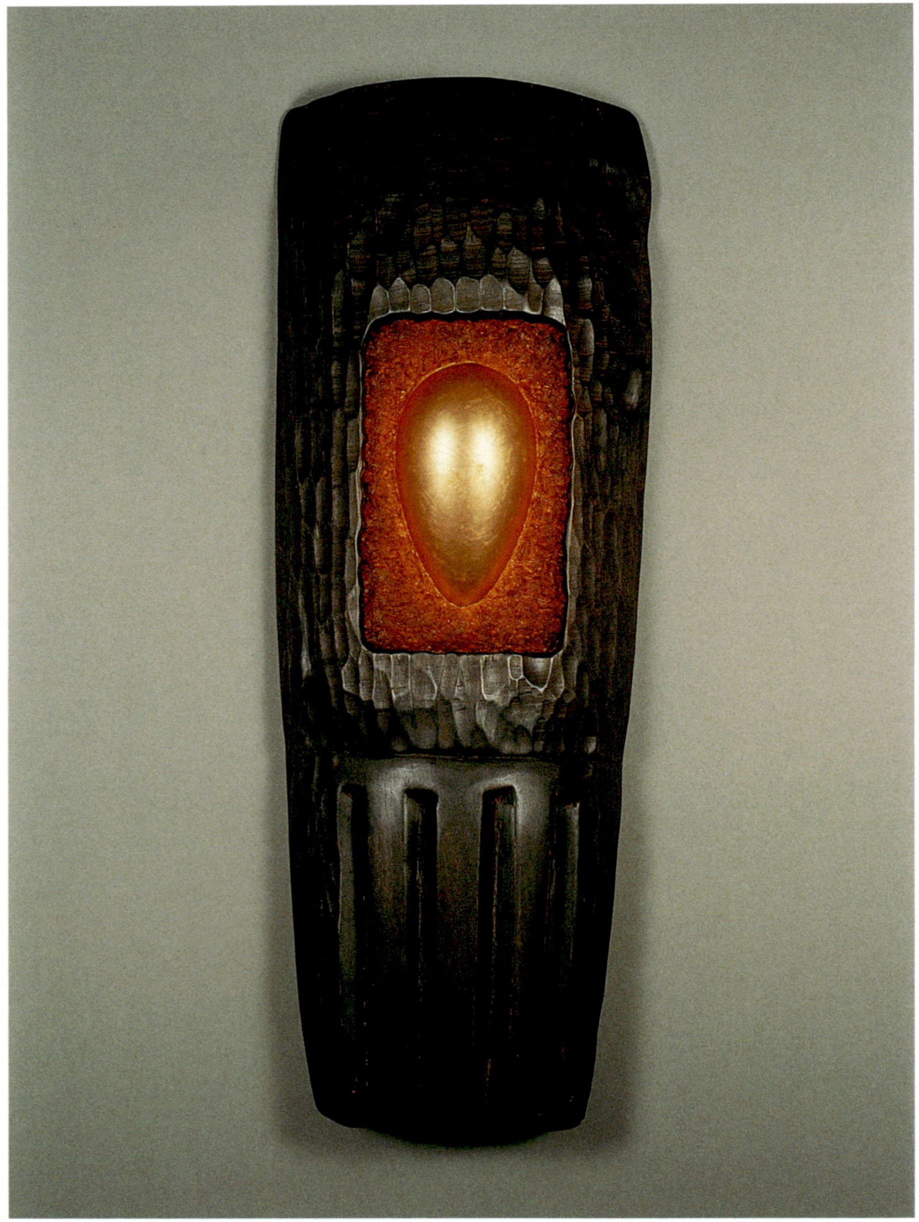

Robert Levin. *Diviner II.* 2004. Wood, glass, copper, 24" h x 4.5" x 6".

Simon Levy

Ashland City, Tennessee, http://simonlevywood.com

Artist's Statement

Commonly, there is an age-old connection between man and tree.

The essence of my work is an artful expression in wood; the visual and tactile qualities of this soulfully useful material are an invitation for the actively open minded participant. Here, the one-of-a-kind vessels and supporting elements offer only a physical resemblance to any functional object. Spontaneously created freehand markings and suggestive abstract shapes interplay with the wood's naturally unique surface features. My intent is to create an inviting space for the curious viewer's imagination.

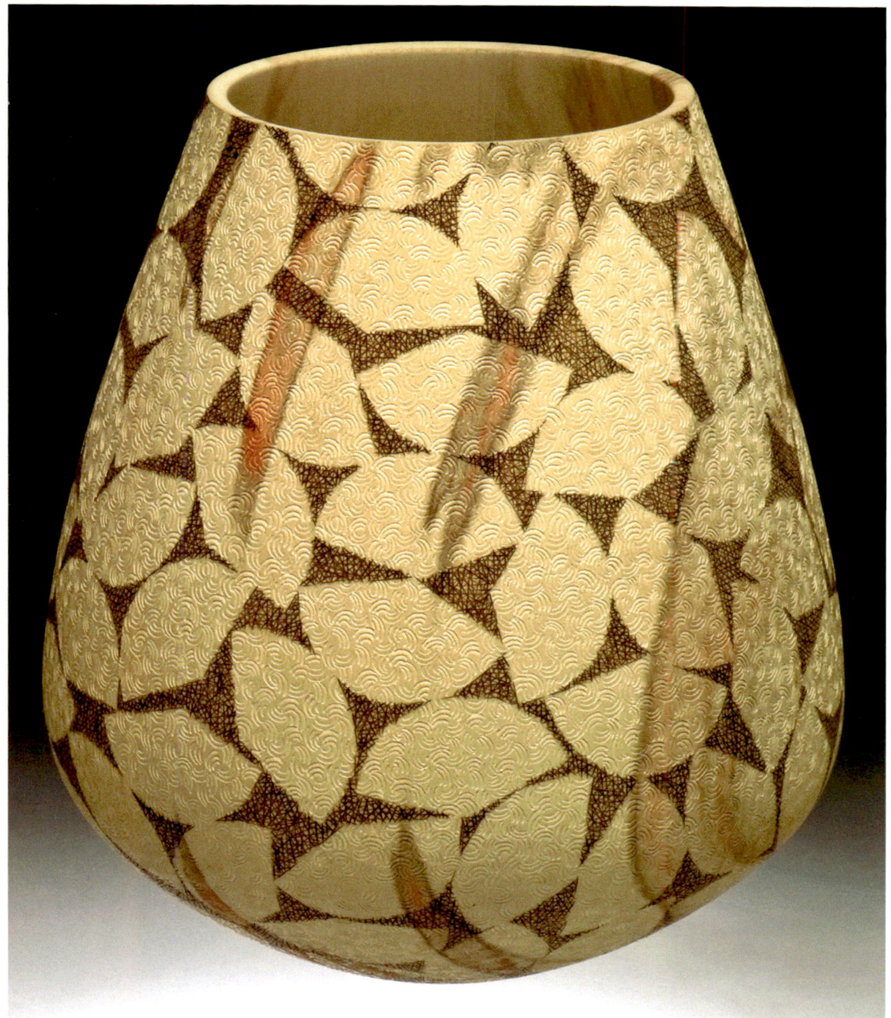

Simon Levy. *Don't Worry Be Happy*. 2008. Vessel, boxelder, turned, pyrography, engraving, 8 1/2" h x 7 1/4" w x 7 1/4" d. *Photography: John S. Cummings*

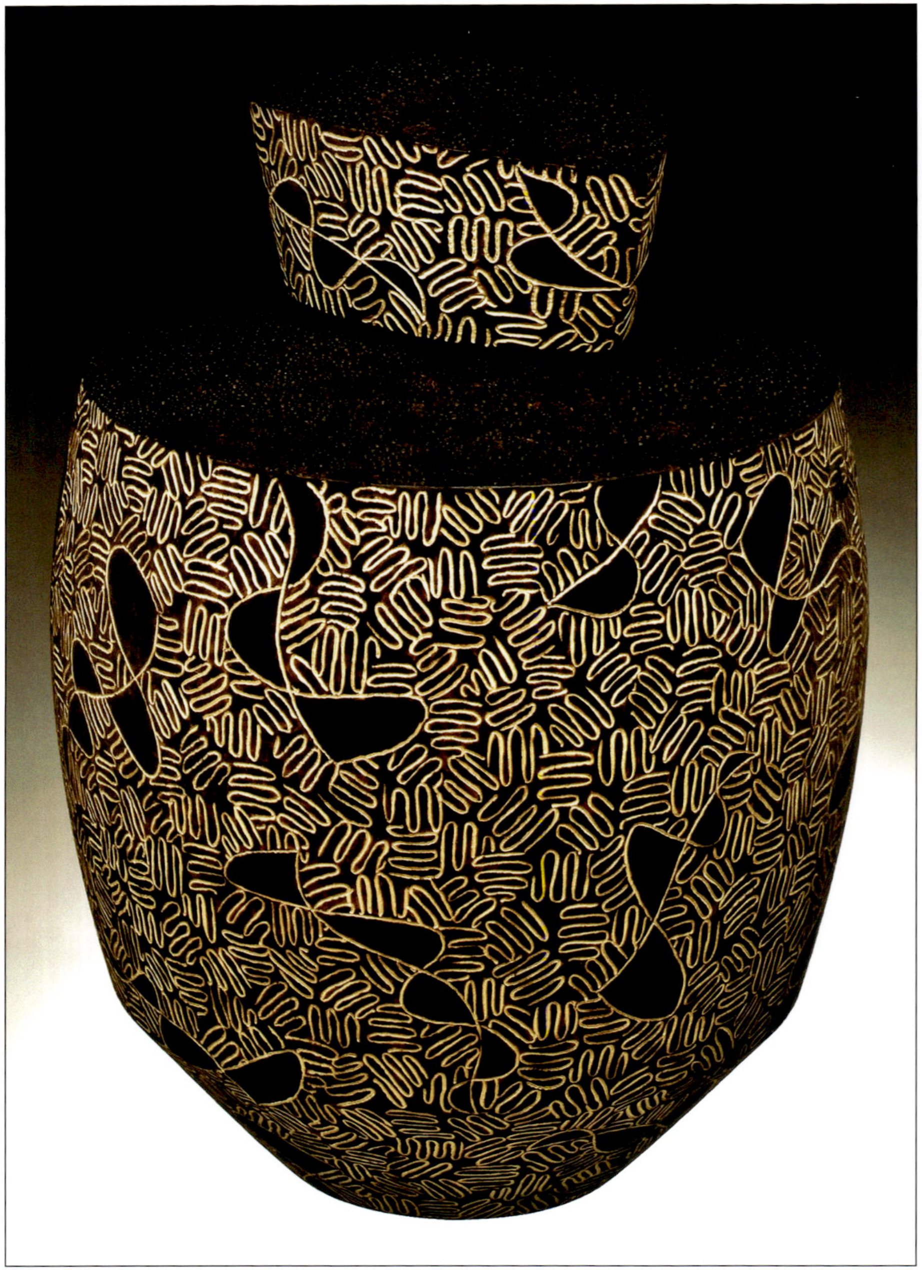

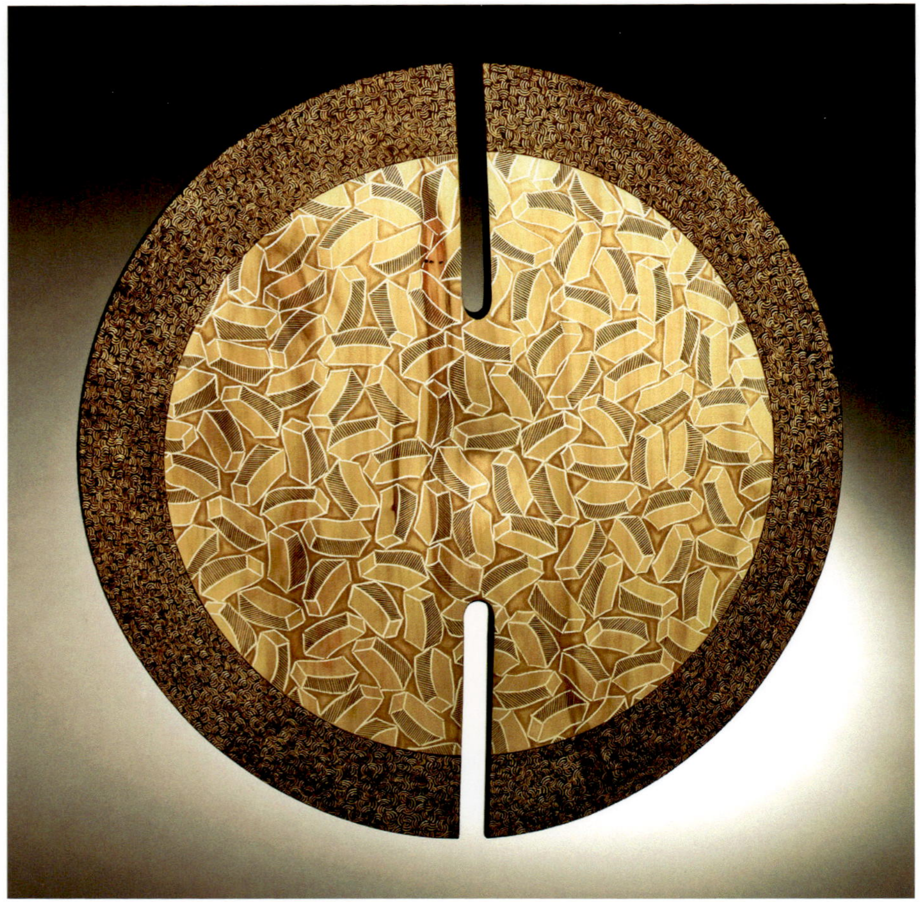

Simon Levy. *Super Nova.* 2009. Wall-mounted Disc, boxelder, turned, pyrography, engraving, pigment, 16" h x 16" w x 2" d. *Collection of Jerry and Gwen Paulson. Photography: John S. Cummings*

Simon Levy. *Around Midnight*. 2008. Lidded Vessel, boxelder, turned, pyrography, engraving, 9" h x 5 3/4" w x 5 3/4" d. *Collection of Ms. Freddi Greenberg. Photography: John S. Cummings*

ARTHUR LIESTMAN

Coquitram, British Columbia, artliestman@shaw.ca

Individual Artwork

The work with which I am most identified is my series of *Puzzling Illusion Vessels* – vessel or bowl forms that each appear to be a three-dimensional jigsaw puzzle that is partly assembled. The jigsaw lines are created using pyrography. Often, loose pieces of the puzzle are displayed with the vessel.

Topless is a 6 1/2" d x 10" h footed hollow vessel made of bigleaf maple burl and walnut. The feet are turned and then bent. I enjoy trying to give my pieces a sense of life, movement, and gesture.

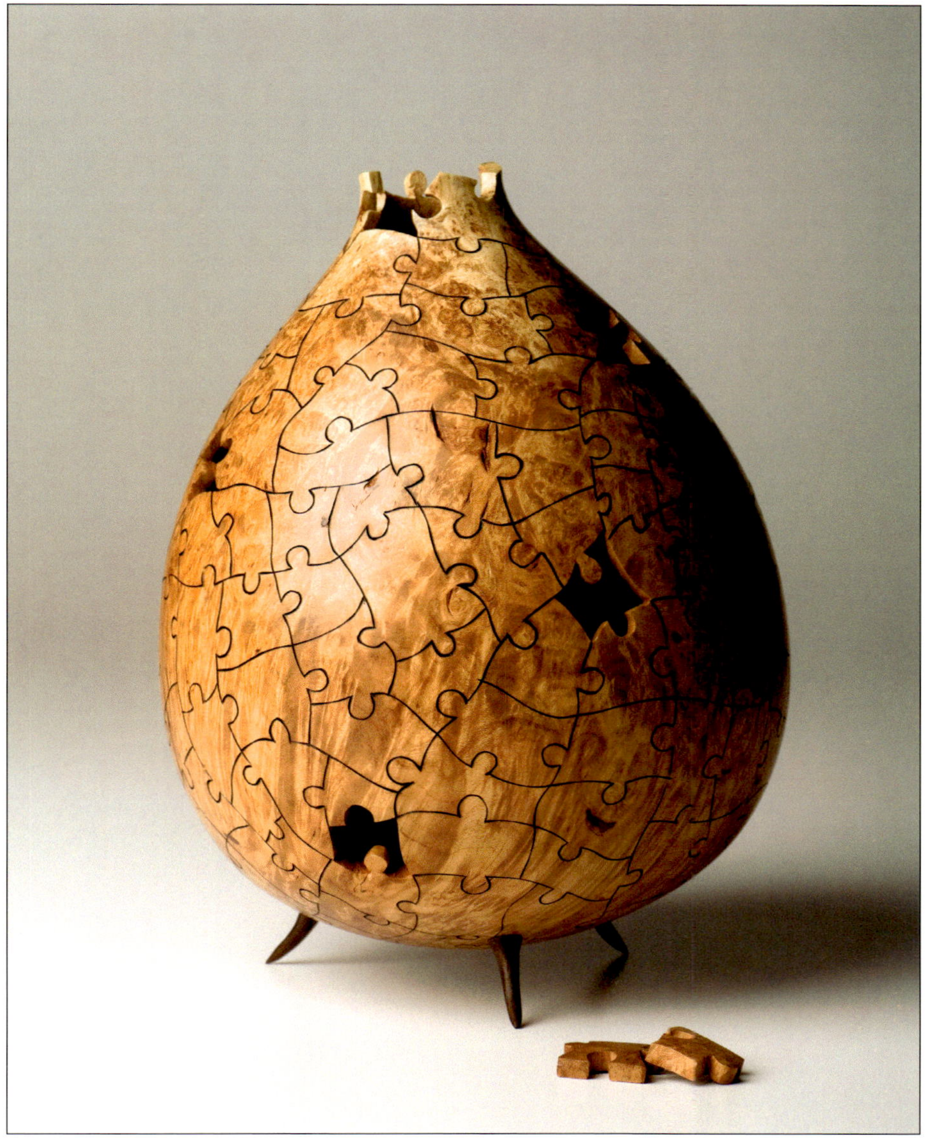

Arthur Liestman. *Topless.* 2008. Footed hollow vessel made of bigleaf maple burl and walnut. The feet are turned and then bent, 6 1/2" d x 10" h. *Photographer: Kenji Nagai*

A request from a collector started my investigation of teapot forms. I have made a series of puzzling illusion teapots and another series of teapots using an old woodturning technique called "therming." The therming technique produces turned objects with multiple curved sides. I like this process as the resulting shape is not so obviously produced on the lathe.

Helga is a 4 7/8" h x 7 1/4" w by 3 1/4" deep thermed teapot made of bigleaf maple burl and ebony.

Recently, I have started to explore a very rough surface texture that gives the illusion of broken layers of stone. The objects have curved surfaces and are hollowed with the surface texture breaking the symmetry of the form and opening up a view of the interior.

Battered and Torn is a 47 3/4" h x 11" w x 7" deep tower made of recycled hemlock and scorched with a propane burner.

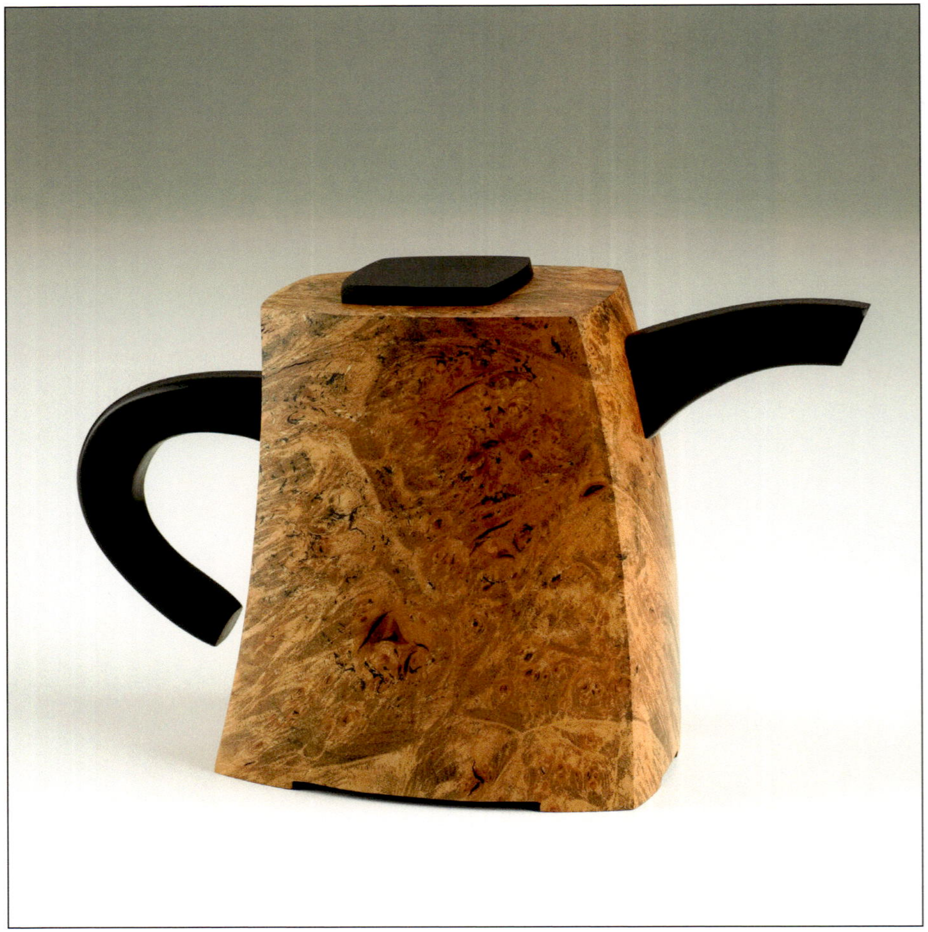

Arthur Liestman. *Helga*. 2008. Teapot made of bigleaf maple burl and ebony. The body of the teapot was turned on four axes and hollowed on a fifth, 4 7/8" h x 7 1/4" w x 3 1/4" deep. *Photographer: Kenji Nagai*

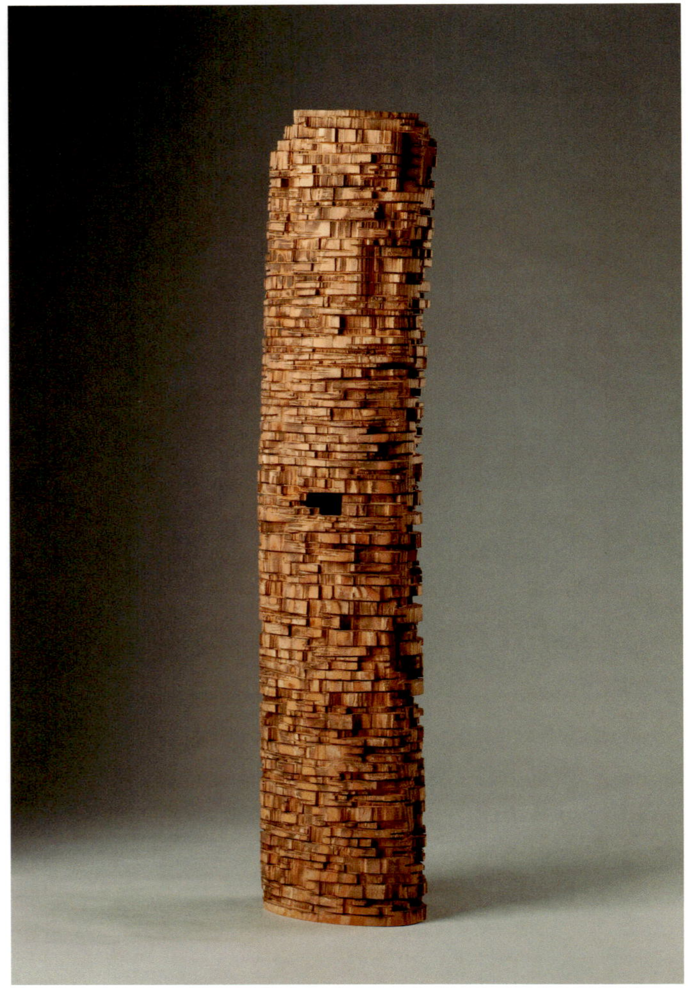

Arthur Liestman. *Battered and Torn.* 2009. Tower made of recycled hemlock and scorched with a propane burner, 47 3/4" h x 11" w x 7" deep. *Photographer: Kenji Nagai*

Arthur Conan Doyle created a partial alphabet of "dancing men" for the Sherlock Holmes story "Adventure of the Dancing Men." These dancing men figures are a substitution code with each position of a dancing figure representing a letter of the alphabet. My dancing men series of vessels and bowls use this alphabet, either piercing the form or incised on its surface. In each case, the title of the piece is written on the piece in dancing men. For me, part of the enjoyment of these pieces is knowing that the dancing men have meaning, but not really being able to "read" the meaning directly.

Endeavor To Persevere is a 2" h x 3 7/8" d dancing men bowl made of bigleaf maple burl.

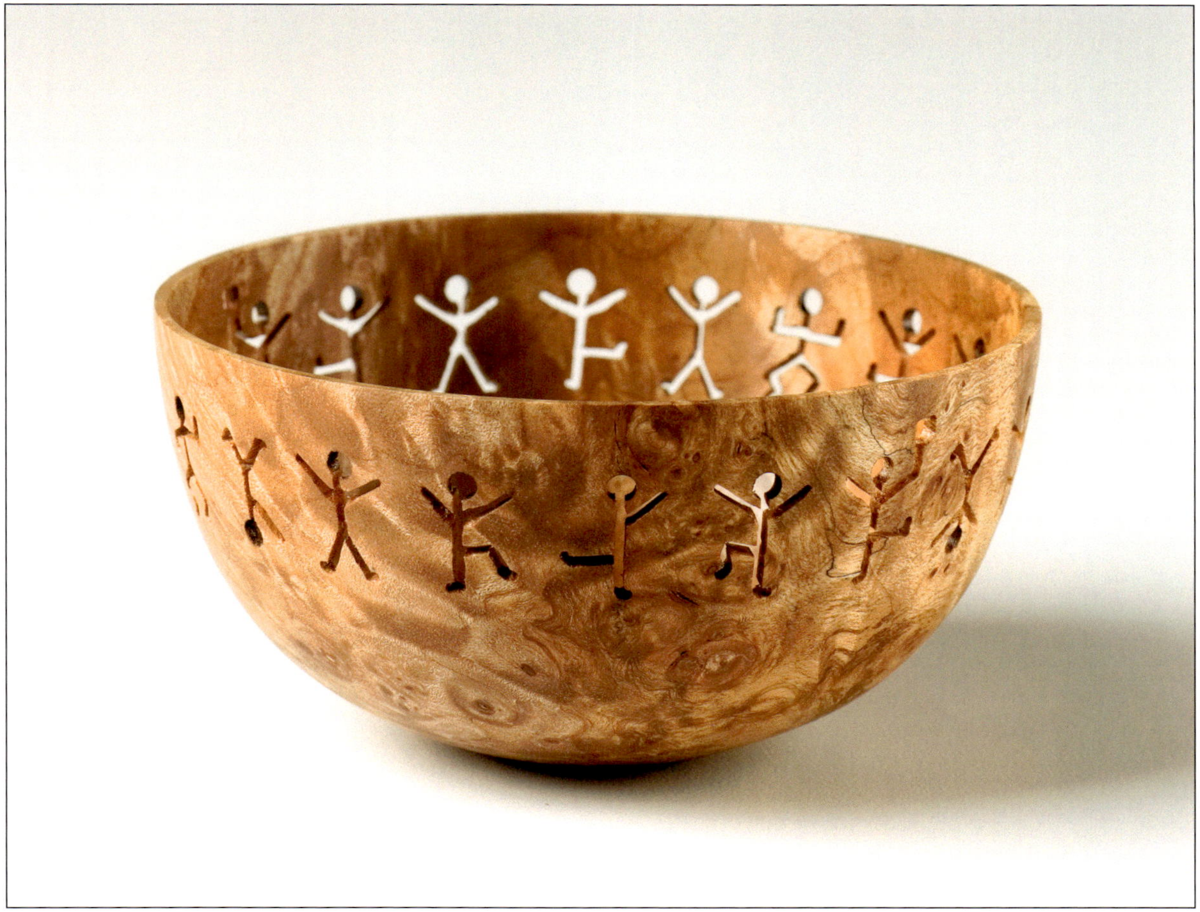

Arthur Liestman. *Endeavor To Persevere*. Dancing men bowl made of bigleaf maple burl. The title of the piece is encoded in the dancing men figures (derived from the code created by Arthur Conan Doyle for the Sherlock Holmes story "Adventure of the Dancing Men"), 2" h x 3 7/8" d. *Photographer: Kenji Nagai*

Robert Lippoth

Haiku, Hawaii, http://robertlippoth.com

Artist's Statement

My design style is a combination of curving, tapering, sculpted forms – sculpture in the form of furniture. Inspiration comes from almost everywhere, including nature, architecture, and artists from all media.

Wood types vary from domestic to exotic hardwoods, but my primary choice for furniture is koa. Koa is endemic to Hawaii. I have not found a wood with such a broad spectrum of color and a wide range of figures. Some koa is visually stunning, which I love to combine with those good designs.

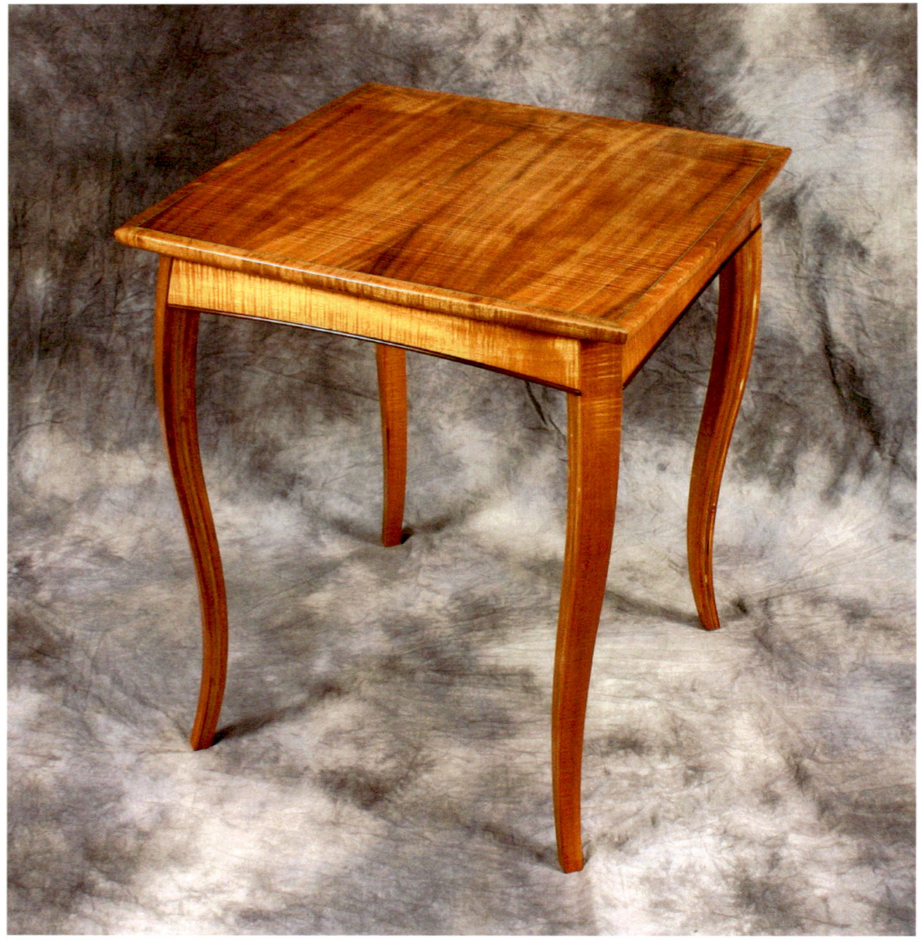

Robert Lippoth. *Dancer.* 2007. Side table, curly koa, rosewood, black dyed costello, holly, legs are tapered bent laminations made with 13 layers, top is bookmatched veneer, black and white inlay detail, solid wood frame, 24" x 24" x 24". *Photographer: Mats Fogelvik*

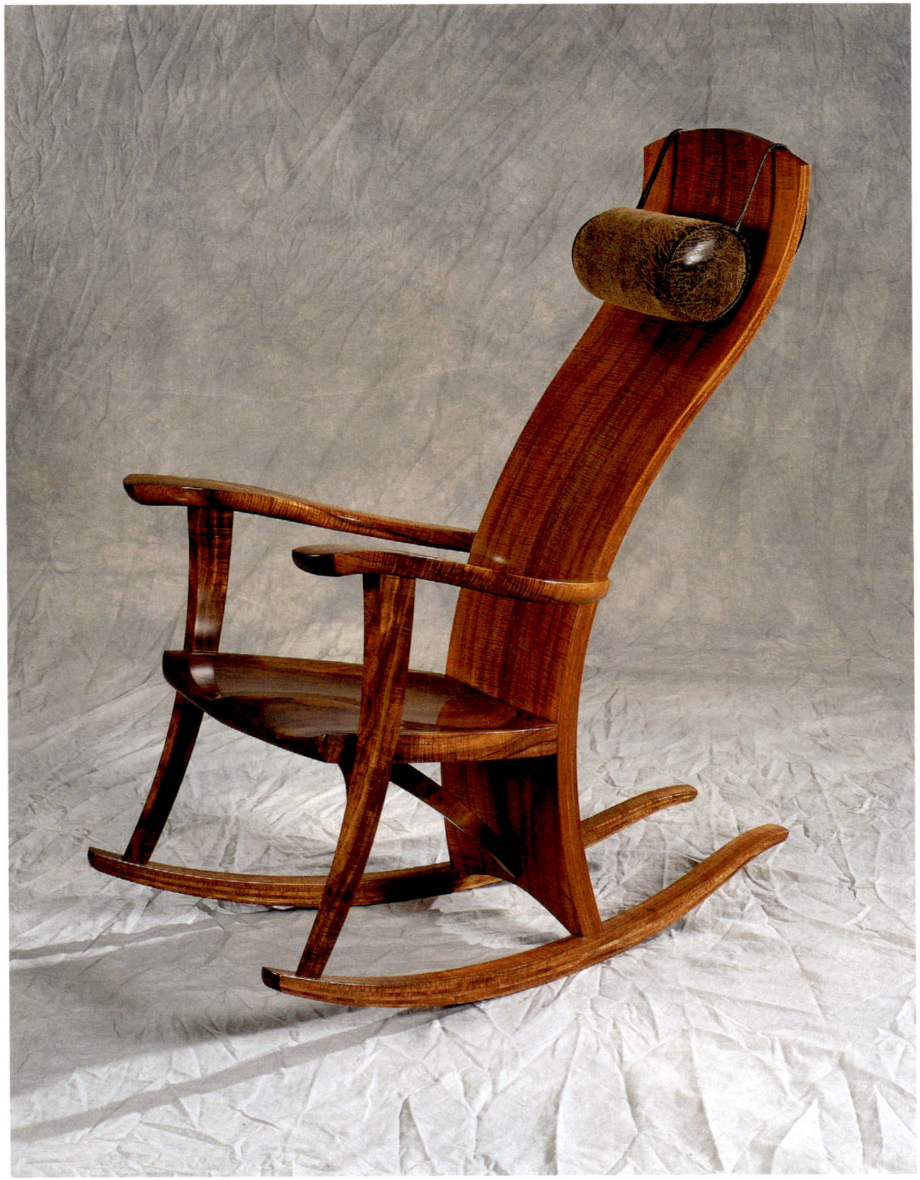

Robert Lippoth. Rocking Chair. 2005. Curly koa, rockers and back is tapered bent laminations, hand shaped solid wood, mortis and tenon joinery, 38" x 25" x 45". *Photographer: Hal Lum*

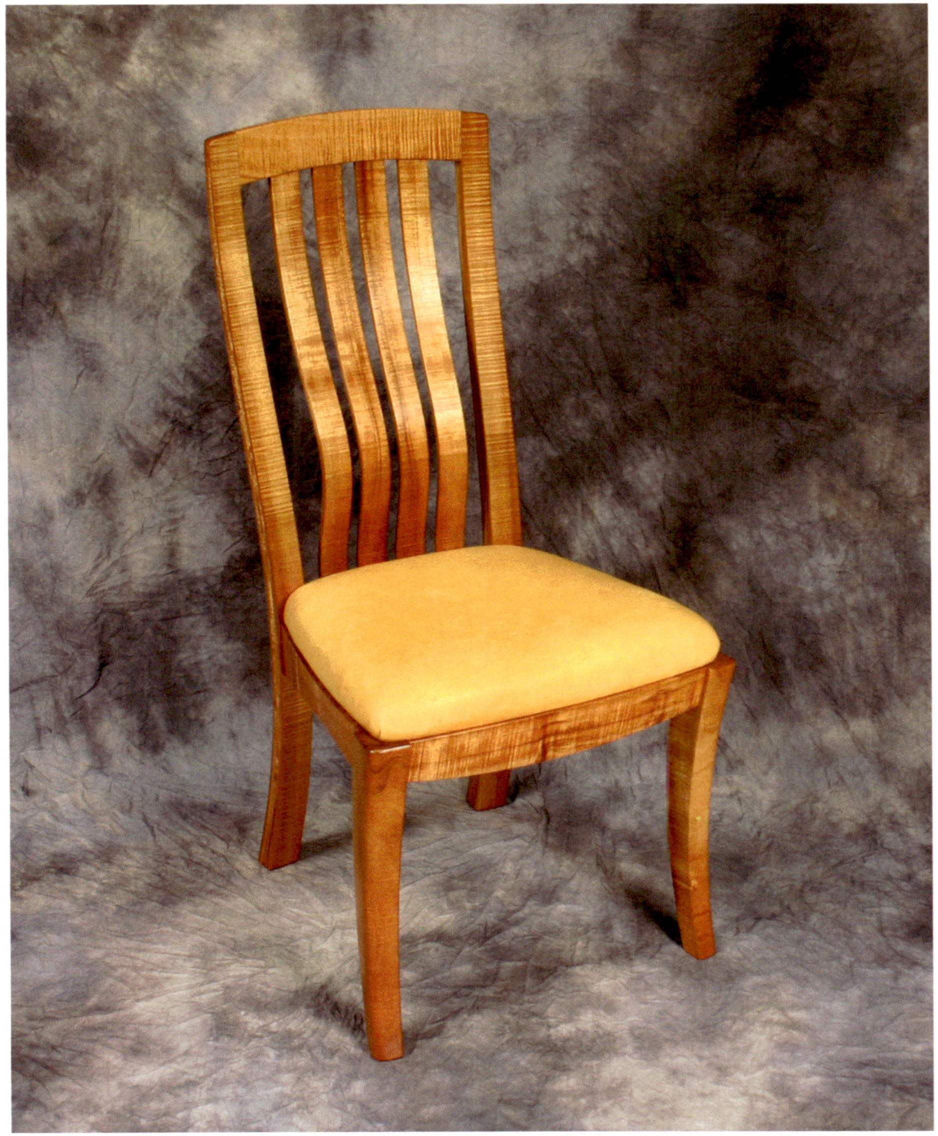

Robert Lippoth. Desk Chair. 2006. Curly koa, buckskin leather, hand-shaped solid wood, mortis and tenon joinery, bent laminated back slats, rear legs are tapered bent laminations, 20" x 19" w x 42". *Photographer: Mats Fogelvik* (above and next page)

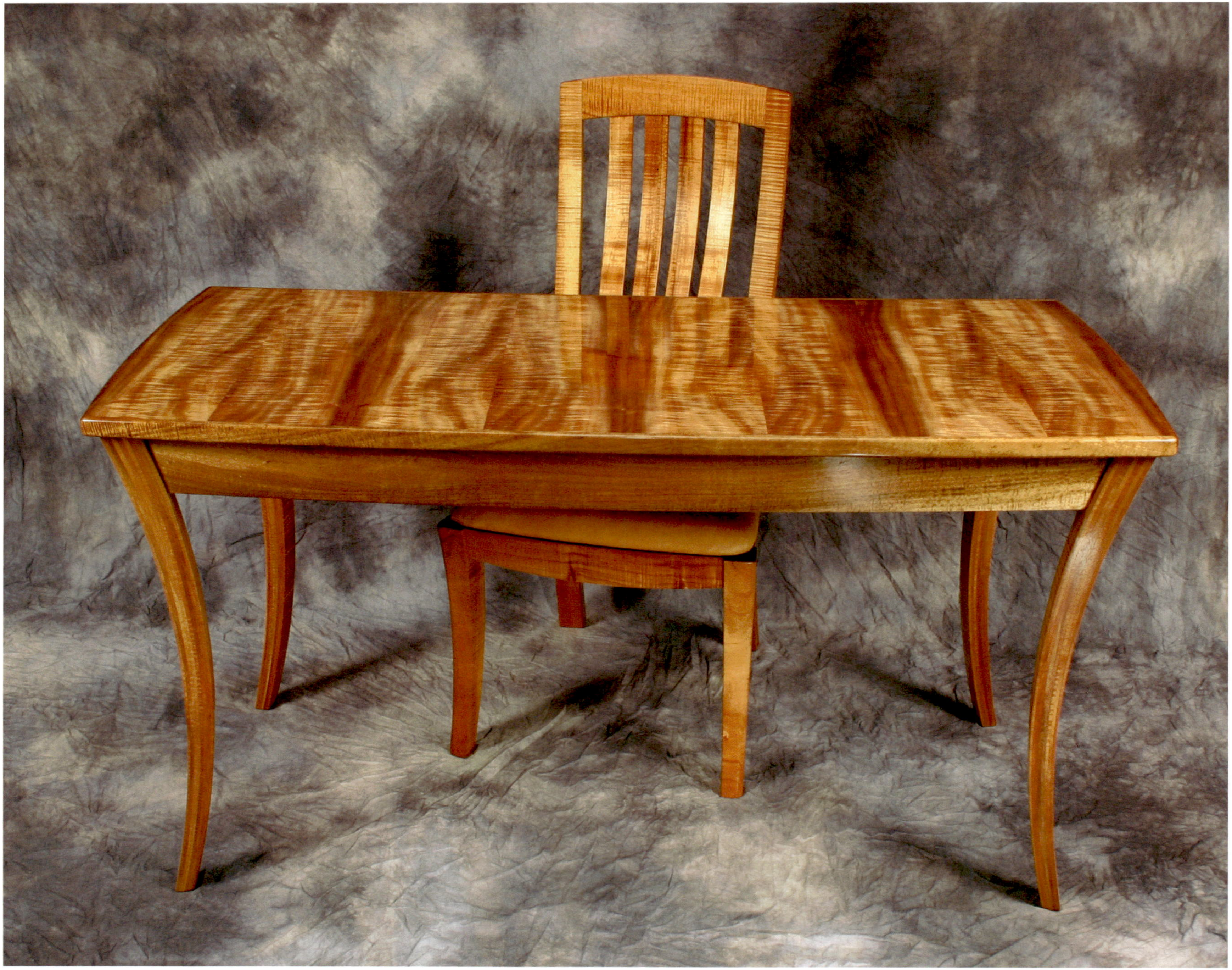

STEVEN LOAR

steven.loar@iup.edu

Individual Artwork

Young Ludwig: Dreaming of the Fifth

Young Ludwig, Dreaming of the Fifth was conceived of, and partially executed, in 1993/94. It was meant to be the big-impact follow-up to *Young Wolfgang,* which is now in the Mint Museum collection. The rough, unresolved turning that is now the *Ludwig* head had been one of several gifts from Stoney Lamar. My career, since then, has been largely shaped by these objects and similar gifts of early offset spindle explorations from Mark Sfirri. As a result, I became one of the initiators of the current trend in collaboration. The *Ludwig* head was one of Stoney's earliest forays into figurative forms as he seriously began his pioneering explorations of large-scale offset turning, circa 1991. It was given to me as a rough unresolved form. I later turned portions of the neck and "ear" to form areas of junction. I also finalized, trued, colored, and finished all of the surfaces. I composed and created all of the rest of the sculpture.

My primary challenge in 2008 was to re-imagine the piece as a whole with new sensibilities; not an easy task. The music had been imagined in a hundred different ways, but never resolved, and the color scheme had never been fully envisioned. As in the past, the great painter James Whistler came to my aid; this time with *The Golden Screen* providing a strategy for the color resolution of the base. Additional compositional help came from Sargeant's painting *Carnation, Lily, Lily, Rose* and Turner's *The Storm (Shipwreck).* The inclusion of the table came from my wanting to make a large-scale sculpture and realizing that a complete in-the-round presentation might be dared.

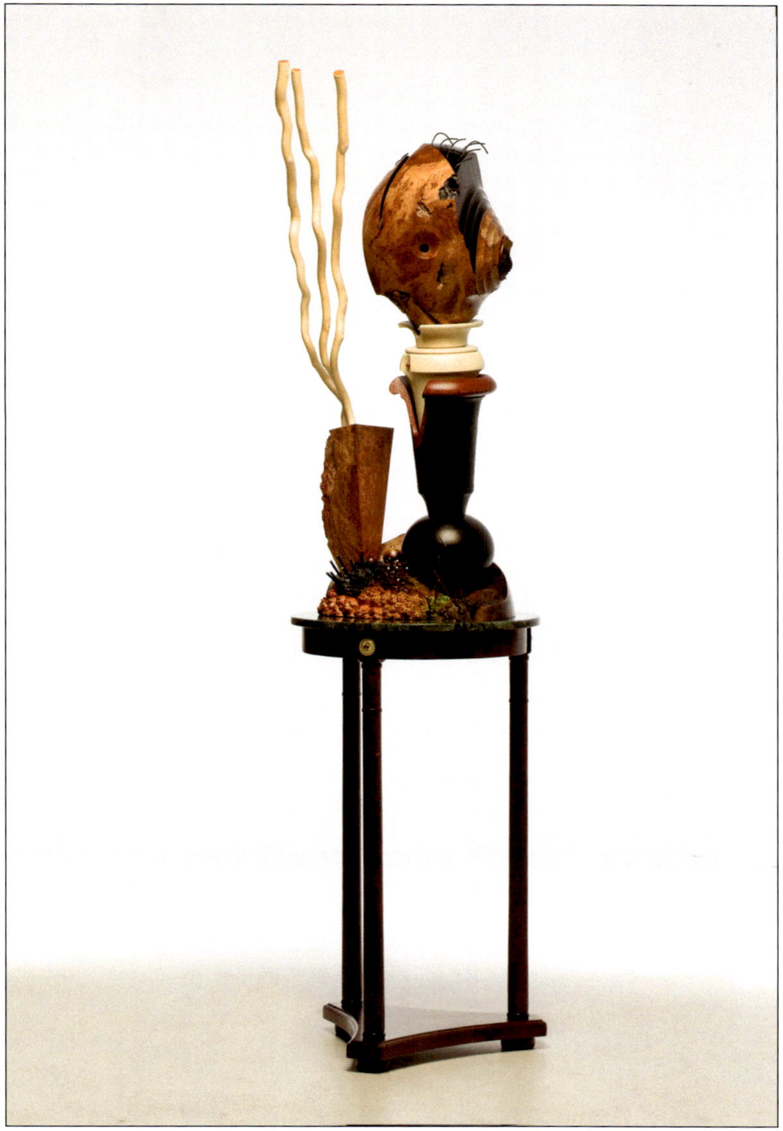

Steve Loar with Stoney Lamar. *Young Ludwig: Dreaming of the Fifth*. Begun in 1993, resumed and finished in 2008. Cherry, walnut, and redwood lace burls, boxelder, oak, curly willow, commercial marble-topped table, mixed media, 80" h x 18" d. *Faux marbling of table base: Kim Conover-Loar. Photographer: Roy Engelbrecht Photography: www.rephoto.net* or *fotodik@sgi.net* (right and next page)

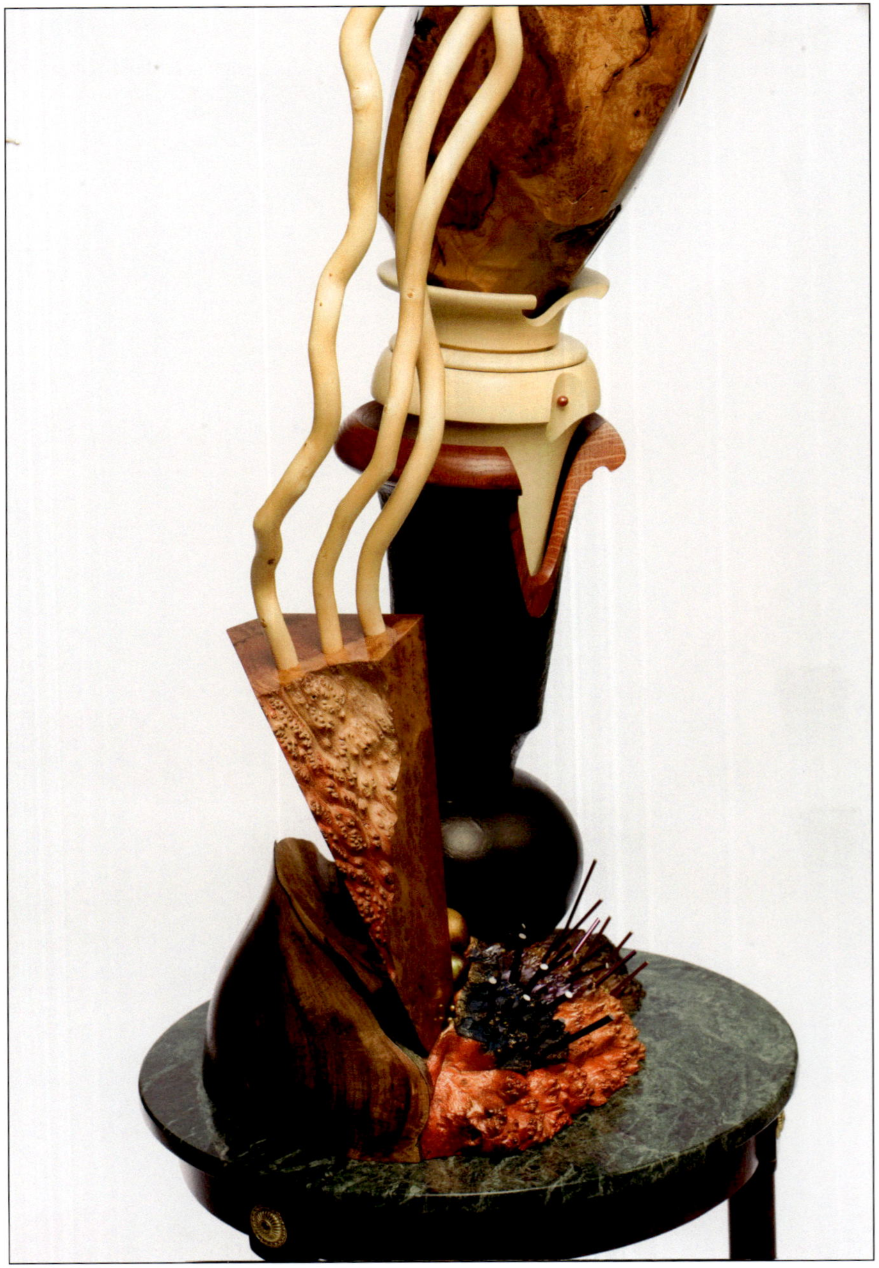

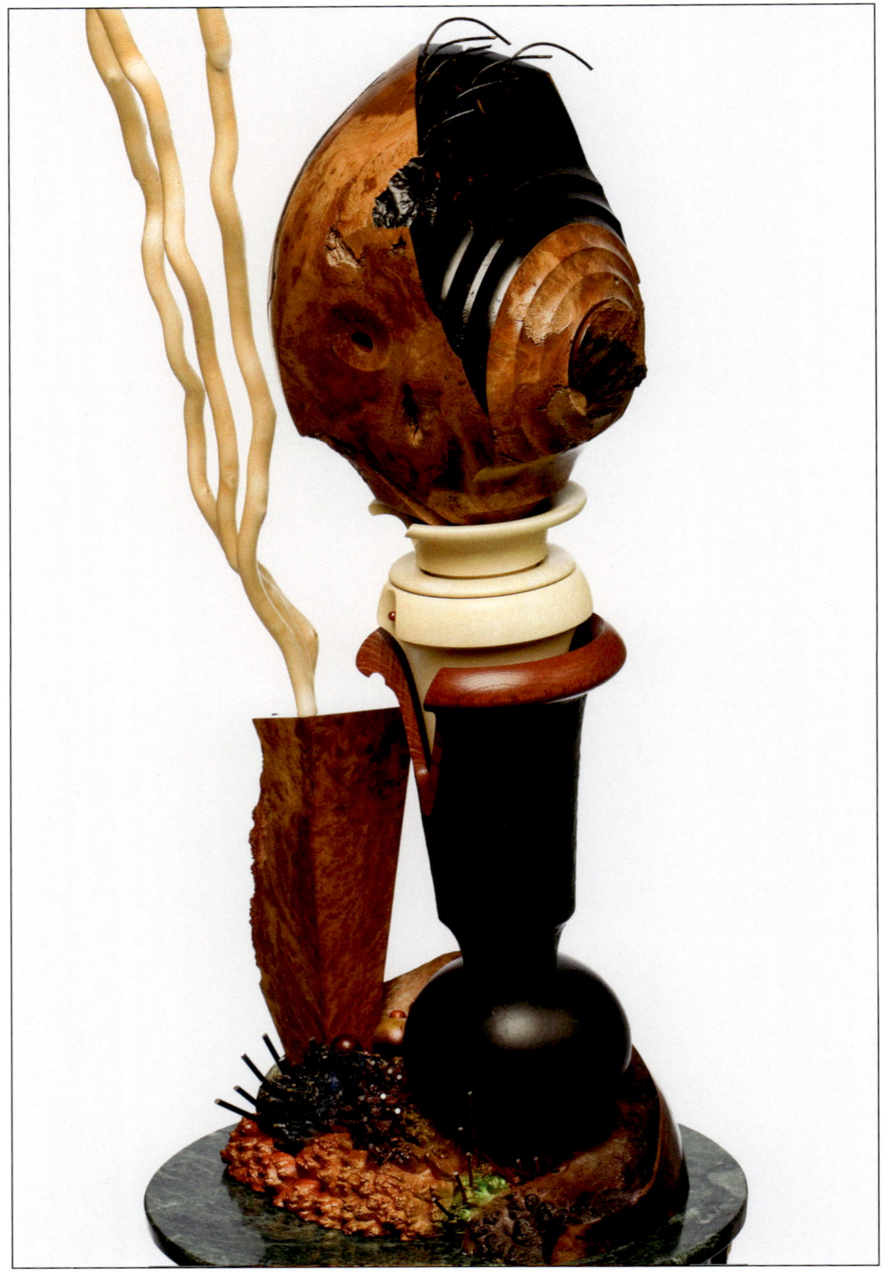

JOHN MAKEPEACE

Dorset, England, www.johnmakepeacefurniture.com

Artist's Statement

Function, structure, and expression are fundamental to each John Makepeace commission, whether for a private home, an historic building or a museum collection.

"As a designer-maker, I am constantly searching for more eloquent concepts for furniture. My objective is to achieve freer, lighter, stronger, and more sculptural forms better suited to their function and more expressive of the materials and craftsmanship involved. My passion is to create masterpieces of fine furniture of our time for current and future generations."

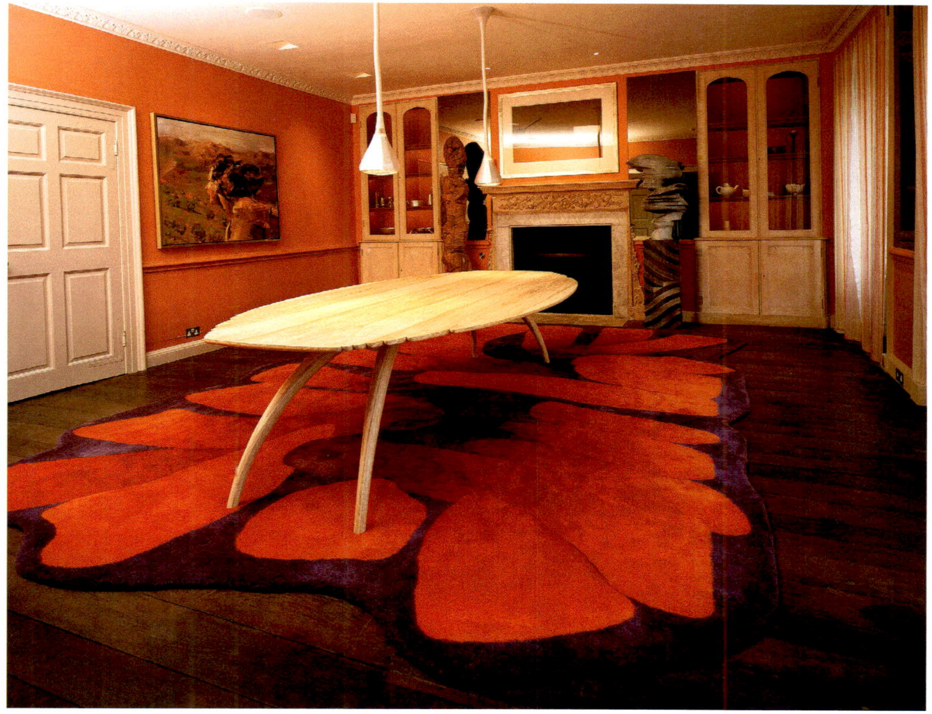

John Makepeace. *Vau!t.* 2004. Designed for a Mediterranean home on Cyprus, the legs arch from end to end, top catilevered off the arch, 300 x 150 x 72 cm. © *John Makepeace*

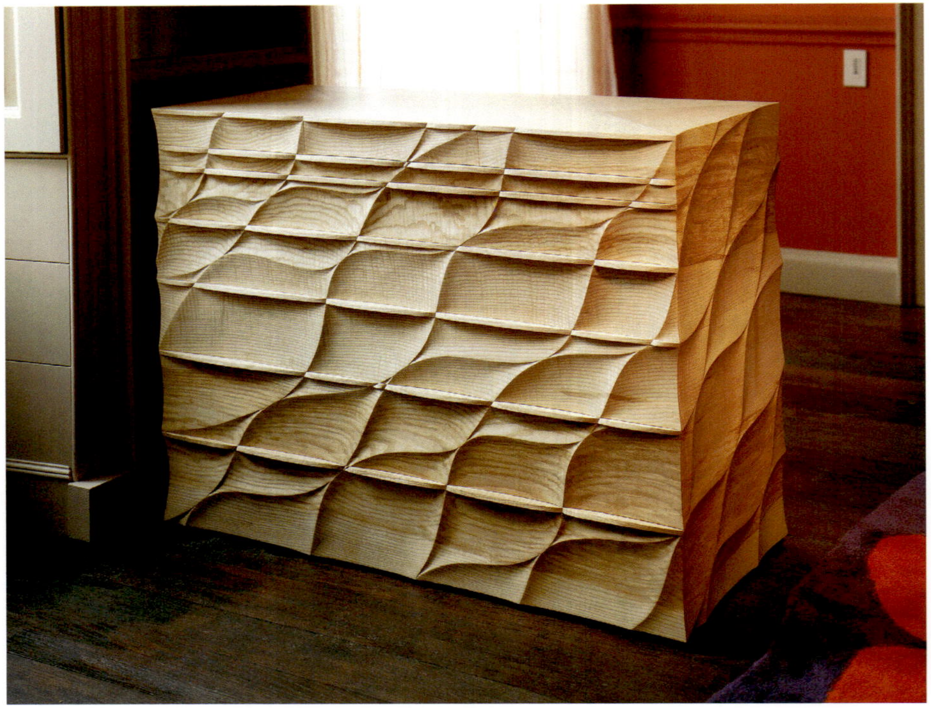

John Makepeace. *Flow*. 2007. Fourth in a series from a single tree of ripple ash, lined with holly wood and cedar, 110 x 48 x 80 cm. © *John Makepeace*

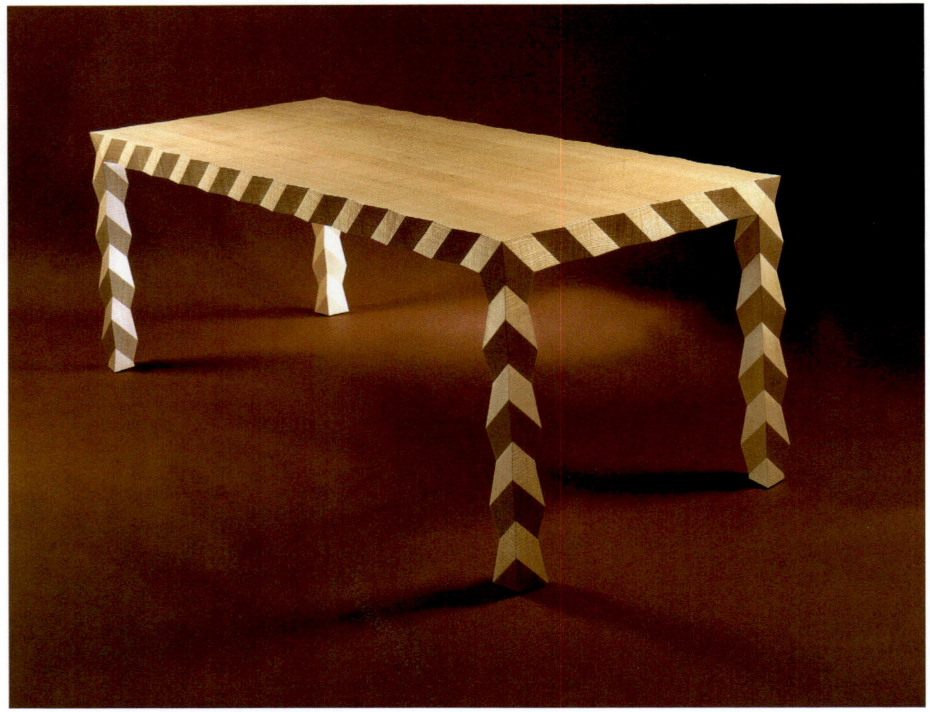

John Makepeace. *Crystal.* 2008. For a new penthouse in Strasbourg, the human rights capital of the world, 180 x 90 x 72 cm. © *John Makepeace*

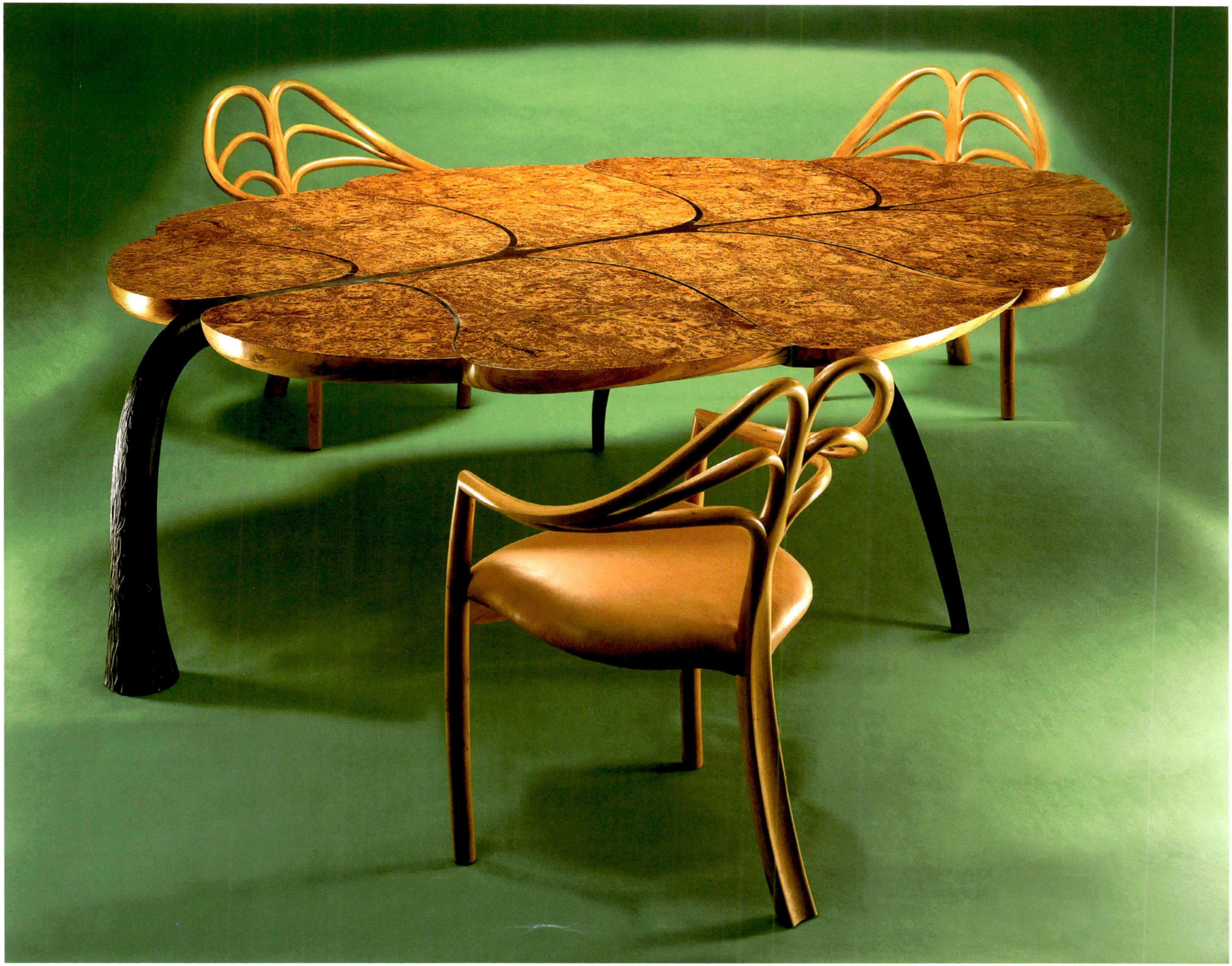

John Makepeace. *Spring.* 2007. For a home in San Antonio, Texas, yew, burr yew, and bronze, only three legs beneath table to seat 10-12, 250 x 190 x 72 cm. © *John Makepeace*

Malcolm Martin & Gaynor Dowling

Stroud, United Kingdom, www.martinanddowling.co.uk

Artists' Statement

We have been working together as carvers for the past twelve years, on projects ranging from public art to small-scale domestic objects. At the heart of our work are our sculptural vessels. These pieces use simple, formal silhouettes as the vehicle for strong and expressive carving using axe and gouge to produce frontal images with surfaces that hold and articulate the light. They are accentuated by the use of liming and scorching.

We use pretty much entirely hand tools to work very traditional carving woods (limewood and oak) in very contemporary ways.

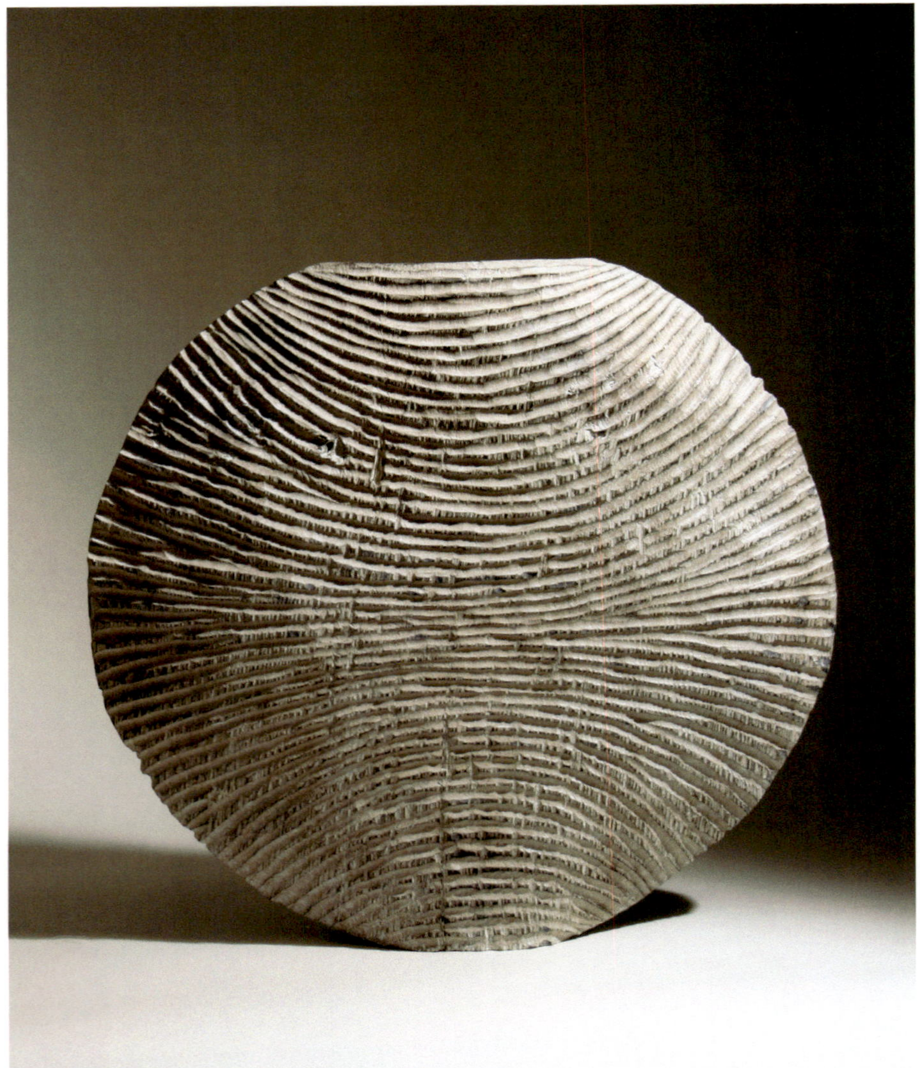

Malcolm Martin & Gaynor Dowling. *Grooved Disc.* 2009. Carved, limed and scorched oak, 25" d x 3" deep.

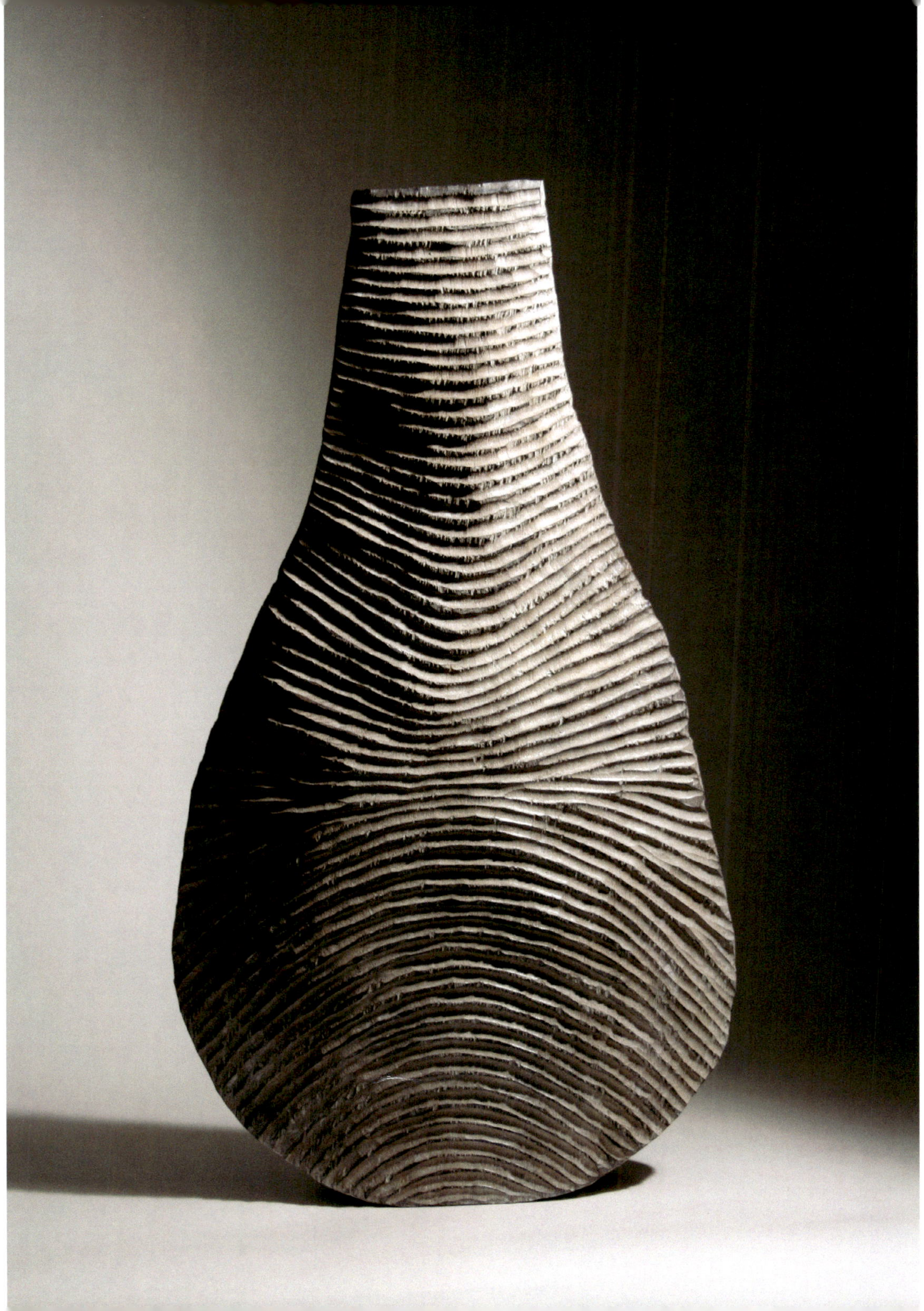

Malcolm Martin & Gaynor Dowling.
Grooved Vessel. 2009. Carved, limed and scorched oak, 30" x 15" x 3".

Damon McIntyre

Seattle, Washington, www.damonmcintyre.com

Artist's Statement

My work is rooted in the traditional craft of woodworking and furniture making, but with a personal twist that can be best described as "a sense of humor." The functional object has always been a springboard for my imagination and furniture provides me with an unending supply of narrative inspiration with which to twist and shape reality into fantasy and back again. Through the use of skewed representation and altered perspective I am able to present to the viewer a world of mystery and invention that piques curiosity and stirs distant memory. Most recently, I have begun to explore light and sound with instruments of observation, which has opened the door to the limitless possibilities that exist when working outside of enclosed spaces.

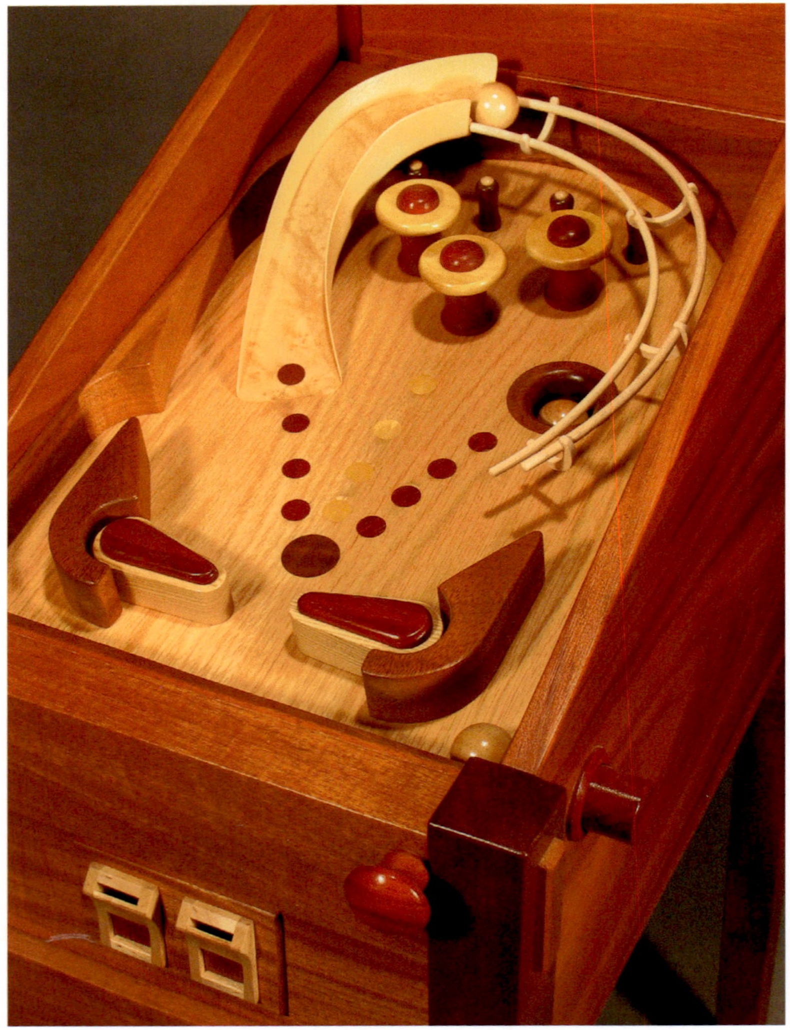

Damon McIntyre. *Pinball Machine*. Various hardwoods, 36" x 24" x 70". (right and opposite page)

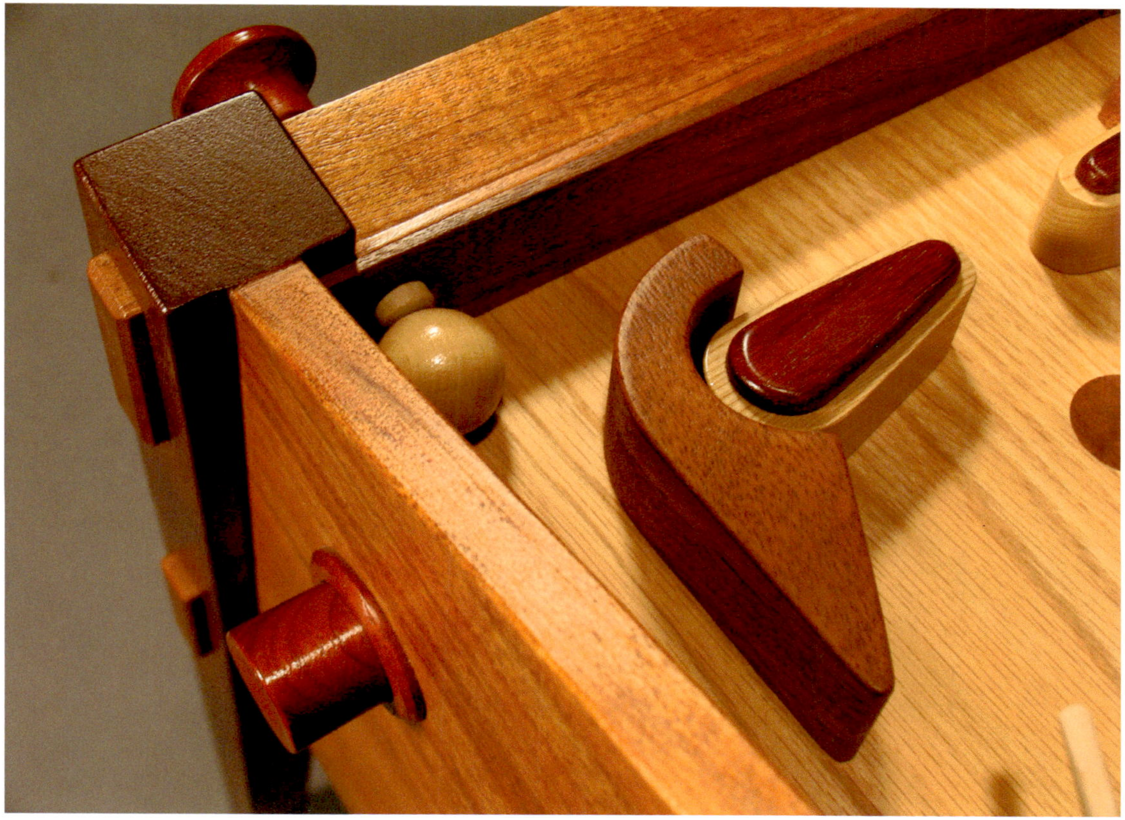

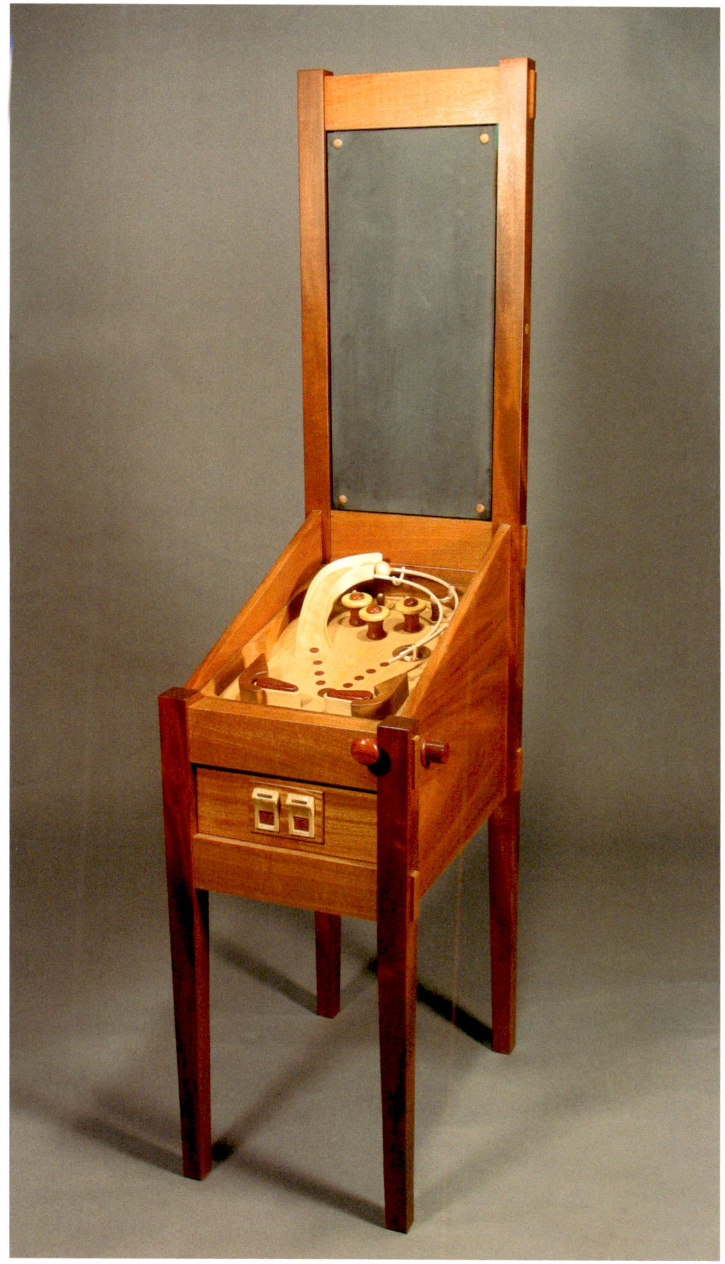

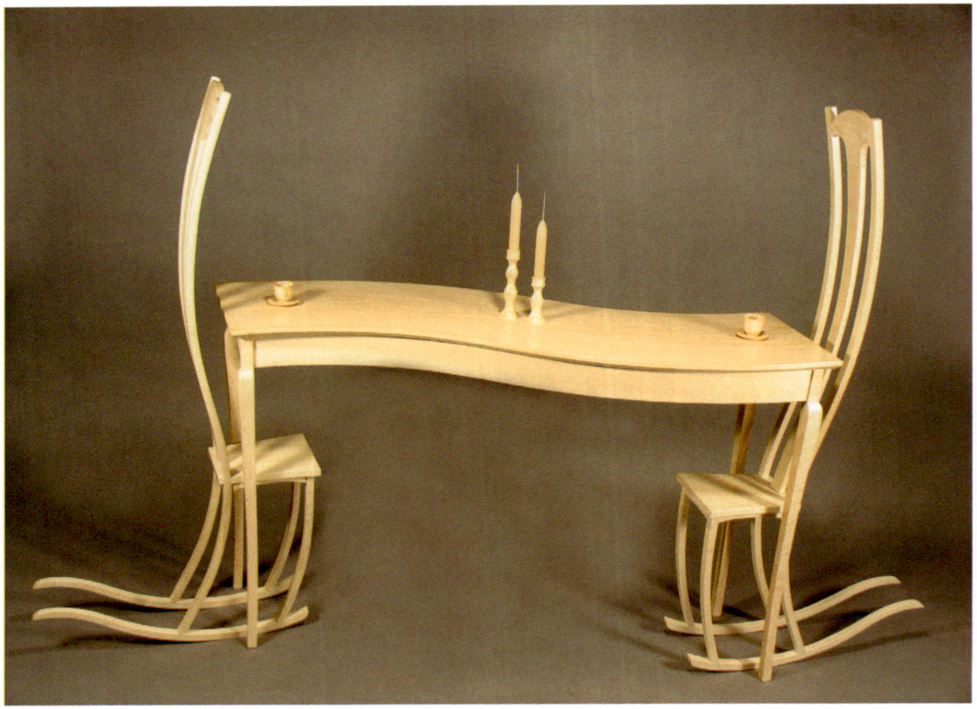

Damon McIntyre. *Tea for Two.* Steam bent oak, bleach, 52" x 16" x 30".

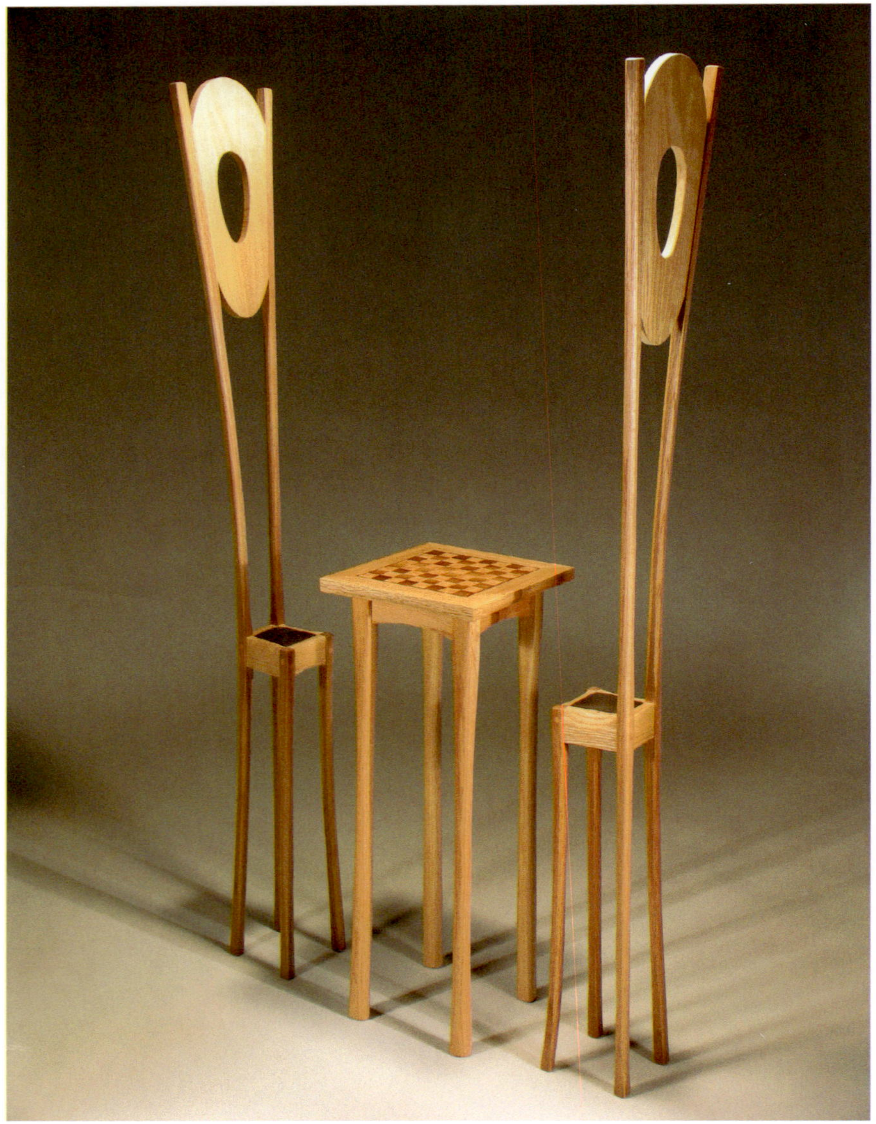

Damon McIntyre. *Your Move.* Steam bent oak, leather, 36" x 12" x 48".

Milo Mirabelli

Port Orchard, Washington, mmirabelli@wavecable.com

Artist's Statement

Milo is a craftsman who produces unique, one-of-a-kind functional and non-functional works of art from various recycled materials and renewable resources. His work addresses the viewers' senses and emotions through sight and touch.

Milo uses his sense of design to work with various media and design elements to bring them to their simplest and most pure form. The combination of sight and touch are the only way the true beauty and depth of the wood and his various creations can be fully experienced. His creativity and design abilities marry with the integrity and personality of the various mediums to come together in a partnership that often leaves the viewer to ponder ... "how did he do that?"

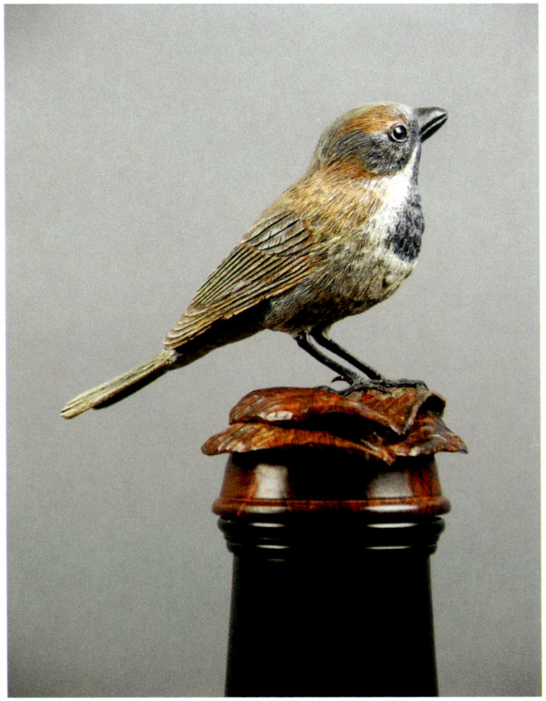

Milo Mirabelli. *Sparrow on Cocobolo*. 2007. Wood sculpture, hand-turned and carved cocobolo wood, tupelo, African blackwood, and acrylic paint, 15" h x 12" w x 5" deep.

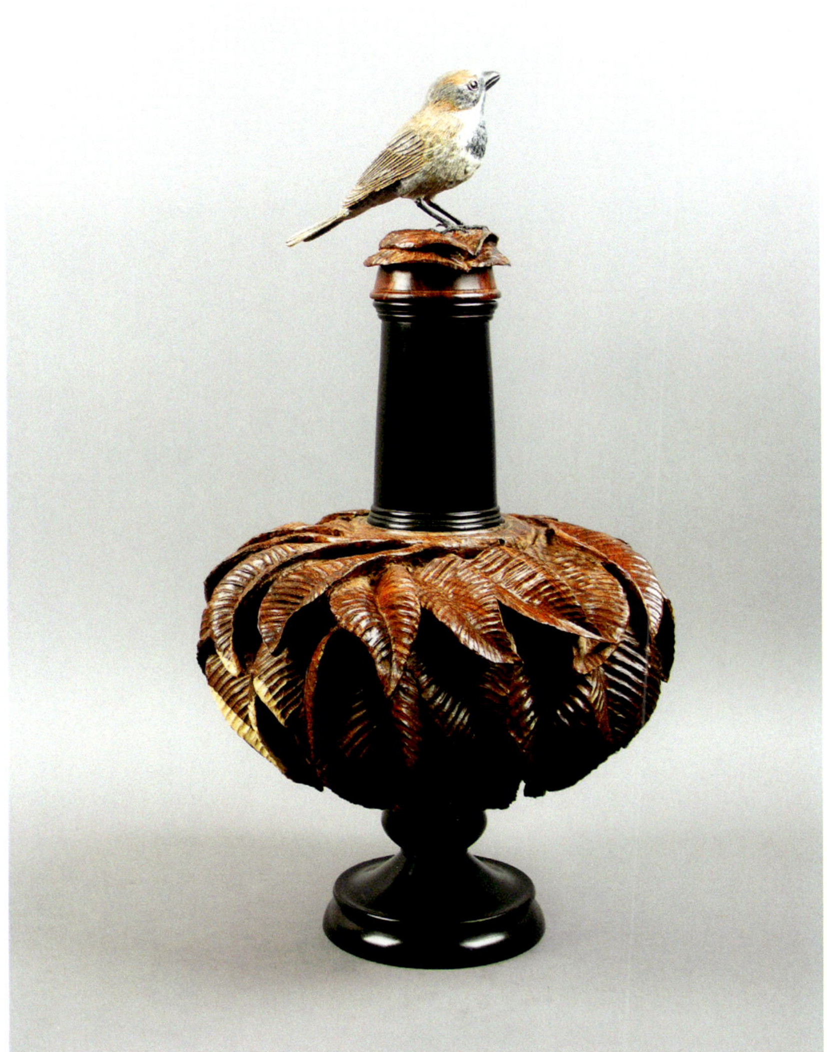

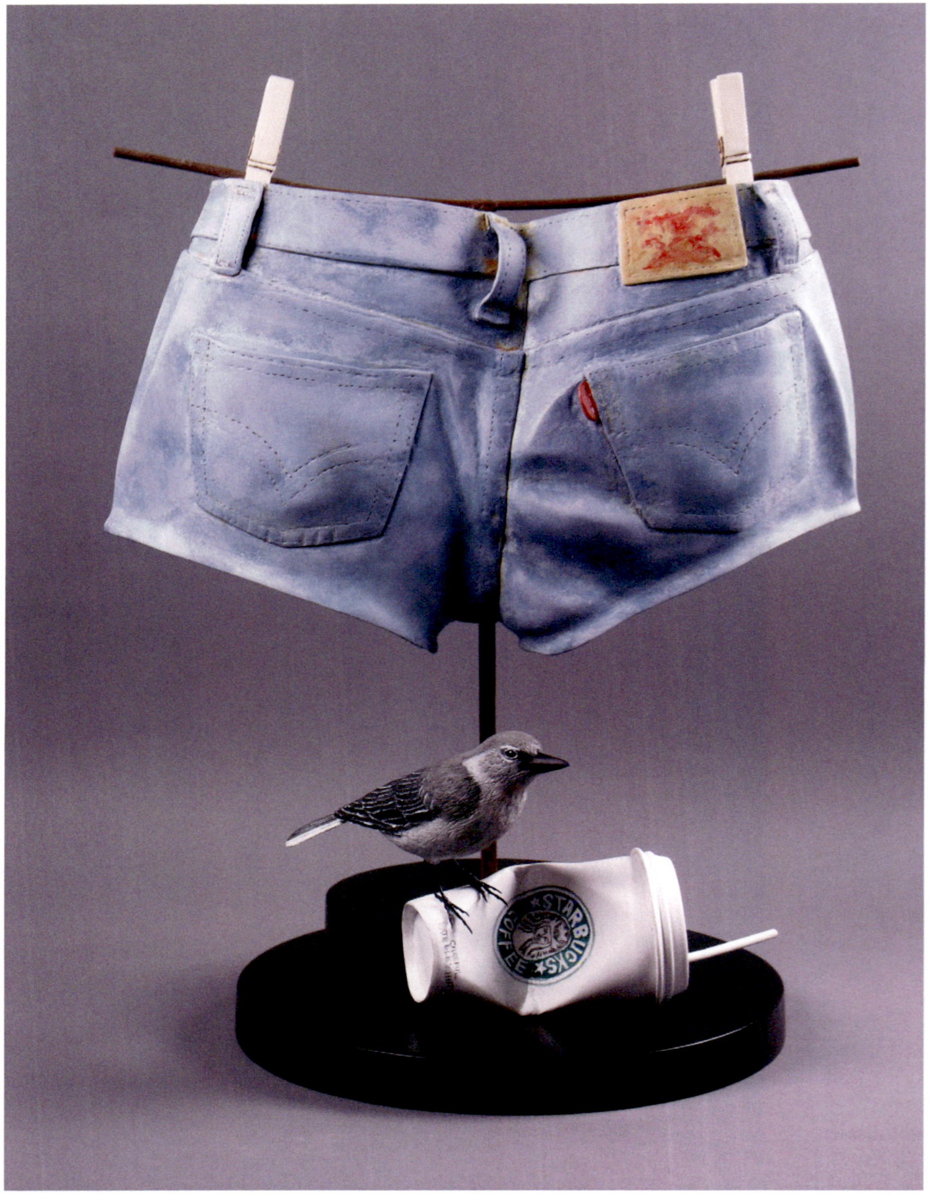

Milo Mirabelli. *Beachcomber.* 2008. Wood sculpture, hand-carved basswood, tupelo, ebonized maple, acrylic paint, 24" h x 19" w x 13 1/2" deep.

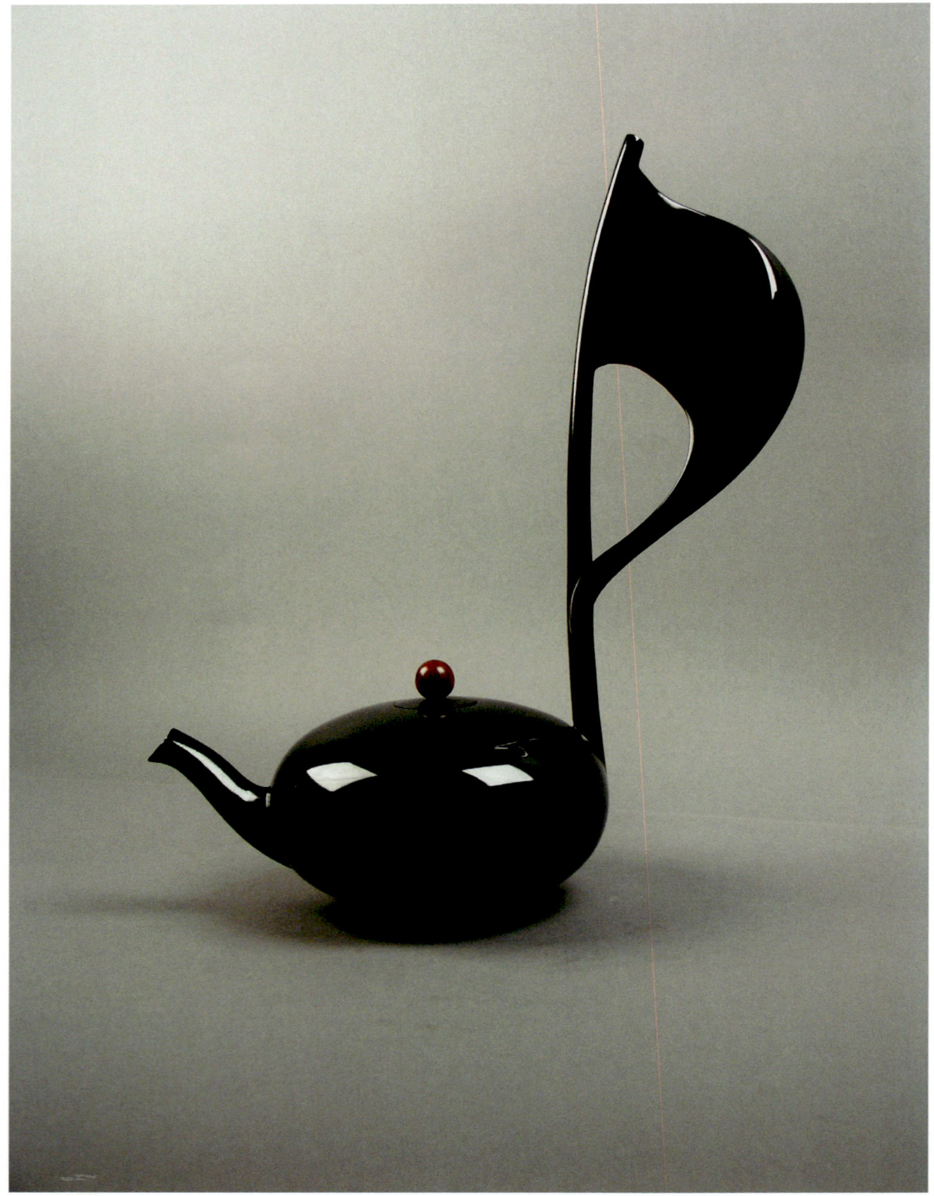

Milo Mirabelli. *Music Note.* 2009. One-of-a-kind teapot, hand-turned and carved basswood, black lacquer, 15" h x 13" w x 6" deep.

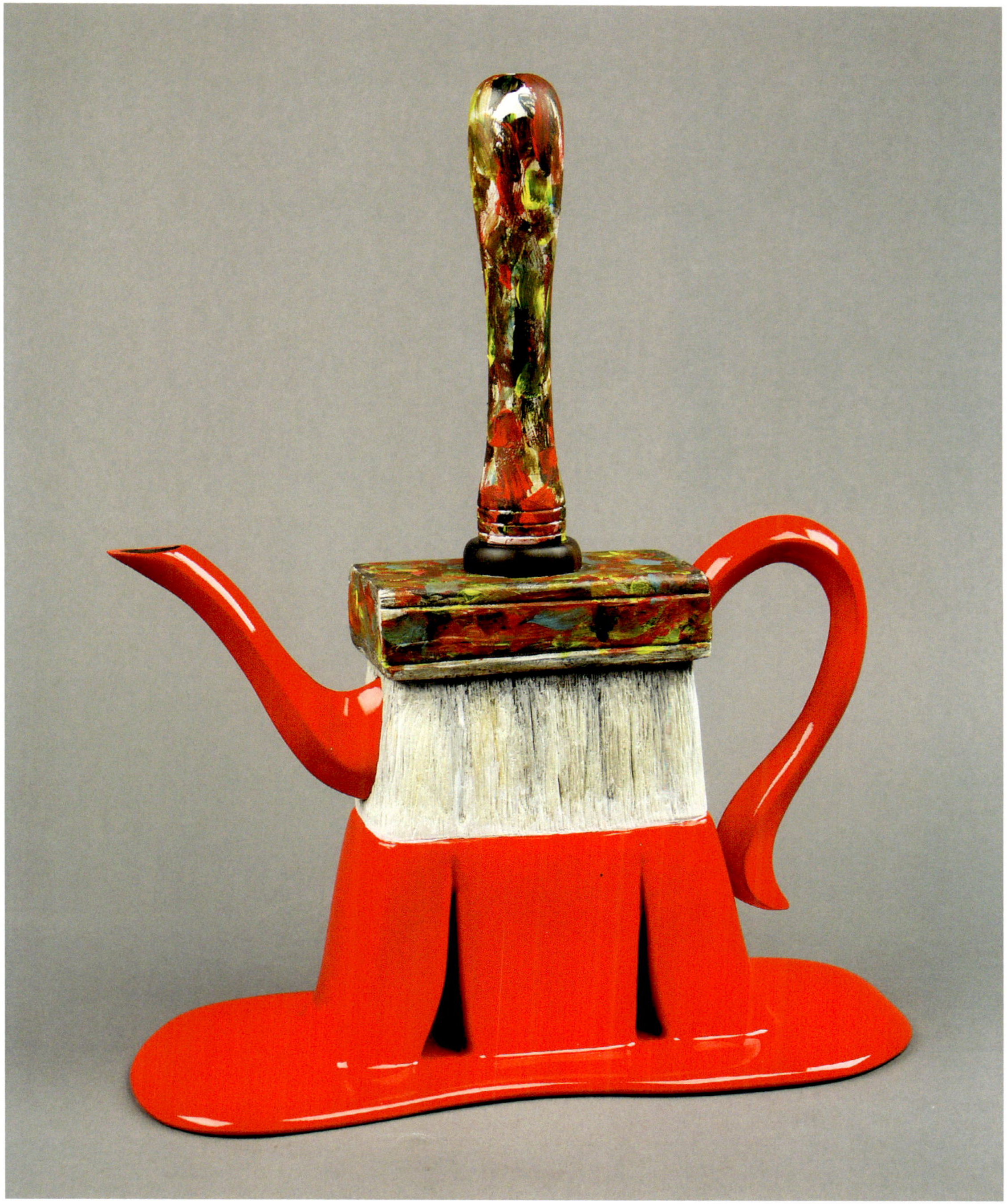

Milo Mirabelli. *Paintbrush.* 2008. Teapot, hand-carved basswood, acrylic paint and red lacquer, 15" h x 12" w x 5" deep.

Michael D. Mode

New Haven, Vermont, www.michaelmode.com

Artist's Statement

My present work concerns forms and surface designs generated via a multi-step lamination process, utilizing the stacking and gluing of angled concentric rings cut from a single laminated plank to produce a rough bowl form which is then refined in shape, smoothed, and finished on the lathe. I use a variety of mostly tropical woods chosen for color, figure, grain, and workability; all colors are natural.

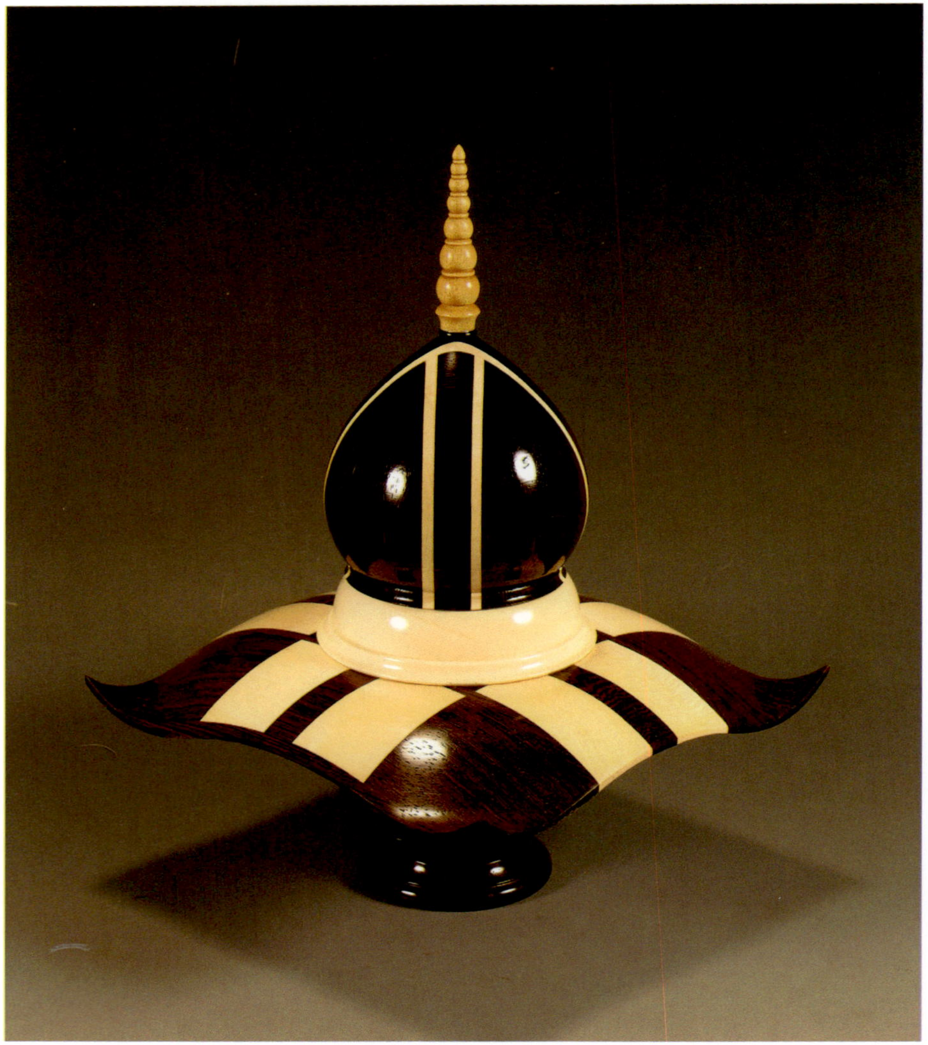

Michael D. Mode. *Dancing Across the Square.* Wenge, holly, ebony & yellowheart, 10" d x 10.5" h. Note: this is a lidded vessel in the architectural style inspired by mugal building in India.

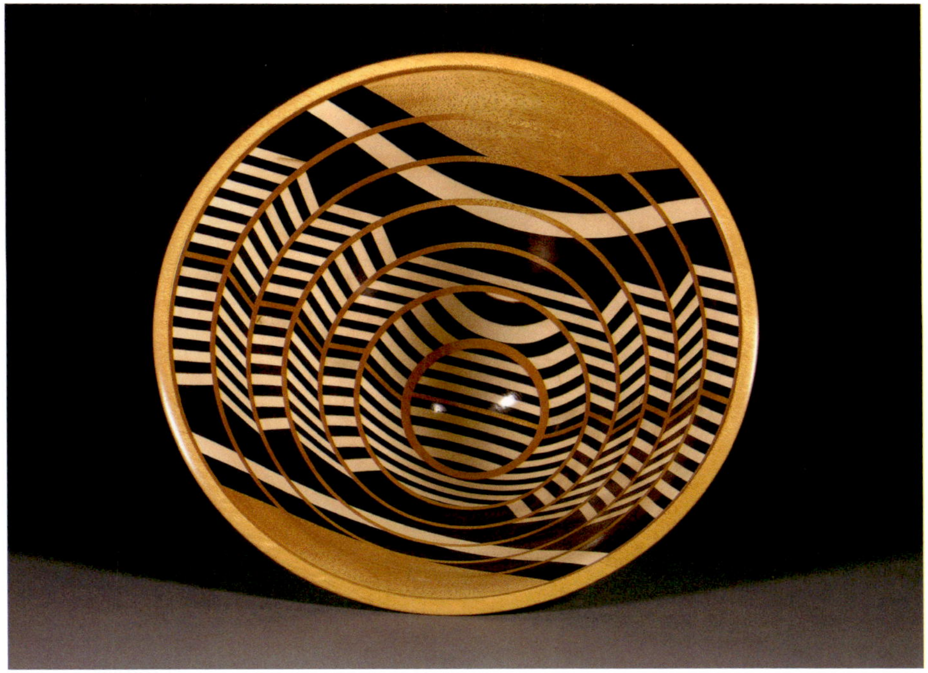

Michael D. Mode. *In the Plaza*. Yellowheart, holly, & wenge, 10.25" d x 7.5" h.

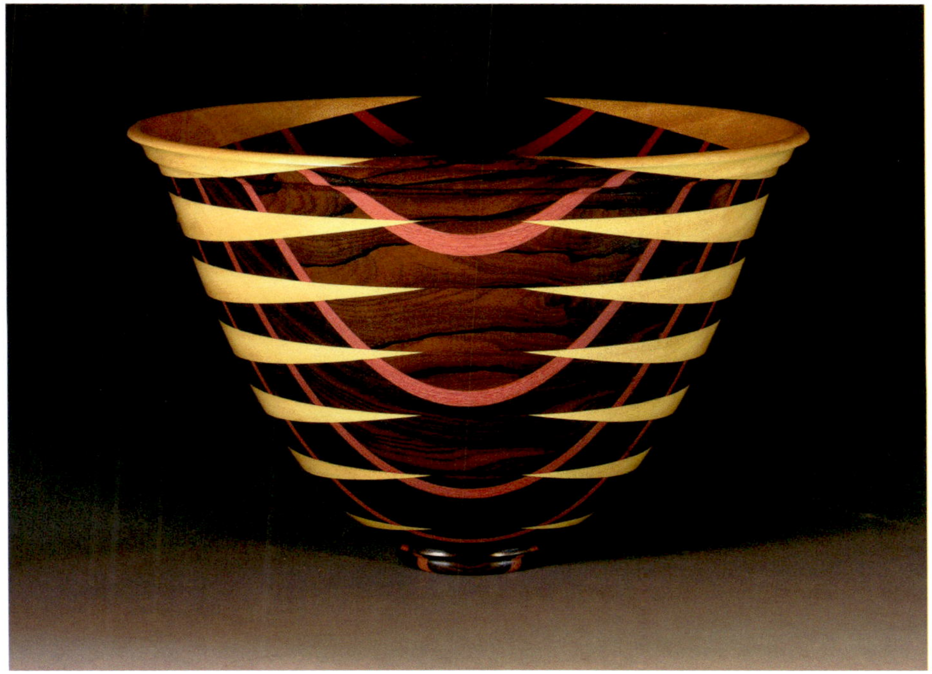

Michael D. Mode. *Needs No Answer.* Ziricote, purpleheart & yellowheart, 12.75 " d x 8.75" h.

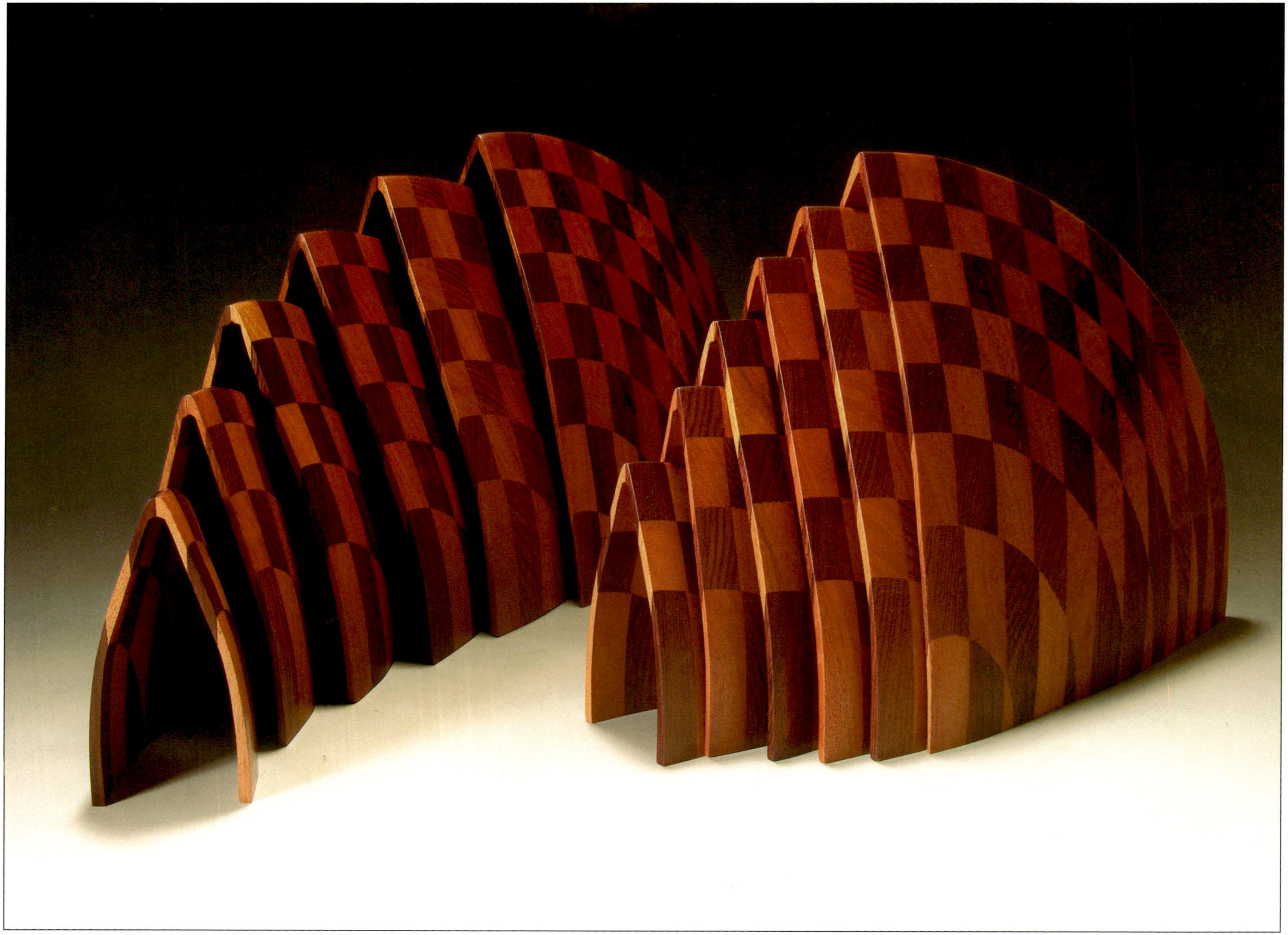

Michael D. Mode. *Walking Cathedrals*. Honduras rosewood & mahogany, maximum height 10". One of a series of multi-part interactive sculptural objects.

Matthew Nauman

Frederick, Maryland, http://matthewnauman.com

Artist's Statement

Throughout the Postmodern era, the interaction of individuals and groups with art and craft mediums has undergone noticeable transformations. By inventing and manipulating conventional mechanisms, I intend for the user(s) to interact with my furniture in order to subvert societal expectations as to how furniture functions. By concealing these mechanisms, I take a simple action of opening and closing a drawer and turn it into an exploration of games and puzzles. Each piece has a sequence of steps; if completed in the prescribed manner, the user's experience will culminate by discovering the internal space(s) of each piece. The books, *Objects and Meaning; New Perspectives on Art and Craft and The Art of Participation*, support my theoretical viewpoints on the continual "crossover" of fine art and craft objects within Postmodernism. By making work that is motivated by design, function, and interaction, the work relates to the generations of the 1980s and '90s due to the growing popularity and demand for innovative technological advancements.

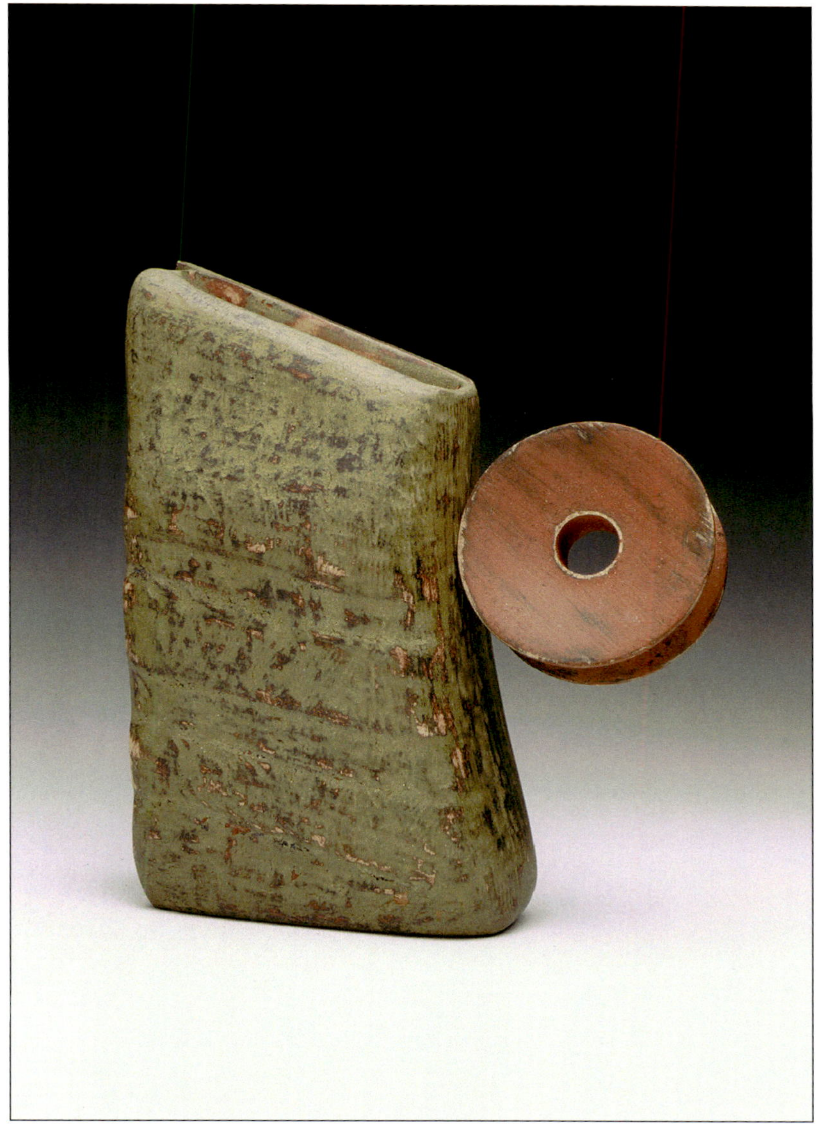

Matthew Nauman. *Vessel #2.* 2007. Maple, brass, milk paint. 8" x 4" x 2". *Photographer: Lynda LaRoche*

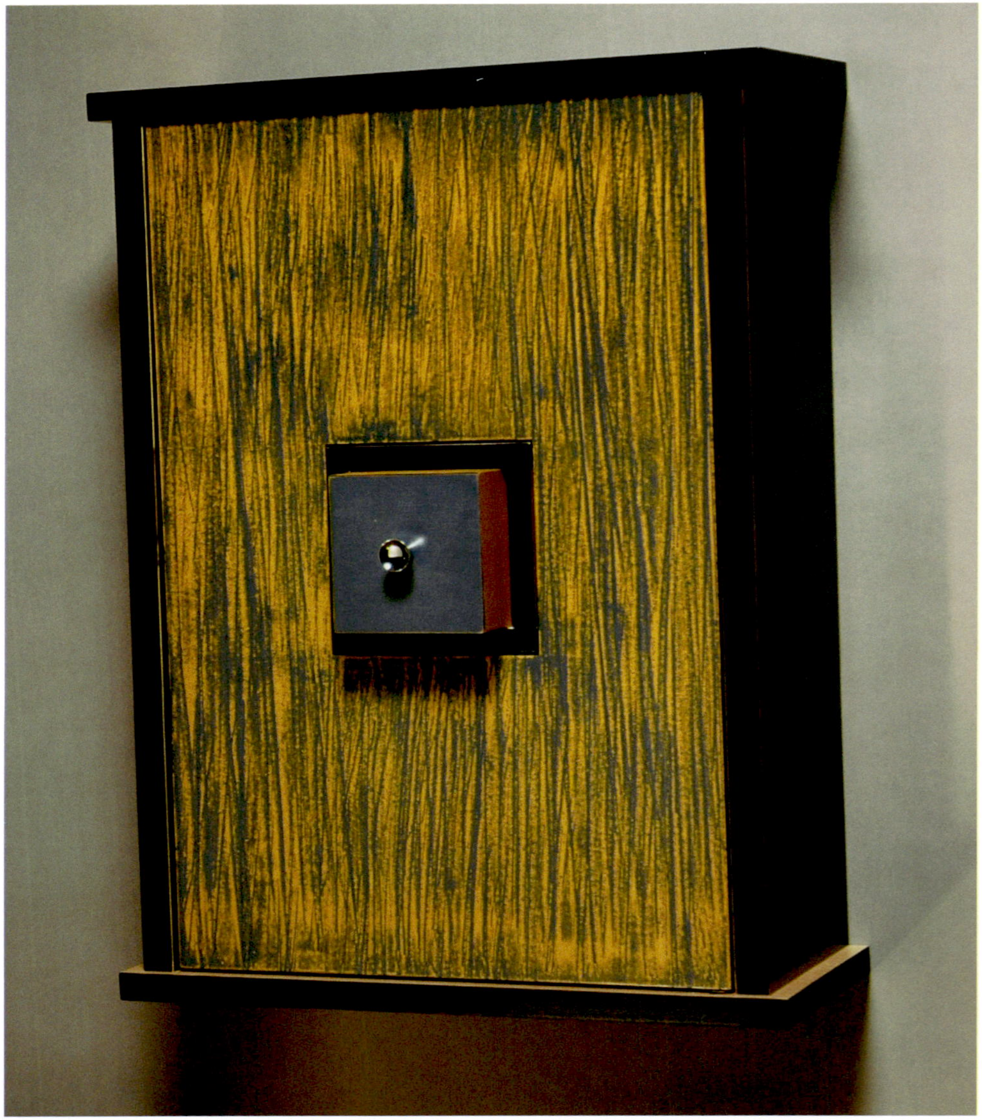
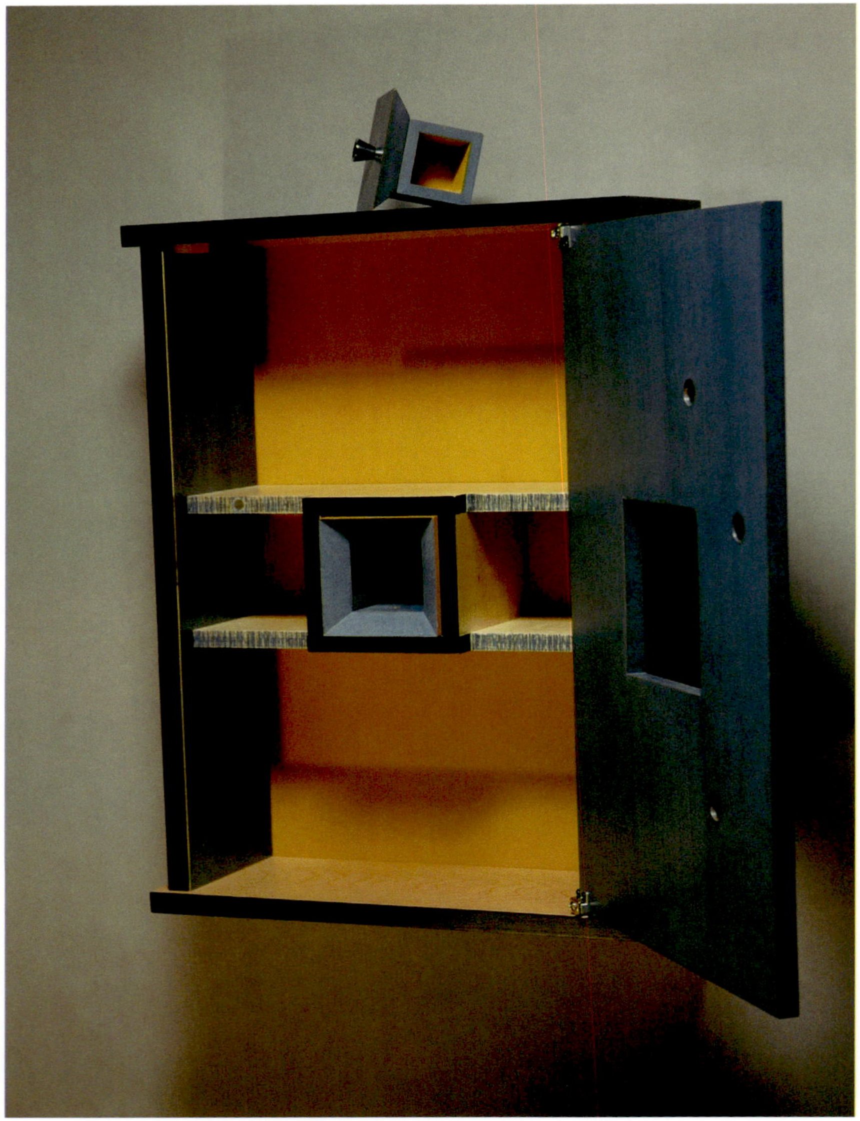

Matthew Nauman. *Door for the Drawer #1.* 2009. Maple, MDF, brass, magnets, milk paint, 24" x 18" x 8".

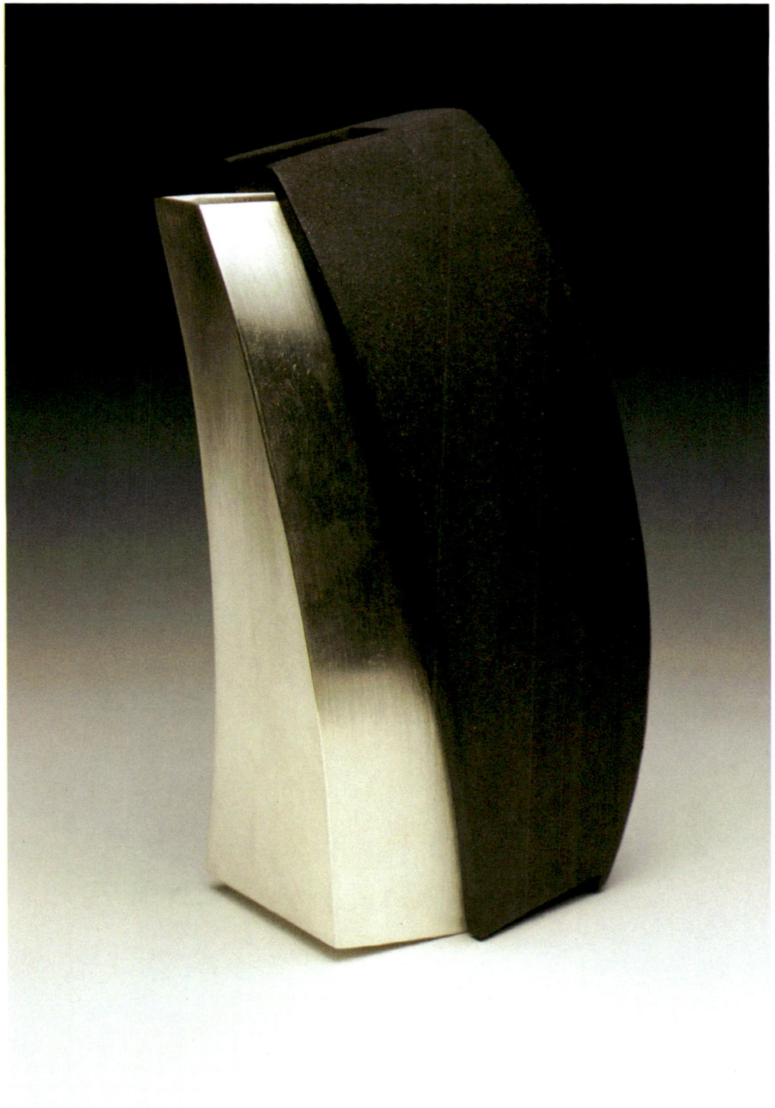

Matthew Nauman. Vessel #3. 2007. Ebonized sassafras, sterling silver, 5 1/2" x 2 1/2" x 2". *Photographer: Lynda LaRoche*

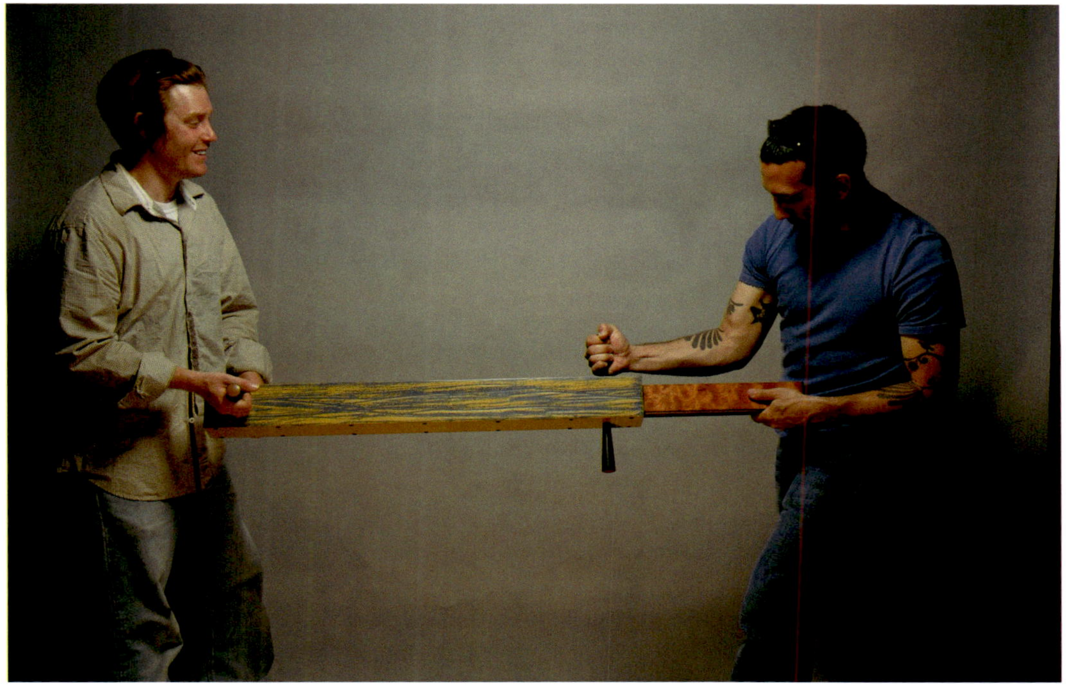

Matthew Nauman. *Give and Take*. 2009. Cherry, tiger maple, bubinga, MDF, brass, milk paint, 72" x 12" x 4".

David Nittmann

Boulder, Colorado, www.davidnittmann.com

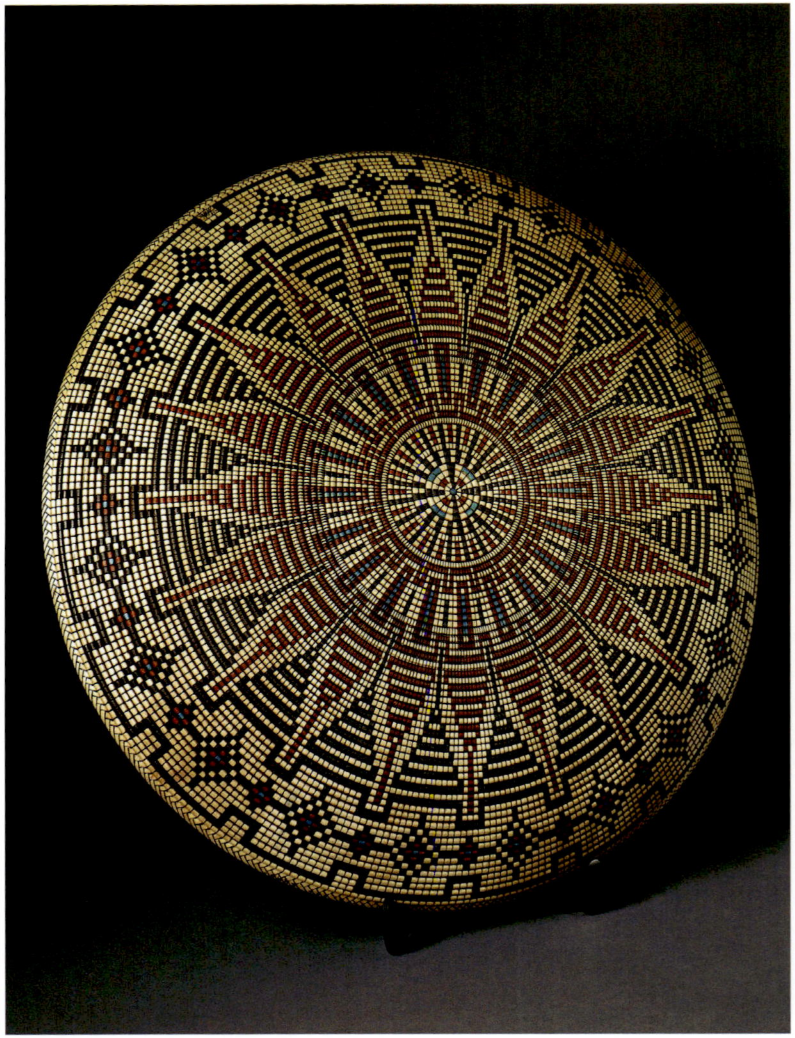

David Nittmann. *El Espiritu de la Flor del Zumo*. Quaking aspen bowl, 21"d x 2-1/2" h.

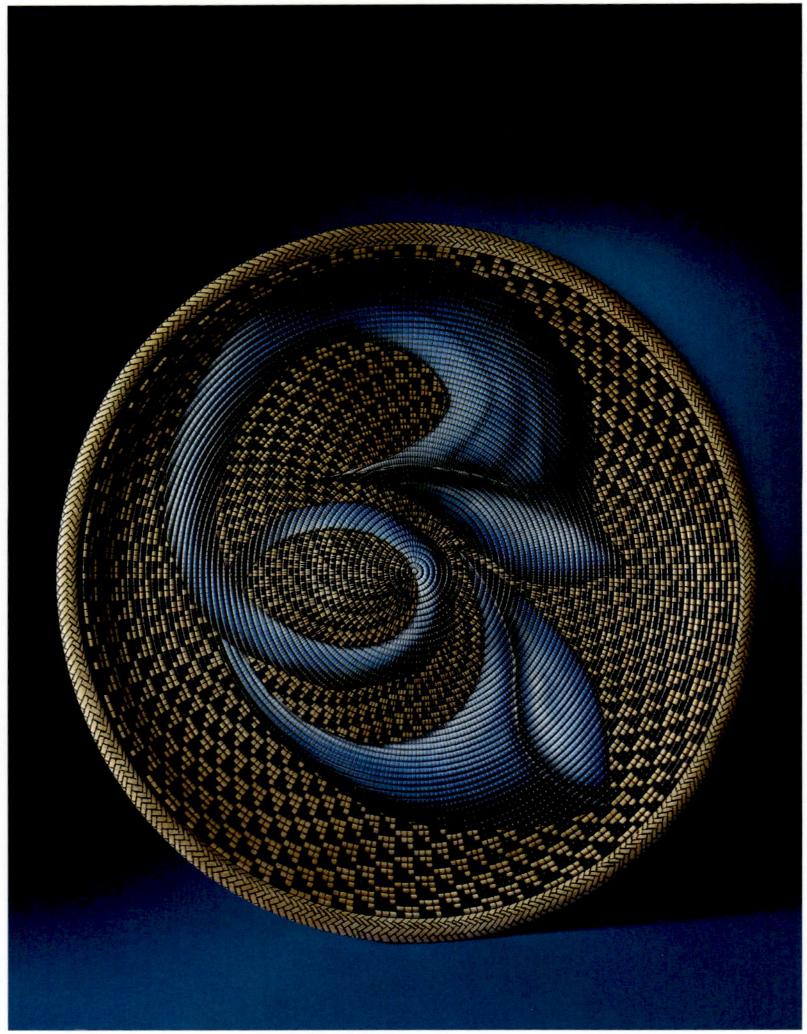

David Nittmann. *Talking Back to the Night.* Maple platter, 21" d x 1-1/4" h.

Robert Ortiz

www.ortizstudios.com

Artist's Statement

My mother and father, born on the island of Vieques, Puerto Rico, came to New York around 1934. I grew up in Greenwich Village where I studied classical piano beginning at age five. The process and discipline of making furniture is not unlike that of making music. Measure upon measure the craftsman builds a piece, one note, one joint at a time. With patience and dedication, the goal is to achieve a well-arranged and orchestrated piece, perhaps even a work of art. Both crafts demand discipline and dedication, attention to detail and nuance, and a respect for the creative process.

Early on in my woodworking career, I was inspired by the works of George Nakashima and Thomas Moser. My furniture incorporates the two major influences that most inform my woodworking. The first is the furniture of the Shaker communities of the early nineteenth century. Theirs is furniture rooted in the "New World," unpretentious, exquisitely proportioned, and examples where ornamentation and beauty are a result of function and joinery.

The second is the aesthetic and temple carpentry that I was introduced to in Mr. Nakashima's book, *The Soul of a Tree.* This work celebrates form and line, detailed and exposed joinery, and a quiet, understated elegance.

The furniture I design and build attempts to marry these two styles in my own interpretation and in a contemporary manner. But while there is a nod to those that have influenced me, my attempt is to create furniture that is approachable, functional, and beautiful.

Individual Artwork

This cherry table is typical of the furniture in my *Sofia Line.* This small table features a single board top and a continuous figured grain pattern in the front apron from which the drawer front is cut. I especially enjoy the interplay of the different curves, i.e., front and side aprons, lower stretchers, and the shelf front. The drawer pull is carved to fit the finger and is made of wenge. I have left the natural edge of the single board top, which measures 17" deep by 22" wide by 7/8" thick. The table stands 28" high.

The *Sofia* end table is a piece that I frequently "customize" to accommodate my client's needs, changing height, width, and depth as need dictates. In order for this to be successful, the overall proportions need to be maintained as well as the proportions of the different elements, leg thickness for example. I have made this table with legs that were anywhere from 1 3/8" square to legs that were 1 3/4" square.

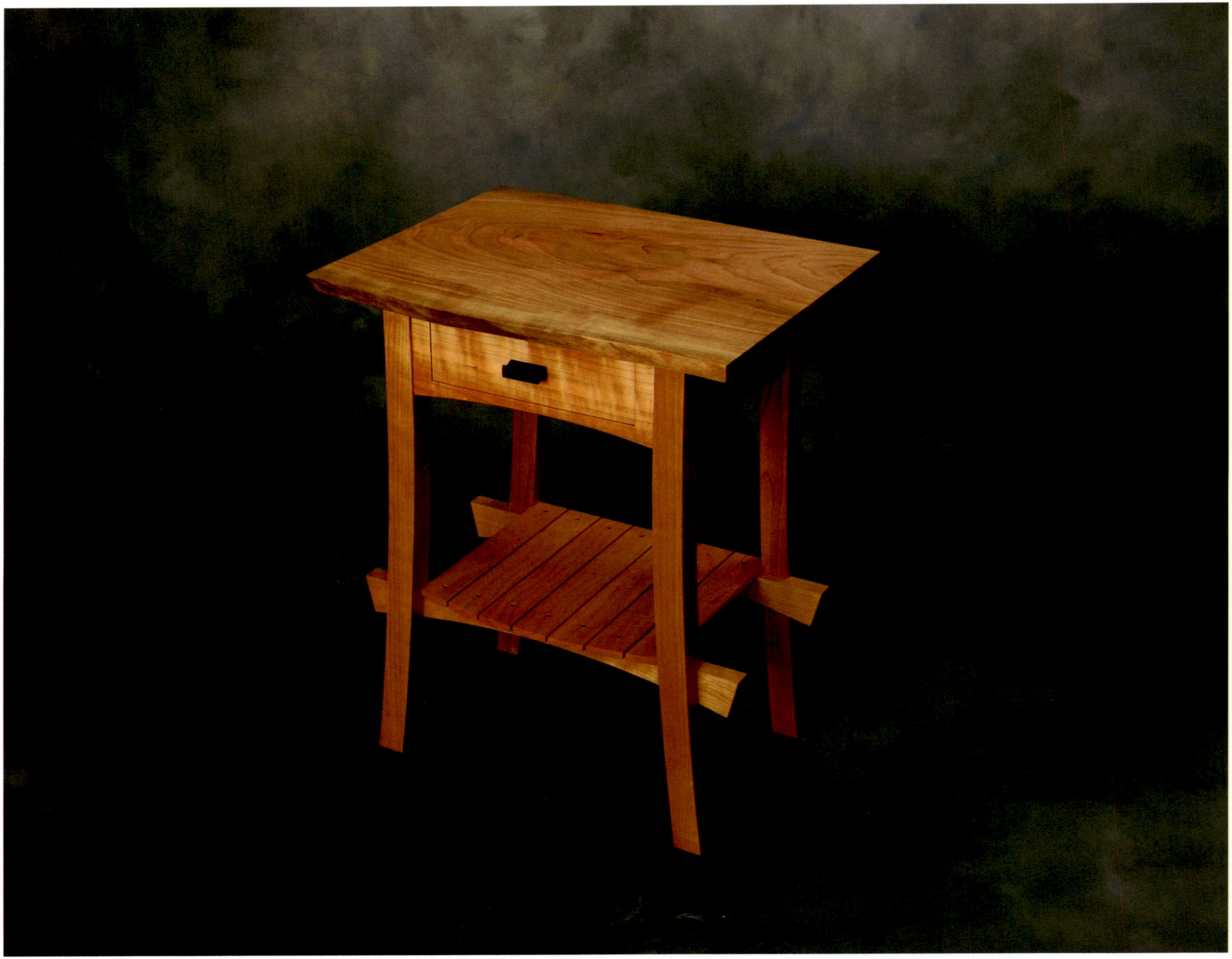

Robert Ortiz. *Sofia* Occasional Table. *Photographer: Tracey O'Connell* (above and opposite page)

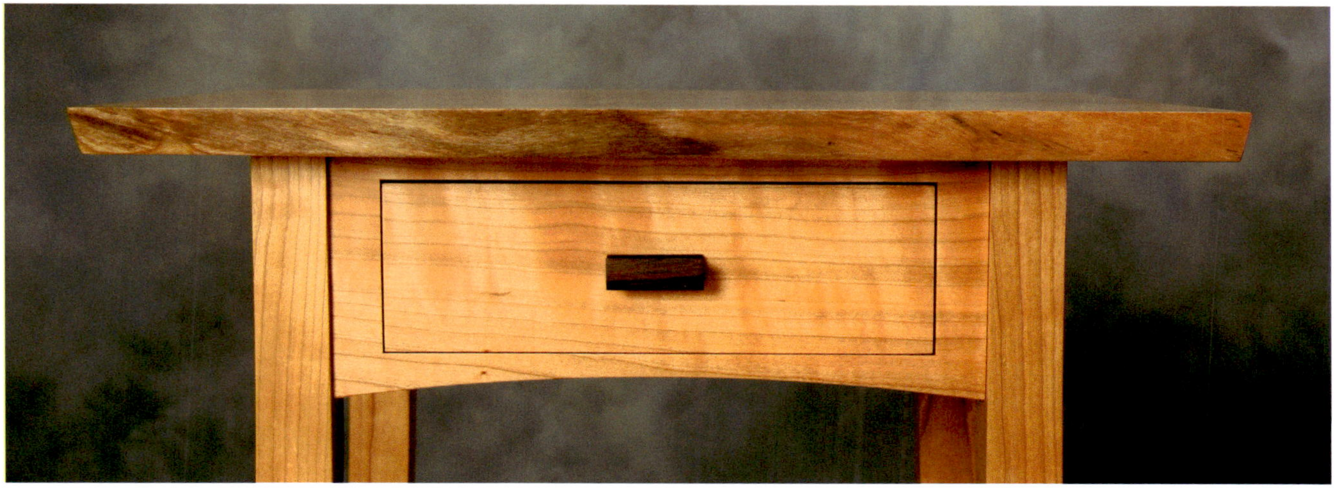

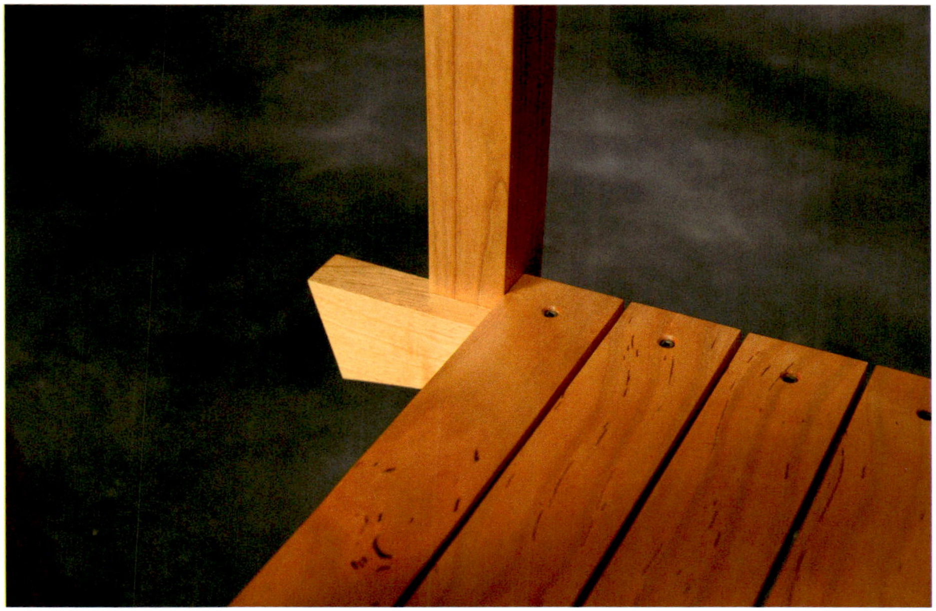

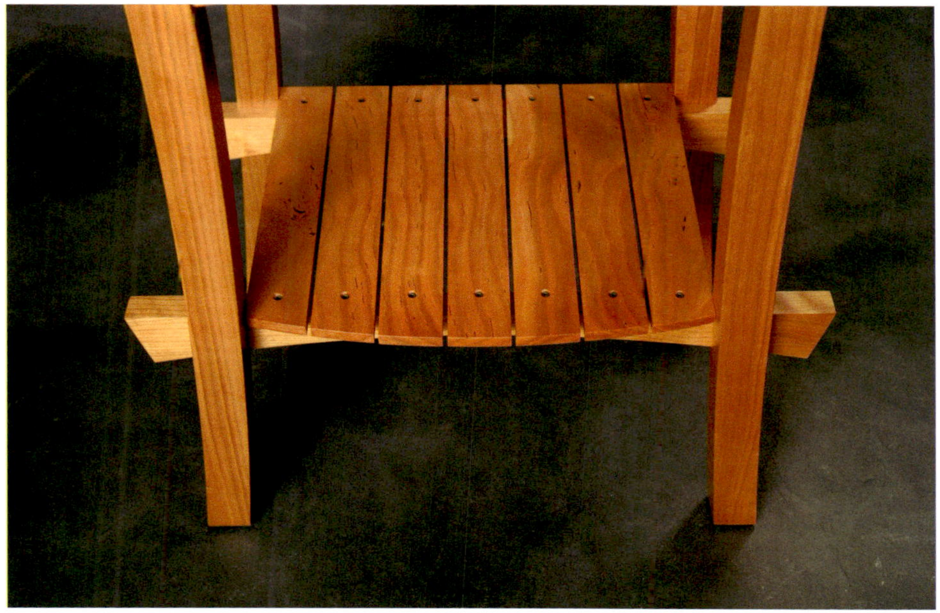

Peter M. Petrochko

Oxford, Connecticut, www.peterpetrochko.com

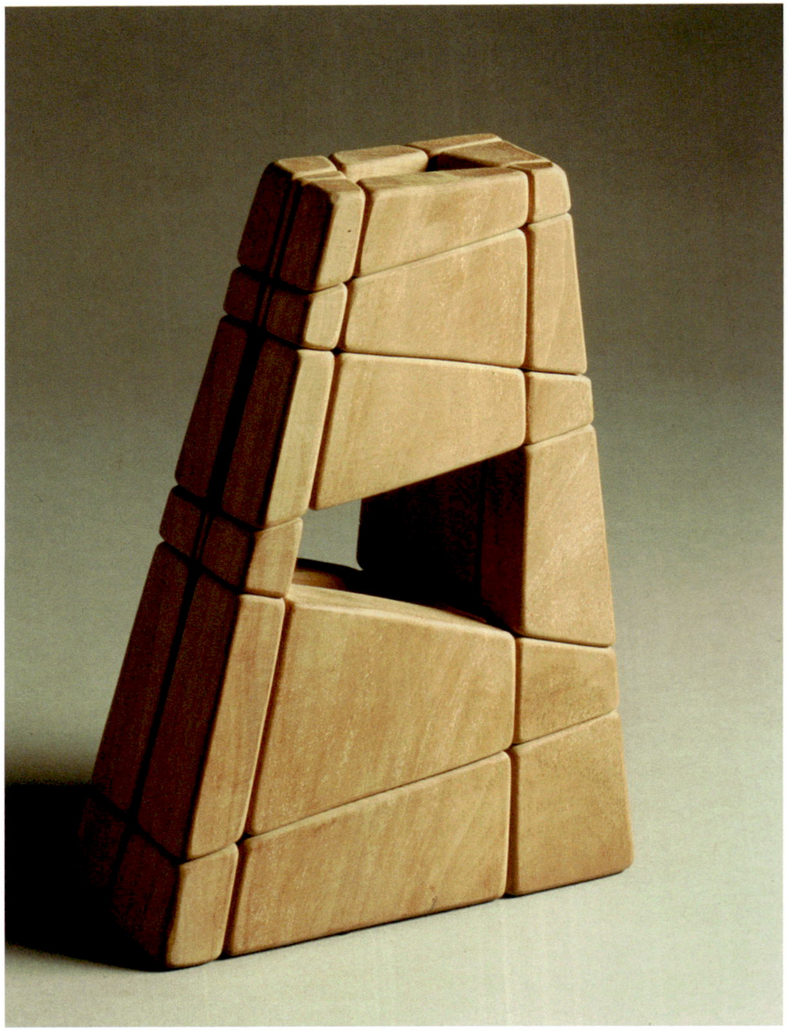

Peter M. Petrochko. Bandsaw/split wood series. Abstract architectural sculpture, Cuban mahogany. This piece plays on space, mass, light, shadow, and form. 12" h x 8" w x 4" d.

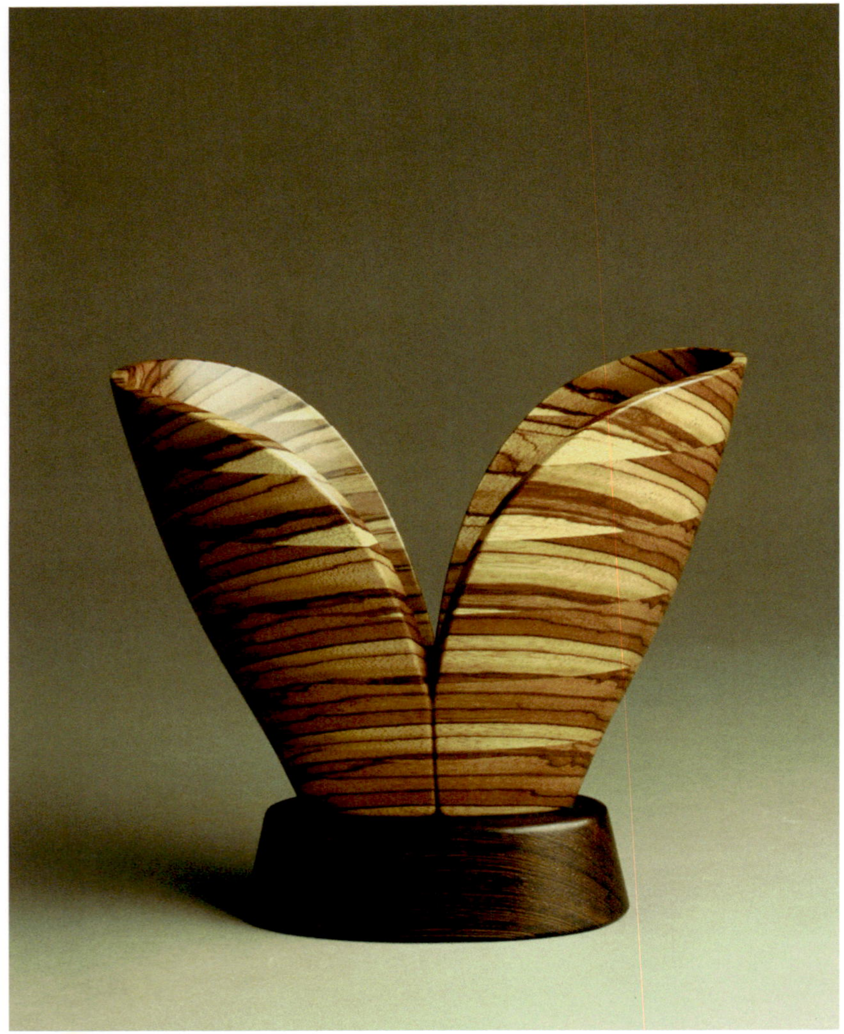

Peter M. Petrochko. Sculpture. Zebrawood (Africa) & wenge – base (Africa), 10" h x 12" w x 5" d.

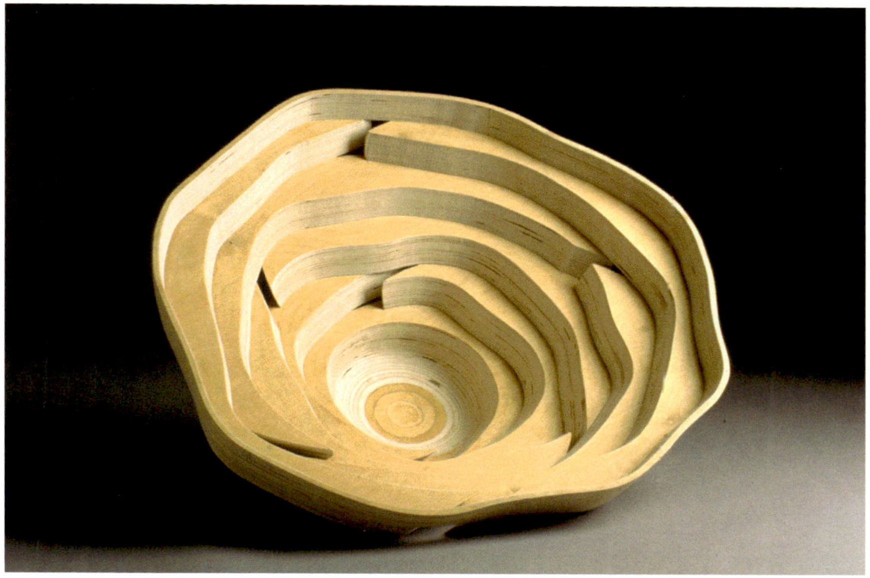

Peter M. Petrochko. Wobble Vessel Series. Baltic birch plywood, 10" h x 27" w x 28" d.

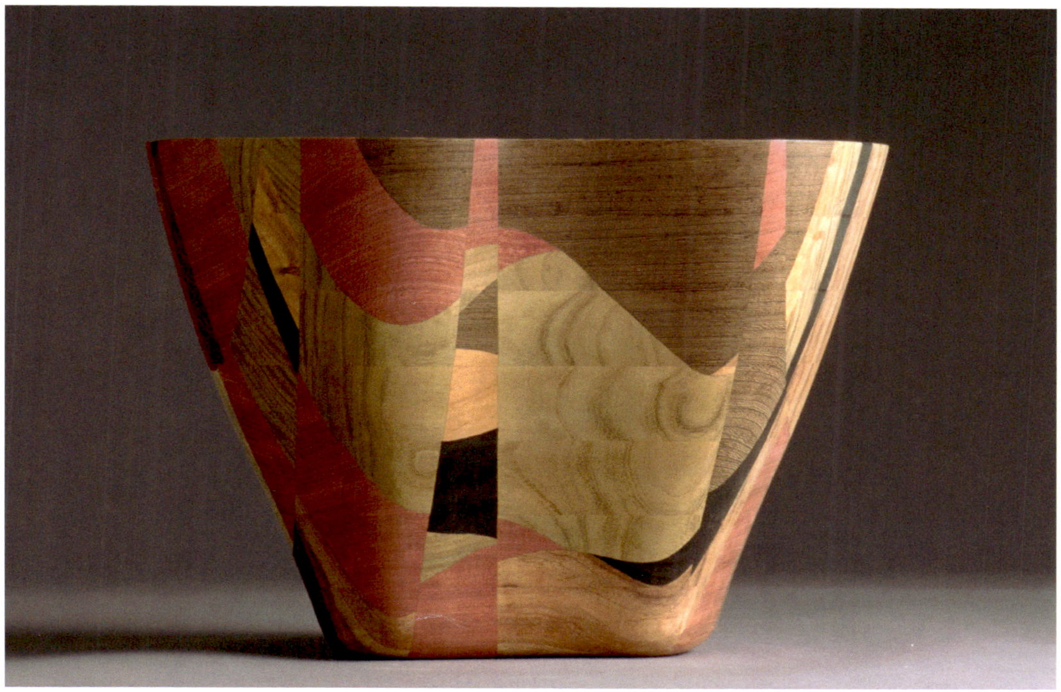

Peter M. Petrochko. Amorphic Tent Series Vessel. American wenge, shedua, ebony, Brazilian purpleheart, and Hawaiian kca, 12" h x 17" w x 12" d.

Binh Pho

Maple Park, Illinois, toriale@msn.com

Artist's Statement

I started turning wood in 1992, learning various techniques from wood turners such as Del Stubbs, Leonard Hartline, Rodger Jacobs, and from watching demonstration at American Association of Woodturners (AAW) symposiums. I like to push the limits, using green wood and turning it to a translucent wall thickness, often including the defective part of the wood in the design to show the character of the material, such as bark inclusions and worm holes. Natural designs, such as worm holes in the wood, offer an exploration of negative space, which I explore further as a means of expressing the unknown and mysterious in using the piercing techniques I learned from the late Frank Sudol. Combining these approaches with my experience in drawing and painting, I came to focus on the surface treatment and embellishment on my turning, using Asian motifs to tell stories, share feelings, and present inspiring scenes and cultural influences.

The greatest breakthrough in my development as an artist was *Challenge VI: Roots: Insights & Inspiration in Contemporary Turned Objects,* organized by the Wood Turning Center in Philadelphia in 2000. I created two pieces for the exhibition about my past and my homeland. Since that time, I have been making pieces to tell my journey to the West, from childhood, growing up through the war, the chaos of exodus in Southeast Asia, escape from communism to find freedom, and the challenges and rewards of my new life in the United States of America. At first, the public response was negative and I often received comments such as, "Why use color, you're covering up the beautiful wood grain" or the criticism that my work contained too much embellishment and content. Yet, I did not give in and kept doing what I love and I still enjoy following my own path as a woodturner. At the same time, it has become obvious that, although I am a product of the field of woodturning and contemporary craft in terms of media and process, my work fits more comfortably into the realm of contemporary art, due to my exploration of concept and narrative.

In creating work, I will often plan and sketch my piece when the inspiration comes into my mind, and then look for a piece of wood to turn a bowl or vessel, which I approach as a three-dimensional canvas. After the vessel is turned and properly dried, I sand the surface smooth and begin to sketch the design. I go on to airbrush the body of the work and pierce the form to compliment the airbrush images. It is the piercing that is my favorite element in the work, as I place messages that are not initially obvious. It is my hope that it will draw the viewer in when they see something, or sense that they see something. It is as if something is not there, yet always present. By using negative space, I explore the presence of the absence.

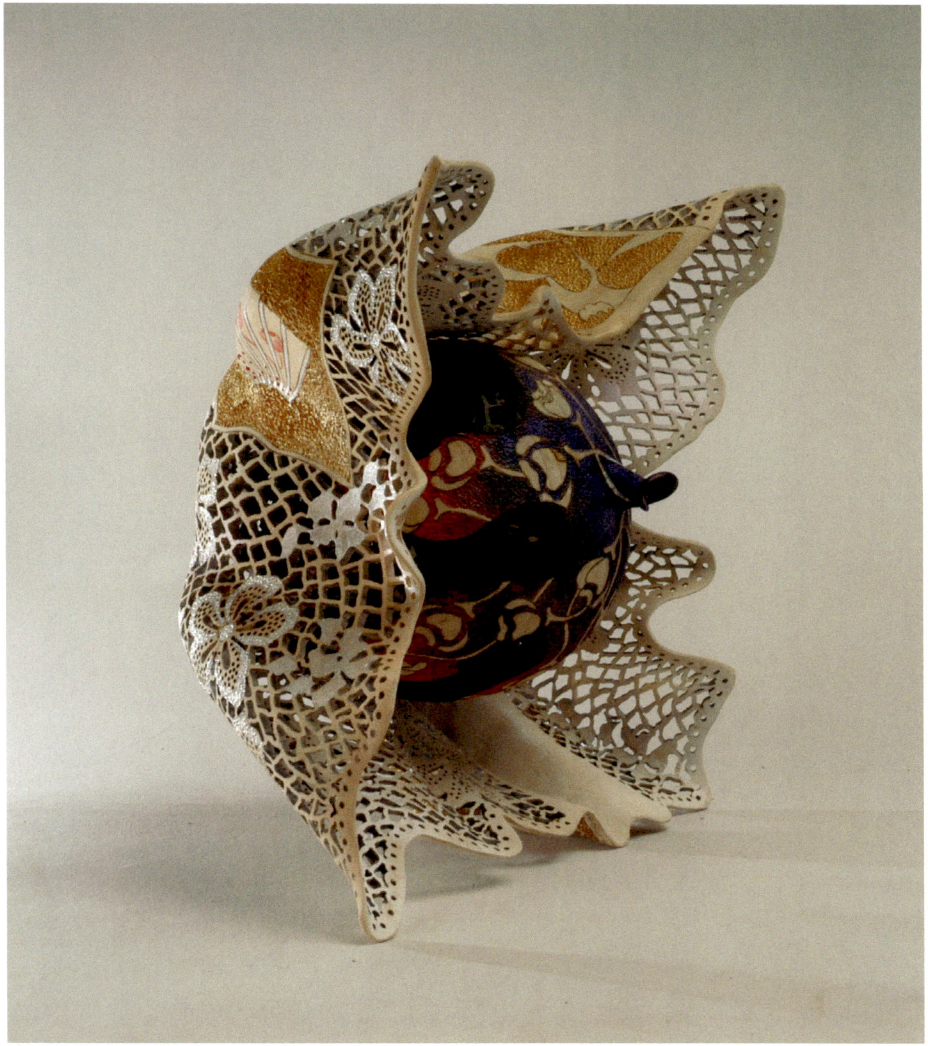

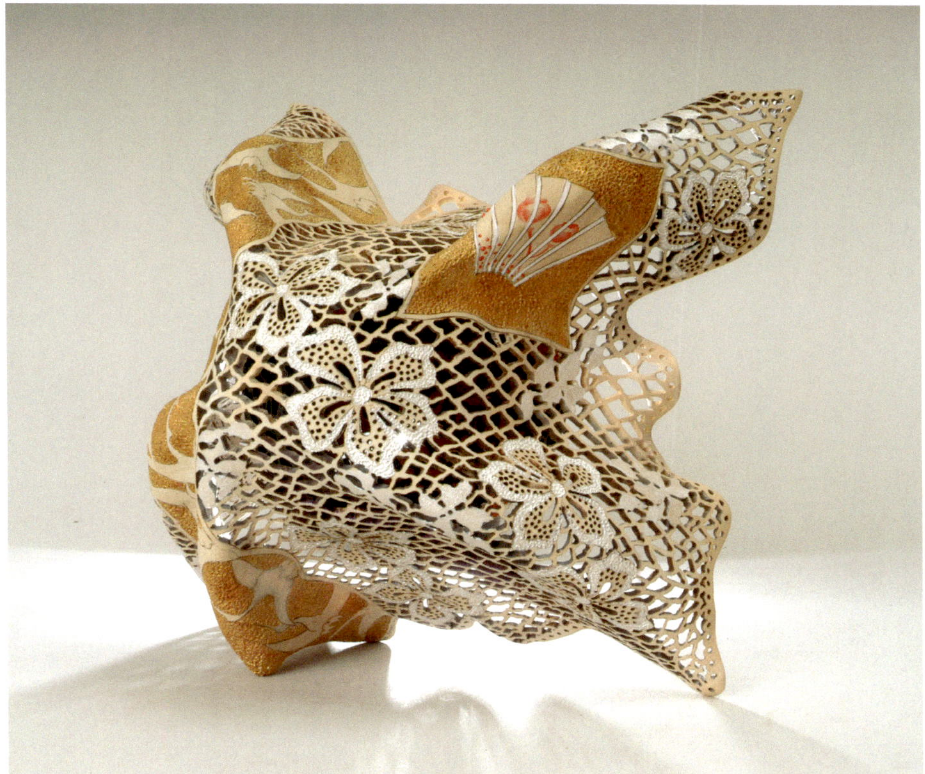

Binh Pho. *Promise.* 2008. boxelder, acrylic paints, turned, pierced and airbrush, 6" x 7" x 3.5". *Collection of Dr, Jim and Elizabeth York.* The promise that Simon gave his Gelkandar that he will not violate the rules of the secret garden.

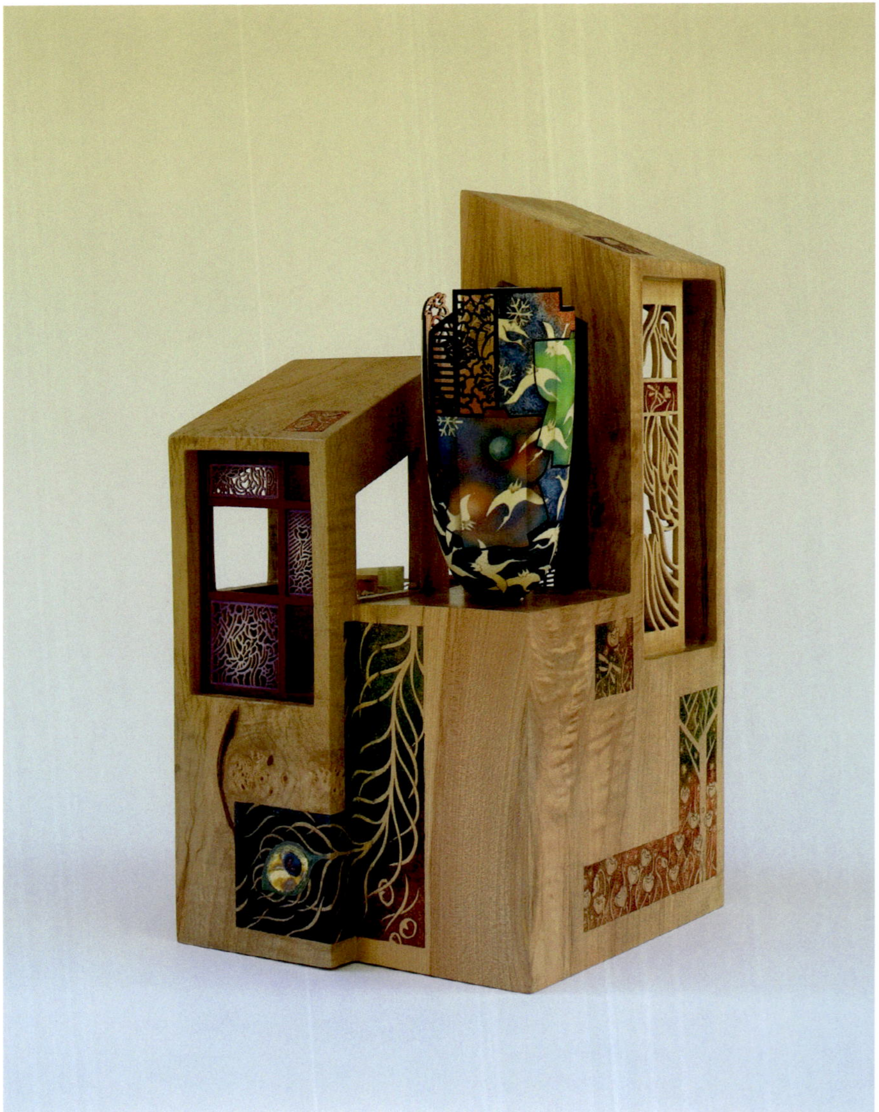

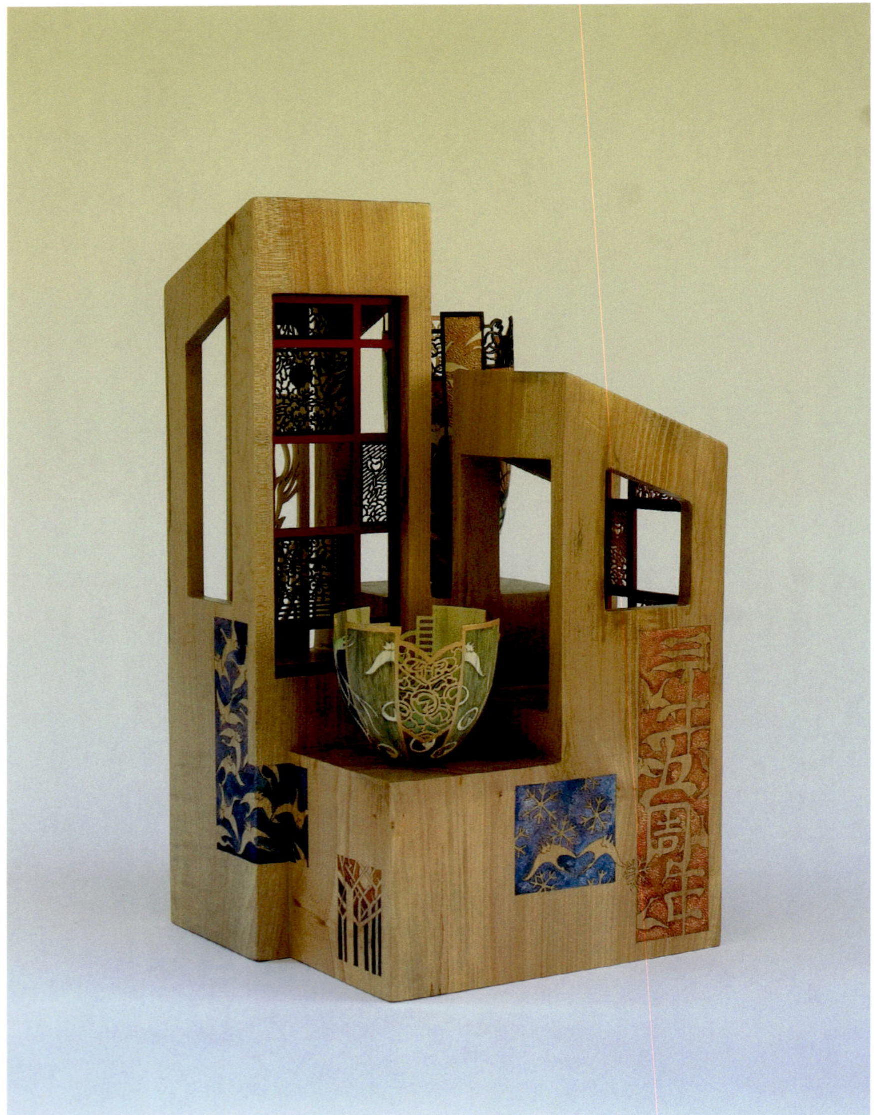

Binh Pho. *Warmth of Winter.* 2008. boxelder, maple, acrylic paints, dye, sculpted, turned, pierced and airbrush, 16" x 8" x 10" each. *Collection of Paul and Sheri Robbins.* Winter, when we always think about the warm places in our life: a fireplace, hot tea, the blanket in our bed… in this piece the warmth of winter is a place like home, loving heart, and memories.

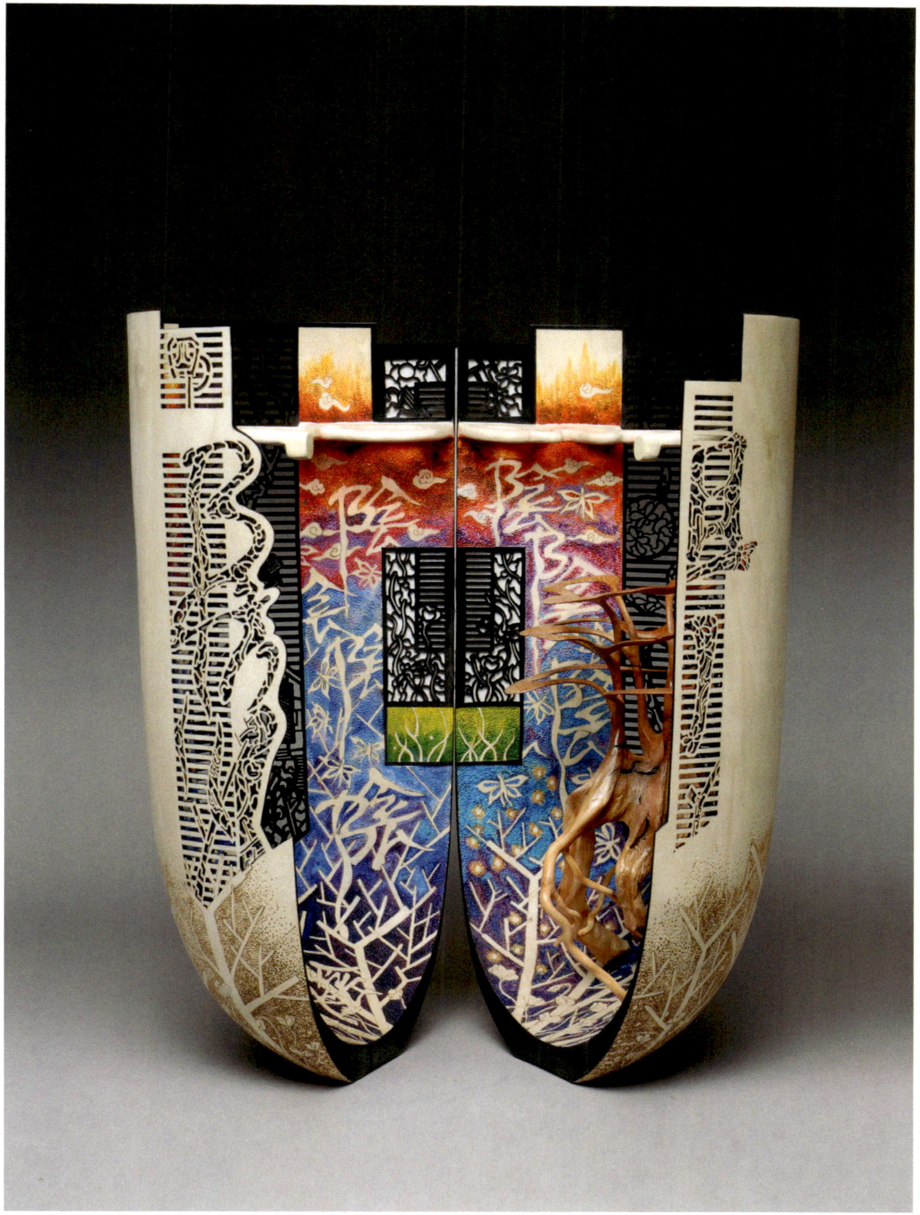

Binh Pho and Alain Mailland. *The Source.* 2009. boxelder, acrylic paints, silk paper, turned, carved, pierced and airbrush, 18" x 9.5" x 9.5" when it is closed. *Photo by David Peters © 09*. The tree is the source of the story "Shadow Of The Turning" and this piece was a collaboration with Alain Mailland, who turned and carved the tree. I created the woods and garden surrounding the tree, which has magical powers, and can be either hidden or revealed, like the Gelkandars.

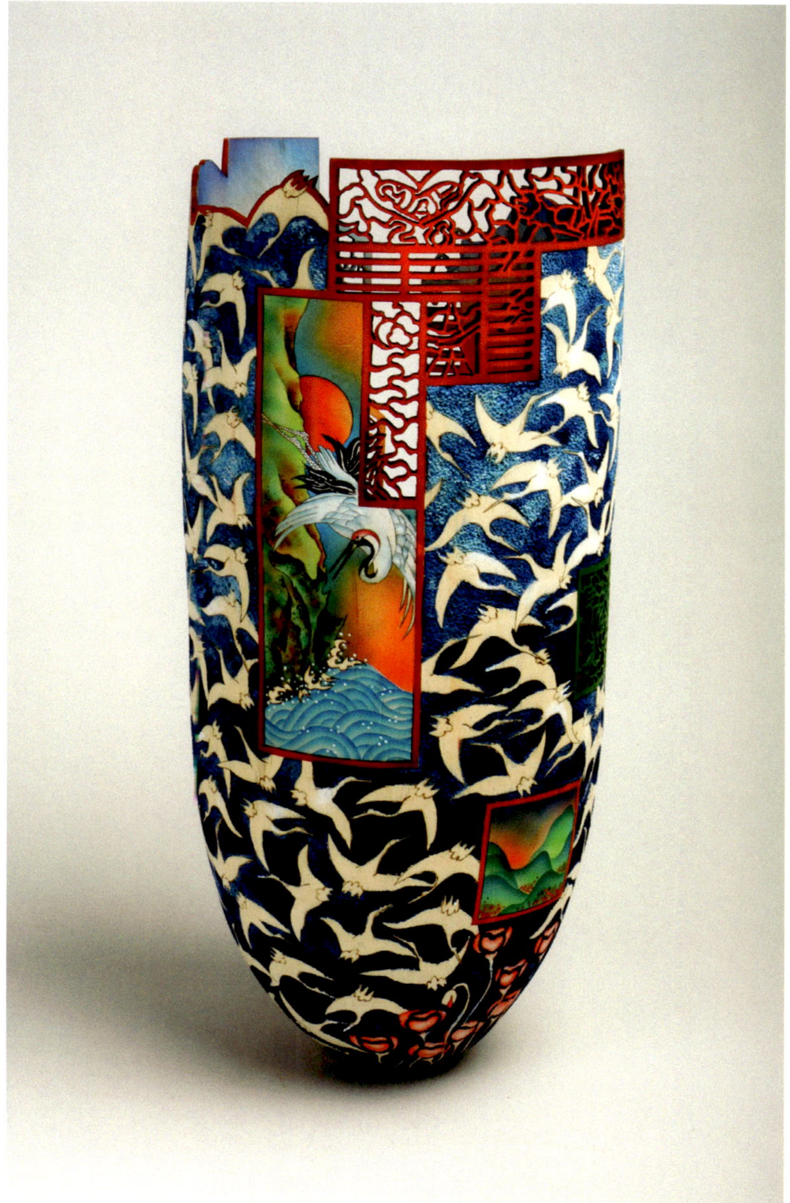

Binh Pho. *Midnight Sun.* 2007. boxelder, acrylic paints, dye, turned, pierced and airbrush, 12" x 4.5" x 4.5". Inspired by the story of two lovers who were cursed by magical power, one is in human form in daylight and the other with the moonlight. They only can be in human form together in the brief moment when the sun rises with the full moon still hanging in the sky.

NORMAN PIROLLO

Ontario, Canada, www.refinededge.com

Artists Statement

With a focus on creating modern, contemporary studio furniture and wood art, a large part of the aesthetic in Norman's designs originates in art deco, modern, and contemporary styles of design. Much of his work can be characterized by up to date variations of these styles with inclusion of design elements from these styles.

The contemporary style of studio furniture Norman creates has simple, clean lines with a combination of subtle and dramatic features while emphasizing original, unique design. His designs combine both rectilinear and curvilinear components and center around both form and function. His wood art is decorative, functional or both.

The design methodology Norman adheres to is both modern and contemporary, utilizing traditional joinery and finishing. Most recently he has delved into mixed media designs, combining both wood and metal into his work, embracing complementary mediums to wood. As an artist, Norman enjoys challenging himself with new techniques and processes, often drawing inspiration from the natural organic forms, which surround us in our environment.

The tendency today is to apply both stain and film finishes to furniture, which mask both the color and texture of the wood and give an artificial appearance to the surface of wood. Norman applies finishes to both protect the wood and maintain the subtle texture.

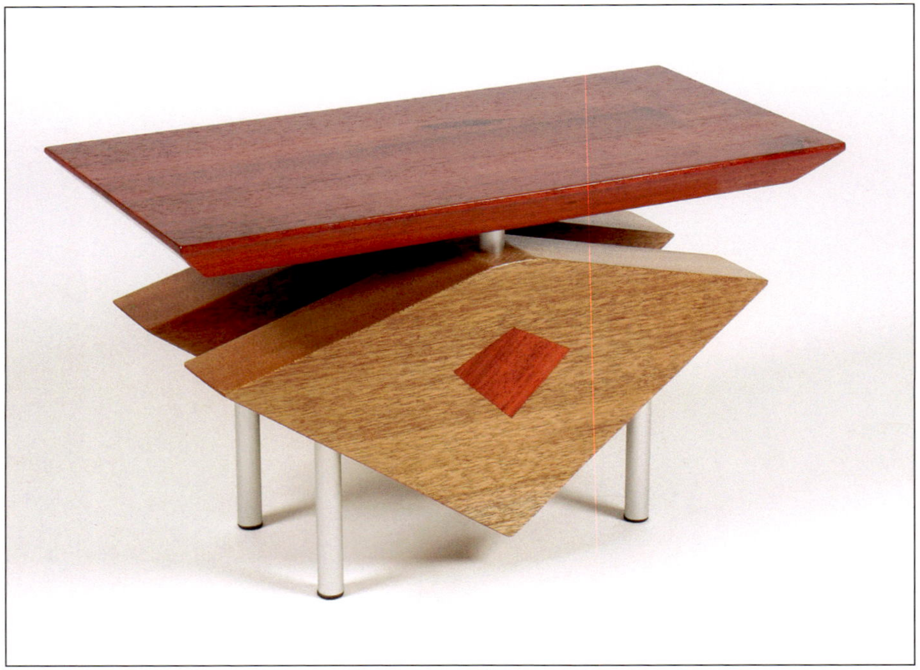

Norman Pirollo. *Diamond Doublet.* 2009. Mahogany, padauk, aluminum, 8.25" h x 13.75" w x 6.7" d. *Photography: Linda Chenard*

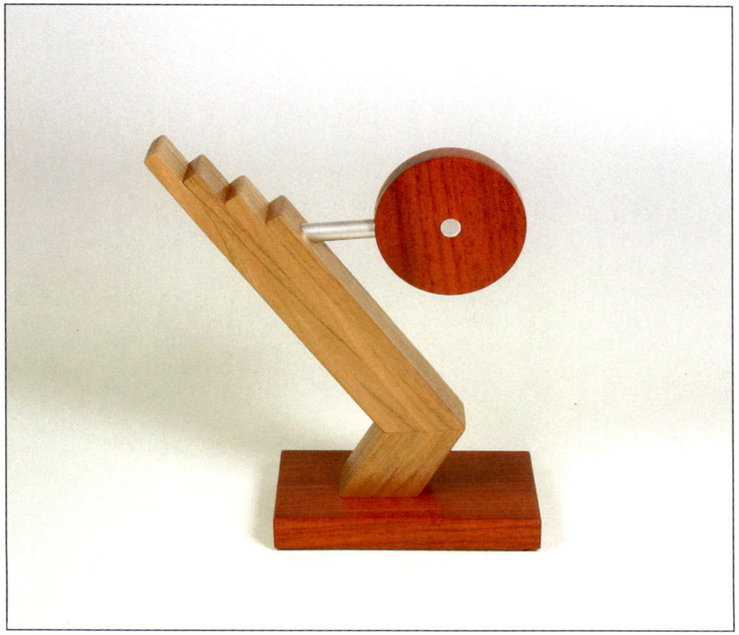

Norman Pirollo. *Equilibrium.* 2009. Padauk, cherry, aluminum, 11" h x 9.8" w x 3.75" d. Photography: Linda Chenard

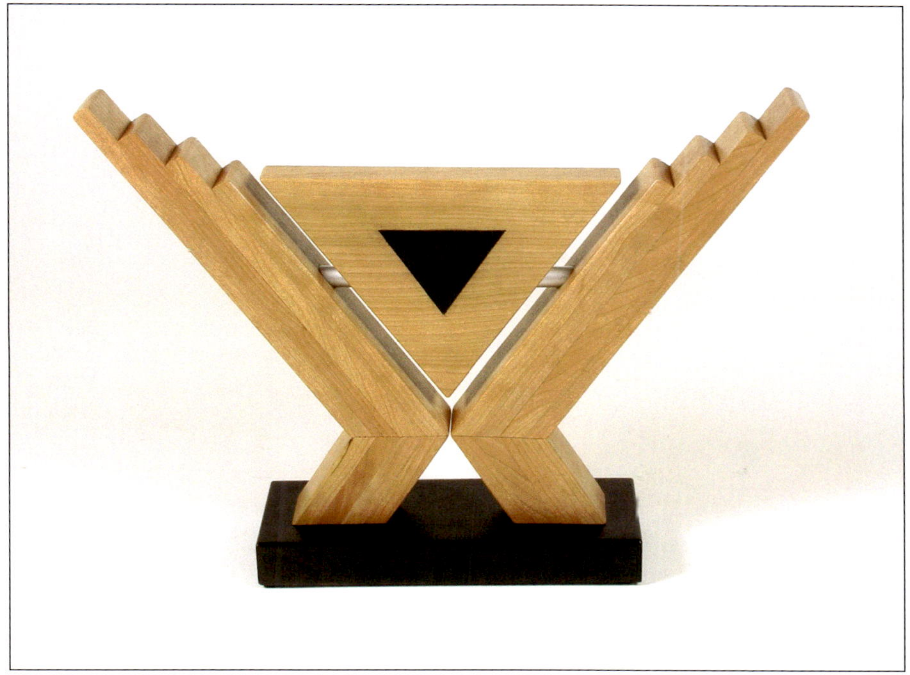

Norman Pirollo. *Reverence.* 2009. Cherry, blackwood, aluminum, 11.4" h x 15.3" w x 3.15" d. *Photography: Linda Chenard*

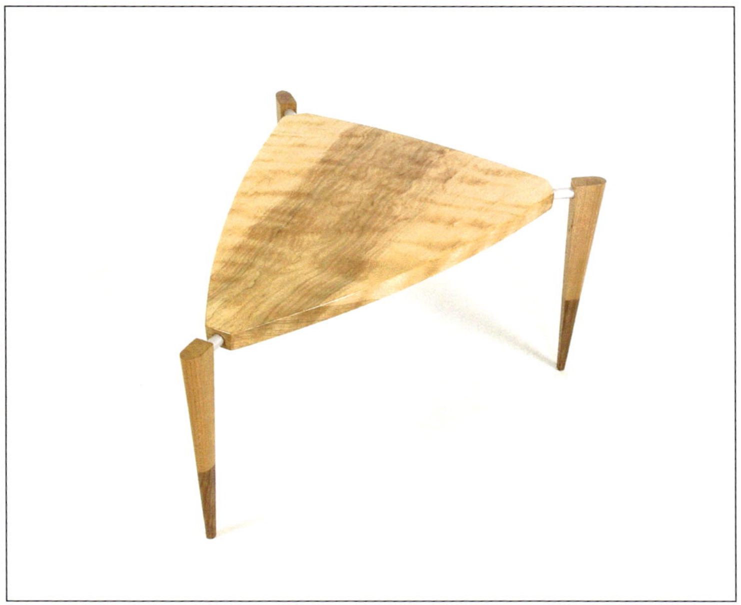

Norman Pirollo. *Trinity Stand.* 2009. Cherry, walnut, flame birch, aluminum, 7.8" h x 13" w x 16" d. *Photography: Linda Chenard*

Harry Pollitt

Santa Fe, New Mexico, http://pollittstudio.com

Artist's Statement

Against the Grain

Commonly, when people inquire how long it takes me to produce a piece, they are incredulous of the time and awed by what they perceive as my patience. Our warp-drive culture has accustomed us to mass production. My work goes against that grain.

Ultimately, my goal is to create beautiful works that are equal to the integrity and quality of the Renaissance Masters while at the same time being contemporary and unique. But I am a restless explorer – loathing repetition. So you will not see sameness of image in my work. My work is a search for the perfect line, plane, form, balance, and structure in cooperation with Nature. Nature has its own ideas and notions about what it wants or will allow. My challenge is to attempt to coax this material to release its secrets and inner beauty.

My work is divided into two major categories. The first half involves "natural sculptures" – forest-found contortions that induce a partnership between my search for the sweeping line and plane and Nature's own rhythm and balance. The second half involves works created from sawmill wood – rough sawn boards that I true-up and laminate into solid structures prior to sculpting. (There is no steaming or bending involved.) This second category allows considerably more freedom to pursue pure design. But in either case, this is labor-intensive handwork where completion is measured in months, not hours. Between major sculptural projects, I occasionally do turned and turned & sculpted works. The lathe affords near instant gratification and presents additional opportunity for artistic adventure & exploration.

Although I appreciate and am drawn to certain styles and periods of art, my art always follows its own course. Many times I will have definite intentions or directions for a piece, but when the work begins, it takes off on its own. This is the headiest trip I know. I just have to "get out of the way" and let it happen. I see a line and pursue it, attempting to release the "sweet spot." I hear swirling symphonic tones as I get close and feel visceral pleasure upon arrival. The inspiration of form and the passion to execute involves interaction with a significantly greater creative force than my own. I do not question that, but humbly accept it into my life and work.

I have selected wood as my medium for three principle reasons. First is the challenge of reduction art. Knowing that there is only one chance to get it right heightens the risk and produces intensity in the work. Second is the ability to work the material into thinner and sharper profiles than stone allows. Third, and perhaps most compelling, is the warmth, color, grain, smell, and sensual tactility of wood.

Individual Artwork

Flug Ober Muotathal

Flug was a design-as-you-go sculpture based upon a doodle that I have sketched since I was a child – free flowing "C" and "S" curves, interlocking and branching. I acquired a 2 x 10 x 10' rough-sawn plank which I then edged and surfaced, butt-jointed two slabs in a V-shape, and then stack-laminated one board on top to provide additional depth for tunneling. I drilled out the knots and then combined the natural flow of grain with my natural flowing doodle in an elaborate dot-to-dot.

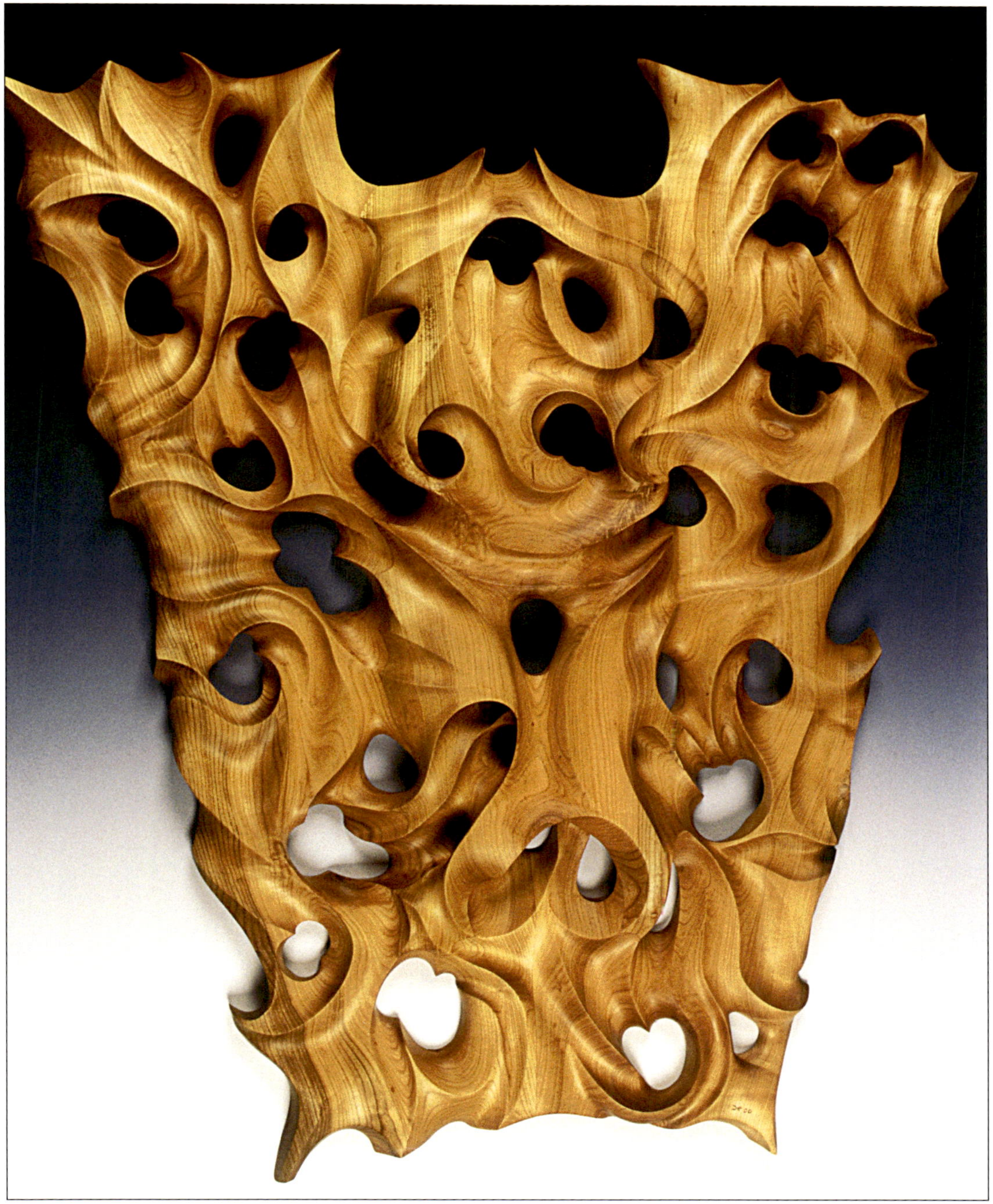

Harry Pollitt. *Flug Ober Muotathal.* 2001. Wall sculpture, Swiss cherry, 3' 10" h x 3' 3" w x 3" deep. *del Mano Gallery. Photographer: Hertzog Fotografin, Switzerland*

Escher Tide

Named after the French artist, M. C. Escher, *Escher Tide* reflects the impossibility of water flowing uphill and downhill simultaneously. It is also part of my ongoing exploration of positive and negative space.

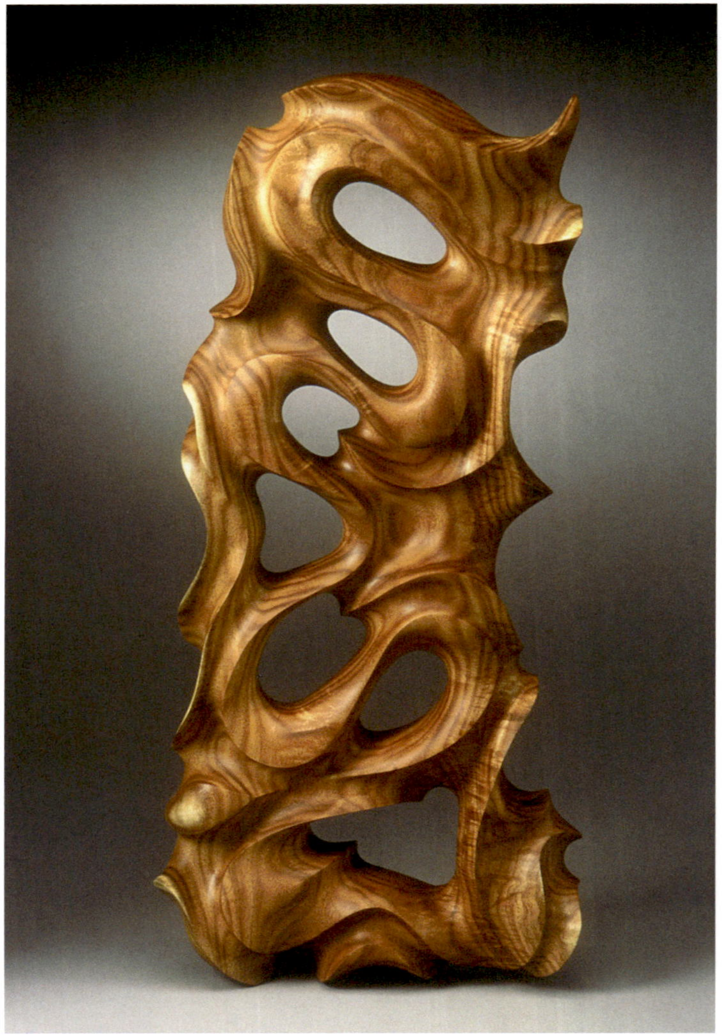

Harry Pollitt. *Escher Tide.* 2002. Wall sculpture, sisso, 2' 3.5" h x 1' 0" w x 2" deep. *Sold to Private Collection. Photographer: Jerry Anthony*

Down Force

I took a roll of stiff ribbon 2" wide, and while uncoiling it from the center, it slipped from my hands, landed on the bench, and cascaded off the sides. *Voilà*! *Down Force* is also a Mobius band 28' long.

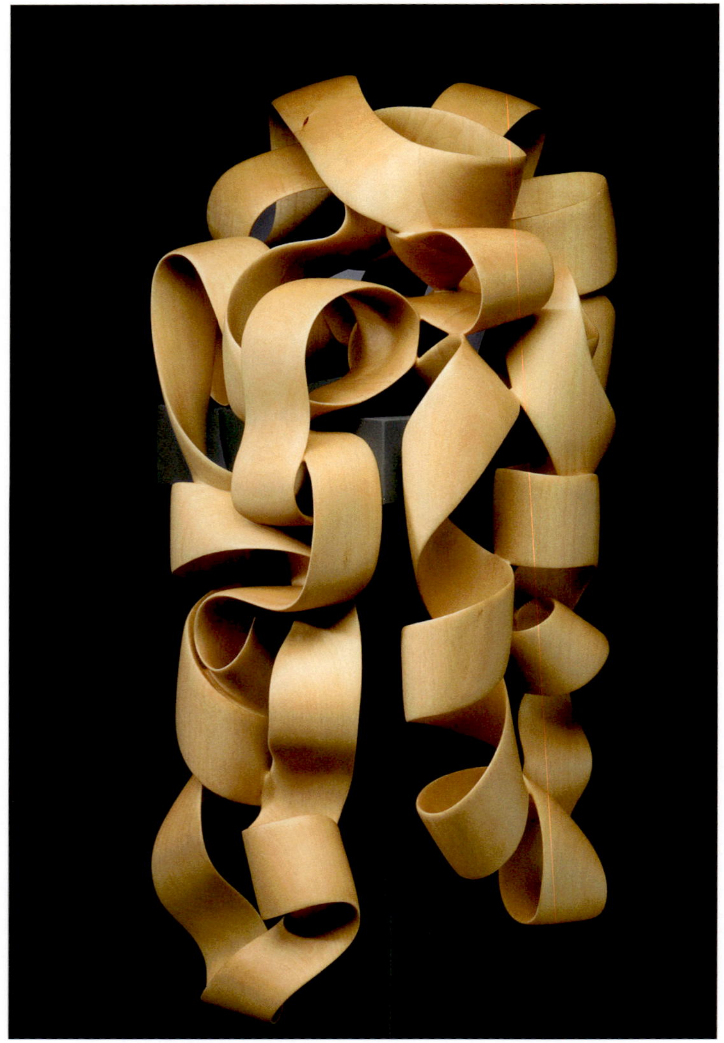

Harry Pollitt. *Down Force.* 2003. Sculpture, basswood, 1' 10" h x 10" w x 10" deep. *Sold to Private Collection. Photographer: Jamie Hart*

Charybdis

A bulbous swelling at ground level of an osage orange tree in a hedge row in Ohio caught my eye. Ying Yang movement in the bark formed the launch point for the entire design. During removal of more than 250 pounds of bark and waste wood, three holes appeared in a rotted center section and seemed ready to expose large worms. Instead, several inches deeper, three 50-caliber muzzle loading rifle balls emerged! Old target practice remnants?

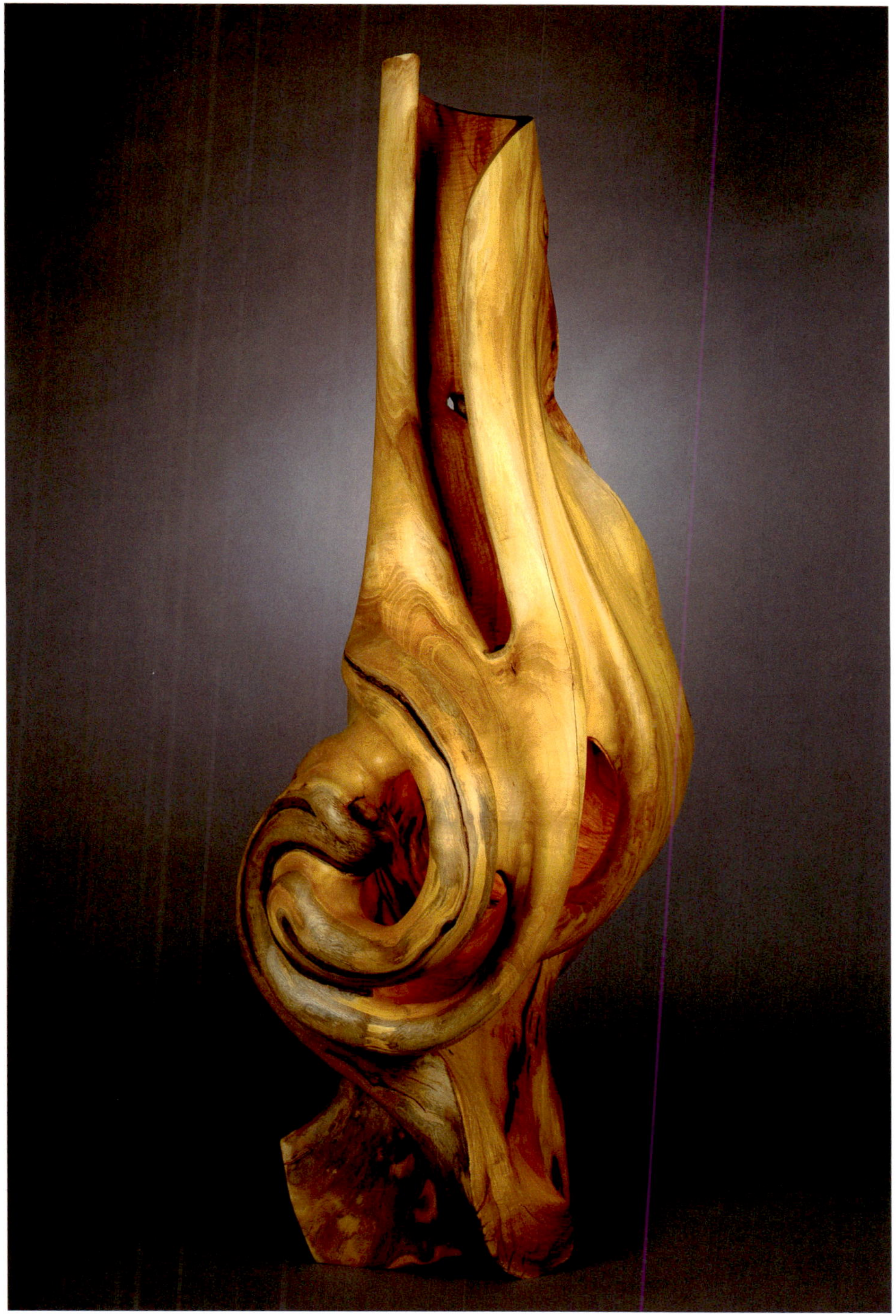

Harry Pollitt. *Charybdis.* 2009. Sculpture, osage orange, 5' 2" h x 2' 3" w x 1' 6" deep. *del Mano Gallery. Photographer: Mark Nohl*

TANIA RADDA

Fountain Hills, Arizona, radda@cox.net

Artist's Statement

These sculptures take on lifelike forms derived from nature, where insects, plants, and animals are presented in larger scale, enabling the viewer to experience a different perspective. Sometimes my work makes reference to ordinary objects that I find appealing; while in other cases it ponders issues that interest me. The work has a cartoonish quality at times, which reflects my love for the world of cartoons and fantasy—a world where the ordinary becomes extraordinary, where clichés are explored, and where the absurd becomes the norm. I have always been fascinated with mankind's persistence in exploring the natural wonders of this world. I enjoy reading and exploring books about plants, animals, and any kind of life. Growing up in Brazil, I experienced up close the fascinating aspects of nature and today I find that by sculpting these pieces, I can continue to explore and study these wonderful life forms. This process keeps my mind open to new discoveries while feeding my spirit with inspiration that keeps me going as an artist. Enjoy and explore my sculptures, and keep in mind that all these pieces are made entirely of wood. No other material has been used.

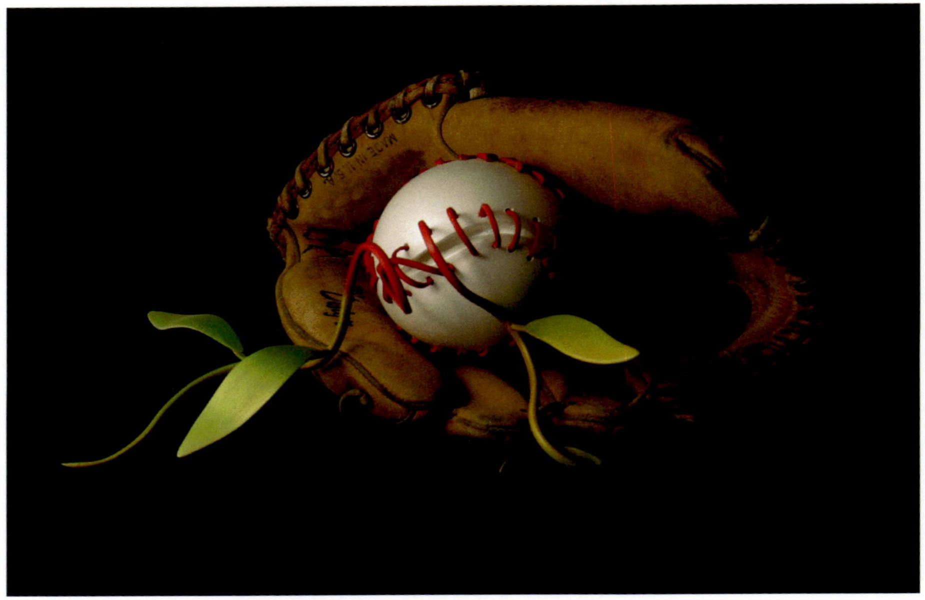

Tania Radda. *Spring Training.* 2006. Basswood, compressed maple, paint, leather, found object-baseball mitt (*Note: The baseball mitt is not made out of wood. The baseball is the carved and created piece.*), turned, carved, bent, 8" l x 7" w x 4" h. This piece represents the end of baseball season. If a baseball had life, this would be the natural progression of the baseball in its environment. (The baseball mitt was introduced to add to the composition, the idea came from my photographer Ken Manicki). *Photographer: Ken Manicki*

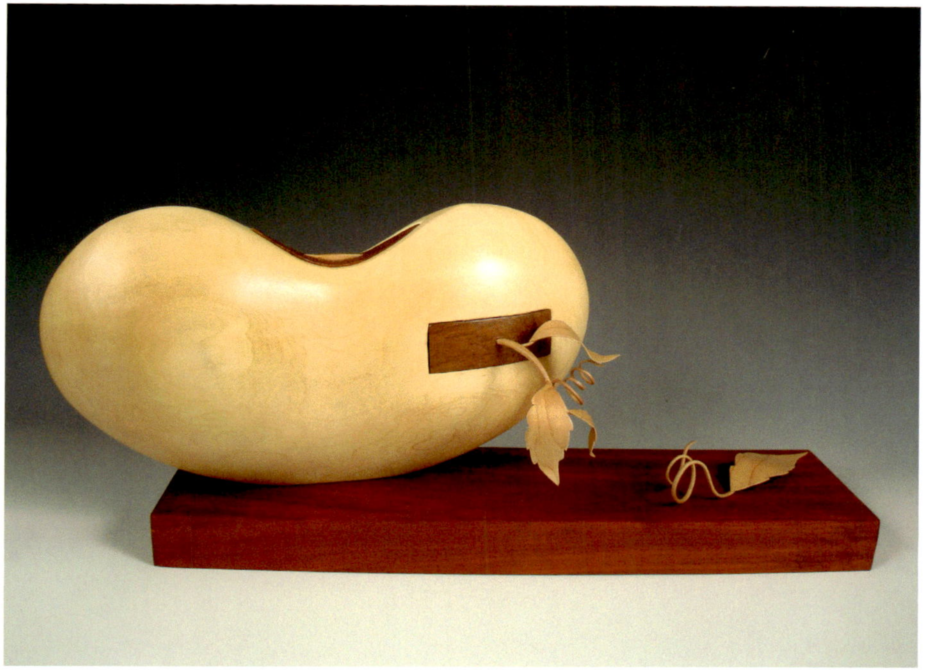

Tania Radda. *Keeping Plentiful*. 2007. Giant lima bean, basswood, compressed cherry, paduk, carved, 5 1/2" d x 25" w x 11" h. I am Brazilian and beans have always been an important part of my culture. I wanted to celebrate the Brazilian cuisine. *Photographer: Ken Manicki*

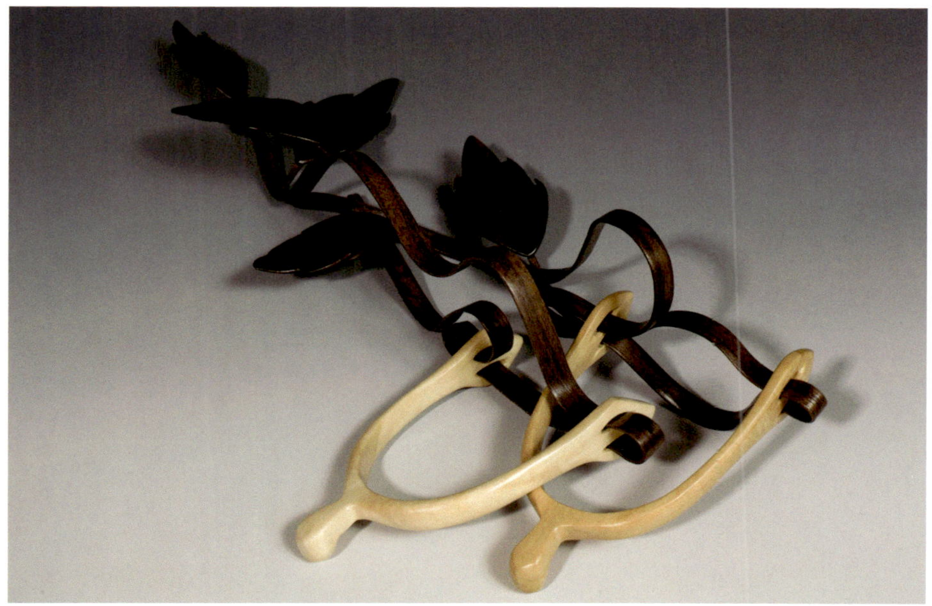

Tania Radda. *Spur of the Moment.* 2008. Basswood, compressed walnut, carved, bent, 4" h x 9" w x 18" d. This piece was created to celebrate the Kentucky Derby. Horses graze the fields and it felt natural to tie the spurs to the green fields in Kentucky. *Photographer: Ken Manicki*

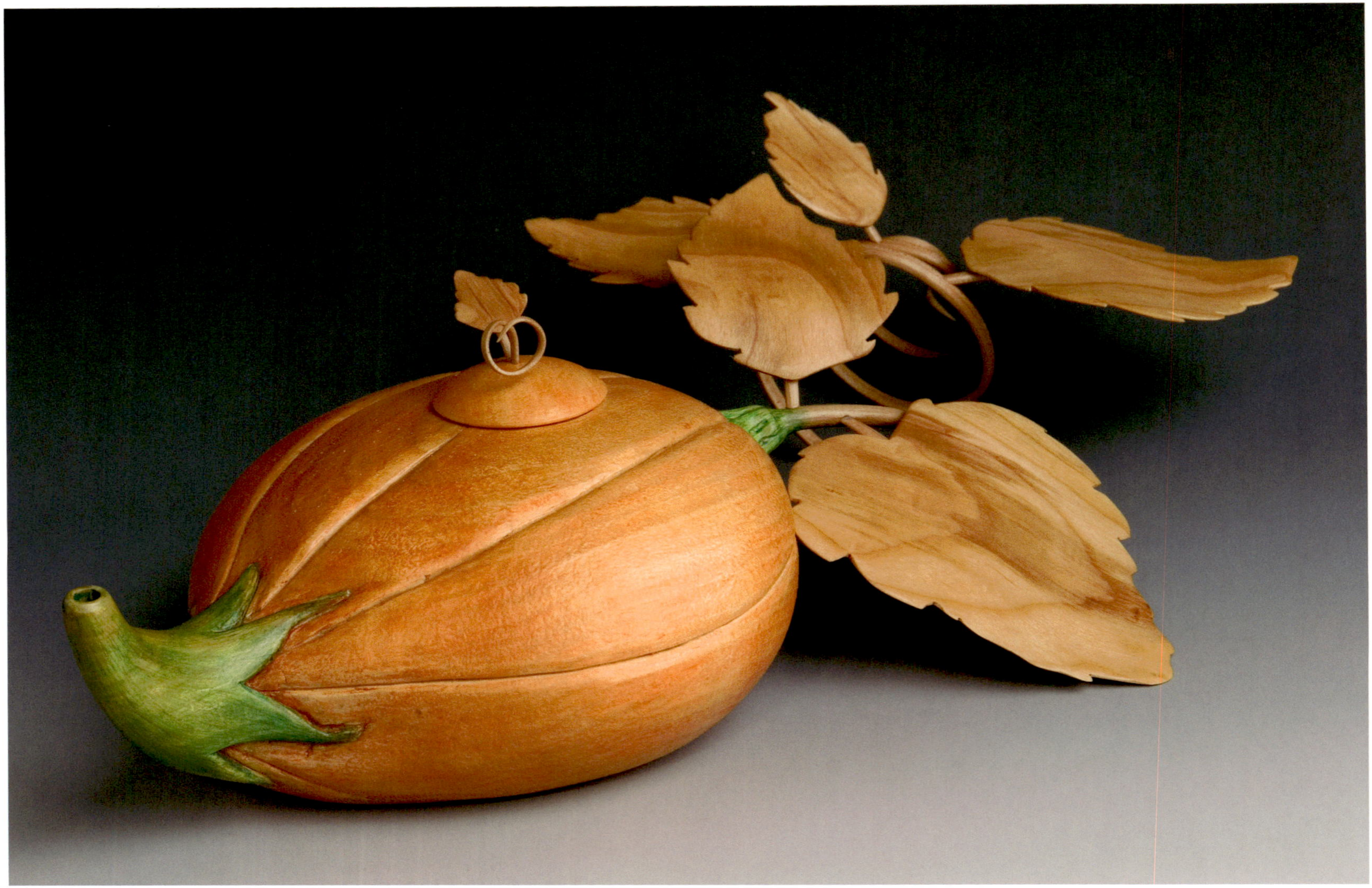

Tania Radda. *Squashed*. 2007. Basswood, compressed cherry, prismacolor pencils, turned and carved, 8" h x 16" w x 17" d. I wanted to create a fun teapot and I enjoy working with squash and pumpkins as a theme for my work. These vegetables are fun and come in a variety of shapes. I wanted to create a pumpkin that had been squashed as a play of words. *Photographer: Ken Manicki*

KALMAN RADVANYI

Queensland, Australia, www.radvanyi.com

Artist's Statement

As a self-taught artist I was born into an artistic family of painters and master craftsman. Learning cabinet making under my father and combining skills from jewelry and gemstone design, I was able to take marquetry into a new realm.

My work is strictly hand-made, seamlessly utilizing ancient techniques to reach the highest level of marquetry. My artwork takes up to eighteen months to complete, incorporating countless pieces of wood and up to 130 types of natural timbers, some over a millennium old.

I see myself as a painter. "I paint with wood." I perceive the finished picture long before I begin; every type of wood, every shade. A painter has to mix paint to accommodate he's ideas, whereas in marquetry the appropriate timber has to be found, the perfect grain, the perfect knot, the perfect shade, so that everything accommodates a perfect result.

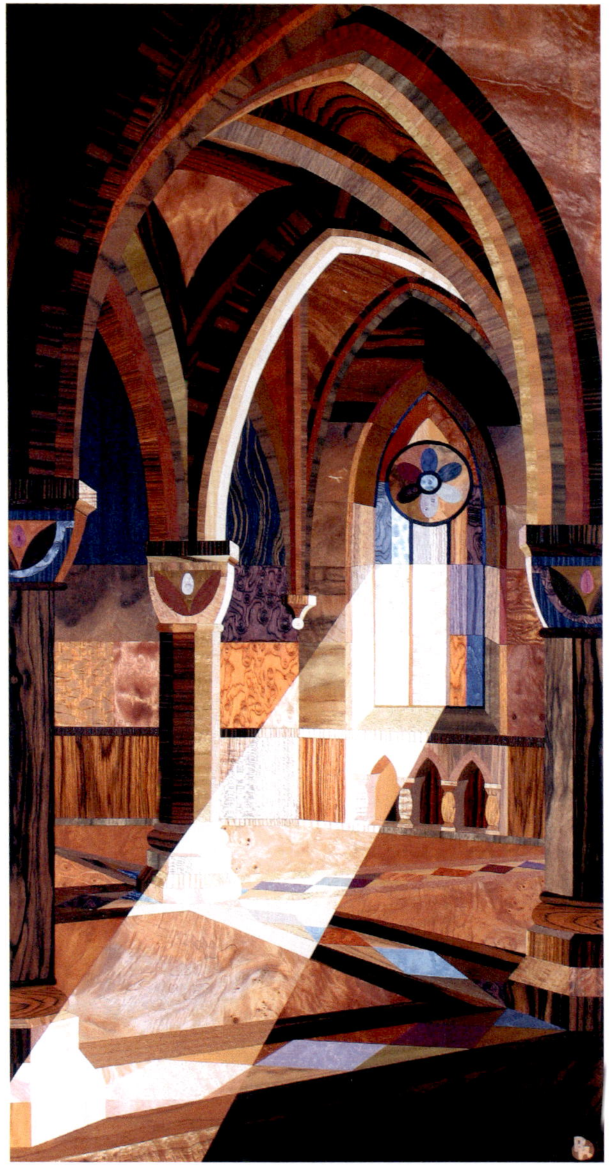

Kalman Radvanyi. *Emerald Cathedral.* Marquetry, 18" x 35".

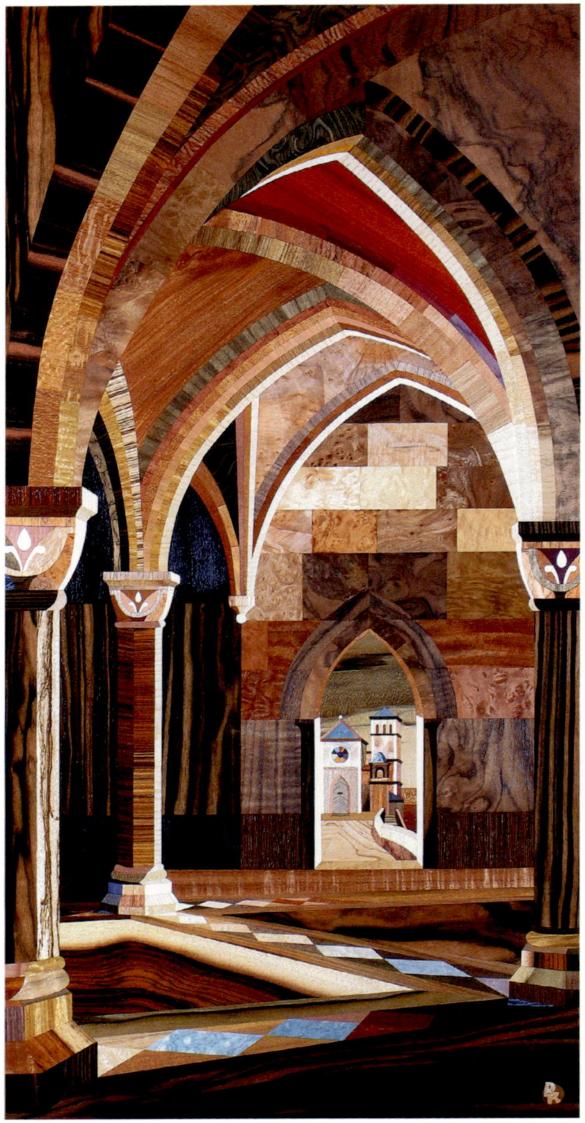

Kalman Radvanyi. *Gothic Castle.* Marquetry, 18" x 35".

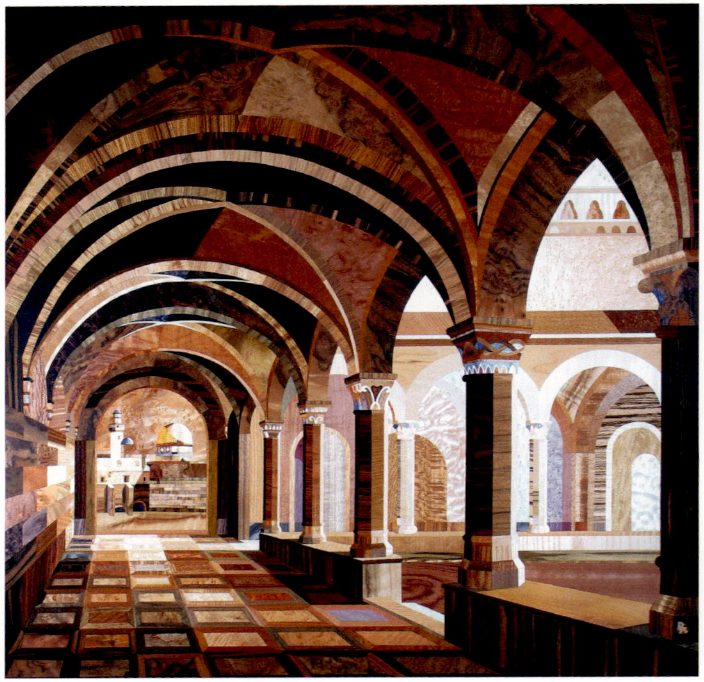

Kalman Radvanyi. *Jerusalem.* Marquetry, 35" x 35".

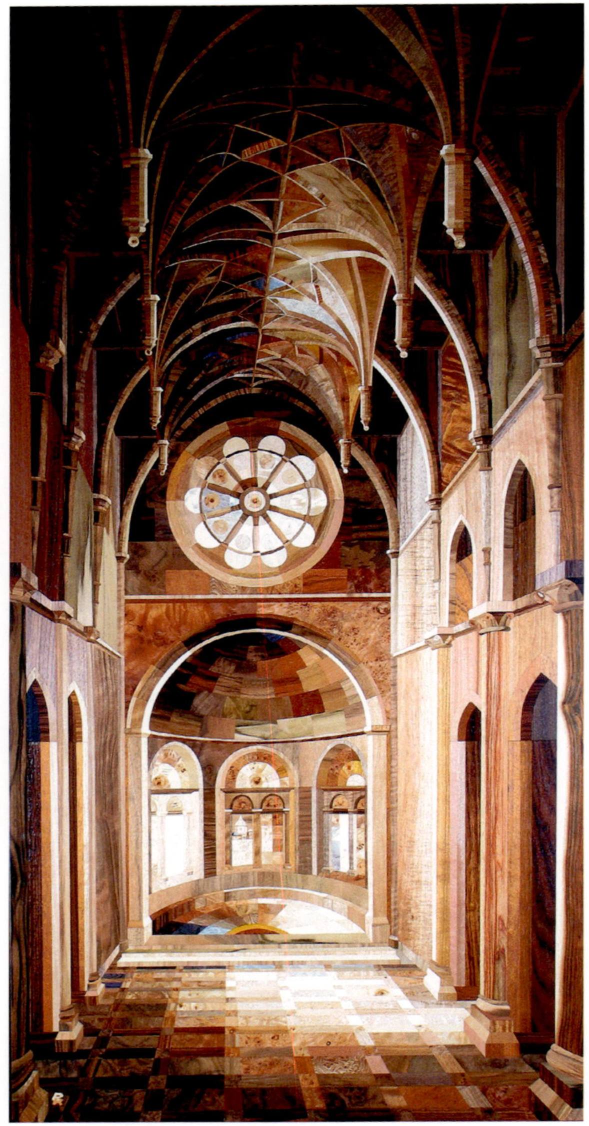

Kalman Radvanyi. *Oxford Castle.* Marquetry, 63" x 35".

Mark Rehmar

O'Brien, Oregon, mail@mrstudio.com

Artist's Statement

My work includes functional objects ranging from small occasional boxes to large furniture items including desks and dining sets. My designs, evolving over the years, have increasingly stressed gentle curves with subtle relations to each other, incorporating an increasing sense of line to complement the rare, highly figured solid woods and veneers I use.

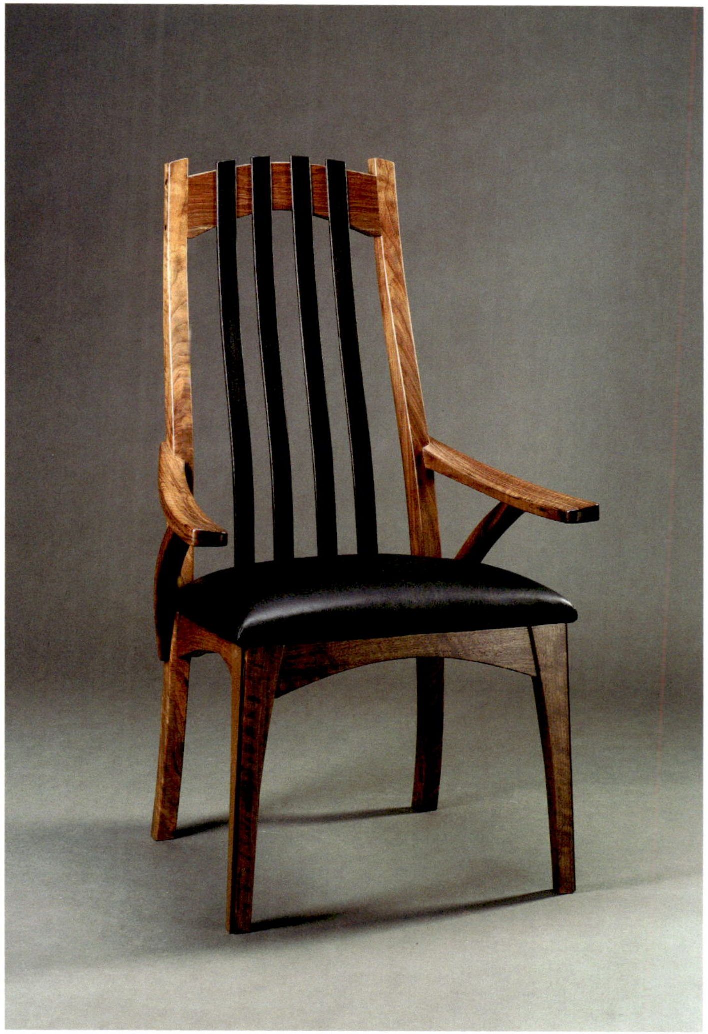

Mark Rehmar. Walnut Arm Chair. Walnut, ebonized poplar, ebony, leather upholstery, finished with catalyzed lacquer, 25" w x 21" deep x 42" h. *Photo credit: Rob Jaffe*

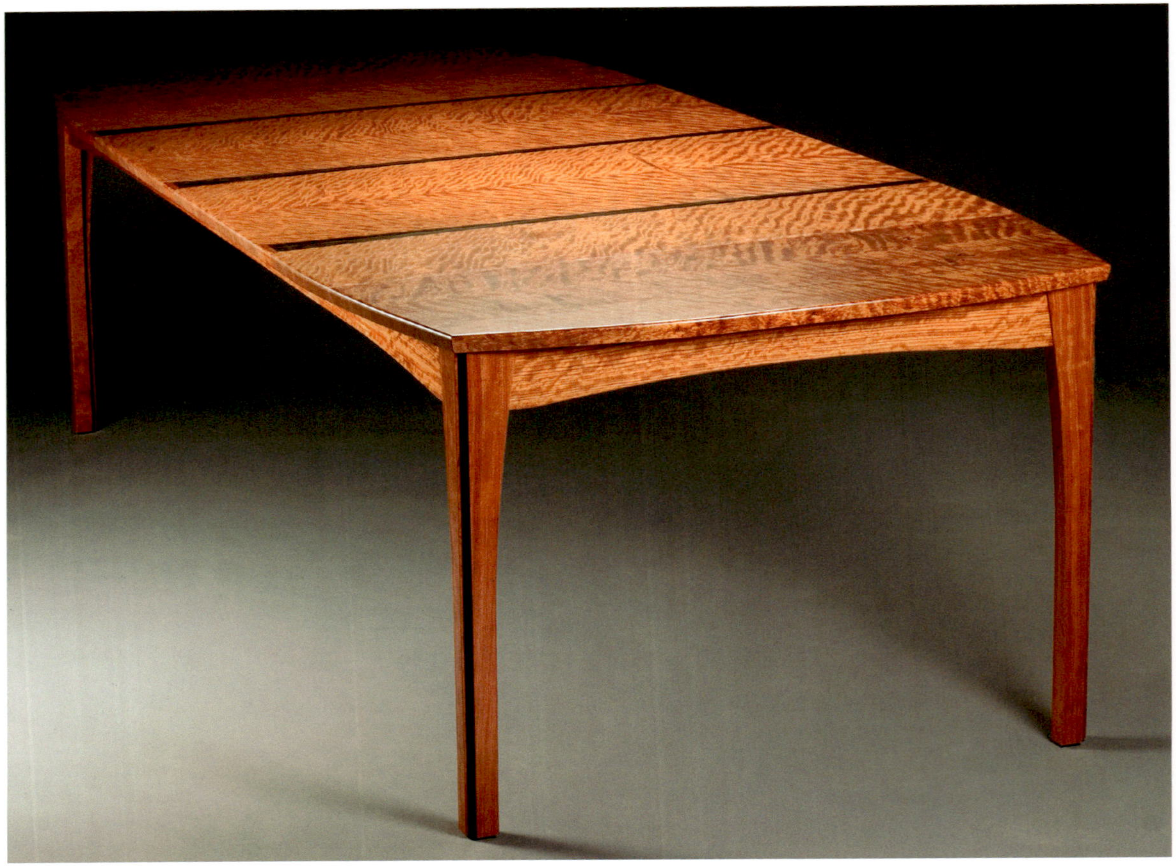

Mark Rehmar. Two Leaf Dining Table. Curly bubinga, ebony, rosewood. The main wood is a matching set of rare figured bubinga. Each leaf provides for a seating at the table. The curved ebony inlays complement the curves of the sides of the table, and resolve the tension that the table curves create. Finished with catalyzed lacquer. 104" l x 43" w x 29" h.

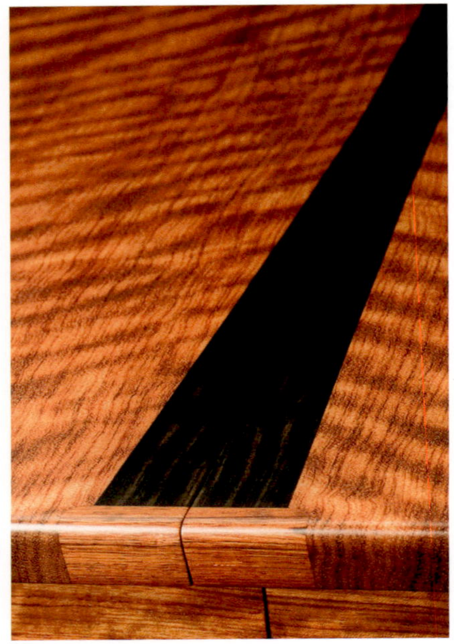

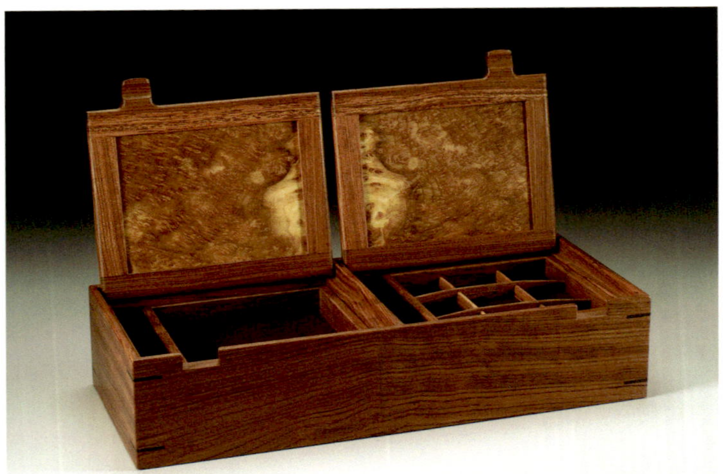

Mark Rehmar. *His 'n Her Jewelry Box*. Bubinga, redwood burl veneer, wenge. The two lids feature book matched panels of redwood burl veneer. Designed originally as a wedding gift, one side has two divided, removable trays and functions as a jewelry chest, while the other side, with a single deeper tray can function as a valet box. (However, as a woman who purchased one at a show recently said, "Once this gets home, this side is mine and the other side is more of mine.") Finished with pure carnauba wax over a special oil. 19" w x 8" d x 4" h. *Photo credit: Rob Jaffe*

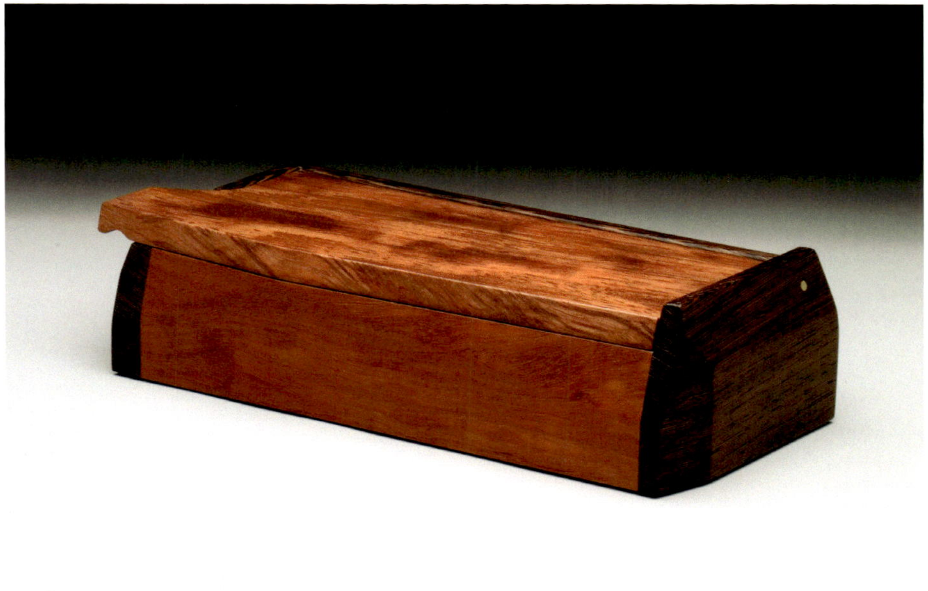

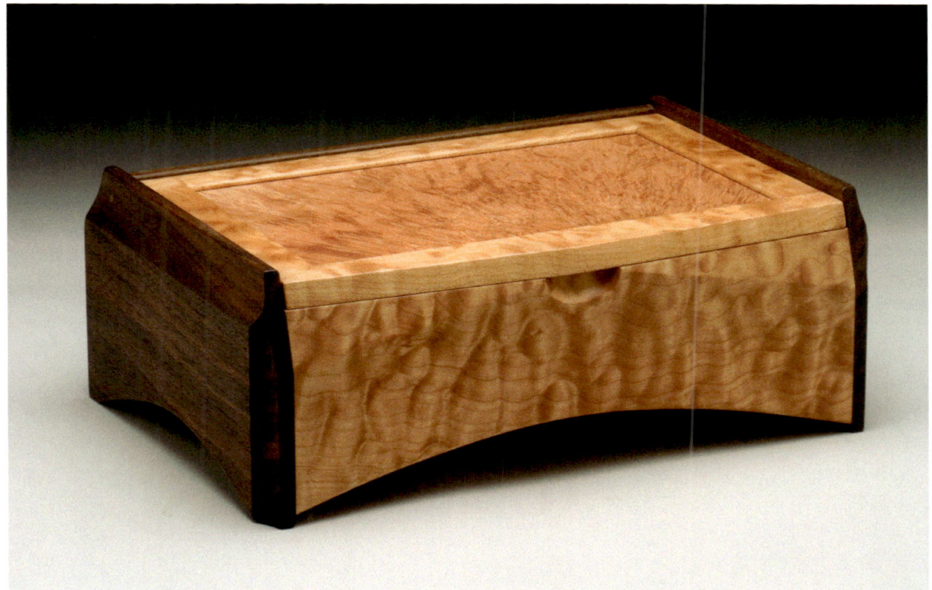

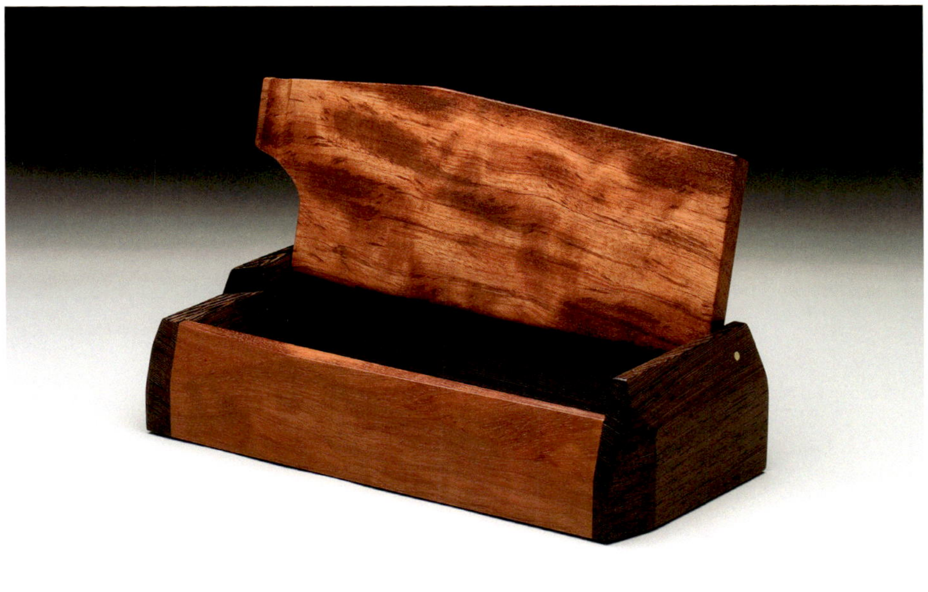

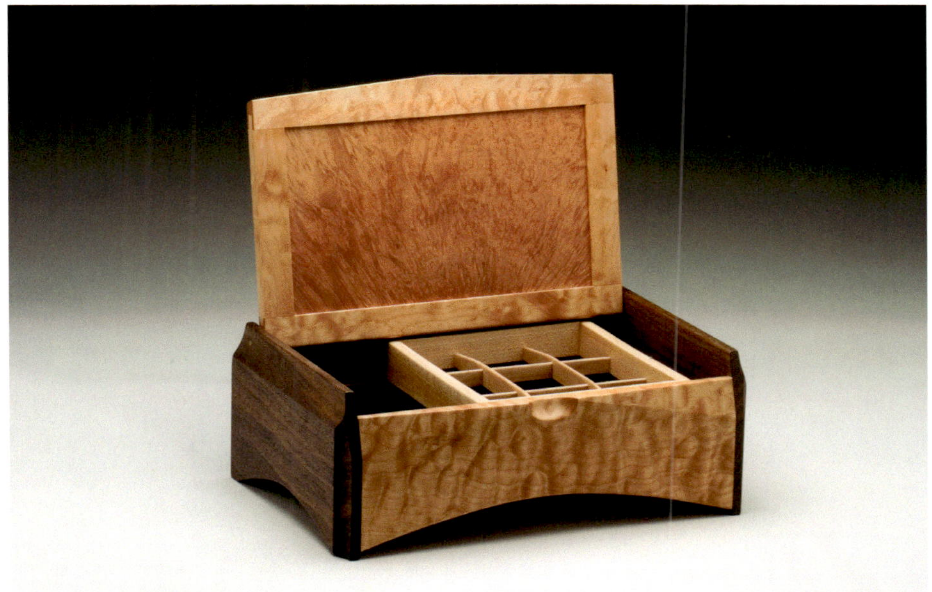

Mark Rehmar. E Series Desk Box. Bubinga and wenge, 11 1/2" x 5" x 3" high. The E Series Desk Box is a dramatically asymmetrical, smaller box. I also make it as a ring box with a padded interior for holding rings.

Mark Rehmar. E Series Jewelry Box. Curly maple and walnut, 13" x 8 1/2" x 5" high. The larger E Series Jewelry Box is a functional Jewelry of Valet Box (the dividers in the tray are removable).

Ken Richards

Maple Valley, Washington

Artist's Statement

When I am witness to things of beauty, I feel an inner glow, a sense of wonder. It is as if my soul is being fed. Some of these objects are made by artists, some by nature. In the work I do, I have the privilege of working with some of nature's beauty. The materials I spend my days with are works of art in themselves. I feel I have a responsibility to do justice to these materials.

I approach each project with the attitude of an artist. I am not just trying to create beautiful furniture. I want to create works of art. I draw inspiration from examples of work created during the reigns of Louis XIV and XV in France. Emile Jacques Ruhlmann also created some incredible pieces in Paris in the early 1900s. I admire the classical styles of the work created by the masters of the past, but it is what they aspired to that inspires me. They worked with the finest materials, and designed pieces that required incredible technical skill to execute. They shot for the stars.

I work alone, and every step of each project gets my personal attention. I am committed to producing the highest level of work I am capable of. It is my goal that the work I create will find a way to express some of that wonderful, soul feeding magic.

Individual Artwork

Demilune Entry Table

A very formal table for a special location, this table is one of a set of four that I made at the same time. I will often do small sets of the same design – but make them from different materials. I enjoy seeing the different personalities the materials bring to the pieces. This is some beautiful imbuya with a rare "pomele" figure. The figured maple was challenging to carve, but I really enjoy the striking contrast of the white maple against the dark brown imbuya.

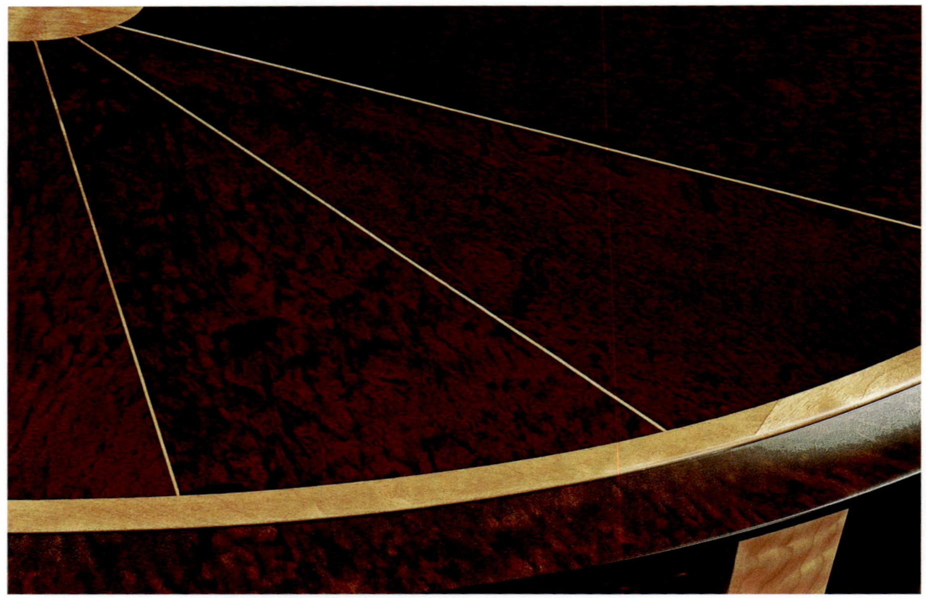

Ken Richards. Demilune Entry Table. Figured imbuya, figured maple, 42" w x 31" h x 14" d. *Photographer: Robert L. McCrory* (above and opposite page)

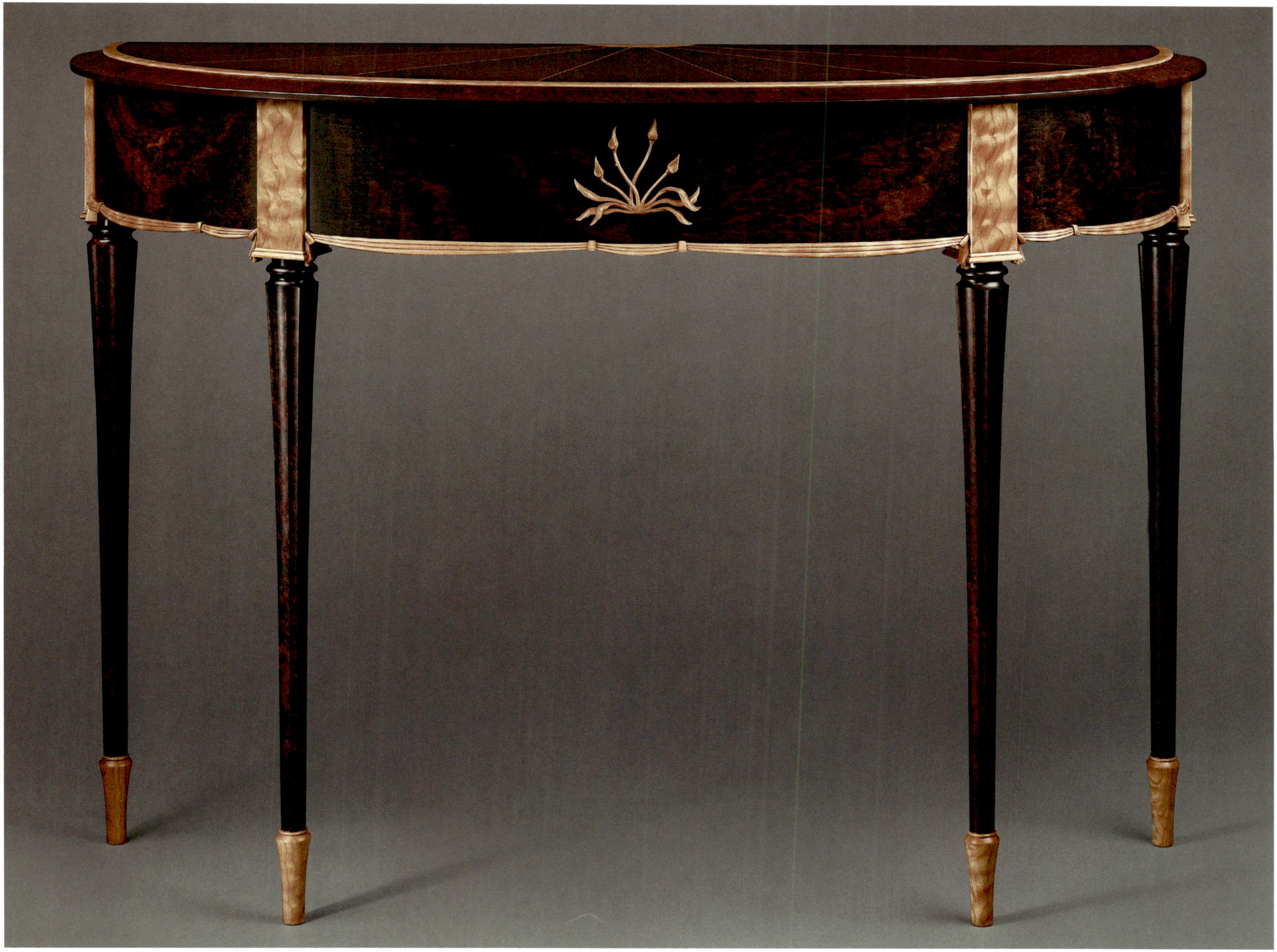

Breakfront Showcase

This cabinet could be used to display many things, but my focus when I designed it was to create a piece that could really show off beautiful art glass.

Both the outside and the center cabinet have low voltage halogen lighting – top and bottom. Upper and lower lights are independently controlled by dimmer switches located in the upper right drawer. Glass shelving is fully adjustable and additional shelving was provided for displaying smaller items. The piece is detailed with lots of fine beading and raised panels. Ebony carvings are set into the corners of the glass doors and the lower ebony molding is detailed with carved and turned components. All drawers are hand dovetailed. Drawer and door pulls are carved ebony pendants mounted to posts and plates I fabricated from solid brass. All six legs are fluted and have turned ebony feet.

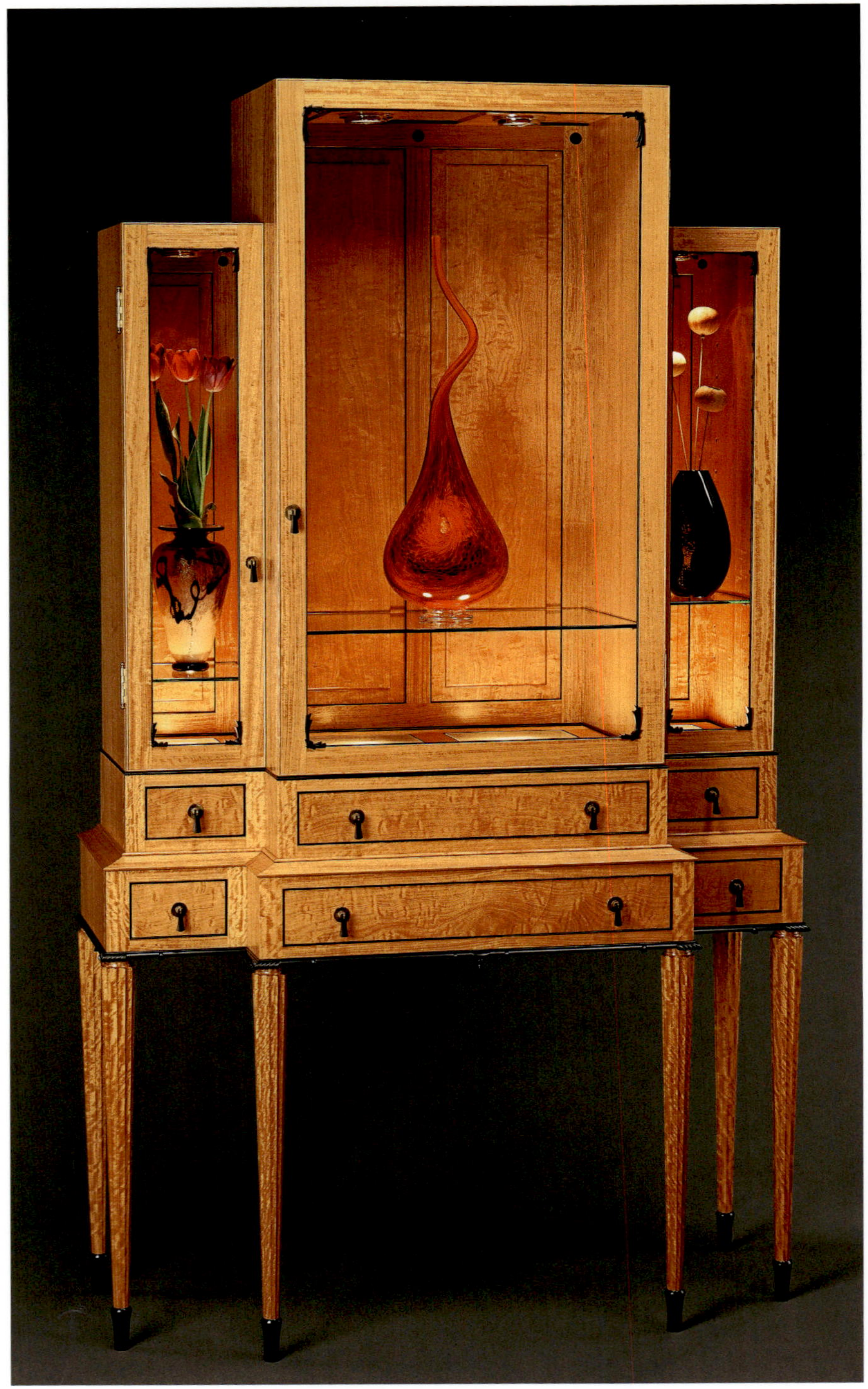

Ken Richards. Breakfront Showcase. Figured Ceylon satinwood, ebony, brass, 42" w x 74" h x 17" D. *Photographer: Robert L. McCrory*

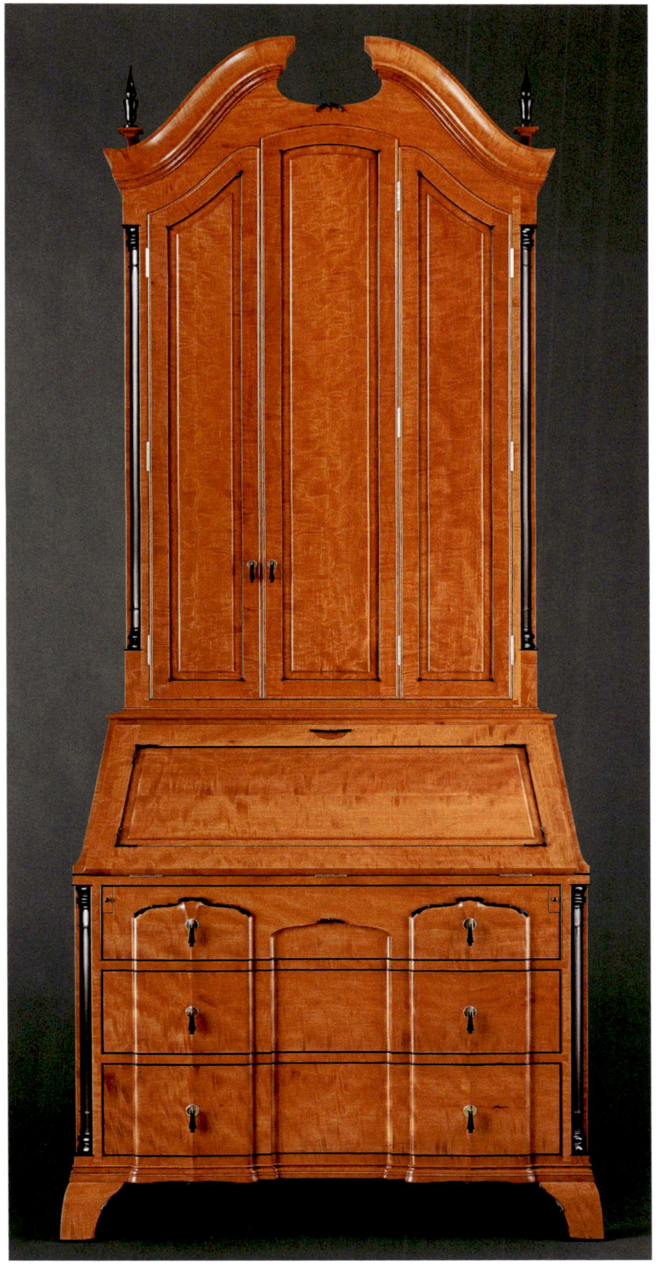

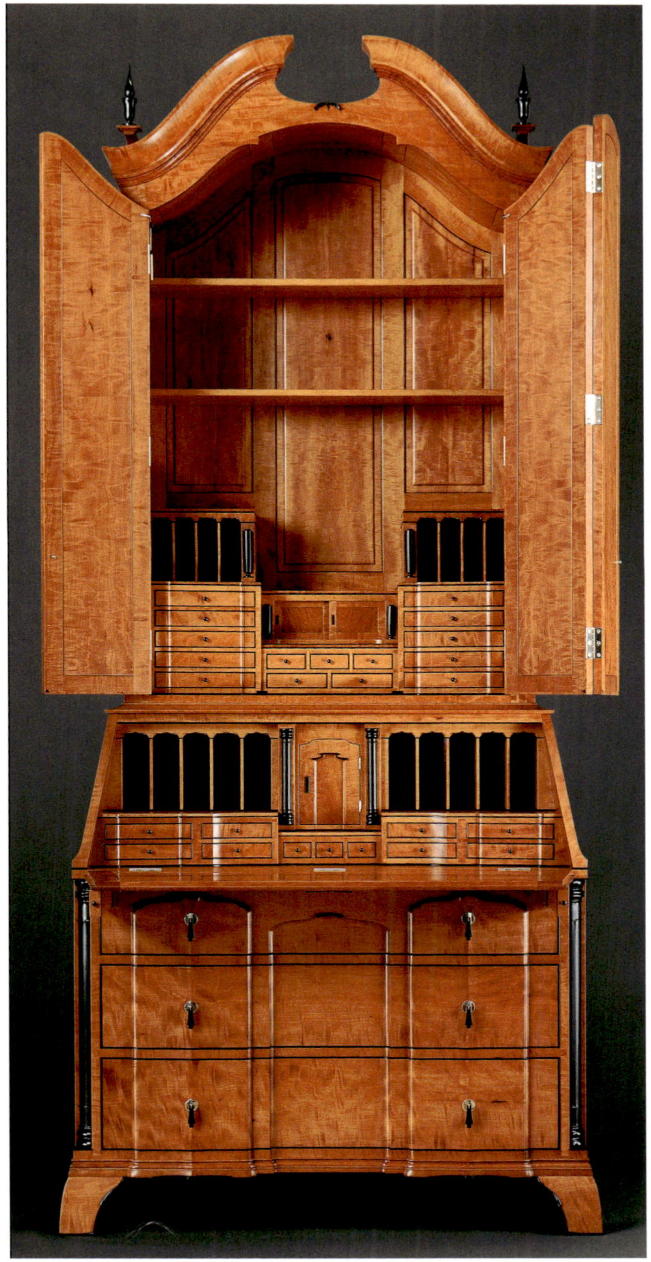

Secretary

A traditional Secretary consists of a lower chest of drawers, middle fall front desk, and upper bookcase. They are considered by many to be the highpoint in the art of furniture making. Creating a piece that brought my contemporary aesthetic to this traditional form was a challenge I looked forward to for many years. When I received a commission for just such a piece, I couldn't resist – I had to do two.

I had a large log of figured European pear in my lumber collection. My customer chose that as the main material for his. Ebony was the obvious choice as an accent material. I also had some special figured African mahogany in stock and decided to use it for the second piece, accenting the mahogany with amboyna burl – one of my favorites. Both pieces are trimmed with sterling silver hardware that was clear coated to prevent tarnishing.

The Secretaries stand close to 9' tall, and are filled with small drawers, pigeon holes, detail carvings, and secret compartments. Much of the 3,000 hours put into each of them was spent on fine detail work. I think they are a good example of what can be achieved when you are given enough time to do something really special. The biggest problem is deciding whether to display them with the doors closed – or open.

Ken Richards. Secretary. Figured European pear, ebony, sterling silver, 44" w x 104" h x 25" d. *Photographer: Robert L. McCrory*

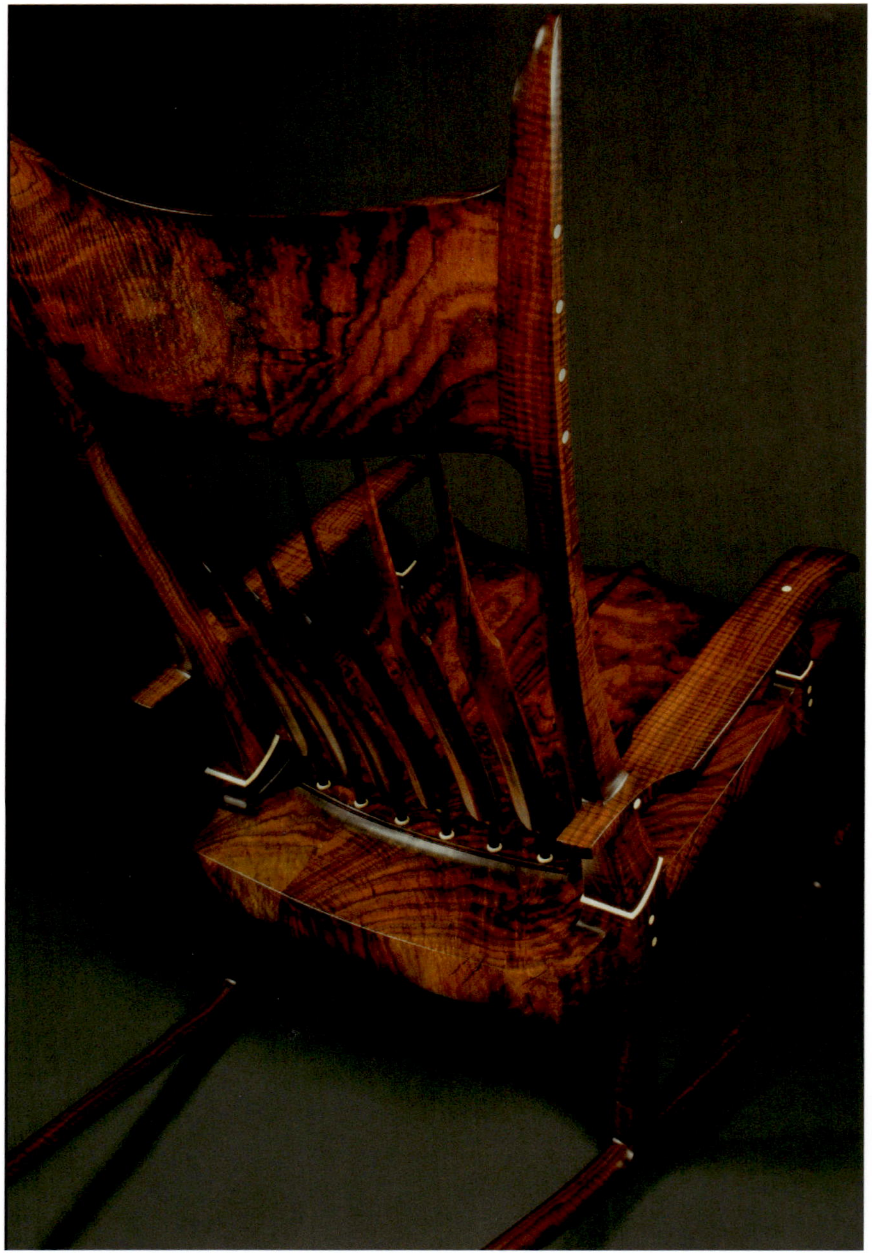

Rocking Chair

The stock for this chair came from two large, thick crotch slabs. The extra thickness (over 3 1/4") allowed me to sculpt more flowing lines and shapes than thinner stock allows. The seat, for instance, has a serpentine shape when viewed from the side and the raised platform at the base of the spindles is sculpted from the same block. The flowing curves and bulbous shape of the crest rail is another area that would not have been possible to create with thinner stock. I appreciate the aesthetics of all the curves but I am also very happy with the level of comfort they bring to the chair. Watching the reactions of people when they sit in it for the first time has been a real pleasure.

The other thing that made these slabs so special is the incredible color and figure. I have had the chair in my home by a window – when the sun shines on it the wood just dances. Very beautiful.

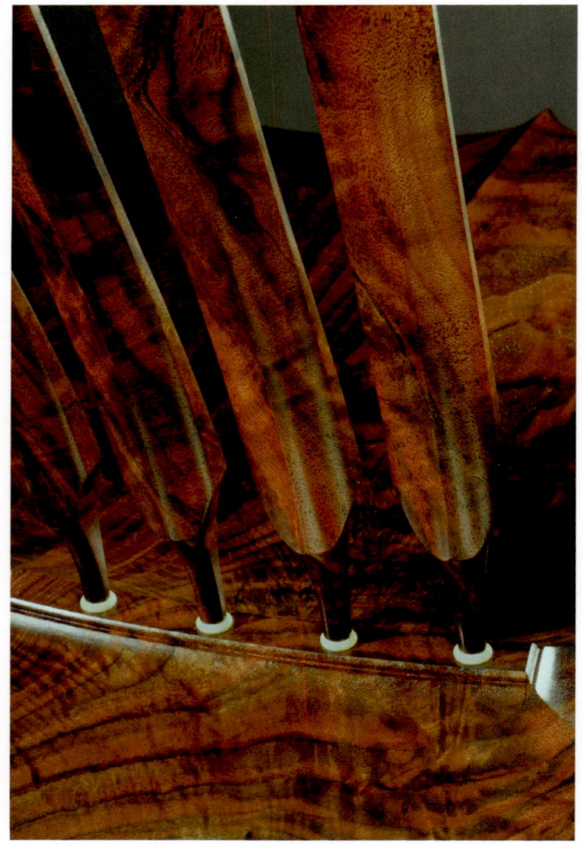

Ken Richards. Rocking Chair. Figured claro walnut, holly, 25" w x 50" h x 45" l.

Joey Richardson

Lincolnshire, England, joeyjoey@btinternet.com

Artist's Statement

Professionally I feel very fortunate to be a female in what is essentially a man's world of woodturning. My style incorporates both the more feminine – the delicate and beautiful – and the more masculine – the big and bold. Combined, these two aspects fully encapsulate and make the most striking use of wood's tactile beauty.

All my pieces are created with passion, and each has its own history and heart. Whenever possible, I use reclaimed local timber. Each piece is individually handcrafted on a lathe, with the cutting, shaping, and sanding all controlled by eye, which gives great originality. Extra diversity is added by my use of piercing, carving, colour, and artwork. I feel excited and fulfilled as each unique piece of turned wood comes alive under my hands, each telling its own story, each allowing the viewer to see into the life of the piece.

Trees are a truly beautiful, vital resource, and wood art allows nature's designs to live on in our homes. Woodturning uses skills that began in the mists of antiquity, as a base for producing essential utility items. When these skills are taken beyond their utilitarian roots with creativity and imagination, and are allied with experiences and a passion from deep within the inner soul, the result transcends craft and rises into the realms of art.

For too long wood has played a supportive role to art in the form of canvas, paper, and frames. Let wood now speak for itself.

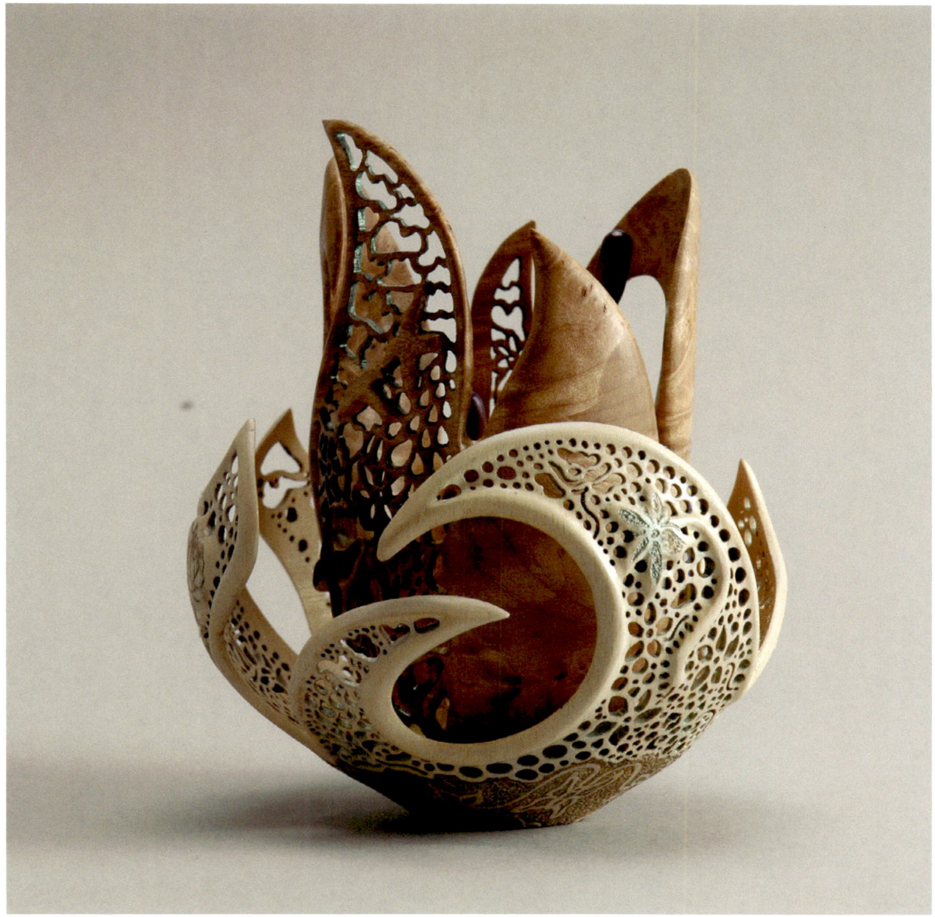

Joey Richardson. *Chance.* 2009. Burl maple, beech, acrylic colors, turned, carved, pierced, 6" x 5" x 5"

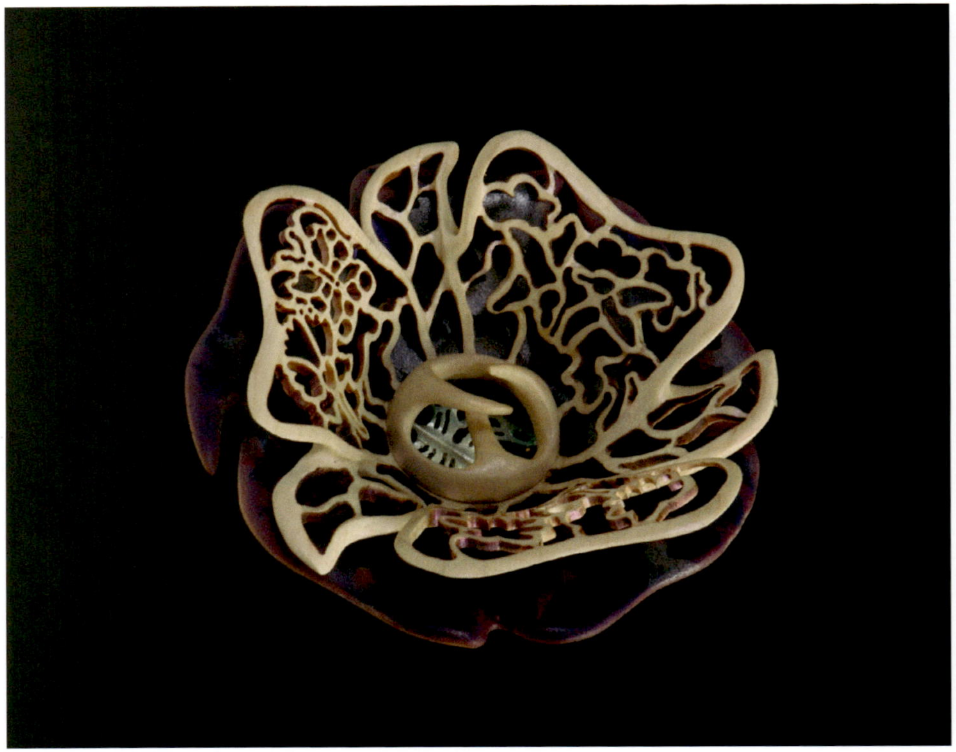

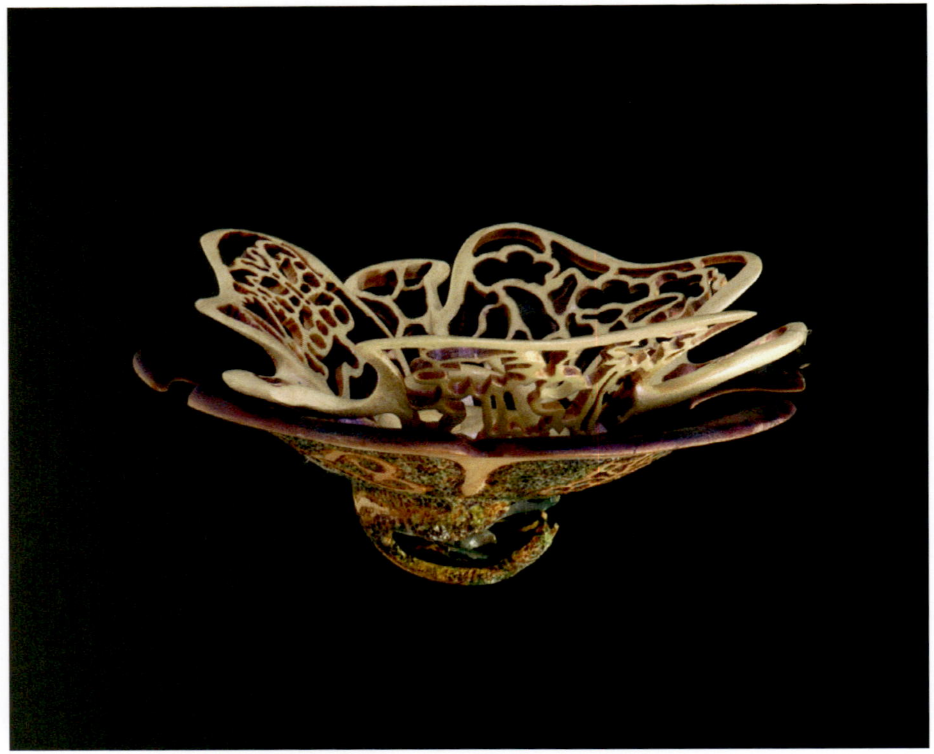

Joey Richardson. *Dancer*. 2008. Sycamore acrylic colors, turned, carved, pierced, airbrushed, 4" x 3" x 3".

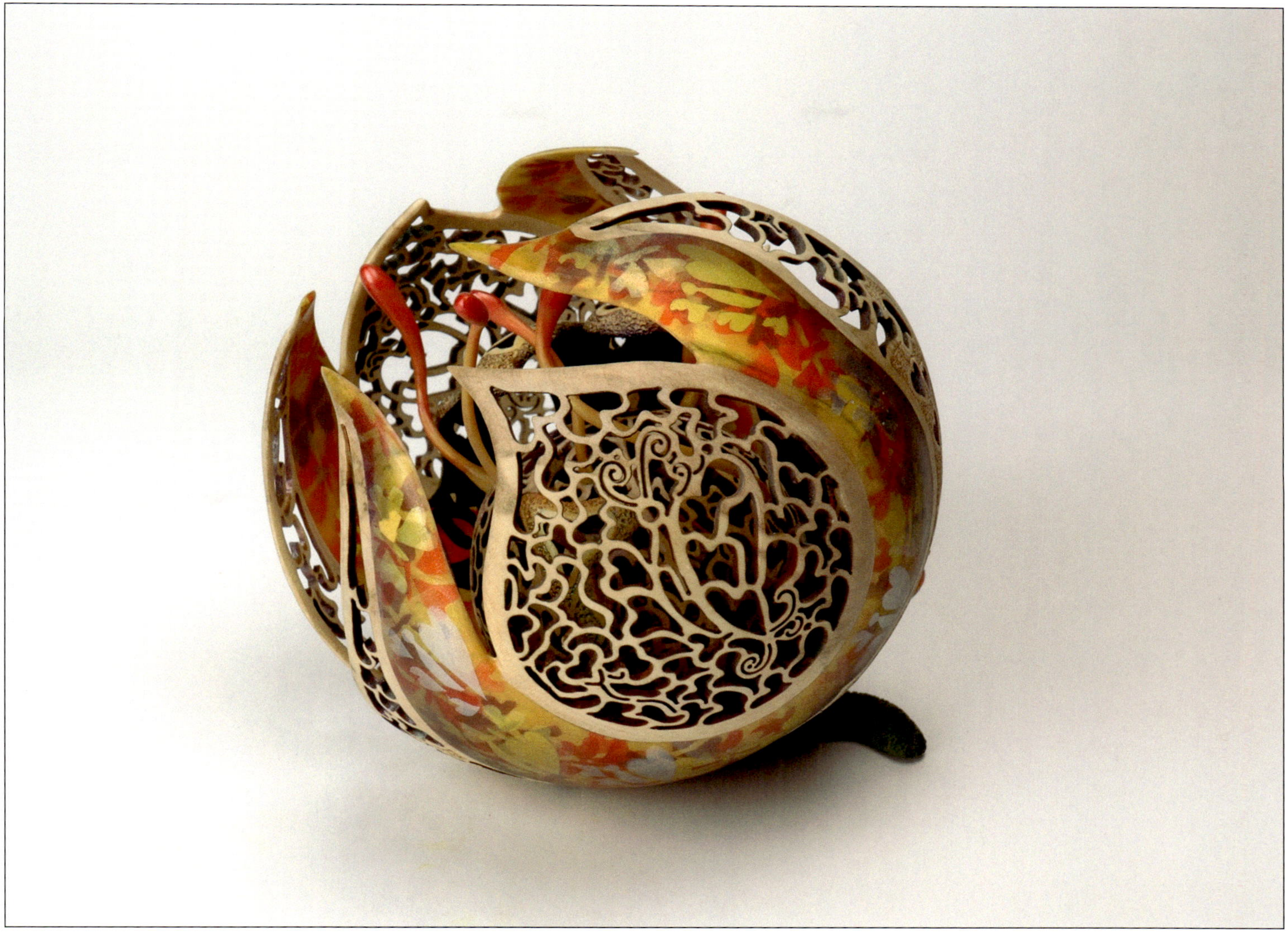

Joey Richardson. *Seed of Love*. 2009. Sycamore acrylic colors, turned, carved, pierced, airbrushed, 6" x 6" x 6".

Scott C. Reuman

Nederland, Colorado, www.conundrumdesigns.com

Artist's Statement

Creativity is the source that sustains and connects all humanity. Without it, there would be no change. With it, we are small but real gods and goddesses.

We are all artists, even if you never pick up paint and brush, chisel and hammer, or pencil and paper. Art is a way of thinking, a way of being, a way of life.

There are certain things I believe deeply: We are all artists. Like the form hidden in the stone awaiting the artist to see and release it, the same is true of the artist in each of us. The artist is there, awaiting release. The older we get, the more forceful the chiseling required, and the more intoxicating the reward.

I also believe in *reciprocity of reverence*. Applied to humans, this principle helps us feel valued, respond positively, and contribute to society. The artist/medium relationship is built of this same bond, fiber upon fiber.

These two things — the hidden art in all of us and a reverence for all things — guide me as woodworker, sculptor, painter, writer, and even in previous "lives" (biomedical engineer and physicist). In a sense, we are all very real gods and goddesses, creating each day with our eyes and minds and hands.

Certain elements of my work repeatedly appear: flowing forms, curves, the contrast of mixed materials, river imagery, and water. Wild things, diversity, human insignificance in the universe, all serve as inspiration.

My work, then, is not contained within a theme. It is instead from within; born in the seat of unconscious, heated in the forge of mind, fueled by a life of observation, and tempered by the heart of soul.

Individual Artwork

Music Stand

Used as a portfolio display, this "music stand" can also hold a dictionary, Bible, special book... Whatever it supports dances on ballerina's legs of cherry.

Can wood sing? Recorders, guitars, violins, pianos, native-American flutes, all are made with wood and one cannot deny their ability to sing. This stand raises the music to a similar level.

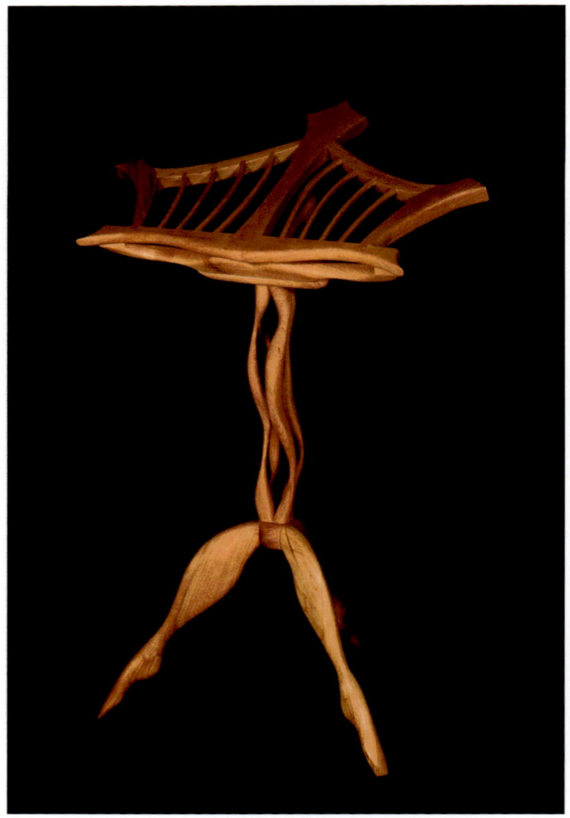

Scott C. Reuman. Music stand. 2003. Cherry, 45" x 30" x 18". © *Scott C. Reuman. Private collection*

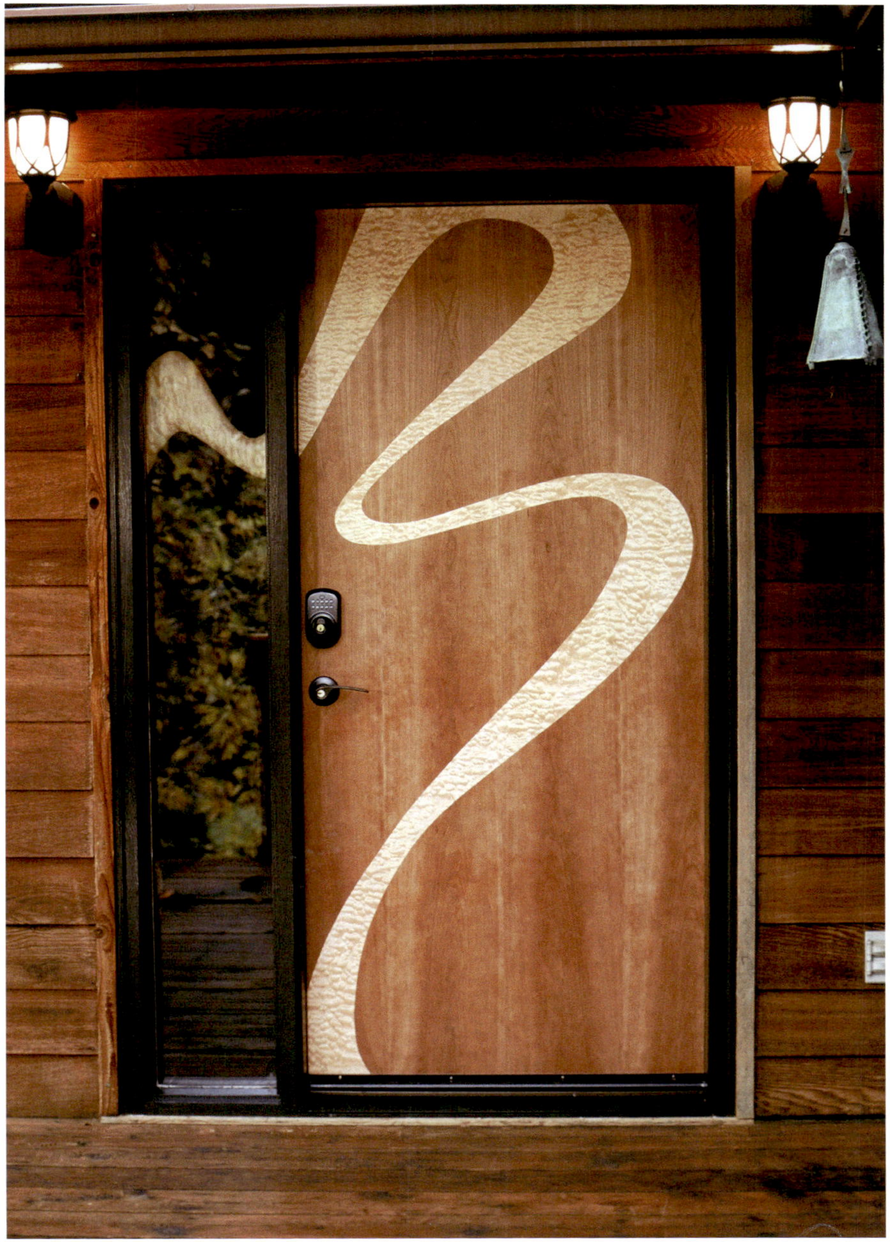

All Who Wander

All Who Wander made a common entry into an invitation. The rectilinear lines of this "normal" house are interrupted, caught in the looping freedom of the door's design. In the sidelight window, solid quilted maple continues the design off the plane of the door and into three dimensions.

When you come home from work or school or a long absence, it's nice to have the family home wave hello and greet you at the front door.

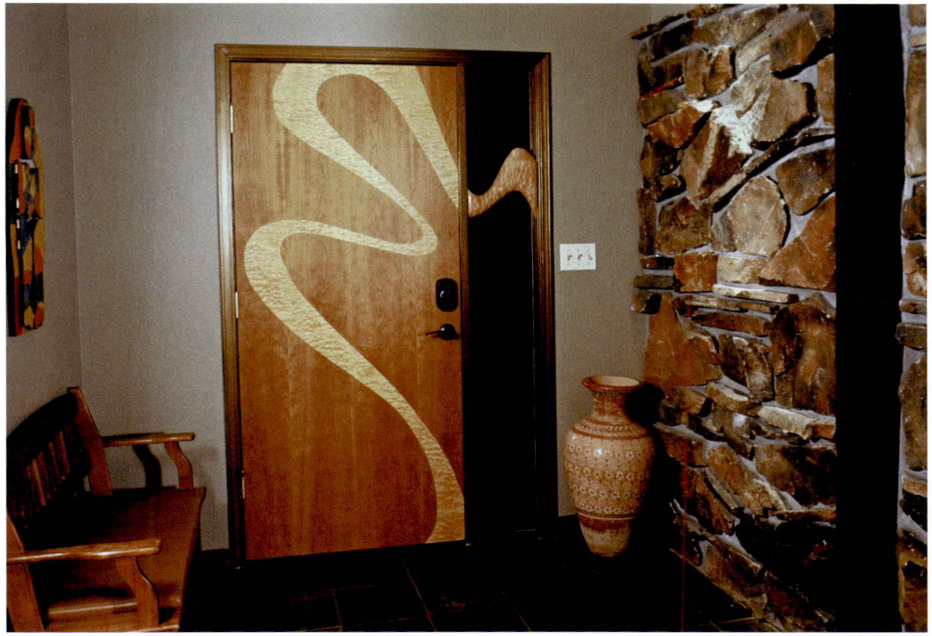

Scott C. Reuman. *All Who Wander.* 2007. Cherry, quilted maple, 84" x 60" x 6". © *Scott C. Reuman. Private collection*

Entertainment Center with River Panel

Built to house stereo and video equipment, the drawers are sized for CDs and DVDs. The River Panel is attached to the wall behind, thus "floats" visually.

How do you build curves into otherwise straight-edged rooms? That was the challenge I gave myself for this commission for a Boulder, Colorado, family. Simultaneously, the form must also serve its function: holding a wide-screen TV and all the electronics and disks and game controllers associated with it. Function. Beauty. Curves in straights. The blue "rivers" meander across the sculpted spherical tabletop support. The bolted center appears to float between the cases sitting solidly on the floor to either side.

The bent parts of the cases are all handmade plywood with cherry and lacewood veneers. This permitted the reveal between drawers to be the same distance in all places.

The client's joy was half the payment.

Scott C. Reuman. Entertainment Center with River Panel (Part of River Series^{tm}). 2008. Cherry, lacewood, pine, dyed resin, 36" x 163" x 28". © *Scott C. Reuman/John Robledo. Private collection*

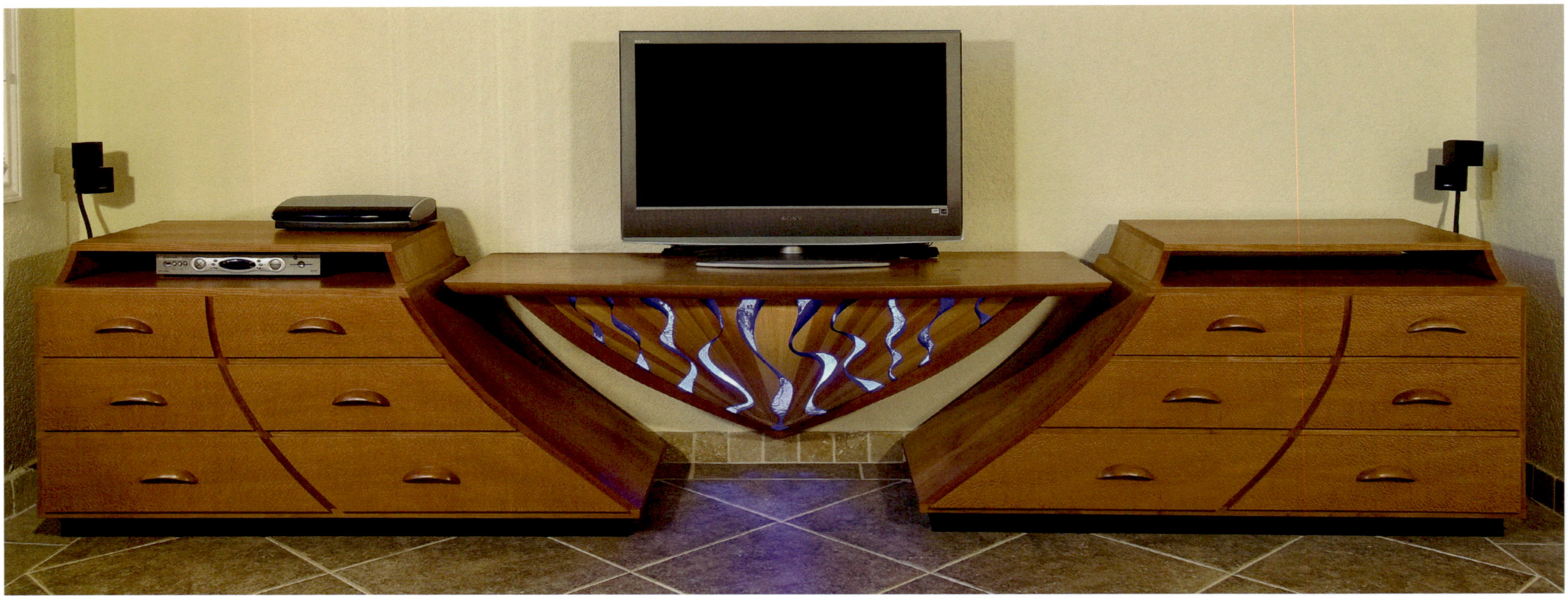

Flight of Stairs

Like salmon swimming upstream to spawn against all odds, this multi-flight sculpture swims its way from the basement to the third floor, nearly 65' total length.

With a stair handrail, there is a functional need and a legal need as defined in the building codes. Working art into the codes can be a challenge. With the completion of this job the County inspector said, "Wow," as he signed the certificate of occupancy.

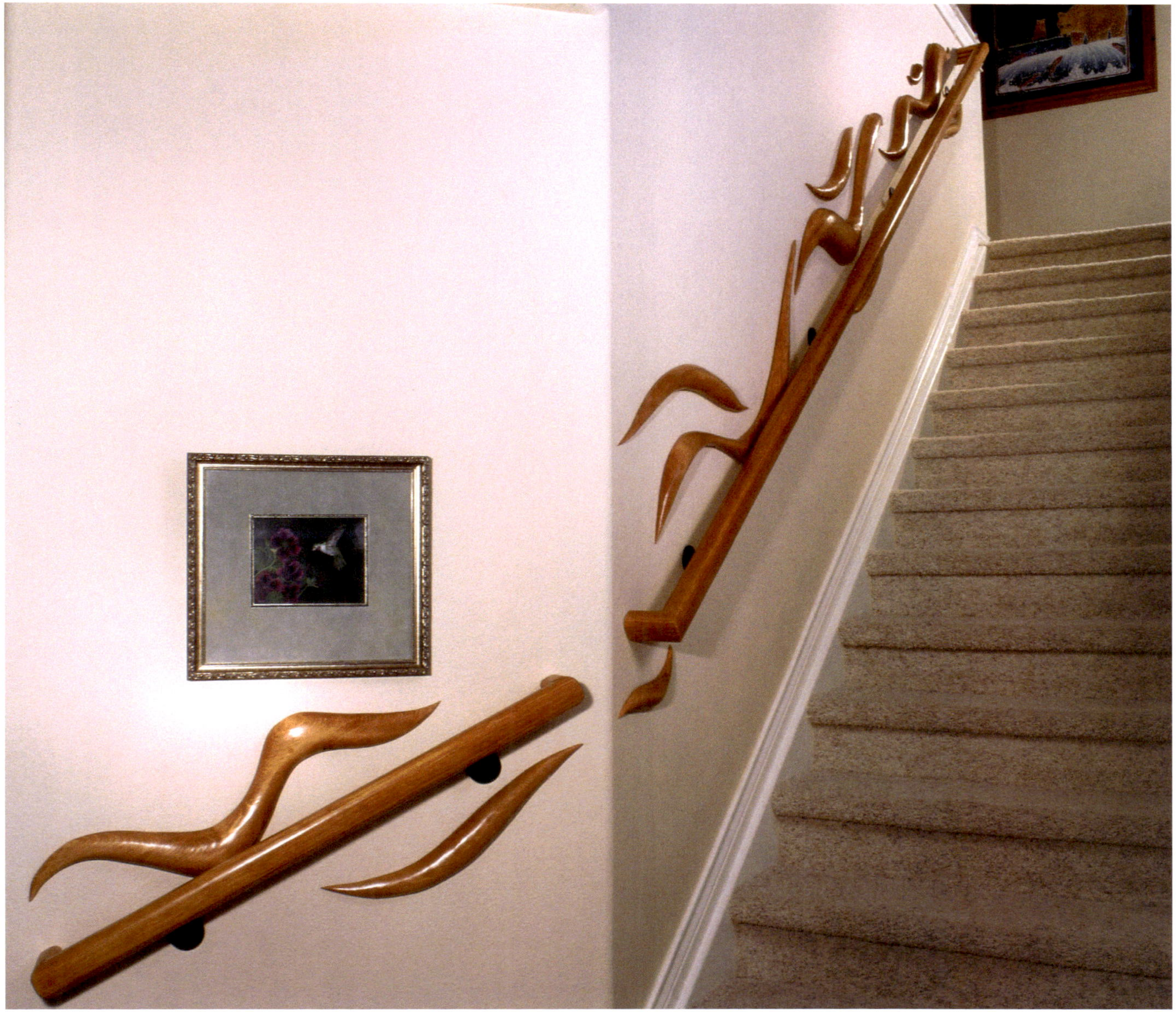

Scott C. Reuman. Flight of Stairs. 2009. Stain, varnish, sculptural handrail actually covers three flights of stairs, about 65' in total length. © *Scott C. Reuman. Private collection*

Jo R. Roessler

www.nojodesign.com

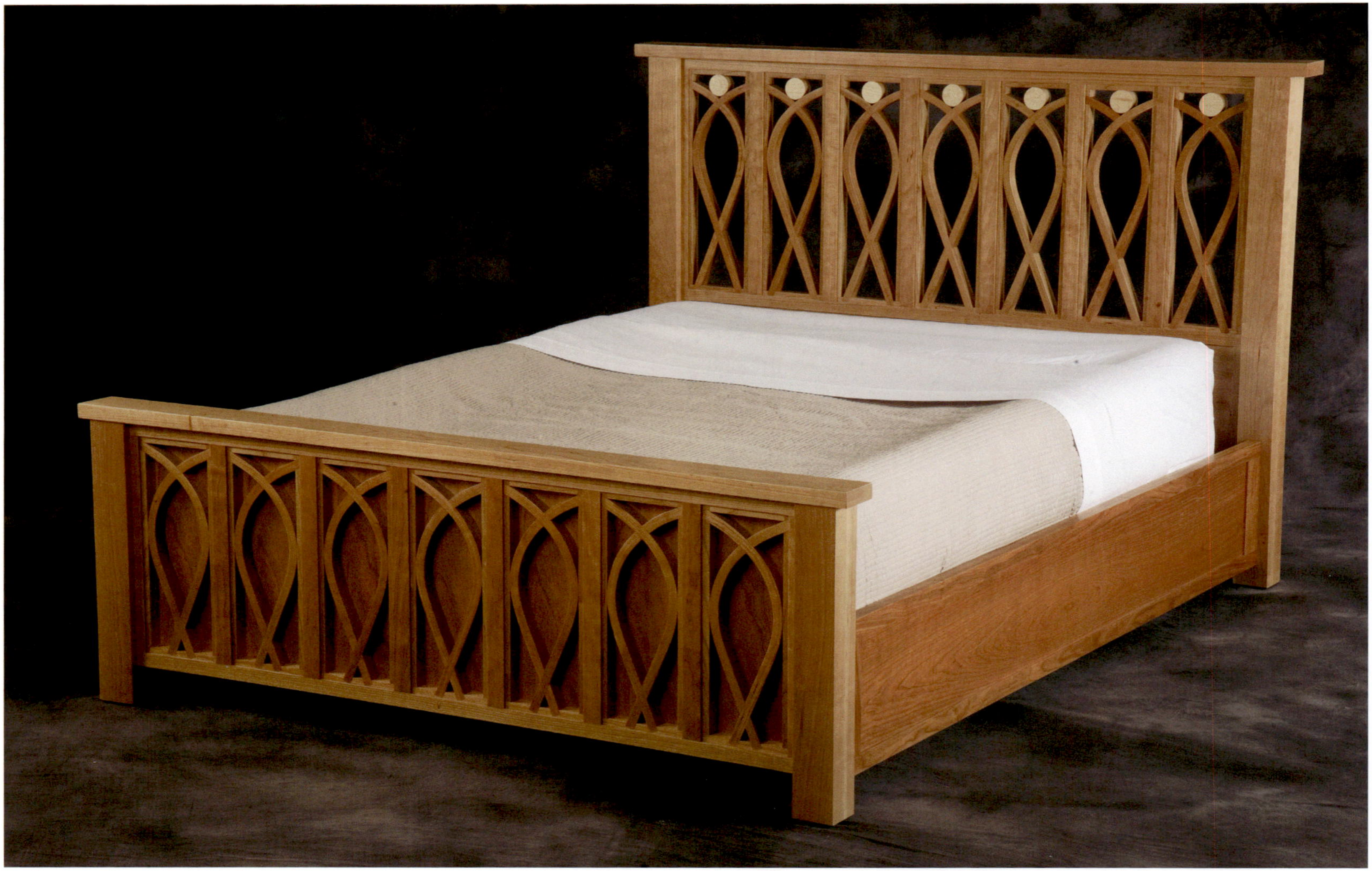

Jo R. Roessler. *Elaine's Bed.* Cherry and birdseye maple, 86" x 76" x 45".

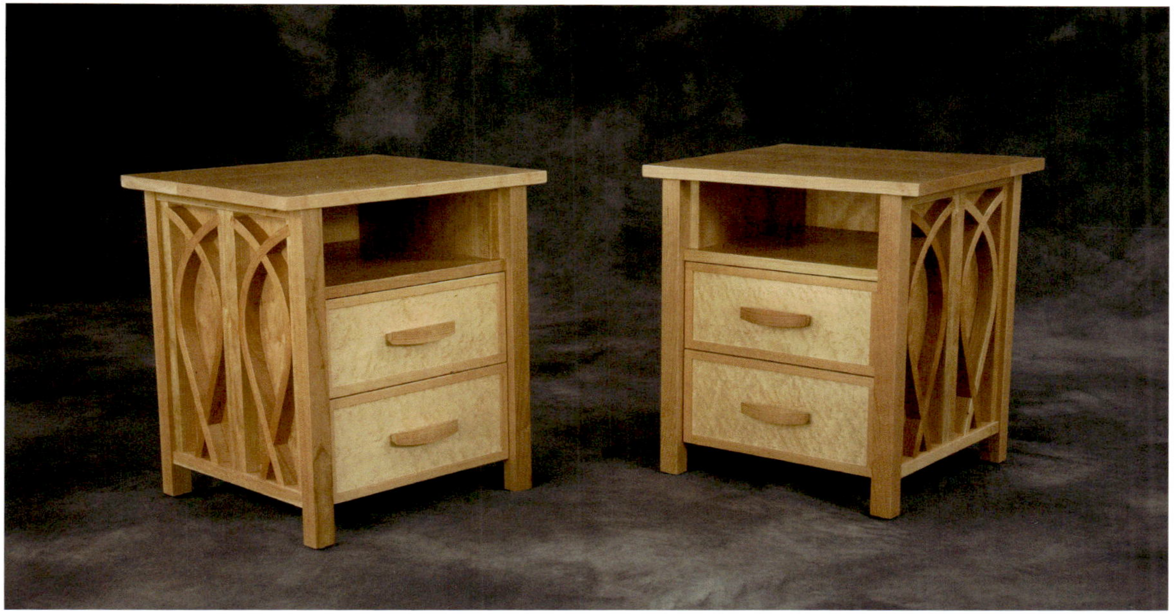

Jo R. Roessler. *Elaine's Beside Tables*. Cherry and birdseye maple, 22" x 20" x 24".

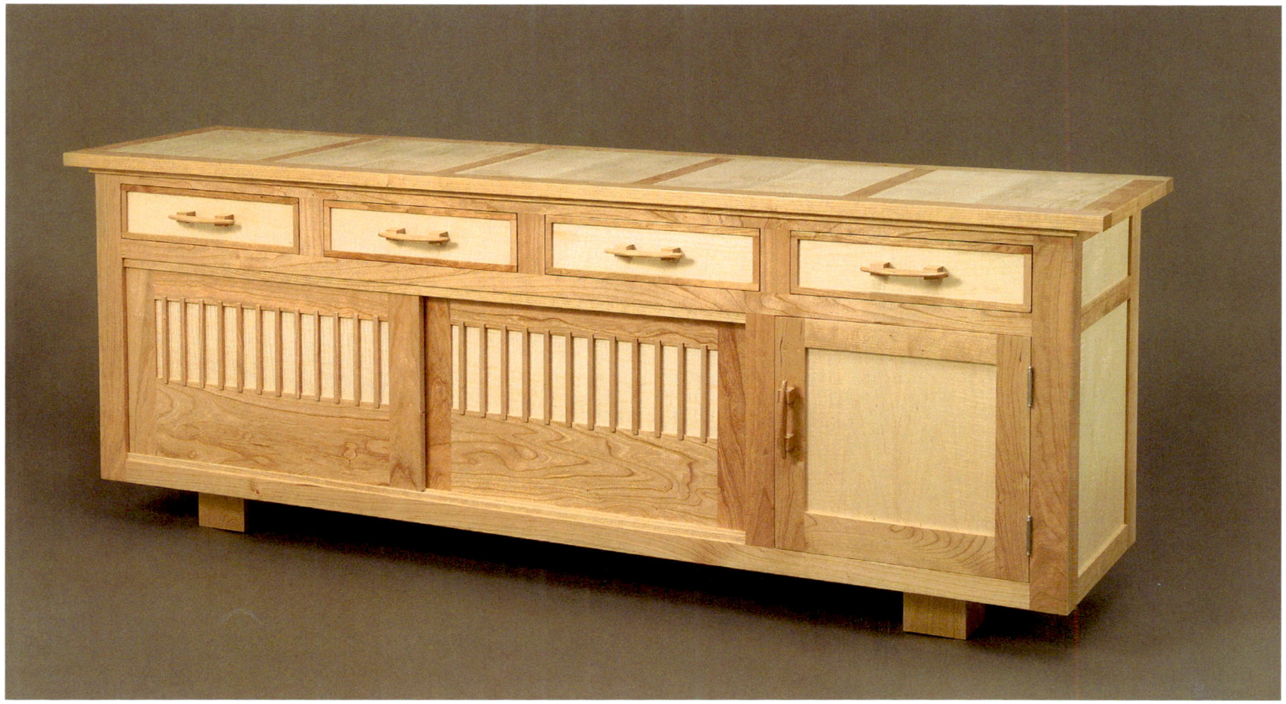

Jo R. Roessler. Studio Sideboard. Cherry and curly maple, 72" x 20" x 30".

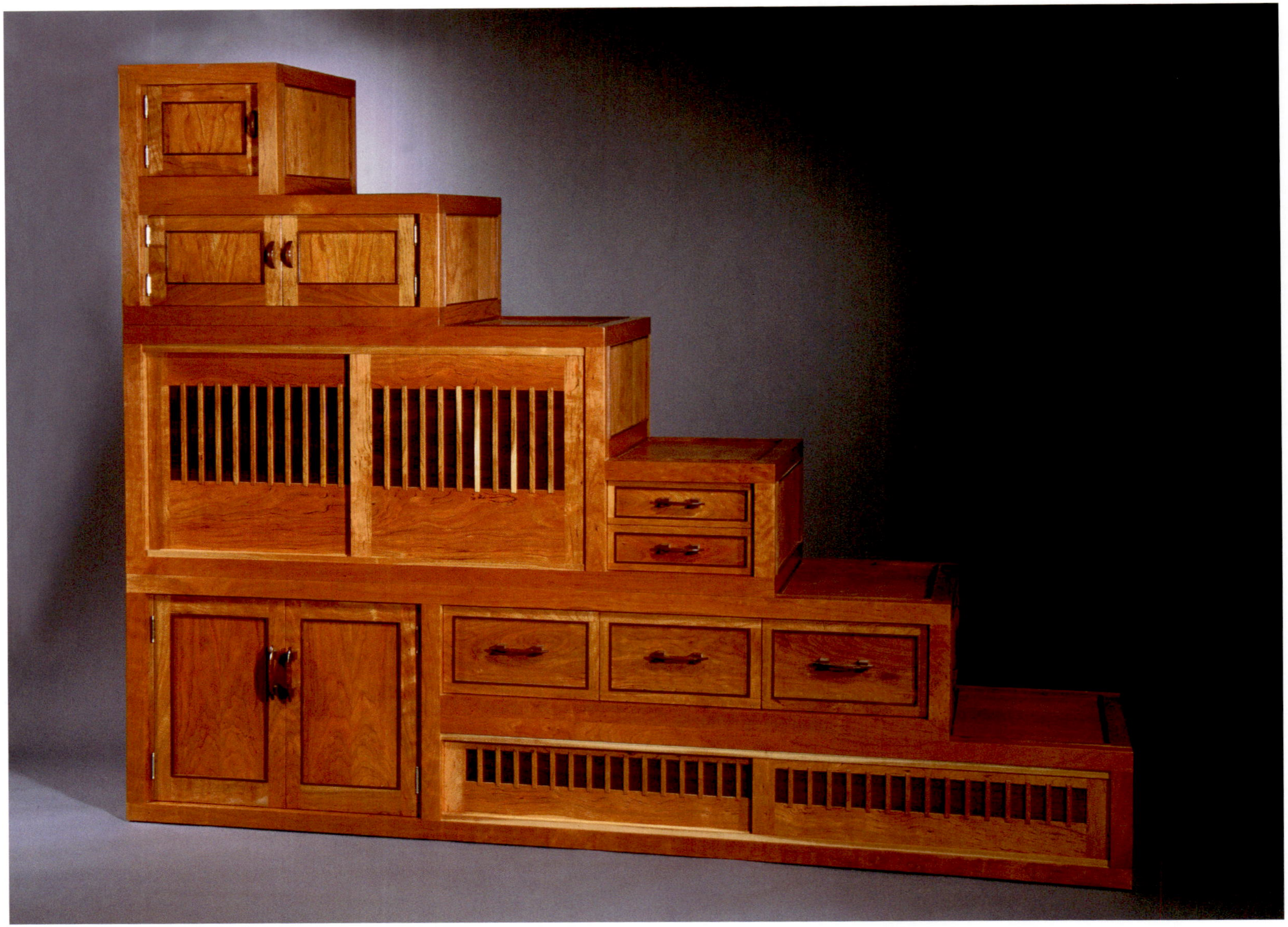

Jo R. Roessler. Tucker Stepped Cabinet. Cherry and walnut, 80" x 72" x 20".

JOSHUA SALESIN

Santa Cruz, California, www.joshuasalesin.com

Individual Artwork

Lighthouse Box

Produced entirely on a 172-year-old ornamental lathe, the *Lighthouse Box* explores finely cut surface ornamentation and pierced-through architectural fretwork in the form of a lighthouse. Fashioned from African blackwood and accented with the natural glow of European boxwood, the design features four "secret" threaded compartments.

Transformations: from seed to tree to wood to me to we shall see...

Everyone understands how trees transform from seeds into woody plants that serve so many important roles in our lives. Trees transform the ecosystem in which they grow and the air we breathe. Their wood is often transformed into building materials for our homes, musical instruments for our pleasure, and art for our soul.

This piece was initially destined to become a clarinet bell. Due to defects in the wood, it was recycled through the lumber trade and I purchased it for my craft. Using an ornamental lathe, I transformed the block of African blackwood into a miniature lighthouse, with finely cut surface ornamentation and pierced-through architectural fretwork.

The piece was fixed in place while a spinning tool was used to make a cut. Then it was repositioned and the next cut made, one after another until the entire surface was decorated. In this way, after more than a thousand individual cuts, the plain piece of wood was transformed beyond a utilitarian object into the realm of decorative arts.

There is another transformation this lighthouse reveals: it becomes four separate screw-fit compartments. Perhaps one of those will someday contain a ring that transforms the lives of those engaged.

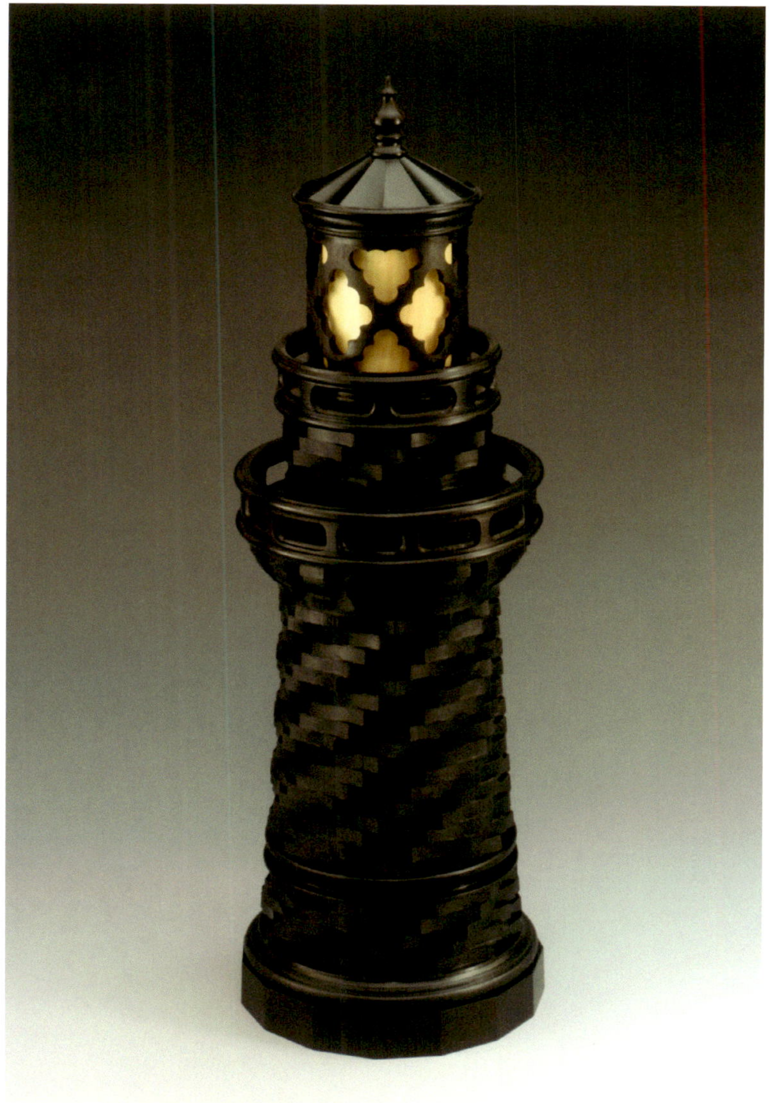

Joshua Salesin. *Lighthouse Box.* 2008. African blackwood, European boxwood, ornamental turning, 6.0" h x 2.0" d.

"Cosmic Burst" Pattern Bowl

Cosmic Burst combines detailed ornamental turning with the natural colors of exotic hardwood. The result is intricate, three-dimensional patterns that interplay with subtle variations of the wood grain.

The work embodies a combination of unique factors: It is created using an antique hand-powered rose engine lathe. The fine finished surface is a direct result of careful cutting without sanding, which requires an "end grain" orientation unusual for larger bowls. This necessitates specially milled wood from the finest section of a tree with straight grain, consistent color, and no defects. The wood is carefully seasoned to prevent cracking and, if successful, ornamental patterning can begin. Each facet is then precisely cut to create the overall artistic plan.

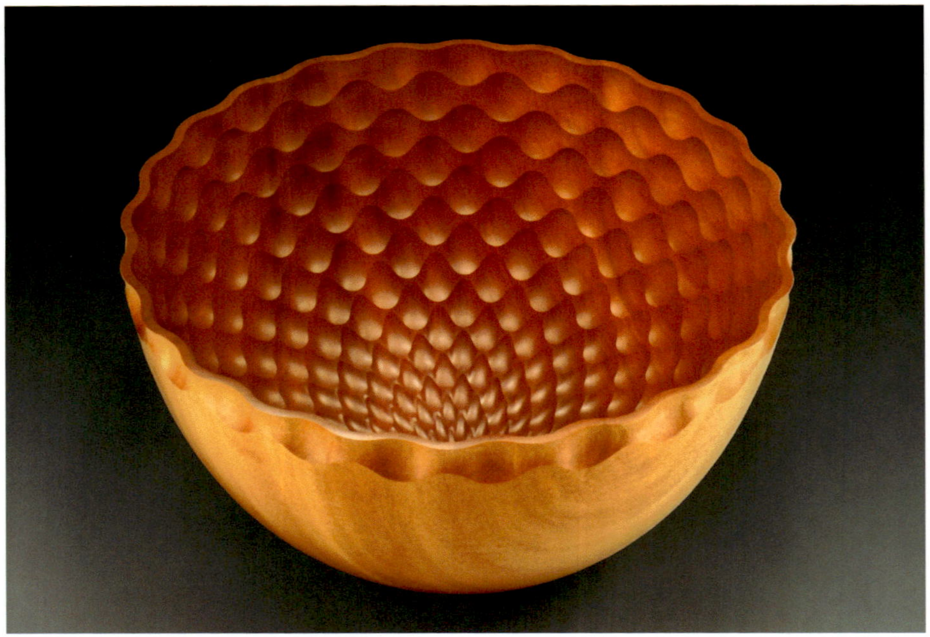

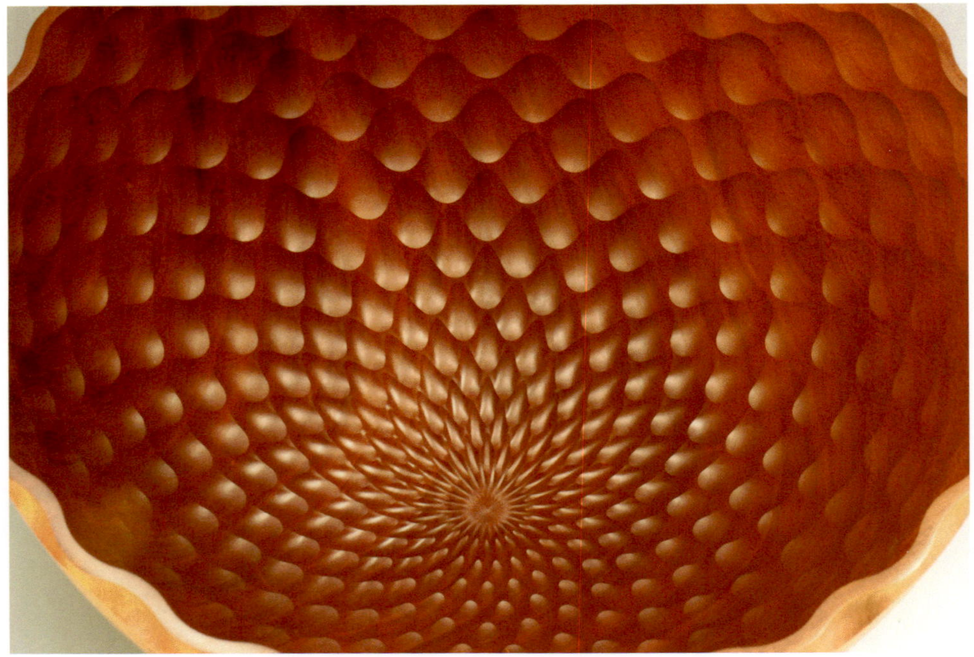

Joshua Salesin. *Cosmic Burst* Pattern Bowl. 2007. Osage orange, ornamental turning, 6.0" h x 9.5" d.

Lattice Boxes

Part Victorian, part victorious, these delightful boxes feature intricate pierced patterns that form lattice windows to a glowing interior. A perfect ring box (plus a small secret compartment) for a very special occasion!

Bumpy Box

This contemporary box design is both a tactile treasure and candy for the eyes. The reciprocated exterior patterns radiate energy and the flowing inner design provides the focal point or center of force – a kind of chakra.

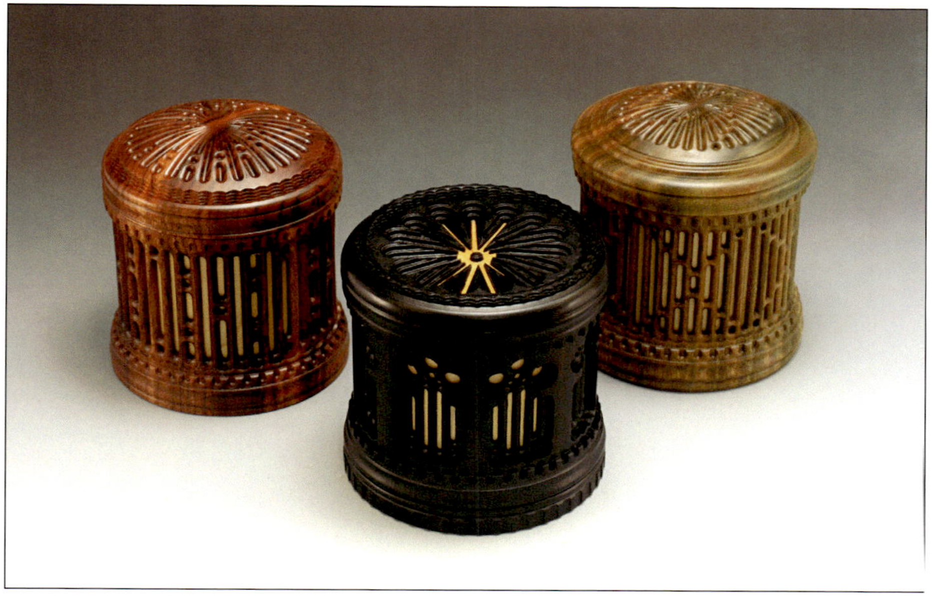

Joshua Salesin. Lattice Boxes. 2008. (L to R) mopane, blackwood, and lignum vitae, with European boxwood inserts, ornamental turning, 2.25" h x 2.0" d. (each).

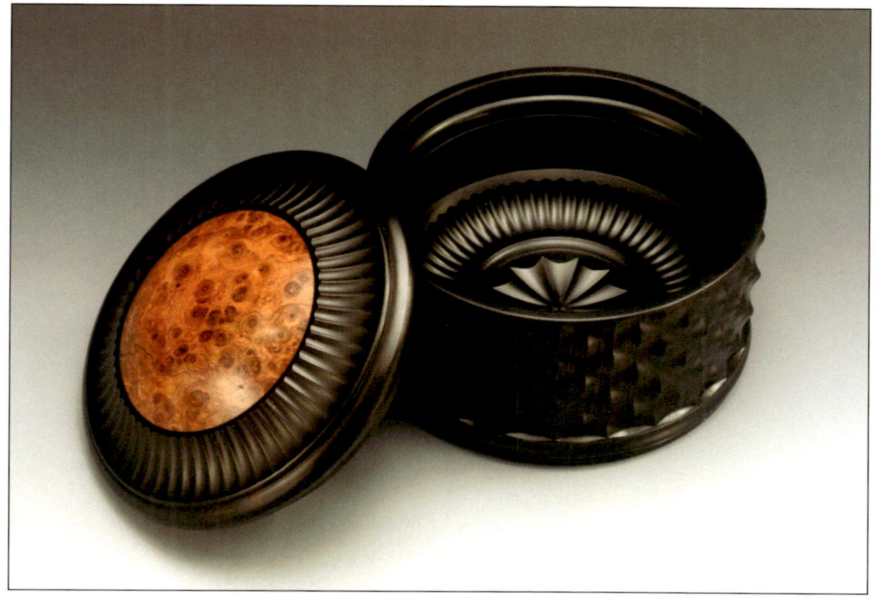

Joshua Salesin. Bumpy Box. 2008. African blackwood, amboyna burl, ornamental turning, 2.25" h x 3.0" d.

Norman Sartorius

Parkersburg, West Virginia, sartorius@verizon.net

Artist's Statement

People look at me rather oddly when I tell them I make non-functional wooden spoons – non-functional in that you wouldn't use them in the kitchen, but functional in that they are objects of beauty. My spoons are sculptures; my sculptures are spoons, not spoons to stir the soup but spoons to stir the soul.

It's the play of heartwood and sapwood, color, unusual grain, knots, textures, or anomalies that suggests the spoons that lie within each piece of wood. The pieces begin with a rough shape on a band saw and are transformed by power carving tools, die grinders, files, and hours of handwork. A finished spoon is as smooth and detailed as a fine piece of jewelry.

I have felt compelled to make spoons since I started woodworking. To me "spoon" is just another category, similar to "bowl," "plate," or "teapot." Within each category are infinite varieties of form, size, texture, abstraction, color, and emotion. The character of the raw pieces of wood and my sensitivity at the time I am working contribute more than my concern for function. Inspiration, for me, is intuitive, and so far I am unable to turn it on at will; however, I am aware when it comes. My goal is to make spoons that people will view as special objects, small treasures that give them pleasure to touch, to look at, to own.

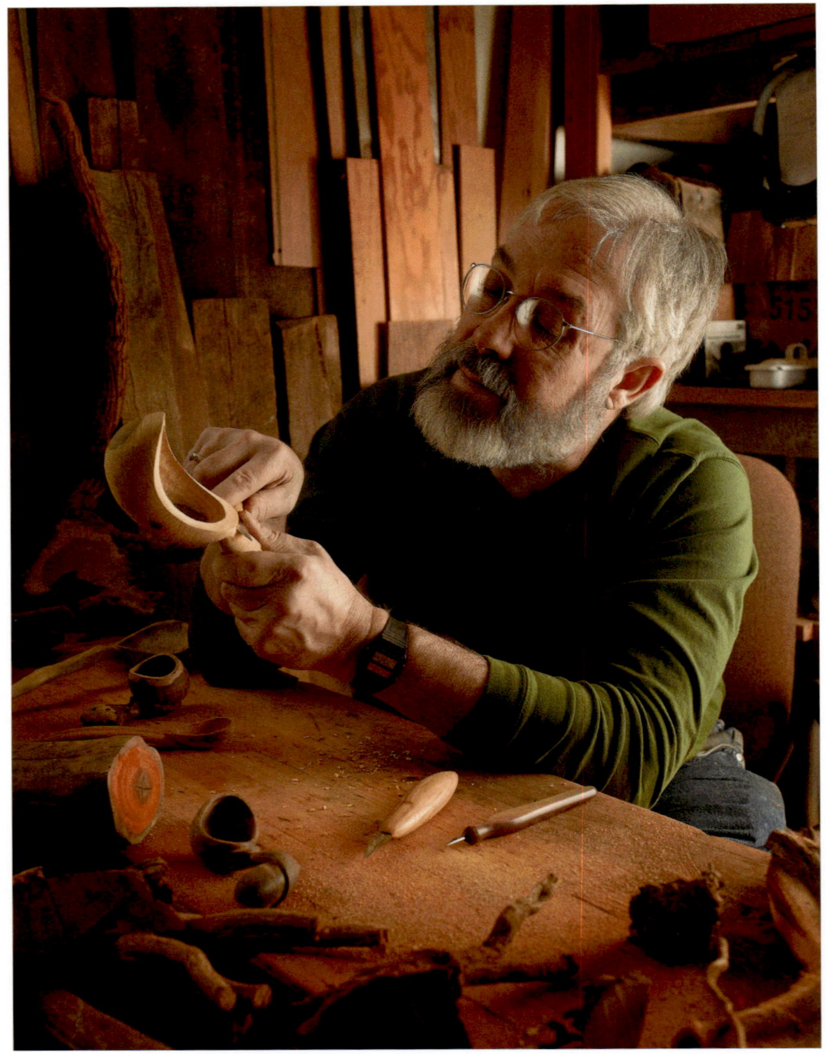

Norman Sartorius. *Norm Seated*. 2006. Refining the transition between the handle and the bowl. *Photographer: Jim Osborn*

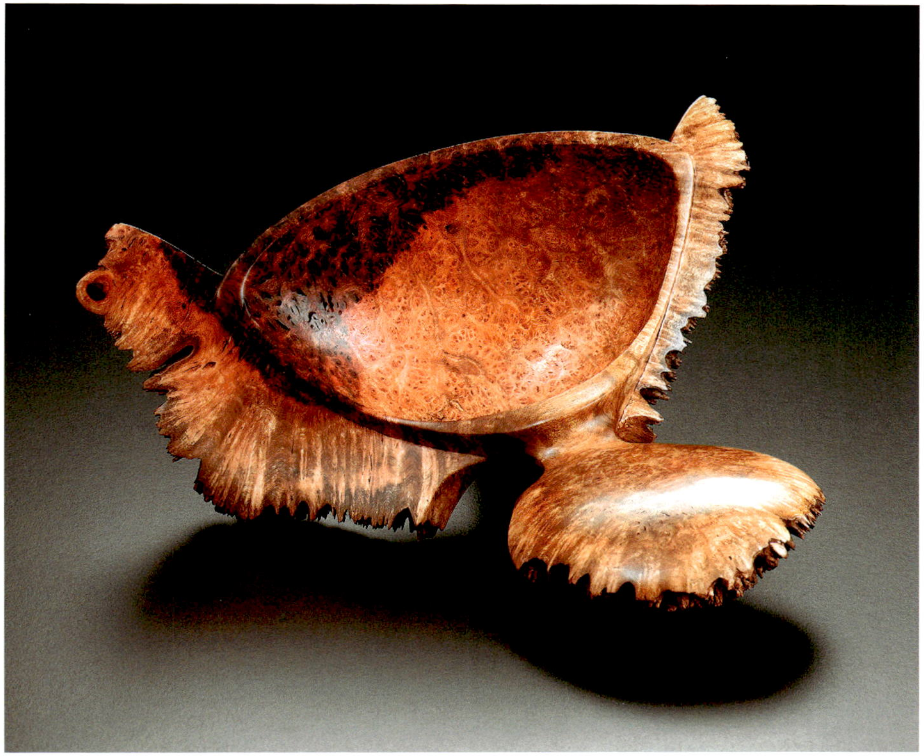

Norman Sartorius. *Bi-Hawk* Che Chen Burl Spoon. 2005. 8.5" x 8" x 3". My son named this spoon, observing that one raised ornamentation was a Mohawk and saying that two would be called a Bi-Hawk. *Collection of Pat McCauley. Photographer: Jim Osborn*

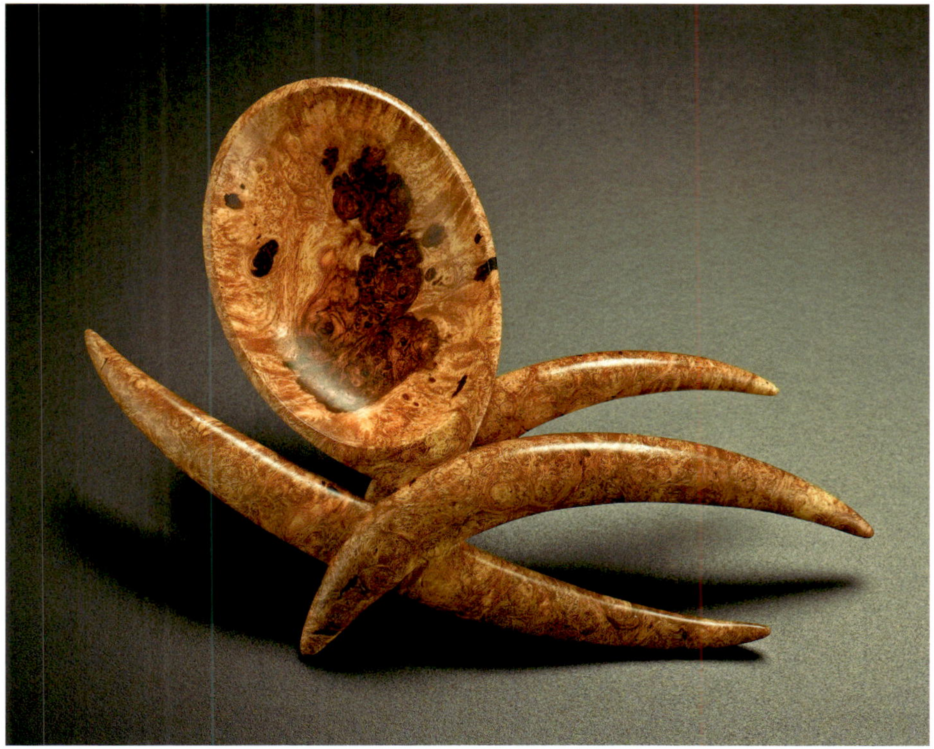

Norman Sartorius. *Cephalopod.* 2008. Honduras rosewood burl, 9" x 6" x 1.5". I loved the sapwood of this burl for its marble-like variation in color. The form is to suggest movement of undersea creatures against the tide. *Collection of Gary Quinlan. Photographer: Jim Osborn*

Norman Sartorius. *Bridge*. 2007. Desert ironwood root, 18" x 7" x 3". I consider this sculpture to be part of my *Spoon Dreams* series. The title *Bridge* suggests the crossing between two styles of work or two states of mind. *Collection of Elizabeth Mai and John Gobrecht. Photographer: Jim Osborn*

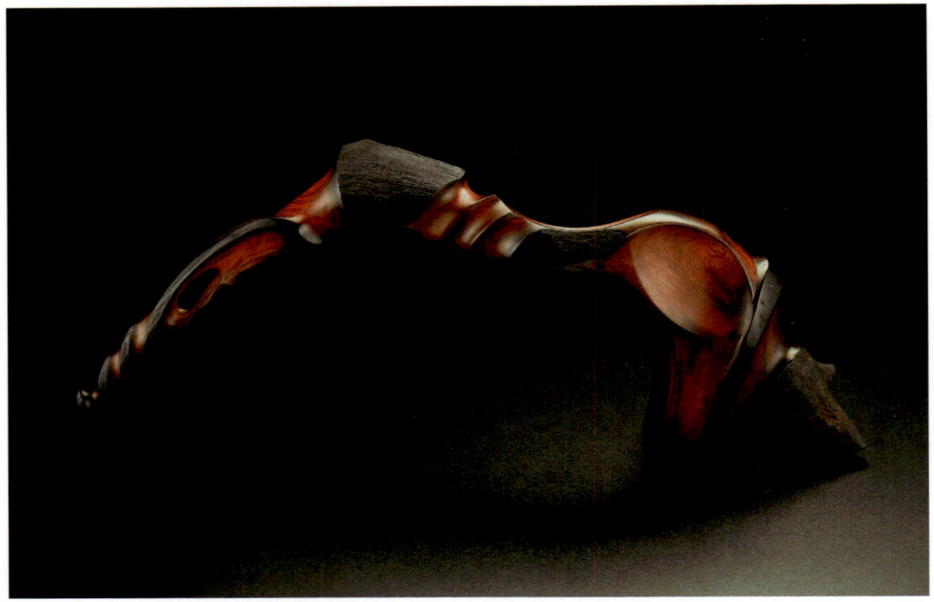

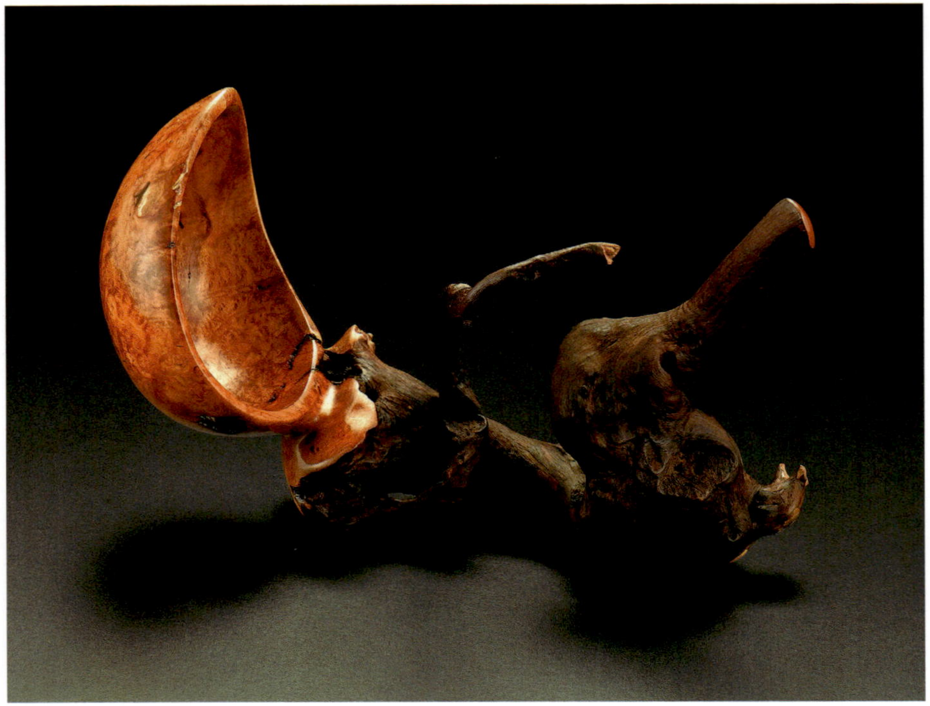

Norman Sartorius. *Pan's Mandrake*. 2007. Mountain Laurel Burl, 8.5" x 5.5" x 4". This spoon resembles the animated mandrake root in the movie Pan's Labyrinth. *Collection of Steve Keeble & Karen Depew. Photographer: Jim Osborn*

Peter Schlech

San Diego, California, www.peterschlech.com

Artist's Statement

Most of my recent work is the result of a process of experimentation and discovery—an attempt to go beyond the bounds of conventional techniques and designs. I also tend to work in series, doing several variations of a particular design and then moving on, as it is all too easy to fall into the seductive traps of repetition or imitation. My aesthetic goals are fairly straightforward—simplicity of design, creative discovery, and the pursuit of wonder. For if we as artists do not impart, if only for a moment, a sense of wonder to the beholder, then we have, perhaps, failed at our task.

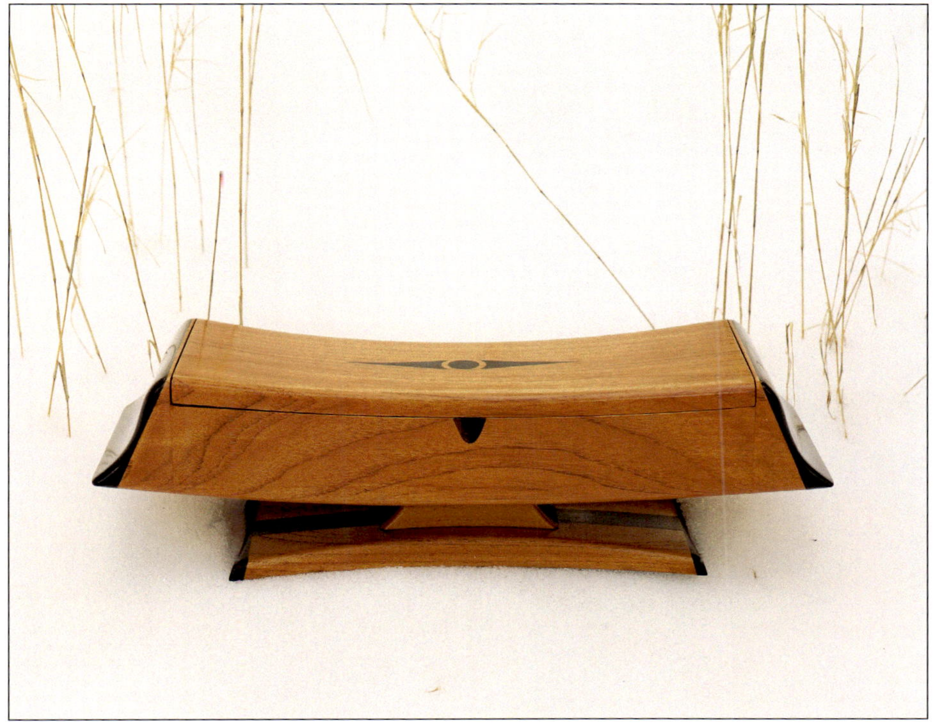

Peter Schlech. Bandsaw Box. 1997. Teak and ebony, one of my first attempts at wood art, 16" x 6" x 4". *Photographer: A. Rogerson*

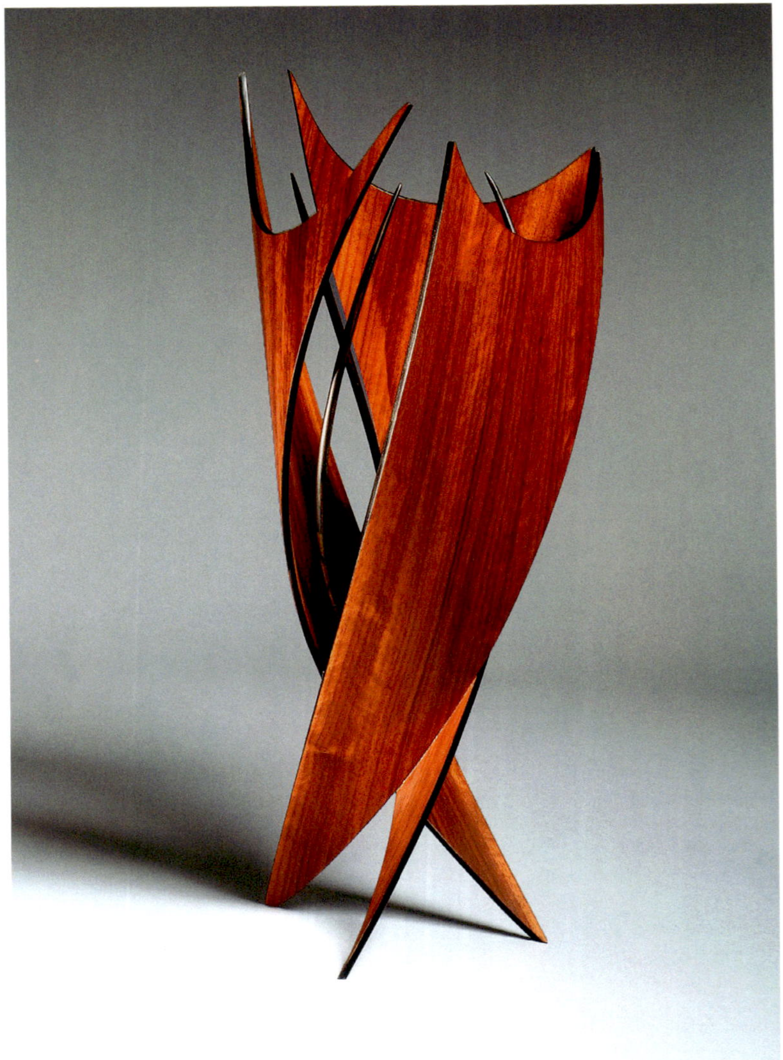

Peter Schlech. *Elizabeth Series#2* 2003. Vessel of laminated and formed padauk veneers with ebony accents.

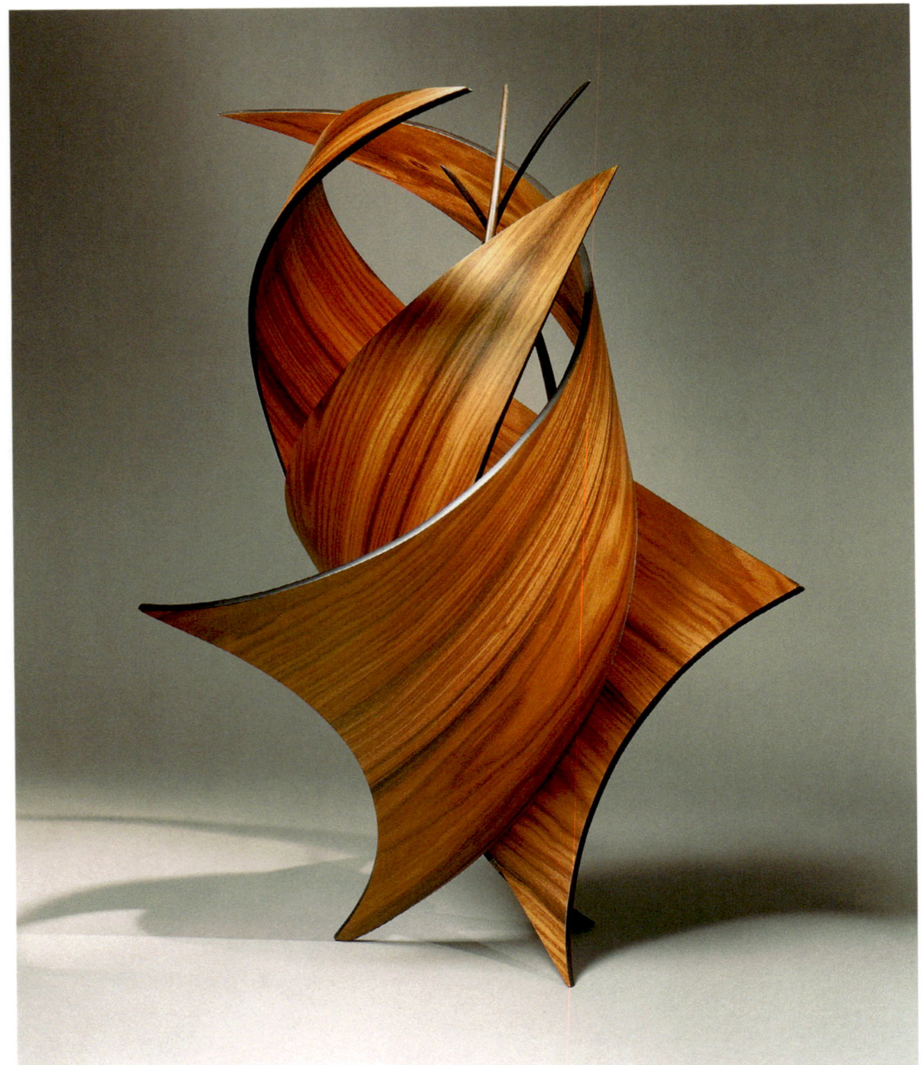

Peter Schlech. *Unisbel series #7.* 2001. Vessel of laminated and formed Brazilian rosewood, 15" x 8" x 7".

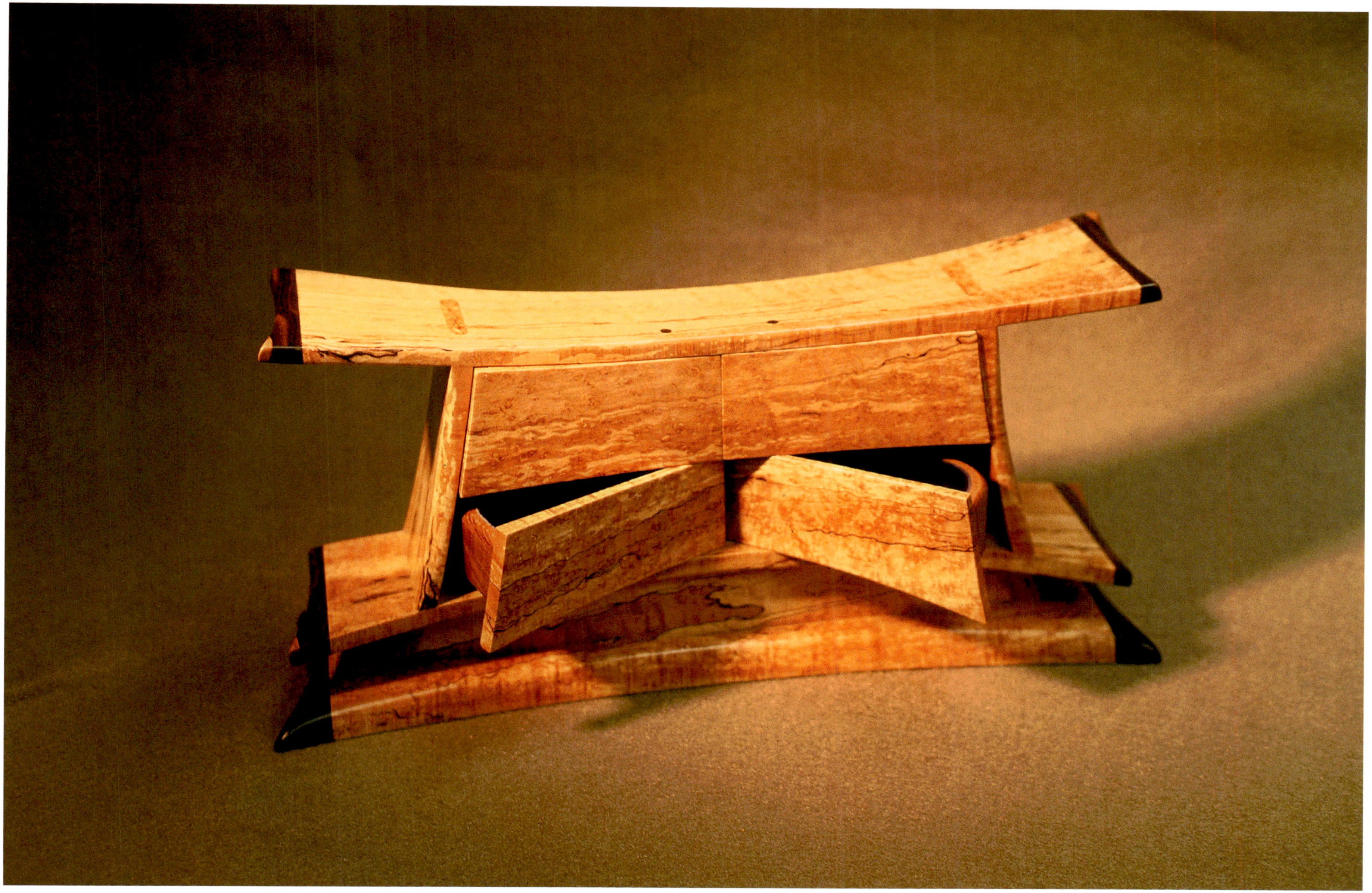

Peter Schlech. *Shinto Series.* 2002 - 2004. Jewelry boxes, spalted and quilted maple with ziricote accents, 14" x 7" x 4".

Brad Sells

Cookeville, Tennessee, www.bradsells.com

Individual Artwork

Eclipse

This pecan tree was harvested from a local doctor's office in my hometown of Cookeville. I made several pieces for the doctors and this piece belongs to the Knoxville Museum of Art.

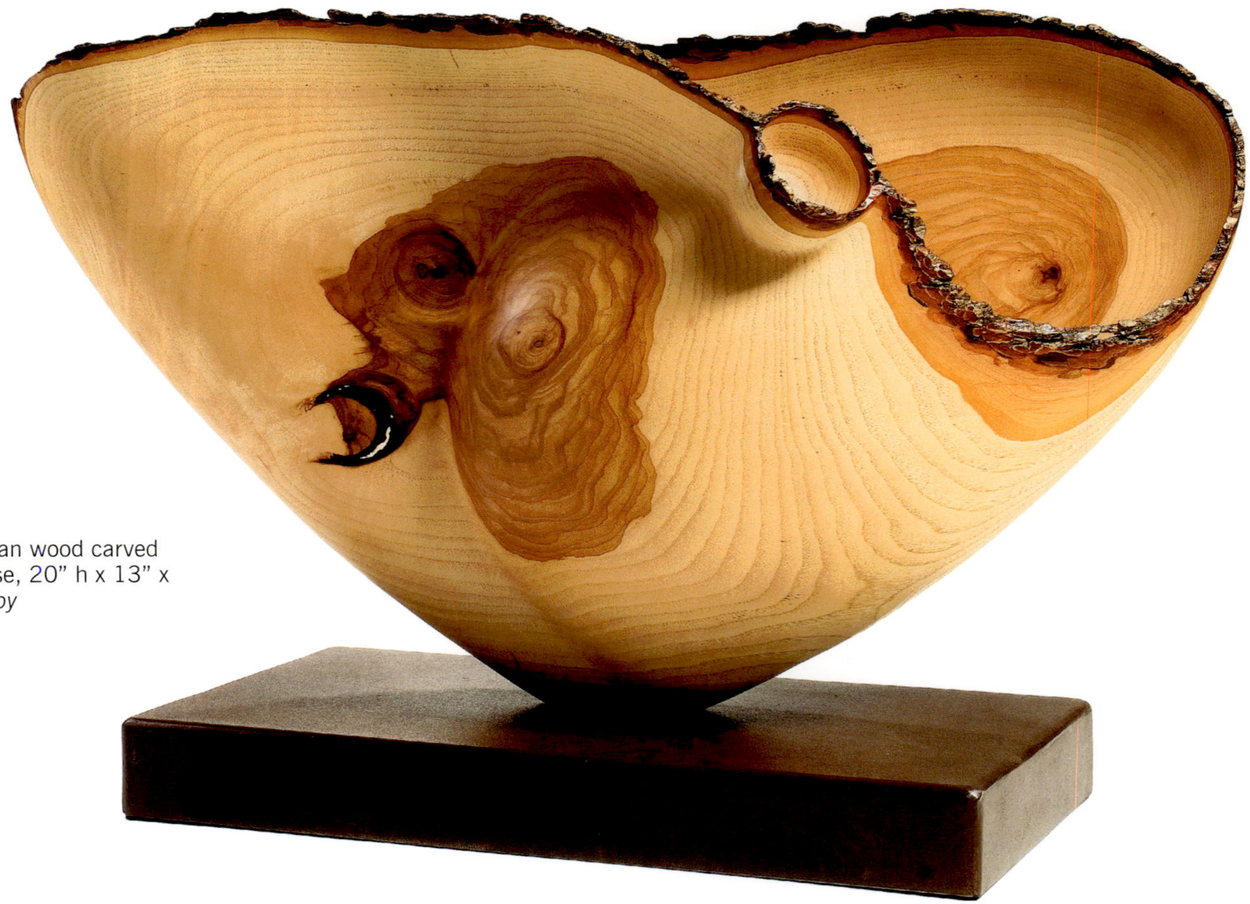

Brad Sells. *Eclipse.* 2007. Pecan wood carved vessel with orbital on metal base, 20" h x 13" x 30". *Photographer: Dan Kellerby*

Peace, Hope, Strength, and Wellness

This commissioned sculpture was done for Cookeville Regional Medical Center. It stands in the lobby of the newly constructed north tower of the hospital. The piece is made mostly from an eighty-year-old blue spruce that grew on the grounds where the tower now stands. The installation depicts a family unit enveloped in a double helix spiral of doves. The sculpture is a symbol of the strength of family. It is my hope as an artist that it promotes a sense of calmness and courage as well as a connection between both the physical and spiritual realms of our existence. The piece took well over a year to create. Over one hundred and fifty butterfly keys hold the logs together.

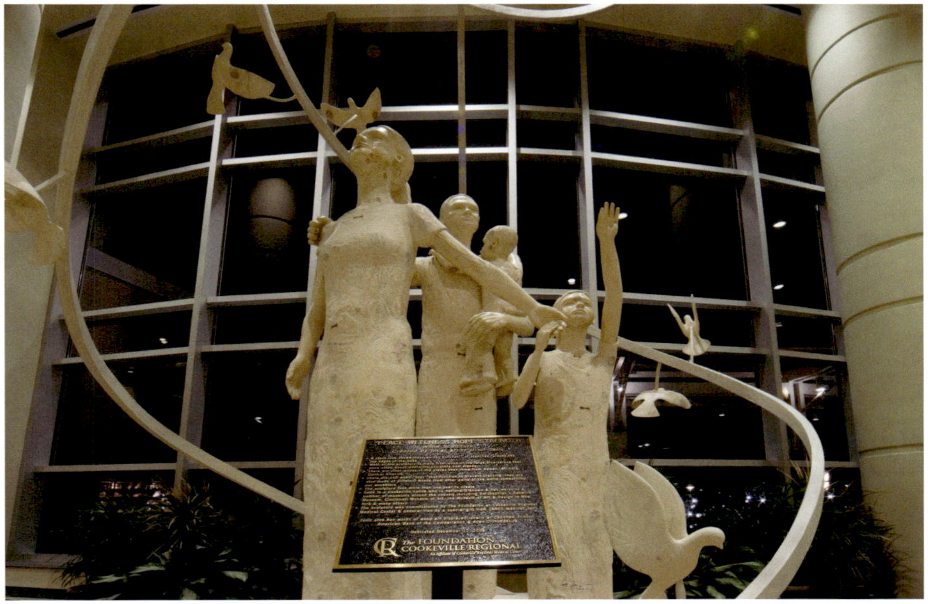

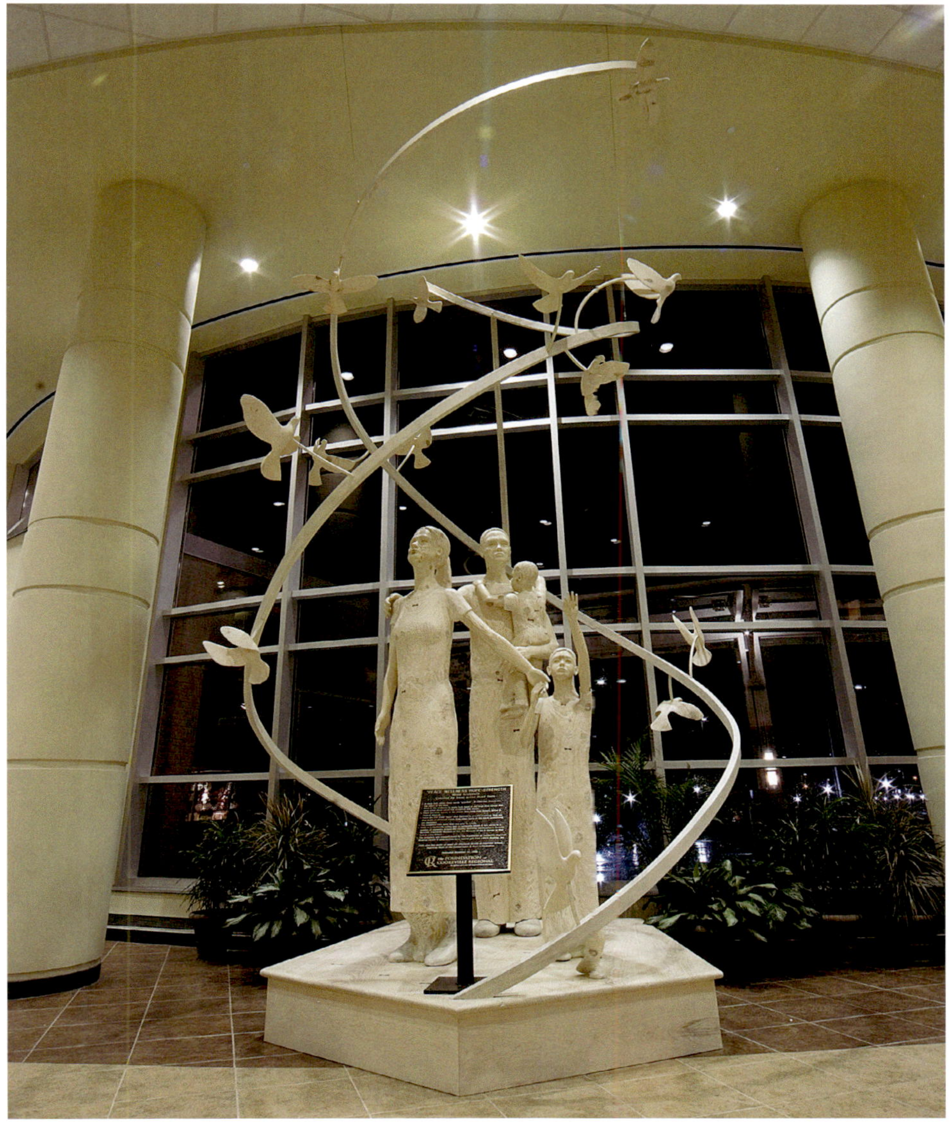

Brad Sells. *Peace, Hope, Strength, and Wellness*. 2008/ Bleached and pigmented blue spruce, 22' h x 10' x 10'. *Photographer: Dan Kellerby*

Where Spirits Dwell

While I was in Hawaii we were working in the big volcano, Mauna Kea. We were in an area at about 7000 feet elevation in the Koa forest. To get to the area that we were salvaging wood, we had to drive off road for about an hour and a half. The tree in this piece had blown down and blocked our way. We had to cut it up to proceed. My assistant, Steven Flatt, and I felt that the tree was an offering from the "spirits that dwell" but did not take any of it until the forester Mike Robinson gave us permission. We did not want any bad karma.

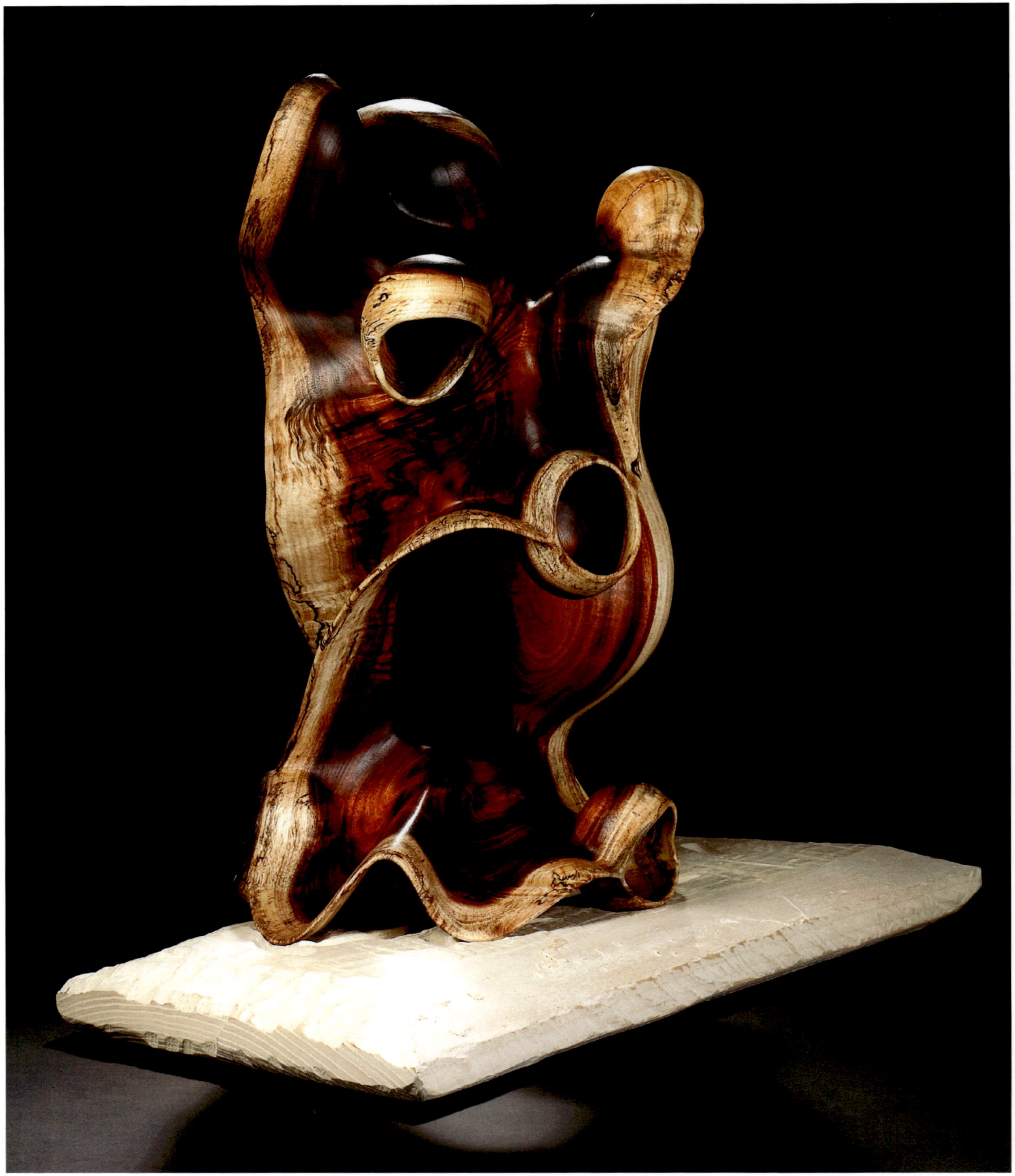

Brad Sells. *Where Spirits Dwell.* Aloha series #43. 2008. Curly koa wood on bleached ash base, 22" h x 13" x 14". *Photographer: John Lucas*

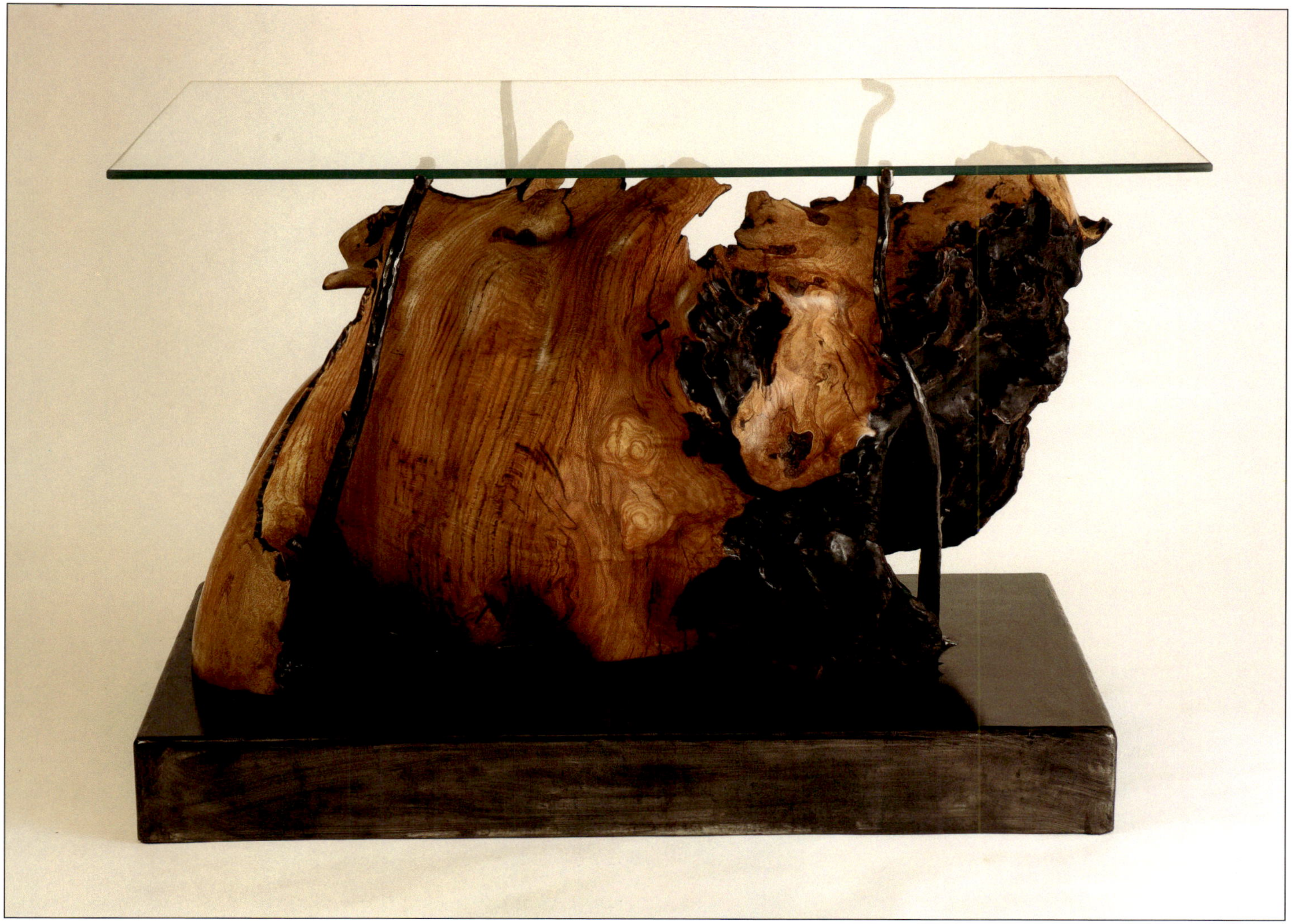

Brad Sells. *Hawk and Sparrow.* Red oak end table with metal base and hand forged supports and glass top, 23" h x 36" x 24". *Photographer: John Lucas*

Hawk and Sparrow

This was a commissioned piece. The tree was taken from the banks of Caney Fork River in Smith County, Tennessee. The five-foot diameter tree had grown around a big limestone boulder. A tornado had blown it down and the wood used was crusty with limestone embedded in it. It was a lot of work to carve and some of the stone was left in the piece. The black areas are burned and interesting due to the way the tree was growing around the block of stone. The piece is titled *Hawk and Sparrow* because the front of the piece has a carved area that looks like a hawk from the top and a sparrow from underneath.

MARK SFIRRI

New Hope, Pennsylvania

Individual Artwork

Allentown Art Museum Bench

This bench was a commission from the Allentown Art Museum in Allentown, Pennsylvania, for public seating. I wanted to incorporate my lathe turned figural forms as legs for a bench. By having the seat curve, I was able to allow enough room for substantial tenons at the tops of the figures. I had made a number of benches before this one and all had bases with much more structure.

Mark Sfirri. *Allentown Art Museum Bench.* 2008. Mahogany and paint, 20" h x 72" w x 20" d. *Photographer: Burns Austin* (below and opposite page)

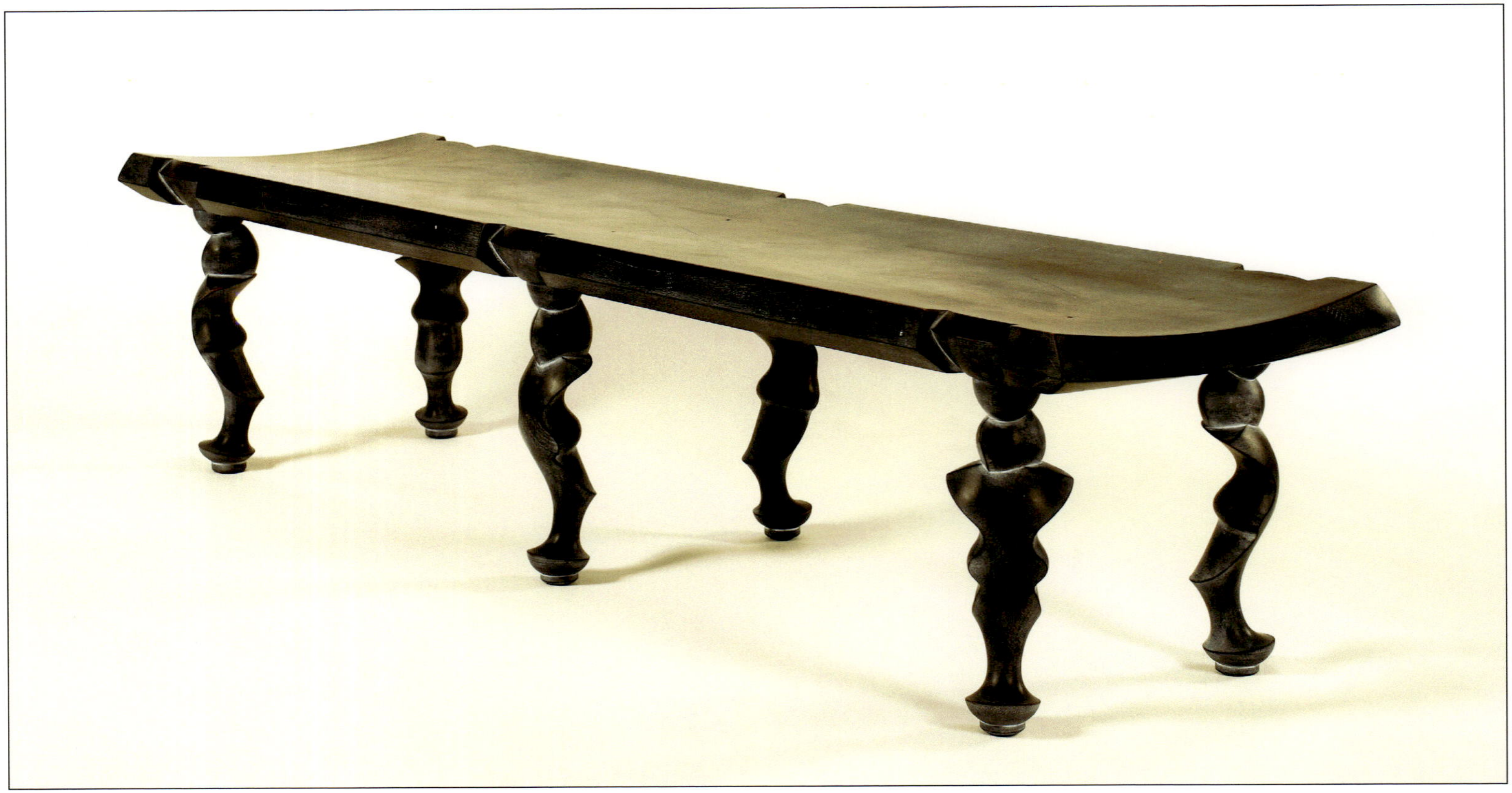

Game Hunting in North America

At the local butcher shop there is a collection of stuffed animal heads, different species, but mostly deer. The heads vary in size somewhat and the antlers vary, some with more points than others, but they sort of look all the same to me. I decided to engage the owner in conversation about them one day. He went into elaborate detail about where exactly in Saskatchewan, Canada, he killed one of them and then how he had to drag it out and get it to someone to mount it. He traveled to upstate New York and hunted another one there. For the butcher, each had a personality and a story and for me, up until that point, they represented more of a repeated wall decoration. It was after that visit that I decided to create my own stories about animals from my visits to various places and that is how the series began. I am not a hunter, but I like the idea of the story of my fictitious animals and I have them mounted and hanging on the wall in a similar fashion to the butcher.

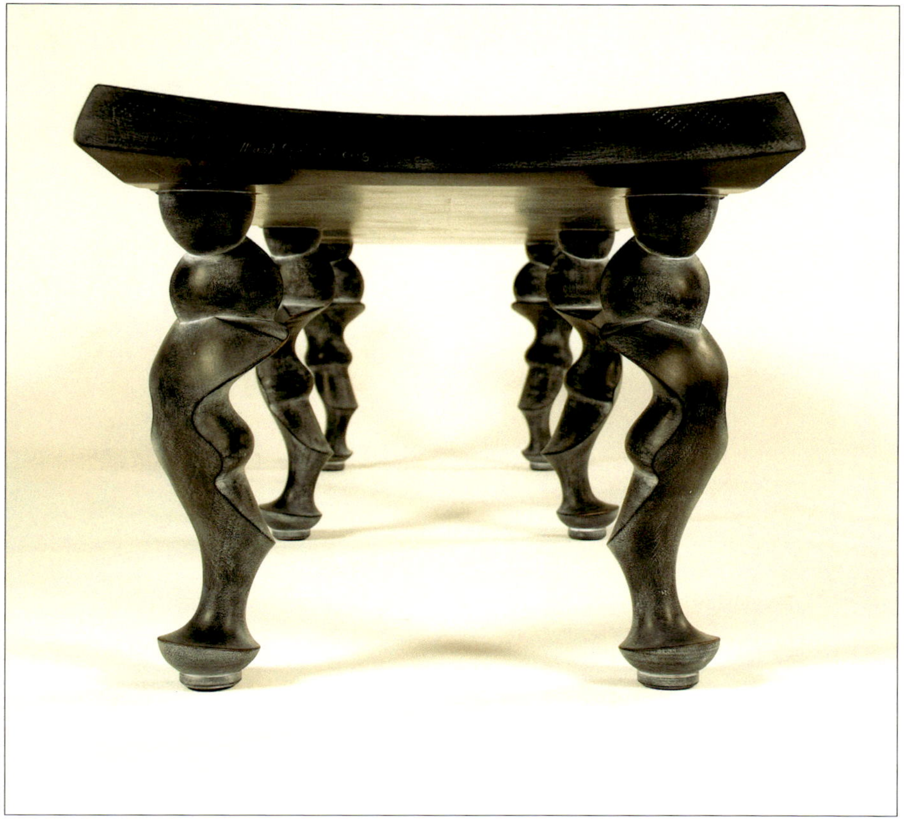

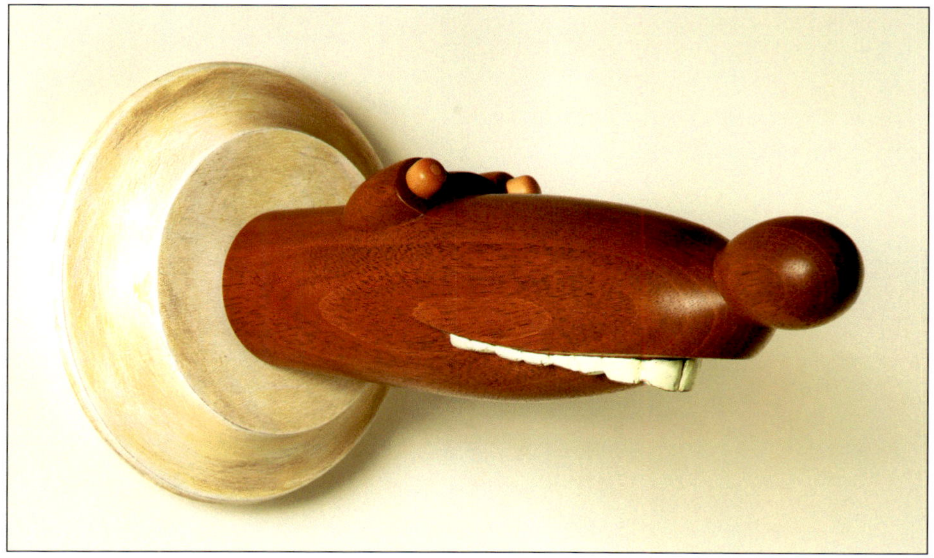

Mark Sfirri. *Big Jim's Camp, Saskatchewan.* 2008. Mahogany and paint, 6" h x 6" w x 12" d.

Rolling Pins

My exploration of a rolling pin form began as a way to demonstrate multi-axis spindle turning. I chose this form as a blank canvas to manipulate. I made several of the same design but never completed them. After 9/11, new words and phrases crept into our country's vocabulary and "homeland security" was one of them. Something clicked and I decided that this was what the title needed to be. The concept is that the real security that one has is the rolling pin that is by the front door in case of a break in. There is a painted apple pie to help with the connection to mom and home. *Branch Rolling Pin* is a mostly turned piece with some carving and the hope was that it would be a blend of the functional turned form and nature.

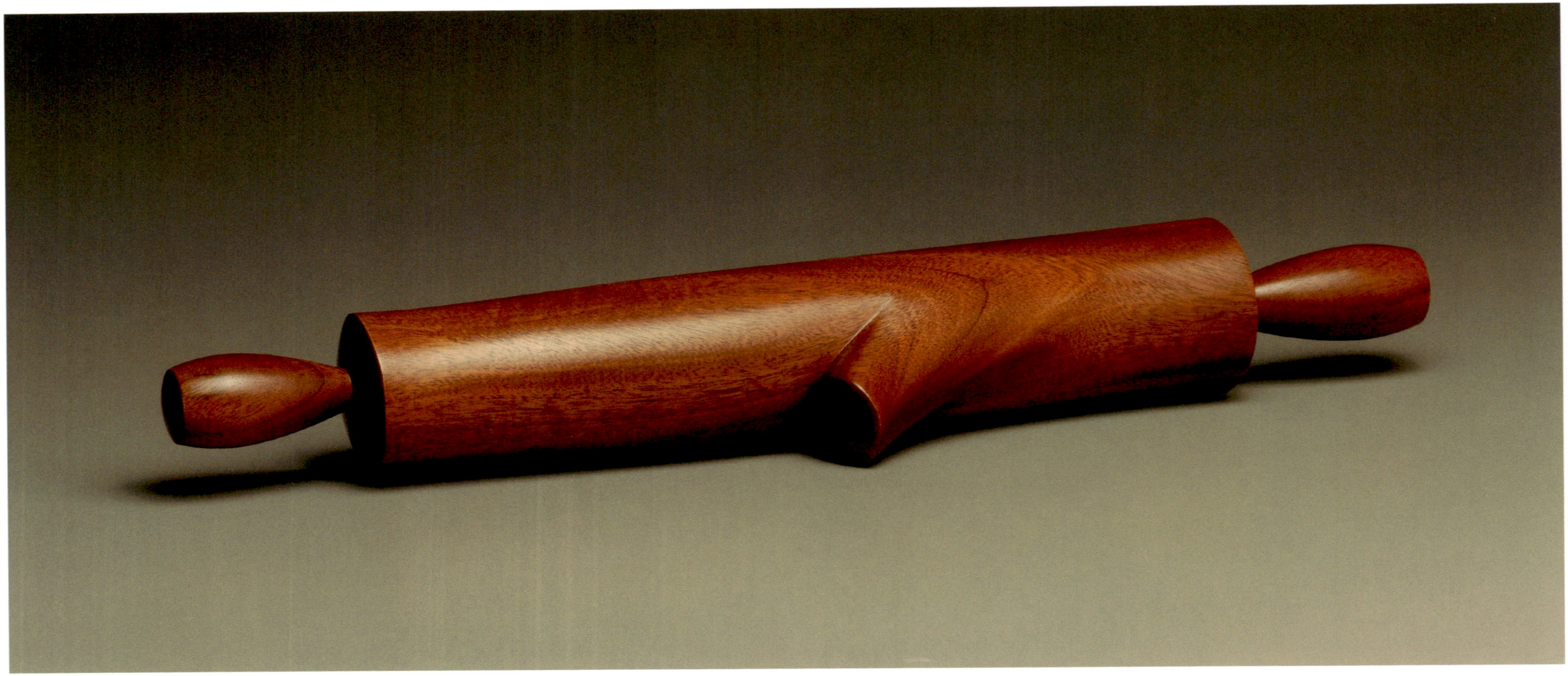

Mark Sfirri. *Branch Rolling Pin.* 2006. Mahogany, 3" h x 4" w x 22" l. *Photographer: John Carlano*

Spoons

I was influenced by the traditional Romanian spoon carving techniques of Zina Burloiu to try making some spoon forms. While that would not be remotely apparent when looking at what I designed and what she made, that was where it started for me. These pieces have bowl forms and handles, but the relationship to spoons and function pretty much ends there. In *Sea of Spoons*, I felt that the individually designed pieces took on an interesting effect when huddled all together and created group motion, akin to a school of fish swimming upstream.

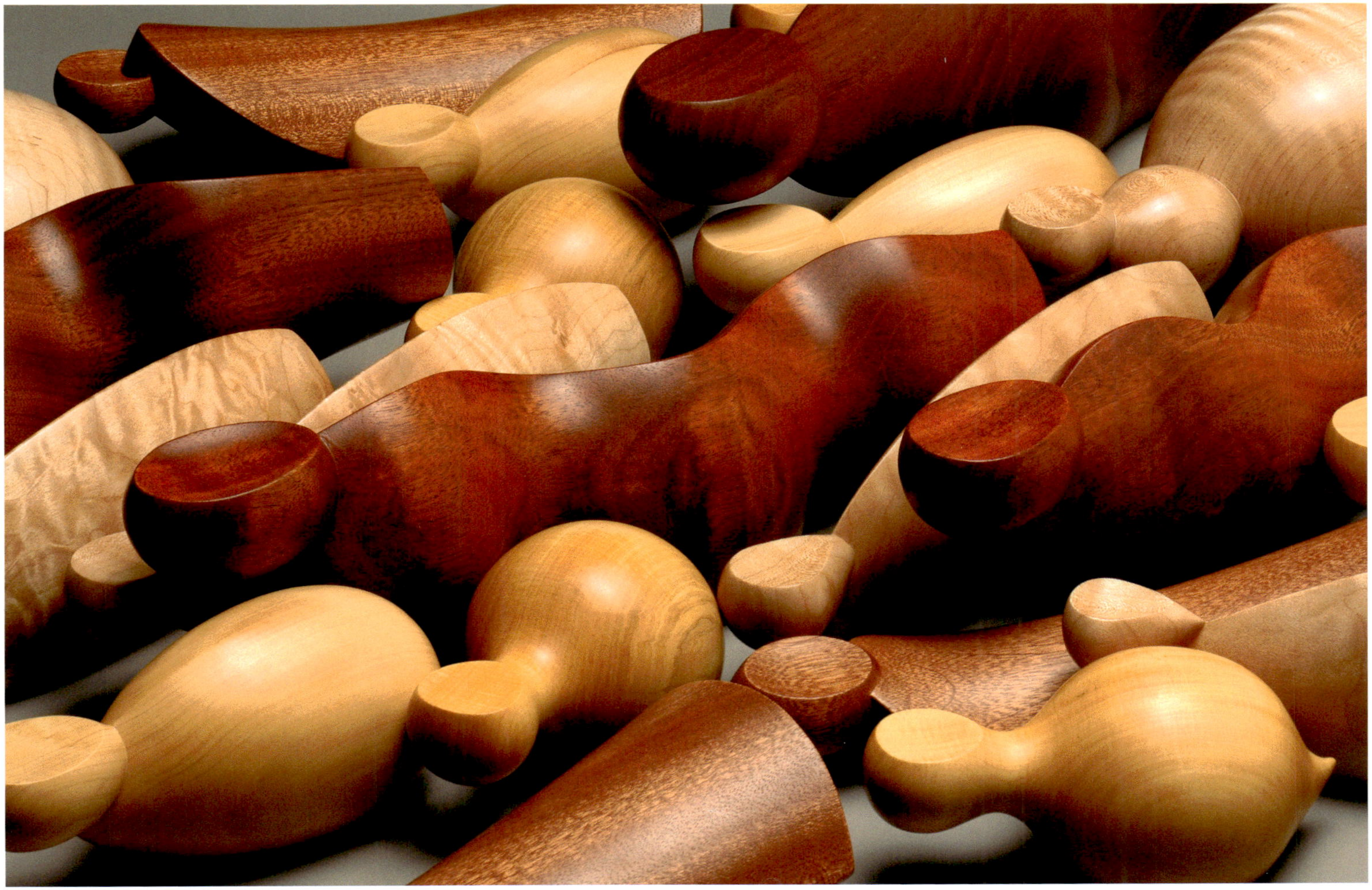

Mark Sfirri. *Sea of Spoons.* 2005. Various hardwoods, all have a natural finish (oil), sizes vary from the smallest: 2 3/4" h x 3" x 5 1/4" to the largest: 4 3/4" h x 3 1/2" x 17 1/2". *Photographer: John Carlano*

Alfred Sils & Carol Richter Sils

http://silsstudios.com

Alfred Sils Artist's Statement

My work has always been defined and influenced by the medium. Wood has been a source of inspiration and satisfaction for me since my childhood. Its graphic figure, tactile qualities, and rich and sensuous aromas have driven me to use form to explore these varied and exciting possibilities. My recent explorations of the use of precious metals in combination with wood have added new dimension to the possibilities.

I have been actively turning since 1980. This area of woodworking allows me to use beautiful woods to design within the constraints of the vessel form. I enjoy the interplay of form and function while utilizing the graphic and tactile qualities of the wood, at times adorned with precious metals, to create vessels and sculptural forms which engage the viewer and encourage connection with function and beauty.

The visual elements of the bowls often remind me of landscapes ranging from desert scenes to the rich earth of the Northeast. By working the texture of the wood and adding to its tactile richness, I hope to accentuate this connection to the land and its myriad visual experiences.

My forms have been heavily influenced by classical ceramics. The vessels of ancient China and Korea have a beauty that is timeless. I have also been influenced by the modern ceramic community and its tendency to explore and push the medium to new levels of expression. In the last analysis, however, it is the visceral excitement of "opening" a new piece of wood that continually renews my senses and provokes my interest. As I get deeper into a new block and discover its grain and figure, I more and more appreciate Michelangelo's descriptions of his feeling as the marble gave way to the beautiful forms he found "trapped" within.

Carol Richter Sils Artist's Statement

The metamorphosis of a lump of clay into controlled forms has long held my fascination. My collaboration with this plastic medium has disclosed those myriad of influential elements of design, color, form, and philosophy, which issue forth during the making process, while the impact of nature and of historical art on my aesthetic choices is revealed through my ever evolving body of work.

The elegant ceramic forms developed by Chinese potters of the Song Dynasty have had a significant influence on my work. The timeless beauty of *Song* is a fountainhead from which I continually draw, while incorporating personal choices in my high-fire porcelain vessels and my low-fire sculptures. I fire my own work and make my own glazes, which are thoughtfully chosen to enhance each piece individually.

Having spent four glorious years at school in southern Indiana, my love of the woods and the effect of sunlight filtering through the forest's canopy of leaves producing a kaleidoscope of colors have enriched the surfaces of my own work. I have always appreciated the changing seasons, which for me, has become a metaphor for evolution of creative concepts and ideas, exploration, discovery, and renewal.

Individual Artwork

Let Reason Ring Series

This series is an example of the combination of ceramics and wood with metal in an exploration of the expressive harmonies of these diverse media. Finding the right balance between the plasticity of Carol's ceramic sculpture and Alfred's subtractive wood techniques is both challenging and enthralling. It requires pushing the boundaries of both media, introducing and inventing new techniques, and even using other materials when the construction and artistic techniques require them.

Technique

The totems are constructed using turned bowls and vases which are, in some cases, deconstructed and carved to form the supporting and framing elements. Classical furniture techniques and joinery are used to make the plinths, the trays that support the ceramic sculpture, and to join the various elements together.

A stoneware clay body has been carved and then hollowed out, thinning enough of the ceramic wall to avoid firing mishaps. Acrylic "washes" provide the surfaces with the suggestion of color and metallic powders have been added to intensify certain areas.

The ceramic sculptures are joined to the wood using epoxy.

Series

The year 2009 is the bicentennial of the birth of Charles Darwin and the one hundred and fiftieth anniversary of his publication of *The Origin of the Species*. Darwin's seminal work introduced reason into our thinking about life on this planet and into our exploration of our own origins, both individually and as a species. It introduced science into the conversation on the origin of life and began the process that led to our understanding of genetic structure, mutation, and of DNA itself. The structure of the double helix and the understanding of its tendency to change has enhanced our understanding of evolution and led to the mapping of the human genome and those of other species. We have used the totem form in this series because it lets us tell the story in a unique and traditional way even as we depart from tradition in mixing two often-incompatible media. This series attempts to explore the effects of our knowledge and our behavior on our future.

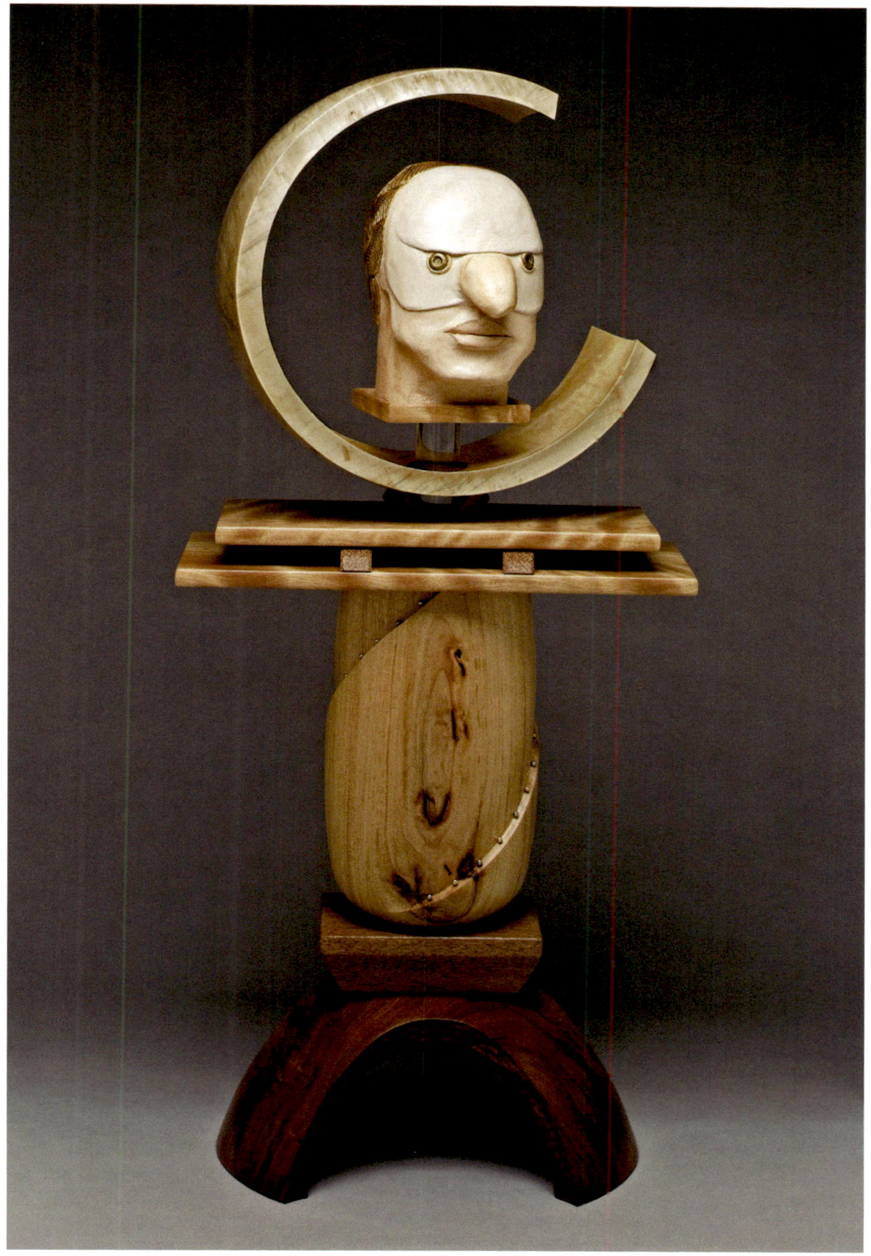

Alfred Sils & Carol Richter Sils. Totem 3: *Autobiology*. Ceramic, black acacia, palm, curly birch, quilted maple, Plexiglas, steel and brass, 39" h x 17" w x 12" d. Mutation brings change to humans and bacteria. People wore masks in the Dark Ages in an attempt to ward off the bacteria, which evolved into invisible invasive killers. Now we put invisible invasive toxins in the environment, which may cause changes in our own DNA. Is the face a mask or could it be the appearance of our new mutation? The double helix, shown on the column in brass and chrome steel, now contains an error. Is it survivable?

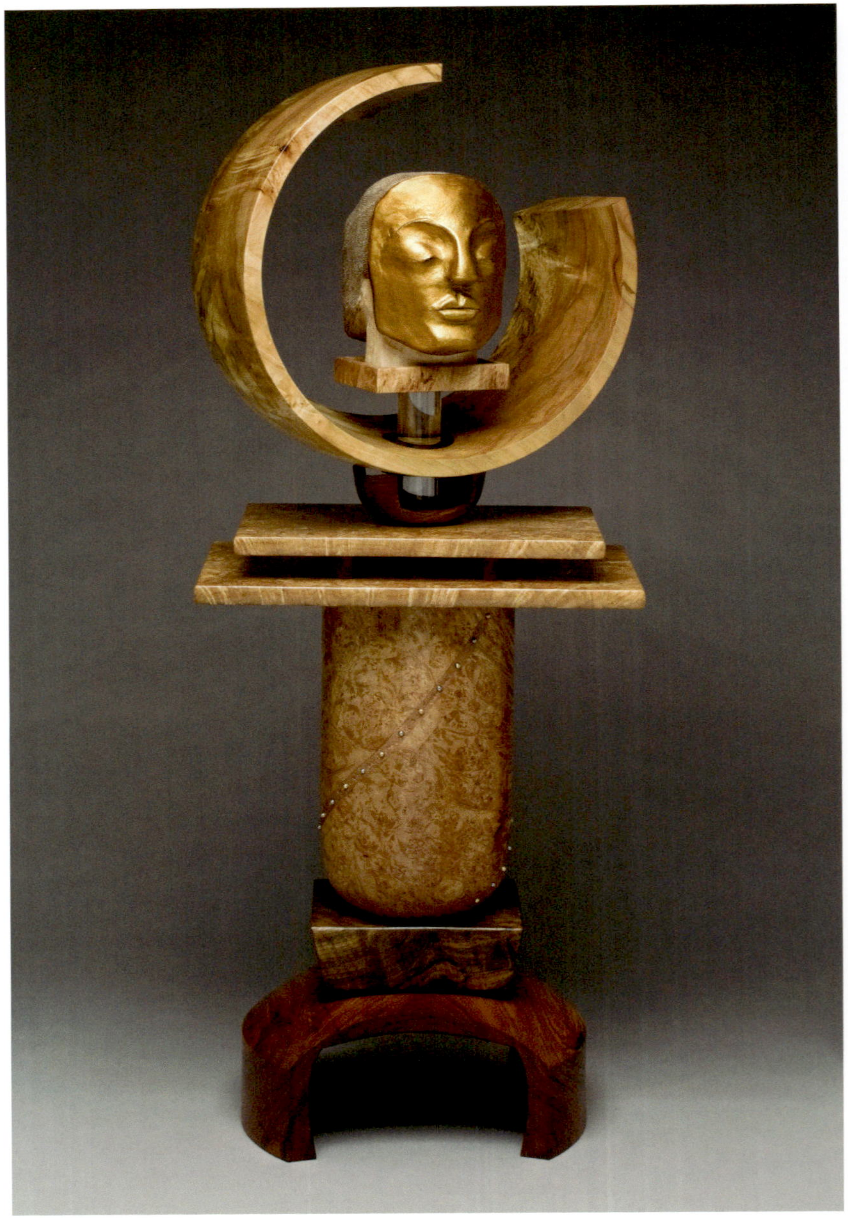

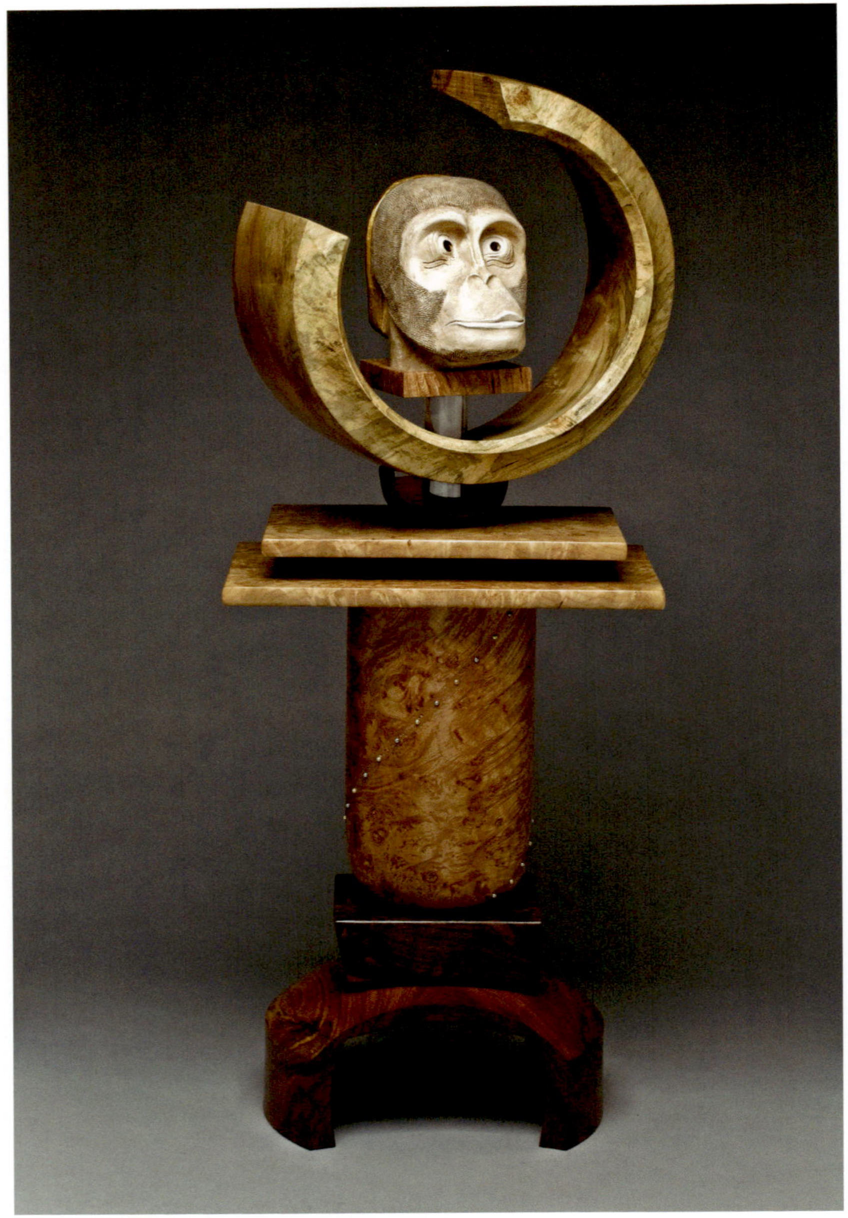

Alfred Sils & Carol Richter Sils. Totem 2: *Who? Me?* Are we just hairless apes? We share 98% of our DNA with the chimp. Is the human face on the back of the chimp's head real or just a mask? Can the human face the future with his eyes closed?

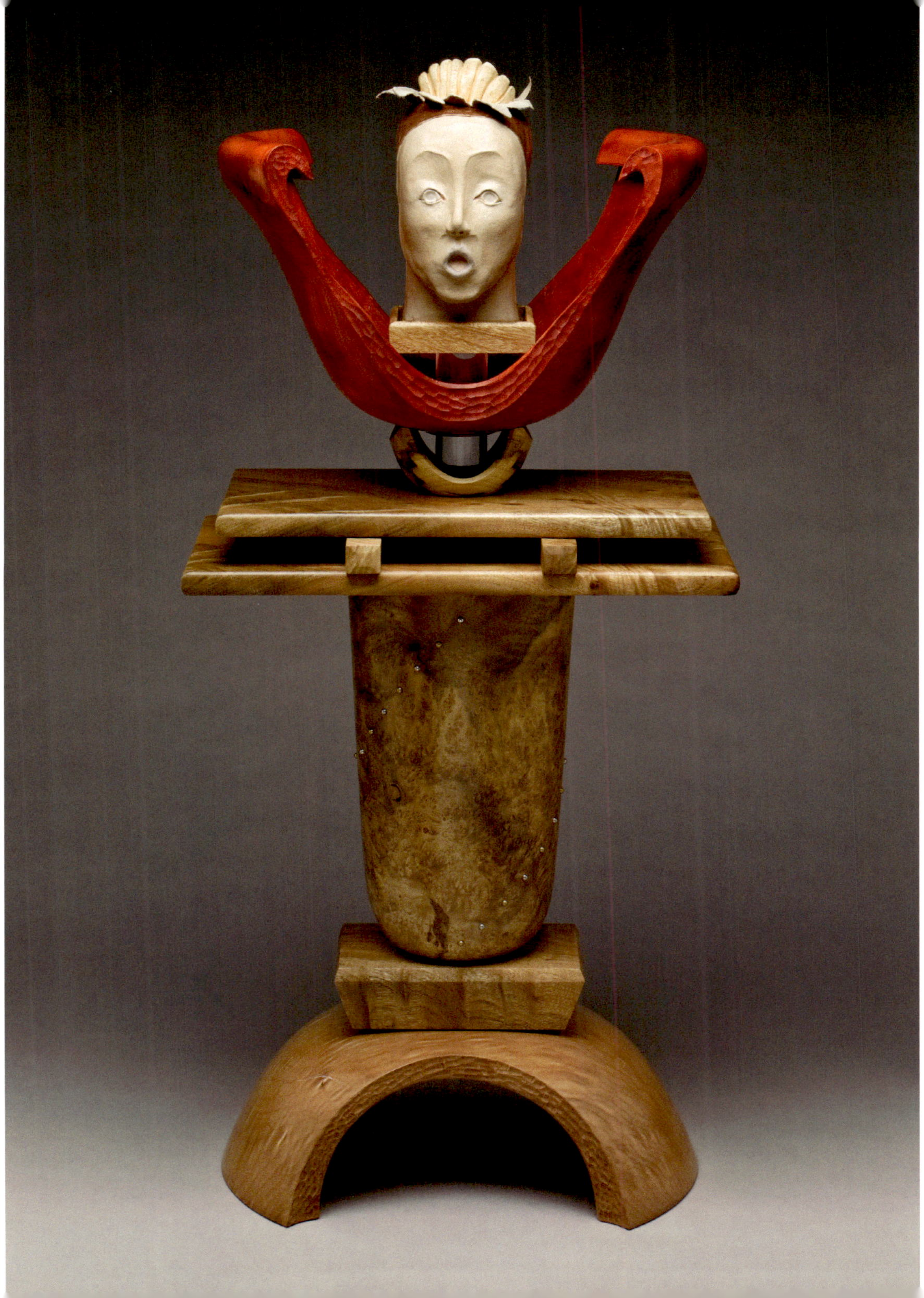

Alfred Sils & Carol Richter Sils. Totem 4: *Brain Storm*. Ceramic, quilted maple, camphor, myrtle burl, magnolia, Plexiglas, steel and brass, 36" h x 16" w x 11" d. We have been taught that our brain is the epitome of the evolutionary process and that it provides the evolutionary advantage that will ensure our permanence. But what if it is an evolutionary detriment? So far we have used it to build larger and more efficient weapons and to despoil our planet. Can our species survive evolutionarily? *Brain Storm*, with its interrupted double helix on the column, depicts the last mushroom cloud.

Steve Sinner

ssinner@mchsi.com

Artist's Statement

Technique and Creative Process

Special techniques and equipment designed and built by the artist are necessary to create each object. It is not unusual to lose a work in progress, and only about half of them can be completed. Any little flaw in the material or the smallest of mistakes during the process will doom the piece to the scrap pile.

Creating a piece begins with fresh cut, or green, wood. It is turned to a cylinder with the wood's pith in the center. The pith is then bored out, leaving a hollow cylinder much thicker than the final work will be. After drying the cylinder to an equilibrium moisture content, which may take months, the cylinder is mounted in a chuck. Boring out the inside to a smooth cylinder is followed by the insertion of a mandrel, which must fit the inside perfectly. While turning the outside of the cylinder to the desired thickness, the mandrel provides support.

After completing the cylinder, the work is moved to a dedicated indexing lathe. A high-speed air powered tool is used to pierce the holes in patterns worked out in advance. Some patterns are developed on the piece by using mathematical formulae, while others may be determined by working out relationships on graph paper. Various sizes of burs allow a wide range of possibilities for creating patterns when combined with variations in spacing and numbering.

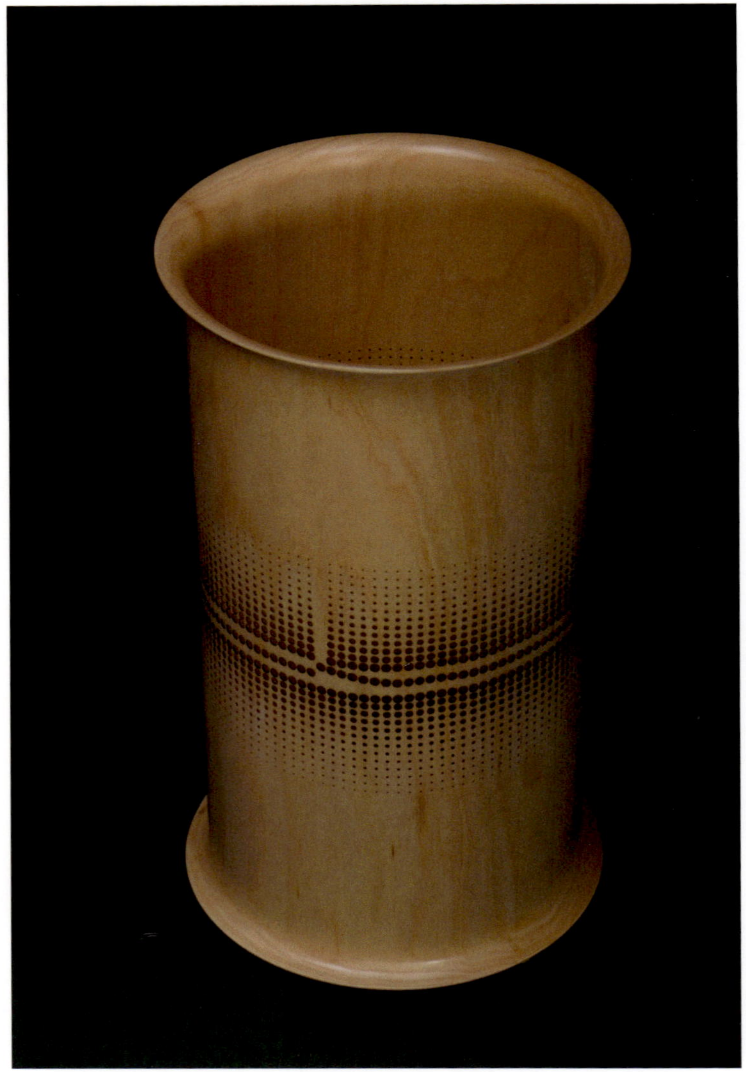

Steve Sinner. *Off Track II.* Sugar maple, 8 3/4" h x 4 7/8" d. This piece references the tendency of a process to drift.

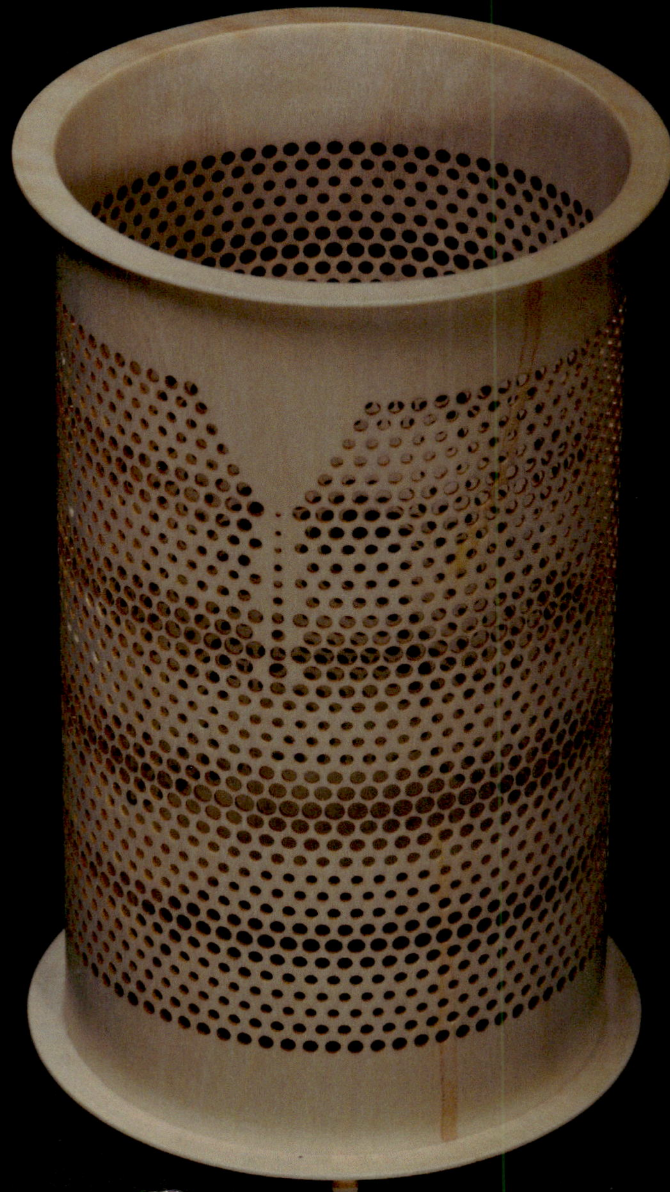

Steve Sinner. *Piercing Piercing A Piercing.* Sugar maple, 4 1/2" h x 2 5/8" d. A needle-shaped set of pierced holes creates a shockwave as it pierces down through the alternating rings of the piece.

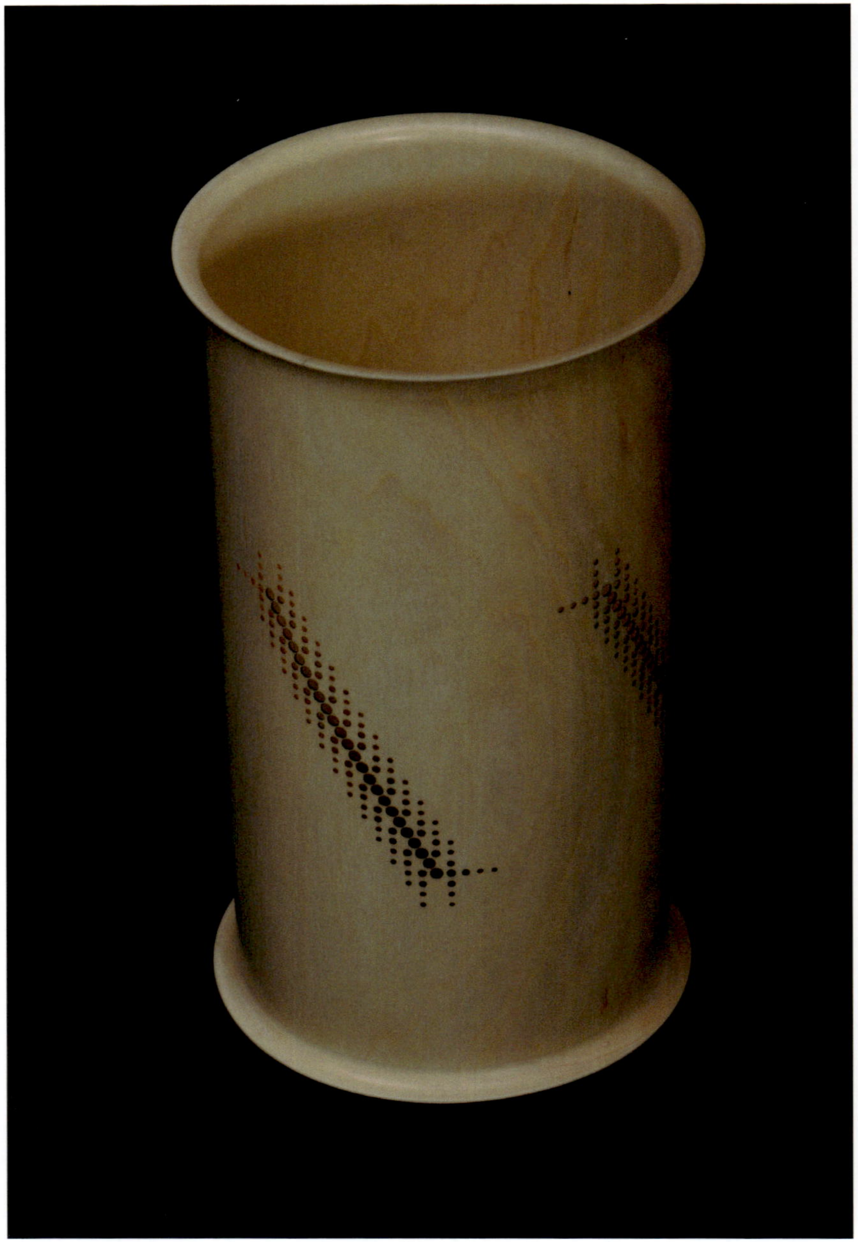

Steve Sinner. *Stardust.* Sugar maple, 8" h x 4 5/16" d. An abstract stellar pattern appears in each quadrant of the work.

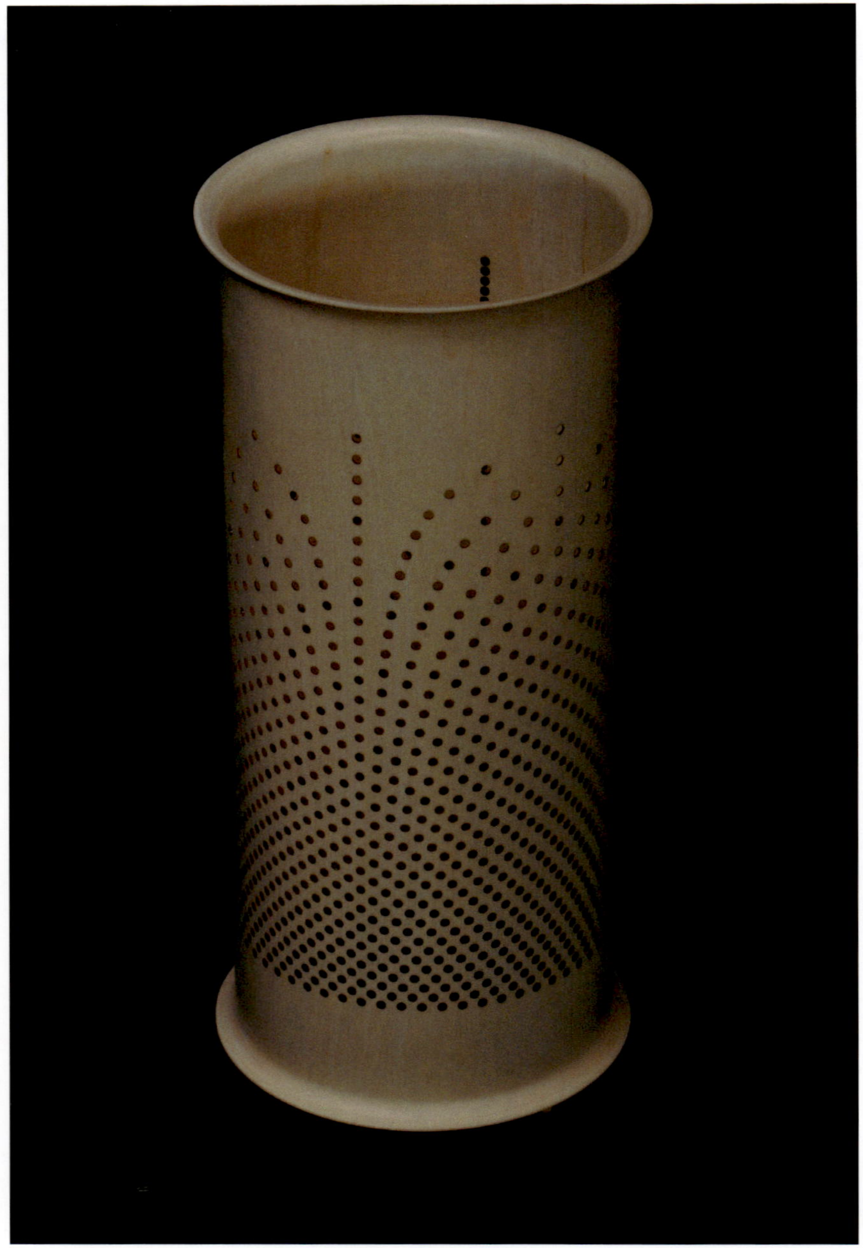

Steve Sinner. *Transition 1-60.* Sugar maple, 8 3/4" h x 3 7/8" d. This pattern develops by starting with a ring of sixty pierced holes and subtracting one from each successive ring, until at the top there is only one hole.

Brent Skidmore

Ashville, North Carolina, www.brentskidmore.com

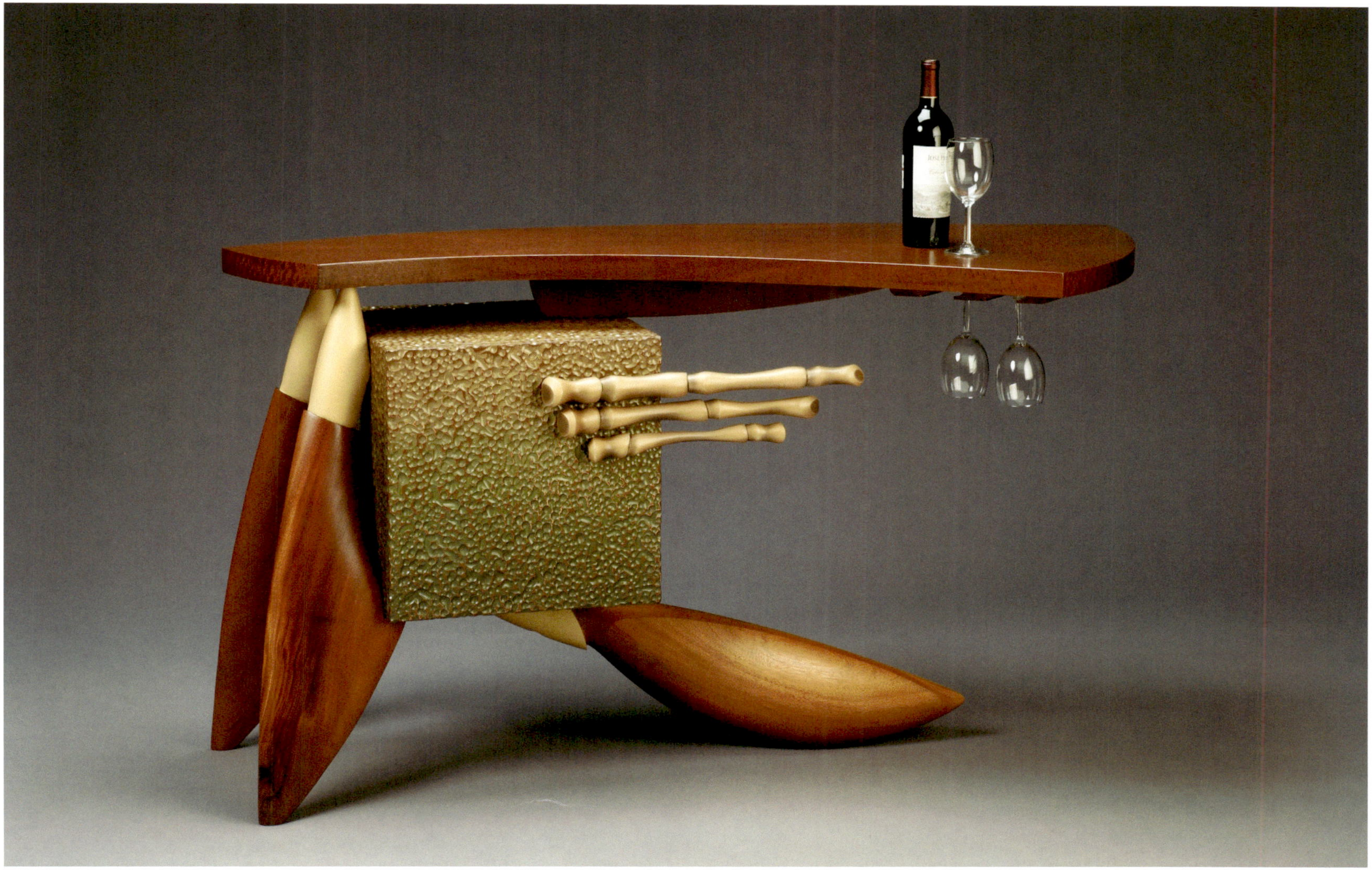

Brent Skidmore. *Bar Bones Boo*. 2003. Pommele sapele, mahogany, birch, poplar, MDF, and acrylic paints, 35" x 58" x 20".

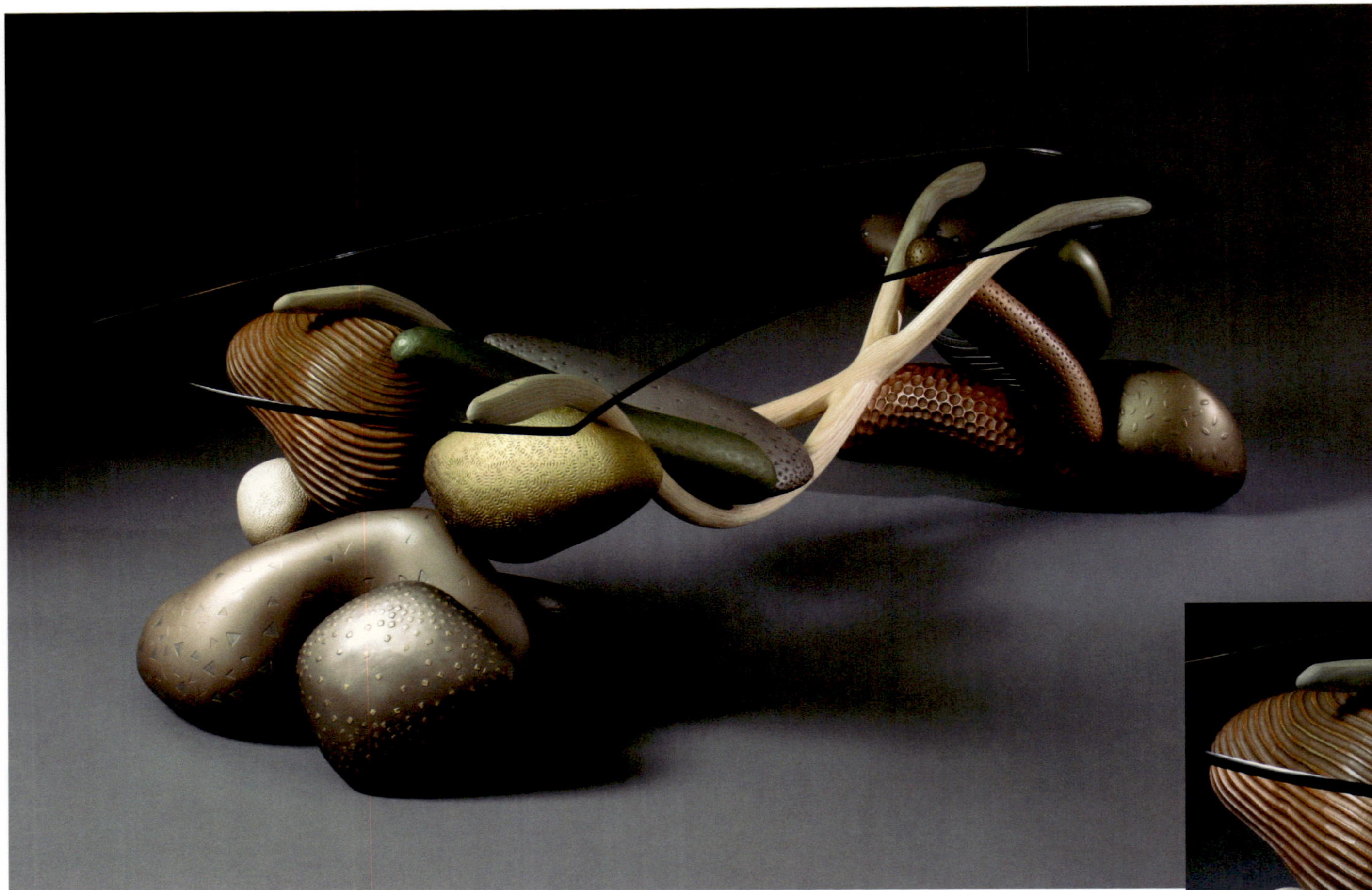

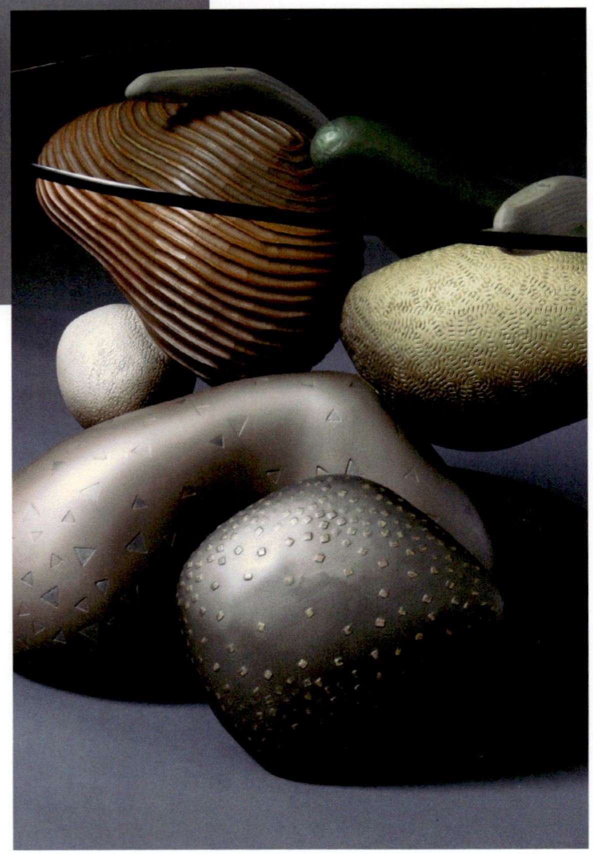

Brent Skidmore. *Low Slung Boulder Table*. 2005. Ash, basswood, acrylic paint, and glass, 53" x 24" x 17".

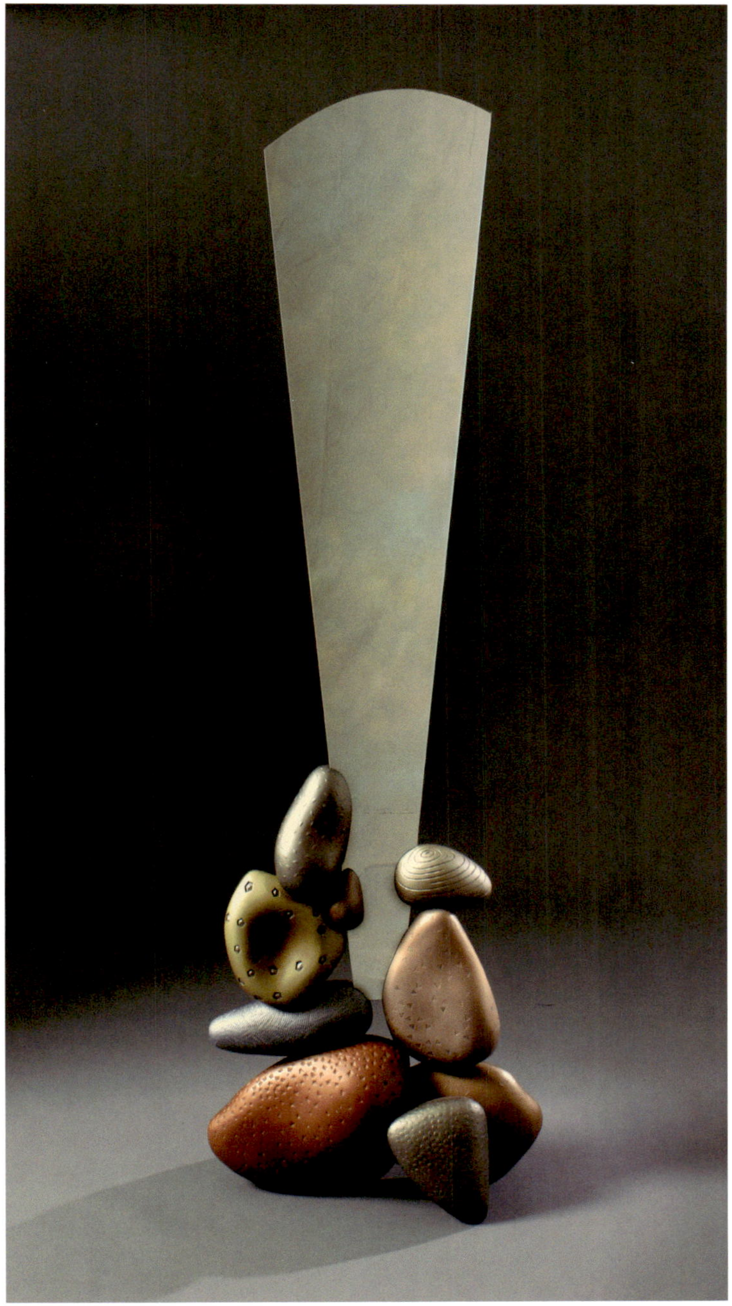

Brent Skidmore. *Maxwell's Mellow Mirror*. 2005. Basswood, mirror & acrylic paint, 65" tall.

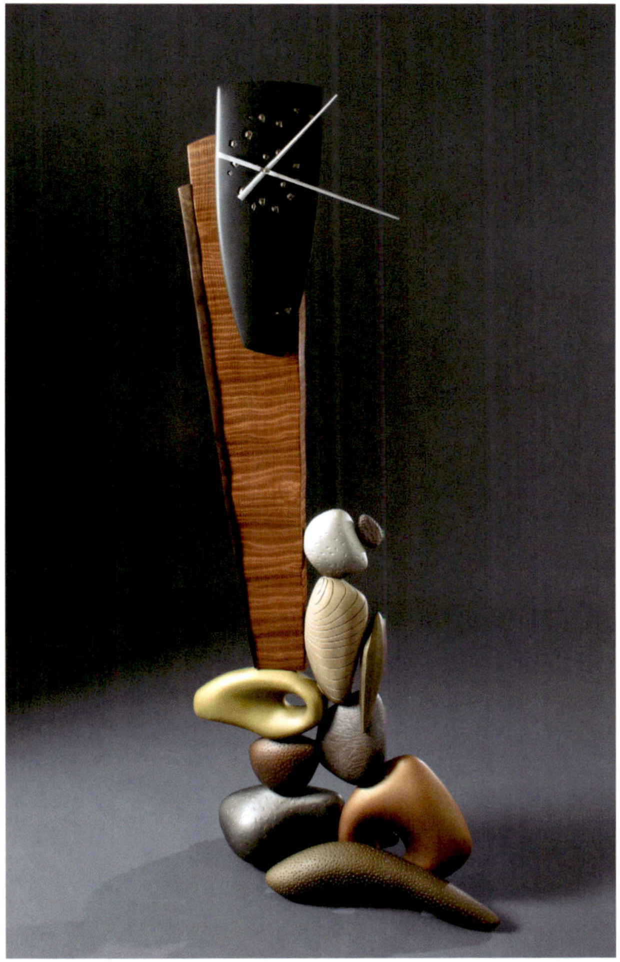

Brent Skidmore. *Stuart's Night Time Canyon Sky*. 2005. Fiddleback redwood, basswood, walnut, and acrylic paints, 72" x 28" x 15"

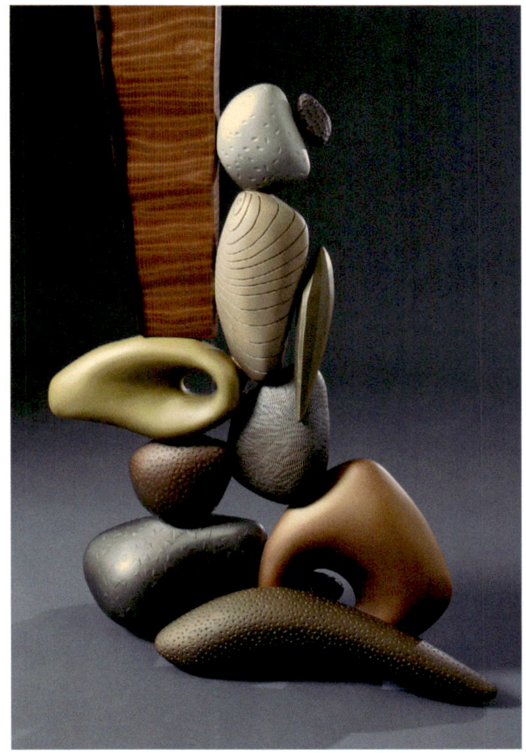

William Smith

wsmith99@gmail.com

Artist's Statement

All of my vessels and sculptural works are created with a process known as Open Segmented Construction. The vessels are made of many small, pie-shaped pieces or segments that are glued together in a configuration similar to brickwork but with small gaps or openings where the vertical mortar would normally be found. These openings make the vessels semitransparent and create wonderful shadow patterns when lighted from above.

I create the patterns by using different types of wood. I currently use a palette of about thirty-five wood varieties. A typical vessel will have between two and five wood species to create the pattern. The *Celtic Knot Bowl* uses three wood species arranged to create the familiar Celtic knot pattern.

To create a vessel, I will cut and glue all of the wood segments. When the glue is dry I then turn the vessel on a wood lathe to the final form. To glue the segments I use a system of jigs and fixtures on a wood lathe. I devised this system in 1996 and it is used by many woodturners today. The work can be tedious and time consuming. The *Celtic Knot Bowl* contains over 1,400 segments and is held together by 5,600 glue joints. Each segment and glue joint must be perfect or it all comes undone during turning.

The piece *Searching For Delphi* is really a hollow vessel. My concept when creating this piece was to take a vessel with a narrow opening and stretch it into a tube closed at one end. This tube was then twisted and folded to form what appears to be a purely sculptural work. The portions of the vessel made from walnut were then burned with a branding iron to create the texture and further blackened with black acrylic paint.

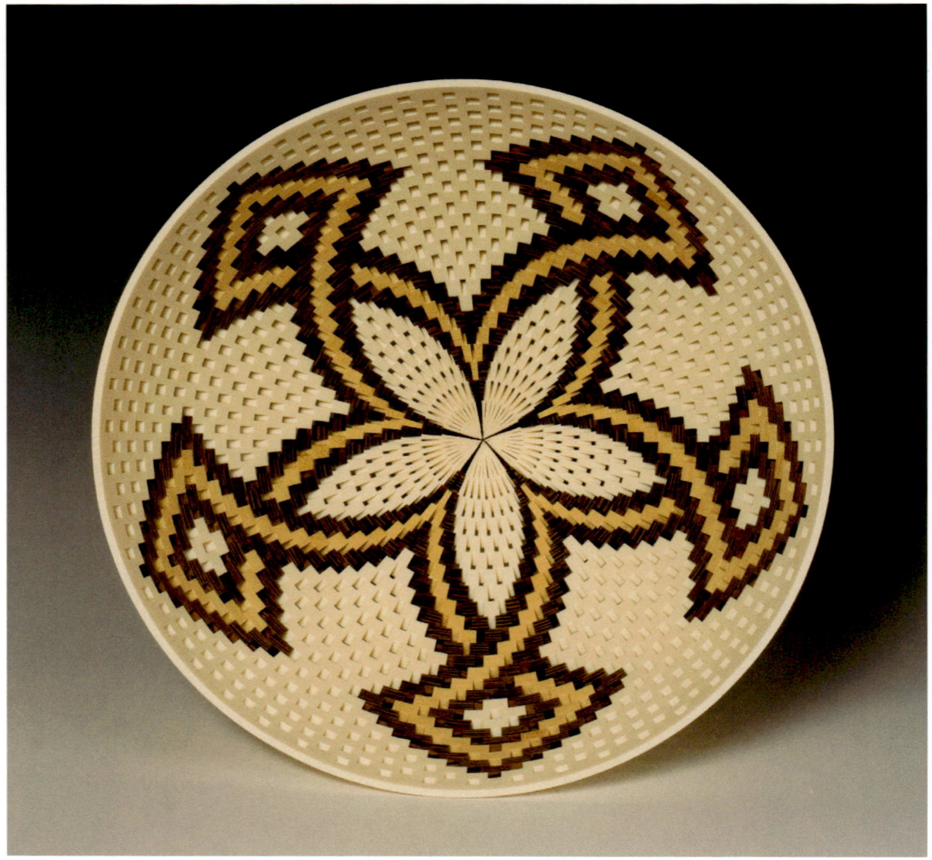

William Smith. *Celtic Knot Bowl.* 2009. Holly, wenge, pau amarello, open segmented, 6.75" d x 3.5" h. (above and opposite page)

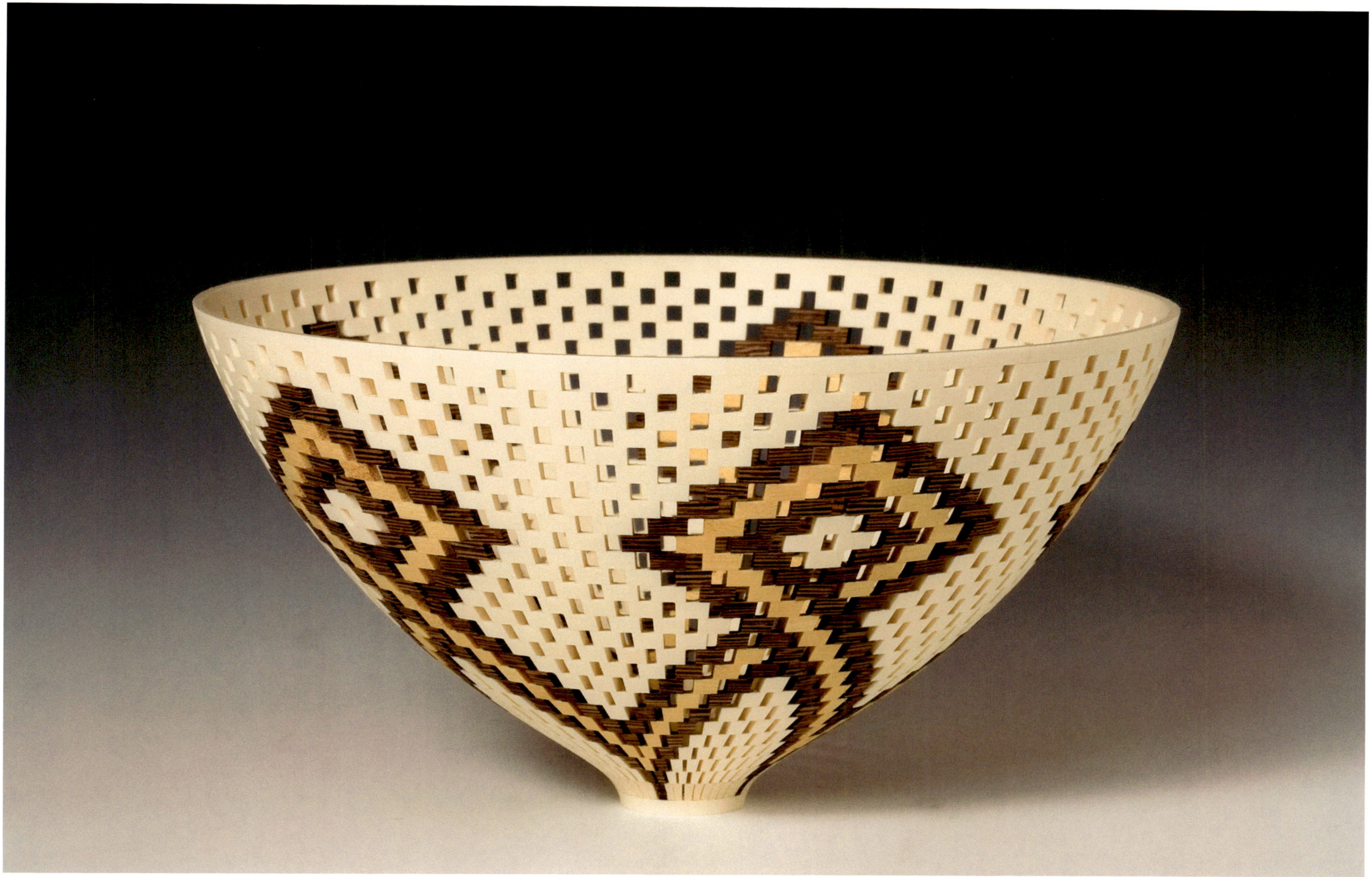

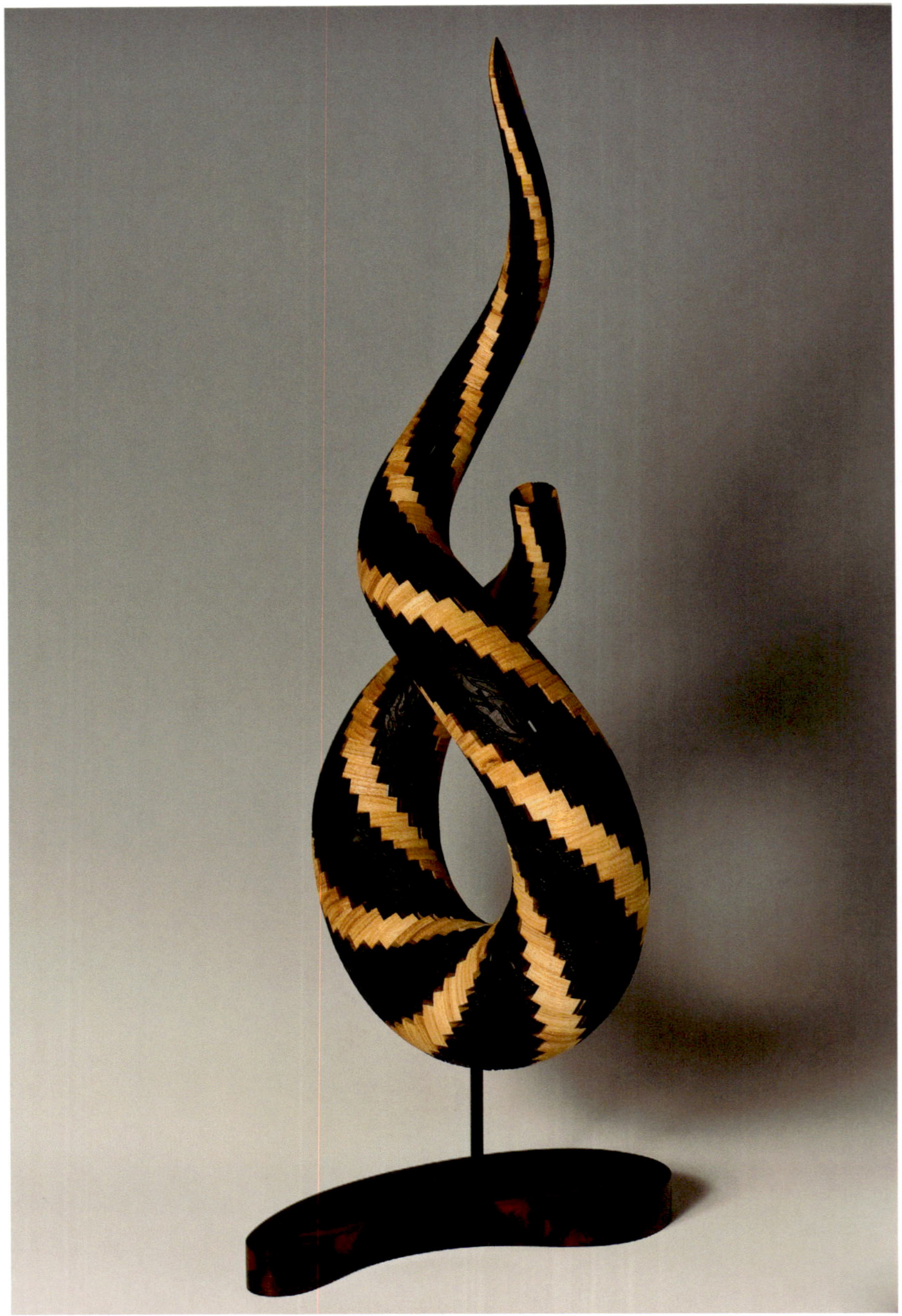

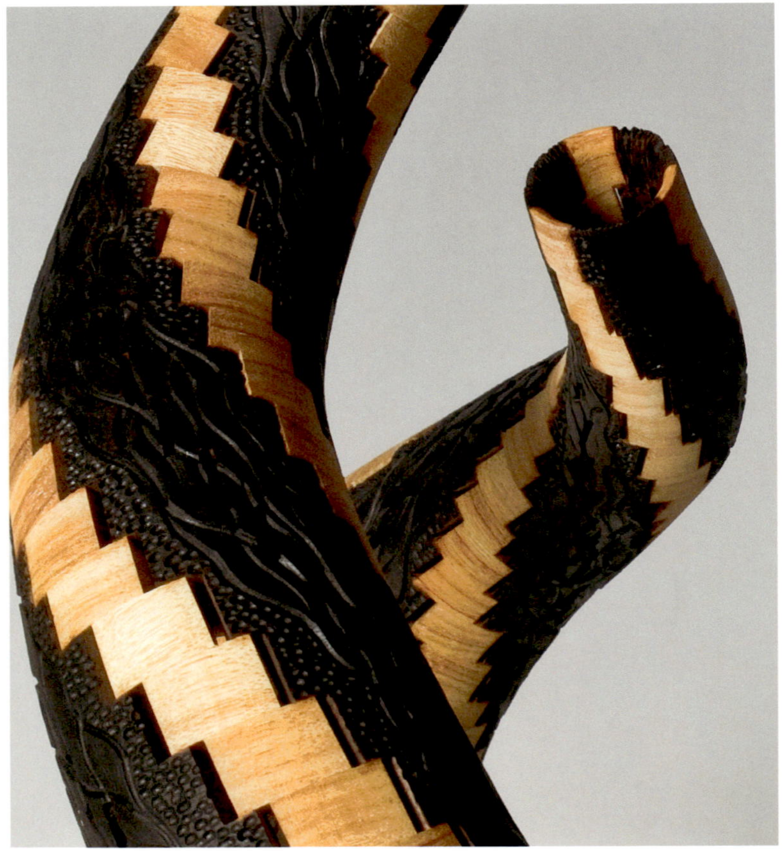

William Smith. *Searching For Delphi.* 2008. Sculpture, canary wood, black walnut, ebony, brass, acrylic paint, open segmented, 10" l x 5" w x 24" h.

ABRAHAM TESSER

Athens, Georgia, www.TesserFurniture.com

Artist's Statement

Designing and building: For me, designing and building furniture is largely solitary and very personal. I struggle with every detail of a design. Is this curve right? Is that part too thick? Will this kind of wood work with that in this context? Do I even have the "right" concept? And then I start again. Finally, when things look like they might work (I am never quite sure) I go from the drawing board to the shop.

Much of the building process is pleasure. It is hard to beat the feeling produced by guiding the transformation of a piece of rough lumber into an elegant, smooth part. And that feeling is dwarfed by seeing the parts come together, nicely and strongly. A bit of oil often makes the piece jump to life! With luck, the piece will be one that captures the eye and invites the hand to touch.

The construction process is not nearly as linear as this description implies. I am constantly redesigning as I am building. The finished piece is unlikely to be what I originally envisioned but a more or less different piece. One resulting from the dialectic involving the original vision and the feedback from eye, hand, brain, and heart associated with the construction process. Murphy's Law is as applicable in the shop as anywhere else. When things go poorly, yet another design opportunity emerges. And when things go well, when a hand plane produces the perfect shaving, when a beautiful shape emerges on the lathe, when a piece of wood that has just been surfaced shows a figure or character that is better than expected, it is indeed thrilling.

There is also a social aspect of designing and building furniture. Others are a source of inspiration and motivation. Interacting with a patron with particular needs and preferences often results in designs that might never otherwise have come to mind. When that works it is a joy. Many others have a very good eye, whether they be design professionals or not, and their suggestions are often invaluable.

Almost nothing pleases me more than learning that others appreciate my work. I want my furniture to be engaging. I'm elated when someone sits in one of my chairs and can't help smiling because the chair is more comfortable than expected; or, when someone reaches down and touches a surface and then reaches down again or asks their partner to touch because it felt good. Wow! Sam Maloof, one of the world's great furniture makers, claims that his favorite piece is always the one he is currently working on. And, so it is for me. Each piece is, for a time, my baby and it is difficult for me to let it go. But it is also gratifying to know that someone likes it enough to have it in his or her home or office.

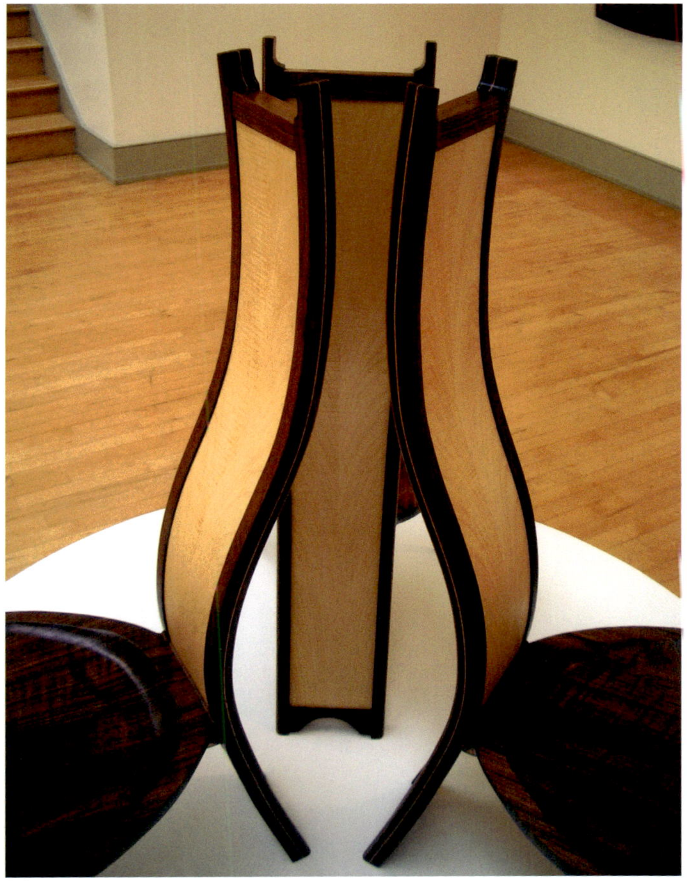

Abraham Tesser. *S-Chairs.* 2006. Curly walnut, book matched Italian sycamore veneer, bending plywood, Danish oil, 23.5" x 20" x 48" per chair; the pedestal is 6' in diameter. (above and next page)

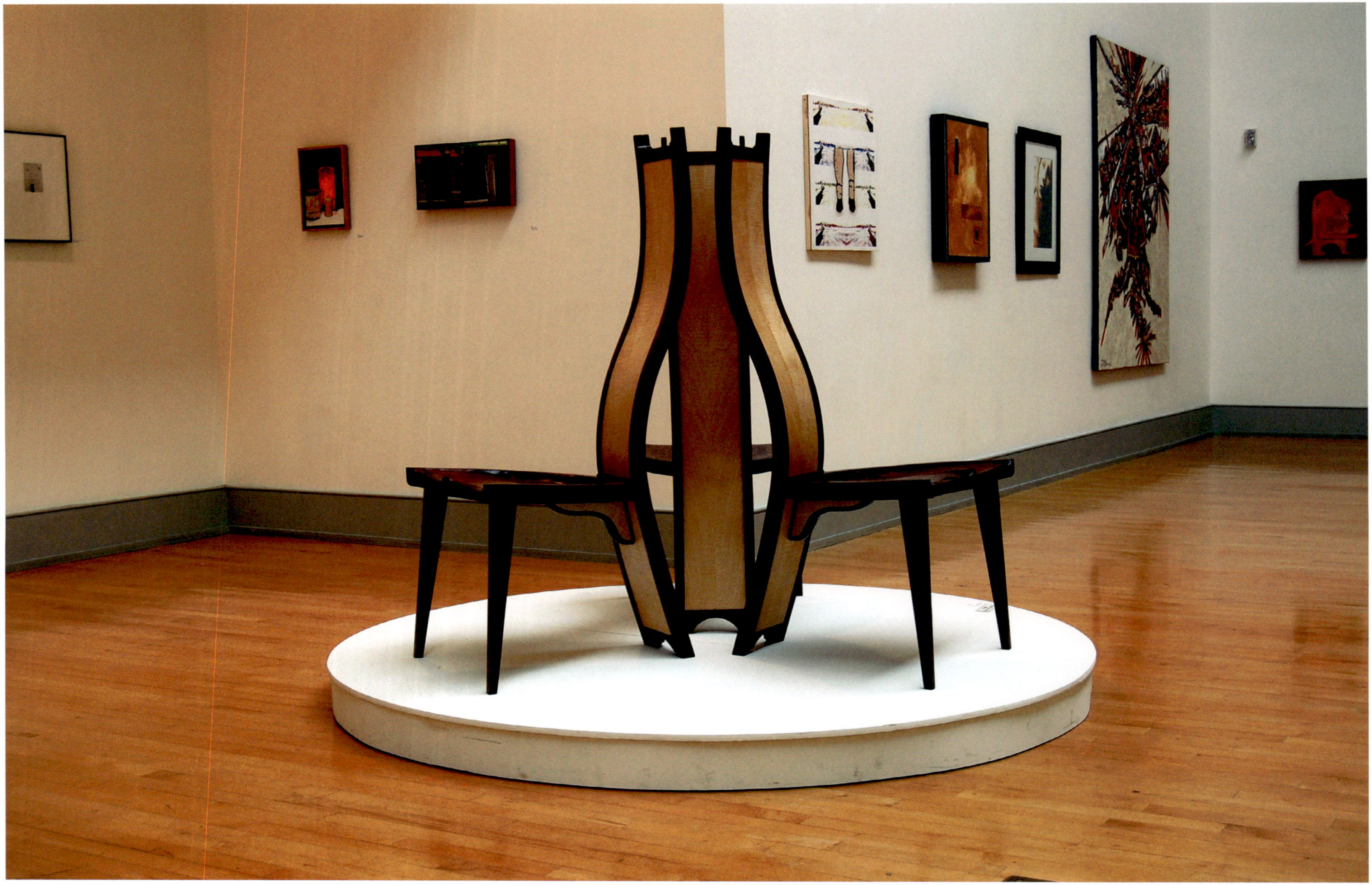

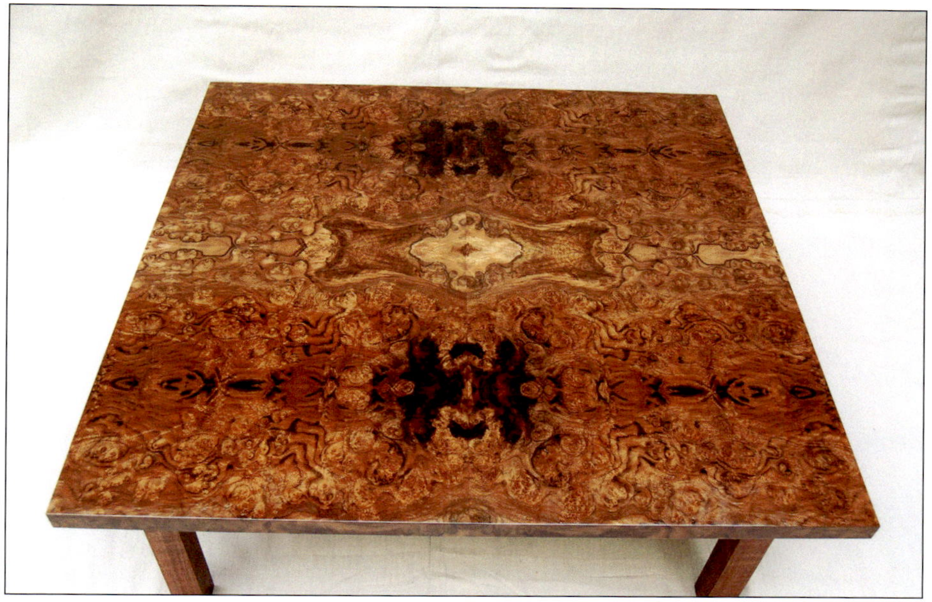

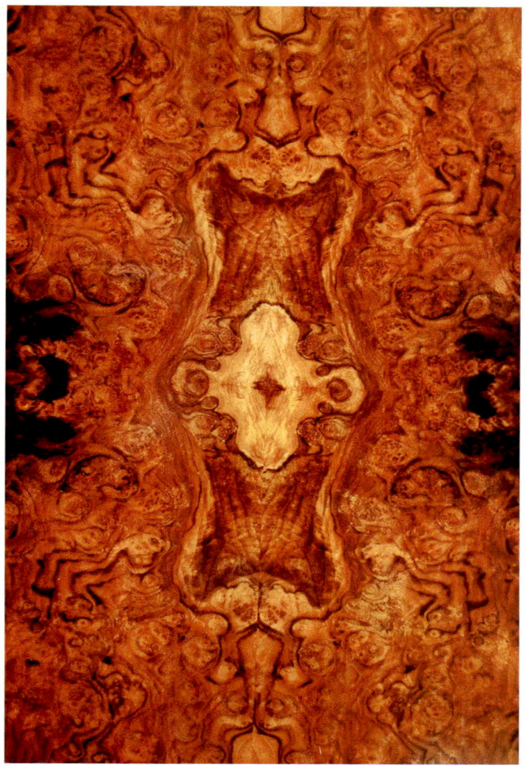

Abraham Tesser. *Craige Table.* 2008. Walnut, walnut burl veneer, rubbing oil with polyurethane, 38" x 38" x 15". *From the collection of Betty Jean Craige*

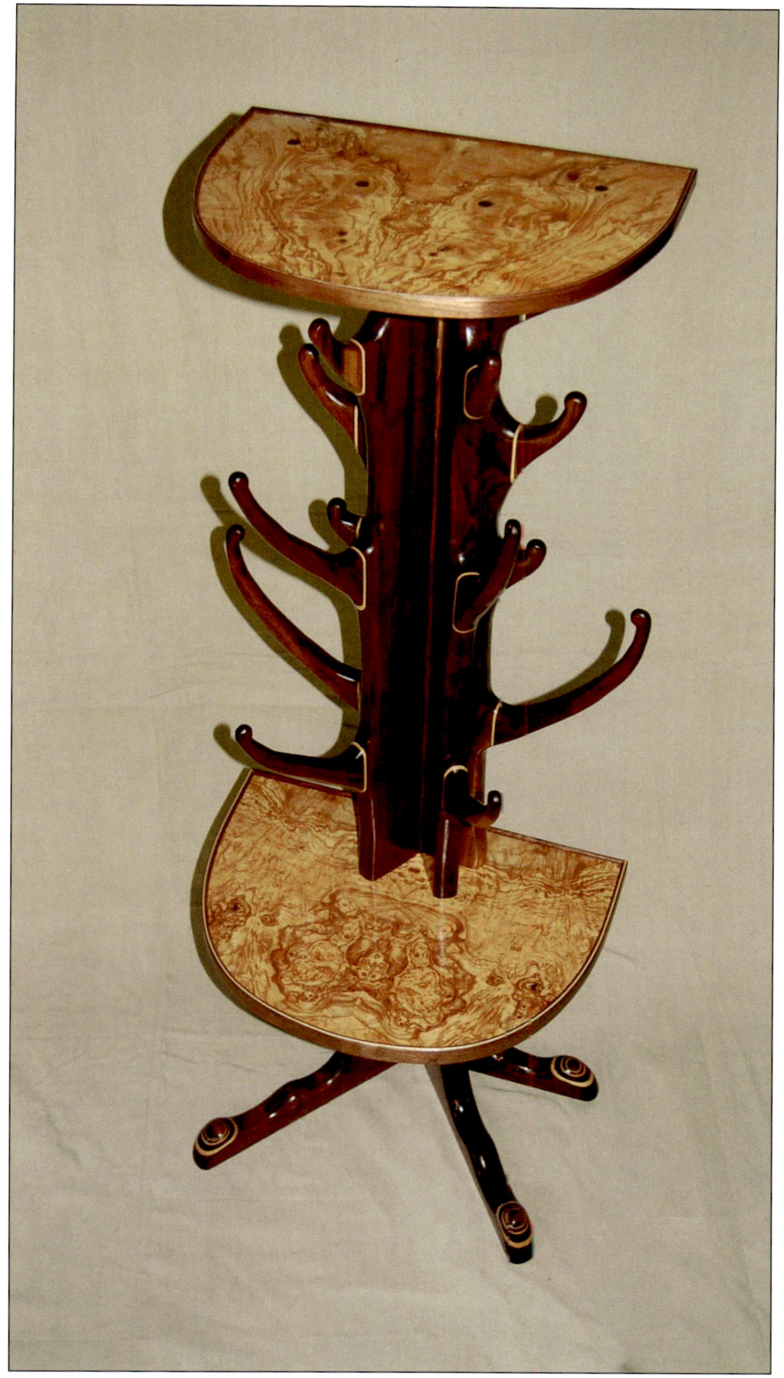

Abraham Tesser. *Kurtz Hat Tree.* 2008. Walnut, maple accents, olive ash burl veneer, oil, 61" h x 22" w x 15" deep. *From the Collection of Carol and Paul Kurtz*

Curt Theobald

Pine Bluffs, Wyoming, cwtheobald@wyoming.com

Artist's Statement

Much of my work is directly related to my life experiences. My creative process begins with putting my ideas into drawings. The drawings help me to define my work and show me any complexities that may happen during construction. The more technically challenging the project gets, the more passionate I become about the piece. Solving the challenge is where my passion lies. Usually I will go through several design changes before I go to the studio. Once I'm satisfied with the design I will construct a prototype. This process allows me to modify any aspects of the piece and work out any design challenges before I begin actual construction of my intended piece. Making the prototype can take up to a week. This consumption of time may seem like overkill, but I don't want any surprises when working with more valuable species of wood.

Individual Artwork

Archaeology Series

While sifting through the archaeological dig of my mind, I assembled fragments into a vessel inspired by a reconstructed Native American artifact.

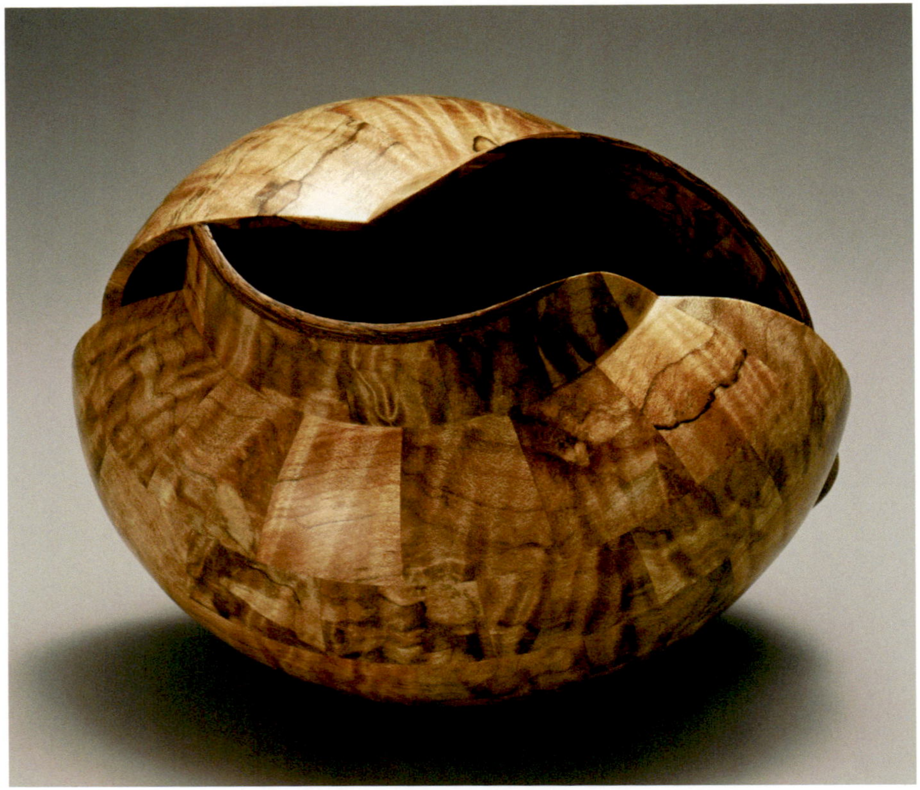

Curt Theobald. *Archaeology Series.* 2005. Spalted maple, panga panga, 6" h x 6" x 7 1/2". *Private collection.*

The Wizard

Wenge is a wood that is very difficult to use. It seems that I cannot pick up a piece of it without getting a splinter. A friend of mine in the UK once called wenge, "A nasty concoction of unusable wood fibers." He might be right; however, the stunning grain patterns in the completed work are worth all the difficulties and challenges the material imposes on me.

Streets of Gold

The apostle John wrote in the Book of Revelation about foundations decorated with every kind of precious stone and a street of pure gold. By peering through the cracks in the wall, you can see the golden glow of the streets.

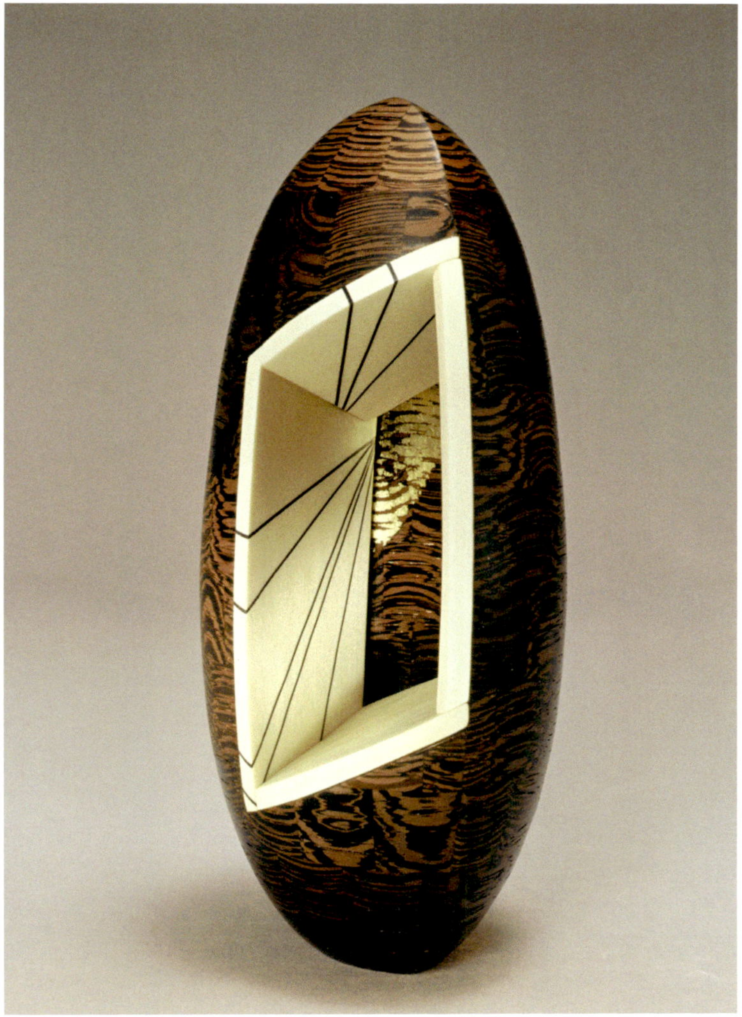

Curt Theobald. *The Wizard*. Wenge, Colorado aspen, gold leaf, 7 1/4" h x 2 1/2" x 3 3/4". *Private collection.*

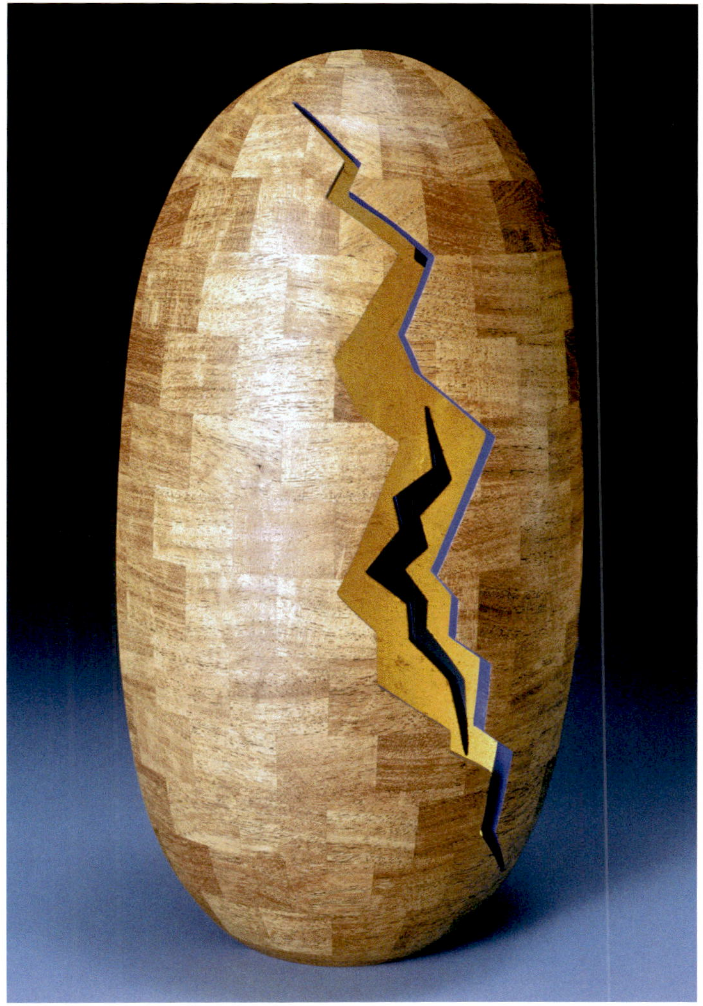

Curt Theobald. *Streets of Gold.* 2006. Mesquite, gold leaf, acrylic paint, 9 1/2" h x 3 1/2" x 5". *Private collection.*

The Promise

This piece was created during our family's long wait for an international adoption to materialize, while the paperwork documenting our approval for this adoption sat half a world away in Beijing, China. The silhouette of the pieces is a teardrop, representing the difficult wait. The trio signifies the promise that someday our daughter would complete our family tree.

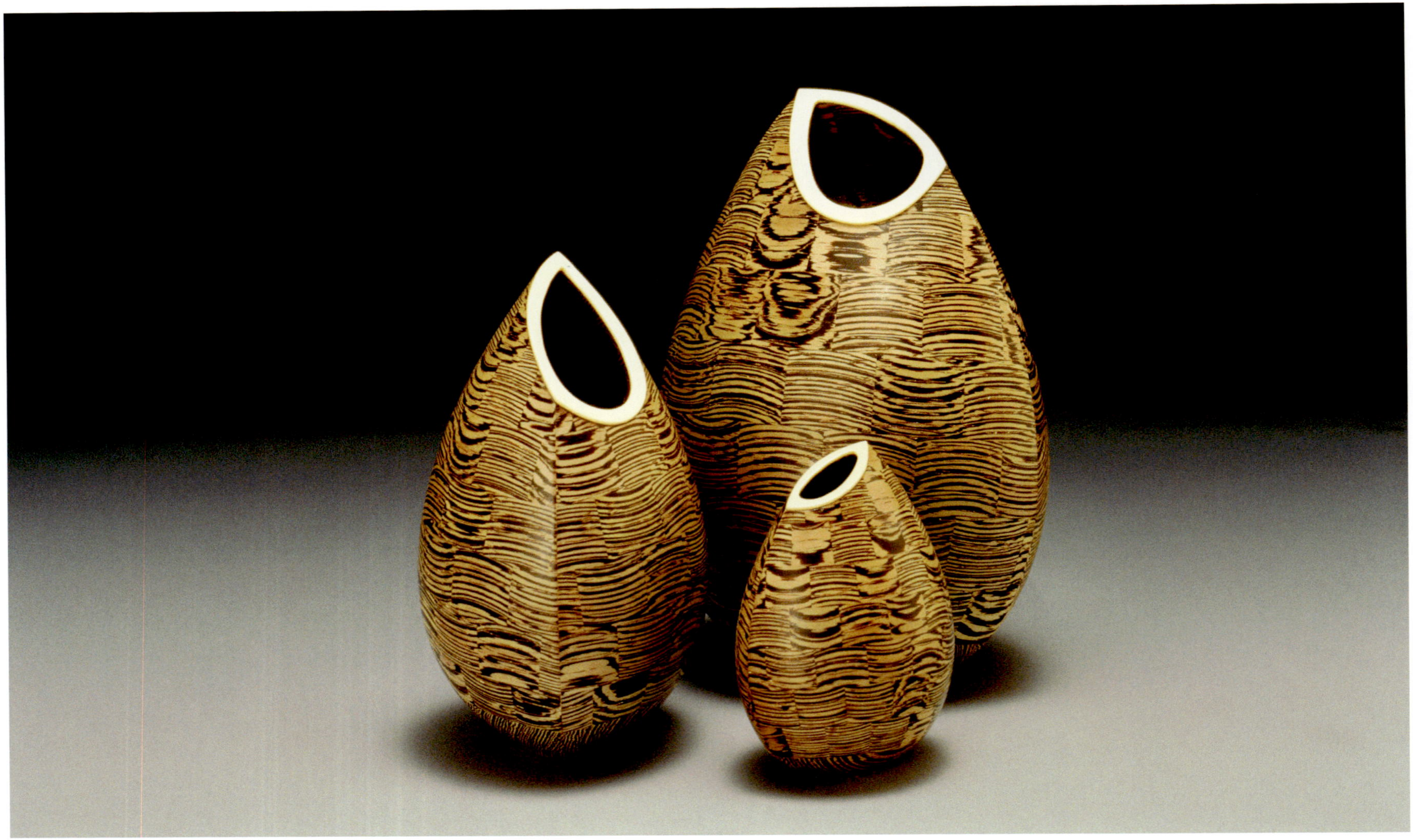

Curt Theobald. *The Promise.* 2007. Wenge, holly, 6 1/4" h x 3 1/2" x 4 1/2"; 5" h x 2 1/2" x 3 1/4"; 3 1/2" h x 1 3/4" x 2 1/8". *Private collection.*

Father Daughter

This series is inspired by the relationship between parents and children. Specific placement of the two elements in the set conveys a sense of emotion. Let your mind run wild with the arrangement of these pieces.

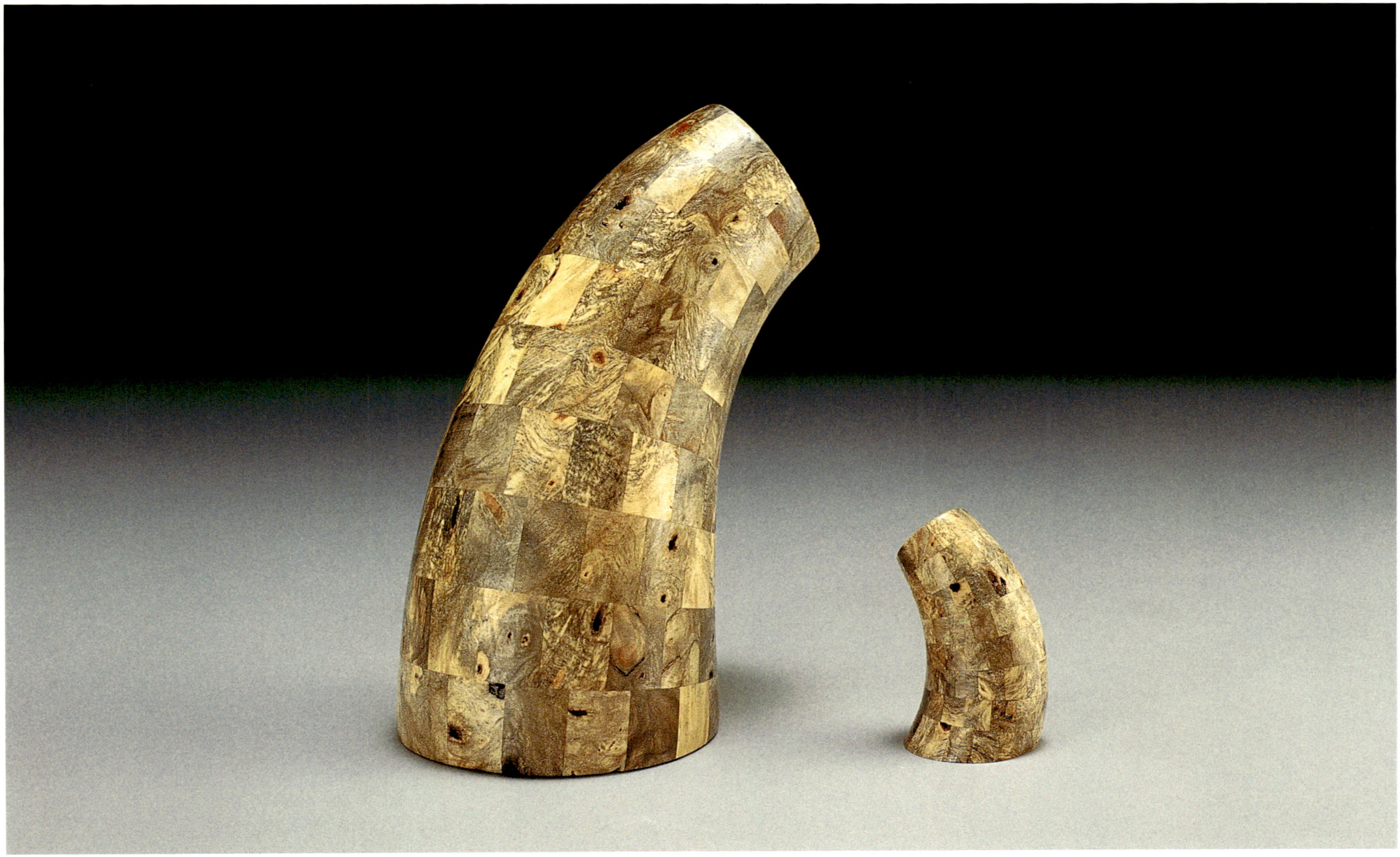

Curt Theobald. *Father Daughter.* 2008. Buckeye burl, 6" h (large piece), 2 1/4" (small piece). *Private collection.*

Craig Thibadeau

San Diego, California, www.ctfinefurniture.com

Artist's Statement

For over a decade I have been quietly taking custom furniture in a new direction in my shop in San Diego. Having studied traditional methods of furniture-making and classical marquetry with some of today's modern masters, I am able to combine beautiful materials, premium craftsmanship, and a touch of artistry to create one-of-a-kind custom furniture of the highest caliber.

As a furniture maker, my work evolves by blending the physical, practical, and artistic needs with my desire to create individual objects with intensity and feeling. To this end I incorporate imagery in the form of flowers, branches, and animals into select pieces of my furniture. I design subtle floral ornamentations, enhancing my furniture with classical marquetry, the ancient art of creating imagery from thin pieces of exotic wood, metal and shell, and applying them to furniture. My marquetry furniture combines the structural geometry of a manmade object with the asymmetry of nature represented in flower and leaf patterns and motifs. I see the addition of decorative marquetry as a doorway into unique and exiting visual forms and more expressive freedom. In this way I attempt to fill the basic need of a functional object with creative detailed work far exceeding expectations.

Individual Artwork

Bubinga Coffee Table

A contemporary Asian styled coffee table with a beautiful book-matched waterfall bubinga veneered top framed in solid wenge. The legs and framework are solid jatoba and it has solid wenge feet. It is finished with highly polished polyester on the top and satin lacquer on the base.

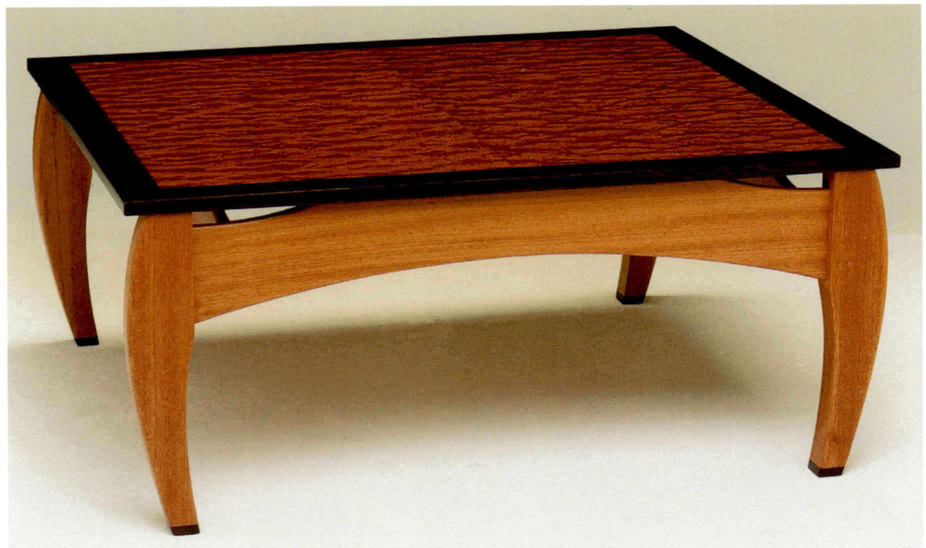

Craig Thibadeau. Bubinga Coffee Table. 2004. Bubinga, wenge, mahogany, and jatoba, wood-veneer and solid, veneering, solid wood joinery, 42" l x 34" w x 17" h. *Photographer: Craig Carlson*

Gardenia Sideboard

A large demilune sideboard with marquetry imagery of gardenia flowers flowing from a central point in the top down the front panels. It has anigre feet and anigre inlay in the legs and mother of pearl and abalone inlayed butterflies in one of the curved doors and the top panel. The curved doors and drawers are bent laminated from layers of poplar plywood and veneer and the wenge legs and trim are a combination of solid wenge and veneer. The cabinet interior and drawers are all made with quartersawn maple. The marquetry veneer for this piece was cut using the Italian packet method and a modern scroll saw. Finished with polyester, conversion varnish and lacquer.

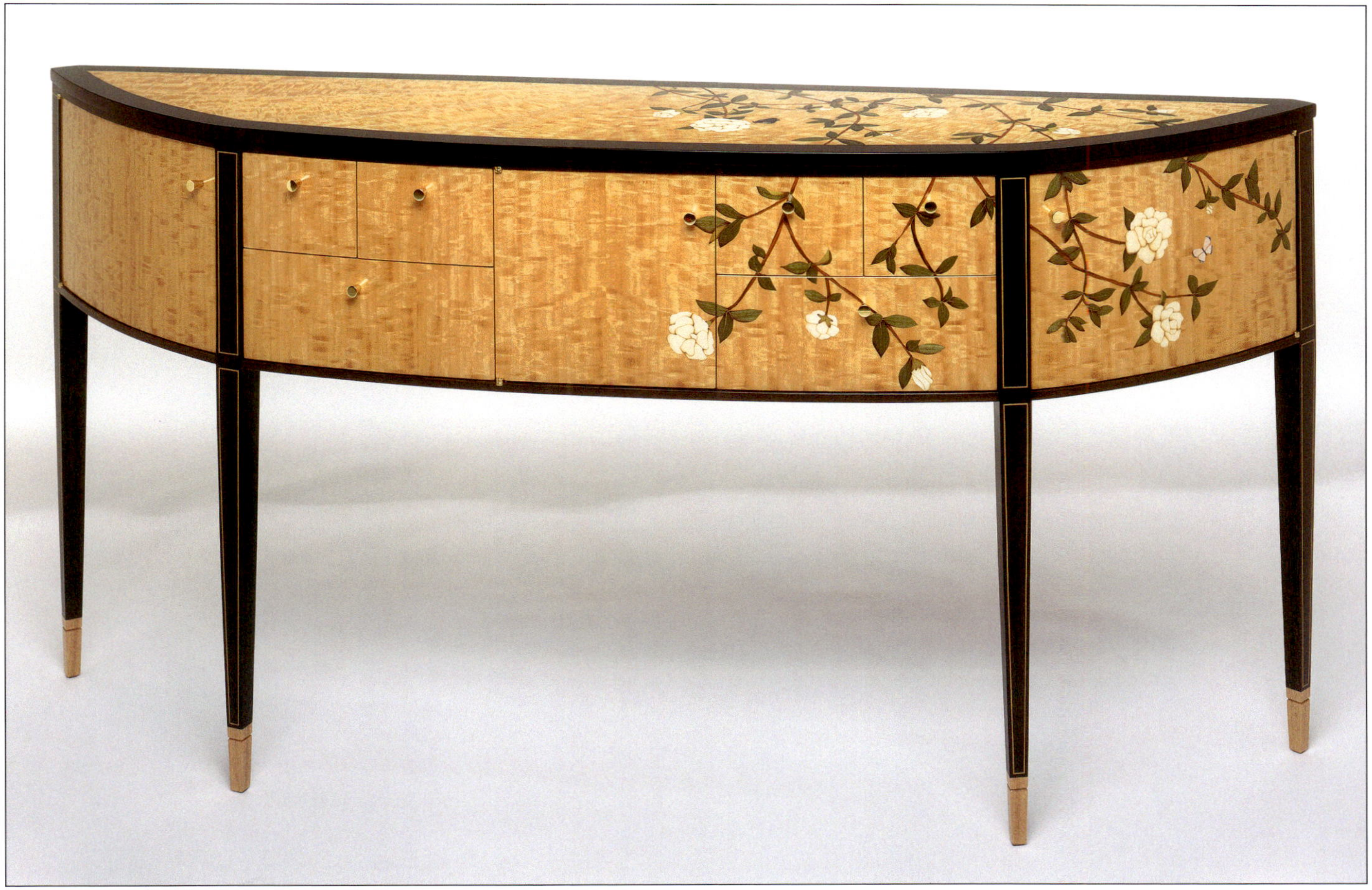

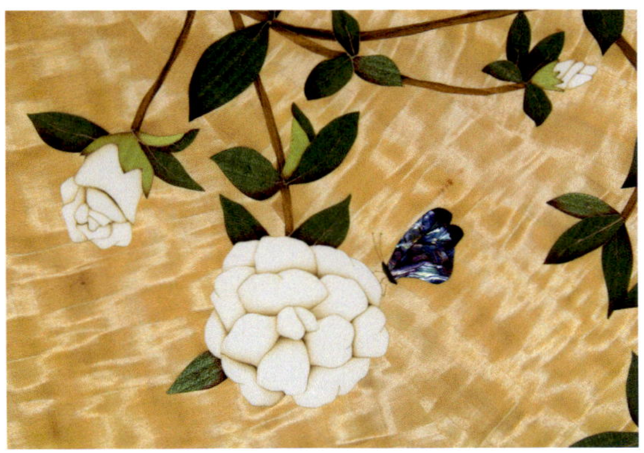

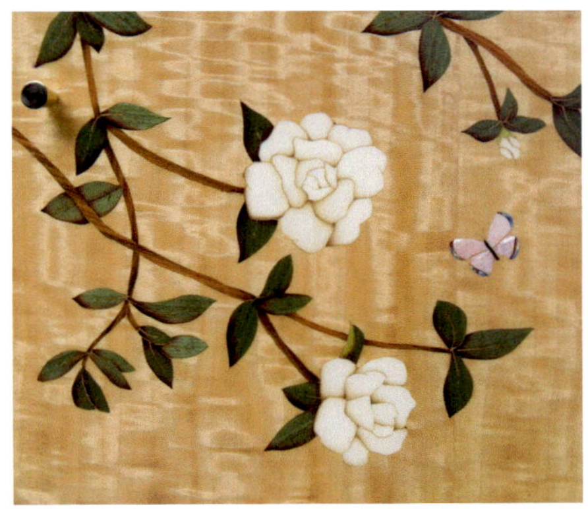

Craig Thibadeau. Gardenia Sideboard. 2007. Cabinet/ Sideboard, Wenge, block figured anigre, quarter sawn maple, ebony, pau ferro, boxwood, maple, poplar, holly, and anigre, wood-solid and veneer, marquetry, veneering, bent lamination, solid wood joinery, and inlay, 72" l x 16" d x 36" h. *Photographer: Craig Carlson*

Myrtle Bench

This Italian Art Deco styled bench has a gentle radiused profile on the feet and a rounded veneered torsion box seat support. The heavy use of curved forms on this bench required some experimentation to create pleasing shapes that could be made repeatedly. The cushion is upholstered in silk fabric. The finish is conversion varnish over polyester fill and the entire bench has been polished to a high gloss. The black detailing is black pigmented lacquer. The myrtle burl veneer was dyed a golden brown color to match the clients existing furniture in this style.

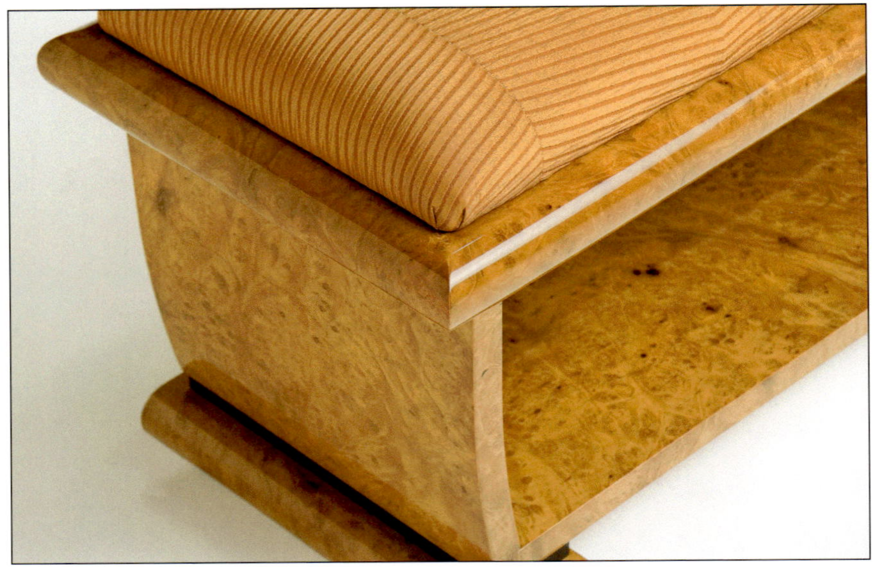

Craig Thibadeau. Myrtle Bench. 2007. Myrtle burl, poplar, and silk fabric, wood-veneer and solid, veneering, bent lamination, and upholstery, 54" l x 16" d x 18" h. *Photographer: Craig Carlson*

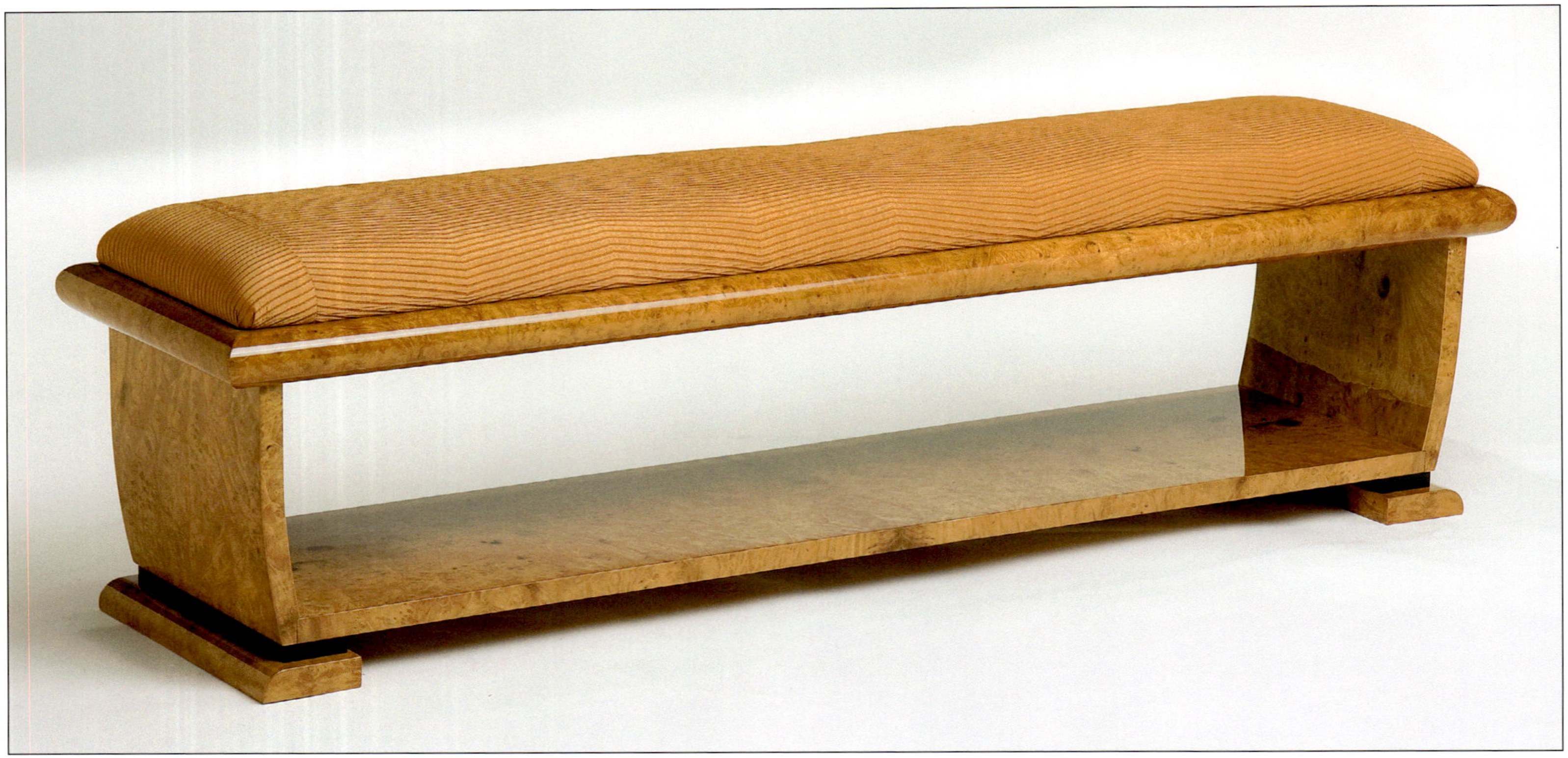

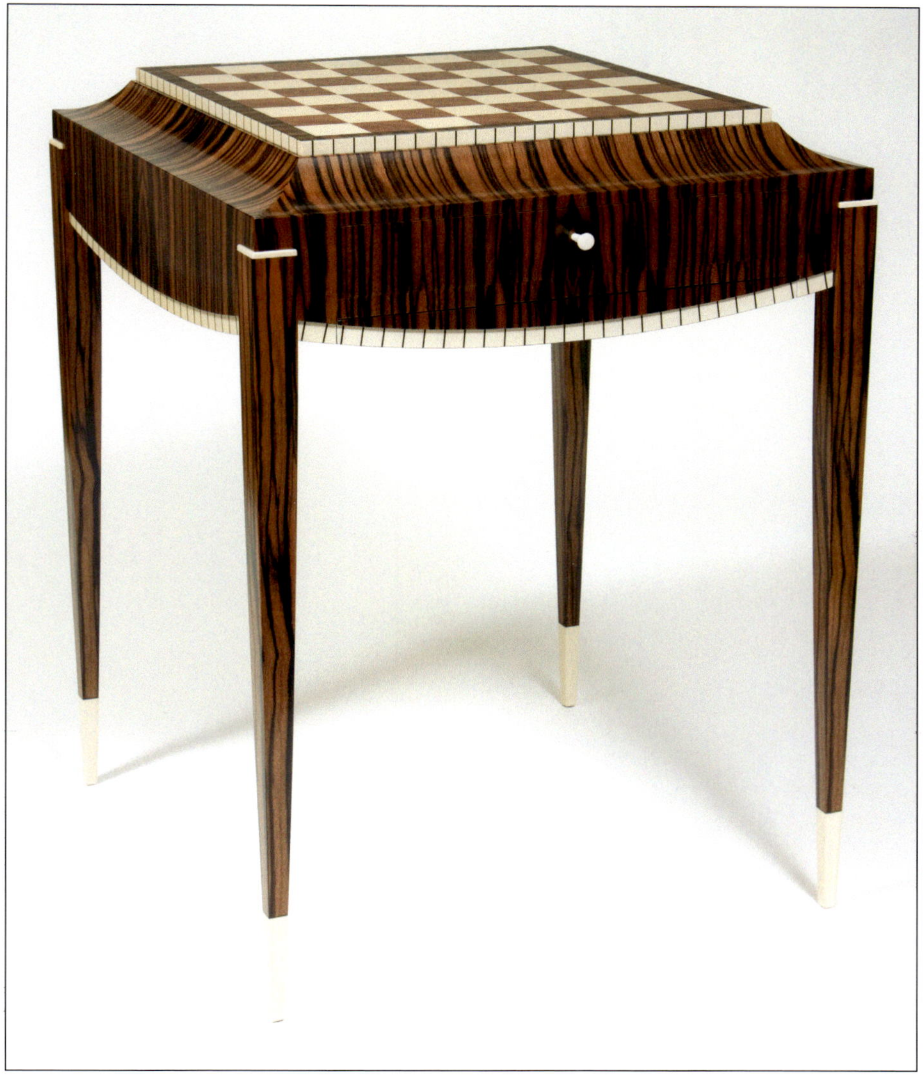

Craig Thibadeau. Chess Table. 2008. Macassar ebony, bubinga, holly, ebony, mother of pearl, and jatoba, wood—solid and veneer, veneering, parquetry, solid wood joinery, and inlay, 27" square x 32" h. *Photographer: Craig Carlson*

Chess Table

An Art Deco-inspired chess table in Macassar ebony with a playing surface of bubinga and holly squares framed with ebony and holly inlay. There is one divided drawer for chess piece storage in jatoba and a slide out tray in ebony decorated with a gently curving pattern of mother of pearl to hold captured pieces during the game. The overall shape of the piece is highlighted by the holly and ebony stringing running along the curved bottom edge of the side panels and around the playing surface. The finish is Bright Rub conversion varnish.

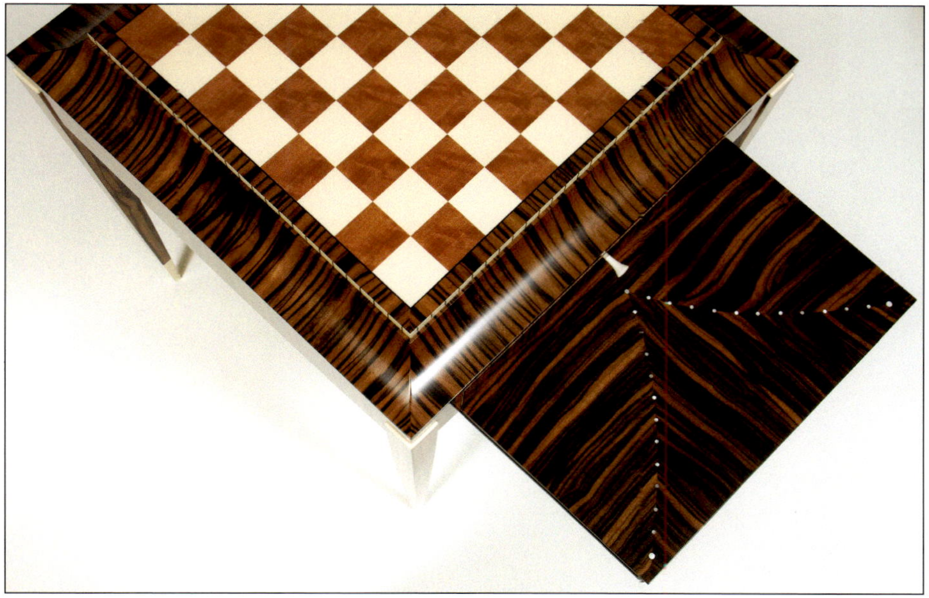

John Thoe

Seattle, Washington

Artist's Statement

I became interested in Baroque and Rococo woodcarving as a student in Norway in 1970. These are styles that rely on curved arcs and ellipses. I realized in the early 1990s that period style furniture was disappearing as an accepted style with promise of a future. Most published furniture and architectural examples in the Seattle area as well as national were contemporary with sleek lines.

My dining furniture is composed of curved arcs and ellipses but not the frills of my earlier work.

Chairs are the one furniture item that can be viewed from all angles and the design must take that into consideration. All my chairs have a similarity that carries in each design.

Viewed horizontally, the geometric shapes of the negative spaces form quadrilateral polygons (two parallel and two non parallel lines). These negative space shapes change as you move around the chair. These negative spaces include the shapes between the spokes or splats and the bottom of the crest rail and the top of the rear rail; spaces formed by the arm rests, legs, and side rail; spaces between the legs under the seat. While some spaces get smaller, others become larger, but the quadrilateral polygons remain constant. The lines of the legs are gentle arcs. The physical shapes of the legs, below and above the seat are, in fact, quadrilateral polygons.

Viewed vertically, from the top, the shapes of the chair are elliptical. The four rails that hold the seat form a half ellipse or half oval, the surface area of the seat. The next higher level of plane is formed by the armrests, which is a more open ellipse. The last level up, the crest rail, opens to a true arc of a circle. One gallery shows these chairs as sculptures.

The contrast of the linear lines in the horizontal view and the ellipse of the vertical view work together much like the white and black keys of a piano. These chairs have very good harmony.

From these upholstered dining chairs I have designed barstools with sculpted wood seats, settees, and sculpted dining chairs.

Chair parts that are paired, front and rear legs, arm rests and side rails are cut from the same length of board. The tops of legs, fronts of side rails, and backs of arm rests line up to each other in the board almost touching. The result is as close to a mirror image of the other part as is possible.

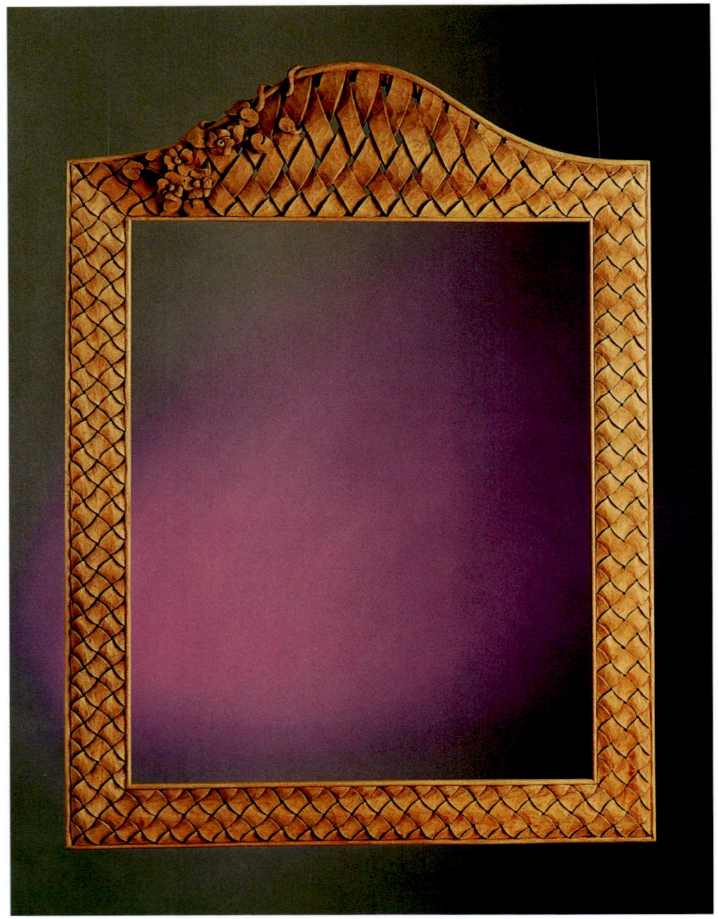

John Thoe. Basket weave with floral vine mirror frame. Honduras mahogany, 46" h x 30" w.

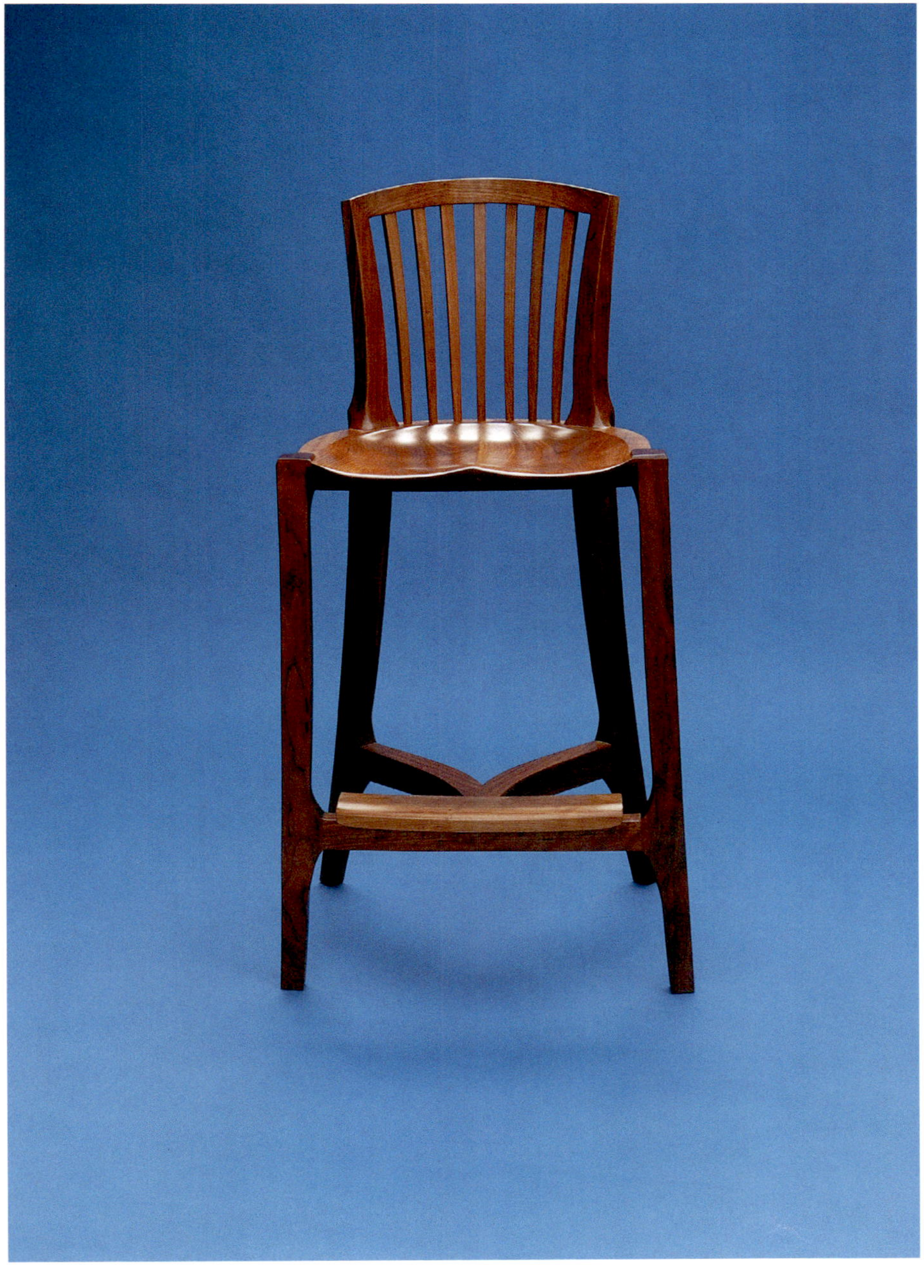

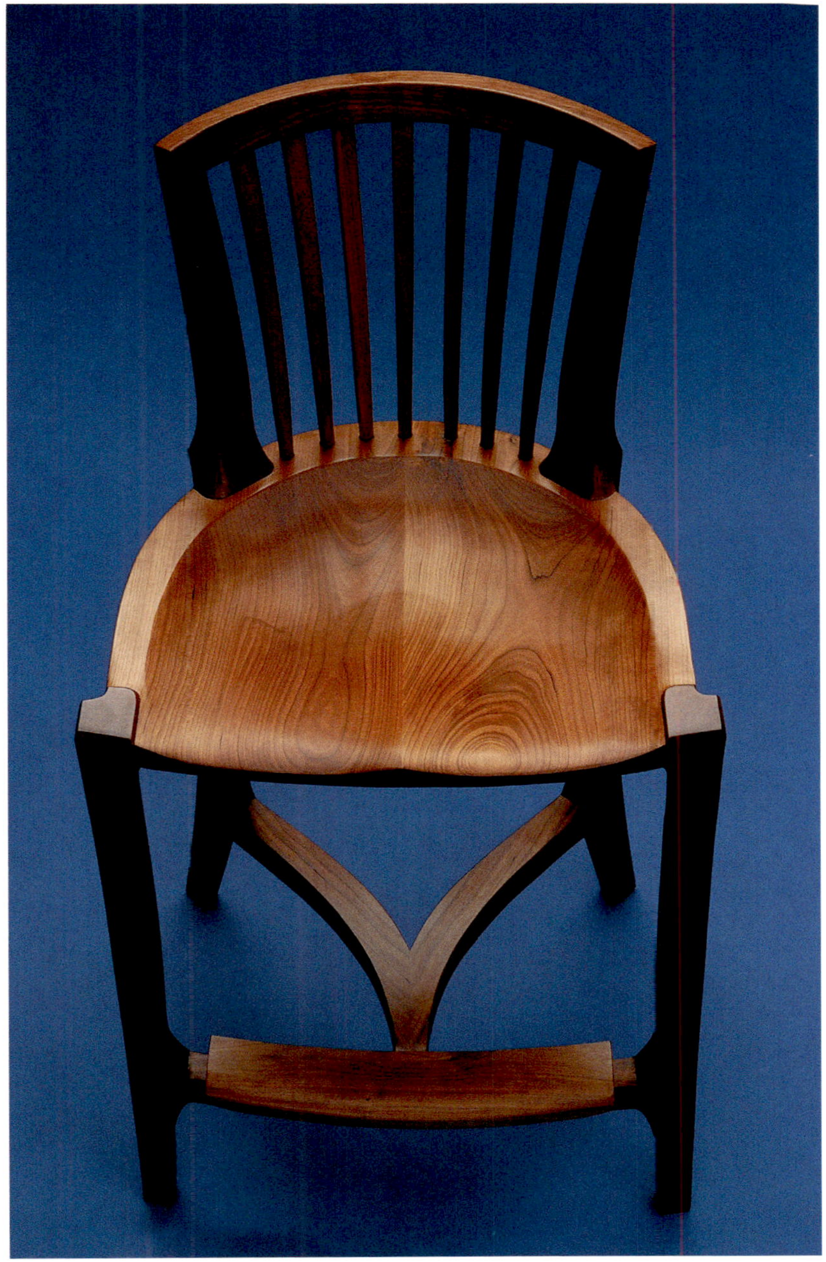

John Thoe. Fan armless bar stool. Cherry, 41" h x 24" w x 24" deep.

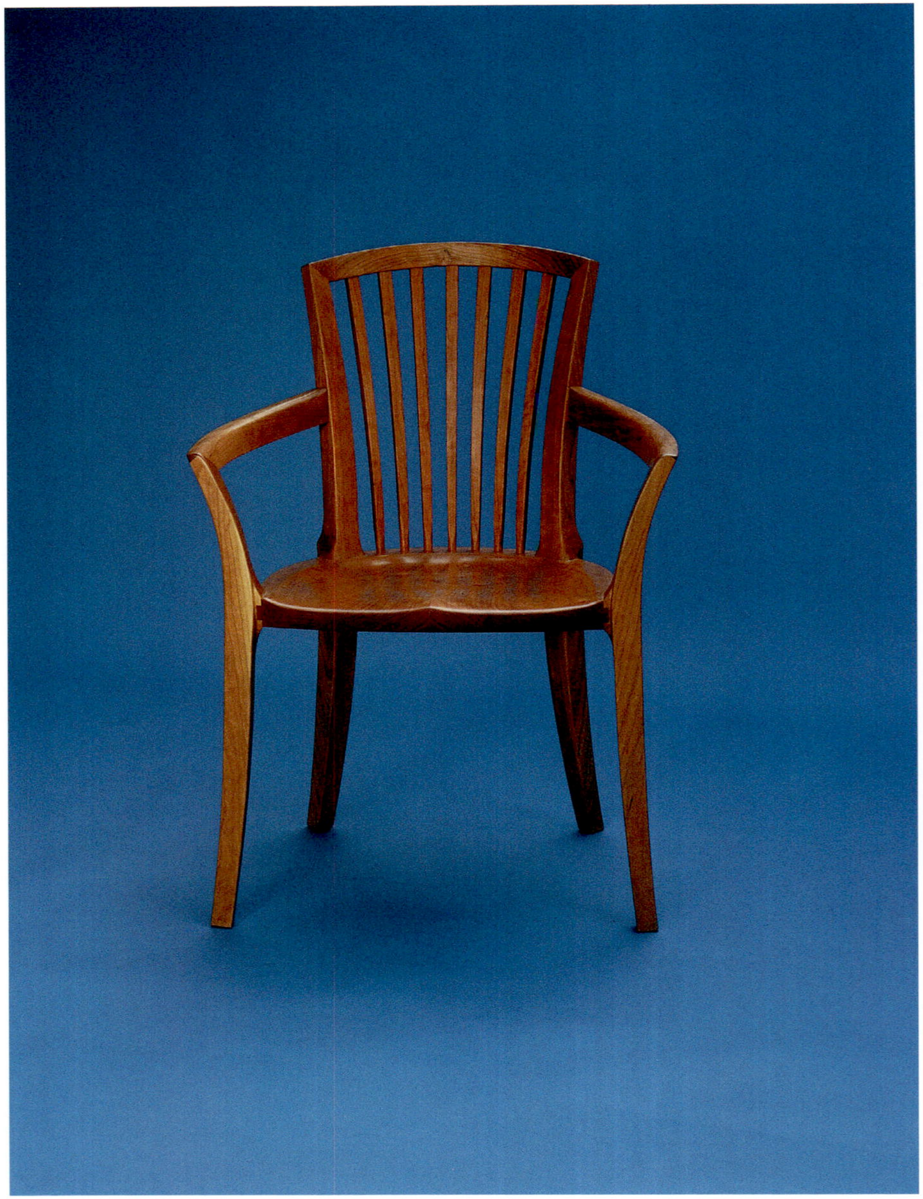

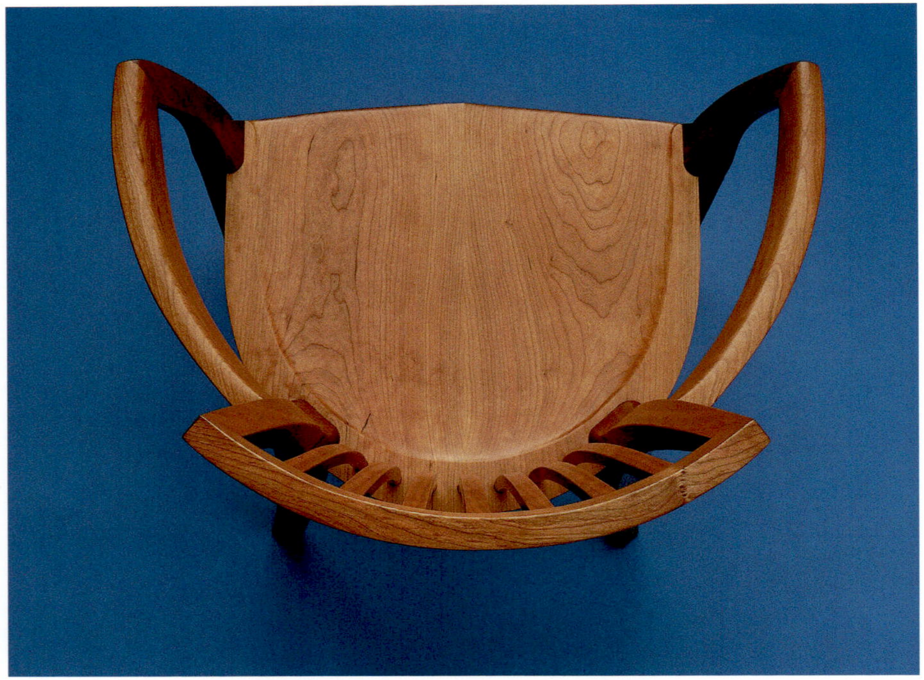

John Thoe. Fan sculpted chair. Cherry, 33" h x 22" w x 23" deep.

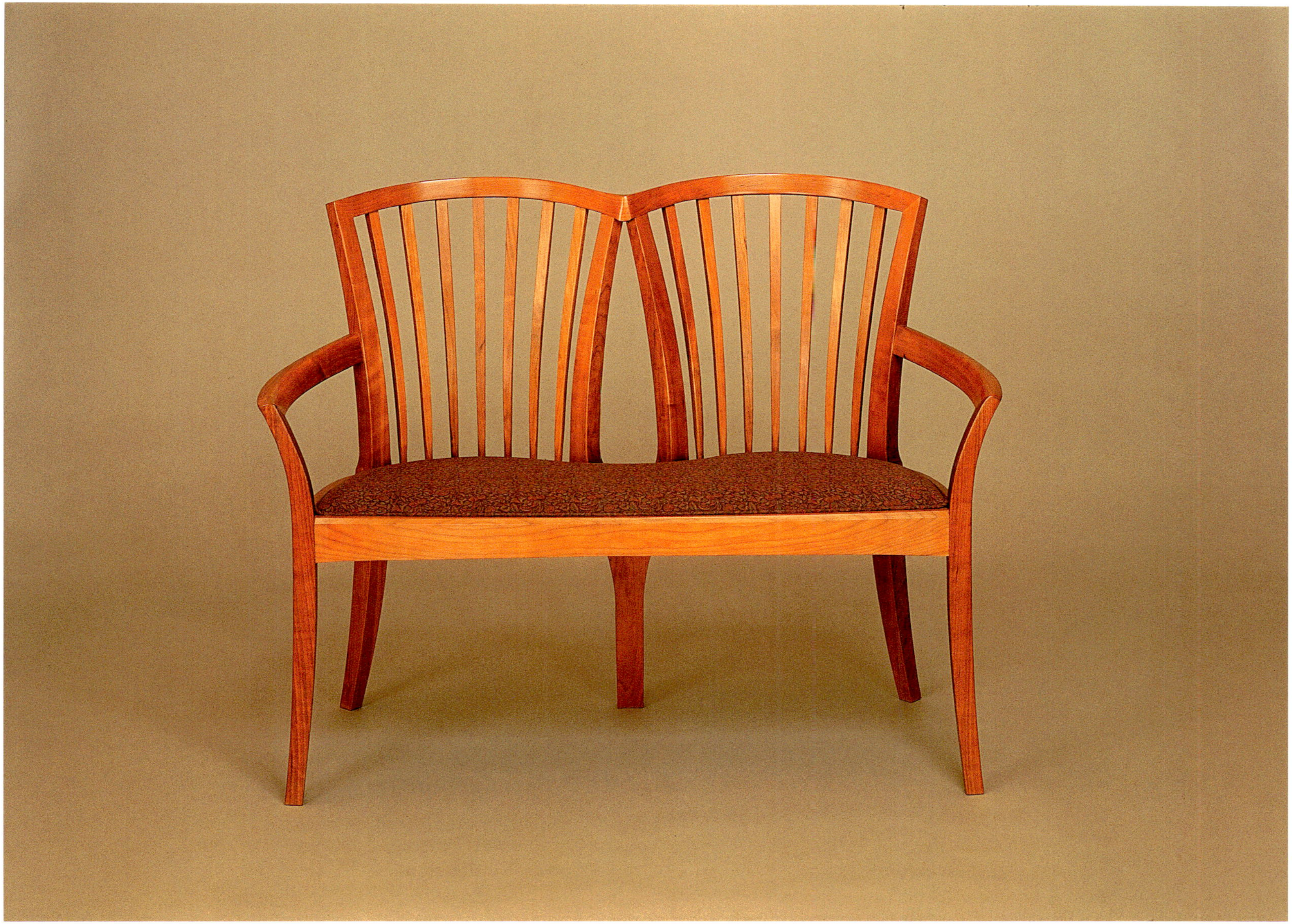

John Thoe. Fan settee. Cherry, 47" w x 24" deep x 35" h.

THOMAS THROOP

New Canaan, Connecticut, www.blackcreekdesigns.com

Individual Artwork

"A Piacere" Music Stand

The head moves up and down and tilts. It has a hand-carved surface creating an additional focal point and visual balance between grain of the pippy elm and the strong graphic form of the base. These music stands are sculptural forms in nature and can stand on their own with or without sheet music. Each has its own special character.

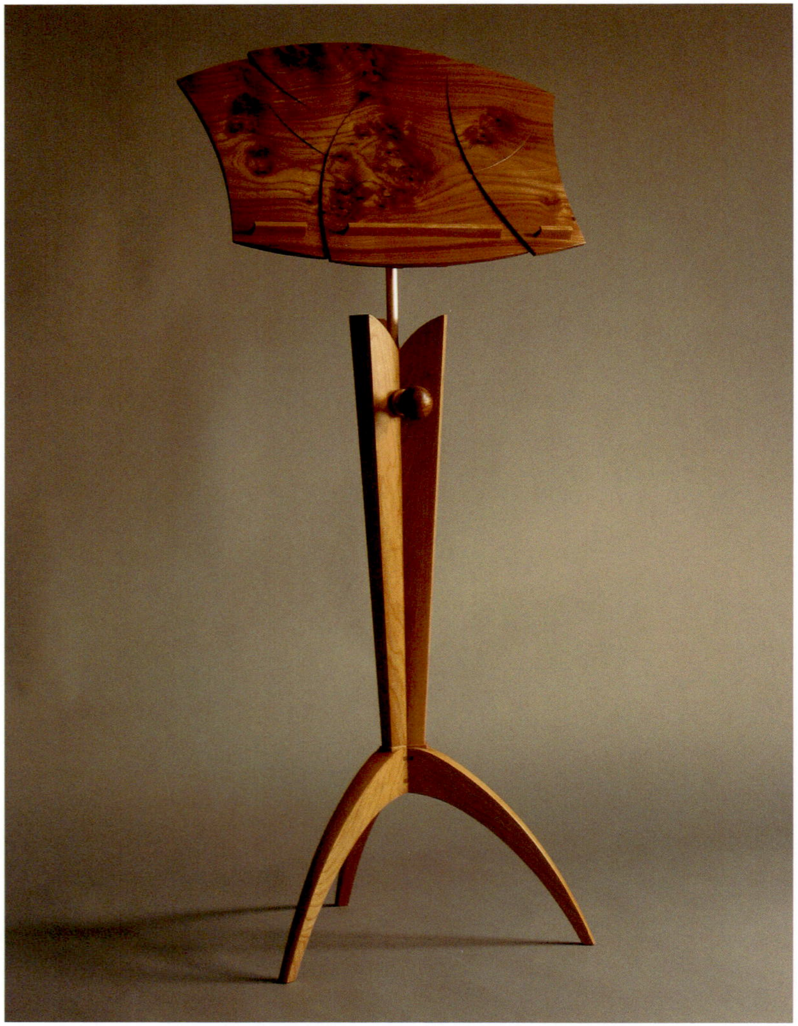

Thomas Throop. *"A Piacere" Music Stand.* Cherry, English pippy elm, brass, 22" w x d 18" d x variable height.

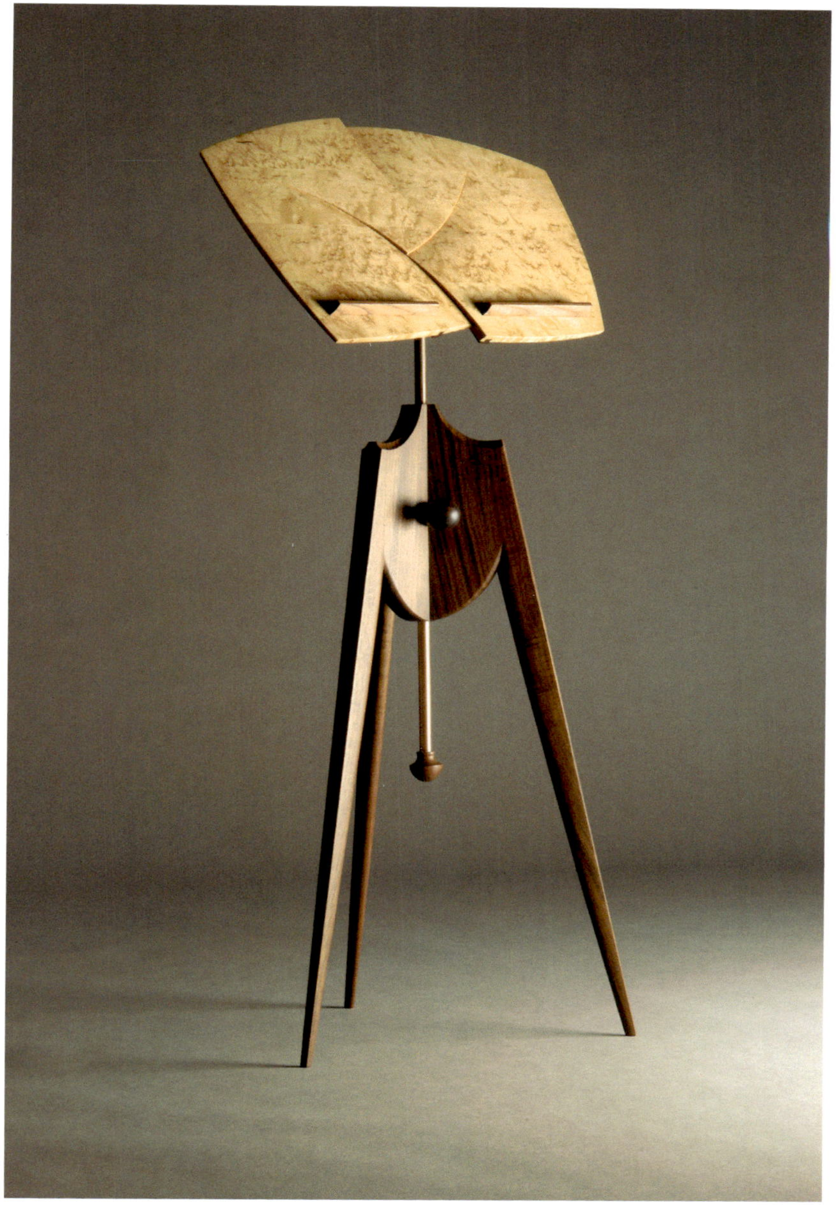

Thomas Throop. *Shakkie Music Stand*. Walnut, birdseye maple, brass, 22" w x 18" d x variable height. *Photographer: Frank Poole*

Saugatuck River Screen

My screens tend to be very graphic. I like the idea of playing with the veneered surfaces of the panels... here, creating a nice visual movement across the three curly maple panels with the imbuya burl. The bubinga frames are constructed with mortise and tenon joinery.

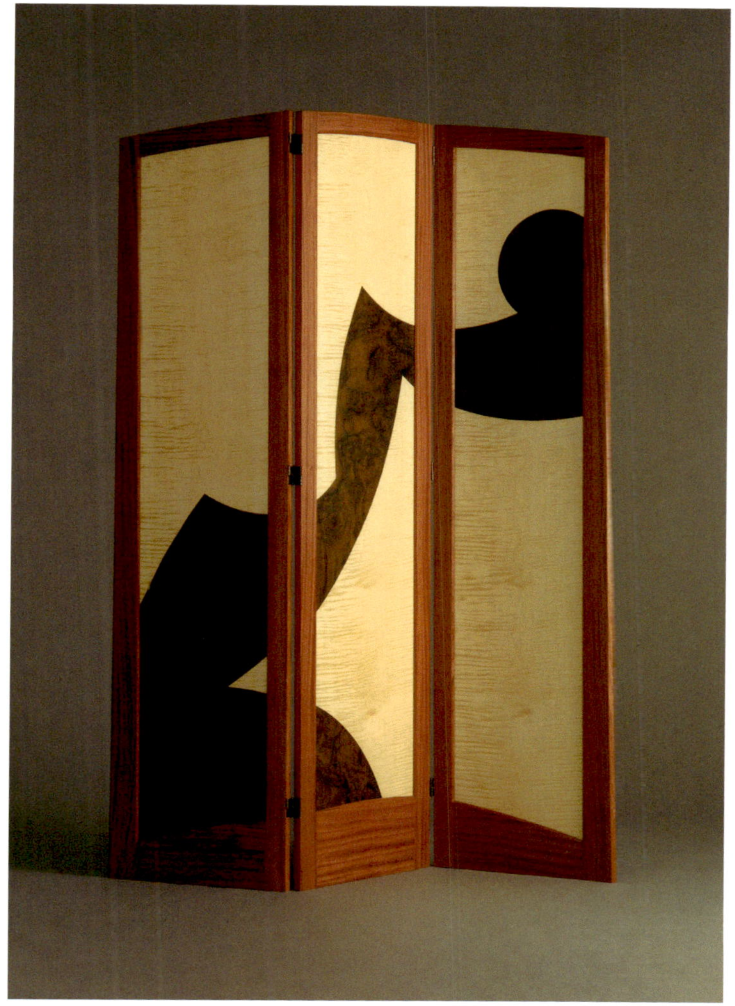

Thomas Throop. *Saugatuck River Screen*. Bubinga, curly maple, imbuya burl, 54" w x 15" d x 73" h. *Photographer: Frank Poole*

Topstone Table

This a traditional trestle table form with carved and shaped feet that create visual stance. The five tiles joining the two top pieces are grafted walnut, cut exactly at the intersection of where the English walnut is grafted onto the American walnut rootstock. The grain here is spectacular where the two walnuts meet. I thought these would be a nice choice to visually and metaphorically bind the two top pieces together.

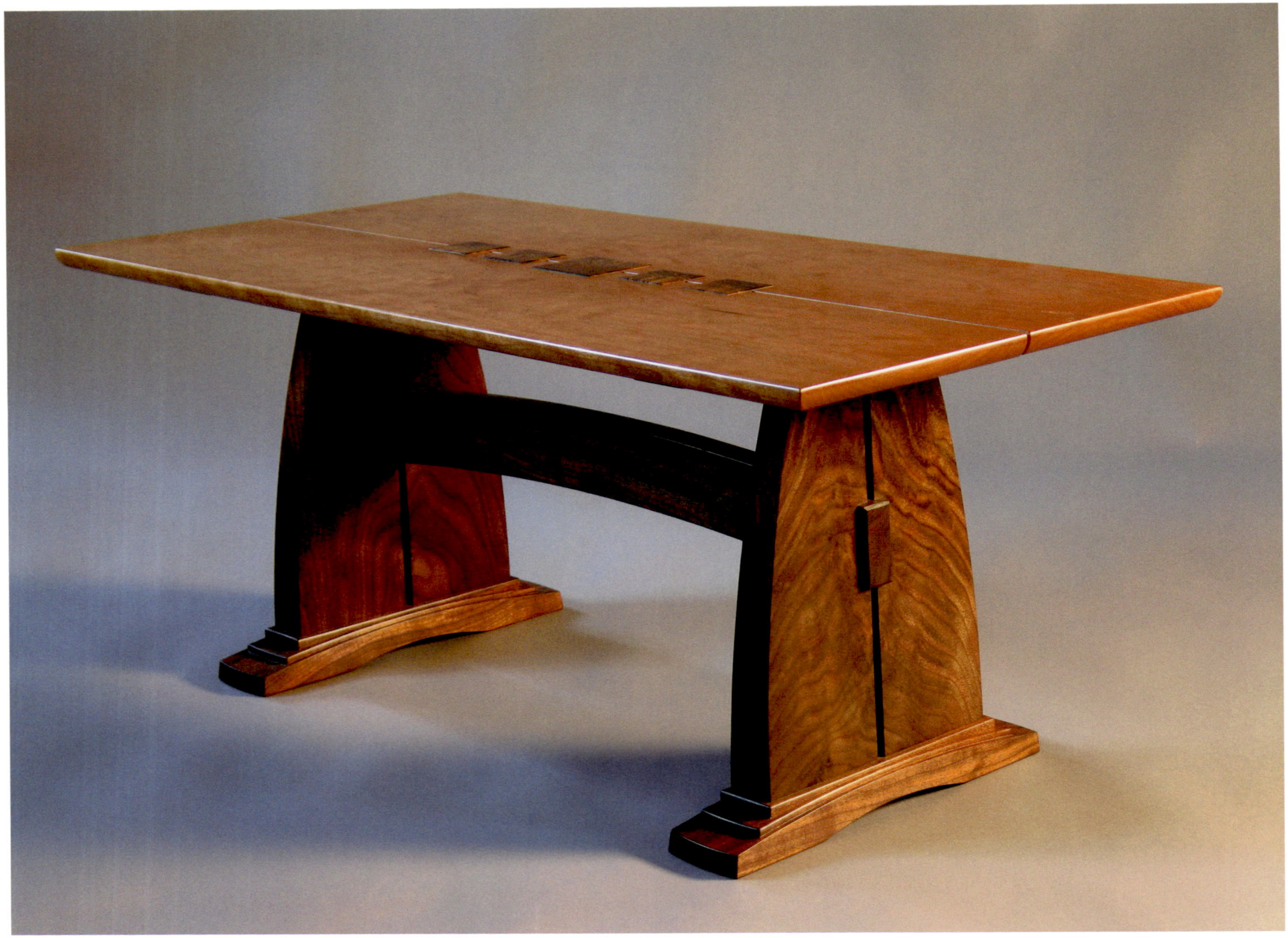

Thomas Throop. *Topstone Table.* Claro walnut, cherry, grafted walnut, 41" w x 21" d x 18" h. *Photographer: Tom Throop*

Keith P. Tompkins

Tivoli, New York

Individual Artwork

Dancing Box

The lid of this box is actually a toy spin-top, made to resemble a dancer with a flared skirt when in motion. It is shown with the pull-handle installed; a string is wrapped around the "waist" and pulled while grasping the handle to set the top in motion. The base resembles a star, which I felt fit the theme of the dancer as a "star" perfectly.

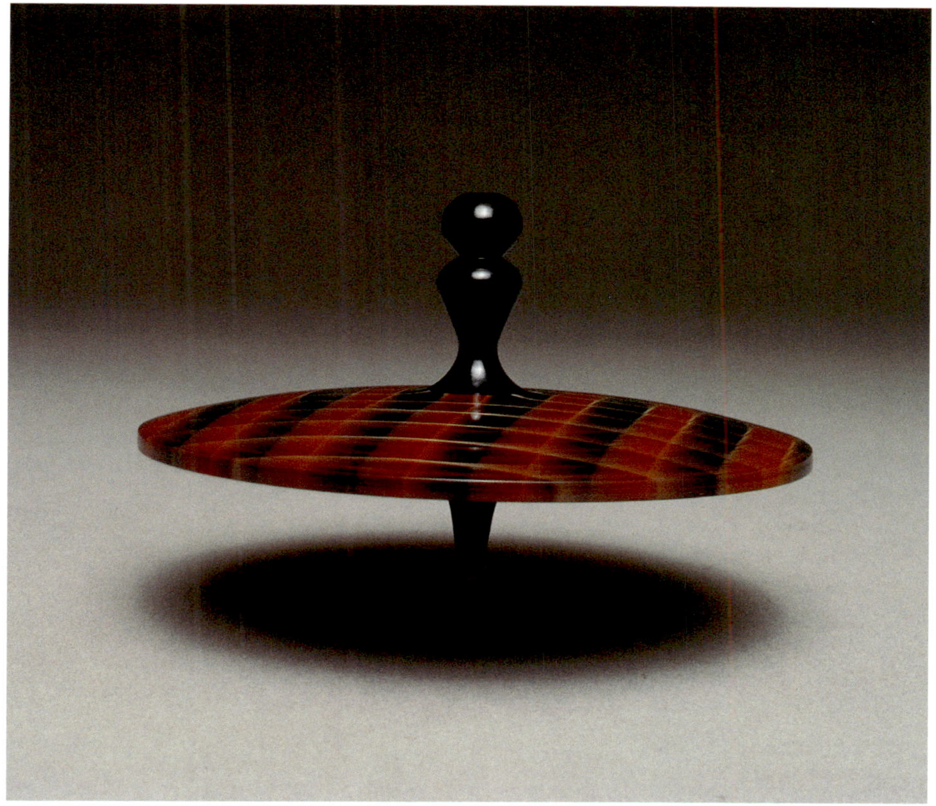

Keith P. Tompkins. *Dancing Box.* Ebonized maple, top: segmented pieces of ebony, maple, bloodwood, and ebonized veneer, 6" w x 6" d x 3" h. *Photo by David Peters © 09*

Merengue

This piece involved combining several turnings to create the diminishing spiral forms, and required turning on several axis points as well. I continued the spiral theme down to the foot with hand-carved details. This piece reminds me of two dancers moving gracefully across the floor as one.

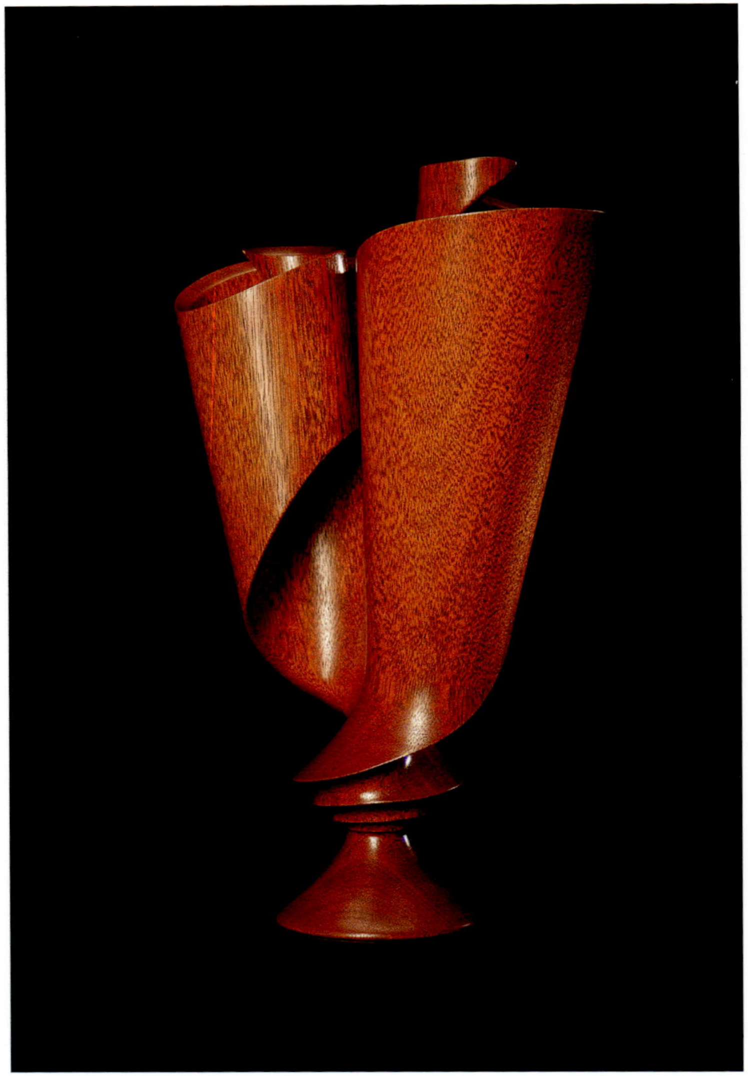

Keith P. Tompkins. *Merengue.* Mahogany, 14" h x 7" w. *Photo: On Location Studio*

Playing Hooky

The acrylic finish is applied with an airbrush. I had just become a grandfather, and decided to turn a collection of hand-made fishing lures for my new grandson. I turned the bodies for the lures from a single piece of stock, one after another. As I worked, it appeared that one piece was chasing the next. I began to laugh aloud; I had inadvertently discovered the inspiration for *Playing Hooky*.

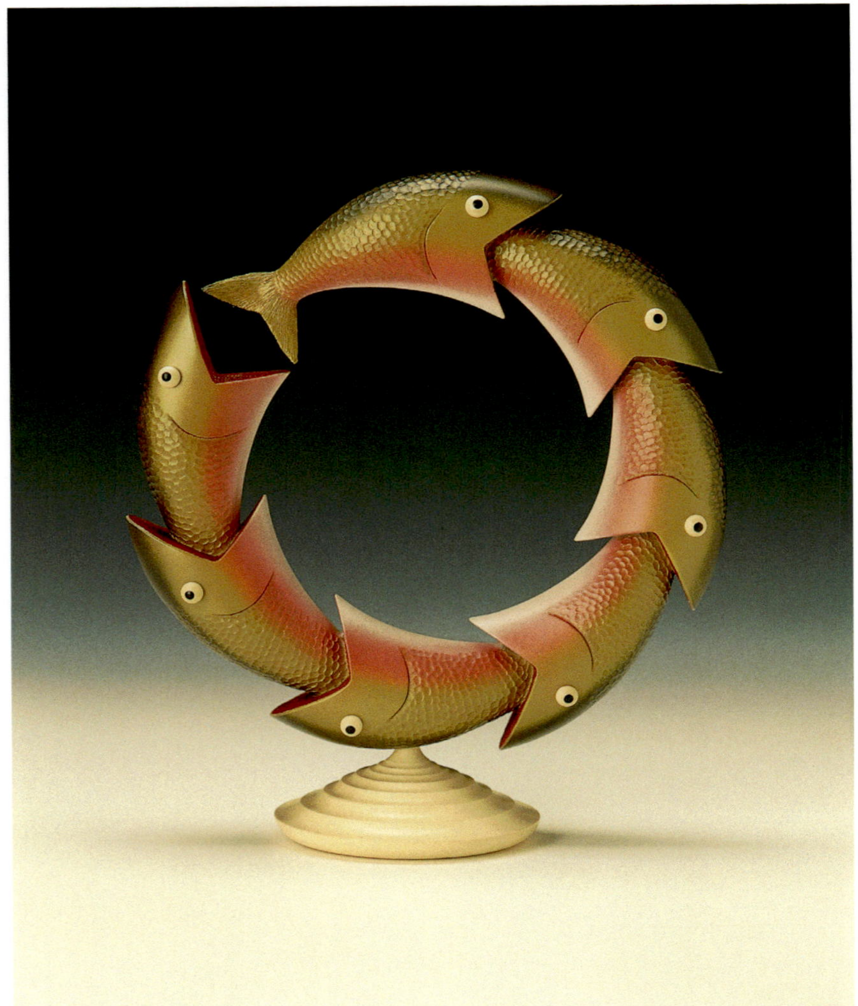

Keith P. Tompkins. *Playing Hooky.* Maple, eyes turned from holly and ebony, 6" d x 7 1/2" h. *Photo: On Location Studio*

Poet's Walk

One of my favorite places is a forest preserve called "Poet's Walk." I go there often; it is a peaceful and tranquil place where I can escape the stresses and demands of everyday life. One brilliant autumn day, as I watched the sun filter through the canopy of leaves, I reached for my sketchbook and began to draw this piece.

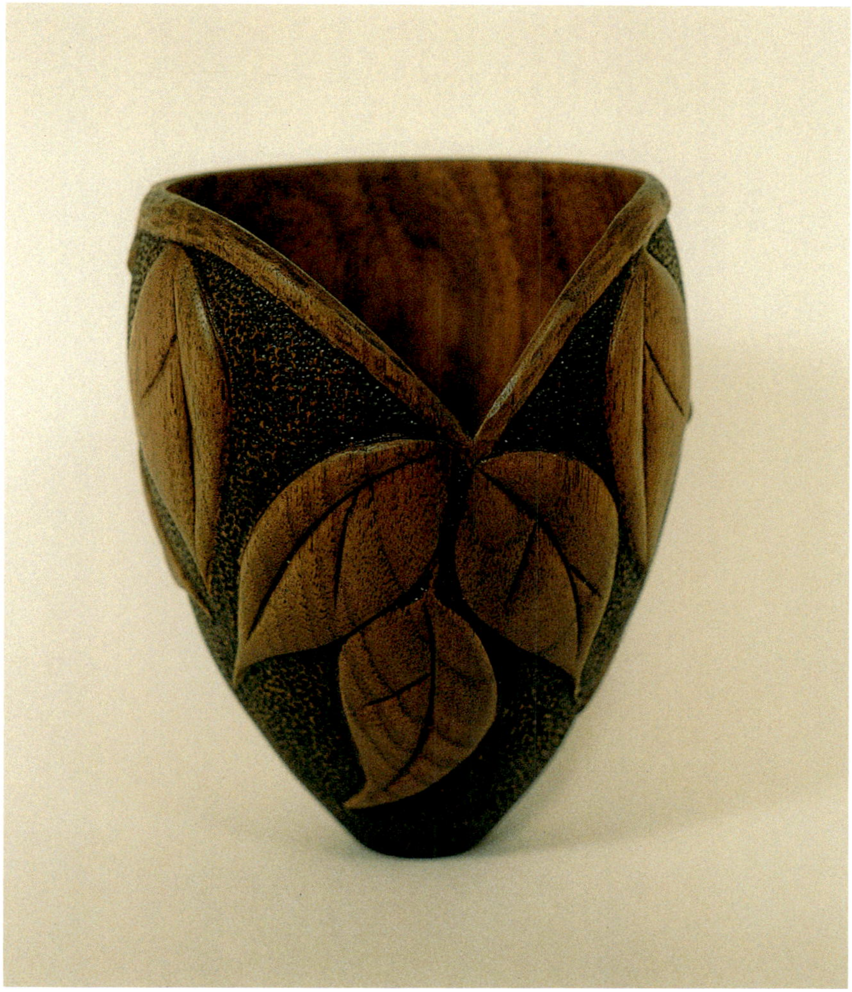

Keith P. Tompkins. *Poet's Walk.* Turned and carved, then textured with a wood burner from black walnut, 6" h x 3" w.

Steppin' Out

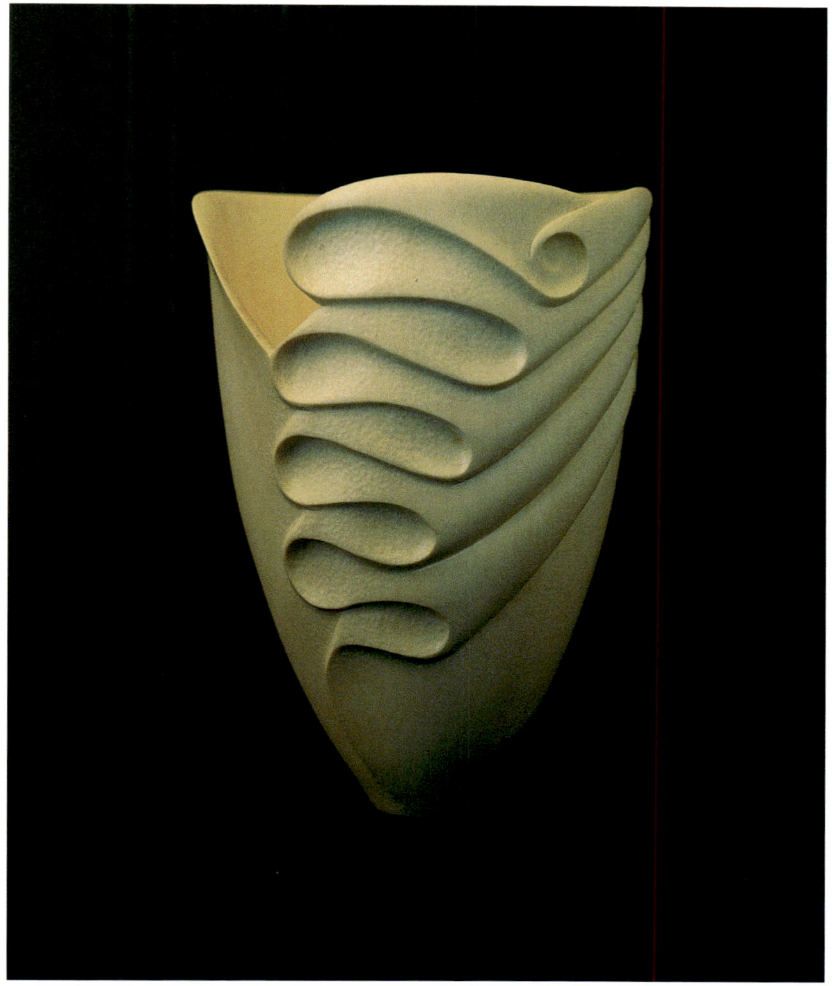

Keith P. Tompkins. *Steppin' Out.* Turned and carved holly, 6" h x 3 1/2" w.

A Winter Rose

All parts of this piece were turned on the lathe, and then details were carved. The blossom required three turnings, combined to form the spiral, the cube was turned as well, and then hollowed, and a threaded ebony insert completed the base. After I completed this piece, I held it behind my back and asked my wife, "Have you ever seen a rose bloom in winter?"

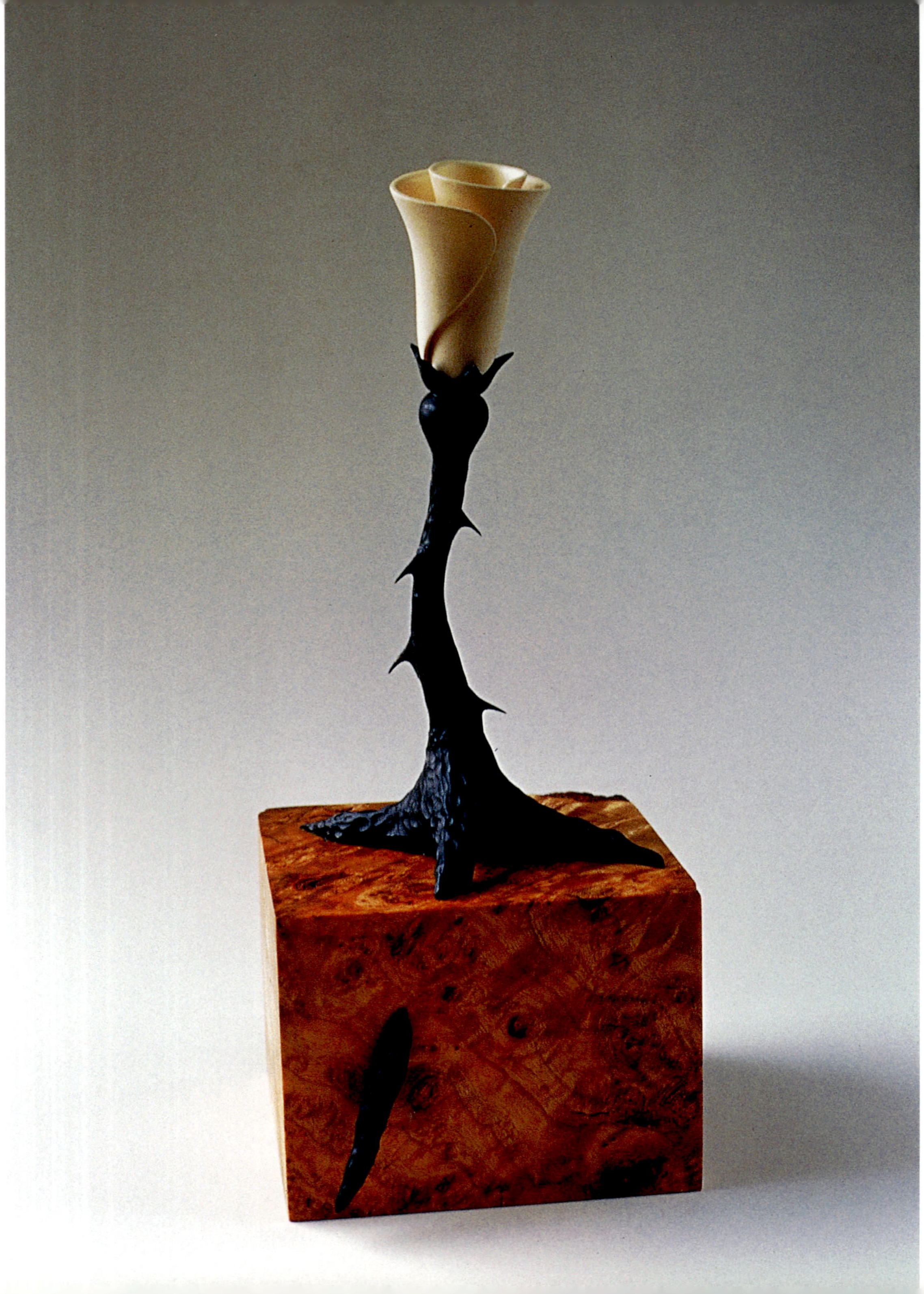

Keith P. Tompkins. *A Winter Rose.* Cherry burl, ebony, and holly, 6" h x 3 1/4" w x 3 1/4" d.

JOËL URRUTY

Hickory, North Carolina, www.joelurruty.com

Artist's Statement

As an artist I strive to create elegant sculptures that capture the true essence of the subject matter. Form, line, and surface are used as the visual language. The figure is abstracted to a minimalist form, void of any superfluous information. The primary material, wood, is often masked by paint to allow the form to take precedence over the material. Monochromatic colors, such as black or white, are often used on the sculptures, allowing light and shadow to play off the subtle shifting facets of the sculptures.

This is what I do. Why I do it, I don't really know. I do know that there is something deep inside that drives me to make these things. Things I don't completely understand myself. But when a piece is finished and it feels right, I know I have done what it was I was suppose to do and move on to the next.

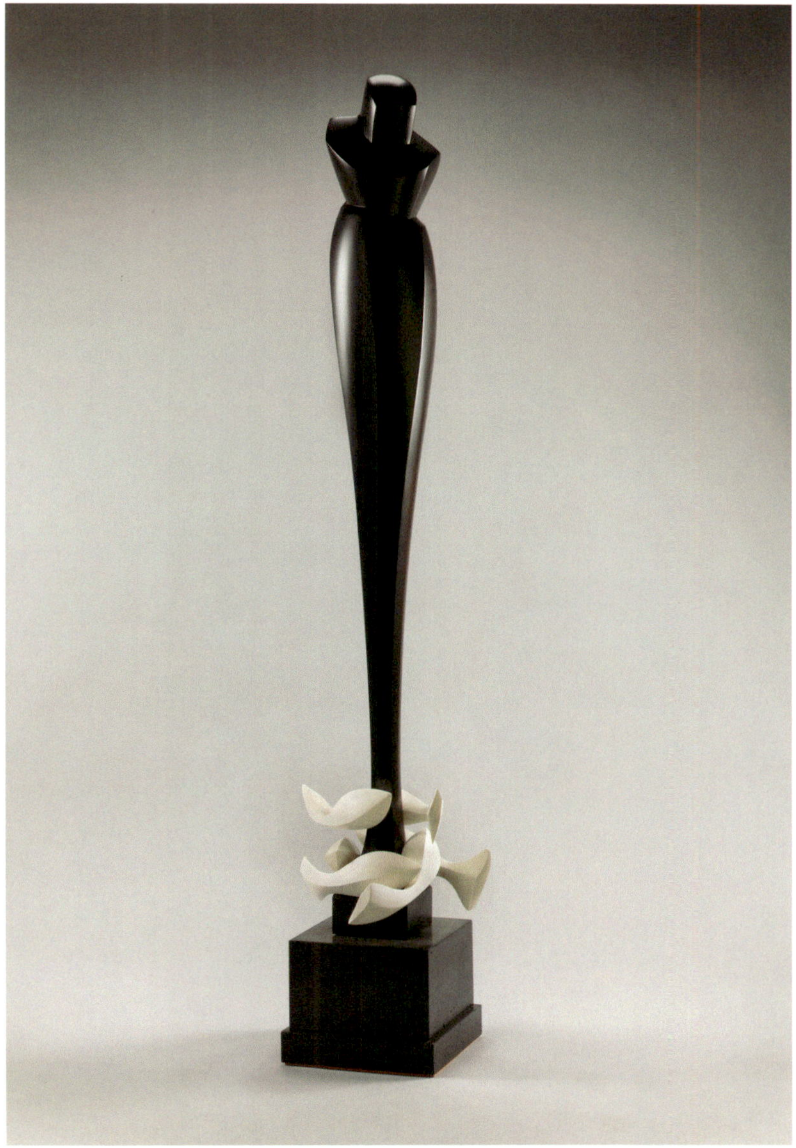

Joël Urruty. *Lady with fish #2.* 2008. Mahogany, bleached ash, milk paint, and concrete, carved and painted wood, 78" x 12" x 12". *Photographer: Tim Barnwell*

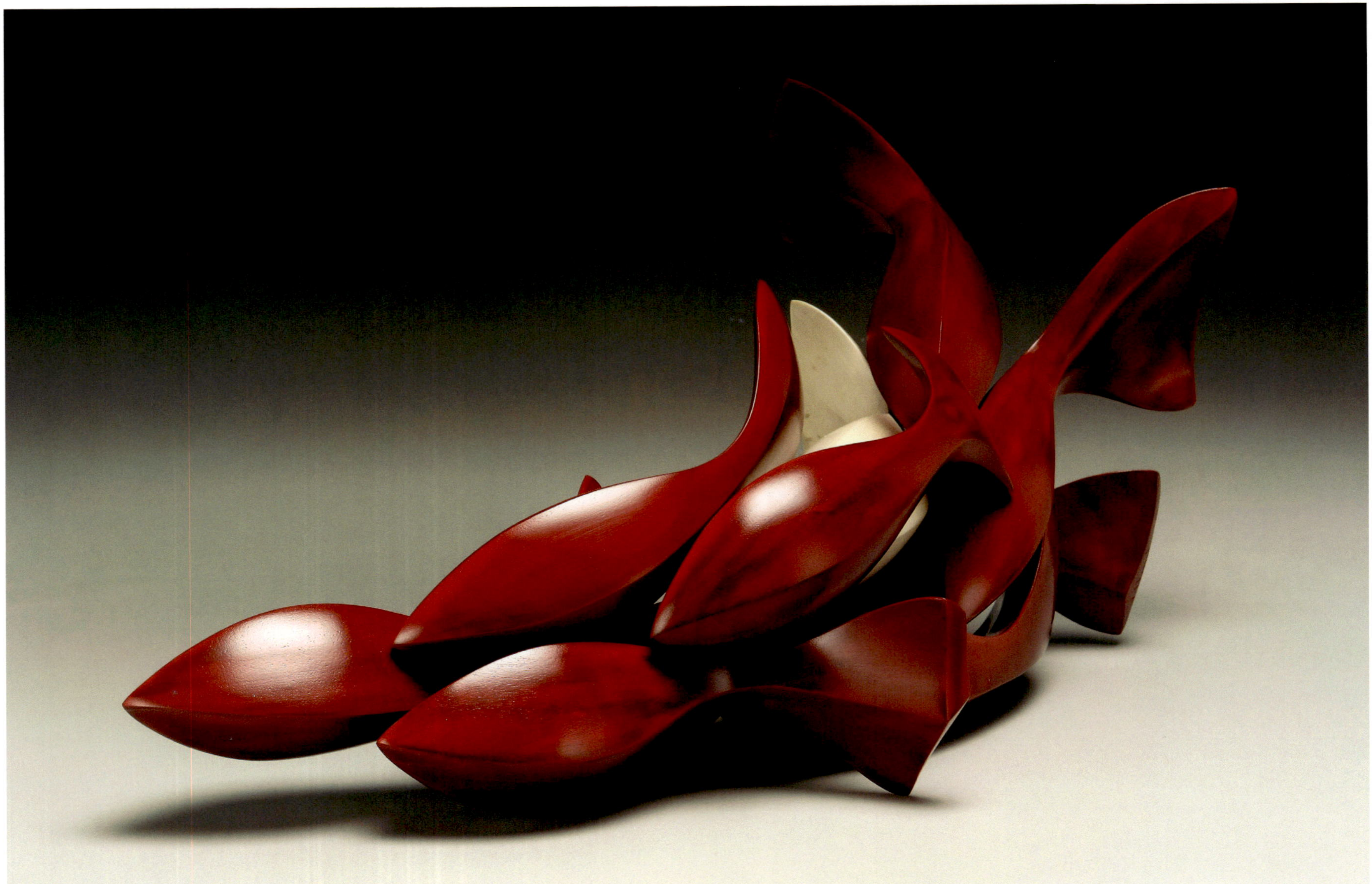

Joël Urruty. *School of fish #8*. 2008. Mahogany and milk paint, carved and painted wood, 15" x 27" x 12". *Photographer: Tim Barnwell*

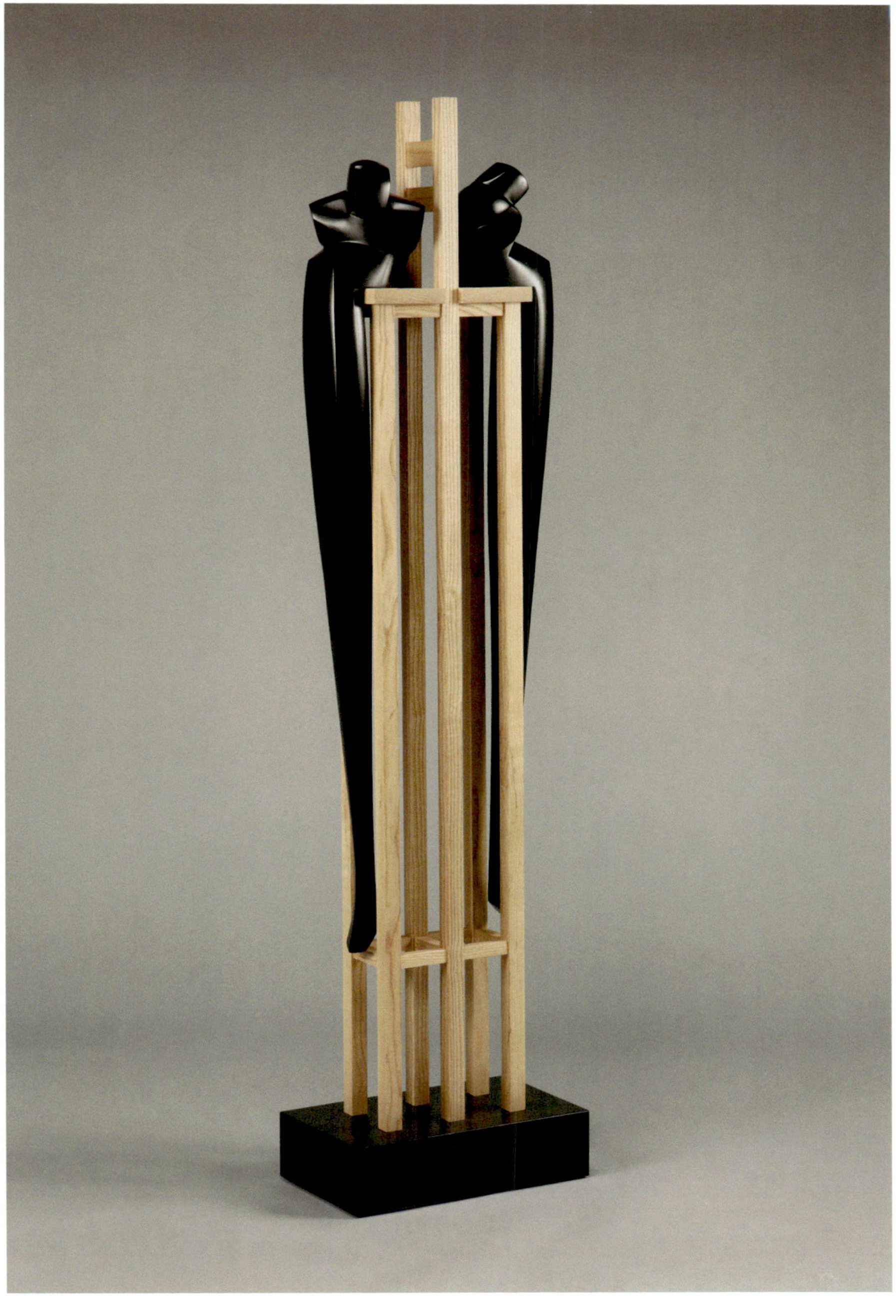

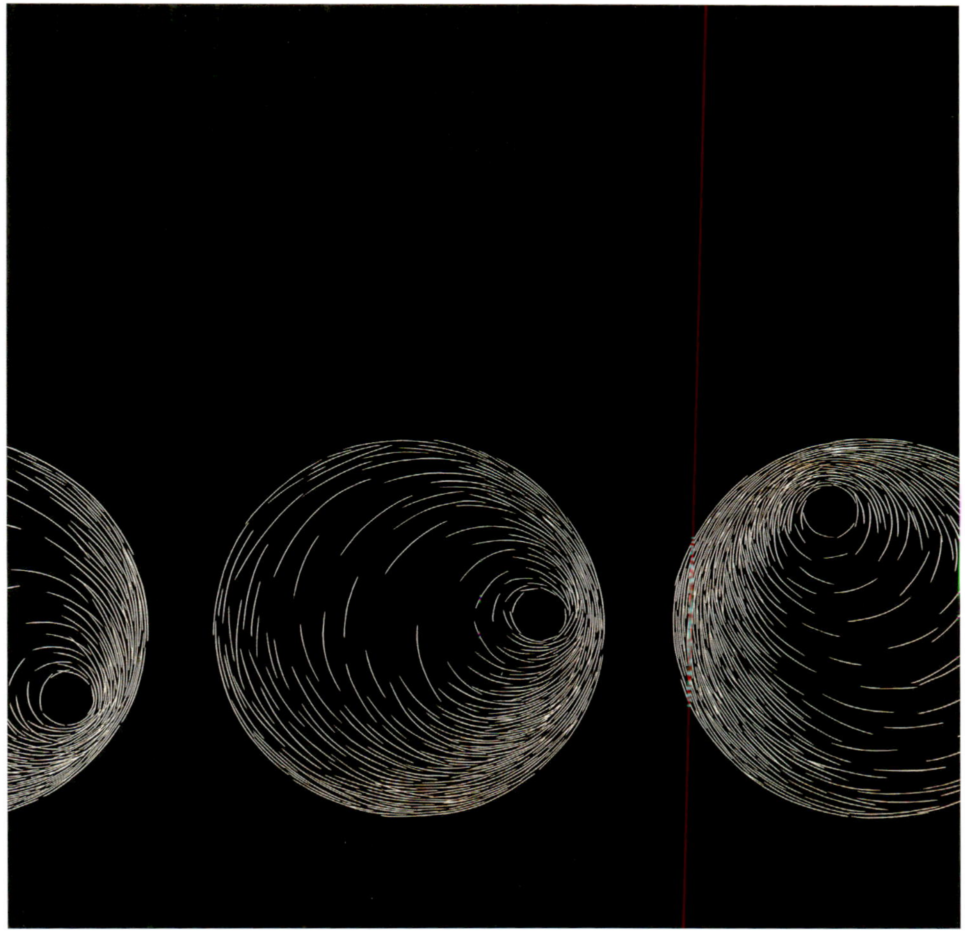

Joël Urruty. *Untitled #9.* 2009. Maple and milk paint, carved and painted wood, 30" x 30" x 2". *Photographer: Tim Barnwell*

Joël Urruty. *Compassion #3.* 2009. Mahogany, ash, milk paint, and concrete, carved and painted wood, 64" x 15" x 9". *Photographer: Tim Barnwell*

Jacques Vesery

Damariscotta, Maine, jvesery@tidewater.net

Artist's Statement

We are touched and influenced every day by many shapes and colors... we look, we listen. I work in wood due to its familiarity, its make up, and qualities... its warmth inspires direction and doesn't inhibit me. The wood becomes my canvas, but it's the engaging convergence of form, proportion, texture, and color that creates the unique spirit and soul with a story to tell. Material and technique then become irrelevant... *"c'est tres important pour moi"*. Each piece of art I create has its own story...we just need to look and listen...

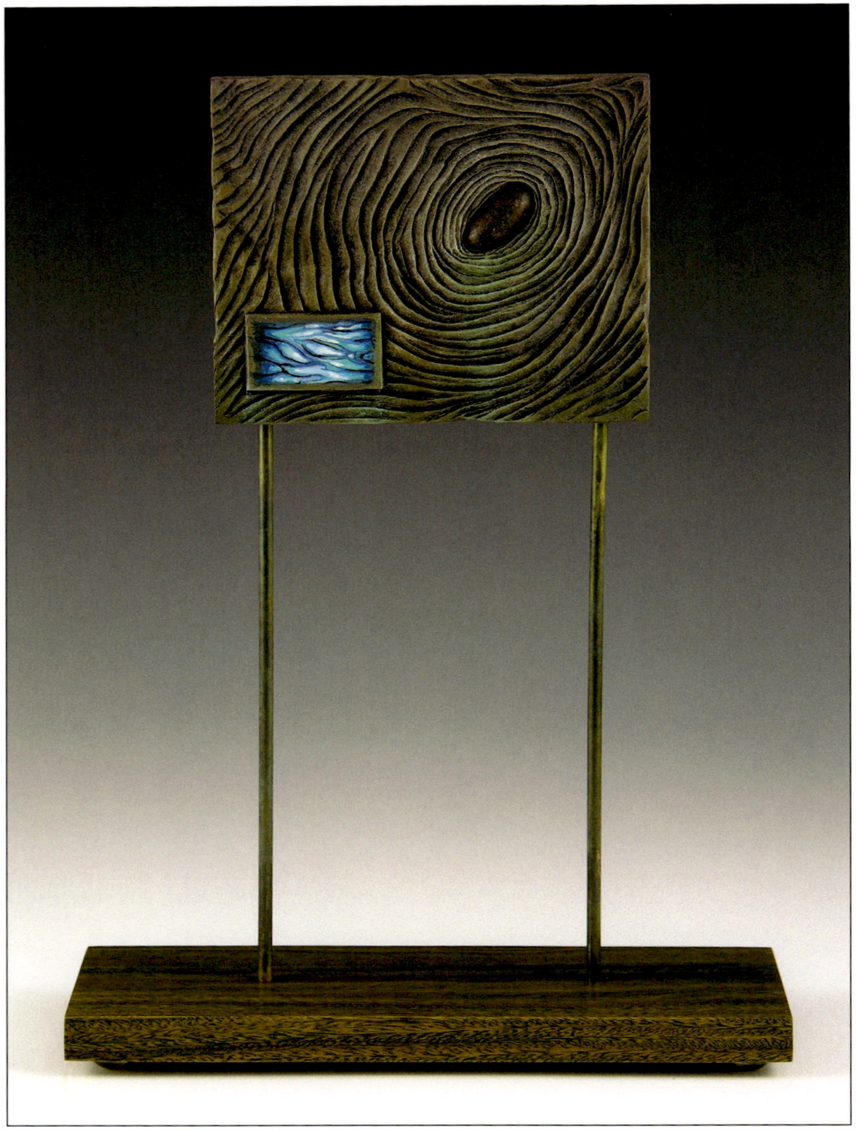

Jacques Vesery. *Ripples.* 2006. Carved/textured cherry, granite, bronze, verawood, acrylic, 8.5" h x 5.5" w x 2.5" d.

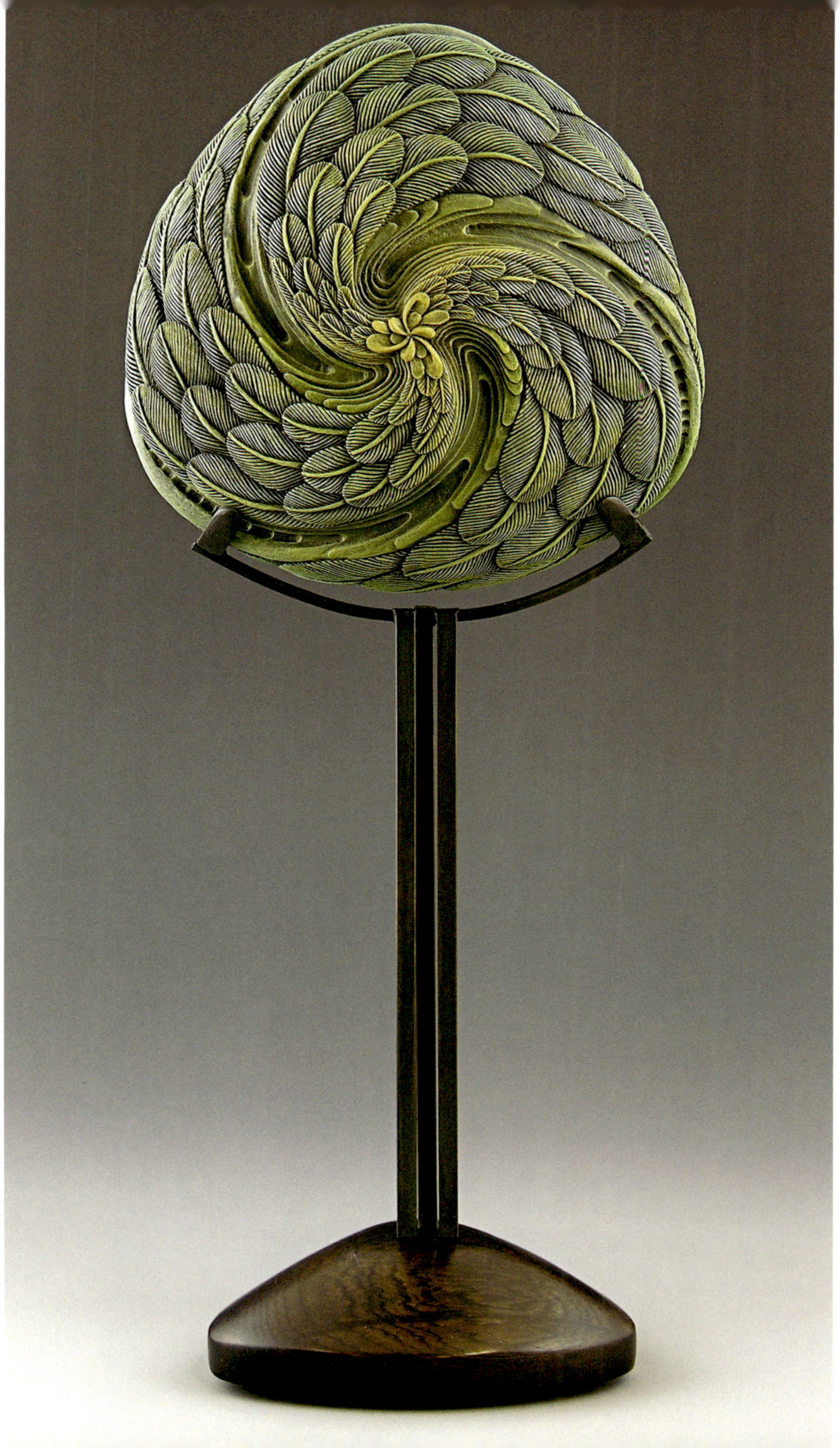

Jacques Vesery. *Une Triade de Mon Moi Intérieur* [*A Triad of My Inner Self*]. 2008. Cherry, acrylics, dyed silver leaf, 6" x 6" x 3".

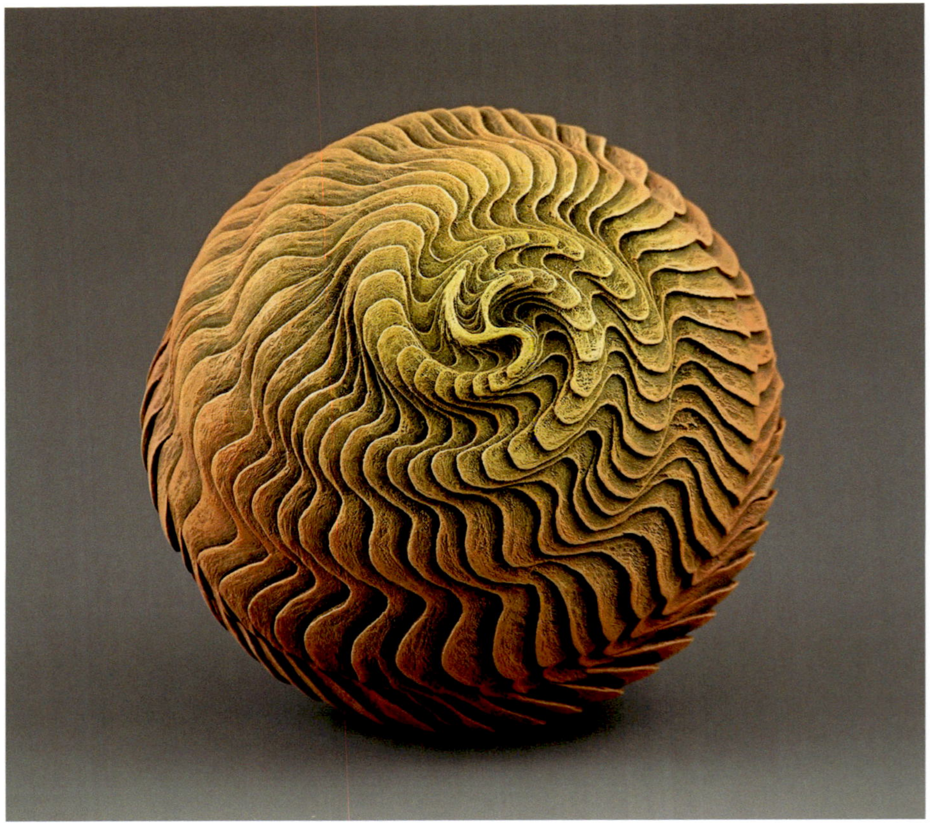

Jacques Vesery. *Eolith in My Garden. Diversity in the Round* series. 2009. Carved/ textured cherry, oak, acrylics, 3" sphere, 5" x 5" base.

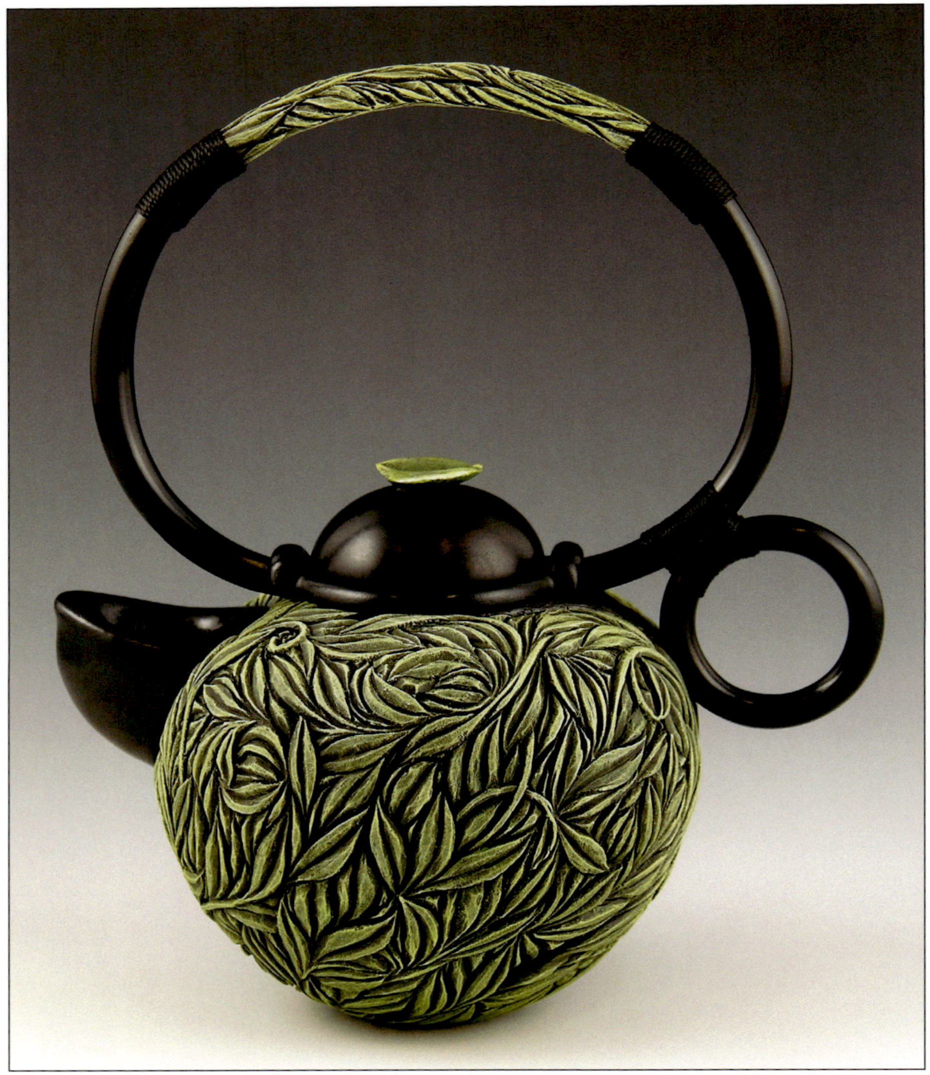

Jacques Vesery. *Printemps Thé au Café du Métro* [*Spring Tea at the Metro Café*]. 2009. Carved/ textured cherry, patinated bronze, acrylics, 4.2" x 6.2" x 4".

Derek Weidman

Green Land, Pennsylvania, derekweidman@hotmail.com

Artist's Statement

There are moments for all artists where a subtle change in perception can have powerful effects on our work. Wherever we happen to find ourselves in these moments, time seems to stop as we reach some epiphany. One such example I have of this in my own work was when the forms that a lathe can produce, such as bowls and vessels, stop dominating the way I looked at the lathe. At first my turning was mostly traditional, bowls and hollow forms, but after classes with Mark Sfirri, I realized the lathe was an extremely powerful sculptural tool. I began exploring the descriptive limits of the lathe, and my first real breakthrough was turning a head on five axes. The head, and face in particular, off the lathe was easily recognizable as a face, but interpreted in a way that I had never seen before. It was a very profound moment for me to finally nurse this piece out of the lathe and essentially have it look back at me. The end result was a novel representation of human anatomy, described in a visual language only the lathe knows how to speak. I have since called the form a "thought" and feel it reflects the fact that it is a conceptualized interpretation of the head, with an emphasis on it being a vessel of the mind.

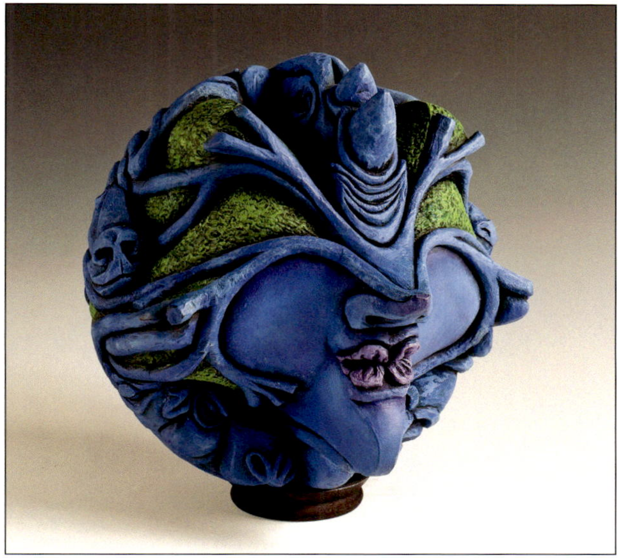

Derek Weidman. *Gaia.* 2007. boxelder, turned on 6 axis, burned, carved, painted with acrylics, 6" x 6' x 6".

Individual Artwork

Gaia

This piece was designed for the Invitational AAW "Sphere" exhibit. The show focused on interpretations of spheres from different wood turners from around the world. I decided to create a representation of Gaia, the goddess of the Earth in Greek mythology, who is both a planet (sphere) and a woman simultaneously. It was that synthesis that made her a perfect character to try and portray for the exhibit. The piece is covered with animals that essentially grow out of the face of Gaia, visually. Instead of focusing on land features, I felt life was a unique quality of Earth to focus on, and used that as my primary motif. The animals used include an elephant, lion, ox, deer, horse, bear, fox, hippo, giraffe, platypus, and a rhino, and were chosen mostly for aesthetic reasons.

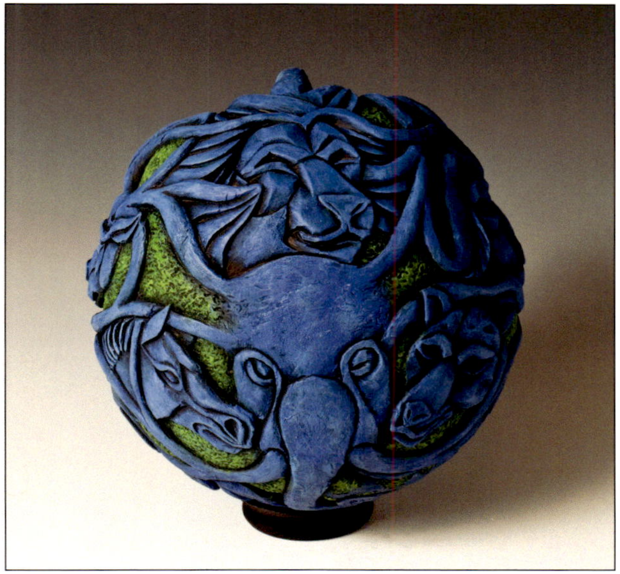

Pan

I often take inspiration from mythology for my work, as the stories of ancient cultures have a certain otherworldly feel to them. These deities exist in concept, with no real physical form, and are perfect subjects for abstracted or surreal representations. The inspiration for Pan has a particular story behind it. I was driving late at night and saw a raccoon, and her babies, trying to cross the street. The other cars on the road kept almost hitting the mother, or the babies. The babies were scared to cross the street, and the mother had to traverse the traffic, from one side of the road to the other, trying to coach the babies across. I stopped my car at somewhat of an angle across the street, and put my four ways on, in hopes that cars that were coming would slow down enough to let them proceed safely. It was late, and the traffic was slowed enough that there were only a few cars coming in the distance. Eventually, the raccoon and her family made the trip safely. We all share a world, were my thoughts, and this piece was my attempt to capture that.

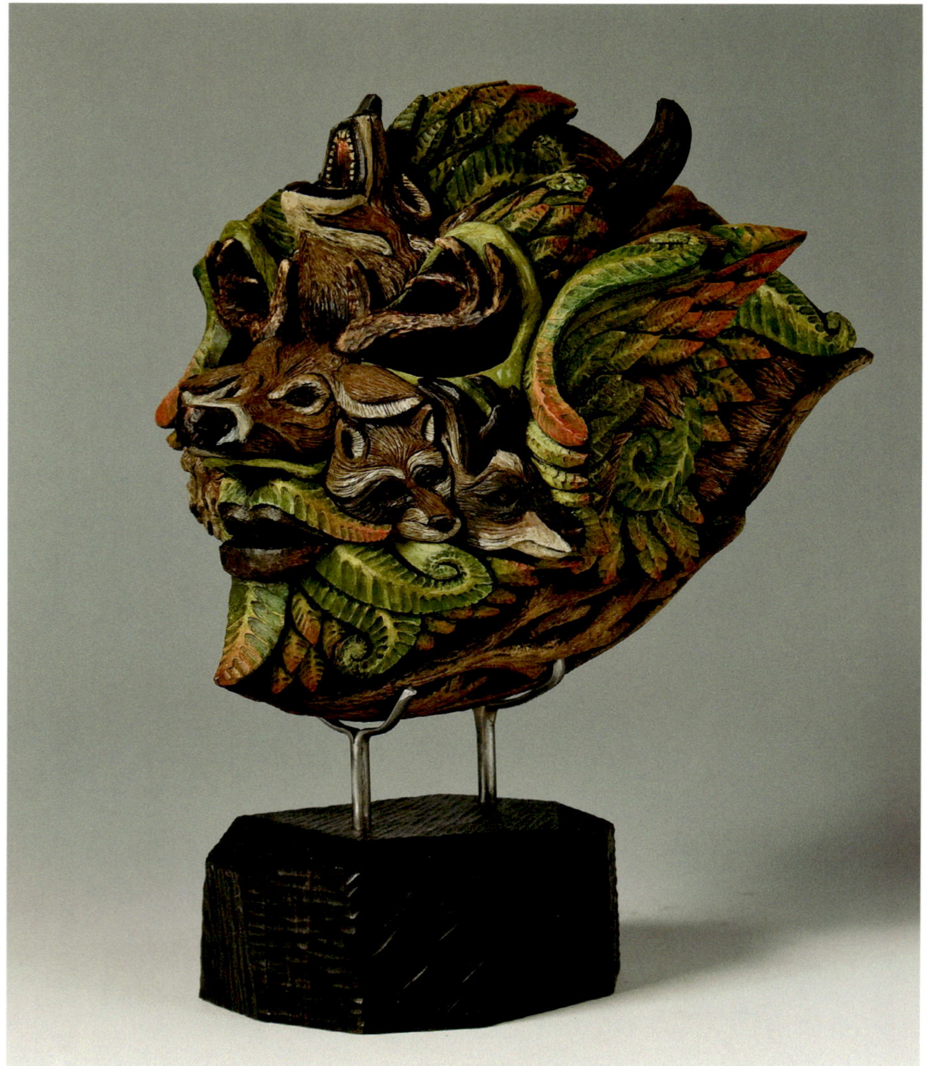

Derek Weidman. *Pan*. 2008. Holly, turned on 6 axis, hollowed, burned, carved, pained with acrylics, 6.5" h x 6.5" w x 7" l.

Dream

I really try to push my work both experimentally and conceptually and this is the first in a series where my *Thought* series changes into a *Dream* series. *Dreams* are a new form I have been working on, similar to my other series of multi-axis turned heads with the difference of distinction being the face bending in on itself. As I continue to explore anatomy through the axis of a lathe, it is always exciting to find new ways to express and interpret ideas with the unique visual and technical vocabulary that the lathe offers. In this piece the front and side of the face is visible from only one vantage point. My reaction to the form was that it was dreamlike, and the carved "skin" on the piece was done in a way that I hoped would enhance and echo that feeling.

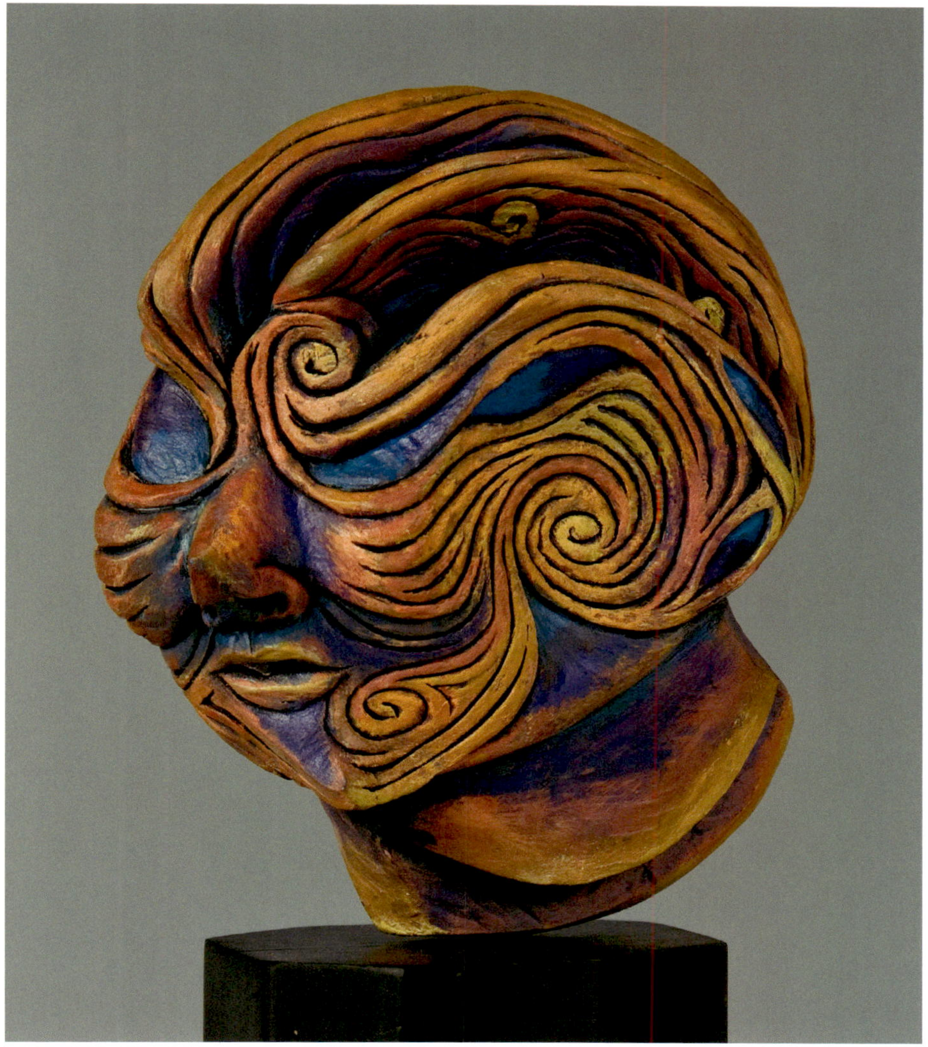

Derek Weidman. *Dream.* 2009. Cherry, turned on 4 axis, burned, carved, painted with acrylics, 4" w x 2.5" l x 7" h.

Molly Winton

turningmaven@hotmail.com

Individual Artwork

Caballos Ascendentes

The vessel was first turned on a wood lathe, forming the exterior first, and then hollowing the interior to match the exterior profile. Once off the lathe, the mustangs are drawn free hand, outlined with a pyrography (woodburning) tool, and the mustang path is textured using another pyrography technique. It is finished by painting black gesso everywhere but the mustangs, and then coated with a matte lacquer to seal and finish the piece.

These pieces are a tribute to the wild mustangs still roaming free, and struggling to survive in a progressively mechanized and technical world. I hope to capture a glimpse of the breathtaking beauty of a herd galloping across an open range, manes and tails flying free in the breeze, completely unfettered.

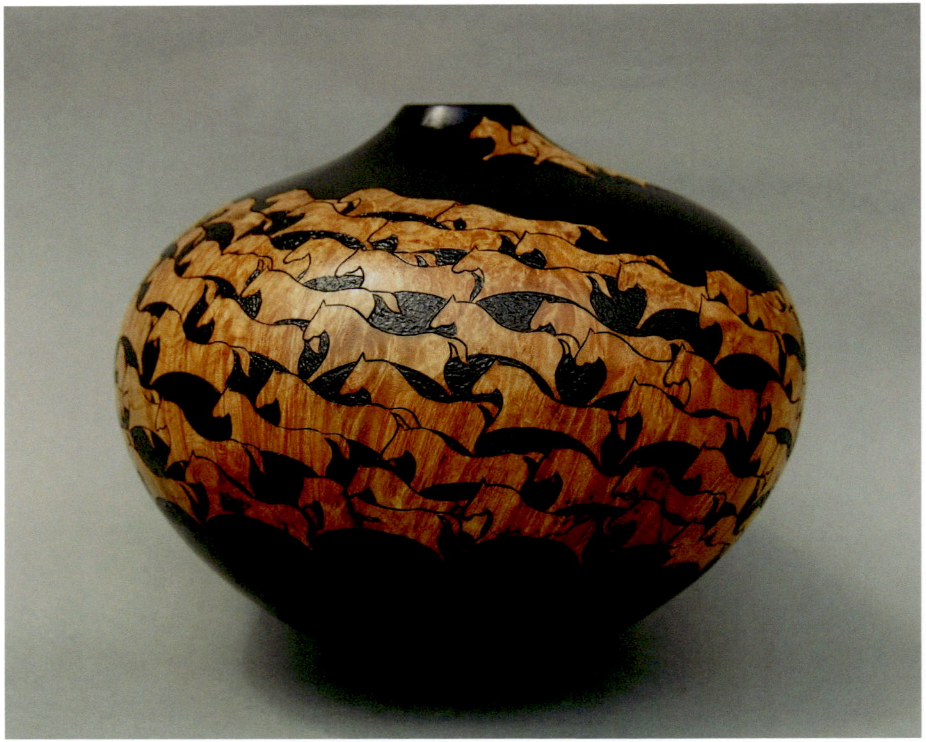

Molly Winton. *Caballos Ascendentes*. 2009. Hollow vessel made of maple burl (wood), using pyrography and gesso, 8" x 8".

Caballos Negros

The vessel was first turned on a wood lathe, forming the exterior first, and then hollowing the interior to match the exterior profile. Off the lathe the base is textured using a homemade coil brand, which burns the imprint into the surface of the wood. Drawing the mustangs free hand and then outlining them using a pyrography pen complete the top portion of the piece. The texture of the negative space between the mustangs is achieved using a different pyrography pen. Once the piece is completed, it is ebonized using an alcohol based black leather dye and finally sprayed with a matte lacquer finish.

The Santa Clara Pueblo, and Mata Ortiz Mexican black on black pottery inspire my black pieces. I have always admired Native American Southwest pottery in their various styles, but the black on black pieces hold a special fascination.

Dzilla

The vessel was turned on a wood lathe forming the exterior, and then hollowing the interior to match the exterior profile. The grooves in the top portion of the vessel are also cut while the piece is on the lathe. Off the lathe the piece is painted with a black gesso surface treatment, and then carved through to the natural wood.

Continued interest in primitive designs has led to further research of some of the world's indigenous cultures. My *Dzilla* series is inspired by the many necklace adornments worn by the married women of the South African Ndebele. I've chosen the designs on the base to represent the continuous spiral of life's journey.

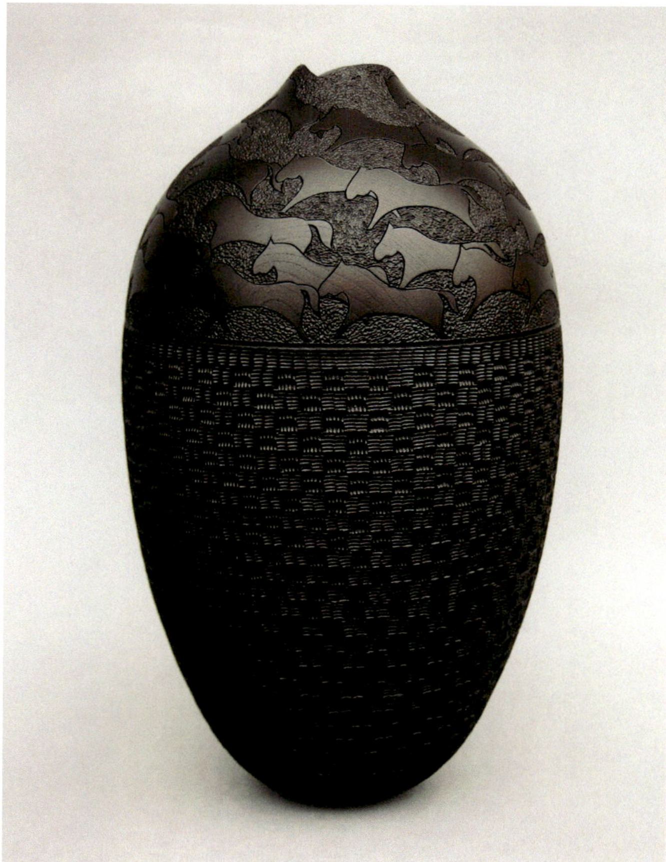

Molly Winton. *Caballos Negros*. 2009. Hollow vessel made from rauli wood, using branding, pyrography, and leather dye, 6" x 10".

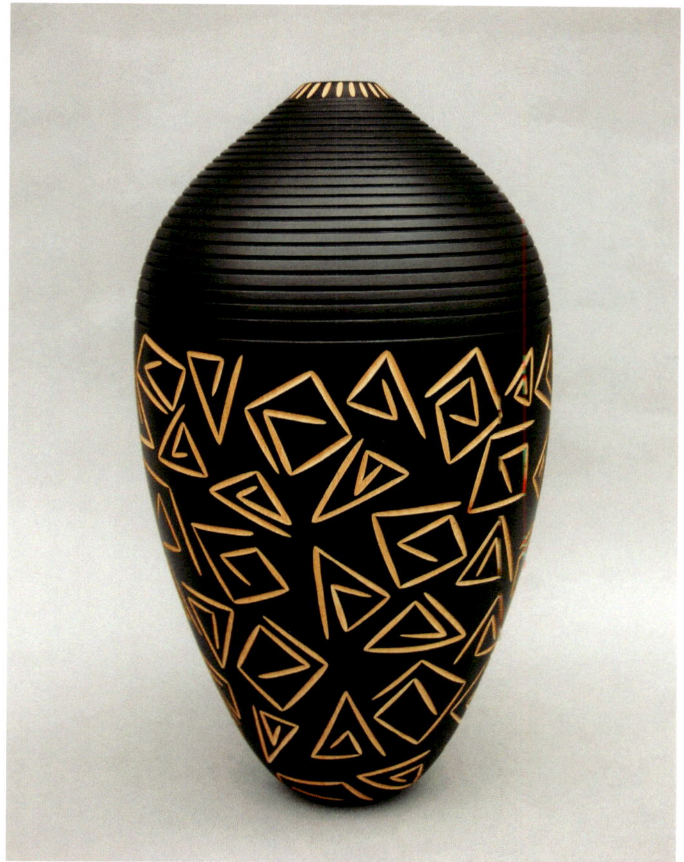

Molly Winton. *Dzilla*. 2009. Hollow vessel made from rauli wood, painted with black gesso, and carved, 8" x 13".

ERIK WOLKEN

ewolken@mindspring.com

Artist's Statement

Much of what I do is inspired by the world around me, both the natural and the manmade. It is often the interplay between simple geometric shapes that I may see in the roof line of a building, the structure of a bridge, or the leaves of a tree that are at the root of my next idea. I seldom know where I am going when I start a piece; it usually starts with a series of rough pencil sketches and a belief that I can somehow divine the meaning of an object in the process of building it.

Individual Artwork

Little Big Man

This piece was the beginning of an exploration in multi-function forms. Sculptural forms that could be turned in different positions so that they could serve more than one purpose, hence its name from one of my favorite books and movies, *Little Big Man*. It was also the start of laminating up large blocks of wood to create forms.

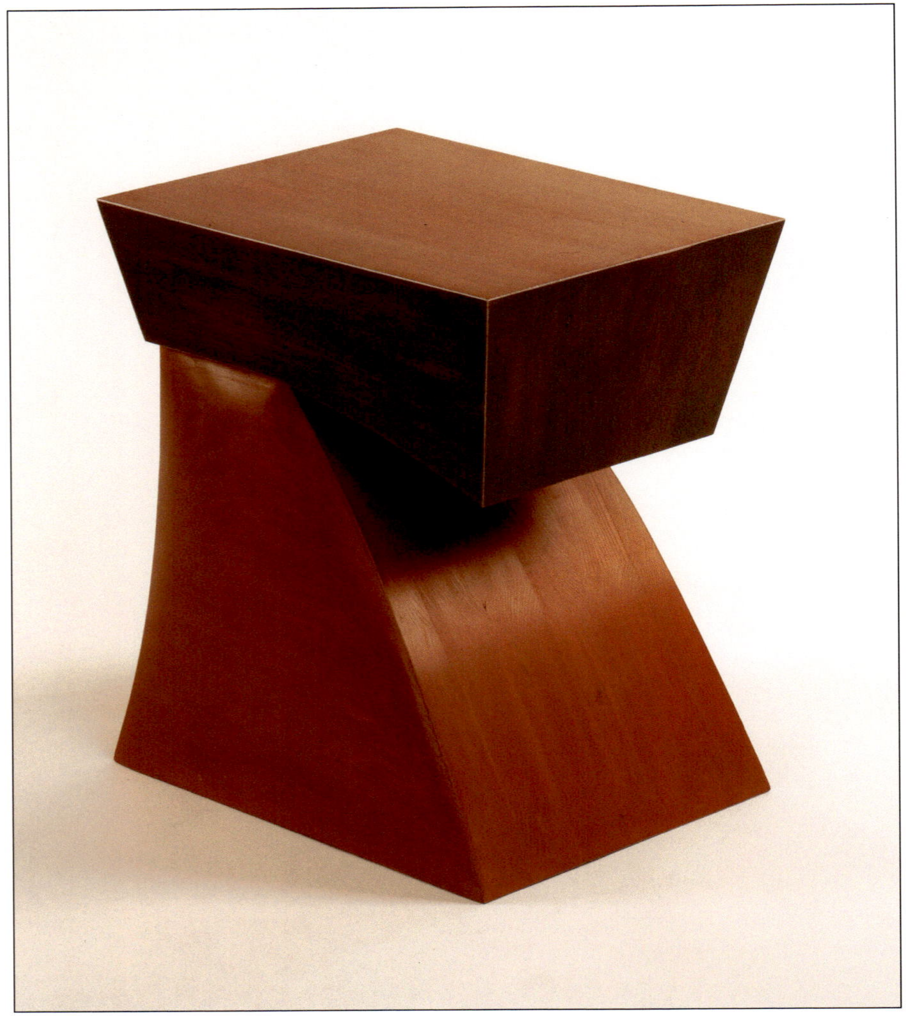

Erik Wolken. *Little Big Man*. 2007. Stool/Table, laminated solid ash, milk paint and hand rubbed oil finish, 14" w x 11" deep x 16" h. (right and opposite page)

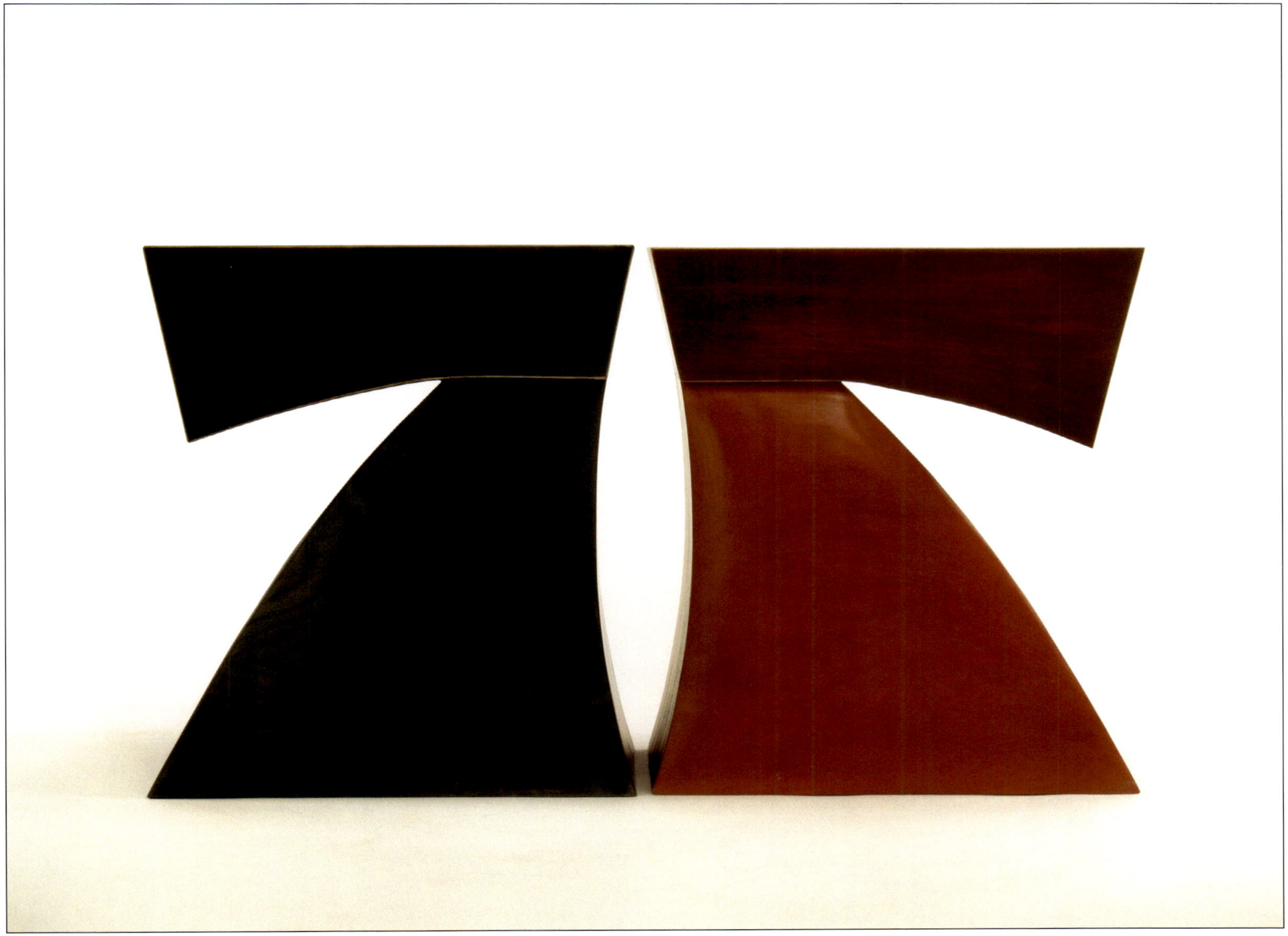

Back in the Saddle Again

This piece was part of a series of sculptural forms made from laminated solid wood so it would have the look and feel of being made from a single block of wood. The name derives from two things, a fascination with the wonderful form of a riding saddle and the fact that this piece was my first new work in two years.

Erik Wolken. *Back in the Saddle Again.* 2008. Bench/Coffee Table, laminated ash, milk paint, pickled finish with lacquer topcoat, 51" l x 12" w x 16.5" h.

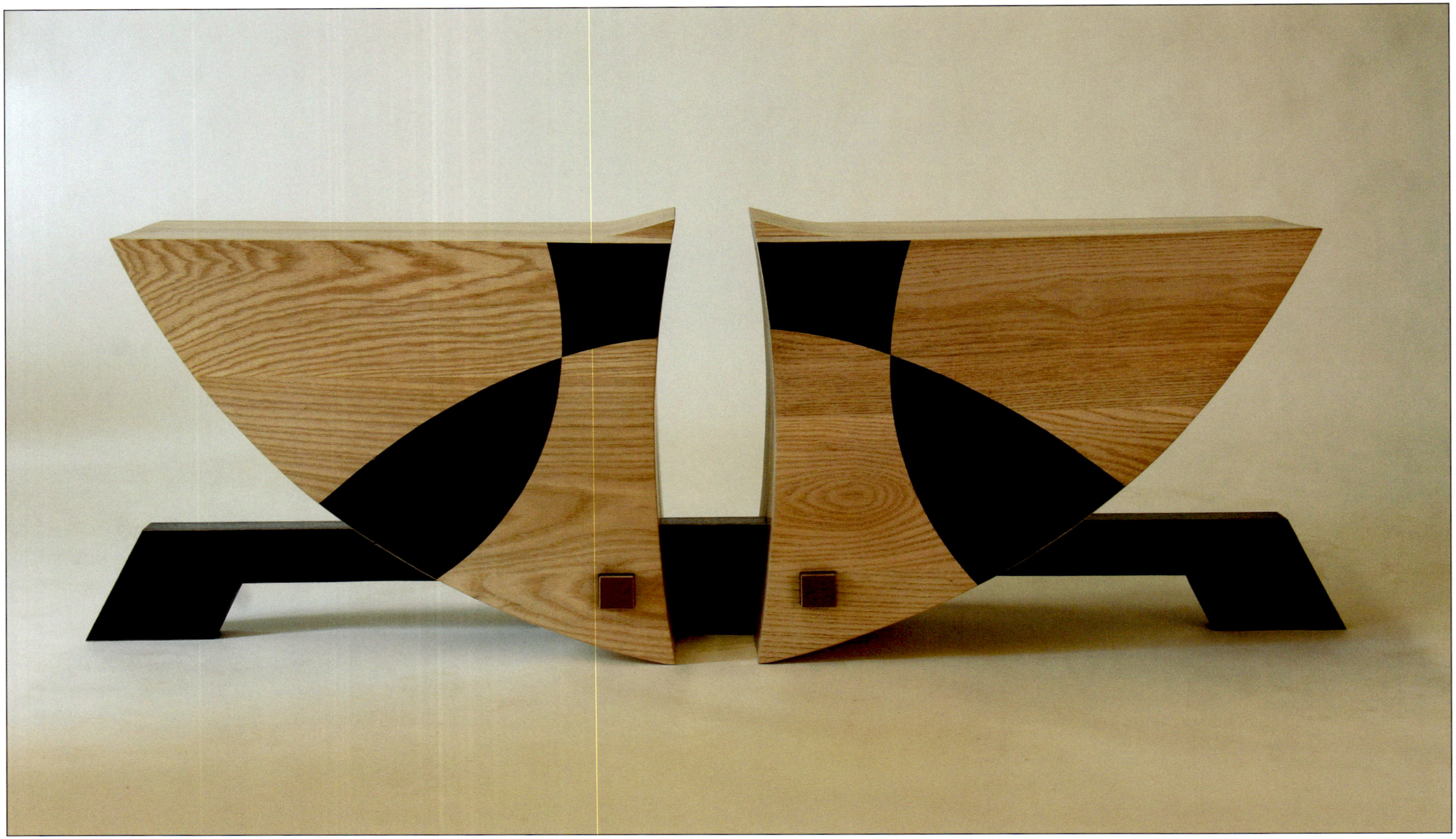

Monitor Rising

This piece and *Back in the Saddle Again* were done in what I call my summer sabbatical, a period of time I have taken over the years when the bank account is full enough that I can take the summer to play with new ideas in the studio.

The form of this table, the leaf form, is something that has appeared in my work in some form for years. The idea for this table was to take that form viewed as a solid mass, again much like *Back in the Saddle*, and with surface decoration. Much like my other work there was no real plan for the surface decoration I just knew I wanted to have three panels or mini canvasses on each side of the piece. As this developed, I realized that the black squares emerging in the orange panels where much like a ship emerging from the sea and the overall form of the piece was much like the Civil War iron clad, the *Monitor,* hence the name *Monitor Rising.*

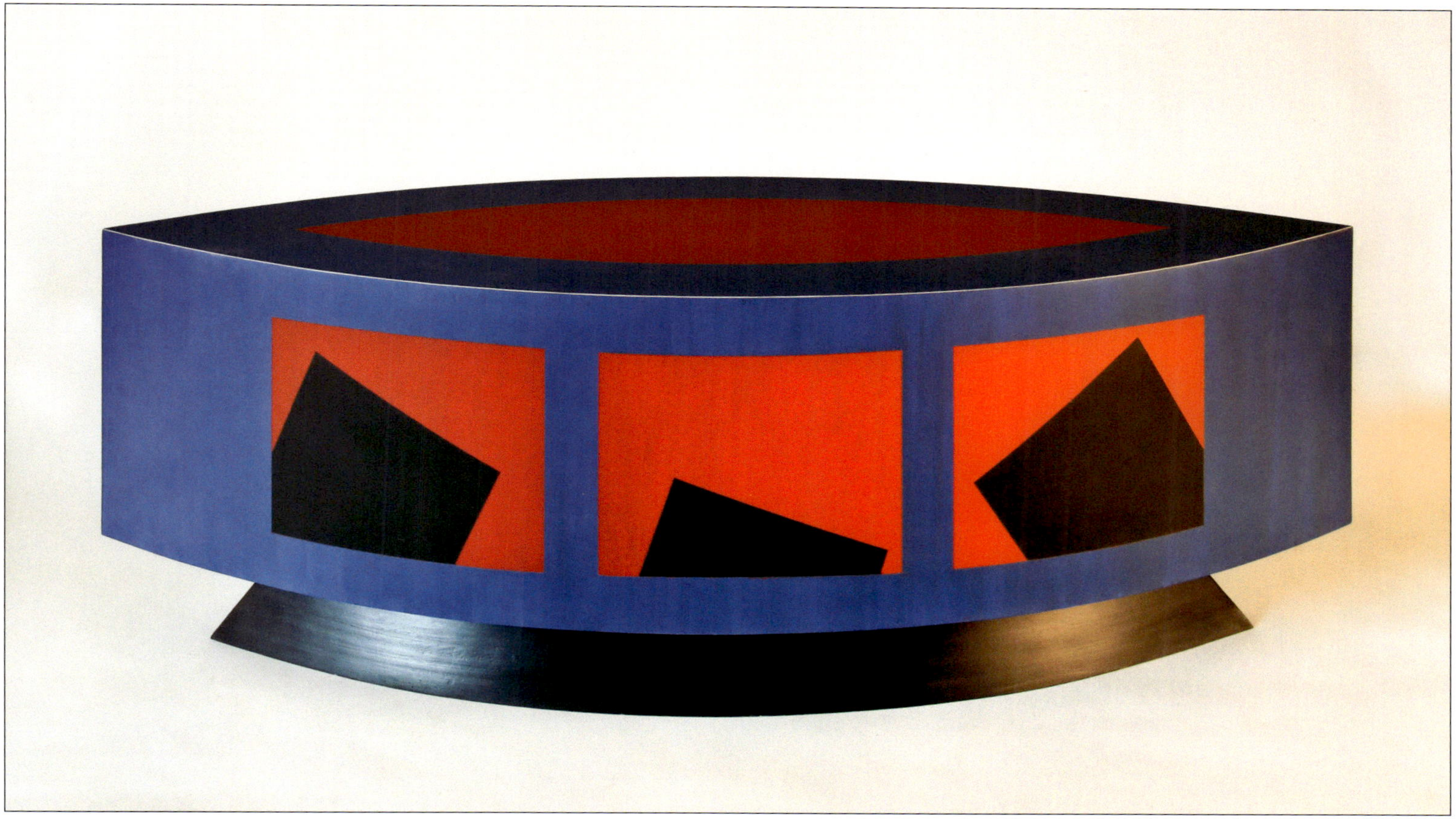

Erik Wolken. *Monitor Rising.* 2008. Coffee Table, bent laminated birch plywood, latex and acrylic paints, 48" l x 16" w x 16" h.

NICO YEKTAI

Sag Harbor, New York, www.nicoyektai.com

Artist's Statement

I consider myself a sculptor making portraits of furniture. I accept function, just as a painter accepts the canvas on which he paints. My goal is to satisfy the function that I have chosen and to express something about myself. I want to create works of art that are bound together by my sense of proportion and my touch with the material. I also want each piece to have its own identity and not be a mere copy of the one that came before it. The nature of this journey is a quest for originality.

Composition is a unique challenge when it comes to furniture. I am aware that the great advantage of this subject is that the history of creative furniture is a fraction of that of sculpture or painting. Therefore originality is easier to attain. I am careful not to be lured in by the newness of this type of art. I want to do something original that is true to the nature of my material and true to my subject. I do not want my ornamentation to be able to be separated from the structure of the piece.

I found my style by allowing each component within a piece of furniture to have its own identity. In a way this mimics the effects of time on furniture. Time usually separates glue joints, warps boards, and people damage furniture. Often I find these defects more interesting than the piece itself. My aesthetic has evolved as a response to these accidents of time. This shifting of planes allows me to push, pull, and facet the components within the piece while it is under construction. This spontaneity helps me create furniture that is as much about me as it is about function. I have left evidence of my control. These are the same issues that a painter has to deal with. Paint takes on its own life as it is applied to a canvas. Paint drips, rolls, and blends in unexpected ways. It is up to the artist to balance these accidents within the composition.

Individual Artwork

Bench #8

The dovetail is one of the fundamental joints of woodworking. For me, it is an invitation to turn that structural detail into the organizing principal of this bench. The dovetails break away from their function by rising and falling to create an intricate composition. It is almost as if tectonic forces have pushed and squeezed them. The facets mellow these violent actions and help create transitions from one part of the bench to another. This energy drives the composition and compels the viewer to walk around the bench looking for more.

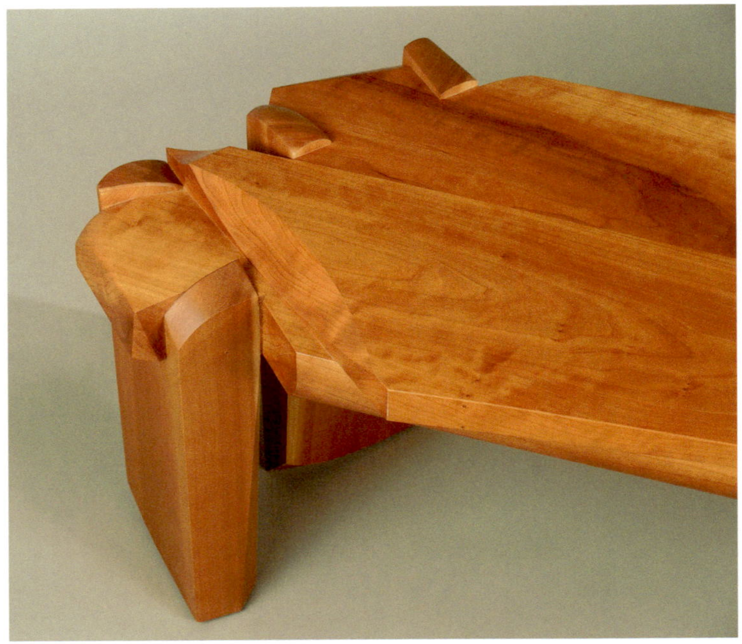

Nico Yektai. *Bench #8.* 2000. Cherry, solid wood construction, dovetails, hand rubbed oil finish, 94" l x 20" w x 18" h. (above and opposite page)

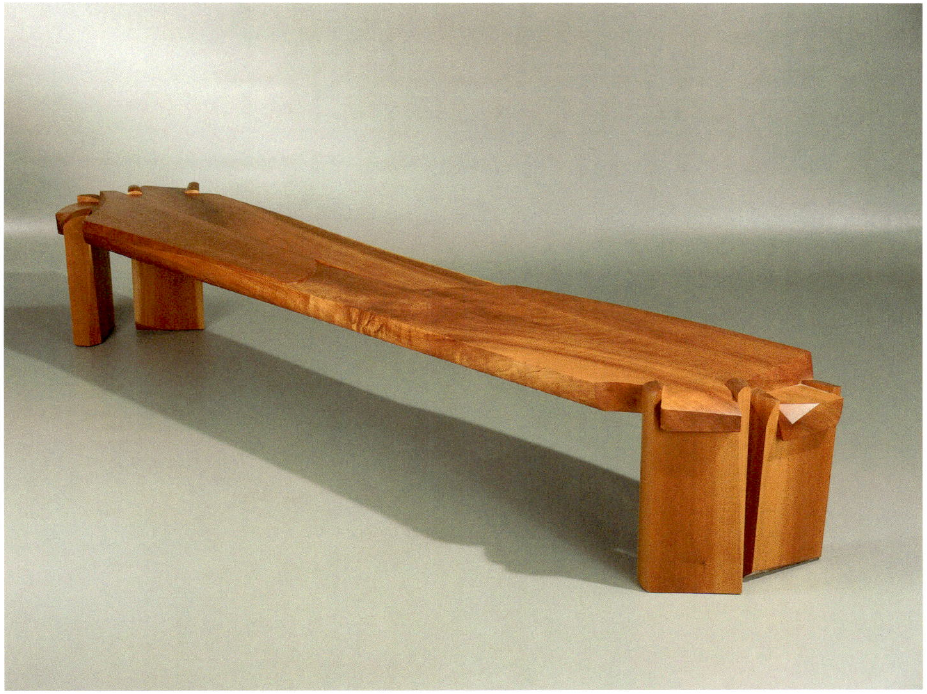

Pedestal Table #5

I often use small pedestal tables as sketches to explore an idea. This table was an attempt to explore bent laminations and the possibilities in a small table. I ended up with some tricky joinery as a result of twisting and turning the curves. I wanted to create the impression of movement as they cradled the tabletop. The relationship of the feet to the floor was very important to me in this piece. I wanted to continue that feeling of movement. My answer was to angle the legs to give the feeling of a dancer on tiptoes. Occasionally I succeed in what I am trying to do. I have caught people tugging on parts of this table as they expect it to continue to move if they could only find the right spot to push.

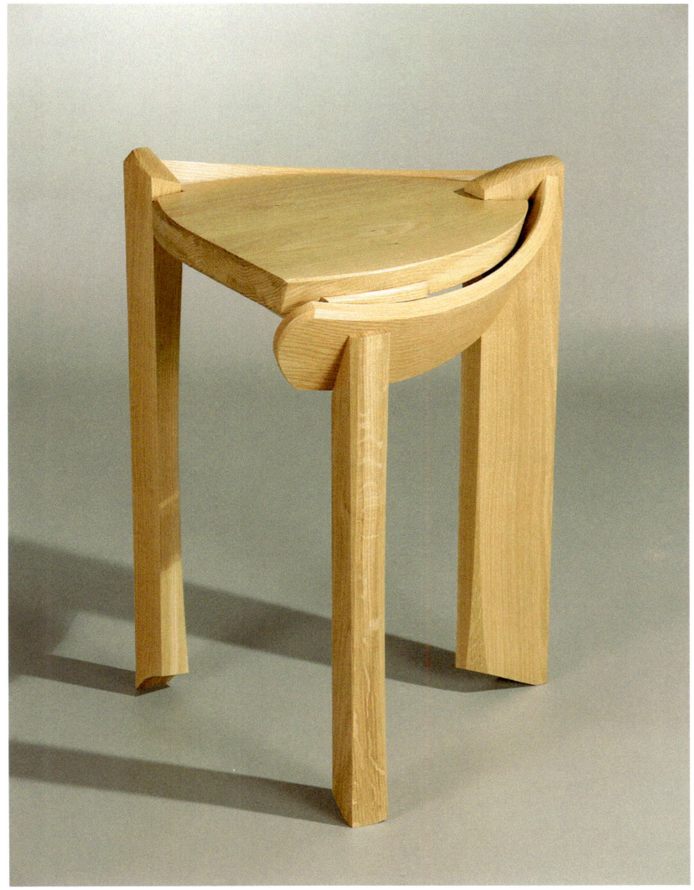

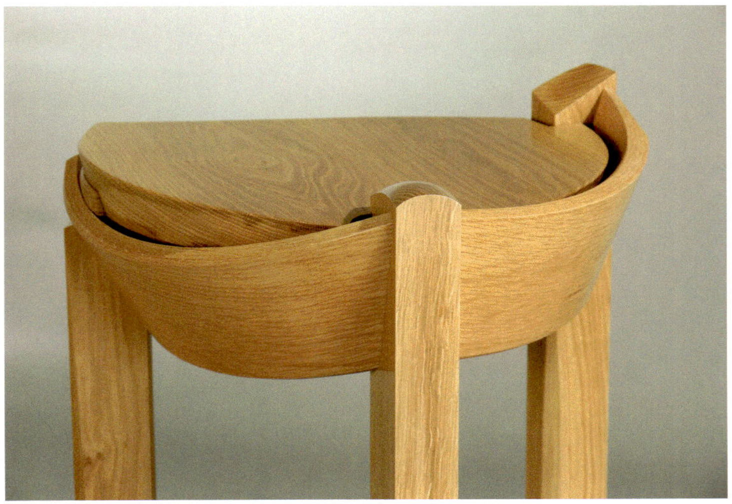

Nico Yektai. *Pedestal Table #5.* 2006. White oak, solid wood construction, mortise and tenon, bent lamination, spray finish, 20" l x 20" w x 30" h.

Dining Table #4

This is not a circular table and it becomes apparent the second that you give it more than a casual glance. The perimeter has been squeezed and stretched to create inviting nooks and gestural sweeps. The leg are not lost under the table, rather they are involved in the sweep of the edge. Legs pop up above the table's edge just as the thickness of the solid maple goes from two inches to four inches. The legs themselves are made up of two pieces of wood, adding yet another structural element that becomes part of the ornamentation of the piece.

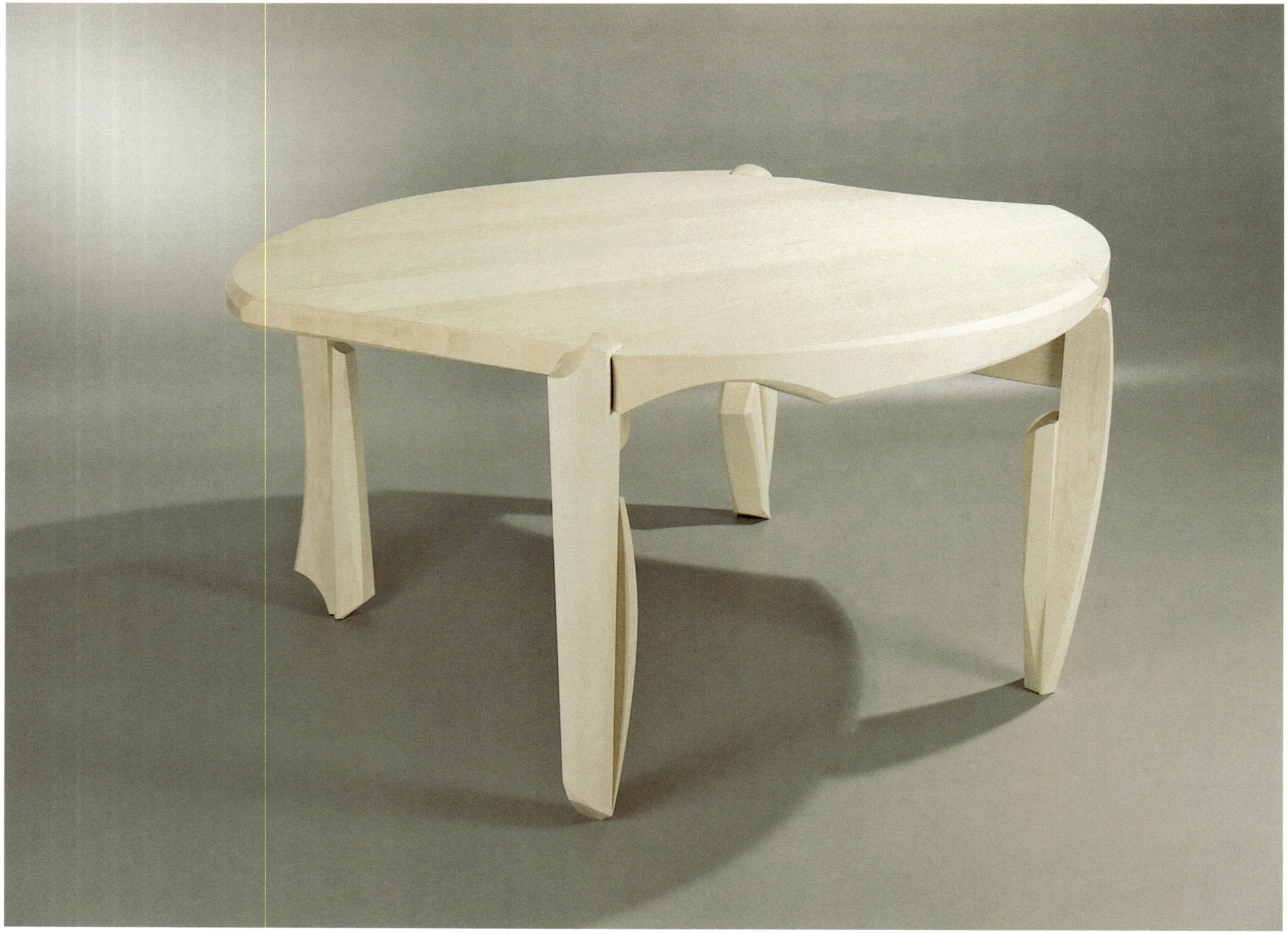

Nico Yektai. *Dining Table #4.* 2008. Maple, solid wood construction, mortise and tenon, steam bent stretchers, water based lacquer, bleach, 60" l x 60" w x 31" h.

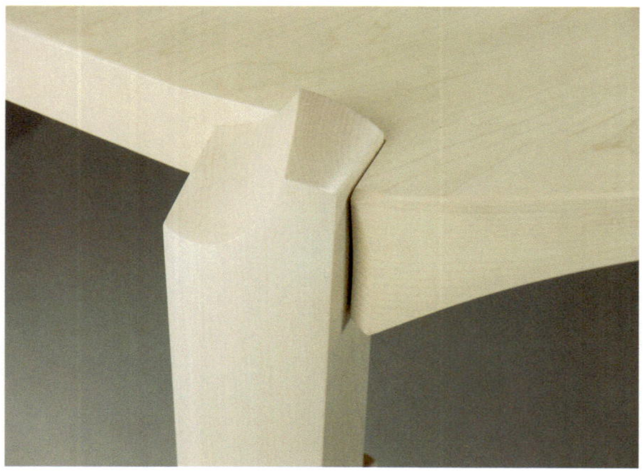

Glass Hall Table

The sweep of the steam bent stretchers are the focal point of this glass topped table. The curves interact with each other differently depending on the perspective of the viewer. This results in the viewer walking around the piece. There are facets that accentuate the curve of the stretchers and offer another level of detail as you get closer to the table. There are only seven separate components that make up this table but together they tell the larger story of my style. Each component within a piece shifts and moves from the conventional, symmetrical position that one would expect. In this way the structure becomes the detail.

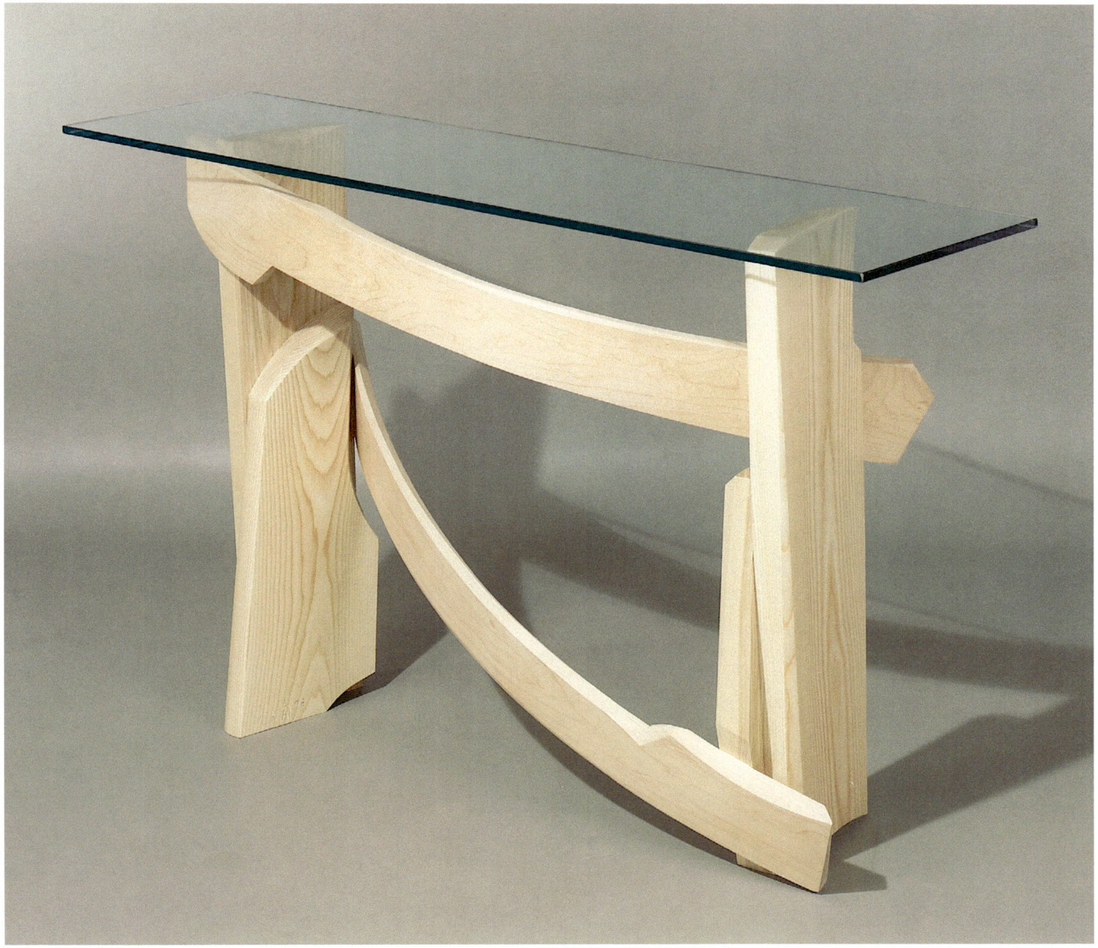

Nico Yektai. *Glass Hall Table.* 2008. Maple, ash and glass, solid wood construction, mortise and tenon, steam bending, water based lacquer, 54" l x 14" w x 35" h.

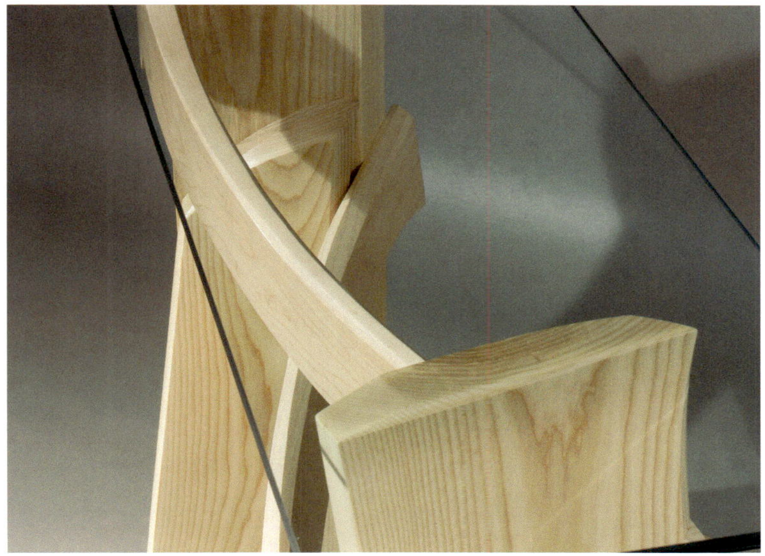

Resources

Galleries

del Mano gallery
W. Los Angeles, CA
www.delmano.com

Hana Coast Gallery
Hana, HI
www.hanacoast.com

Ironwood Gallery
Ridgefield, CT
www.ironwoodgallery.com

Northwest Fine Woodworking
Seattle, WA
www.nwfinewoodworking.com

The Wood Turning Center
Philadelphia, PA
www.woodturningcenter.org

Craft and Furniture Shows

American Craft Council Show
New York, NY
www.craftcouncil.org

Wood Working Show Redwood College
Fort Bragg, CA
www.crfinefurniture.com

Calendar of Shows

Contact the shows for dates and times.
For the Wood Working Shows:
info@thewoodworkingshows.com

Fine Art & Craft Show
January
Gold Canyon, AZ
www.dixiegreenpromotions.com

Fine Art & Craft Show
January
Carefree, AZ
www.dixiegreenpromotions.com

Wood Working Show Baltimore
January
Timonium, MD

Wood Working Show New England
January
W. Springfield, MA

Wood Working Show Columbus
January
Columbus, OH

Wood Working Show Indianapolis
January
Indianapolis, IN

Wood Working Show Atlanta
January
Norcross, GA

Fine Art & Craft Show
January
Carefree, AZ
www.dixiegreenpromotions.com

Huff Promotions
January
Pennsylvania
www.huffspromos.com

American Craft Council Show
February
Baltimore, MD
www.craftcouncil.org

Wood Working Show Milwaukee
February
West Allis, WI

Wood Working Show St. Louis
February
Collinsville, IL

Wood Working Show Kansas City
February
Overland Park, KS

Wood Working Show Somerset
February
Somerset, NJ

Wood Working Show Detroit
February
Taylor, MI

American Craft Council Show
March
Atlanta, GA
www.craftcouncil.org

The Philadelphia Invitational Furniture Show
March
Philadelphia, PA
www.pffshow.com

Wood Working Show Reading
March
Reading, PA

Wood Working Show Fredericksburg
March
Fredericksburg, VA

Wood Working Show Tampa
March
N. Tampa, FL

American Craft Council Show
April
St. Paul, MN
www.craftcouncil.org

Smithsonian Craft Show
April
Washington, DC
www.smithsoniancraftshow.org

Wood Working Show Chantilly
April
Chantilly, VA

Wood Working Show Houston
April
Katy, TX

Wood Working Show Huntsville
April
Huntsville, AL

International Contemporary Furniture Fair
May
New York City, NY
www.icff.com

Grany Wood Art Fest
June
Anamosa, IA
grantwoodartfestival.anamosachamber.org

American Craft Council Show
August
San Francisco, CA
www.craftcouncil.org

Arts & Crafts San Francisco
August
San Francisco, CA

Arts & Crafts San Francisco
August
San Francisco, CA

October fest
September
Columbus, OH

Pearl Fine Arts & Crafts
September
North Blocks, OR
www.artinthepearl.com

Home for the Holidays A+C show
October or November
Canton, OH

Philadelphia Museum of Art Craft Show
November
Philadelphia, PA
www.pmacraftshow.org

Washington Craft Show
November
Washington, DC
www.craftsamericashows.com

Society of Fine Arts (SOFA) Chicago
November

Phila Museum of Art Craft Show
November
Phila, PA
www.pmacraftshow.org/artists-wood/

Furniture Societies

American Association of Woodturners
Shore View, MN

American Society of Furniture Designers
High Point, NC

Boston Design Center
Boston, MA
www.bostondesign.com

William Morris Society
Washington, DC
www.morrissociety.org

Schools and Universities with Woodworking Instruction

Academy of Art University
79 New Montgomery Street
San Francisco, CA
www.academyart.edu

Alpine School of Woodcarving
225 Vine Avenue
Park Ridge, IL 60068
(847) 692-2822
www.chipcarving.com

Ambrose Pollack
Carmel, CA 93923
(831) 625-6554
www.ambrosepollock.com

American School of French Marquetry
W. Patrick Edwards
3815 Utah Street
San Diego, CA 92104
619-298-0864
www.wpatrickedwards.com

American School of Lutherie
449 Allan Court
Healdsburg, CA 95448
707-431-9530
www.americanschoolofflutherie.com

American Sycamore Retreat
7559 E County Road 950 S.
Cloverdale, IN.46120
(765) 795-4044
www.americansycamoreretreat.com.

American Woodworking Academy
1304 W. Lark Industrial Dr.
Fenton, MO 63026
(636) 240-1804
www.awacademy.com.

American Woodcarving School
21 Pompton Plains Crossroad
Wayne, NJ 07470
973-835-8555
americanwoodcarving.com

Anderson Ranch Arts Center
5263 Owl Creek Rd.
Snowmass Village, CO 81615
970-923-3181
andersonranch.org

Arizona State University
Herberger College of the Arts
PO Box 871505 Tempe, AZ 85287
480-965-3468
www.art.awu.edu

Arrowmont School of Arts & Crafts
556 Parkway
Gatlinburg, TN 37738
(865) 436-5860
www.arrowmont.org.

Arts Wood Shop & School of Woodworking
240 Portage Rd.
Niagra Falls, NY 14303
716-285-1814
www.awsnf.com/

Asheville Woodworking School
91 Biltmore Avenue
Asheville, NC 28801
828-252-8088
ashevillehardware.com

Ashworth College
430 Technology Parkway
Norcross, Georgia 30092
800-957-5412
www.ashworthcollege.edu

Augusta Heritage Center
David & Elkins College
100 Campus Drive
Elkins, WV 26241
800-624-3157
www.augustaheritage.com

Barnard Woodworking School
Dale Barnard
1714 E. Owl Hollow Road
Paoli, IN 47454
812-723-3461
www.daleswoodshopclasses.com

Ben Hobbs Furniture Making Classes
Ben or Jackie Hobbs
948 Pender Road
Hertford, NC 27944
252-426-7815
www.hobbsfurniture.com

Black Hills School of Woodworking
105 Spruce Lane
Spearfish, SD 57783
605-591-2947
www.bhsw.org

Boston Architectural College
320 Newbury Street
Boston, MA 02115
(617) 262-5000
www.the-bac.edu

Boston Woodworking Co, Ltd.
Mark Arnold School of Fine Furniture Making
423-A South Galena Road
Sunbury, OH 43074
740-972-6304
www.bostonwoodworking.com

Brookfield Craft Center
P.O. Box 122 Route 25
Brookfield, CT 06804-0122
203-775-4525
www.brookfieldcraftcenter.com

Bucks County Community College
Mark Sfirri or Jon Alley
Swamp Road
Newtown, PA 18940
215-968-8425
www.bucks.edu

California College of the Arts
San Francisco and Oakland
800-447-1ART
www.cca.edu/

Calvo Woodcarving School
David Calvo
186 East Main St.
Gloucester, MA 01930
978-283-0231
www.davidcalvo.com/woodcarving__classes.html

Cedar Lakes Crafts Center
Gloria Gregorich
HC 88, Box 21
Ripley, WV 25271
304-372-7860
www.cedarlakes.com

Center for Furniture Craftsmanship
25 Mill St.
Rockport, Maine 04856
207-594-5611
www.woodschool.org

Center for Turning and Furniture Design
Steven Loar or Christopher Weiland
Indiana University of Pennsylvania
Department of Art
Sprowls Hall, Room 115
470 South Eleventh Street
Indiana, PA 15705
724-357-2538
www.arts.iup.edu

Cerritos College
111150 E. Alondra Blvd
Norwalk, CA 90650
562-860-2451, ext. 2986
www.cerritos.edu/wood

Chidwick School of Fine Woodworking
Andy Chidwick
146 Crooked Pine Rd.
Stevensville, MT 59870
406/546-7130
www.chidwickchairs.com

Coeur d'Alene School of Woodworking
Skip Gillespie
4951 Building Center Drive
Coeur d'Alene, ID 83815
208-755-9902
www.cdawoodworkingschool.net

College of the Redwoods
7351 Tompkins Hill Rd.
Eureka, CA 95501
800-641-0400
www.redwoods.edu/

College of the Redwoods
440 Alger Street
Fort Bragg, CA 95437
707-964-7056
www.crfinefurniture.com

Connecticut Valley School of Woodworking
Bob Van Dyke
249 Spencer Street
Manchester, CT 06040
860-647-0303
www.schoolofwoodworking.com

Conover Workshops
18125 Madison Road
P.O. Box 679
Parkman, OH 44080
(440) 548-3491
www.conoverworkshops.com/

Country Workshops Woodworking School
990 Black Pine Ridge Road
Marshall, NC 28753
828-656-2280
www.countryworkshops.org/

Craft Alliance Education Center
Ron Diefenbacher
6640 Delmar Blvd.
St. Louis, MO 63130
314-725-1177
www.diefenb@networkusa.net

Dakota County Technical College
Mitch Kohanek
The National Institute of Wood Finishing
1300 145th Street East (County Road 42)
Rosemount, MN 55068
651-423-8301
www.dctc.mnscu.edu

Dana Robes Wood Craftsmen
Eric Gesler or Chris McGrody
Box 707 Lower Shaker Village
Enfield, NH 03748
603-632-5385
www.danarobes.com

David Finck
161 Hickory Trail Banner
Elk, NC 28604
828-963-6504
www.davidfinck.com

Durham School for Early American Trades
Rick Bihlmeyer
230 Maple Ave.
Durham, CT 06422
860-349-8872

Fashion Institute of Technology
Dr. Hugh R. Crean
227 W. 27th St.
New York, NY 10001
212-217-7823

Fine Art Woodcarving
Thomas Golding
Main St.Route 30
P.O. Box 302
Newfare, VT 05345
802-365-7255
www.carving@souer.net

Furniture Institute of Massachusetts
Bevely, MA 01915
978-922-0615
www.furnituremakingclasses.com

Furnituremaking Workshops
Jeff Miller J.
Miller Handcrafted Furniture
1774 W. Lunt Ave. Chicago, IL 60626
773-761-3311
www.furnituremaking.com

Go Figured Fine Furniture
Randall Bowling
900 Old Trents Ferry Road
Lynchburg, VA 24503
434-426-8281
www.gofigured.com

Great Ned! Woodworks
1842 SE 1st Street
Redmond, OR 97756
541-923-0808

Greenwoodworking
Jennie Alexander
1406 Light Street
Baltimore, MD 21230
410-685-4375
www.greenwoodworking.com/

Gregory Paolini Design LLC
Gregory Paolini
Waynesville, NC
828-627-3948
www.gregorypaolini.com

Grew-Sheridan Studio
3450 Third Street, #5E
San Francisco, CA 94124
415-824-6161

Gwinnett Woodworkers Assoc.
Stone Mountain Power Tools/Kentec
535 Indian Trail Road
Lilburn GA, 30047
(770) 925-3674
www.gwinnettwoodworkers.com/

Haystack Mountain School of Crafts
Stuart Kestenbaum
P.O. Box 518
Deer Isle, ME 04627
207-348-2306
www.haystack@haystack-mtn.org

Haywood Community College
Freedlander Drive
Clyde, NC 28721-9454
704-627-2821

Heartwood School of Art
James Mellick
15040 Maple Ridge Road
Milford Center, OH 43045
937-349-8408
www.urec.net/users/jmellick

Hennepin Technical College
Gayle Johnson
Brooklyn Park Campus
9000 Brooklyn Blvd.
Brooklyn Park, MN 55445
800-345-4655
www.hennepintech.edu

Hennepin Technical College
Gayle Johnson
Eden Prairie Campus
9200 Flying Cloud Drive
Eden Prarie, MN 55347

Highland Woodworking
1045 North Highland Avenue, NE
Atlanta, GA 30306
800-241-6748
www.highlandwoodworking.com

Hobbs Furniture Classes
948 Pender Road
Hertford, NC 27944
252-426-1593
hobbs@hobbsfurniture.com

Homestead Woodworking School
52 Bald Hill Road
Newmarket, NH 03857
(603) 659-2345
www.woodschool@comcast.net

Ivan Whillock Studio
122 NE First Avenue
PO Box 611
Faribault, MN 55021
888-901-8099
www.willcock.com

J D Lohr School of Woodworking
Jeffry Lohr
242 N. Limerick Road
Schwenksville, PA 19473
610-287-7802
www.jdlohrwood.com

Jeffrey Greene Design Studio
3853 Old Easton Road
Doylestown, PA 18901
215-348-5232

J. Miller Handcrafted Furniture
1774 W. Lunt Avenue
Chicago, IL 60626.
(773) 761-3311.
www.furnituremaking.com

John C. Campbell Folk School
1 Folk School Road
Brasstown, NC 28902
800-365-5724
www.folkschool.org

Kelly Mehler School of Woodworking
Kelly Mehler
PO Box 786
Berea, KY 40403
859-986-5540
www.kellymehler.com

Kent State University
Kent, OH 44242
330-672-3000
www.kent.edu

Landmark Logworks
Redmond Manierre
3489 Landmark Road
The Plains, VA 20198
540-687-4124

Laney College
900 Fallon Street
Oakland, CA 94607
510-834-5740
www.laney.peralta.edu

Long Island School of Classical Woodcarving & Woodworking
Walter T Connolly
74 W. Hoffman Ave.
Lindenhurst, NY 11757
631-225-1666
www.web.me.com/walterc530

Lonnie Bird's School of Fine Woodworking
Lonnie Bird
1145 Carolina Drive
Dandridge, TN 37725
www.lonniebird.com

Luthiers School of the Rockies
Harry Fleishman
4500 Whitney Place
Boulder, CO 80303
303-499-1614
www.guitars@henge.com

Makeville Studio
119 8th Street Unit 208
Brooklyn, NY 11215
917-873-5542
www.makeville.com

Marc Adams School of Woodworking
Marc Adams
5504 E. 500 North
Franklin, IN 46131
317-535-4013
www.marcadams.com

Mark Supik Woodturning Workshops
Mark Supik
1 N. Haven Street
Baltimore, MD 21224
410-732-8414
www.marksupikco.com

Masterpiece School of Furniture
541 S. Franklin St
Fort Bragg, CA 95437
707-964-8798
www.masterpieceschool.com

McLaughlin Woods
Tom McLaughlin
336 Baptist Road
Canterbury, NH 03224-2513
603-783-9700
www.experiencewoodworking.com

Mike Siemsen's School of Woodworking
9912 Green Lake Trail
Chisago City, MN 55013
651-257-9166
www.schoolofwood.com

Minneapolis College of Art and Design
2501 Stevens Ave.
Minneapolis, MN 55404
(612) 874-3700
www.mcad.edu/

Minneapolis Community and Technical College
Mark Lindstrom
1501 Hennepin Avenue
Minneapolis, MN 55403
612-659-6076
www.minneapolis.edu

Mt Diablo Unified School District
Adult Education, Judy Sosnowski
One Santa Barbara Road, #210
Pleasant Hill, CA 94523
925-682-8000, ext. 3911
www.mdaewoodworking.com

New England School of Architecture Woodworking
Margaret Larson
One Cottage St
Easthampton, MA 01027
413-527-6103
www.nesaw.com

Nora Hall, Woodcarver
PO Box 237
Cloverdale, OR 97112
503-392-3415
www.norahall.com

North Bennet Street School
Robert Delaney
39 North Bennet St.
Boston, MA 02113
617-227-0155
www.nbss.org

Northern Michigan University
Department of Art and Design
William Leete
1401 Presque Isle Ave.
Marquette, MI 49855
906-227-2194
art.nmu.edu/department/wood.html

North House Folk School
PO Box 759 Grand Marais, MN 55604
218-387-9762
www.northhouse.org

Olney Central College
Rick Hartom
305 North West St.
Olney, IL 62450
618-395-7777, ext. 2540
www.hartom@advant.com

Oregon School of Arts & Crafts
8245 SW Barnes Road
Portland, OR 97225
503-297-5544, ext. 117
www.ocac.edu

Orth Furniture Apprenticeship
David Orth
20817 Bunker Hill Road
Marengo, IL 60152
815-943-4099
www.OrthFurniture.com

Oyster Bamboo Rod Making Classes
193 Toccoa River Forest
Mineral Bluff, GA 30559
706-374-4239
www.oysterbamboo.com

Palomar College
1140 West Mission Road
San Marcos CA 92069
760-744-1150
www.palomar.edu

Penland School of Crafts
P.O. Box 37
Penland, NC 28765
704-765-2359
www.penland.org

Peters Valley Craft Education Center
Jennifer Brooks
19 Kuhn Road
Layton, NJ 07851
973-948-5200
www.pvcrafts.org

Philadelphia Furniture Workshop
Alan Turner or Mario Rodriguez

5212 Pulaski Ave
Philadelphia, PA 19144-4015
215-849-5174
www.philadelphiafurnitureworkshop.com

Philadelphia Windsor Chair Workshops
Jim Rendi
P.O. Box 67
Earlville, PA 19519
610-689-4717
www.philadelphiawindsor.com

Pleasant Hill Education Center Wood Shop
One Santa Barbara Rd. Room 208
Pleasant Hill, CA 94523
925-937-1530 Ext.3990
www.diablowoodworkers.com

Pocahontas Woods, Inc
John Friel
503 3rd Avenue
Marlinton, WV 24954
304-799-6985
www.pocahontaswoods.com

Port Townsend School of Woodworking
200 Battery Way
Fort Worden State Park
Port Townsend, WA 98368
360-344-4455
www.ptwoodschool.com

Purchase College School of the Arts
School of Art+Design
State University of New York
Dennis FitzGerald
735 Anderson Hill Road
Purchase, NY 10577
914.251.6763
www.purchase.edu/Departments/AcademicPrograms/Art/ArtDesign/

Randall O'Donnell Classical Institute
Randall O'Donnell
Early American Design & Hand Tool Techniques
2380 Turning Tree Drive
Nashville, IN 47448
812-988-1380
www.randallodonnell.com

Red Rocks School of Fine Woodworking and Lutherie
Rand Richards
Red Rocks Community College
13300 W 6th Ave
Lakewood, CO 80465
www.rrcc.edu/finewood/

Rhode Island School of Design
Rosanne Somerson
2 College St.
Providence, RI 02903
401-454-6373
www.risd.edu

Rich Johnson's Woodturning Center
14979 Joanne Ave.
San Jose, CA 95127
408-254-8485
Rich@latheart.com

Rockingham Community College
Winifert Lawson-Graves
P.O. Box 38
Wentworth, NC 27375-0038
336-342-4261 ext. 178
www.rcc.cc.nc.us

Santa Fe Community College
Fine Woodworking Program
6401 Richards Ave.
Santa Fe, NM 87505
505-428-1726
www.sfccnm.edu

Savannah College of Art and Design
P.O. Box 3146
Savannah, GA 31402-3146
912.525.4727
www.scad.edu

School for American Crafts
Rochester Institute of Technology
Bob Schmitz
1 Lomb Memorial Drive
Rochester, NY 14623
www.rit.edu/~652www/

School of Classical Woodworking
Ian Agrell
319 Dolan Avenue
Mill Valley, CA 94941
415-381-9474
www.agrellandthorpe.com

Seattle Central Community College
Wood Construction Center
2310 S. Lane Street
Seatttle, WA 98144
206-587-4915
www.woodconstruction.org

Shelburne Art Center
P.O. Box 52
Shelburne, VT 05482
802-985-3648
www.shelburnartcenter.org

Snow Farm The New England Craft Program
Tom O' Malley
5 Clary Rd.
Williamsburg, MA 01096
413-268-3101
www.snowfarm.org

Southern Union State Community College
1701 Lafayette Parkway
Opelika, AL 36801
334-745-6437
www.suscc.cc.al.us

Spring Harvest School of Fine Woodworking
George Huron
1523 East Commerce St.
San Antonio, TX 78205
210-232-2899
www.springharvestfww.com

Tennessee Technological University
Appalachian Center for Crafts
Ward Doubet
1560 Craft Center Drive
Smithville, TN 37166
615-597-6801

Thaddeus Stevens College of Technology
Steve Latta or Rob Tobias
750 East King Street
Lancaster, PA 17602
717-299-7733
www.stevenstech.org

The Acanthus Workshop, LLC
Charles or Lorraine Bender
244 Ellis Woods Road
East Coventry, PA 19465
610-970-5862
www.acanthus.com

The American School of French Marquetry
North Park,
San Diego, CA
www.wpatrickedwards.com

The Breed School
American 18th Century Furniture By Hand
13 Liberty Street
South Berwick, ME 03908
603-749-6231
www.allanbreed.com

The Center for Essential Education School of Woodworking
Paul Sellers
608 Dry Creek Rd.
Waco, TX 76705
254-799-1480
www.cfeeschool.com

The Center for Furniture Craftsmanship
25 Mill St.
Rockport, Maine 04856
207-594-5611
www.woodschool.org

The Dogwood Institute School of Fine Woodworking
Ronald G. Peyton
1640 Mid-Broadwell Rd., Ste 200
Alpharetta, GA 30004
800-533-2440
www.dogwoodwoodworking.com

The Eliot School of Fine and Applied Arts
24 Eliot St.
Jamiaca Plains, MA 02130
617.524.3313
www.eliotschool.org

The Furniture Institute of Massachusetts
Philip C. Lowe
116 Water Street
Beverly, MA 01915
978-922-0615
www.furnituremakingclasses.com

The Heartwood School
Will Beemer
Johnson Hill Rd.
Washington, MA 01223
413-623-6677
www.heartwoodschool.com

The Landing School
Wade Elliott, Director of Admissions
PO Box 1490
Kennebunkport, ME 04046
207-985-7976
www.landingschool.edu

The Northwest Woodworking Studio
Gary Rogowski
1002 SE 8th Avenue Portland, OR 97214
503-284-1644
www.northwestwoodworking.com

The Preservation Education Institute
PO Box 21
Windsor, VT 05089
802-674-6752
www.preservationworks.org

The University of Akron
302-Buchtel Common
Akron, OH 44325
330-972-7111
www.uakron.edu/

The Vermont Woodworking School
148 Main Street
Cambridge, VT 05444
802-849-2013
www.vermontwoodworkingschool.com

The Wild Earth School
George or Emily Vondriska
924 County Road N.
Hudson, WI 54016
715-749-9011
www.aboutwildearth.com

The Windsor Institute
Mike Dunbar
44 Timber Swamp Road
Hampton, NH 03842
603-929-9801
www.thewindsorinstitute.com

The Wood School
Tim Clark
53 Sears Lane
Burlington, VT 05401
802-864-4454

The Woodworker Academy
Jack P. Shallow
1731 Clement Ave.
Alameda, CA 94501
510-521-1623
www.woodworkeracademy.com

The Woodworkers Club
Nick Suttora
4950 Wyaconda Road
Rockville, MD 20852
301-984-9033
www.woodworkersclub.com

The Woodworking School
Roger Goad
5813 152nd Ave. Ct. E. #104
Sumner, WA. 98390
253-862-6571
www.thewoodworkingschool.com

The University of Maine
Wood Design and Craftsmanship -
Barry Goodell
5755 Nutting Hall
Orono, ME 04469
207-359-4651
www.woodscience.umaine,edu

University of Rio Grande
Fine Woodworking
Eric Matson
218 North College Ave.
Rio Grande, OH 45674
740-245-7441
www.rio.edu

West Virginia Wood Technology Center
Paul Schreffler
10 Eleventh St.
Elkins, WV 26241
304-637-0803
www.wvwoodtech.com

White River Artisans School
P. O. Box 308
Cotter, AR, 72626
870-435-2600

William Ng Woodworks School of Fine Wookworking
1340 N. Dynamics St. #H
Anaheim, CA 92806
714-993-4215
www.wnwoodworks.com

Willow Tree Academy
Joe Trippi
12413 Stark Rd.
Livonia, MI 48150
734-679-6330
www.willowtreeacademy.com

Windsor Studio and Fine Joinery Workshop
Jim Rubino
Obernburg, New York,

Woodenboat
Rich Hilsinger
Naskeag Road
P.O. Box 78
Brooklin, ME 04616
207-359-4651
www.woodenboat.com

Woodsmith Store Woodworking Seminars
Joel Hess
10320 Hickman Road
Clive, IA 50325
515-875-7107
www.woodworkingseminars.com

Woodturning School
Ken Keoughan, Director
10 Cappalletti Drive
Damariscotta, ME 04543
PO Box 190
Friendship, ME 04547
207-563-2345
www.woodturningschool.org

Wm. B. Sayre, Inc.
Bill Sayre
One Cottage St.
Easthampton, MA 01027
413-527-0202

Worcester Center for Crafts
Tom O' Malley Professional Craft Studies
25 Sagamore Rd.
Worcester, MA 01605
508-753-8183, ext. 3014
www.WorcesterCraftCenter.org

Yestermorrow Design/Build School
Peter Walcott
Route 100 RR1 Box 97-5
Warren, VT 05674
888-496-5541
www.yestermorrow.org

INDEX